Perspectives in Family and Community Health

Karen A. Saucier, RN, PhD
Associate Professor
Assistant Director/Undergraduate Programs
University of Southern Mississippi
School of Nursing
Hattiesburg, Mississippi

St. Louis Baltimore Boston Chicago London Philadelphia Sydney Toronto

Dedicated to Publishing Excellence

Editor: N. Darlene Como
Editorial Assistant: Barbara M. Carroll
Project Supervisor: Barbara Merritt
Designer: Susan Lane

Printed in the United States of America

Mosby–Year Book, Inc.
11830 Westline Industrial Drive
St. Louis, MO 63146

International Standard Book Code: 0-8016-4338-4

GW/DC 9 8 7 6 5 4 3 2 1

Contributing Authors

Elizabeth Anderson, RNC, DrPH
Chair and Professor
Department of Community Health and Gerontology
School of Nursing
University of Texas—Galveston
Galveston, TX

John Barkey, BA, MA
Senior Research Associate
U.S. HMO Dental Consultants, Inc.
Cleveland, OH

Heather Becker, PhD
Research Scientist
Center for Health Care Research and Evaluation
School of Nursing
The University of Texas at Austin
Austin, TX

Andrea S. Berne, CPNP, MPH
Child Health Planning Analyst
Office of Child Health Planning
New York City Department of Health
New York, NY

Michael Blauner, BA, MA
Doctoral Candidate
Advanced Studies Program
School of Applied Social Sciences
Case Western Reserve University
Cleveland, OH

Marie Annette Brown, RN, PhD, ARNP
Assistant Professor and Coordinator of the Primary Health Care Pathway
Department of Community Health Care Systems
School of Nursing
University of Washington
Seattle, WA

Helen A. Bush, RN, PhD
Professor
College of Nursing
Texas Woman's University
Denton, TX

Angeline Bushy, RN, PhD
Assistant Professor
Division of Community Health
College of Nursing
University of Utah
Salt Lake City, UT

Robert N. Butler, MD
Brookdale Professor and Chair of the Gerald and May Ellen Ritter Department of Geriatrics and Adult Development
Mount Sinai Medical Center
New York, NY

Patricia G. Butterfield, RN, MS
Doctoral Candidate
School of Nursing
Oregon Health Sciences University
Portland, OR

Ruth Carey, RN, MPH
Assistant Professor
Alternative and Continuing Education—Health Sciences and Gerontology
Spring Arbor College
Spring Arbor, MI

Shu-Pi C. Chen, RN, DrPh
Department of Public Health Nursing
College of Nursing
University of Illinois at Chicago
Chicago, IL

Chandice Harris Covington, RN, PhD
Assistant Professor
College of Nursing
Wayne State University
Detroit, MI

Karen Cox, RN, PHN
District Public Health Nurse
Bellflower Health Center
Los Angeles County Health Services
Los Angeles, CA

Candy Dato, RN, CS, MS
Administrative Coordinator
St. Luke's — Roosevelt Hospital Center
New York, NY

Carol Ann Diemert, RN, MS
Community Health Faculty
School of Nursing
University of Minnesota
Minneapolis, MN

Mary Ann Draye, RN, ARNP, MPH, FNP
Assistant Professor
Primary Health Care Program
School of Nursing
University of Washington
Seattle, WA

Mary E. Duffy, RN, PhD
Associate Professor
Department of Social and Behavioral Science
College of Nursing
University of Utah
Salt Lake City, UT

Charlene Dye, RN, PHN
District Nursing Director
Bellflower Health Center
Los Angeles County Health Services
Los Angeles, CA

Ruth Enestvedt, RN, MS
Community Health Faculty
School of Nursing
University of Minnesota
Minneapolis, MN

Wayne A. Ewing, MDiv, PhD
Psychotherapist in Private Practice
Denver, CO

Beverly C. Flynn, RN, PhD
Professor and Director
Institute of Action Research for Community Health
Department of Community Health Nursing
School of Nursing
Indiana University
Indianapolis, IN

Stephen S. Fox, PhD
Professor, Department of Psychology
University of Iowa
Iowa City, IA

Sheana Whelan Funkhouser, RN, MN
Research Specialist
Nursing Research and Education
City of Hope National Medical Center
Duarte, CA

Helen Grace, RN, PhD, FAAN
Program Director in Health
W.K. Kellogg Foundation
Battle Creek, MI

Joanne M. Hall, RN, MA
PhD Candidate
School of Nursing
University of California — San Francisco
San Francisco, CA

Robert Halpern, PhD
Erikson Institute
Chicago, IL

Patti Hamilton, RN, PhD
Associate Professor
College of Nursing
Texas Woman's University
Denton, TX

Sixten S.R. Haraldson, DrMed, MPH
Professor of International Development
Clark University
Worcester, MA
Former Director of the Nordic School of Public Health, Sweden

Anne Helton, RN, MS
Clinical Associate for the Prevention of Battering During Pregnancy Program (underwritten by Educational Grant CPE-86 from the March of Dimes–Birth Defects Foundation)

Alan L. Hull, PhD
Assistant Professor of Medicine
Director, Educational Component
Northeast Ohio Multipurpose Arthritis Center
Case Western Reserve University School of Medicine
Cleveland, OH

Judith B. Igoe, RN, MS, FAAN
Associate Professor and Director
School Health Programs
University of Colorado Health Sciences Center
Denver, CO

Marguerite M. Jackson, RN, MS, CIC
Director, Medical Center Epidemiology Unit
Assistant Clinical Professor of Community and Family Medicine
University of California—San Diego
San Diego, CA

Jeanine L. Johns, RN, MS, ANP
Lecturer, University of Michigan at Ann Arbor
Student in the Doctoral Program in Nursing
Wayne State University
Detroit, MI

Bonnie Kellogg, RN
Associate Professor
Department of Nursing
California State University
Long Beach, CA

Richard D. Lamm, LLB
Former Governor of Colorado (1975-1987)
Director, Center for Public Policy and Contemporary Issues
University of Denver
Denver, CO

Cheryl Ann Lapp, RN, MPH, MA
Community Health Faculty
School of Nursing
University of Minnesota
Minneapolis, MN

Madeleine M. Leininger, RN, PhD, LHD, DS, FAAN, CTN
Professor of Nursing and Anthropology
College of Nursing
Wayne State University
Detroit, MI

Judith J. Liebman, RN, BS, MSLS, MSN
Director of Staff Development
Montefiore Home
Cleveland, OH

Louisa M. Lundgren, RN, MS
College of Nursing
University of Illinois at Chicago
Chicago, IL

Patricia Lynch, RN, MBA, CIC
Epidemiology Department
Harborview Medical Center;
Clinical Instructor
School of Community Medicine and Public Health
University of Washington
Seattle, WA

Joan K. Magilvy, RN, PhD
Associate Professor
School of Nursing
University of Colorado Health Sciences Center
Denver, CO

Diana J. Mason, RN, C, PhD
Assistant Director of Nursing for Education and Research
Beth Israel Medical Center
New York, NY

Lillian McCreight, RN, MPH
Director of Assessment and Quality Assurance
South Carolina Department of Health and Environmental Control
Columbia, SC

Judith McFarlane, RNC, DrPh
Professor
College of Nursing
Texas Woman's University
Denton, TX

Rose McKay, RN, EdD
Formerly Faculty Member
School of Nursing
University of Colorado
Denver, CO

Jo McNeil, RN, MN
State Director of Public Health Nursing
Virginia Department of Health
Richmond, VA

John H. Milsum, ScD
Acting Director
Institute of Health Promotion Research
University of British Columbia
Vancouver, BC

Debra K. Moser, RN, MN
Research Nurse
School of Nursing and Department of Cardiology
University of California—Los Angeles
Los Angeles, CA

Roland W. Moskowitz, MD
Professor of Medicine
Department of Medicine
Case Western Reserve University
Director, Division of Rheumatic Diseases
University Hospitals of Cleveland;
Director, Northeast Ohio Multipurpose Arthritis Center
Cleveland, OH

Denise C. Murphy, RN, DrPh
Seminarian
Zen Mountain Monastery
New York

Julie Cowan Novak, RN, MA, CPNP, DNSc
Associate Professor
School of Nursing
San Diego State University;
Associate Clinical Professor
School of Medicine
University of California—San Diego
San Diego, CA

Dorothy S. Oda, RN, DNSc, FAAN
Professor and Department Chair
School of Nursing
University of California—San Francisco
San Francisco, CA

Mary Peoples-Sheps, RN, DrPh
Associate Professor
Curriculum in Public Health Nursing
School of Public Health
University of North Carolina
Chapel Hill, NC

Betty Pesznecker, RN, MN
Associate Professor Emeritus
Community Health Care Systems
School of Nursing
University of Washington
Seattle, WA

Margaret Rafferty, RN, MA, MPH, CS
Assistant Professor
School of Nursing
Long Island College Hospital
Brooklyn, NY

Dixie W. Ray, MPA
Department of Community Health Nursing
School of Nursing Graduate Program
Indiana University
Indianapolis, IN

JoAnn Bell Reckling, RN, MN, MA Phil
Doctoral Student
School of Nursing
University of Kansas
Kansas City, KS

Bonita R. Reinert, RN, MSN, ANP-C, PhD
Assistant Professor
School of Nursing
University of Southern Mississippi
Hattiesburg, MS

Denise Ribble, RN, BSN, MPA
Psychiatric Nurse III
Middletown Psychiatric Center
Middletown, NY
Co-Chairperson
Orange County AIDS Task Force

Molly A. Rose, RN, MSN
Assistant Professor
Department of Nursing
LaSalle University
Philadelphia, PA

Greta Rosenow, RN, PHN
District Public Health Nurse
Bellflower Health Center
Los Angeles County Health Services
Los Angeles, CA

Marla E. Salmon, RN, ScD, FAAN
Chairman and Professor (on leave)
Curriculum in Public Health Nursing
School of Public Health
University of North Carolina
Chapel Hill, NC
Director, Division of Nursing
Bureau of Health Professions
Health and Human Services
Rockville, MD

Dolores Sands, RN, PhD
Dean, School of Nursing
The University of Texas at Austin
Austin, TX

Phyllis R. Schultz, RN, PhD
Associate Professor
Former Faculty Member
School of Nursing
University of Colorado Health Sciences Center
Denver, CO
Faculty Member
School of Nursing
University of Washington
Seattle, WA

Mary Segall, RN, PhD
Former Faculty Member
School of Nursing
University of Colorado
Denver, CO
Faculty Member
Case Western Reserve University
Cleveland, OH

Patricia E. Stevens, RN, BSN, MA
PhD Candidate, School of Nursing
University of California — San Francisco
San Francisco, CA

Alexa K. Stuifbergen, RN, PhD
Assistant Professor
School of Nursing
The University of Texas at Austin
Austin, TX

Sandra S. Sweeney, RN, PhD
Professor, School of Nursing
University of Wisconsin — Eau Claire
Eau Claire, WI

Toni Tripp-Reimer, RN, PhD, FAAN
Professor and Director
Office for Nursing Research Development and Utilization
College of Nursing
University of Iowa
Iowa City, IA

Patience Vanderbush, MA, MSPH
Medical Writer/Editor
Clinical Research International
Research Triangle Park, NC

Paul J. Vignos, Jr., MD
Professor Emeritus, Department of Medicine
Case Western Reserve University
Director, Muscle Disease Center
University Hospitals of Cleveland
Cleveland, OH

Kathleen M. Waybrant, RN, MN, FNP
Family Nurse Practitioner
Douglas County Health Department
Roseburg, OR

Carolyn A. Williams, RN, PhD, FAAN
Dean and Professor
College of Nursing
University of Kentucky
Lexington, KY

Karen E. Witt, RN, MSN
Assistant Professor, School of Nursing
University of Wisconsin — Eau Claire
Eau Claire, WI

Consultants

Elizabeth T. Anderson, RNC, DrPH
Chair and Professor
Department of Community Health and Gerontology
School of Nursing
University of Texas—Galveston
Galveston, TX

Judith A. Barton, RN, PhD
Assistant Professor
School of Nursing
University of Colorado Health Sciences Center
Denver, CO

Mary Bear, RN, PhD
Assistant Professor
College of Nursing
University of Florida
Orlando, FL

Kaye Bender, RN, MS
Director of Public Health Nursing and
Chief of Special Staff
Mississippi State Department of Health
Jackson, MS

Anne Bolin, PhD
Assistant Professor of Anthropology
Elon College
Elon College, NC

Linda Lee Daniel, RN, MN
Associate Professor
Community Health Nursing
University of Michigan
Ann Arbor, MI

Sister Rosemary Donley, RN, PhD, FAAN
Executive Vice President
The Catholic University of America
Washington, DC

Cora Hinds, RN, BScN, MScN, EdD
Associate Professor
Faculty of Health Sciences
School of Nursing
University of Ottawa
Ottawa, Canada

Joan E. Johnston, RNC, PhD
Assistant Professor
School of Nursing
University of Texas—Galveston
Galveston, TX

Kathleen L. Keller, RN, PhD, CS
Associate Professor
School of Nursing
California State University—Long Beach
Long Beach, CA

Marjorie Keller, RN, DNS
Associate Professor
College of Nursing
University of Kentucky
Lexington, KY

Carole D. Kelly, RN, MS
Assistant Clinical Professor
School of Nursing
University of California—San Francisco
San Francisco, CA

Janet Kenney, RN, PhD
Associate Professor
College of Nursing
Arizona State University
Tempe, AZ

Jerri Laube-Morgan, RN, PhD, FAAN
Professor, School of Nursing
University of Southern Mississippi
Hattiesburg, MS

Jane Parker-Conrad, RN, PhD
Joanna Johnson Chair in Occupational Health Nursing
Associate Professor
School of Nursing
University of Wisconsin—Milwaukee
Milwaukee, WI

Kathleen Russell, RN, MSN
Assistant Professor
School of Nursing
Ball State University
Muncie, IN

Iris Shannon, RN, PhD
Associate Professor
College of Nursing
Rush University
Chicago, IL

Cecilia Tiller, DSN, RN
Assistant Professor
Department of Parent-Child Nursing
School of Nursing
The Medical College of Georgia
Augusta, GA

Preface

Community health nursing has evolved into a complex, multifaceted nursing specialty that is constantly challenged by an ever-changing health care delivery system. As a caring profession, nursing historically has been committed to assisting people to become healthy and self-sufficient. Community health nursing, which evolved from public health nursing, has responded to changes in society to include the care of such diverse populations as school children, workers, AIDS clients, and the homeless. As a broad field, community health nursing is affected by structural changes in society to a greater degree than other nursing specialties. To understand contemporary community health nursing practice, the nurse must keep current regarding social trends, nursing's development as a profession, health needs, and recent changes in a health care delivery system in a changing and diverse culture.

Perspectives in Family and Community Health focuses on the nature of community health nursing in the context of today's society. The purpose of this anthology is to provide nursing students, nurse educators, and practicing nurses with the most current perspectives regarding health care and community health nursing. The articles included were carefully selected to represent a variety of contemporary topics relevant to community health and community health nursing practice. This text was developed to assist nursing students who need to understand the concepts of wellness, family, community, disease prevention, and health promotion whatever their future field of nursing practice. Nurse educators can effectively use this text to keep up with current development and approaches in health care. The text can be equally relevant for practicing community health nurses in the field who want and need to stay abreast of current influences on their nursing practice.

Articles were chosen from numerous scholarly sources on a variety of topics related to community health and community health nursing practice. The articles provide in-depth analysis of important issues, research, theory, and applied nursing practice relevant to contemporary community health nursing. The text can be effectively used as a companion to a community health text. In courses where previous community health nursing knowledge is expected, it can be used as a primary community health nursing text. The readings provide the baccalaureate or graduate student with critical perspectives of community health nurse specialists, educators, and researchers, as well as those of other community health specialists. Articles were selected from community health literature to demonstrate the holistic and interdisciplinary nature of the diverse field of community health nursing. Basic and advanced selections appropriate for both baccalaureate nursing students and those in graduate study in community health nursing are included.

Recommendations for articles to consider for inclusion were provided by our panel of consultants, including community health educators and specialists in the field. The consultants' recommendations were augmented by my own extensive review of the community health and community health nursing literature. In all, nearly 200 articles were initially considered. I made the first selections to exclude approximately half of these articles, primarily those that were of secondary importance and/or that addressed topics already covered by other articles. Several of our consultants were then asked to review this collection of articles and recommend articles for inclusion in the final manuscript. Since numerous excellent articles were appropriate, space limitations made final article selections very difficult. Articles were carefully chosen for their relevance to contemporary practice, their readability, and their usefulness in facilitating classroom discussion. To assist readers in gaining access to the community health literature we researched in preparing this text, I have included a list of suggested additional readings at the end of each of the text's eight parts. These reading lists contain many fine articles that had to be omitted because of space limitations.

To reflect major aspects of community health nursing practice, the text is organized into eight parts: (1) an introduction to the context of community health nursing, including the social, political, and economic factors influencing contemporary health care in our society, as well as an examination of trends that may affect community health nursing practice in the future; (2) the conceptual foundations for nursing care at the community level, including models for practice, theory development, and the use of conceptual models in nursing practice; (3) diverse community health nursing roles, including their function, process, and practice settings; (4) current issues affecting community health and nursing practice, including leadership, risk management, ethics, and self-care; (5) community-centered nursing practice, which focuses on aggregate health and group-centered health care; (6) cultural influences affecting community health nursing care; (7) family health care and nursing intervention, including assessment and care of diverse family structures; and (8) special health needs of high-risk, vulnerable populations and implications for the community health nurse.

Many persons have contributed to the development and completion of this book. I would like to thank the authors of the articles, as well as their publishers, who granted me permission to reprint their published articles. Invaluable contributions were made by numerous nursing colleagues, both in practice and in educational settings, who provided important feedback regarding the focus and evaluation of this text. Those who participated most directly are listed as consultants to the book. I owe a special acknowledgement to the nursing students in my classes for their contributions and ideas for the book. My appreciation goes also to the staff and administration of Delta State University and the University of Southern Mississippi for their encouragement in this project. I am especially grateful to Virginia Foley and Brenda Mixon for their time, effort, and support. Special thanks go to Darlene Como, Senior Editor at Mosby–Year Book, for her patience, ideas, and help in seeing this book become a reality. I am also indebted to Barbara Carroll, Editorial Assistant at Mosby–Year Book, for coordinating reprint permissions and consultants' suggestions for the book. I would like to thank my family and friends who have sustained me throughout this endeavor, especially my husband, Chris Lundy, for his unwavering support and encouragement.

Karen A. Saucier

Contents

PART VII FAMILY AND COMMUNITY HEALTH NURSING PRACTICE

PART VIII HEALTH CARE OF VULNERABLE POPULATIONS

PART I

THE CONTEXT OF COMMUNITY HEALTH NURSING PRACTICE

Community health nurses must understand the structure and scope of the health care delivery system in which they operate in order to plan effective nursing interventions. The nature of community health nursing requires that the practitioner utilize knowledge of current social, political, economic, and technological influences. Considering the social context is important as community health nurses plan care for populations with specific health needs.

A society's particular health care delivery system reflects its values regarding health and human services, including social and philosophical views on its responsibilities in maintaining its members' health. Health care in the United States has often been described as a "non-system" because of the fragmentation and frequent inaccessibility of existing services. Although the U.S. is one of the world's most technologically advanced societies, health care is often unavailable, inaccessible, and inadequate for many of its residents. An estimated 15 percent of the U.S. population have poor or no access to health care. Cardiovascular disease, cancer, and accidents, each associated with personal lifestyles... continue to be the most common causes of death, yet we still utilize most of our resources on acute and episodic health care rather than preventive health measures.

Community health nurses must be aware of the historical, contemporary, and future context of health care if they are to be effective change agents. The articles selected for Part One consider the nature of community health nursing, historical influences on community health nursing practice, various viewpoints concerning the most significant problems in the health care system, and trends that may influence the future of community health nursing.

CHAPTER 1

Community Health Nursing—What is It?

Carolyn A. Williams, RN, PhD, FAAN

When we talk about community health nursing today, what do we mean? Many nurses in both education and service seem to be in a conceptual and semantic muddle about the nature of community nursing practice: What it is or should be, whether it constitutes or should constitute a specialty, and—if it is a specialty—how it is distinct from other specialties. Even community health nurses have some trouble with the concept; while there is evidence of renewed interest in increasing the amount and types of personal health services provided by community-based agencies, it is questionable whether such services are being planned, delivered, and assessed in a manner consistent with public health philosophy.

One way, perhaps, to diminish some of this confusion and ambivalence is to look again at those fundamental concepts and approaches that have traditionally been a part of public health practice and note their contemporary relevance. Although such a review may not resolve the dilemma, it may stimulate thinking about skills and approaches to bring about more responsible and effective participation by nurses in decision making related to health care delivery.

At present, there are three key barriers to effective integration of preventive and therapeutic community health services and to the planning, delivery, and evaluation of nursing services that are in touch with community needs, include appropriate consumer participation, and give attention to the natural history of the problems being addressed. Two of the barriers are conceptual ones: first, defining public health nursing practice solely in terms of *where* care takes place and/or whether or not the provider functions in a family-oriented fashion, and second, failing to understand the distinction between the respective foci of clinical nursing and medicine, on the one hand, and public health practice, on the other. The third barrier, in part a legacy of the first two, is an organizational one: paucity of service settings in which the individualistic clinical approach of nursing and medicine and the basic public health strategy of dealing with aggregates are effectively merged and practiced.

Reprinted from *Nursing Outlook,* Vol. 25, No. 4, with permission of American Journal of Nursing © 1977.

WHY SUCH BARRIERS?

Many nurses tend to view care settings other than inpatient hospital units as community settings and to define the nursing care which takes place there as community nursing. Some even consider community nursing so defined as a specialty! Such distinctions are less than helpful, and for several reasons.

First, a very narrow definition of community results when one leaves acute care institutions and meaningful articulation between such institutions and other delivery systems out of the picture. Second, although such distinctions may once have enjoyed some validity, other specialty areas in nursing are now preparing students to consider family factors and to practice in extra-hospital situations. The result is a blurring of specialties and the emergence, particularly in graduate education, of confusion about the focus of community nursing. Finally, and most important, the distinctions cited do not appropriately reflect the essence of public health practice, its relationship to other specialty areas, and its relevance in addressing health-related problems in a rational manner.

Further, in viewing direct care services provided outside of institutional settings as community health practice, those responsible for education and service programs have either completely neglected or seriously de-emphasized the distinction between the foci of clinical nursing and medicine, on the one hand, and public health practice, on the other. *And they are different.* In clinical nursing or medicine the individual patient or family is the unit of care, whereas the central feature of public health practice, according to Sidney Kark is, ". . . focus on the health of population groups (aggregates) such as . . . [those in a defined] community".[1]

Both nursing and medical education focus primarily on preparing professionals to make decisions at the individual patient level. Students are taught to assess the health status of individuals, to make appropriate decisions regarding the care each patient or client should receive, and to see that such care is provided through their own efforts or those of others. Considerably less attention is given to defining problems and proposing solutions at the group or aggregate level, and the transition to this kind of approach may be difficult.

While the integration of community health concepts into basic nursing programs might have been expected to facilitate such thinking, the teaching has frequently emphasized individualistic approaches as opposed to methods of defining problems and assessing impact at aggregate levels. As a result, the graduates are not familiar with group-level decision making, nor are they explicitly aware of the relationship between decisions made at the aggregate level and those made at the patient-provider encounter level.

DISTINGUISHING AGGREGATES OR GROUPS

Group, as defined here, is not limited to an interacting entity — a sociological term — although in some cases it may be. Rather it refers to an aggregate of individuals who have in common one or more personal or environmental characteristics. Some of these characteristics may mean that a group is at high risk of developing specific health problems: for instance, those with hypertension and thereby at greater risk of developing a stroke or coronary heart disease, or those persons living alone who are discharged from an institution to home and may therefore have a lower potential for dealing with a variety of circumstances. Other characteristics may be positively associated with specific problems — that is, black males have a higher prevalence rate of hypertension than white males.

Aggregates can be determined at many levels. Thus, for certain health-related decisions (Medicare), individuals over 65 years throughout the country can be grouped. Locally, decisions about aggregates are made by community agencies in establishing criteria for admission to service and for the types of services which will be offered.

Such a focus on groups or aggregates, however, is not reflected in movements such as the development of expanded roles for nurses and training programs in family medicine. Instead, these developments represent efforts to strengthen the clinical aspect of *personal* health service programs. While they have often resulted in more available, accessible, and acceptable structures for health care delivery at community health centers, rural satellite clinics, and health maintenance organizations, they have also tended to perpetuate the episodically oriented, patient demand, provider response approach to care.

In such situations, patients *select themselves* into the care system, and the provider's role is to deal with what the patients bring to them. No one worries about the relationship between the individual patient's problems and the problems within the community as a whole or within select subpopulations. As the clinical components of these programs are strengthened, individualistic and, less frequently, family-oriented approaches seem to be emphasized to the detriment of a population (aggregate) or community orientation, which would serve to put the clinical services into proper perspective. Although individual or even family-oriented clinical services are necessary for dealing with the personal health service needs of populations, they are not enough!

In 1974, Sheps commented:

> It is difficult to find an official or unofficial health agency which is clearly taking on the tasks of monitoring, protecting, and restoring the health of the population; it is not a simple matter to find one that is placing proper emphasis on prevention, and reflects, in its program, the understanding that there are major forces in the way people live that affect their health. These are the problems which public health must address in the future by encompassing the whole area of the environment, patterns of living, and opportunities for the full development of human beings both physically and mentally.[2]

Obviously, Sheps was sketching in broad terms a mandate for the entire field of public health, while the focus of nursing is primarily on two of its components—the promotion of health-related behaviors and the provision of personal health services to members of populations or communities. His comments, however, raise several questions: Why is it unusual to see evidence of public health practice? How would a personal health program that is consistent with a public health philosophy differ from one that is not? And, finally, why isn't there more evidence of personal health programming in which clinical and community dimensions have been appropriately merged?

Despite the fact that it is not easy to change or improve the environment, such efforts may be easier to conceptualize at the community level than are personal health service programs. The need, the relevance—indeed, the potential—in personal health service programs for obtaining group-level data—by conducting a community diagnosis, for instance, or monitoring the health status over time of those receiving care in a particular program—appear to be less obvious. Yet, if the concept of public health practice is to have meaning in the area of personal health care services, it must be operationalized in relevant and viable practice terms which are clear to all.

One approach is to develop an epidemiology in practice orientation similar to that described by Kark.[3] Such an orientation stresses the need to anticipate and estimate the extent of personal health problems at the community level, without limiting the problem definition to only those subgroups seeking care. Such programs, it is suggested, should have a scientific basis and thus reflect what is known about the natural history of the problems being addressed. Further, such an approach demands a continuing surveillance of the delivery system—the types of services given, to whom, and at what points in the natural history of the problem—just as the status of an individual patient would be monitored. And it also suggests that the relationship between services provided and health status changes, both in those served and in the overall target population, should be assessed.

That it *is* possible to take an aggregate approach with personal health service programs is attested to by the following examples.

Many agencies have difficulty in estimating the relationship between those who need a service and those who are already receiving the service. Unfortunately, most agencies simply accept those who are referred to them, without considering the biases operating in the referral system which may bring to attention only a subset of those in need. Another difficulty lies in obtaining an estimate of the need for prevention or for help in maintaining function, rather than an estimate of the requirements for care after an illness event.

In order to deal with these problems, a county health department in the midwest conducted a community diagnosis as a first step in restructuring its nursing services.[4] Through a systematic, rigorous survey of a sample carefully chosen to be representative of community residents 65 years and older, staff were able to document the status of this population in terms of health conditions as reported, physical functioning, social isolation, and accessibility of medical care. On the basis of these diagnostic data, they projected that their services were reaching only about 25 percent of the people in that age group who could potentially profit from them. And because of other data gathered, they were able to estimate where those in greatest need could be found. These data are being used in restructuring and refocusing the nursing program.

POPULATIONS AT RISK

In another county health department, the focus was on a school population.[5,6] The services provided to school children were a responsibility of the department's public health nursing staff. Because of time limitations, however, and with the exceptions of hearing and vision programs, the nurses' school-related responsibilities were frequently limited to one-time episodic encounters with individual children referred by teachers or principals or occasionally self-referred. Response to such service needs may be necessary; however, persisting in these activities would result in an unbalanced program, with insufficient preventive services. Further, children with problems unidentified by the teacher, principal, or themselves often did not come to the attention of the nurse at all. Aware of this fact, the health department decided to continue the usual services provided to the schools while also conducting a pilot program that was preventive in nature and directed to a defined group of children.

How could children with needs or at risk of developing problems be identified? Industrial studies have shown that a small proportion of persons are responsible for the majority of illness in work groups.[7] Further, a recent school study indicated that a good predictor of a pupil's future absences is his previous year's absence record.[8] The significant point here is that at least 80 percent of school absences have been found to be for health reasons.[9,10] It was therefore decided that identification of children with a high record of absences would be a reasonable way of defining a group who would be at high risk for future episodes of illness and absence and who, as a group, might have more basic health problems than children with a history of low absence. And it was further decided that this was a group to whom nursing services could be profitably directed.

In order to evaluate the services, the design of the program called for a comparison of results in one population to those in a control population. Two groups of high absence children comparable in factors thought to be associated with absence experience were therefore selected. One group received professional nursing services, the control group did not, and the results were documented in terms of change in absence status.

At the beginning of the school year, the nurses assigned to the experimental groups made a family-centered assessment of each high absence pupil as soon as possible. In the process, the nurses were expected to assess and identify possible explanations for the previous year's absence, determine the child's current health status, and assist the family in recognizing and coping with problems or situations which might result in future difficulties.

On completion of the study, it was found that (1) children with high absence records had many needs for preventive and corrective action; (2) the difference in absence experienced between the two groups had meaning both statistically and practically; and (3) while about 99 percent of the 302 children in the experimental group actually received services only 12 or 3.9 percent of the 302 children in the control group ever came to the attention of the nurse. In other words, if one accepts the notion that high absence children are a group with either problems or potential problems, it is interesting that where there was not an explicit attempt to identify such children, only a small proportion came to the attention of the nurse.

Clearly, the preceding examples demonstrate movement toward systematic community health practice in the area of personal health services. In both cases there was a conscious focus on aggregates or subpopulations, which served to direct clinical care services.

An example of the benefits derived from targeting services to a specific group is suggested from data generated in a midwifery project.[11] The project, which served the segment of a community who contributed greatly to the community's overall prematurity and infant mortality rates (those who utilized the county hospital in which the program was based), reported important favorable changes in rates for those who delivered at the county hospital. However, a year after termination of the nurse-midwifery services the county neonatal mortality rate showed a dramatic increase to 30.0 (per 1,000 live births) from 17.6 during the last year of the program. This shift in county-level rates suggests that the subpopulation in the county contributing the most to high rates is the subpopulation the program served.

In summary, much more attention needs to be given to the distinction between diagnosis, treatment, and evaluation at the individual patient level (the focus of clinical nursing) and at the aggregate level (the focus of public health). And, after acknowledging the distinction, we need to consider carefully what it means to think in aggregate terms and how clinical and aggregate approaches interrelate.

Such thinking is not only the route to more effective service, which is directed to those most likely to benefit, but it is necessary if we are to implement appropriate priorities for clinical practice. In addition, this type of thinking is necessary for the development and effective use of a knowledge base for practice—that is, the appropriate generation and application of research findings. Finally, such an approach is essential to meaningful collaboration with other disciplines and to the actualization of leadership in health care delivery.

COMMUNITY HEALTH PRACTICE SKILLS

Although a group orientation is an essential feature of public health, other characteristics also distinguish community health practice from clinical orientations. For instance, careful consideration must be given to the health status of *many* aggregates. These aggregates may be defined in various ways—infants during their first year, expectant mothers, children of school age, the older population, or those who have just experienced the death of a spouse. A public health orientation demands attention to multiple and sometimes overlapping aggregates as opposed to concern for only one or two specific subgroups, as in the case of clinical specialties such as midwifery or pediatrics.

Further, if practice is to be consistent with public health philosophy, attention must be given to the influence of environmental factors (physical, biological, and sociocultural) on the health of populations, and priority must be given to preventive and health maintenance strategies over curative strategies.

The skills necessary to deal with aggregates, particularly multiple aggregates, are different from those needed for clinical practice. Although some persons may be prepared to function effectively at both levels, it is questionable how realistic such an expectation could be. In the past, failure to recognize this distinction has led to neglect or merely superficial development of skills for dealing with decision making at the aggregate level. Learning these skills is as demanding and time-consuming as developing advanced clinical skills. Therefore, within service settings, it seems reasonable to have both types of skills represented on the staff. Since it may be impossible to have both types of skills in the same person, then communication and collaboration among the staff should be emphasized.

The examples used in this paper focused on the application of selected analytical and measurement skills in both epidemiology and biostatistics to programming for the delivery of personal health services. However, as the following recommendation on higher education for public health points out, such skills represent only one of several deemed essential for public health practice.

> In order to produce professional personnel with the appropriate knowledge, skills, and perspective so that they might deal effectively with the new challenges in public health, all institutions providing higher education for public health should build their educational programs on the unique knowledge base for public health. This combines the three elements central and generic to public health with content from many related fields such as medicine and other patient care disciplines; economics, political science, and sociology; biology and the physical sciences. The elements central to public health are the measurement and analytic sciences of epidemiology and biostatistics; social policy and the history and philosophy of public health; and the principles of management and organization for public health. This knowledge base may be modified and expanded with changes in the nature and scope of health problems and the techniques used to deal with them, but an appropriate mix of its central elements with selected related fields is crucial to the effectiveness of any program of higher education for public health.[12]

From a service perspective, it is clear that if nurses are going to have a meaningful role in making policy decisions that deal with aggregates and thus share in determining the boundaries within which direct care providers shall function, nursing educators must give attention to turning out graduates with skill in one of the three areas central to public health practice. Historically, graduate nursing programs in both schools of nursing and of public health have offered programs in nursing administration and nursing supervision. Yet it can be argued that those programs have not given sufficient attention to such matters as policy analysis and development and the use of epidemiology in making practice decisions.

What about the future? Although I did not intend to carve out a specialty area for community health nursing, the potential of approaches long associated with public health practice indicate a need for a broader perspective in the preparation of nurses at the graduate level. In addition to programs to prepare direct care providers such as nurse practitioners, much more attention must be given to the preparation of nurses at the master's and doctoral levels whose focus will be on aggregate level decision-making. Although not completely separate, the two types of skills are different.

Further, just as direct care clinicians may concentrate on the care of one type of patient defined in terms of age or problems, those preparing for aggregate decision making may focus on developing one of the variety of skills necessary at that level. In addition, there is a serious need for (1) providing core content in the aggregate level skills for those focusing on preparing for specific clinical roles, and (2) developing practice models which clearly demonstrate effective collaboration between clinical approaches and strategies for dealing with aggregates. This is necessary if nursing is to prepare a cadre of professionals who have not only developed skill in their own areas of decision making but who appreciate the context of their practice and can work in a complementary manner with others.

REFERENCES

1. Kark, S. *Epidemiology and Community Medicine.* New York: Appleton-Century-Crofts, 1974. P. 319.
2. Sheps, C. G. Crisis in Schools of Public Health: The Issues. *The Body Politic* (School of Public Health at the University of North Carolina, Chapel Hill) 2:3, 1974.
3. Kark, *op. cit.*
4. Managan, D., et al. Older Adults: A Community Survey of Health Needs. *Nurs. Res.* 23:426, 1974.
5. Tuthill, R. W., et al. Evaluating a School Health Program Focused on High Absence Pupils: A Research Design. *Am. J. Public Health* 62:40, 1972.
6. Long, G. V., et al. Evaluation of a School Health Program Directed to Children with History of High Absence: A Focus for Nursing Intervention. *Am. J. Public Health* 65:388, 1975.
7. Hinkle, L. E., Jr., et al. Continuity of Patterns of Illness and the Prediction of Future Health. *J. Occup. Med.* 3:417, 1961.
8. Roberts, D. E., et al. Epidemiological Analysis in School Populations as a Basis for Change in School Nursing Practice. *Am. J. Public Health* 59:2157, 1969.
9. Rogers, K. D., and Reese, G. Health Studies—Presumably Normal High School Students: 2. Absence from School. *Am. J. Dis. Child* 109:9, 1965.
10. School Absenteeism. *Stat. Bull.* (Metropolitan Life) 31:4, 1950.
11. Levy, B. S., et al. Reducing Neonatal Mortality Rate with Nurse-Midwives. *Am. J. Obstet. Gynecol.* 109:53, 1971.
12. Milbank Memorial Fund. *Commission on Higher Education for Public Health.* Cecil G. Sheps, Chairman,. New York. Prodist, 1976, Recommendation No. 3. pp. 74–75.

CHAPTER **2**

The Social Mandate and Historical Basis for Nursing's Role in Health Promotion

Julie Cowan Novak, RN, MA, CPNP, DNSc

Nursing is concerned with the adaptation of individuals and groups to actual as well as potential health problems, the environments that influence the individual's health, and the nursing interventions that promote health.[1] Schlotfeldt[2] defines nursing as "assessing and enhancing the general health status, health assets, and health potentials of human beings." Both definitions of nursing emphasize the promotion of health, which is defined by Pender[3] "as activities directed toward developing resources of clients that maintain or enhance well being and self actualization." Nursing's renewed emphasis on health promotion had its roots in the teachings of Florence Nightingale. However, in the 20th century, this unique concern was preempted by an illness orientation that was dependent on other professions for existence and on hospitals for training (education) and sustenance. This article documents the social mandate and historical basis for nursing's role in health promotion from the mid-19th century to the present.

Florence Nightingale's Views on Health Promotion

Historians acknowledge Florence Nightingale as the founder of modern nursing and one of the world's greatest humanitarians.[4] Nursing's tradition of espousing health promotion is directly attributable to her. She clearly articulated nursing's practice domain.[5] Nursing's basic philosophy was defined by Nightingale[6] as "the same laws of health or of nursing, for they are in reality the same, obtain among the well as among the sick. . . ." She believed nurses must put the patient in the best condition for nature to act upon him or her.[7] Nightingale identified basic principles of nursing, such as creating those conditions in which the restoration and preservation of health and the prevention of disease and injury were possible.[4] She stated that "health is not only to be well, but to use well every power that we have."[6] She perceived the nurse as the key to establishing a healthy, disease-free citizenry. "She visualized the nurse as primary care agent, the nation's first bulwark in health maintenance, in the promotion of wellness, and in the prevention of disease."[4] Nightingale stated, "One duty of every nurse certainly is prevention."[6]

Nightingale's early interest in the prevention of disease transmission among the troops of the Crimea raised important questions about the impact of the environment and the prevention of ill health in the nonaffected. When she was called to the Crimean War in 1854 by Sir Sidney Herbert, the British Secretary of State for War, the death rate in the military hospitals was 42 per cent. In six months, she, her group of nurses, and others, including the Sanitary

Reprinted from *Journal of Professional Nursing,* Vol. 4, No. 2, with permission of W.B. Saunders Co. © 1988.

Commission, had reduced the death rate to 2.2 per cent.[8] She established programs directly affecting the health and welfare of the British soldiers. The initiation of effective laundry, housing, nutrition, physical fitness, and recreational facilities for the British soldiers was among her far reaching reforms. Her Crimean experience forged her belief in the value of cleanliness into a "rigid, inflexible dogma of sanitation."[4] She proposed that nursing was a significant way to improve the health of the British population, which was the source of the British Army.[9]

In her writings on rural nursing, Nightingale, an early proponent of health as a rightful sphere for women, contended that "since God did not mean mothers to be always accompanied by doctors the health of the nation depended on womankind, that women should be instructed in the 'art of health' and the person to best accomplish this instruction was the nurse in the home."[7] She wrote of the importance of teaching the cottage mothers specific, proper sanitation methods, and she discussed child health teaching that could be done by the "health missioners" under the supervision of the district nurse. She spoke of the importance of removing the things that cause disease: dirt, drink, diet, damp draughts, drains. She demonstrated a knowledge of child development, a field not yet in existence, with her statement that "a child learns before it is three whether it shall obey its mother or not. And before it is seven its character is a good way to being formed."[8]

Nightingale's concern for all aspects of environmental health was exemplified when she advocated, "As for the workshops, work people should remember health is their only capital, and they should come to an understanding among themselves not only to have the means to secure pure air in their places of work, which is one of the prime agents of health. Denial would be worth a 'trade union,' almost worth a strike."[8]

Nursing's Social Mandate for Health Promotion

In the latter part of the 19th century, three forces stimulated interest in community health throughout Western Europe and the New World. First among these movements was a deepening consciousness and a spirit of reformism on the part of social philanthropists to the problems affecting the lives of many people. Social problems such as poverty, inadequate housing, evils of the industrial revolution, child labor, deplorable prison conditions, and lack of opportunity for education for the general public were paramount. Another major force was the development of medicine from an emphasis on cure to the beginnings of disease prevention. The third significant movement was the development of nursing as a profession and a discipline.[4] Brainerd[10] asserted that the "new humanity" taught disease is not a visitation from an angered God but is the result of people's own carelessness in not following the right principles of hygiene, sanitation, and healthful living.

In the 18th century, health care in the original colonies was provided by wives and mothers in their own homes and by untrained servants in hospitals.[5] Lemuel Shattuck (1793-1859) was an early American public health reformer and a former teacher who sold books. In 1842, he was instrumental in achieving the passage of a law in Massachusetts that resulted in statewide registration of vital statistics. In 1845, he compiled and published a census of Boston that encouraged and stimulated accurate reporting of statistics in the United States. His census presented the shocking facts of a high mortality rate with an extremely high infant and maternal mortality rate.[11]

Shattuck's greatest achievement came in 1850, when his report was published by the Massachusetts Sanitary Commission.[11] The Shattuck Report, one of the first public health documents in the United States, was an important milestone in the evaluation of the field of public health. It earned Shattuck the title, Father of Public Health. He recommended state and local health departments or boards of health be organized, he established the need for sanitary surveys, and he recommended that Massachusetts General Hospital and other similar institutions educate nurses to care for the sick.[11] There was no immediate societal response to the recommendation about educating nurses, although there had been earlier efforts to train women as nurses. American-trained nurses emerged as a formalized system of work in 1873, as part of the reform era that followed the Civil War.[12] Many socially responsive upper-class reformers, with the leadership of Shattuck and others, enhanced an upsurge in the social consciousness during a period of enormous social change in America. The events of the previous ten years—the Crimean War, the educational endeavors of Florence Nightingale, and the Civil War with the development of the Sanitary Commission in 1861—had also focused attention on the necessity for nurses and on the importance of an educational system in which to prepare them (Palmer I, personal communication, 1987).

Early images of public health nurses, conducting infant immunization clinics, case finding, and providing health education for the prevention of tuberculosis and other diseases are also part of nursing's rich heritage in health promotion. In the United States, visiting nursing began its development in Philadelphia in 1839.[13] In 1877, the Women's Branch of the New York City Mission sent its first trained nurses into the homes of the indigent. In 1890, 21 cities used visiting nurses.[8] By 1892 the Nurse's Settlement House in New York City was serving people from all socioeconomic and ethnic groups. In 1892, because of a large volume, the Settlement House was moved to Henry Street with the help of philanthropist Jacob Schiff and others. Soon nine graduate nurses were living at Henry Street, including Lavinia Dock.[14] In the first five years, the staff at Henry Street, led by Lillian Wald and Mary Brewster, cared for over 196,000 persons.[15]

The extensive absenteeism of children from school due to illness and their readily correctible health problems led Lillian Wald in 1902 to conduct a school nurse experiment. Wald believed that nurses could help improve the health and attendance of school children.[16] School nursing was institutionalized soon thereafter. Statistical comparison of the numbers of students excluded with communicable disease in the New York City Schools before and after the hiring of school nurses revealed a 90 per cent decrease in the number of necessary exclusions.[17] This experiment had a dramatic impact on the school budget at the time and still has implications today.

By 1909, the Henry Street Settlement had grown from two nurses to a large organization with many departments.[18] In the same year, at the suggestion of Wald, who was concerned with the health of the worker, the Metropolitan Life Insurance Company organized its Visiting Nurse Department and entered into an agreement with the Henry Street Settlement. After a successful three-month trial period, policy holders in 14 cities were receiving the services of the visiting nurses. By 1912, 589 Metropolitan Nursing Centers were established[8] for the purpose of preventing disability or premature death. These programs continued after World War II, when changing social, economic, and health conditions made them no longer feasible. Many communities, however, had learned the value of nursing services and took over their support through public and private means.

Progressive reform also steered public health fervor toward an intense concern for child welfare. The 1909 White House conference produced disturbing data on infant and maternal mortality rates in the United States. It was estimated that 300,000 children under one year of age died each year in the United States, and at least half of these deaths were preventable. By 1910, milk stations for the distribution of clean, safe milk existed in 31 cities. From milk dispensaries, these stations often evolved into health promotion centers as the emphasis on health education and screening examinations grew.[8]

The public's concern with disease control and the widely accepted germ theory spawned a number of lay organizations that took up battle against single diseases. These associations offered new opportunities in health promotion. Antivenereal disease campaigns stressed health education, case finding, and treatment. Public health reformers began to shift attention from the larger urban environment to the home setting.

Restraining legislation for child labor was also initiated. The Children's Bureau, founded in 1912 through Lillian Wald's influence, gave organizational form and tax funding to child welfare services.[19] Later that year, the National Organization of Public Health Nursing was formed with Wald as its first president.

The growing sense of social injustice was exemplified in the development of the Red Cross at the Geneva Convention, and the establishment of the American Red Cross in 1881 led to the care of the sick at home. In 1912, at Lillian Wald's suggestion, the Red Cross established a rural nursing service to provide nurses to care for the sick and to give instruction in sanitation and hygiene in the homes of people living in rural areas. Wald secured financial support for this program. As a result of these health promotion efforts, areas served by rural nurses showed decreases in infant mortality and the general death rate, as well as improvements in sanitation, hygiene, and nutrition.[8]

Industrial nursing was also created at the turn of the century. In 1895, Proctor, the Governor of Vermont, who held a high regard for visiting nursing services, introduced "district nursing" into several villages whose residents comprised employees of his Vermont Marble Company. In its early form, industrial nursing placed minimal emphasis on the care of injuries, but rather stressed health promotion activities implemented in the employees' homes.[20]

By 1912, the public health nursing movement could look with pride to two decades of major impact on the health of the nation's citizens. Because of their efforts, there were significant declines in the incidence of tuberculosis, diarrheal diseases of children, and typhoid fever—campaigns in which public health nurses had played an active role.

Inadequate maternity care and actions taken to improve this care greatly influenced the development of nurse-midwifery in this country.[21] In 1910, nurse Margaret Sanger began her historic fight for the right of families to limit their size, the rights of women to health care and personal choice, and the rights of children to be loved and wanted. Sanger[22] stated, "The first right of every child is to be wanted—to be desired with an intensity of love that gives it its title of being and joyful impulse of life." In 1916, Sanger organized the Planned Parenthood Foundation of America, which established hundreds of family planning centers throughout the United States.[21]

The War Effort

Although involvement in World War I checked most progressive health reform, it gave the movement a message of urgency. The health status of recruits provided a snapshot of the health of the nation. Physical examination of these recruits on induction revealed that 29 per cent were physically unfit for military duty. Epidemiologic studies revealed a high rejection rate from rural areas due to a higher incidence of tuberculosis and typhoid.[19] The war also spurred efforts to confront venereal disease, with ever vigilant public health nurses playing the major role in case finding. At the time, the incidence of gonorrhea was estimated to be in the range of 40 to 60 per cent in the entire male population. In response to this staggering finding, Congress passed the Chamberlain-Kahn Act of 1918, which provided funding to state-administered programs of education, case finding, and treatment.[19]

Adelaid Nutting, Annie Goodrich, and Lillian Wald met in 1917 to determine methods of providing effective nursing service to the military. Twenty-two thousand nurses entered the nursing corps from 1917 to 1919. Goodrich[15] wrote if this number could be "encompassed for the service of preventive medicine, one might predict as remarkable an influence upon community health, as the introduction barely a half a century ago of the service of the student nurse into the hospital."[16] Although nurses would never forget the nightmare of treating mass casualties of the fighting and diseases abroad, as well as the influenza epidemic at home, they would remember their crucial battles to save lives and "lighten the toll of war and pestilence."[8]

Health Promotion in the 1920s and 1930s

During the 1920s, the primary duties of the public health nurse moved to advising and instructing people on how to avoid illness through personal hygiene. Large-scale health demonstrations, supported by philanthropic foundations, insurance companies, or state funds, provided intensive programs of health education. The goal was to impress upon communities the importance of health promotion so that the program might be permanently adopted by the demonstration community. In 1921, Congress passed the Sheppard-Towner Act for federal aid for maternal and child health.[21] The funding was distributed nationwide through the state departments of health. Supporters of the bill reminded their audiences that 29 per cent of military inductees were unfit for military service and pointed out that healthy children would grow into healthy adults, the mothers and soldiers of the next generation. This approach, reminiscent of Nightingale's, was successful and resulted in organized prenatal and infant care programs in 45 states.

This constituency provided an excellent audience for the health promotion message. The focus on child rearing gave nurses access to entire families, which improved opportunities for case finding and health education. As a result, maternal and infant welfare programs became the primary activity of public health nurses through the 1920s and 1930s. Throughout the lifetime of this legislative act, three million home visits were made to 700,000 expectant mothers and four million infants. The infant mortality rate dropped from 100/1000 live births in 1915 to 69/1000 live births in 1926. Opposition to the program was led by Senator Reed of Missouri and others, who were supported by the American Medical Association. These opponents asserted that the program was "unsound in policy, wasteful, extravagant, and promoted communism" (Palmer I, personal communication, 1986). Sadly, the program was not renewed after the Congress allowed it to lapse in 1929.[8]

In 1925, Mary Breckenridge, a nurse-midwife, organized the Frontier Nursing Service in southeastern Kentucky. Because no quality nurse midwifery programs were available in the United States until the 1930s, the early nurses received their training in England and Scotland. The nurse-midwives gave antepartal, intrapartal, and postpartal care and provided child health visits. During these visits, diet, cleanliness, sanitation, and preventive care were discussed. In 1932, Dr. Louis Dublin,[23] of Metropolitan Life, studied the first 1000 deliveries of the Frontier Nursing Service. He concluded that none of the women had died as a direct result of pregnancy or labor. The two deaths in the series were secondary to chronic heart disease. He asserted, "If such a service were available to the women of the country there would be a saving of 10,000 mothers' lives a year in the United States; there would be 30,000 less stillbirths and 30,000 children alive at the end of the first month of life."[23]

Unemployment, increasing rapidly after the stock market crash of 1929, created a major relief problem in the United States. In 1930, almost four million people were unemployed, and the failure of over 1400 banks by 1932 created major financial crises. People, including nurses, had no money for food, clothing, shelter, or health care. Payment for nursing care in the home was recognized as a legitimate relief expenditure under the Federal Emergency Relief Administration (FERA) in consultation with the United States Public Health Service. In West Virginia, the Relief Nursing Service began in 1933 to meet the nursing care needs of families on relief and to meet the employment needs of nurses. This was essentially a visiting nurse program. Fundamental services included bedside nursing care, health supervision for the family, arrangement of medical and hospital care for emergencies and obstetrical cases, health supervision of children in relief nurseries, and caring for patients with tuberculosis. In many counties, classes were offered in parenting, home care, and first aid.[8]

The Social Security Act of 1935 and its amendments in succeeding years included provisions for public assistance, social services, and a means of strengthening family life. The provisions affected maternal and child health programs throughout the country, rural and urban. A number of nurses who were involved in the work relief projects were eager to acquire formal public health training. During the first year of the Social Security program, 1100 nurses received stipends to study at universities offering public health nursing programs. In 1934, only 7 per cent of the more than 5000 employed public health nurses had completed an approved postgraduate program. Within two years after the implementation of the Social Security Act, 2304 public health nurses received postgraduate training in public health nursing.[8]

With the heightened attention to health promotion and preventive care, nurses aligned with the public health movement looked toward a promising future. The traditional conception of nursing as Christian service was recalled. One manual urged nurses to lead the great procession toward the "promised land of municipal health." During this era, public health nurses described their relationships with patients in terms reminiscent of traditional private duty nurses' sense of womanly duty and intimate involvement with patients.[24] The language also reflected the growing professionalism of reform. Nurses sought a more scientific method, a rational approach to the goal of better health. In its funding and philosophy, health promotion programs moved from their charitable origins toward a view of health as a concern of the state, a method of ensuring national productivity and security.[19] Manuals emphasized health education as the special contribution of the public health nurse, minimizing the traditional tasks of bedside nursing:

"The nurse who tends the sick only, and teaches nothing and prevents nothing, is abortive in her work."[24]

Public health nurses and private physicians were divided by fundamentally different social visions. Many physicians clung to a paternalistic approach to reform. The 1934 National Organization of Public Health Nursing survey explored physician's objections to public health programs. The data revealed that medical resistance was strongest against staff-supported boards of education. School nurses attended to students of all income levels, arousing the doctors' age-old fears of competition for the health care dollar. School nursing programs, funded by local governments, were also a red flag to physicians. Doctors reacted more favorably to visiting nurses associations, which serve predominantly poor clientele, dependent on private sources of funding, and frequently based on standing orders from physicians.[25]

The 1920s and 1930s was a time of delicate balance for public health nurses. The distance of public health from mainstream medicine had revealed opportunities. The success of the public health movement undermined its special character in the 1940s and 1950s. As public health became more acceptable, it was absorbed into the growing hospital system and into the philosophy of mainstream curative medicine. With this cooptation in public health, many nurses lost autonomy; they were forced to return to subordinate positions in a bureaucratic system of delivery.[19] Once powerful, nursing departments of public health were absorbed into the larger umbrella department of health under physician control.

The Nation's Health in the 1940s

During the period from 1923 to 1943, the average life expectancy in the United States rose from 55 to 65 years. The average newborn baby could expect to live a decade longer than a child born during World War I. Despite this achievement, the results of the local Selective Service Boards and induction centers indicated that the health of the nation's young men was no better at the start of World War II than it had been during World War I.[8]

World War II, like World War I, led to centralization of medical services in support of the military. Servicemen's families became eligible for a broad program of maternity and infant care. In 1941, an emergency health and sanitation bill was passed that provided funds to supplement public health nursing services for the families of workers in major defense industries.[8] Nurses played important roles both at home and abroad throughout World War II.

Federal Mandate for Health Promotion

Recent trends in legislation at the national level are part of the press and priority both nurses and our nation face in the current and coming century. A national agenda identifies goals of reducing morbidity and premature mortality in all age groups. Nursing's heritage in health promotion has affected our current health priorities. It is from history that we gain our vision and mission of our future. Green[26] organized recent history into four eras of federal investment in health. Era one, the 1940s and 50s, was characterized by resource development with federal government resources such as personnel, facilities, and knowledge. Personnel were developed through the provision of the health manpower and public health manpower training acts and facilities development through the Hill-Burton Act. Emphasis was on medical or disease care, not health care or health promotion. Knowledge was developed through the establishment of the National Institutes of Health in 1945. Today, the National Institutes of Health constitute the most powerful and most generously budgeted institution within the Public Health Service. Once again, however, knowledge development within this institution was primarily biomedical.[26] The dominant medical ideology in the United States in the 40 years following World War II has focused on cure rather than prevention or health promotion.

Era two, the 1960s, was an age of ferment, with the federal government fighting poverty with visions of a Great Society.[26] Emphasis turned to redistribution of resources. Medicare and Medicaid were passed, greatly improving the health-purchasing power of the poor and medically indigent. Neighborhood health centers sprang up, and "comprehensive" health planning occurred along with comprehensive mental health centers. This was an era of consumer involvement and consumer advisory groups. Era two inflated the medical (not health) care dollar higher than the general inflation rate.[26]

Cost containment is central to the third era, the 1970s and 80s, as health care is big business in the United States.[26] "Capping" medical care spending has become a primary objective. The significance of patient education was rediscovered in the 1970s as an alternative regulatory approach to cost containment. In 1971, the President's Commission on Health Education was appointed to advise the Administration on health education. Multiple task forces and committees between 1972 and 1976 culminated in the passage of the National Health Information and Health Promotion Act of 1976.[26] In the same era, the Health Maintenance Organization Act was passed, which specified that preventive and educational services were formally required for health maintenance organizations receiving federal certification. Again, in 1971, the President's Commission on Health Education recommended the establishment of the National Center for Health Education.[27] In 1974, the National Health Planning and Resource Development Act declared public health education a national health priority. The Office of Health Information and Health Promotion in the Department of Health, Education, and Welfare was established by PL-317. Interestingly, a century ago, Florence Nightingale advocated health education for the public, control and prevention of disease, sanitation, and the institutionalization of health agencies as a governmental obligation.

During the 1970s, the maturation of nursing saw a growing emphasis on theory development, research, and doctoral education. A developing segment of the profession saw itself as entirely different from the nurse of the previous era. No longer did they accept the widespread assumption that nursing was a lesser profession than medicine and subservient to it.[8]

An evolving role that placed an emphasis on health promotion, autonomy, and advanced education for nurses was that of the "nurse practitioner." This title was first used in a demonstration project at the University of Colorado, codirected by Loretta Ford, RN, and Henry Silver, MD. This grant-funded project was designed to prepare nurses to give comprehensive well-child care, to give anticipatory guidance and health promotion in ambulatory settings, and to make sophisticated clinical judgments when seeing children with common childhood illnesses.[28]

A study to evaluate the pediatric nurse practitioner program confirmed the value of the new role. By the late 1960s and early 1970s, nurse practitioners had assumed national visibility to consumers, other health professionals, and legislators. Practice patterns regained some of the autonomy enjoyed by early public health nurses and the Frontier Nursing Service. As the movement gained momentum, Elliott Richardson, Secretary of the Department of Health, Education, and Welfare, requested a group of leaders in health care to examine the possibilities of nursing role expansion. The resulting report, Extending the Scope of Nursing Practice, concluded that enlarging the nurse's role was essential for providing equal access to health services for all citizens. The committee urged establishment of curricular innovations by health education centers and increased financial support for nursing education.[29]

Era four, the 1980s, is the era of disease prevention and health promotion in the United States.[26] Marked by the publications of Healthy People and Objectives for the Nation, this is the era of not only promise but also of fruition for primary health promotion in our country.[30] After years of a disease-oriented health care system in this country, nursing's ongoing commitment to health promotion is receiving increasing support due to consumer demand.

Conclusion

Nightingale's strong foundation, the impressive accomplishments of the public health nursing leaders, and extensive community nursing services, have all contributed to nursing's role in health promotion. Nursing's emphasis must be on comprehensive health promotion rather than on patchwork remedies.[31] Nursing is on its way toward becoming recognized as a well-defined, academic discipline whose practitioners are making significant contributions toward improving the health status of all persons, thus attaining the health objectives of the nation. The Surgeon General in 1980 asserted that half of the mortality in the United States is due to an unhealthy lifestyle. Our nation needs a cadre of professionals whose role is to appraise and enhance the health status, health assets, and health potentials of all humans.[32] Nurses are the health professionals to take that role.

Acknowledgment

The author thanks Irene Palmer, RN, PhD, University of San Diego Phillip Hahn School of Nursing, for her review and editorial assistance with this article.

REFERENCES

1. American Nurses' Association: Social Policy Statement. Kansas City, American Nurses' Association, 1980
2. Schlotfeldt R: Nursing in the future. Nurs Outlook 29:295-301, 1982
3. Pender N: Health promotion and illness prevention. *In* Werley H, and Fitzpatrick J (eds): Annual Review of Nursing Research. New York, Springer, 1984, p 84
4. Palmer I: From whence we came. *In* Chaska N (ed): The Nursing Profession: A Time to Speak. New York, McGraw-Hill, 1983
5. Schlotfeldt R: Critical issues in nursing practice, education, and research. Occup Health Nurs 32:11-16
6. Nightingale F: Notes on Nursing: What It Is and What It Is Not. London, Harrison, 1860
7. Seymer L: Selected Writings of Florence Nightingale. New York, MacMillan, 1954, pp 353-386
8. Kalisch P, Kalisch B: The Advance of American Nursing, ed 2. Boston, Little Brown & Co, 1986
9. Palmer I: Florence Nightingale: reformer, reactionary, researcher. Nurs Res 26:84-89, 1977
10. Brainerd A: The Evolution of Public Health Nursing. Philadelphia, Saunders, 1922, p 102
11. Shattuck L: Report of the Sanitary Commission of the State of Massachusetts. Boston, Massachusetts Sanitary Commission, 1850, p 228
12. Baer E: Nursing's divided house—an historical view. Nurs Res 34:32-38, 1985
13. Palmer I: Origins of the education of nurses. Nurs Forum 22:102-110
14. Wald L: Windows on Henry Street. Boston, Little, Brown & Company 1934
15. Goodrich A: The social and ethical significance of nursing. New York, MacMillan, 1932
16. Dock L: School nurse experiment in New York. Am J Nurs 2:108-110
17. Gardner M: Public Health Nursing, ed 2. New York, MacMillan, 1926
18. Wald L: House on Henry Street. New York, Holt, 1934
19. Melosh B: The Physician's Hand. Philadelphia, Temple University, 1982
20. Brown M: Nursing in occupational health. Public Health Rep 79:967-972, 1964
21. Varney H: Nurse Midwifery, ed 2. Boston, Blackwell, 1987
22. Sanger M: The New Motherhood. London, Jonathan Cape, 1922, p 58
23. Dublin L: The Effect of Life Conservation on the Mortality of the Metropolitan Life Insurance Company. New York, Metropolitan Life Insurance Company, 1917, p 11
24. Gardner M: Public Health Nursing, ed 3. New York, MacMillan, 1936
25. National Organization of Public Health Nursing: Survey of Public Health Nursing: Administration and Practice. New York, Commonwealth Fund, 1934, p 131
26. Green L: Emerging Federal Perspectives on Health Promotion. Health Promotion Monographs. New York, Teachers College, 1981, pp 11-13
27. Green L, Drueter M, Deeds S, et al: Health Education Planning: A Diagnostic Approach. Palo Alto, CA, Mayfield, 1980
28. Silver H, Ford L, Stearly S: A program to increase health care for children: the PNP program. Pediatrics 39: 756-760, 1967
29. Department of Health, Education, and Welfare: Extending the scope of nursing practice. Washington, DC, Department of Health, Education, and Welfare, HSM 73-2037, 1971
30. Surgeon General: Healthy People: The Surgeon General's Report on Health Promotion and Disease Prevention. Washington, DC, Department of Public Health and Human Service, 1980
31. Murray R, Zentner J: Nursing Concepts for Health Promotion. Englewood Cliffs, NJ, Prentice Hall, 1979, p 17
32. Schlotfeldt R: A brave new nursing world. AACN-NLN 82:1-13, 1982

CHAPTER **3**

The Ten Commandments of Health Care

Richard D. Lamm, LLB

An admiral in the navy was on the high seas when, all of a sudden, a little blip showed up on his ship's radar screen. The admiral told his ensign, "Tell that ship to change its course fifteen degrees." A message came back on the radio, "You change your course fifteen degrees." The admiral said, "Tell that ship that we're the United States Navy and to change its course by fifteen degrees." The word came back on the radio, "You change your course by fifteen degrees." At this, the admiral himself got on the radio and said, "I am an admiral in the United States Navy. Change your course fifteen degrees." The word came back, "You change your course fifteen degrees. I am a lighthouse."

It's a perfect parable, at least for my views. I believe the United States is heading for shoals. It's true that this can be prevented; we can change our course. But if we don't change our course, we are heading for shoals. The only way to really avoid those shoals is to take on some sacred cows, to address some political taboos, and to really get involved in some areas that in the past have been too sacrosanct. We must crawl into the no man's land of politics where, I believe, unfortunately, a lot of the solutions lie.

It's a vastly different America we are seeing right now from when people of my generation graduated from high school. When we graduated from high school, most of us took the generational baton from our parents, looked over our shoulders, and saw that there was nobody else in sight. The United States had 44 percent of the world's economy when I graduated from high school in 1953. When my son graduated from high school this past June, he got out to an America that is now the world's largest debtor nation. The United States has the slowest rate of productivity growth of any of the industrialized nations. Its politicians borrow twenty cents out of every federal dollar they spend. It has massive back debts. I believe very strongly that, if we are going to rejuvenate America, we must, in fact, deal with some of these sensitive subjects.

What types of things are we talking about? The average enlisted person in the military retires at the age of thirty-nine; the average officer retires at forty-three. Both retire with indexed pensions and health care coverage. You can't retire people at the age of thirty-nine when they live into their eighties! In the United States, incredible amounts of money are spent not only on service-connected disabilities but on nonservice-connected disabilities for veterans. Eleven cents out of every dollar in America is spent on health care. If capital is the stored flexibility we possess with which to build our children and our grandchildren a better life, then you have to look at where that capital goes. It's the Willie Sutton theory of bankrobbers: you go where the money is.

Consequently, like a lot of other people in public policy, I have simply looked at the health care area and

Reprinted from *The Humanist,* May/June 1987, with permission of the American Humanist Association.

asked, "How can we make it more efficient? Where is the money going? How do we use this capital that we have to build our children a better life?" It is my own personal opinion that my generation—those of us in our fifties and beyond—have been prodigal parents. I believe that, in fact, we have built up systems that are unsustainable for the indefinite future, whether it's pension systems, health care, or whatever else. To me, it is almost a moral issue: how can one generation heap that kind of burden and moral debt on another generation?

Schopenhauer says, "Every man confuses the limits of his mind with the limits of the world." Perhaps I do, too. But nevertheless, from the viewpoint of somebody who has been in public policy for twelve years and to illustrate my concern, I would like to offer you what I consider to be the "Ten Commandments of Health Care."

I. HUMANS CANNOT LIVE BY HEALTH CARE ALONE

Just as people cannot live by bread alone, a society cannot live by health care alone. But that is almost exactly where we seem to be going in the United States. We have other, desperately important functions in which we must invest to create the kind of world we want to leave for our children and our grandchildren. We must invest in education, infrastructure, and retooling America. Where are we going to get the jobs for our children? Yet, this problem is ignored while our whole system is tilting toward health care and toward the military.

When I entered high school in 1950, health care represented 45.9 percent of what our society spent on education. This past year, it was over 100 percent. We have many important things to do with our limited societal resources. Health care is certainly one of them, but it isn't the only one. Yet, it is the one to which we give so much precedence that it almost dominates all the others. One of the governors calls health care the Pac Man of his budget. In my opinion, like the fading southern family in a William Faulkner novel that takes sick and ceases to work, we are treating illness at the expense of our livelihood.

We spend more than a billion dollars a day for health care while our bridges are falling down, our teachers are underpaid, and our industrial plants are rusty. This simply can't continue. There is something fundamentally unsustainable about a society that moves its basic value-producing industries overseas yet continues to manufacture artificial hearts at home. We have money to give smokers heart transplants but no money to retool our steel mills. We train more doctors and lawyers than we need but fewer teachers. On any given day, 30 to 40 percent of the hospital beds in America are empty, but our classrooms are overcrowded and our transportation systems are deteriorating. We are great at treating sick people, but we are not very great at treating a sick economy. And we are not succeeding in international trade. When you really look around and try to find the industries the United States is succeeding in, you discover that they are very few and far between.

I believe one of the challenges of America's future is to invest our scarce resources wisely. To do this, we must be realistic, we must ask heretical questions, and we must question the sanctity of sacred cows. We simply cannot stand back and let one segment of our economy—no matter which one it is—dominate all the others. When you look at where America is spending its resources, you see health care.

Like the person who carries a first aid kit, the weight of which gives him or her blisters, our health care system has become part solution, part problem. We wouldn't want to be without it, but it has become a heavy burden. It is definitely interfering with the public's ability to invest in our public goods and with private industry's ability to retool itself. Health care insurance now costs U.S. corporations approximately $125 billion per year, which is 50 percent of their profits before taxes. That's money that is desperately needed elsewhere.

II. HONOR NOT ONLY THY DOCTOR AND THY HOSPITAL BUT THY PUBLIC HEALTH NURSE AND THY SEWAGE DISPOSAL PLANT WORKER

This is startling, perhaps, but, when you start looking at how you buy health for a society, you do not start with doctors and hospitals. With all due respect to doctors and hospitals, which are immensely important, there is little correlation between how much money is spent on doctors and hospitals and how healthy a society is. We are too easily seduced into thinking that health care means doctors and hospitals, when actually the great advances in health care have been made in sanitation, pasteurization, chlorination, and refrigeration. Screen windows to keep out mosquitoes were an incredible health advancement. Public health officials have saved more lives than hospitals.

If we look at how we can improve the health of the average American, we find a similar figure. The greatest causes of *premature* mortality, not of total mortality, are very simple: smoking, drinking too much, eating the wrong things, and not wearing a seat belt. If you really want to know how to make America healthy, start attacking those things. Those are four things an individual has within his or her control, and three of them are things you do with your mouth. The mouth is the most dangerous organ in the body.

It becomes clear that there are many paths to health, and certainly doctors and hospitals are one of them. I would rather have a dollar-per-pack tax on cigarettes than I would another $100 billion put into health care. The number of people in America who die from smoking is equivalent to the number who would be killed if a 747 crashed every day. Look at the alternatives available. Give me some of those empty hospital beds in return for locking up some drunk drivers and I'll save more lives than the hospitals would. A mandatory seat belt law would probably save more lives than most medical procedures.

America has to look at what it is getting for its money. The United States spends $2,000 per capita on health care, Great Britain spends $500 per capita, Singapore spends $200, and all three have the same mortality and morbidity rates. You're going to say that these figures don't include cataract operations and hip replacements, and you're right. But I'll tell you again, mortality and morbidity rates are an immensely important yardstick. There is an inverse correlation in our industrialized world between how many doctors there are and how healthy that society is. West Germany has the largest number of doctors per capita; they've got the worst health statistics. The Japanese have the least number of doctors per capita; they're the healthiest. There are many ways to attain health, and society has to look objectively and ask how we can get the most bang for our buck.

III. LOVE THY NEIGHBOR

But one cannot bankrupt America by giving to one's neighbor all of the medicine that is technologically available. We are not wealthy enough to base our health care system on the assumption that we can give everything that medical genius has invented to all of the people in our country. I believe strongly that the United States must ration medicine. We already ration health care. In the comic strip *Peanuts,* Linus says, "There's no issue so big you can't run away from it."

But the genius of medicine has outpaced America's ability to pay; *The Painful Presumption* by William Schwartz and Henry Aaron tells us that. Rudolf Klein, a very thoughtful observer from England, says, "Rationing is inherent under any health care system." Representatives from Oregon Health Decisions, a statewide health policy group, say:

> We cannot live under the idea that we can give everybody all the health care that they need. Rationing of health care is inevitable because society cannot or will not pay for all of the services modern medicine can provide. People in this state must search their hearts and their pocketbooks and decide what level of health care can be guaranteed to the poor, the unemployed, the elderly, and others who depend upon publicly funded health services.

They point out that we already ration medicine. We ration it chronologically, economically, geographically, politically, scientifically, and by disease.

In short, rationing is not a future possibility—it is a present reality. The ancient Greeks said, "To know all to ask is to know half." I believe that, if we start asking the right questions, we vastly improve our chances of coming up with the right answers. If we ask ourselves how to avoid rationing, I believe that we do our society an injustice. If we ask how we might allocate finite resources to meet an infinite demand and do it compassionately and justly, then I believe we can increase rather than decrease medical care in our most basic areas. In short, rationing can be described in the same words Mark Twain used about Wagner's music: "It's not as bad as it sounds."

IV. SPEND THY HEALTH MONEY WHERE IT WILL BUY THE MOST HEALTH CARE

I believe very strongly that in certain instances we are looking for ways to maximize our health care dollars. Humana Hospital's budget for the artificial heart is roughly equivalent to what society spent on eradicating smallpox. Consider the difference between the two. The fact is, we have a system that seems to give the health care dollar to highly dramatic technology while a third of the children in America have never seen a dentist and 20 percent of them haven't had their polio shots. In 1982, the Robert Wood Johnson Foundation found that 12 percent of all Americans—one in eight—have serious problems with access to health care. In the same year, the foundation also found that one million families had at least one member who had been refused health care.

Lester Thurow talks about an exercise for doctors in which every time an expensive procedure is ordered, the doctor responsible for making such an order would have to pick an American worker to be sentenced to a period of slavery long enough to pay the medical bill for that procedure. Victor Fuchs suggests that physicians have always practiced within constraints and, as long as rationing was implicit, they were tolerant. Rationing at the individual patient's bedside can continue to remain implicit if the patient-physician-family nucleus has accepted the economic, social, and moral importance of national restraint. All of society must understand that we can't do everything for everybody. Theologian Harvey Cox says, "Not to decide is to decide." So, in fact, by avoiding these issues, we *are* deciding.

V. NEITHER OVER-DOCTOR NOR OVER-LAWYER SOCIETY

Forty percent of the Rhodes Scholars in this country go to law school. Japan trains one thousand engineers for every one hundred lawyers. We train one thousand lawyers for every one hundred engineers. Which society in a technologically based, information-based market is going to succeed? The one that trains lawyers? I've read a little bit of history and I have yet to find an example in history in which a nation has sued its way to greatness. But the same thing applies to the field of medicine. It is estimated that there may be as many as 145,000 more physicians than needed by the year 2000. A study by Duke University points out the fact that every excess doctor, or every doctor in practice, increases the nation's health care costs by $300,000 annually. Thus, on an average career spanning forty years, a single physician would create health care costs of some $12 million. We've got to limit the number of people going into medicine and law.

Likewise, defensive medicine hangs like a sword of Damocles over the medical profession. Hospital bankruptcies in a lot of areas in America ought to be put under the "Good News Today" column of the newspapers. There are 200,000 excess hospital beds in the United States. That's equivalent to at least 1,000 hospitals out there that we don't need, that we've overbuilt. Some studies show that one-third of the people in hospital beds don't need to be there.

I really believe that there is no way we are going to come to grips with this problem until we also look at some of these areas that aren't going to go away. One of the toughest of these is what Victor Fuchs calls "flat-of-the-curve-medicine"—those medical procedures which are the highest in cost but achieve little or no improvement in health status. He says that they must be reduced or eliminated. We must demand that professional anxieties and licensing authorities establish norms and standards for diagnostic and therapeutic practice that encompass both costs and medicine. We're going to have to come up with some sort of concept of cost-effective medicine.

VI. DO NOT KILL NOR STRIVE OFFICIOUSLY TO KEEP ALIVE

We must look much more maturely at these sensitive issues. Victor Fuchs says that, in a number of areas, one of our assumptions is that we should spend any amount of money if a life is at stake. I governed a state that has many plane crashes because of its high mountains. There were 101 crashes in Colorado in

1985. Was I supposed to close the schools and penitentiaries and send people out looking for crash survivors because a life might be at stake? It sounds so good, but, in fact, when you're faced with that situation, what you have to do is the best you can. You must balance the tragedy to be averted with the resources available.

Consequently, I think we need to discuss death and dying much more candidly and openly. We treat death as if it were optional. People talk about the right to die as if they have the right to refuse to die. Shakespeare said, "We all owe God a death." Once we stop treating death as an enemy and start recognizing it as an inevitability, we can save massive resources. Today, patients with massive strokes are saved from death but live for years in a comatose state. Others with metastatic cancer are subject to a myriad of studies and therapies that add little to their longevity.

I think we must look rationally at the phenomenal amount of resources we spend on the last few weeks of people's lives, only to prolong suffering. We simply cannot afford a system in which, on the way out the door, we take $100,000 to $200,000 of our children's limited resources to give us a couple of extra days of pain-wracked existence. If you can make people better, terrific. But in American medicine, it often seems to be against the law to die in peace. Most elderly don't fear death as much as they do the pain and suffering and degradation and loss of economy that our Faustian bargains have brought to them.

VII. HONOR THY MOTHER AND FATHER, BUT ALSO HONOR THY CHILDREN

The way the whole health care system is slanted toward the benefit of my generation is another sensitive subject. When my wife and I bought our first home, our house payments were forty-nine dollars per month. A recent congressional study concluded that less than 50 percent of the people under thirty are going to be able to buy their own homes. I would suggest that one of the great issues of the future is going to be intergenerational equity. Our children are going to wake up one day and find out how badly we screwed things up.

I don't question the need to give both the young and the elderly access to preventative and primary care, but, when it comes to limited resources that cannot be made available to everyone, I approach the problem in a very personal way. I have a fifteen-year-old daughter. If there is a limited resource and you have to decide between my fifteen-year-old daughter and me, give it to my daughter. I'm not being a hero, but my daughter has 60.4 statistical years ahead of her and I have 28.1 statistical years ahead of me. Such a policy is not age discrimination; it's a common sense answer to the question of who should get any limited resources.

This leads me into the question of Medicare, an ultimate sacred cow. When Medicare was passed in 1965, the elderly were disproportionately poor. There was every good reason in Congress to vote for Medicare then. But the elderly are no longer disproportionately poor. In 1970, 23 percent of the elderly were poor and 12 percent of the children were poor. Today, 12 percent of the elderly are poor and 23 percent of the children are poor. Yet, we give 254,000 millionaires Medicare while we're closing well-baby clinics.

The aged are not a static group; it is a status through which we all will go one day. We cannot change our gender or our race, but we all age daily. In a marvelously egalitarian way, time takes its toll on all of us. The elderly are the same people—at a different stage of their lives—about whom we worry while we deny prenatal care to pregnant women. I believe we must weigh the marvels of our health care technologies against other less visible but more cost-effective strategies. Everybody pulls for the Barney Clarks and the Baby Fayes and the marvelous technology that helps them. But we don't hear about the 33 percent of American women who don't receive prenatal care in their first trimester. Stalin was horribly right when he said, "One man's death, that's a tragedy. A million men's death, that's a statistic." We look at the individual and we ignore the statistics. The money we spent on the heart transplant for Mr. Schroeder could have been far more productively spent on the replacement of heart valves for two hundred patients or for prenatal care for that one-third of American women who currently receive none in the first trimester of pregnancy.

VIII. DO NOT COVET THY NEIGHBOR'S WIFE'S ARTIFICIAL HEART

In the area of artificial organs, I would announce right now that, until other needs are met, no taxpayer money should be spent on artificial organs. Are we going to wait until a politically active group of chronic heart patients—many of them smokers—wheel a bunch of artificial heart recipients before a congressional committee, their hearts literally and figuratively in their hands, and plea for the taxpayers to save their lives by providing publicly paid artificial hearts? Is that how we want to set our health care priorities?

I am not a medical Luddite. I admire the miracles of medicine. But I contrast cornea transplants, cataract operations, and hip replacements—all of which add tremendously to the quality of life for many elderly people—to artificial hearts. We should continue to experiment with artificial hearts; medical science must not be stifled or hampered from experimenting. Medical science has made some of its greatest discoveries from the unexpected. I object only to the taxpayers being forced to pay for this at the expense of other, more beneficial health care programs. This occurred in California in 1985 when it was decided that organ transplants would be funded while 200,000 low-income people were knocked off Medi-Cal. That is not a good trade.

The National Institutes of Health called for greatly expanded federal research efforts to develop a fully implantable permanent artificial heart. Such devices, it said, "could provide a significant increase in lifespan, with an acceptable quality of life, for 17,000 to 35,000 patients below the age of 70 annually." The group estimated its annual cost would be up to $5 billion!

This would be a staggering price to pay for the few people who would benefit. It would add significantly to the cost of health insurance premiums for all of us. It would eat into the budgets for Medicare and Medicaid. But, most significantly, it wouldn't do a thing to prevent heart disease in the first place. And if we think we would be able to add availability of the artificial heart to other programs and still pay for them all, we are tragically mistaken.

IX. DO NOT WORSHIP GRAVEN IMAGES OF HIGH TECHNOLOGY

My criticism is not of high technology. There certainly are high technologies that deserve to be worshipped and certainly deserve to be respected. My criticism is aimed at the mindless way in which we invent certain high technologies and then are forced to use them while foregoing many more high-benefit procedures and technologies that could save so many more lives. An artificial heart is a high-technology, low-benefit invention because its cost is very high and it only benefits a few people.

The ultimate goal to which this society should apply its high technology is the understanding of the mechanisms that are the underlying causes of disease. In Medusa and the Snail, Lewis Thomas wrote that the diseases that were the greatest menace to human health when he was a medical student on the wards of Boston City Hospital fifty years ago were, "in the order of degree of fear they caused in the public mind, tertiary syphilis of the brain, pulmonary tuberculosis, and acute rheumatic fever. Also, of course, poliomyelitis." He points out that because of classical clinical research, they "have nearly vanished as public health problems, and the vanishing involved the expenditure of pennies compared to what we'd be spending if they were still with us."

Now, *that* is true high-technology medicine.

But just as we would never have cured polio by putting all our money into artificial lungs, so also we will not understand and cure heart disease if we put our money into artificial hearts. In a world of limited resources, such choices become clear.

I do not have a tenth commandment. But let me conclude with an anecdote. I am reminded of a story that came out of the Second World War when rationing was widespread. A man went into a restaurant, ordered a cup of coffee, and then asked for more sugar. The waitress cast a cynical eye on him and said, "Stir what you have." I believe that is what America must do with its medical care expenses: we must stir better the more than $1 billion per day that we put into health care already. There is not enough money, and we can buy an incredible amount of health if we utilize our resources better.

The great genius of democracy is that, once we start asking the right questions, we can all get together to come up with the answers. We really do have to develop a concept of appropriate care or some sort of cost-effective medicine. I know that is difficult. I know that when a doctor is treating a patient at the bedside he or she is not required to balance the federal budget—total dedication to the patient is the first priority. But this doesn't mean that we still can't find ways to set standards, perhaps through professional organizations, which can develop cost-effective medicine.

Clearly, we can stop training so many doctors and lawyers. We can, via tort reform, give some protection to the physicians against the incredible cost of malpractice insurance. Let me share with you a curse that comes out of Mexico to be used only if you hate somebody very much: "May your life be filled with lawyers!"

We can close hospitals and reduce the number of hospital beds and intensive care units. We can regionalize some of the high-technology medicine. We can push for alternate delivery systems. There are many things we can do, but the issue boils down to this: what kind of world are we going to leave our children and grandchildren? Health care *is* a very high priority, but it isn't the *only* priority. It can't be a monopoly. By working together, we can find ways to delivery more health care to more people at a lower cost.

CHAPTER **4**

Can Health Care Costs Be Contained?

Helen Grace, RN, PhD, FAAN

Medical care costs continue to rise at a rate of 10% per year—far exceeding the inflation rate. Medical care costs consume 12.7% of the gross national product (GNP) and are expected to rise to 15% by the end of the century. The increasing consumption of the GNP for medical care services means that resources are being shifted from other areas of need, such as housing and social services. Despite the alarming rise in medical care costs, the general public seems remarkably unconcerned. As Reinhardt (1981) summarized the situation, "The notion continues to spread that health care is one of those commodities to which every citizen in a civilized society is entitled regardless of ability to pay. This sentiment now threatens to engulf *all* technically available health care regardless of its costs."

Despite the continued rise in the costs of medical care, . . . it is estimated that 65 million Americans, or one in four, are either uninsured or underinsured. Thirty-five million Americans have neither private nor public insurance, and another 30 million have minimal coverage.

Ironically, despite this high rate of expenditure for medical care in the United States, the health of the people as measured by a number of standards is not good. Infant mortality rates, particularly among blacks, are alarmingly high.

Reprinted from *Nursing & Health Care*, Vol. 11, No. 3, with permission of National League for Nursing © 1990.

Assessment of progress in meeting health goals for the nation for 1990 points to similar problems in the health of adolescents, minorities of all age groups, and the elderly.

This article will first analyze the factors contributing to the high cost of medical care. It will then offer what this author is convinced are the only viable, long-term solutions if medical care costs are to be contained.

The High Cost of Medical Care

There are four major contributors to the escalation of medical care costs:

1. the overcapacity of hospitals
2. a surplus of highly specialized providers
3. the inequitable financing of health care services
4. the passive role of the health care consumer

Hospitals

The first hospitals were designed to care for those who had no families. They were directed toward *care* of patients and not *cure*. After World War II, with advances in technology and anesthesia and the inflow of public dollars, the focus of hospitals quickly shifted to cure. As Renn (1987) notes:

> The Hill-Burton program, begun in 1946, provided a massive infusion of federal and state governmental

> monies, and helped construct over 400,000 hospital beds between then and the early 1970s. The most current data indicate that there are now just under 5,800 community hospitals containing nearly 1 million beds. Community hospitals admitted slightly less than 36 million patients in 1985 . . . with an average length of stay of 7.4 days. The average hospital's occupancy rate, a measure of the industry's capacity being utilized was 64 percent. Hospitals now employ 3.6 million people, or about one out of every 30 U.S. workers.

Until 1977 there was a continuing increase in demand for hospital beds; the demand plateaued until 1982, and since that time, there has been a steady decline in both number of admissions and length of stay. Renn (1987) attributes this decline to four factors:

1. The change in incentives that has resulted from moving from a retrospective reimbursement system that paid for actual costs of treatment to a prospective payment system that provides payment based upon average costs of treatment for patients within a particular diagnostic category.
2. Growth in capitated financing arrangements that provide disincentives for admitting patients to hospitals.
3. A proliferation of treatment settings that can substitute for hospitalization.
4. The increased burden of cost sharing which shifts part of the cost of care directly to the patient (p. 51).

Despite decreased use of hospitals, profit in the overall hospital industry has increased. Schramm reports, "Although hospital occupancy declined by 12 percent in the first year of prospective payment, profits doubled and reached record levels. In 1984, hospital profits were 6.2 percent of total revenues—three times higher than a decade earlier" (Schramm and Gabel, 1988).

How can the increase in profitability of hospitals be explained? First, the estimated costs of treatment for diagnostic related groups overestimated the actual costs, and certain hospitals profited on the treatment of particular categories of patients. Fast turnover of patients increases the profitability of hospitals.

And even though the number of hospital beds being occupied was less, most hospitals remained open. Costs of patient care cover the overhead for keeping these facilities open and were included in the rate-setting formulas. Renn estimates that in 1984 there was an excess of 140,000 beds, or roughly 800 average-sized community hospitals (Renn, 1987, p. 9).

The decline in numbers of patients in private hospitals has been achieved in some instances, by: keeping out patients likely to be most costly, shifting costs for the care of patients from private nonprofit hospitals to public hospitals, and discharging patients earlier, shifting costs from the hospital to the family and community.

Physician Influence on Health Care Costs

Factors contributing to the escalating cost of medical care are the high incomes that physicians make, the increase in numbers of physicians, overspecialization of practice, and the phenominal power physicians have over patients in the decision making process. In noting that medical care costs in the United States are three times those in Britain and five times that of Japan, Menzel raises the question of whether we are getting our money's worth. He notes that physicians make twice and sometimes up to five times that of other professionals with equal training.

Menzel concludes, "It is utterly hypocritical for doctors, health care administrators, academic analysts, and policymakers to close their eyes to the level of doctors' income amidst an otherwise vigorous concern for making health care worth the increasing money we pay for it (Menzel, 1986).

Under normal marketplace conditions, an increase in the supply of physicians would serve to drive the income of physicians downward and also address another problem, that of maldistribution of physicians. For example, Massachusetts has 308 physicians per 100,000 residents, while Mississippi has less than half that number per resident, 122 per 100,000. A Michigan study of the health professions indicates that increases in the total number of physicians results in a concentration of physicians in urban areas. The costs of medical care rise proportionately to the number of physicians practicing in an area. While the number of physicians has increased dramatically in

Michigan since 1960, there are more counties in Michigan without physicians in 1985 than there were in 1960.

One of the reasons for the escalation of costs is the increased specialization of physicians. The more highly specialized the physicians, the higher the consumption rate of health care services to support specialty practice. Renn (1987) cautions:

> If physicians continue to make most of the allocative decisions in the delivery system, if the emphasis on treatment in acute care inpatient settings persists and if payment mechanisms continue to insulate physicians from the financial risks associated with their decisions—then growth in the supply of physicians will probably translate into corresponding growth in health care spending (p. 25).

While the fees charged by physicians for services account for only 20% of medical costs, decisions made by physicians represent 80% of expenditures. Physicians decide when, how, and for how long patients are to be hospitalized, and medically treated. One of the problems related to the physician's decision making and health care costs is that the physician holds that the physician-client relationship is "sacred" and that no one should interfere with the physician's rights to care for each individual patient, including ordering the tests and treatments defined as necessary for "good" patient care regardless of their costs. The problem with this is the physician is looking at care from the perspective of only the individual patients that come through the door to his or her practice and does not have to weigh the values of individual patient treatment against the broader question of the need of all people within the United States, including the privileged and the poor.

Financing of Medical Care Services

A further complication in controlling health care costs surrounds the way in which medical care services are financed. Payment usually comes from a third party rather than the individual. Public payers—federal, state, or local governments—paid slightly more than 40% of medical care expenditures in 1985, while private insurance supplied an additional 31%. Direct out-of-pocket payments by patients accounted for 27%.

One of the unique features of U.S. health care financing has been the role of private insurance. Starting in 1929, Blue Cross plans became a major force in the financing of medical care. One of the unique features of these plans was that they were originally provider-based and involved service agreements with all of the providers in an area. Rashi Fein (1986) clarifies, "Blue Cross and similar plans were brought into being by hospital representatives with active support of the A.H.A. . . . acting in response to serious problems they and their patients faced: how should hospital bills be paid and how should stable hospital revenues be assured?" The insurance plans were largely for the benefit of hospitals and physicians, and only secondarily for the welfare of patients.

The interlocking relationships between physicians, hospitals, and insurers have dominated decision making regarding the financing of health care; rather than the interests of the patient. Renn notes, "Physicians and hospital representatives often dominate the plans' boards of directors and see the plans, like most participants, as a means of ensuring the financial solvency of the community's providers" (Fein, 1986, p. 27). Blue Cross established the approach of reimbursing hospitals on a retrospective, cost-plus basis, thus building in disincentives for economy. Payment of bills related to hospitalization also built in incentives for physicians to hospitalize patients and thus contributed to the over-building of hospital facilities.

Another complicating facet of this scene was the ability of insurance companies to link with businesses so that the provision of health insurance became a major part of the benefits paid to workers. Thus, the worker began to see the provision of health care insurance and, thereby, the assurance of the economic viability of hospitals and of physicians, as part of the benefits to be expected. Until recent years, the employer has accepted this obligation, until the costs have escalated to a point beyond the ability of the employer to pay. Currently, 10% of the cost of a U.S. automobile goes to pay the health care costs of workers. Employers are saying that they can no longer pay the cost, and are requiring the employees pay a portion of their medical care costs. This is partially a factor considered responsible for reduced utilization of health care services. Initiated in 1966, the Medicare program provides a number of health care benefits to the elderly covered by the Social Security system. Twenty-eight percent of the income of hospitals currently comes from Medicare. Medicare extended to the elderly the concepts established by Blue Cross-Blue Shield for working people and brought the financing for these services into the federal government. Thus, public funding was used to support the private offering of services of physicians and hospitals. Fein (1986) writes:

> Medicare paid hospitals retrospectively on the basis of the costs incurred by covered beneficiaries at participating providers and paid physicians their reasonable, customary, and prevailing fees. While originally resisted by organized medicine as an instance of the federal government becoming an intervening force between the physician and his or her patient, Medicare payments have become a major source of income for both physicians and hospitals. In addition to paying physicians and hospitals, Medicare became a major stimulant for capital growth without reference to community needs and priorities or regional planning efforts (p. 9).

While insurers of public sources pay for over 70% of health care costs, Renn points out, "Ultimately individuals pay for all health care expenditures . . . consumers, workers, and taxpayers, with the dollars taking merely different routes to the providers" (Fein, 1986). If this is so, why are consumers not more involved in the debates about reducing medical care costs?

Consumer Participation

Since much of the cost of care for those without adequate insurance coverage under the prospective payment system was paid for by overcharging for the actual costs of care, much of this cost was subsidized by insurers and indirectly by consumers. This was a hidden problem until the change to a prospective payment system. Now the costs of care for the uninsured and underinsured cannot be paid for this way. As a result, some worry that a two-, three-, or four-tiered system of medical care is emerging. Thurow (1985) has labeled these three levels as follows: one for people on government assistance, a second for workers having employer-paid plans, and another for the wealthy who can afford the private health care market. To this Reinhardt (1987) has added a fourth tier at the bottom for indigent patients who have no insurance. The result of this separation into tiers, according to Maureim (1988), is that "each tier is increasingly forced to care for its own patients using only the resources available to that tier. And as each lower tier is less well-founded than that above, a serious question arises: Should physicians still be expected to deliver the (roughly) same standard of care to all patients regardless of their resources?" As this debate regarding differential treatment dependent upon ability to pay emerges, medical care costs continue to escalate far beyond other costs in our economy.

Since physicians and hospitals primarily control the goods of medical care, the consumer has little choice over the types of treatment he or she receives. Although there are a number of options, the consumer is purposefully kept ignorant, and, therefore, the decision-making control is in the hands of the provider. As a result, the most costly form of treatment is usually that provided. Too often even with basic medical care knowledge, the consumer assumes that the "doctor knows best" and rarely challenges the prescriptions that are made. Reinhardt (1981) further observes that while physicians are always resisting intrusion of government into their relationships with patients, they are not adverse to using regulations to restrict the practice of other less costly practitioners. Restriction of licensure and controlling payment for other service providers constrains less costly care.

Increasingly the public is becoming more knowledgeable about the issues related to costs of medical care. We are confronted by hard choices. Do we continue to address problems of medical care costs by withholding services from those who cannot pay? What are the long-range consequences of this approach? What is the legacy that we will leave our children if we opt to deny services that could prevent illness and instead pay the costs associated with chronic illness and disability? Fein (1986) summarizes the challenges for us:

> Health care and the way we pay for it is a matter of efficiency, and today's system is inefficient. Health care and the way we pay for it is a matter of equity, and today's system is inequitable. We can do better; and, since we can, we should. Will we? It depends upon whether enough of us are concerned about costs, recognize that a less costly

system will free resources for other private and public purposes, and support the notion of health care budgets. It also depends upon whether enough of us care enough to work at translating concepts of decentness, humaneness, cooperation, universality, and justice into actions that would protect all members of the American family. At stake is not only your health care system, but the very nature of our society. While it may appear that in this scenario the consumer is a passive participant, the health care dilemma has indeed been consumer driven and is a reflection of 1) The American inclination to prefer being "fixed" as opposed to "avoiding getting broken," and 2) The American inclination to deify doctors and to assume that the most expensive advice/care is the best. This fascination with high technology continues to fuel the system and technology creates its own demand (pp. 221-222).

Enthoven and Kronick (1989, p. 30) have characterized the situation of rising health care costs and decreased access as a "paradox of excess and deprivation." While it is possible to describe the current situation in great detail, what are the avenues for addressing the problem? Two recent proposals have been set forth and have received widespread attention, particularly in the medical community.

Enthoven and Kronick have proposed universal health insurance coupled with managed competition in which the insurers (private and public) contract with competing health plans to "manage a process of informed cost-conscious consumer choice that rewards providers who deliver high quality care economically" (p. 30). The costs of implementation of their plan would be $15 billion in additional costs in the first year (3% of GNP) as a time increase. Long range, this approach is projected to decrease the *rate of escalation* of health care costs, but does not hold forth the promise of decreased cost (Enthoven & Kronick, 1989, p. 37).

An alternative approach "a national health program for the United States" has been proposed by Himmelstein and White on behalf of a working group of physicians. To summarize the central elements of this proposal:

We propose a national health program that would 1) fully cover everyone under a single, comprehensive public insurance program; 2) pay hospitals and nursing homes a total (global) annual amount to cover all operating expenses; 3) fund capital costs through separate appropriations; 4) pay for physicians services and ambulatory services in any of three ways: through fee-for-service payments with a simplified fee schedule and mandatory acceptance of the national health program as the total payment for a service or procedure (assignment), through global budgets for hospitals or clinics, or on a per capita basis (capitation); 5) be funded, at least initially, for the same sources as at present with all payments disbursed from a single pool; and 6) contain costs through saving on billing and bureaucracy, improved health planning, and the ability of the national program, as the single payer for services, to establish overall funding limits.

It is important to note that this proposal does not address any changes in practices of either hospitals or physicians, but merely proposes a way of paying for them. Neither does this proposal address anything other than the payment for physicians, hospitals, and nursing homes.

While both proposals contain very important potential strategies for paying for the high cost of medical care, it is important to bear in mind that both continue to emphasize the interests of the *providers,* the hospitals, and physicians in how the bills will be paid for as business as usual; the interests of the consumer for more appropriate care are secondary. Second, these proposals continue to focus upon *medical* care. Although the terminology health care is used, these proposals do not address broader issues of *health* care. While some might argue that truly expanding the definition from *medical* to *health* care would further escalate the problem, an alternative argument is that if *health* care were provided, the medical care system would be utilized more appropriately, thereby reducing costs.

Medical care focuses on the diagnosis and treatment of disease, while health care has as its aim the well-being of the individual and family at an optimal level of health. Within this broader framework, the individual and the family have primary responsibility for maintaining health with support from health care specialists. While individuals still will experience illness that will require expert care and treatment, a broader orientation to health care would result in earlier identification of problems at a less acute stage, and, therefore, the treatment would be less costly. Furthermore, a reduction in chronic diseases, most of which are preventable, and maintenance of mobility as people age would do much to reduce costs of care in the long run. For example, in the area of maternal child care, there is growing evidence that early prenatal care that is comprehensive in nature, including provision for adequate nutrition, social services support, and health education, reduces infant mortality, increases infant birth weight, and reduces numbers of damaged (mentally and physically) infants. Rough data drawn from one midsize community indicates that providing such comprehensive services to about 500 uninsured and underinsured mothers by a nurse-managed clinic using nurse midwives will cost about $250,000 over the available compensation for such care from both public and private sources. However, the local community hospital has experienced a total decline in demand for a neonatal intensive care unit, a "savings" to the hospital of $650,000. While simple mathematical calculations would lead to a conclusion that $400,000 had been saved, if one looks at this from a provider perspective (hospital and physician), the conclusion is somewhat different. The hospital looks at this scenario as a loss of revenue, in that the $650,000 previously spent on neonatal intensive care was collectible revenue. From the physicians' point of view, these "savings" were largely a result of services provided by nutritionists, social workers, nurses, and midwives. Physicians' revenues, both for obstetrical and pediatric care, were reduced.

Similar examples could be drawn from well-child care, women's health, and care of the elderly. *Returning responsibility for health care to the individual and family, engaging a wide range of specialists in supportive roles to the individual and family, demystifying health and illness through education of the public, and using the medical care system appropriately to treat only acute diseases are the long-range solutions to the problem of escalating medical care costs.*

If this be so, what are the steps toward change in this direction? First, there need to be some carefully controlled demonstration projects, such as that described above, which illustrate the benefits to be achieved by comprehensive *health* care. Some examples of such studies are beginning to appear in the literature. Producing data, however, is merely the first step. These data then must be made known to those who pay the bills—ultimately, everyone in this country. In the scenario related to prenatal care, nothing will change in the community if the financing for expanded prenatal care to create this degree of long-range improvement is left to the decision making of the providers. These data need to be translated and publicized so that citizens of the community know the choices that are open to them, so that ultimately they can make informed decisions as to how health care is to be provided. In this community, the $400,000 that could be saved through adequate prenatal care could result in reduction of dollars going for insurance, either directly or indirectly, and it could be redirected toward other pressing societal issues.

Nurses have a crucial role to play in creating change. First, movement from a medical care system to health care requires nursing intervention and leadership. Nurses can set up the demonstrations that lead to necessary data and publicize these findings to individuals and policymakers. Ultimately, a revolution of the citizenry is the only force to create change in a democracy. Nursing has the capacity to educate the consumer to create such changes.

A second essential component is to articulate clearly the components of health care, enlist individual responsibility for maintenance of health, and clearly describe the supportive roles of health specialists in promoting individual health, including that of nurses. The myth that anything less than care provided by physicians is second-best must be dispelled. In fact, there is mounting evidence that for health care, the physician is perhaps the least qualified.

At the heart of change is the need for the consumer to be educated, and nurses have the expertise to provide this education.

What hinders this type of change? First, nurses have been socialized to be co-conspirators with hospitals and doctors in maintaining the current medical care system. They have been reticent to let the public know of the unnecessary and damaging high-technology invasive procedures that are being done every day in the interests of the medical care system. Nurses are intimidated and fearful of loss of jobs when the hospital is their main employer, and all avenues for practice independent of physicians or hospitals are constrained. With nurses comprising the largest number of health care workers in the United States (1.8 million, estimated), collectively the profession has the capacity to speak with "one loud voice." Second, energies of the profession have become focused on the profession itself rather than on the issues of health care for people. Fragmentation of the profession results in a feeling of abandonment on the part of nurses engaged in practice, who feel that leadership is preoccupied with the self-interests of the profession. If nurses could unite, with a common concern for health care for people at affordable costs, they have the capacity to join with consumers to create such change and thereby "heal" themselves.

In summary, change is possible. Such change depends on (1) a fundamental change from a focus on a medical care delivery system to participatory health care for people; (2) breaking the monopoly of hospitals, physicians, and insurers in the decision-making process that preserves the current system; (3) engaging the consumer in assuming greater responsibility for personal health and decision-making regarding broader health policy issues; and (4) greater involvement of nurses and other health-related specialists in joining with the consumer in supportive roles and relationships with an emphasis upon health promotion/disease prevention. Nurses are central in making the difference. The ability to become "one strong voice" on behalf of the U.S. public is essential if nursing is going to be a force for positive change.

REFERENCES

The doctor's dilemma. (1911, 1971). In *Shaw's Collected Plays with Their Preferences.*

Eisenberg, J. W. (1968). *Doctors' decisions and the cost of medical care.* Ann Arbor, MI; Health Administration Press Perspectives.

Enthoven, A. & Kronick, R. (1989). A consumer-choice health plan for the 1990's, *New England Journal of Medicine, 320*(1); 30.

Fein, R. (1986). *Medical care medical costs: Search for a health insurance policy.* Cambridge, MA: Harvard University Press.

The health of America's children. (1987).

Himmelstein, D. U., & Woolhandler, S. *New England Journal of Medicine, 320*(2); 102-108.

Maureim, E. H. (1986). Cost Containment: Challenging fidelity & justice: *Hastings Center Report, 18*(6); 22.

Menzel, P. T. (1986). *Medical costs, moral choices.* New Haven CT: Yale University Press.

Michigan State Health Plan 1983-1987. Volume III, Health Personnel.

Reinhardt, U. W. (1981). Health insurance and cost containment policies: The experience abroad. Mancur Olson (Ed.), *A new approach to the economics of health care* (p. 151). Washington and London: American Enterprise Institute for Public Policy Research.

Reinhardt, U. W. (1987). Health insurance for the nation's poor. *Health Affairs, 6*(1); 101-112.

Renn, S. (1987). Health care delivery in the 1980s. In Schramm, C. (Ed.), *Health care and its costs: Can the U.S. afford adequate health.* New York: W. W. Norton & Co.

Schramm, C. J., & Gabel, J. (1988). Prospective payment: Some retrospective observations. *New England Journal of Medicine, 318*(25);1682.

Thurow, L. C. (1985). *Medicine vs. economics. New England Journal of Medicine, 313*(10):611-614.

CHAPTER 5

Does Nursing Have the Power to Change the Health Care System?

Sandra S. Sweeney, RN, PhD
Karen E. Witt, RN, MSN

This chapter asks, "Does nursing have the power to change the health care system?" The question is neither new nor original, but the issues have become increasingly important to the profession, given the dramatic changes that have taken place in health care organizations and delivery of services throughout the industry. This is particularly true for the more drastic changes that have occurred during the past 5 years. While some are writing of the current crises confronting the profession of nursing,[20] others note the unparalleled opportunities such changes can bring if nurses mobilize and capitalize on the challenges being placed before them.[12,21,28,37]

The turmoil and chaos surrounding the American health care delivery system today have sparked a renewed interest in the concept of power, particularly by nurses who are concerned not only about their own or their profession's interests but also about the quality of care received by consumers. This chapter analyzes both the positive and the negative implications of using power to change the health care system and suggests obstacles nurses can expect to confront should they demand change. Power is conceptually defined, and actual and potential relationships that exist between the concept of power and the profession of nursing are illustrated.

The framework used to organize and structure the debate was selected from the seminal work published by Berle.[8] Berle considers power to be a "universal experience and a human attribute of man with five discernible natural laws."[8] The laws of power are as follows:

1. Power invariably fills any vacuum in human organization.
2. Power is invariably personal.
3. Power is invariably based on a system of ideals or a philosophy.
4. Power is exercised through, and depends on, institutions.
5. Power is invariably confronted with, and acts in the presence of, a field of responsibility.

Laws, by definition, allow generalizations while also providing a structure for logical reasoning. Berle's laws[8] seemed to provide an appropriate framework for the question raised in this chapter. Each law will be briefly restated followed by an amplification of the law and the argument in which power and its relationship to the profession of nursing is debated relative to our contemporary health care delivery system. The literature on power is replete with definitions, none of which seemed inclusive enough for the purposes of this debate.

Reprinted from *Current Issues in Nursing,* J. C. McCloskey and H. K. Grace, eds., with permission of Mosby-Year Book, Inc.

Therefore, we synthesized the following conceptual definition of power for use in this chapter:

> Power is an ability to employ effort toward attaining specific ends. It exists as either a stimulus, state, or response and is situationally specific. Power is experienced internally or externally and is consciously or unconsciously employed in symmetrical or asymmetrical equations. It emerges in a specific form and is constrained at microcosmic or macrocosmic levels. Power emerges, can be used or diffused, has sustenance requirements, is subject to challenge, possesses limitations, and may be either won or lost by election, expiration, resignation, or expulsion. Power is a universal attribute of humans and is governed by five invariant natural laws.

NURSING DOES NOT HAVE THE POWER TO CHANGE THE HEALTH CARE SYSTEM

To repeat Berle's first law: "Power invariably fills any vacuum in human organization. As between chaos and power, the latter always prevails."[8] The health care industry has enjoyed several decades of public-supported expansion and substantial freedom in self-governance but now finds itself facing radical change. Impending changes are occurring in access, finance, organizational ownership, management, payment systems, and limited hospital stays. In addition, there are movements by consumers to encourage, if not mandate, agencies at local, state, and national levels to impose more prescriptive, not restrictive, policies to improve and protect the rights of all citizens to affordable, quality health care. The possibility of enforced changes is creating a chaotic situation at best while simultaneously producing even larger numbers of individuals whose health care needs remain unmet.

Berle maintains, "when a vacuum occurs at any level of the power structure, the immediate result is to throw power downward to the next lower institutional echelon."[8] The changes in health care delivery in the United States during the past 5 years, combined with the increasing plight of the homeless, greater numbers of uninsured and underinsured, the increasing needs of a chronically ill and aging population, and shortened hospital stays might lead one to think that nursing has accumulated unprecedented power by now; but nursing's services have not been demanded by those in positions to recognize how valuable nurses can be to an organization. Indeed, instead of delegating power downward from hospital administrators and physicians to competent nurses, the medical profession has proposed instead a new category of health provider, the registered care technologist (RCT), who is supposed to replace nurses at the bedside and provide effective, efficient quality care after only a 9-month course of instruction![1] While the American Medical Association (AMA) has been busy formalizing the RCT proposal, there has also been a slow but steady trend toward shifting the responsibility for caring for individuals who need close monitoring from institutions to homes or day-care facilities; this is also a movement away from care given by professional nurses toward family members or other less prepared health care workers. If nurses have the power to change or influence health care, why have they not emerged with a new mantle of power?

Lynaugh and Fagin[28] list five paradoxes—characteristics of the profession—that pose dilemmas nurses have had to face throughout history. One of the dilemmas is that our society has systematically undervalued care, particularly the care given by nurses. Now, especially, with prospective payment systems, increased acuity levels, earlier discharges, increased technology, improved pharmaceutical agents, and longer life spans, the assumption that nurses can substitute for family members or servants is being reversed to suggest that family members and servants can substitute for nurses. Nursing will not be able to reverse this trend until it can document its efficiency and effectiveness in dollars and cents. Although there may be a general unwillingness of health care policymakers to think of quality nursing care in terms of a monetary value, nursing's inability to document its relative merit is also largely responsible for contributing to the profession's weak power base when issues of health care are addressed and policies formulated. Reverby[38] concurs with the problems contemporary nursing faces in attempting to care for a society that refuses to value caring.

Nurses cannot hope to change the health care delivery system in this country until they are entitled to receive monetary compensation for their services, particularly in the realm of third-party reimbursement. At present, thousands of nurses are providing care to hundreds of thousands of American citizens in need of professional services. However, the nursing care being provided is either unreimbursed or, worse, being paid to a health care organization or physician! Even when armed with statistical estimates of their cost-effectiveness, nurses have been unable to marshall the support necessary to achieve (1) recognition of the financial worth of their work, and (2) the right to receive direct payment for their services. Andrews[5] states, "Conservative estimates suggest even if nonphysician providers undertook the readily delegable portions of adult primary and pediatric primary care, between one-half billion and one billion dollars would be saved annually, cutting 19 to 49 percent of the total primary care provider bill," and further, "an examination of 58 different health care tasks indicated that the costs averaged $8.13 when the tasks were performed by a nurse practitioner and $16.48 when performed by a physician."[5] Nurses must find mechanisms through which existing reimbursement systems can be revised. They must unite their economic capacity with their professional capabilities if they are to wield the power necessary to change the health care system.

Finally, I believe nurses must be able to overcome their own conflicts and divisions, beginning with the problem of what level of educational preparation should be required for entry into practice, before there is any hope of coalescing power and influencing change in areas outside the profession. Currently, the entry into practice issue is perceived by many nurses and others as a major source of division. Even though people understand the history behind the current controversy, they remain polarized over the proposed solutions. The education for beginning practice issue is further confounded by issues of gender and a history of being an oppressed group.[28,39] Unless and until the philosophical and practice components of nursing's constituencies are able to focus their energies on combating the problem in the health care system instead of fighting with each other, nursing will never succeed in garnering the power it needs to effect change in a health care system already too accustomed to male control and physician domination.

Berle's second law suggests power "is invariably personal; that there is no such thing as class power, elite power, or group power; although classes, elites, and groups may be the processes of organization by which power is lodged in individuals."[8] Nurses and nursing are in double jeopardy when it comes to describing potential power bases using this law. First of all, nurses have rarely, if ever, found a common interest that they as individuals or collectively through the processes of organization have fought to preserve, protect, or alter. It may be argued that various speciality groups of nurses have been somewhat successful in effecting change; however, as a group or class of professionals, nurses have not used their collectivity to pursue either institutional or professional goals or objectives. At present, there seems to be a unified and organized reaction among nurses and their organizations to vehemently oppose the registered care technologist proposal being advanced by the American Medical Association.[2] If this effort is successful, it may provide the impetus nursing needs to formulate future policies and agendas that have the potential to enlist the broad-based support from among its membership and ensure the power that accompanies strength in numbers.

This debate is about the present, however, not the future. If nurses are to effectively implement the law of power described above, they must first recognize the need to develop personal power. May[30] argues one's denial "of the importance of power commits oneself to continued helplessness . . . and manifests itself in depression and self-hatred as one's psychological growth is thwarted by an unwillingness to exert influence and affirm one's own worth." How can nurses who care and are concerned about the needs of the unserved patient-clients fully express their concerns when faced with the possible loss of their jobs? How can nurses confront hospital administrators and refuse to stay at home "on-call" for $1.50 an hour when policies are implemented by their head nurses or supervisors? How can individual professional nurses fight for quality care when they are unable or unwilling to unite to openly express their outrage and concern or to enlist the public's awareness to arouse support for change? Perhaps it is because many nurses lack personal power, the power one invests in oneself—self-esteem, self-respect, and self-confidence. Nurses do not seem to possess the personal power needed to go forward, and without it, they will not have the ability to know when to lead or when to follow, both essential strategies in the appropriate utilization of power.

Nurses either have not developed or have not been able to sustain a keen sense of their individual responsibilities as professionals, which further impedes their ability to attain personal and professional goals. Nurses cannot expect to wield power until they join a professional organization or group in which their individual and collective agendas can be put into motion. Although many nurses talk of our collective numbers — the largest group of health professionals in the United States — those numbers become unimportant when legislators, physicians, and corporations are quick to note that the American Nurses' Association (ANA) currently represents only about 10% of all nurses in America.[4] Organizations are composed of individuals, but without their support, it is difficult, if not impossible, for organizations to make their members see the potential power in numbers.

Another obstacle for nurses and their organizations in their quest for a strong power base is a tendency to fight battles reactively rather than proactively. Nurses need to anticipate and propose changes that will work to their benefit rather than to resist change. Nurses have a long history of accommodation, particularly in relation to external forces, such as coping with the revolving cycle of shortages, accepting temporary staff nurses from external agencies, accepting one-time bonuses in lieu of annual salary increases, and accepting decisions made and enforced by nonnursing personnel. This process of accommodation is typical of a group that perceives itself to be powerless and helpless. "Individuals who do not perceive themselves to be in control of material, social or intellectual resources are generally found to act passively and believe that luck or chance controls their fate."[23] If nurses expect to possess power and be able to actualize it as individuals and through groups and organizations, they must be prepared to identify and follow a new group of individuals who will lead them into proactive postures.

Nurses who want themselves, their group, and the profession to have power must also be willing to pay the price; that is, there must be a commitment to finance such efforts. Nurses do not readily part with their hard-earned money and usually want to be informed of exactly how funds have been spent.[42] When nursing has an established financial foundation, it will then be able to represent individuals and organizations and to promote and actualize its programs and agendas.

"Power is based on a system of ideals or a philosophy. Two ingredients of power are inseparable . . . an idea system, a philosophy . . . and . . . an institutional structure transmitting the will of the power holder," states the third law of power.[8] Nursing's system of ideals and philosophical premises can be traced to the beginning of civilization, but they have become more closely aligned within an occupational structure since the Florence Nightingale era. A typical dictionary definition of nursing today continues to suggest nursing means to suckle, take care of, nourish, foster, or to serve as a nurse.[43] Although nurses do take care of others in need, nourish when necessary, foster independence when possible, and serve client-publics as part of their functions, such descriptors fail to convey a unique set of ideals or philosophical posture conducive to establishing a strong competitive power base in today's health care arena.

Nurses have a long history of struggling to legitimize themselves and the work they do to the societies they serve. Whether nurses have served well in either military or civilian sectors, their contributions have frequently gone unrecognized, if not unnoticed. Recent struggles have involved nursing's attempts to move from occupational to professional status, from hospital-based programs of education to university settings, from dependent to independent or interdependent practice opportunities, and from modalities of trial and error to sophisticated methodologies including the formulation of conceptual or theoretical models. Each of these changes, however, has been greeted with distrust, misgiving, and suspicion both from within and without the nursing community. Thus our diversity and lack of agreement in identifying common ideals and philosophical postures has prevented the profession from being able to develop the power necessary to effect change in many of the institutions in which nurses function.

It has been suggested by Norris[34] that the nursing community has agreed on four phenomena unique to the discipline: nursing, patient, health, and environment. If this were indeed true, then nursing would have a framework on which to begin structuring a system of ideals, a philosophy, and a common will among its membership. However, in reality, it seems only a small number of nurses actually accept or are even aware that these concepts exist, let alone subscribe to the belief that they are the foundation of nursing's theory and practice. The issue is further confounded when one analyzes the increasing number of conceptual/theoretical models published for and by nurses relative to the discipline. Each theory has its own terminology, definitions, framework, and philosophical message and its relationship to nursing theory and practice. These diverse positions may provide academicians with an opportunity to discuss, debate, and verify the relative merits of each contribution, but they do little to stimulate or convince the greater majority of practicing nurses that there is any relationship between the theoretical conceptions of nursing and the daily work world encountered by staff nurses.

Ideologies speak with one voice and espouse a common philosophy. As long as nurse academicians and theorists continue to speak a language unaccepted, impractical, and difficult to apply by practitioners, it will be impossible for the profession as a whole to champion a united cause. Nursing needs to address the concerns, contexts, and interests of both academic and practicing nurses if there is to be any hope of establishing common bonds and shared ideals. As long as nurses remain a group of health care providers who cannot extend their historical traditions of caring and nurturing and consolidate their existing estranged positions, they will continue to be powerless in both the academic and health care institutional environments.

Nursing must determine who or what institution will identify and communicate its ideals, philosophy, and structure. Organizations espousing nursing's interests now number close to 50, and all lack sufficient membership to truly represent the profession as a whole. Unions are attempting to organize and represent the profession, but many question whether agreement is possible given the professional-union dichotomy in purposes, objectives, and philosophies. Individual nurses cannot be expected to operate alone without the collective support of colleagues and leaders. There are those who speak of the opportunities available to nurses now,[35,37] but who will lead, coalesce, and unite the community of nurses to make the opportunities a reality?

Berle's fourth law states: "Power is exercised through and depends on institutions. Power is invariably organized and transmitted through institutions."[8] The profession of nursing has been closely associated with hospitals since its immigration from England. Although in Britain, Florence Nightingale may have insisted on separating nursing education from formalized institutions such as hospitals, such divisions did not accompany the establishment of educational programs in the United States. Whether the affiliations nursing education established with hospitals are to blame for many of our current problems, the fact remains that relatively few nurses have achieved success either as independent practitioners or as pioneers in entrepreneurial enterprises. The vast majority of nurses continue to work within hospitals or institutions closely affiliated with hospital-based centers of control.

Harriman suggests:

> Organizational policies award power to individuals who can exert influence upward and outward in the organization. This power is based on achieving credibility and creating dependency through the control of resources of supply, information and knowledge. The more critical one's activities are to the organization's success and survival, the more dependent other elements of the organization and the more power is generated.[16]

If Harriman is correct, then one can only deduce that nurses employed in hospitals and related institutions are unable to exert influence within the organization, lack credibility, are not able to create situations requiring dependency on their work by others, and do not have control over critical resources such as supply, knowledge, or information! Assuming this scenario to be correct, how realistic is it for nurses to expect to exert influence on institutional policy-making?

Until the arrival of home health care, the only service patients received in hospitals that could not have been offered almost equally well on the outside was nursing care. Logic suggests, therefore, that professional nurses would command significant organizational power within hospital-based complexes. But the fact remains that they have not nor do they now. One explanation for this is offered by Reverby, who implies that the endorsement and utilization of scientific management theory and its techniques by nurses during the middle of this century led to the unanticipated consequence of dividing patient care into many individualized tasks. It became easy, therefore, to delegate specific responsibilities to others, many of whom were relatively untrained workers earning wages substantially lower than those earned by professional nurses. "Nurses found themselves often doing the same work as nurse aides or licensed practical nurses and trying desperately to define and justify what the differences were between their skills.[38]

Task differentiation and subsequent rationalization of what constitutes professional nursing services have prompted hospital administrators to continue to hire individuals with meager nursing preparation as substitutes for registered nurses. Administrators can do this as long as they are able to meet their specific regulatory agencies' minimum requirements regarding supervision by professional nurses. The continued diffusion of tasks among so many categories of workers undermines nursing's ability to effectively influence institutional policy because it remains unable to demonstrate its unique contributions to the organization's mission.

Hickson and others proposed a strategic contingencies theory, with a hypothesis that three variables governed a subunit's power within an organization: (1) centrality—the degree of interdependence and indispensability; (2) substitutability—the possibility of easy replacement by others; and (3) coping with uncertainty—the ability to handle inevitable and unpredictable occurrences.[19] It is difficult to argue that nursing care should not be central to most care-providing institutions, such as hospitals, nursing homes, and public health and home health agencies. It is not difficult, however, to see that nursing has been unable to make others realize the centrality of its services. Nurses are hard pressed to define their area of expertise, demonstrate significant findings to support their knowledge base or clinical practice, and determine who among the more than 2.5 million individuals engaged in the practice of nursing are considered to be the professionals.[13]

The next assault on nursing's credibility and status within health care institutions may very well come from physicians. Given the projected oversupply of physicians, there is reason to suspect physicians may attempt to resume responsibility for tasks previously delegated to nurses, or at the very least attempt to further restrict nurses from initiating independent interventions they now provide patient-clients under their care. Nurses will have to determine what they want their roles and responsibilities to be if they expect to escape what Ginzberg calls the "rising protectionism of the medical profession."[13]

The credibility of professional nursing has also been diminished by nurses who reject graduate study in favor of the more "attractive," "exciting," and, most important, "lucrative" areas of business administration, psychology, counseling, and so forth. This disregard for the need to study advanced nursing suggests to nurses and others that there is nothing to be gained professionally, personally, or monetarily from further preparation in one's chosen profession. Indeed, nurses are frequently encouraged not to pursue graduate study in nursing by the very people who have benefited most by hiring less prepared individuals to replace nurses at the bedside, who seem to have the view that a nurse is a nurse is a nurse! Such views diminish even further the idea that nurses should develop areas of specialization and place a low value on furthering one's education. As long as nurses willingly succumb to such advice and perceive success as being possible only outside the profession of nursing, they will not be able to convey a sense of the importance of nursing because they themselves do not see its importance. A professional whose practice boundaries are being threatened externally and who cannot envision a potential future internally will be unable to project a credible image, garner power, or earn respect from either constituency.

"Power is invariably confronted with and acts in the presence of a field of responsibility."[8] A field of responsibility is further defined by Berle as "aggregates made up of tiny or great power organisms to whom the powerholder is responsible."[8] Given this context, it will be difficult for nursing to ever create a cohesive field of responsibility, because the profession is composed of large numbers of relatively small aggregates, each perceiving itself as unique and somewhat removed from the larger population of registered nurses, which now numbers more than 1.5 million individuals. The field of responsibility, rather than addressing the common needs and rights of nurses generally, is more frequently perceived as belonging to specialty practice areas, special interests groups, or those having particular educational credentials. This wide diversity only serves to dilute and diminish the parameters within which a field of responsibility can exist and survive.

Nursing's early endeavors to reach consensus on what constituted its field of responsibility consisted of attempts to create formal organizations that would represent and speak for the emerging profession. The leaders of the time, Robb, Nutting, Dock, Wald, and Stewart, believed that power would accompany strength of purpose and courage of convictions when large numbers of nurses attempted to achieve common goals and objectives. Today, however, the contemporary organizations that have evolved from those early efforts no longer possess the memberships necessary to justify any claim to speak for professional nursing. Indeed, the overwhelming lack of participation by nurses in their professional organizations is frequently used by opposing groups to refute agendas for change proposed by nursing's leadership.

"Nursing's power base originates at the bedside."[24] Practice, then, should define nursing's field of responsibility. Although this may seem ideal, practicing nurses must identify and document nursing's role and field of responsibility as opposed to the responsibilities ascribed to them by other health care professionals. Thus practicing nurses must be immune to the dictates of others if they are to formulate their own parameters of practice. This may not be feasible given the overwhelming workloads being managed by most nurses in today's health care institutions. Nurses are actively engaged in determining parameters of practice as evidenced by the National Implementation Project[32] and the Nursing Knowledge Project.[14] Whether or not the findings of these efforts will be accepted and endorsed by practicing nurses, however, remains open to question.

If nursing's field of responsibility is to emanate from practice, then the way nurses view power in the workplace and in relation to one another will have to undergo change and modification. Although the number of studies exploring the concept of power and nurses in hospital organizations is limited, findings by Heineken suggest nurse executives and staff nurses hold quite different perspectives regarding at least two areas of power: "(1) the power that is associated with political abilities and (2) the power that is needed to maintain control and autonomy. . . . Nurse executives scored significantly higher than nurses holding lower level positions on both dimensions."[17] Findings such as these have significant consequences for nursing practice. For example, these findings suggest executives will attempt to cultivate political alliances, use power to influence decisions, have a higher and different span of influence, and be perceived as the institution's leaders and role models for nursing. Staff nurses, on the other hand, will not have political interests; will have fewer power connections with which to use their influence, establish strong working relationships among their peers, other health care workers, and their patient-clients; and will be perceived as the followers and implementors of policy-level decision making.[17] These differences in perceptions of power, control, and autonomy must be resolved if both clusters of nurses are going to arrive at some measure of agreement regarding a common field of responsibility. Further, if these discrepancies reflect one community of nurses, imagine how much greater they must be in the total aggregate!

Studies such as Heineken's, however, do carry a message and a vision for the future of nursing that must not be overlooked. The findings deserve careful analysis because they may hold the key to defining nursing's field of responsibility. The responses of nurses to these findings, however, must come from the total community to implement new directions and recommendations. Continued fragmentation will not breed success.

NURSING DOES HAVE THE POWER TO CHANGE THE HEALTH CARE SYSTEM

There is no doubt that the profession of nursing has the power to change the health care system! Nursing has always had the power to effect change but perhaps has hesitated to challenge existing systems in institutions designed to provide primarily acute and medically dictated care. Now, however, we would argue that nurses not only have an opportunity to change health care delivery services, but they have a professional responsibility to do so. Berle clearly states as his first law of power: "Power invariably fills any vacuum in human organization. As between chaos and power, the latter always prevails."[8]

One of the most disturbing realities confronting American society today concerns the organization, distribution, availability, and access of health care services to individuals in need. It is, indeed, a contradiction to recognize that although this country's "health care system may now be capable of providing quality health care to all segments of our society, that we are no longer sure we can afford to do so."[15] This dilemma has resulted, we believe, from the vacuum and chaos that resulted from the introduction of diagnosis-related group (DRG) categorizations that formed the foundation for the prospective reimbursement payment system initiated in 1983. Berle maintains that whenever chaos and power coexist power will always prevail; to date, the drastic effects this revolutionary change has had for the delivery of nursing care seem to suggest that nursing lacks the power to make a difference in health care. However, before nurses can effect change, they must be knowledgeable, informed, and willing to assume the risks incumbent with any initiative designed to challenge existing conditions.

When the diagnosis-related group–prospective payment system was first initiated, hospital administrators were quick to bemoan the catastrophic effects the system would have on the state of hospital finances. Nurses were summoned to many meetings in which the deleterious effects of the impending policies were discussed and strategies delineating how various components of nursing service departments would be expected to respond were carefully outlined. Cutbacks would have to be made in staffing levels, full-time employees would have to reduce their employment status to .5 or .8 time, and ancillary personnel would be severely reduced or, in some cases, eliminated from the workforce. Nurses at all levels of the organization complied with the mandates, simultaneously complaining about being overworked, underpaid, forced to care for more patients than could possibly be managed with any measure of safety, and becoming more and more disenchanted with their ability to function in a professional capacity. This scenario, one of my colleagues suggested, is hardly the portrait of a profession with power.

Why, if nursing has power, does such exploitation occur? It occurs, we will argue, because rather than pursue the power inherent in knowledge, it is easier to embrace the powerlessness of compliance; rather than challenge the "facts" being presented, it is easier to accept administrative dictates; and rather than pursue common goals, objectives, and perhaps avenues of accommodation that would work to nursing's advantage, it is easier to adopt a reactive posture and expect solutions to come from the organization's hierarchy rather than from within the professional complement of nurses. It is conceivable that professional nurses could have responded to the preceding situation in an entirely different manner. For example, if a committee of nurses charged with maintaining quality assurance and/or patient care standards in the nursing service department had obtained, analyzed, and evaluated the policy statements generated by the Health Care Financing Administration regarding prospective payment, it might have been able to counteract the dictates made by hospital administrators, enlist the assistance of physicians, and propose alternative strategies that would have met the intent of the policy changes but not at the expense of patient care.

One example of nursing's failure to capitalize on these policy changes occurred in the area of patient discharge. While nurses were lamenting the numerous instances in which patients in poor condition were being discharged too early, it was Ralph Nader who pushed for the addition of an advocacy clause that would guarantee patients the right of appeal and the right to a hearing if they felt they were being discharged too soon. Well-informed nurses could have served the patients equally well, but even today many nurses remain unaware of such provisions in the policy. In this instance, therefore, power remained with hospital administrators.

Today nurses have more opportunities than ever to capitalize on the chaos in the health care system in the United States. The prospective payment system remains in effect for many facilities, and similar systems will probably soon be initiated by other paying agencies, such as private insurance companies and health maintenance organizations. Nurses must become informed on all aspects and consequences of such payment systems if they expect to improve the quality of care being provided consumers. Nursing must continue to develop and improve data-base systems that clearly document its role in delivering quality, cost-effective care. Although progress has been made in this area, more needs to be done.

The next decade will present other opportunities to nurses to exercise their influence and power. There will be a continued decline in mortality rates, continued increases in the morbidity rates, and the number of aging Americans will continue to expand at an exponential rate, as will the projected costs of health care.[12] Nurses have the knowledge, skills, and abilities to manage and cope with these potential problems and patient populations.

Nurses need to initiate and implement creative strategies if they are to assume a major role in caring for these segments of the population. Nurses need to become familiar with economic concepts such as supply and demand, production functions, product lines, and product-line management; in addition they must learn to cost out their services if they are going to state their case effectively and remain a viable component of the health care system of the future. The potential for chaos exists in many segments of the health care arena, not just in traditional health care delivery settings. At present, many individuals in the greatest need of health care are not able to get it: the homeless, the poor, the disadvantaged, the unemployed, and the elderly. Another group, the uninsured, is also quickly making its presence known. Nurses can serve these publics as well and perhaps even better than other health care providers and should expand efforts to assist these groups in formalized ways through nursing clinics, community health agencies, or other innovative mechanisms and structures.

Nurses comprise the largest single group of health care providers in this country. The educational level of its practitioners continues to increase steadily, and nurses remain the professionals who continue to have the greatest amount of contact with the patient-client. The changes in health care policies to date have not limited the practice of nursing as much as they have endangered traditional opportunities enjoyed by medicine. Fagin reports:

> "In the past five years, health care costs have risen at a rate almost three times that of the general inflation rate . . . and . . . according to a report from the Office of Technology Assessment, the increases are due to an intensification of services, expanded availability and use of costly diagnostic and treatment services, and sophisticated technologies.[12]

Physician services were responsible for 20% of all health-related expenditures in 1984, and the rate has continued to grow at approximately 14% each year since.[12]

Costs such as these cannot continue to escalate. Nurses provide an attractive care alternative because of their unique knowledge, skills, and ability to deal with their client-patients' responses to actual and potential health problems. Legislators, unions, and the public at large are beginning to support the idea of nurses having new roles designed to provide necessary health care services. If nurses do not respond and capitalize on the dramatic changes occurring in the health care marketplace, other providers will no doubt manage to fill the vacuum, as can be seen in the recent proposals by physicians to introduce yet another health care provider — the registered care technician.[1] Nurses cannot be content to sit back and watch while other health care providers act.[12] If nurses will accept the opportunities available to them, they will not only assist in bringing order out of chaos, but also will acquire the power necessary to significantly influence and change the health care delivery system of this country.

Berle's second law states: "Power is invariably personal. There is no such thing as class power, elite power, or group power; although classes, elites, and groups may be processes of organization by which power is lodged in individuals."[8] This law mandates that before nurses can use the power they have, they must first recognize and internalize their capacity for holding power as individuals. Historically, however, nurses have been content to invest their power collectively in such organizations as the American Society of Superintendents of Training Schools of Nursing — the forerunner of the National League for Nursing, — and the Nurses' Associated Alumnae of the United States and Canada — better known now as the American Nurses' Association.

Although nurses must maintain a strong sense of professional identity through membership in professional organizations, they must simultaneously promote efforts designed to enhance their individual sense of worth. Feminist authors have described power as having two dimensions: power-over and power-within.[26] Power-over reinforces the traditional forms of power so often described in the organizational literature and encompasses such concepts as bureaucracy, control, vertical lines of authority and decision making descending from above. Nurses have some familiarity with the basic tenets of a power-over dimension. The power-within dimension, however, suggests power can exist on a horizontal plane and recognizes all individuals have some part or role in decision making in encouraging the establishment of cooperative rather than competitive relationships.[26]

Nurses need to appreciate the power they possess as employees. Patrellis noted, "To believe you are powerless is the beginning of your downfall . . . supervisors need to feel their employees have what it takes to accomplish the organization's objectives . . . your supervisor needs you . . . when you realize mutual dependence exists, and you can provide what is needed . . . you have power."[36] Nurses are professionals who are frequently employed by organizations. The proximity of the professional nurse to the patient-client in most health care organizations is an enviable one and can be useful as a source of power. In brief, the success of those institutions whose primary mission is patient care, is dependent upon the quality of the nursing services rendered. Rather than lamenting a salaried employee status, nurses need to find ways to channel their unique and important contributions into strategies designed to improve relationships with hospital administrators and governing boards, increase the opportunities for interdependent working relationships with other employee health care providers, strive to achieve win-win situations, and ultimately enjoy the benefits that consistently accrue with outstanding levels of performance.[36]

Nurses can further cultivate and enhance their personal power by developing a sense of their ability to communicate using nonverbal behavior and dress. Power is, indeed, communicated by one's nonverbal behavior, whether it results from illusion, perception, or one's self-confidence, dress, or mannerisms.[25] Lamar illustrates the power of nonverbal behavior when she gives the following negative example:

> Ms. A., the Vice President or Director of Nursing arrives to an administrative committee meeting 10 minutes late wearing a well-worn and slightly snug white uniform. She is carrying a stack of file folders, each filled with paper. The meeting has already begun and she pulls up a chair to the table. She offers her usual apologies as she shuffles papers in an attempt to find the material being discussed and that which she is expected to present.[25]

Who among us has not worked with such an individual, and what lasting impressions have we formed of this person's capabilities? Certainly the image of power is not paramount in such individuals. Therefore, nurses should be aware of what Lamar identifies as impression management as one means of increasing an individual's personal power.[36]

Another component of personal power is the ability to analyze and tend to the language individuals use to communicate with others in the workplace. Language is the means by which humans communicate and interpret ideas, emotions, and experiences.

> "Words captivate and compel, or hobble and bag. . . . Words rich in meaning generate excitement, and the use of metaphors can give added meaning to work. . . . nurses need to give added attention to the use and subtleties of language, to the need to develop strong linguistic skills, to remain sensitive to the values implicit in varying lexicons, and to appreciate the discretions often "implied" in verbal and written forms of communication if they expect to strengthen their overall ability to improve their performance and acquire power."[18]

Communication is highly valued as an integral element of the nursing process. Nurses focus on the need to develop excellent communication skills, but as Henry and LeClair note: "While communication is widely discussed in nursing . . . language and the recognition that words have different meanings for different people" is frequently neglected.[18] Nurses work with different kinds of people on a daily basis: patients, and their families, colleagues, and other health professionals—and may need to use different words with different people, recognizing that the words selected may also have different meanings for different people. Quality care, for example, might "mean timely and courteous service to clients; holistic assessment and family education to nurses; and an appropriate per case cost and reimbursement to finance officers."[18] Developing their language use and analysis skills in the workplace could lead to an increase in power and influence.

Finally, if nurses are to utilize personal power, they must distinguish between using personal power as a form of self-aggrandizement and using personal power to achieve the goals of the organization. Booth argues quite persuasively that individuals who must achieve personal goals at the expense of others will find themselves consistently involved in tenuous situations, rendered powerless, and displaced within a given period of time.[9] Power accrues, however, when individuals use personal power to achieve the goals of the organization. These individuals derive satisfaction from seeing others achieve; they reward talent and eventually build teams in which power is shared. Thus the group gains influence and is able to foster reciprocal loyalties and relationships between the organization and employee groups.

Nurses must, therefore, endorse attempts to promote the cultivation of personal power, keeping in mind the need to articulate personal power with professional and organizational goals. Once individual nurses recognize our sense of professional identity and accept, maintain, and defend our common interests, particularly in relation to our workplace, then we will indeed demonstrate our power to change the conditions under which we presently practice.

The third law of power identified by Berle states: "Power is invariably based upon a system of ideals or a philosophy."[8] Throughout its history nursing has been guided by concepts that have exemplified its ideals and philosophical foundations. Concepts such as caring, health, nursing, environment, and individuality have remained dominant concerns among nurses who perceive their task as assisting patient-clients to attain, maintain, or regain health through the "diagnosis and treatment of human responses to actual or potential health problems."[34] Indeed, although these concepts can be gleaned from the early writings of Nightingale, they are present in the published works of contemporary nurse theorists.

Ideologies serve to communicate visions, doctrines, ideas, manners, or a set of characteristics subscribed to by individuals, groups, or programs. Ideologies often draw individuals and groups together whenever there is consensus about an issue or the need to appear united in order to achieve definite goals. They can form a basis upon which individuals or groups structure their thinking or attempt to convince others to share in particular views of life or specific cultural norms. Rokeach suggests there are three major ideological belief systems: (1) descriptive-existential, (2) evaluative, and (3) prescriptive-proscriptive. Descriptive-existential beliefs are those capable of being either true or false; evaluative beliefs offer judgments regarding the goodness or badness of an object or topic; and prescriptive-proscriptive beliefs are those that judge the degree of desirability or undesirability of the means or ends of specific actions.[40] Ideologies often incorporate personal, social, and moral aspects of one's visions, doctrines, ideas, programs, or agendas.

Nurses have generally not subscribed to the descriptive-existential belief system, perhaps because of the difficulties in establishing the rightness or wrongness of specific actions in a fluid profession such as nursing. Nurses have, however, utilized both the evaluative and prescriptive-proscriptive belief systems in conceptualizing and operationalizing their ideological and philosophical positions. Nursing has evolved from early perceptions describing it as "woman's work" to recognition as a professional discipline.

Although nursing's basic ideologies, as outlined in the concepts stated above, have remained remarkably intact throughout the professionalization journey, numerous internal disagreements have served to distract nurses, diverting their efforts from the profession as a whole toward more specialized group constituencies. Although nurses themselves may have understood the issues being debated and the need to resolve their differences internally, other groups such as consumers, physicians, and other health care providers have become increasingly confused about what nurses view as their visions, doctrines, and missions of caring.

Recently, the AMA proposed introducing the registered care technologist into the health care system. These individuals would be prepared to function in acute-care facilities after having received a minimum of 9 months of instructional and practical preparation.[1] Nurses have focused on such issues as the minimum educational preparation necessary to practice professional nursing, entry into practice, licensure requirements, titling, and appropriate roles and responsibilities; the AMA proposal, however, presents a clear challenge to nursing's evaluative and prescriptive-proscriptive belief systems. Nurses from all constituencies have been quick to respond to the proposal, describing it as poorly conceived, and a most undesirable means of solving the problem of providing quality care.

There is no doubt that the caring ideology espoused by nurses embodies power! The need to maintain quality care has emerged as a focal point in arguing against the AMA proposal. Nurses everywhere are being urged by their individual organizations to renew their commitment to the profession first and to individual specialized concerns second. "Professional bonding," based upon a set of mutual ideals, has become a reality as evidenced by the united stand taken at a recent summit meeting by nurses representing 46 national nursing organizations, all of whom endorsed a position opposing the AMA proposal.[2] Now is the time for nurses and the profession to reach a new consensus regarding the direction the profession should take and the methods by which success can be achieved. Only by reaffirming nursing's basic ideologies can nurses realize their potential in providing care, while simultaneously experiencing a sense of completeness that comes from fulfilling work. The power inherent in ideologies can be used by nurses to display their talents to consumers, physicians, and other health care providers.

"Power is exercised through, and depends on institutions," states Berle's fourth invarient law of power.[8] *Institutions* refer to a set of established practices or systems and organizations with a particular purpose. Institutions have two facets: (1) they have organized patterns of roles, the behaviors of which are often enforced by using positive and negative sanctions; and (2) there are patterned habits of thought learned by individuals assigned to perform the roles deemed necessary for the institutions effective and efficient functioning.[11]

Nurses have historically practiced their profession within a variety of institutional structures, although hospitals, clinics, physician's offices, and schools have been the key locations. Unfortunately, structure often dictates function, and institutions such as those listed above have tended to dictate the roles and functions to nursing within parameters largely influenced and dominated by the intrinsic medical establishment. Added to these restrictions were those imposed by legal definitions of what constituted nursing care and the requirement in some instances that nurses be supervised by a physician, dentist, or podiatrist! Even today, many of these institutions continue to ignore the independent functions and professional services nursing is capable of providing consumers.

Nursing has begun to initiate actions designed to modify, if not replace, some of the traditional structures that have prevented nursing from becoming an institution in its own right, responsible for determining its own parameters of practice. Many state nursing associations have obtained legislative support to revise state nurse practice acts to reflect an enlightened perspective of nursing practice using definitions of professional nursing such as the one suggested by the ANA. It is highly likely that the changing health care delivery scene will facilitate more of these efforts and will enlarge significantly nursing's power to serve patient-client populations in ever-expanding roles.

Bakalis maintains that power must combine with purpose in a harmonious relationship to achieve effective action and that institutions, no less than people, must possess the right combination of both in order to operate effectively.[6] Nursing has published a very clear statement of purpose in "The Social Policy Statement."[3] Keeping that purpose in focus, nurses must combine their strong sense of professional identity with their knowledge of the organizations in which they work in order to exercise their power through the use of organizational processes. Hickson and others proposed three variables that when blended together govern the power a subunit has within any single organization: centrality, substitutability, and coping with uncertainty. Centrality refers to the extent to which a subunit's activities connect with other organizational units and the degree to which other units' operations would be affected should the subunit stop functioning. Substitutability refers to how easily members of any given subunit can be replaced either from within or from outside the organization; and coping with uncertainty is defined as the ability of a subunit to respond effectively and efficiently to anticipated or, more often, unanticipated events that may confront the organization. The theory argues that the more a subunit can remain central, reduce its vulnerability to substitutability, and constructively cope with uncertainty, the more power it will accrue relative to other subunits in the organization.[19]

If Hickson and others[19] are correct, then their theory offers a framework easily adapted to those institutional structures most frequently encountered by nurses in their work situations. In most health care institutions, nurses are not just a central component of the organization but the primary element of most services provided patient-client consumers. Perhaps it is time to recognize this important position and to develop strategies that illustrate how crucial the delivery of nursing care really is in meeting institutional objectives. It was interesting to note that specific positions such as discharge planners, utilization reviewers, and admission workers were viewed as holding a central place in many health care institutions and were in fact recommended as choice positions for "social workers" seeking to accrue strategic organizational power.[10] Nurses might do well to reclaim these functions, which, when combined with the roles and responsibilities already ascribed to nurses, should ensure both a central role in the organization and the power that accompanies it.

A second source of power evolves around the notion of substitutability: the vulnerability to replacement by someone from within or without the institution.[19] Nurses have long suffered from the perception that a nurse is a nurse is a nurse. Hospitals and other care organizations continue to hire, assign, and even promote nurses without demanding appropriate educational and experiential credentials. The designated float nurse or float pool provides another example of how nurses have been viewed as easily substituted commodities within organizational structures. Perhaps nurses should consider the notion of substitutability in a new light and rather than be victimized by it, replace it with nurse-designated categories of substitutability to ensure safe practice. For example, perhaps critical care nurses could be cross-leveled with emergency room nurses, labor room and delivery nurses with operating room nurses, and intermediate level surgical or medical nurses with their staff nurse counterparts. Perhaps it is time to rebel against nurses being supplied by external employment agencies and insist on personnel who are loyal to the nurses within the institution. If substitutability is managed properly and purposely, it can provide nurses with immeasurable power.

Coping with uncertainty, the third variable in strategies for developing organization power,[19] should not pose any problems for the average nurse working in most health care delivery systems today, because nurses are known to be masters of adaptation and improvisation, especially in using resources creatively. However, nursing's responses to uncertainty have tended to be more reactive than anticipative in most instances. A slight philosophical adjustment by most nurses would enable them to garner increased organizational power by adopting proactive anticipatory postures designed to improve their own services by enhancing the organization as a whole as it, too, copes with an ever-changing health care arena.

Nurses have a comprehensive awareness of all aspects of the increasingly complex health care industry, as well as its strengths and weaknesses. They are also aware of the needs and concerns of clients, have the capability of using leverage to better shape and improve the system, and therefore must resign themselves to fighting to maintain principles of care with those forces that threaten to undermine and dilute the quality of nursing care.[27] A new health paradigm is materializing in this country in which the emphasis is shifting rapidly from the cell to society, from illness care to wellness care, from institutional care to home care, from physician care to team care, from individual-focused care to group-centered care, from specialty knowledge to general knowledge, and from holistic to humanistic care.[29]

Changing opportunities such as these are giving the profession of nursing new challenges and new possibilities for work within institutional structures. Now is the time for nurses to solidify their posture of centrality, identify, acceptable surrogates for substitutability, and demonstrate their ability to anticipate and cope with uncertainty. Once nurses assume more responsibility for practice and believe that they are indispensable resources for health care institutions, they will acquire and solidify the power bases required not only to effect change in health care institutions, but also to become a force actively engaged in determining the structure and functions such organizations will have relative to the delivery of health care.

Berle's fifth and last law of power states: "Power is invariably confronted with, and acts in the presence of, a field of responsibility."[8] A field of responsibility implies, by definition, the power to perform tasks or duties and to fulfill obligations to those individuals who expect and trust they will receive quality care. Acceptance of a field of responsibility signifies acceptance of a commitment to being fully accountable to one's designated duties and obligations.

Nursing's field of responsibility has been historically defined by Nightingale as manipulation of the patient's environment, attending to the patient's needs, and observing the patient's condition in order to assist restorative processes.[33] The ANA definition of nursing's field of responsibility suggests "nursing is the diagnosis and treatment of human responses to actual or potential health problems."[3] Finally, contemporary nurse models such as one proposed by Loomis and Wood extend the ANA's definition to include four major categories specifying groups of actual or potential health problems, designate six categories of human responses, and stipulate how nurses' clinical decisions evolve from the data being assessed within four prototypes of care-giving situations.[27] If these three definitions are merged, the result provides individuals and the profession with a clear notion of what constitutes nursing's field of responsibility.

The one variable not included in the preceding delineation of nursing's field of responsibility is that of setting. Unfortunately, nursing has traditionally allowed its field of responsibility to be defined within organizational settings and has, therefore, found its field of responsibility often being defined by hospital administrators, physicians, and even unions rather than by the nurses themselves. Adopting and subscribing to a field of responsibility independent from organization contexts permits nurses to perform professionally, with commitment, and assuming full accountability for their role in providing care. Nurses must divorce their responsibilities from settings if they wish to accumulate the power to perform nursing tasks and duties independently or even interdependently with other health care professionals.

Naisbitt suggests the new health paradigm is shifting from medically administered care to self-care and from institutional help to ambulatory or home-based assistance. This transition to a self-help/self-care paradigm features prevention, wellness, and the need to assume personal responsibility for one's health.[31] This paradigm shift also opens new settings and new opportunities for the practice of nursing. With a clearly defined field of responsibility such as the one proposed above, there is no reason why nurses cannot enlarge the scope of their responsibilities and fully meet the challenges always available to those who seek and accept them.

Nurses now have an opportunity to respond to changing health needs and populations; indeed, nurses have already indicated how they would change health care delivery in this country. Nurses maintain they would establish programs in which nurses assume primary responsibility for well maternity clinics and birthing centers; they would also establish and maintain managed-care programs for the mentally impaired, the developmentally disabled, the physically disabled, and the frail elderly. Nurses suggest a renewed emphasis on promoting health and would institute rigorous programs in school systems, where problems could be screened early and programs could be designed to foster healthy life styles. Nurses feel they can better serve their clients in home nursing situations if they assume full responsibility for referring their patient-clients to needed services, because physicians rarely know the available options. Nurses have proposed a multitiered system of healthcare in which they could serve in a variety of roles; nurse-practitioners would assess clients, treat them when appropriate, and refer them to the medical community when necessary; nurses would reestablish the control of home care in the tradition of Wald; and obviously nurses would lobby, finance, and work collectively to alter the legislative statutes currently preventing many of these changes from occurring.[21] These changes are possible given a clear statement and collective endorsement of a field of responsibility.

The acceptance of a field of responsibility would

provide not only a strong sense of personal and professional identity, but also the motivation to support their common interests. Berle states:

> Members of a group must realize that their interest is common . . . and they must be willing to accept, maintain, and defend that common interest . . . or risk being divided against each other to the detriment of their common interests . . . let members ask themselves when they conceive of the existence of any they, whether they consider themselves within it . . . the they many times never becomes a we . . . and when an individual speaks of we he/she thinks of himself/herself as a member of an organizational body with common attributes.[8]

The diversity of opinion that seems to pervade so many issues in nursing today might not assume the same level of prominence if nurses agreed on the basic parameters that form the boundaries of a field of responsibility.

A field of responsibility is also based on scientific knowledge and a scientifically based practice theory.[45] Knowledge is frequently recognized as one source of power. Nurses can now identify the major phenomena unique to their field of responsibility and have made rapid advances in recent years in clarifying their concepts and verifying assessment and intervention modalities by conducting sound programs of research. These efforts not only must continue, but also must enlist the support of all nurses if they are to find their way from the research laboratory or journal into practice.

Nurses must continue their education beyond the baccalaureate degree and pursue graduate study at both the master's and doctoral levels. The state of nursing's knowledge is rapidly advancing primarily because of the increased sophistication of research being conducted. Advanced study provides nurses with the processes by which they can organize and communicate their nursing knowledge to other health care professionals to effect change in the delivery of care. Advanced educational preparation provides nurses with specialized knowledge and skills that structure and improve the delivery of quality nursing care while simultaneously documenting its cost-effectiveness. The additional preparation provided by advanced training allows nurses to develop a philosophy and set of beliefs that can withstand the assaults on care dictated by institutional administrators, finance officers, and physicians; and the addition of graduate-level degrees offers the credibility associated with exacting and difficult work that is voluntary rather than work that is mandatory for entry-level positions. Finally, those nurses who complete graduate study have the security of knowing they are at least as well, if not better, prepared in their chosen field of study as many of their colleagues in other health related professions. What power and confidence! If nurses sought graduate study as the norm rather than the exception, there would be increases in salaries, responsibilities, roles, credibility, and accountability—and nurses would have a major role in establishing institutional policies. In fact, we have often wondered if the advice given to nurses not to pursue graduate work in nursing may not be just another ploy to prevent nurses from gaining full control of their work environments.

Given the power of knowledge and its role in guiding practice, nursing could determine how, where, and when it might extend its field of responsibility beyond existing boundaries and settings. Nursing has the ability and resources to offer comprehensive health care in conjunction with other health care providers. Nursing can respond to the challenges coming before it and will continue to change accordingly, but it must do so with vision, purpose, and a field of responsibility if it is to be successful.

SUMMARY

This chapter has considered the question, "Does nursing have the power to change the health care delivery system? Power is a perceptual entity, and although power is perceptual so also is perception power. How one perceives power, then, is a delicate portion of all interactions and is a crucial component of how one receives, transmits, integrates, and reacts in any given situation.

Willman notes a new generation of nurses is emerging: nurses who are creative rather than conforming; initiating rather than reacting; assertive rather than passive; change agents, not retardants; political activists, not victims; and independent, not dependent.[44] Today a new set of career opportunities is available in nursing. The future belongs to the visionary—to those who can create new configurations to respond to new demands and who have the courage to follow their vision.[41] Perhaps the time has come for nurses to cease their discussions and concern for power and instead direct their energies toward assuming enlarged roles in a rapidly changing health care environment. Perhaps returning to traditional values of caring, humanity, and recapturing the spirit of nursing will ultimately provide more power than is currently imaginable. Nursing has an opportunity to institutionalize itself as an integral component of the health care system when so many health care providers are voicing concern over and competing for resources. Nursing's primary resources are the aggregate of nurses themselves combined with their patient-clients.

Nursing has previously demonstrated its ability to make a significant difference in health care; there is no reason why it should not do so in the future. However, nurses must keep in perspective and balance the role of power and its related concepts, for as Benner notes:

> When power, status, autonomy, and wealth are preferred characteristics . . . [used to select or define a profession] . . . who can understand wanting to be a nurse? Only those who have participated in the triumph of the human spirit in circumstances as extreme as birth and death. Only those who have the courage to master the technology now used for cure and the virtuosity to provide care that makes the modern cures accessible, safe, humane, and healing.[7]

Need we say more? We think not.

REFERENCES

1. Am J Nurs: "News" 88(8):1131, 1988.
2. Am J Nurs: "News" 88(12):1716, 1988.
3. American Nurses' Association: Nursing: a social policy statement, Kansas City, Mo, 1980, The Association.
4. American Nurses' Association: personal communication, Kansas City, Mo, 1989.
5. Andrews L: Health care providers: the future marketplace and regulations, J Prof Nurs 2(1):51, 1986.
6. Bakalis MJ: Power and purpose, Phi Delta Kappan 65(1):7, 1983.
7. Benner P: Taken from Vital Signs Calendar, Menlo Park, Calif. 1989, Addison-Wesley Co., Inc.
8. Berle AA: Power, New York, 1969, Harcourt, Brace, and World.
9. Booth RZ: Power: a negative or positive force in relationships? Nurs Admin Quart 7(4):10, 1983.
10. Chernesky RH and Territo T: Sources of organizational power for women in the health care field, Soc Work Health Care 12(4)93, 1987.
11. Dugger WM: Power: an institutional framework of analysis, J Econ Issues 14(4):897, 1980.
12. Fagin CM: Opening the door on nursing's cost advantage, Nurs and Health Care 7(7):353, 1986.
13. Ginzberg E. The economics of health care and the future of nursing, J Nurs Admin 11(3):31, 32, 1981.
14. Gorman S and Clark N: Power and effective nursing practice, Nurs Outlook 34(3):129, 1986.
15. Gunn IP: Nursing innovations help reach traditional goals, Nurs and Health Care 7(7):359, 1986.
16. Harriman A: Women/men/management, New York, 1985, Prager Publishers.
17. Heineken J: Power-conflicting views, J Nurs Admin 15(11):36, 1985.
18. Henry B and LeClair H: Language, leadership, and power, J Nurs Admin 17(1):19, 1987.
19. Hickson D and others: A strategic contingencies theory of organizational power, Admin Sci Quart 16:216, 1971.
20. Holcombe B: Nurses fight back, Ms. 16(12):72, June 1988.
21. Huey FL: How nurses would change V.S. health care, Amer J Nurs 52:1482, 1988.
22. Kalish BJ: The promise of power, Nurs Outlook 22(1):42, 1978.
23. Kipnis D: The powerholders, Chicago, 1976, Univ of Chicago Press.
24. Kuhn R: Gaining power through practice, Heart and Lung 14(b):22A, 1985.
25. Lamar EK: Communicating personal power through nonverbal behavior, J Nurs Admin 15(1):41, 1985.
26. Lind A, Wilburn S, and Pate E: Power from within: feminism and the ethical decision-making process in nursing, Nurs Admin Quart April 1986, p. 50.
27. Loomis ME and Wood DJ: Cure: the potential outcome of nursing care, Image 15(1):4, 1983.
28. Lynaugh JE and Fagin CM: Nursing comes of age, Image 20(4):184, 1988.

29. McCormick KA: Preparing nurses for the technologic future, Nurs and Health Care 4(7):379, 1983.
30. May R: Power and innocence: a search for the sources of violence, New York, 1982, WW Norton & Co.
31. Naisbitt J: Megatrends, New York, 1982, Warner Books.
32. National Implementation Project. De Back, V. The nation's nurses: A credible profession doing an incredible job. No date.
33. Nightingale F: Notes on nursing, New York, 1969, Dover Publications.
34. Norris CM: Nursing theory: state of the art; projections for the future. Paper presented at the University of Wisconsin-Eau Claire, April 8, 1983.
35. Ostrander VR: Consumers look to nurses for affordable quality care, Nurs and Health Care 7(7):369, 1986.
36. Patrellis AJ: Your power as an employee, Supervisory Management 30(4):37, April 1985.
37. Peck SB: Nursing: on the cutting edge of opportunity, Nurs and Health Care 7(7):365, 1986.
38. Reverby S: Ordered to care: the dilemma of American nursing 1850-1945, New York, 1987, Cambridge Univ Press.
39. Roberts SJ: Oppressed group behavior: implications for nursing, Adv in Nurs Sci 5(4):21, 1983.
40. Rokeach M: The nature of human values, New York, 1973, The Free Press.
41. Smith G: The new health care economy: opportunities for nurse entrepreneurs, Nurs Outlook 35(4):182, 1987.
42. Sweeney SS: An analysis of selected exchange relations and transactions between a college of nursing and a selected public—its alumni, doctoral dissertation, Iowa City, 1982, University of Iowa.
43. Webster's Ninth New Collegiate Dictionary, Springfield, Mass, 1985, Merriam-Webster Inc.
44. Willman MD: Change and power. In Stevens KR, editor: Power and influence, New York, 1983, John Wiley & Sons.
45. Wooldridge PJ and others: Behavioral science and nursing theory, St. Louis, 1983, The CV Mosby Co.

CHAPTER **6**

The Future of Public Health

Lillian McCreight, RN, MPH

What is the status of the U.S. public health system? Are public health agencies and departments around the country able to act effectively against threats to the public well-being? If not, what barriers stand in their way? These were some of the questions addressed in *The Future of Public Health,* which reports on a study carried out by the Institute of Medicine (IOM), an arm of the National Academy of Science. The IOM, which was created in 1970 to study health policy issues, released the report in August 1988.

The study was supported by the Kellogg Foundation, with additional funding from the Centers for Disease Control and the Health Resources Administration of the U.S. Department of Health and Human Services. The concerns and questions on which the study focused were first articulated by members of the Association of State and Territorial Health Officials who were gravely concerned about what they saw in the public health system.

The 26 members of the study committee, who came from across the United States, represented many different disciplines and multiple perspectives, reflecting the diversity of public health. The committee had representatives from medicine, nursing, social work, and mental health, and also included health economists, historians, epidemiologists, and environmentalists. Many of them had federal, state, and local governmental experience.

Data collection included a review of existing databases, papers commissioned and presented on topics of particular interest, public hearings, and site visits. Four widely publicized public hearings were held across the country; people were invited to come and talk about their concerns and interests in public health.

Committee members made site visits to six states chosen for diversity in size, population, demographics, geography, and organization of their public health system. During these site visits, committee members and staff observed and talked with hundreds of persons representing a wide range of perspectives and interests. These people included employees of official public health agencies; representatives of voluntary health agencies; nurses, physicians, and other health professionals in other practice settings; and members of other disciplines with an interest in health. The contacts, however, were not limited to health professionals. Committee members talked with legislators, county councilmen and commissioners, legislative staff, community leaders, consumers of health services, and private citizens.

An enormous amount of data was collected through these interviews. Certain questions were asked of every person interviewed. In addition, tracer issues such as teen pregnancy, AIDS, environmental toxins, and Alzheimer's disease were used to get interviewees to speak specifically about problems and processes in public health. For example, an interviewer might ask a local public health nurse, "Tell me about teen pregnancy here. Do you have a problem?" Then the interviewer would listen for the system's dimensions of the response: whether and how a problem had been identified, how the public's atten-

Reprinted from *Nursing Outlook,* Vol. 37, No. 5, with permission

tion and support for action were engaged, what plans were made to alleviate the problem, what actions were being taken, and how progress was being evaluated. By listening to people talk about specific, concrete issues, the interviewers got a full description of the system. Computer technology was then used to search the narrative data for key words and phrases that would identify themes in the interviews.

The committee worked for more than two years and completed a draft report in the fall of 1987. In the time between the final committee work and publication of the report, the study went through a strenous peer review process, which is part of all National Academy of Science studies. After some modifications were made as a result of that process, the study was released in August 1988.

The report begins with a description of the problems and concerns that prompted the study, all of which culminated in a fear that the infrastructure of public health is suffering from neglect and that this country may not be able to marshal the forces necessary to address the public health problems facing us, such as AIDS and environmental toxins.

The report goes on to describe the ideal public health system envisioned by the committee as a standard against which to balance and measure the facts found in the study. It provides a brief review of the history of public health, acknowledging the major gains in health status and in protection of the population's health through public health measures and giving credit for those accomplishments.

The report then describes the public health system as the committee found it, highlights some of the barriers to effective action, gives conclusions, and offers recommendations. This article focuses on some of the barriers and the recommendations for overcoming them.

Barriers to Action

The mission and content of public health

The barriers made up several clusters, one of which was the lack of consensus on the mission and content of public health. In the ideal world, public health would have a clearly defined mission and everyone would agree on what public health is and is not. The committee did not find such agreement.

One of the questions the committee members asked each person they interviewed was, "What is your definition of public health?" Almost universally, the first response was, "Do you mean what public health agencies do, or what really is public health?" That response demonstrated that when we talk about the public health system, we are not talking only about what public health agencies do; we are talking about all of the dimensions of our society that have an impact on the public's health. The committee's recommendations include a mission statement that says, "The mission of public health is fulfilling society's interest in assuring conditions in which people can be healthy." Numerous roles and players are essential if that mission is to be accomplished.

Indigent Care. One area in which there was lack of consensus about the content of public health was responsibility for indigent care. One has only to look around the country at where responsibility for indigent care is organizationally located in the states to see the diversity of opinion.

The Medicaid program is considered the major initiative taken by states, in partnership with the federal government, to address needs of the indigent for health care. The differences in placement of responsibility for Medicaid reflect the lack of consensus on whether or not indigent care is a public health activity. For example, in some states the Medicaid program is located in the Department of Health, while in other states it is located in the Department of Social Services. In still other states, there is a completely separate Medicaid agency.

The committee found that the location of the Medicaid program was considered by many to be a double-edged sword. In states where the Medicaid program was located in the Department of Health, people often described it as a steamroller that overwhelmed other public health initiatives by the size and complexity of its programming, and its budget. Others felt that the preventive and broad social aspects of public health were getting lost in the attention given to the Medicaid program.

On the other hand, in states where the Medicaid program was housed outside of the state's public health agency, people experienced considerable frustration because resources that might have been brought to bear on preventing health problems were unavailable to them. In these states, the Medicaid program tended to focus almost entirely on payments for institutional care and physician services, with little attention to prevention of health problems and some of the other dimensions of health care.

While recognizing that both organizational choices have pros and cons, the committee clearly favored placing organizational responsibility for indigent care in the public health arena. The committee also recognized that the problem of indigent care will not be solved by individual states; there must be a federal initiative if universal access to care is to be ensured. The desirability of universal access to care was never in question for the people interviewed; the issue was how to accomplish this. People also discussed the problem of a single state attempting to provide universal access and thereby becoming a magnet for people in surrounding states who lacked access to care. The state offering universal access would soon become overburdened and unable to sustain the program.

While clearly stating its belief that responsibility for universal access to care lies with the federal government, the committee acknowledged that until a solution is found, the responsibility will rest with public health agencies, which must fill the gaps and be providers of last resort for persons without other access to care. This provider role is legitimate and viable and reinforces the desirability of locating responsibility for indigent care in public health.

Environmental Health. Public health's relationship to environmental health was a second area of disagreement over content. Here too the committee found enormous diversity in the organization of states' environmental agencies.

One of the clearest examples of the dilemmas created by the organizational smorgasbord came from an interview with a man who had responsibility within the local public health agency for eight to ten environmental health programs, each one of which was accountable to a different state agency. When the environmental director was confronted with a problem in his local area requiring immediate attention, such as a spill of potentially toxic materials along a roadway, the shuffle would begin as to who would provide the guidance, authority, and technical assistance needed to take action. How the problem was named (e.g., toxics, drinking water, ground water, hazardous waste, solid waste) determined which agency was accountable and there was usually prolonged inaction during the attempts to fix responsibility. The environmental director found himself advocating for local ordinances that would clarify his authority to act, despite his knowledge that the problems were rarely limited to one locality.

The committee's recommendations strongly state the need to maintain an organizational link between public health and environmental health. This link is of unquestioned benefit in investigating and addressing the health impact of environmental protection. In one state where health and environmental responsibilities *are* combined, the citizens' perception that their health is being adversely affected by something in the environment (e.g., the water supply or emissions from a nearby industry) gets a joint response. The environmental staff may intensify its monitoring activities, while the medical epidemiology team assesses the symptoms and patterns of illness in the population. When a problem is found, there is a double-pronged strategy for correction, and when concerns are unfounded, environmental staff have the expertise of physicians, nurses, and health educators to help interpret the findings for the community and allay unnecessary fears.

The committee recommendation notes that the combination of public health and environmental agencies allows use of the skills of people traditionally working in health agencies, like health educators, to raise the public's awareness of environmental risks, to help convey the concept of relative risk, and to demonstrate how individual choices can modify health risks.

Mental Health. The third area of disagreement about the content of public health centered on the relationship of public health to mental health. Some reasons why mental health has become separate from public health in many states are clear. For example, certain constituencies have sought organizational visibility for mental health to make it easier to advocate attention and resources for specific problems. Also, at one time treatment of mental illness became so institutionally focused that people found it hard to relate mental health to other more community-based public health activities. However, what the committee heard from mental health and public health practitioners around the country pointed to a real need to draw on mental health expertise in addressing a number of public health problems.

The advantages of such a partnership are obvious for problems like alcohol and drug abuse and their relationship to motor vehicle accidents and domestic violence. The very disturbing patterns of child and spouse abuse and their impact on infant health and mortality have been vividly illustrated in studies on battering during pregnancy and the link between battering and low birthweight.

The committee recommended linking mental health expertise to public health expertise to address some of these problems, beginning by making such links locally. Even with the different organizational arrangements in each state, local partnerships have the potential for a positive impact on the health of the population.

Education. The final area in which there was a lack of consensus on content relates to public health's role in encouraging healthful behaviors through education and modification of the social environment. For many, the suggestion that such actions were not a part of public health was heresy. Those persons viewed education and programs to facilitate behavior change as major tools for affecting health problems related to individual choices and lifestyles. However, others questioned whether such activities belong in public health or in education.

The disagreement centered on whether the hard science of public health (e.g., epidemiologic studies, laboratory findings) is compromised by the intermingling of "soft" behavioral and social science content. The committee recommended both attention in practice to the behavioral influences on health and strengthening of the behavioral and social science content in educational programs that prepare individuals for public health practice.

The essential work of public health agencies

The second cluster of barriers to effective action revolved around the essential work of public health agencies. The committee identified three essential functions of these agencies: assessment and surveillance, policy development, and assurance of access to the benefits of public health.

Assessment and Surveillance. The assessment and surveillance function of public health agencies involves assembling data to determine the status of the public's health, including existing, emerging, and anticipated threats that should be a focus of public health action. The same databases provide the measures needed to assess progress toward improved health status. The impediments to this function identified by the committee include fragmented data collection (exacerbated by some of the organizational fragmentation described earlier), gaps in data, and lack of support for the assessment and surveillance function. The organizational identity for a major portion of this function is in vital records and health statistics. Although in some states this unit is close to the policy and decision-making level, in others it is buried under several layers of bureaucracy, or virtually invisible on the organizational chart.

Policy Development. This function of public health agencies should ideally be characterized by a coherent, comprehensive, and inclusive process for setting health policy direction for the state. The committee found that policy direction was most often fragmented by structure and driven by single issues or crises. In one state the committee visited, all the legislative time and attention were being given to one individual's need for a heart transplant, to the exclusion of broad public health needs.

Policy development is also complicated by the need to reach agreement on interventions that the community will accept for modifying the social environment to benefit health. The issues raised during this process are not limited to issues of professional or organizational responsibility, but also include conflicts between the value of protecting the public's health and that of protecting individual freedom of choice. Examples include seat belt laws, tax increases on tobacco to limit its economic accessibility to young people, and AIDS and sex education in the schools. These value conflicts should be debated and resolved in the context of health policy choices, and the responsibility for setting health policy lies with public health agencies.

Some specific recommendations in the study address state health agencies' review of health statutes that are in fact statements of health policy. These recommendations call for adequate legal authority to protect the public's health, and laws that allow use of public health methodologies in addressing or preventing problems. Veterans of the recent flurry of legislation around AIDS will appreciate the necessity of the guardian and leadership roles of public health agencies in defining laws that adequately protect health, and in pointing out where proposed statutes run counter to the achievement of public health goals and the most effective use of public health resources.

Assurance of Access to Benefits of Public Health. The third area of public health agency function described by the study was assurance of access to the benefits of public health. This again raises the issue of universal access. The committee's recommendations address access not only to medical care but also to a broad range of public health benefits. There are places in this country where a person who is unsure of the safety of the drinking water cannot locate help in making that determination. The committee found that accessibility to public health services varied enormously across the country, from fully staffed, comprehensive health departments to places where there may be a public health nurse who appears every two to four weeks or where there are no identifiable public health programs at all.

The committee strongly advocated a local public health presence everywhere in the country. That does not mean having a fully staffed health department in every community; however, citizens should be aware of where to call and they should know that they will get a response when they have concerns about the health of their community. Further, even in the absence of calls, the citizens need to know that someone is paying attention to basic public health services.

Specifying "basic" services posed a dilemma for the committee. There was ready agreement among its members that certain basic services should be assured everywhere in the country (e.g., protection against communicable disease, safe drinking water, safe disposal of waste). Beyond these, the committee agreed that the basic services that need to be assured depend on what health threats exist in a given community. The committee therefore avoided proposing a list of basic services that could be limiting. We chose instead to reference the table of contents of the *Model Standards for Community Health** and to challenge states and localities to tailor that list to their own needs, choosing among priorities and supporting those choices in their allocation of resources.

The committee chose the word "assurance" carefully to communicate that public health agencies need not be the provider of all the services seen as essential. Rather, assurance implies that the assessment function will provide information on all the needs that affect people's health in a given area. The goal will be meeting all of those needs, regardless of who the providers are.

The committee's report also uses a stronger word, "guarantee," in the belief that states should identify services so critical to the public's health that the state or public health agency should guarantee meeting all the needs for those services. For example, at least one state currently guarantees adequate treatment for anyone with active tuberculosis. The guarantee extends beyond follow-up of contacts and the offer of treatment to the provision of supervised therapy and, when necessary, state-paid hospitalization. In another state, infant mortality is considered to be such a critical problem that every pregnant woman is guaranteed prenatal care. The committee encourages states to do the analysis and priority determination that can lead to similar limited guarantees.

Public health leadership

Another cluster of barriers to effective action identified by the committee involved the issue of public health leadership. Ideally, public health leaders would be technically competent in the substance of public health issues, and would have management abilities, communication skills, skills in the public decision-making process (including its political aspects), and the ability to marshal constituencies for effective action. This ideal is not what the committee found.

Conflict Between Technical and Political Expertise. One of the biggest barriers to effective leadership was found to be the interaction of public health technical

* American Public Health Association, Association of State and Territorial Health Officials, National Association of County Health Officials, U.S. Conference of Local Health Officials, U.S. Department of Health and Human Services, Public Health Service. *Model Standards: A Guide for Community Preventive Health Services.* American Public Health Association, Washington, DC, 1985.

expertise with the political process. Public health professionals, who are often able to see a solution for a problem, expressed frustration with legislators for not passing enabling legislation or regulations, or with elected county officials for not supporting the solutions with resources. On the other hand, political leaders described their frustration at the unresponsiveness of "those eggheads over at the department of health who have ideas that will never work in the real world." The tension and conflict reflected in these two points of view present a major dilemma for effective leadership. The report addresses the need to develop leaders with the skills to articulate public health problems and translate solutions in ways that make them marketable and acceptable in the political environment.

The committee also recognized that the ability of leaders to resolve the political/technical conflict requires not only a set of skills but also the belief that political accountability is an essential, healthy part of democracy. We need public health leaders who recognize the essential role of political accountability and include the necessary political skills and attitudes in their sphere of activity and influence.

A second barrier to effective leadership is lack of continuity of leadership in public health. State health officer positions in particular are characterized by frequent turnover; in 1987, the median tenure for state health officers was only two years. There are a variety of reasons for this, including political/technical conflict, inadequate pay, effects of reorganization, frustration with the structure of decision making, and low professional prestige.

Moreover, in many states, when a new governor is elected, all the state agency heads are replaced. The qualifications of the new appointees depend entirely on whether or not the governor deliberately seeks people known to be qualified leaders in public health. It is entirely arbitrary. Consequently, in such systems, the type of individuals selected for leadership positions varies considerably. In one state the committee visited, for example, the political appointment process extended through the three top layers of state agencies, and it was only four or five layers down in the organization that the public health professionals who carried out programs on an ongoing basis could be found.

In such situations, professionals stated that, "We just keep doing those things that are not controversial and not difficult to implement. We can't get anything new started or get tough and sensitive issues addressed." Another frequent response was, "This administration is really not helpful, but they will disappear and maybe the next one will be better." Both responses reflect the frustration and lack of productivity that can result when people are just doing ordinary tasks and waiting out a bad time.

Although the committee did not carry out a comprehensive study of the federal government, it did identify a necessary role of *national* leadership in public health, not only in guaranteeing universal access, but also in identifying and taking public positions on specific health problems and in allocating funds to accomplish national public health objectives. The Association of State and Territorial Health Officials (ASTHO) has drafted a proposed bill for introduction in Congress that would fund preventive initiatives to address these national public health objectives. The funding would be on a capitation basis calculated at $4.00 per person, which totals something over a billion dollars. Although this amount may seem enormous, it would represent only a small proportion of the total this nation spends on health care. This is just one example of a concrete initiative that is an appropriate role for national leadership.

National leadership can also build constituencies to support both appropriate action and the development of a public health research and data base. While a National Institute of Health may not be necessary in every state, the additional knowledge that comes from research is needed. Support for research and dissemination of findings are other important roles for federal leadership.

The committee acknowledged that both historically and in recent years, some national leadership has been provided, such as the positions taken by Surgeon General Koop in support of public health efforts. They stressed, however, that public support should not depend on one individual, but should be institutionalized and made consistent and reliable. The committee therefore recommended that a task force be appointed to examine the structure and process of the federal government and identify ways to foster a national leadership role supportive of public health efforts.

Lack of Communication Between Public Health and Medicine. Another barrier to effective leadership was found to be the poor relationship between public health and medicine. In the ideal public health system, each would contribute its expertise in a partnership to influence health problems. The committee instead found a lack of communication, with recognized leaders in the medical community unaware of most public health activities.

Therefore, the committee report advocates building a partnership between medicine and public health. Recent experience in one state health agency, which collaborated with private practice obstetricians to solve problems of access to obstetrical care, has shown that such a partnership can be productive. The health commissioner in that state convened a task force that developed workable solutions to the physicians' problems and promoted public health objectives as well.

Lack of Community Organization. The task force example leads to the final barrier to effective leadership identified by the committee—the lack of community organization for effective public health action. Community organization is needed to build coalitions and encourage special interest groups to combine their efforts so that problems are seen as community problems rather than as health department problems.

The structure and organization of public health

A fourth set of barriers was found in the structure and organization of public health. Ideally, there would be a single, coherent organization with all public health factions in organizational alignment. In reality, public health is practiced in a deliberately complex set of organizational and jurisdictional relationships. The committee's recommendations emphasized the state role, because the state has the responsibility for health (since that is not one of the powers specifically designated to the federal government in the Constitution). The phrase used in the report is "the state is where the health buck stops." The states cannot abdicate their responsibility for health actions not taken at the federal or local levels of government. States are responsible for the health of the public regardless of what the other players in the public health system are doing or not doing.

The committee, however, does strongly support delegation of functions by the state to local health entities. In addition, the state has a responsibility to build the capacity of local health departments so that delegation is effective. Where capacity cannot be developed locally, or where local public health programs are absent, the state must assume responsibility.

The committee further advocates the creation or re-creation of state and local health councils. The term "council" was deliberately chosen to avoid confusion with "boards of health." The latter, which have now largely disappeared, were predominantly made up of physicians and functioned without input from consumers. Public health councils, on the other hand, would be made up of people who are consumer-oriented, as well as community leaders. Local and state councils would provide oversight for the work of the official public health agency, representing the eyes and ears of the community, and giving the agency feedback on community needs and community responses to public health initiatives. Council members would also become advocates for public health in their respective spheres of influence.

Finally, councils could specify qualifications for leadership positions in the agency and make recommendations on the appointment of leaders as a way of buffering some of the political aspects of the selection process.

Another structural and organizational issue relates to the creation in some states of health and human service "super agencies." About half of the states have combined health and social service agencies. In the states with super- or umbrella-agency structures, public health is perceived by policymakers as predominantly a welfare program, with public health's relevance to broader societal issues diminished. In these states, coordination of services to individual clients was emphasized, while less attention was given to the broad, population-based functions of public health. Usually, administrative generalists with no formal health background or expertise were appointed as agency heads, while the experts in health were subordinated in both the organizational structure and policy-making process. Overall, the committee found that agencies of this type were less attuned to a broad vision of public health.

While affirming that coordination of services for individual clients is a critical function, the committee questioned whether a broad organizational structure is the most effective way to achieve that objective. We concluded that the interests of public health are best served if public health activities are kept organizationally separate from the income-maintenance programs that are the major component of social service agencies.

Deficits in capacity to conduct programs

The fifth and final set of barriers to effective action described in the report are deficits in the capacity to operate programs. An ideal public health system would have an adequate knowledge base, enough well-trained personnel, technical expertise, strong constituency support, competent management, and fiscal resources that match existing needs. That is not what the committee found.

Inadequate Knowledge Base. Public health decisions are almost always made with incomplete data. The available facts are collected and weighed in the light of possible implications, and the best decision possible is made. The report makes a strong plea for ongoing development of public health's knowledge base, even while recognizing that it is very difficult to support research in what are largely service agencies. In this context, universities play an important role in conducting research that is relevant to health problems in their communities. Public health agencies could enlarge the public health knowledge base by building research linkages with universities.

Lack of Well-Trained Personnel. Most workers and some leaders in public health have no formal education in the field. Even those who have some technical expertise and preparation may lack management skills. The committee's recommendations send a strong message to schools of public health about education for the practice of public health. The committee did not hold the unrealistic expectation that everyone who works in a public health agency should have a master's degree in public health. However, collaboration between public health agencies and schools of public health to provide meaningful continuing education for existing public health practitioners is not only realistic, but essential.

The committee's recommendations on educational content for public health practice principally target schools of public health and departments of preventive medicine; however, they are also directed to colleges of nursing, schools of social work, nutrition programs, and any other educational institution that prepares health professionals to play a role in public health. The committee urges that public health content be included in the curriculum of every health professional. Collective efforts can have an enormous impact on improving the content of educational programs and also in strengthening public health practice.

Shortage of Technical Expertise. In examining the issue of qualified personnel, the committee identified not only deficits in the preparation of existing practitioners, but actual shortages in some areas, such as epidemiology. The report expresses concern that too few epidemiologists are available, not only in the area of communicable diseases but also in the application of basic public health science to the problems of infant mortality and emerging environmental issues.

Weak Constituency Support and Inadequate Fiscal Resources. The recommendations on capacity building emphasized the need to develop constituencies for public health and build fiscal support for public health efforts. There is an obvious link between the report's other recommendations and the need for fiscal support. Political support of specific initiatives like the ASTHO legislation previously mentioned and candidates with strong public health agendas is needed. If attention is given to the issues of leadership, constituency building, and making the public health agenda understandable and acceptable to the public, it is likely that some of the fiscal support issues will be addressed. As public health's assessment and database functions develop and it becomes easier to see and to measure, through research, the impact of public health interventions, answers to the questions of policy-makers and resource allocators on the costs and benefits of their investments in public health will also become clearer.

Notwithstanding the diversity of the public health system and its problems, the committee found a core of support, expertise, and willingness to take on tough problems that will provide a foundation on which a stronger public health system can be built. The report's impact will be measured by the seriousness with which its findings and recommendations are considered by all the components of the broad public health system.

Suggested Additional Readings for Part I

The context of community health nursing practice

Anderson RC: Ethical issues in health promotion and health education, *AAOHN J* 35(5):220-223, 1987.

Aroskar M: The interface of ethics and politics in nursing, *Nurs Outlook* 35(6):268-272, 1987.

Davis K and Rowland D: Uninsured and underserved: inequities in health care in the United States. In Lee PR and Estes CL, editors: The nation's health, Jones & Bartlett, 298-308, 1990.

Holleran C: Nursing beyond national boundaries: the 21st century, *Nurs Outlook* 36(2):72-75, 1988.

Kerley LJ: The escalating health care costs of AIDS: who will pay? *Nurs Forum* 25(1):5-14, 1990.

Maglacas A: Health for all: nursing's role, *Nurs Outlook* 36(2): 66-71, 1988.

Maraldo PJ: Home care should be the heart of a nursing-sponsored national health plan, *Nurs & Health Care* 10(6): 301-304, 1989.

Masson V: If new graduates went to the community first, *Nurs Outlook* 36(4):172-173, 1988.

McCreight L: The future of public health, *Nurs Outlook* 37(5): 219-225, 1989.

Millenson M: Health care in America, *Mod Healthcare*, Sept 1988.

Millenson M: Beyond medicare, *Consumer Rep* 375-391, June 1988.

Moccia P: Re-claiming our communities, *Nurs Outlook* 38(2):73-77, 1990.

Monteiro LA: Florence Nightingale on public health nursing, *Am J Public Health* 75(2):181-185, Feb. 1985.

Montgomery P: At risk: the hidden cost of neglecting public health, *Common Cause* 29-33, March/April 1989.

Reinhardt VE: Economics, ethics and the American health care system, *The New Physician*, Oct 1985.

Reinhardt VE: Rationing the health care surplus: An American tragedy, *Nurs Economics* 4(3):101-108, 1986.

Schnell E: Lessons from the Canadian health care system, *Nurs Economics* 7(6):306-309, 1989.

Smith JB: Levels of public health, *Public Health Nurs* 2(3): 138-144, 1985.

Tansey E and Lentz J: Generalists in a specialized profession, *Nurs Outlook* 36(4):174-178, 1988.

Watson J: The moral failure of the patriarchy, *Nurs Outlook* 38(2):62-66, 1990.

White MS: Construct for public health nursing, *Nurs Outlook*, 527-530, Nov-Dec 1982.

Wilson LM: The American revolution in health care, *AAOHN J* 36(10):402-420, Oct 1988.

PART II

CONCEPTUAL MODELS FOR COMMUNITY HEALTH NURSING PRACTICE

Conceptual models for practice are necessary in community health nursing as we strive to enhance our credibility as a profession. Part II presents several models, because no one conceptual model is appropriate for all nursing practice in community health.

Conceptual models are a necessary part of theory development in nursing and serve as components of the foundation of community nursing practice. Conceptual models guide community health nursing practice by providing direction and organizing information in a meaningful way. The selection and use of a particular model are determined by the focus of the model and the unique needs of the target population. The chosen model is then used to guide the community health nurse in utilizing the nursing process to promote health for individuals, families, and communities.

Conceptual models in nursing generally describe relationships and interactions among the four essential components of person, environment, health, and nursing. The articles presented in Part II detail perspectives of one or more of these primary concepts. Each selected article describes the concepts' relationships and interactive patterns as they apply to community health. Each model presented describes a unique perspective of health and nursing and their relationship to family, community, and society. The articles in this part present a particular emphasis on the environment's positive and negative influences on community inhabitants.

The articles selected illustrate current conceptual models in nursing and the social sciences. This section also includes epidemiology, because of its historical significance and usefulness in understanding community health problems. Evaluation of theoretical and conceptual models is essential. This important aspect of community health programs is illustrated in Part II as it deals with quality assurance in community health nursing.

CHAPTER 7

Community-as-Client: A Model for Practice

Elizabeth Anderson, RNC, DrPH
Judith McFarlane, RNC, DrPH
Anne Helton, RN, MS

The use of models to guide practice, education and research in nursing has been standard practice for some time.[1,2] During the past several years, models of community health practice have appeared as well.[3-5] The Community-as-Client model, an adaptation of the Neuman Health Care Systems model, is an effort to put into practice the definition of public health nursing as a synthesis of public health and nursing.[6,7]

The four central concepts, person, health, environment and nursing, form the basis for any conceptual model of nursing.[8] Each is defined in the box at right to provide a foundation for the more specific description of the Community-as-Client model.

According to this model, the community has eight major subsystems: recreation, safety and transportation, communication, education, health and social services, economics, politics and government, and the physical environment. The core or basic structure of the community is its people, their values, beliefs, culture, religion, laws and mores. Within a boundary (usually geopolitical), the people and subsystems in dynamic interaction comprise the whole of the community. As a system, this whole represents more than simply the sum of its parts.

Reprinted from *Nursing Outlook,* Vol. 34, No. 5, with permission of American Journal of Nursing, © 1986.

Definitions of concepts central to the community-as-client model

Person

The community; all persons who reside within a defined geopolitical boundary or who share a common characteristic.

Environment

All the conditions, circumstances and influences surrounding and affecting the development of the community, which is, in and of itself, also part of the environment.

Health

Competence to function; a definable state of equilibrium in which subsystems are in harmony so that the whole can perform at its maximum potential.

Nursing

A profession that brings a unique, holistic view to the community and contributes to the health of the community by participating in the community assessment; identifying and diagnosing problems amenable to nursing intervention; planning for the alleviation of community health problems; carrying out nursing interventions in conjunction with others; and evaluating the effect of those interventions on the community's health.

Surrounding the community is its *normal line of defense* or the level of health the community has reached over time. The normal line of defense may include characteristics such as high immunity, low infant mortality or middle class socioeconomic status. It includes the usual patterns of coping, along with problem-solving capabilities: it represents the community's health.

The outermost "buffer zone," the community's *flexible line of defense,* represents a dynamic level of health resulting from a temporary response to stressors. This temporary response may be a neighborhood mobilization against an environmental stressor such as flooding or legislative activity aimed at prohibiting "adult" bookstores near schools.

Stressors in the community are tension-producing stimuli that have the potential of causing disequilibrium in the system. They result in disruption of the community by penetrating the flexible and normal lines of defense. Inadequate, inaccessible, or unaffordable services are stressors for a community.

Within the community are *lines of resistance,* internal mechanisms that act to defend against stressors. An evening recreational program for youth created to decrease vandalism and a free-standing, no-fee health clinic to diagnose and treat sexually transmitted diseases are examples of lines of resistance. Lines of resistance exist in each of the subsystems and represent the community's strengths.

The *degree of reaction* is the amount of disequilibrium or disruption that results from the stressors impinging upon the community's lines of defense. The degree of reaction may be reflected in mortality and morbidity rates, unemployment, or crime statistics, to name a few examples.

An analysis of the data gathered through assessment of the basic structure (core), the normal and flexible lines of defense, lines of resistance, and identification of stressors, along with the degree of reaction, provides the community nursing diagnosis.

The community nursing diagnosis gives direction to nursing's goals and interventions (Figure 7-1). The goal is derived from the stressors and may include the elimination or diminution of the stressor or the strengthening of the community's ability to resist the stressor through strengthening the lines of defense. By measuring the degree of reaction, the nurse can plan interventions to strengthen the community's lines of resistance. Primary prevention is used to strengthen the lines of defense so stressors cannot penetrate or to interfere by attacking the stressor. Secondary prevention, applied after a stressor has penetrated, supports the lines of defense and resistance to minimize the degree of reaction to the stressor. Tertiary prevention is used after stressor penetration and a degree of reaction have occurred, bringing about system disequilibrium. Tertiary prevention is aimed at preventing further disequilibrium and reestablishing the equilibrium of the system.

In the Community-as-Client model, these interventions are applied in the community so that relationships are dynamic, reciprocal and interactive. The system is open so that all components comprise a part of the system's environment, are found in the environment, and are also affected by it and all other parts of the system.

An analysis using Johnson's "essential units" of a conceptual model for nursing summarizes the Community-as-Client model (see box on page 62).[9] The goal is system equilibrium (a healthy community) and includes the preservation and promotion of community health. The model target or "patient" is the total community system, the aggregate, and as such includes individuals and families. The role of the actor (nurse) is to help the community attain, regain, maintain and promote health. The nurse contributes to the regulation and control of system responses to stressors. The intervention focus is the actual or potential disequilibrium or an inability of the community to function, and the intervention mode comprises the three levels of prevention: primary, secondary and tertiary. The intended consequences in this model include a strengthened normal line of defense, an increased resistance to stressors, and a diminished degree of reaction to stressors.

The Community-as-Client model is multidimensional and holistic. It includes all variables affecting a community's response to stressors. Nursing intervention is aimed at preventing actual or potential disruption of equilibrium.

Application

The Community-as-Client nursing model was applied in the community of Rosemont. Each of the eight

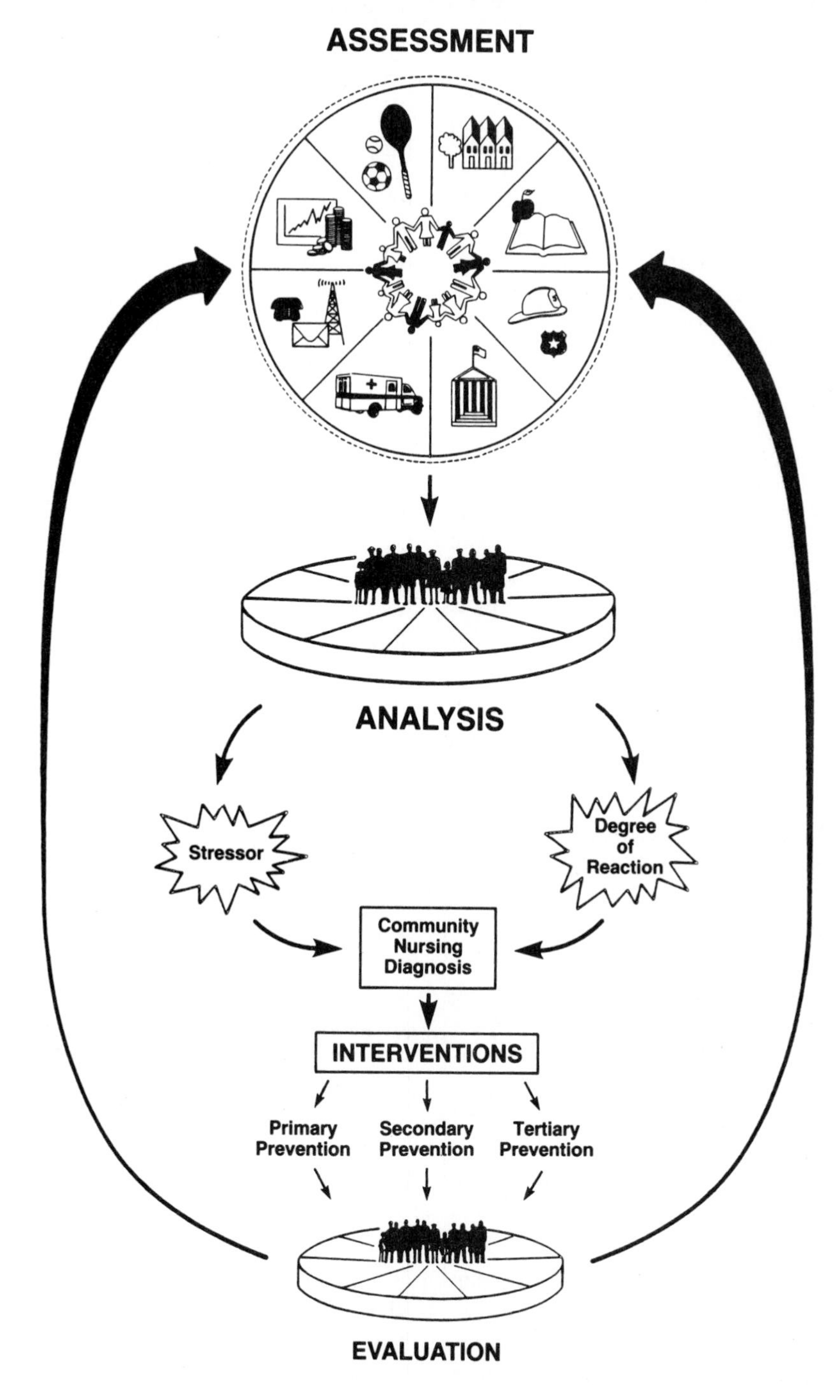

FIGURE 7-1
The community-as-client model.

Community-as-client model application of Johnson's "Essential Units of a Nursing Model"

Essential unit	Community-as-client model
Goal	System equilibrium
Target	Total community system
Actor's role	Assist to attain, regain, maintain and promote health
Source of difficulty	Stressors
Intervention mode	Inability of community to function
Intervention focus	Prevention (3 levels)
Consequences intended	Strengthen normal line of defense; increase resistance to stressors; decrease degree of reaction

subsystems and the core provided a framework for assessment and analysis (see Figure 7-1). Following assessment, the data were analyzed to determine community health needs and community strengths, as well as to identify patterns of health responses and trends in the use of health care services. After each system was analyzed and its relationship to the health of the community appraised, safety emerged as the primary concern of the residents.

Residents of Rosemont, especially women and the elderly, repeatedly voiced concern about their personal safety. Indeed, when police records were evaluated, the episodes of burglary had increased by 31 percent between 1982 and 1984 and robbery by 67 percent during the same period. Episodes of assault in the community had increased by 135 percent.

Further analysis revealed that 75 percent of the victims were women. Generally these women had been assaulted by a man with whom they were sharing or had shared an intimate relationship, usually a spouse. Frequently the assault victims required emergency medical care. (Assault or battering is defined as a physical attack and will be referred to throughout the remainder of this paper as battering). The National Clearinghouse on Domestic Violence estimates that three to four million American women are battered each year by their husbands, ex-husbands, boyfriends, or lovers, and episodes of severe and repeated battering are estimated to affect 10 to 50 percent of all married couples.[10,11] Roy estimates that violence against wives will occur at least once in two-thirds of all marriages.[12] (The wide variation in data stems from lack of reporting, imprecise police records, and a variety of studies using differentpopulations.) A national sample survey of 22,000 families found that 16 out of every 100 couples have violent confrontations during the course of a year and 4 of every 100 wives were seriously beaten during the same period.[13] Battering tends to escalate in severity over time. Stark reports that 21 percent of the 2,676 women treated in one emergency department were at risk of abuse. At risk was defined as positive, probable or suggestive of battering.[14]

Surfacing throughout the literature on battered women are reports of mutilation and violence inflicted during pregnancy. A study by Gelles reported that 25 percent of all women battered are struck during pregnancy.[15] Research by Stacy and Schupe concerning 542 women entering shelters found 42 percent had been battered during pregnancy.[16] The women reported blows to the abdomen and genitals. Stark reported from a review of trauma histories of 2,676 women treated in an emergency service that 15 percent of the women at risk of battering had had at least one spontaneous abortion compared to 8 percent of the unbattered women.[17] In the same study, Stark found that battered women often begin to use drugs or alcohol after a battering incident in an attempt to cope. The effects of alcohol and/or drug abuse on the pregnant woman and unborn child are well documented.

The etiologies of battering are multifactorial and range from psychopathology, to learned socioculturally acceptable behavior, to alcohol or drug abuse, to abuse as a child, to oppression of women in general. The more violence a person sees or experiences as a child, the more likely one is to act violently to others. Once the batterer has hit a woman, some barrier seems to be broken and the anger and violence are likely to increase.

Returning to the Community-as-Client model and the analysis of the assessment data, a documented *degree of reaction* of the community was increased battering of women. *Stressors* acting as possible etiological antecedents of the *reaction* include learned gender role behaviors, low self-esteem, high dependency needs, substance abuse, a history of exposure to violence as a child, and community acceptance of violence. Therefore, the community nursing diagnosis was increased battering of women related to low self-esteem, substance abuse, high dependency needs, a history of exposure to violence as a child, and community acceptance of violence.

The next phases of the model are planning and intervention. Nursing interventions serve to help the community attain, regain, maintain, and promote health as well as contribute to regulating and controlling the community's response to stressors. However, to what community aggregate(s) are interventions directed? Teenagers? Families? Pregnant women? Equally important, in what setting? Clinics? Emergency rooms? Community centers?

To plan a community-focused program, we needed information on the prevalence of battering in Rosemont as well as the characteristics of the affected women. (National statistics are primarily from battered women in shelters, and there are no published reports on the prevalence of battering among pregnant women.) Because most healthy women have frequent scheduled contacts with nurses only during pregnancy and because the literature documented that pregnant women were at risk of battering, a prevalence study of battering during pregnancy was completed. A total of 112 women randomly selected from public and private prenatal clinics were asked if they had been battered prior to or during their present pregnancy and if they had sought treatment for injuries.[18] The women were asked to mark the location of battering on a body map. The women ranged in age from 18 to 37 years and were white, black, and Hispanic. Seventy-six percent of the women were at least five months pregnant, the majority were married, 75 percent had graduated from high school, and 46 percent had completed some college. The findings were as follows:

- 21 percent of the women reported having been battered before or during the current pregnancy;
- 11 percent demonstrated behaviors suggestive of battering, including standing to leave the interview prematurely, lack of eye cont interviewer, and comments such a men?" or "Not recently, he hasn'
- 6 percent reported threats of batt

A total of 38 percent of the women had experienced or were at risk of battering. Of the 23 battered women, 42 percent reported battering during their current pregnancy and 21 percent had sought medical treatment for injuries resulting from the battering.

Battered women report a significantly greater family history of violence than unbattered women. The survey identified the women at highest risk of battering during pregnancy as those women who had previously been battered. As a result, a prevention program focusing on pregnant women was proposed. Using the model as a guide, Table 7-1 presents the nursing interventions for the primary, secondary, and tertiary levels of prevention for both the community and health care providers.

Once nursing interventions were established, a three-year implementation schedule was suggested. A grant proposal was submitted to the March of Dimes for funding of a communitywide program to prevent the battering of pregnant women and promote violence-free relationships. In August of 1985, the grant was funded and the program was begun.

The Prevention of Battering During Pregnancy program is a communitywide educational program focused on health care professionals and the general public. A slide-tape program, "Prevention of Battering During Pregnancy," was developed to educate health care providers about the problem. The 19-minute program includes information on normal conflict as opposed to battering, definition and types of battering, cycle of violence, battering during pregnancy, roots of violence to women, effects of battering over time, and a guide for assessment and intervention that can be used by all health care providers in working with pregnant women. Pre- and post-tests designed to measure changes in knowledge and attitudes accompany the slide-tape presentation. Follow-up interviews also help to determine program impact. To date, the Prevention of Battering During Pregnancy program has been presented to over 1,000 health care providers.

The slide-tape program is available from the March of Dimes Birth Defects Foundation. Other materials

TABLE 7-1
Primary, secondary, and tertiary interventions to prevent battering during pregnancy for the community and health providers

LEVEL OF PREVENTION	COMMUNITY	HEALTH PROVIDERS
	Use Public Service Announcements and Media Presentations to:	*Use Educational Seminars to:*
Primary	Increase the public's awareness of the problems of battering and the cycle of behaviors that precede and follow battering. Increase the public's knowledge of available community resources and services for women at risk of or experiencing battering. Prepare the public to self-refer to appropriate community resources. Prepare the public to become involved in working toward the decrease of violence.	Increase understanding about the circumstances that place a woman at risk of battering and the cycle of behaviors that precede and follow battering. Increase understanding about existing community resources and services for the woman at risk of or experiencing battering.
	Prepare the Public to Use a Family Violence Risk-Assessment Guide to:	*Prepare the Health Provider to:*
Secondary	Self-screen and refer to appropriate community resources. Screen and refer family and friends to appropriate community resources.	Screen all women for actual or potential battering and refer the woman at risk of or experiencing battering to appropriate resources.
	Prepare the Public to:	
Tertiary	Lobby for adequate shelter facilities and therapy programs for battered women, their children, and the batterer.	Provide therapy, counseling, and rehabilitation services to battered women, their children and the batterer.

include a brochure designed for pregnant women, a poster for the general public, and a protocol of care booklet for the health care provider. Public service announcements on battering during pregnancy are being aired on local television. Other programs include "Relationships without Violence" for school-age youngsters and a "Family Violence Risk Assessment Tool" for the community at large.

This real-life example shows how the Community-as-Client model can be applied in public health nursing practice to a wide variety of problems that affect the well-being of a specific population.

REFERENCES

1. Fawcett, J. *Analysis and Evaluation of Conceptual Models of Nursing.* Philadelphia, F.A. Davis, 1983.
2. Fitzpatrick, J. J., and Whall, A. *Conceptual Models of Nursing Analysis and Application* Bowie, MD, Brady Communications Co., 1983.
3. Braden, C. J. *The Focus and Limits of Community Health Nursing.* Norwalk, CT, Appleton-Century-Crofts, 1983.
4. McKay, R., and Segall, M. Methods and models for the aggregate. *Nurs Outlook.* 31:328-334, Nov.-Dec. 1983.
5. White, M. S Construct for public health nursing. *Nurs Outlook.* 30:527-530, Nov.-Dec. 1982.

6. Neuman, B. *The Neuman Systems Model Application to Nursing Education and Practice.* Norwalk, CT, Appleton-Century-Crofts, 1982.
7. American Nurses' Association. *A Conceptual Model of Community Health Nursing.* (Publ. No. CH-10) Kansas City, The Association, 1980, p. 2.
8. Fawcett, *op. cit.* p. 5.
9. Johnson, D. Unpublished lecture notes. In *Conceptual Models for Nursing Practice.* 2nd edition edited by J. P. Riehl and C. Roy, Norwalk, CT, Appleton-Century-Crofts, 1980, p. 7.
10. National Clearinghouse on Domestic Violence. *Wife Abuse in the Medical Setting and Introduction for Health Personnel.* (Monograph series No. 7) Rockville, MD, The Clearinghouse, 1981.
11. Langley, R., and Levy, R. C. *Wife Beating: The Silent Crisis.* New York, E.P. Dutton, 1977.
12. Roy, M., ed. *Battered Women: A Psychosocial Study.* New York, Van Nostrand, 1977.
13. Straus, M. A., et al. *Behind Closed Doors: Violence in the American Family.* Garden City, NY, Doubleday & Co., 1980. (paperback 1981).
14. Stark, E., et al. Wife abuse in the medical setting. *Domestic Violence.* (Monograph series No. 7) Rockville, MD: National Clearinghouse on Domestic Violence, 1981.
15. Gelles, R. J. *The Violent Home: A Study of Physical Aggression Between Husbands and Wives.* Beverly Hills, CA, Sage Publications, 1974.
16. Stacey, W. A., and Schupe, A. *The Family Secret.* Boston, Beacon Press, 1983.
17. Stark, et al. *op. cit.,* pp. 15-16.
18. Helton, A. *Battering During Pregnancy: A Prevalence Study in a Metropolitan Area.* Denton, TX, Texas Woman's University, 1985 (Unpublished master's thesis).

CHAPTER **8**

Thinking Upstream: Nurturing a Conceptual Understanding of the Societal Context of Health Behavior

Patricia G. Butterfield, RN, MS

Despite acknowledgement that an understanding of population health is essential in professional nursing, descriptions of one-to-one relationships predominate in the literature read by most nurses. Such portrayals often emphasize the evolution of the relationship between nurse and client with minimal attention to forces outside the relationship that have been paramount in shaping the client's health behaviors. Yet for most people their cultural heritage, social roles, and economic situation have a far more profound influence on health behaviors than do interactions with any health care professional. Examination of nursing problems from a "think small" perspective[1(p504)] fosters inadequate consideration of these social, environmental, and political determinants of health. This perspective results not only in a restricted range of intervention possibilities for the nurse, but also in a distorted impression of clients' behaviors. An understanding of the complex social, political, and economic forces that shape people's lives is necessary for nurses to promote health in individuals and groups. If nurses are not given an opportunity to appreciate the gestalt of populations and societies, they will be unable to develop a basis for analyzing problems.

Reprinted from *Advances in Nursing Science,* Vol. 12, No. 2, with permission of Aspen Publishers, Inc., © 1990.

This article addresses the issue of overreliance on theories that define nursing primarily in terms of a one-to-one relationship and the inherent conflict between these theories and the goal of enabling nurses to promote health through population-based interventions.

NURSING'S ROLE IN PUSHING UPSTREAM

In his description of the frustrations of medical practice, McKinlay[2] uses the image of a swiftly flowing river to represent illness. In this analogy, physicians are so caught up in rescuing victims from the river that they have no time to look upstream to see who is pushing their patients into the perilous waters. The author uses this example to demonstrate the ultimate futility of "downstream endeavors,"[2(p9)] which are characterized by short-term, individual-based interventions, and he challenges health care providers to focus more of their energies "upstream, where the real problems lie."[2(p9)] Upstream endeavors focus on modifying economic, political, and environmental factors that have been shown to be the precursors of poor health throughout the world. Although the analogy cites medical practice, it also aptly describes the dilemmas of a considerable portion of nursing practice. And while nursing has a rich historical record of providing preventive and population-based care, the current American health system, which emphasizes episodic and individual-based care, has done woefully little to stem the tide of chronic illness, to which 70% of the American population succumbs.

What is the cost of a continued emphasis on a microscopic perspective? How does a theoretical focus on the individual preclude understanding of a larger perspective? Dreher[1] maintains that a conservative scope of practice often uses psychologic theories to explain patterns of health and health care. In this mode of practice, low compliance, broken appointments, and reluctance to participate in care are all attributed to motivation or attitude problems on the part of the client. Nurses are charged with the responsibility of altering client attitudes toward health, rather than altering the system itself, "even though such negative attitudes may well be a realistic appraisal of health care."[1(p505)] Greater emphasis is paid to the psychologic symptoms of poor health than to socioeconomic causes; "indeed the symptoms are being taken as its causes."[1(p505)] The nurse who views the world from such a perspective does not entertain the possibility of working to alter the system itself or empowering clients to do so.

Involvement in social reform is considered to be within the realm of nursing practice.[3] Dreher[1] acknowledges the historical role of public health nurses in facilitating social change and notes that social involvement and activism are expected of nurses in this area of practice. The American Nurses' Association (ANA) Social Policy Statement delineates, among other social concerns, the "provision for the public health through use of preventive and environmental measures and increased assumption of responsibility by individuals, families, and other groups"[3(p4)] and addresses nursing's role in response to those concerns. However, in her review of the document, White[4] notes an incongruence between nursing's social concerns, which clearly transcend individual-based practice, and the description of nursing as "a practice in which interpersonal closeness of the professional kind develops and aids the investigation and discussion of problems, as nurse and patient (or family or group) seek jointly to resolve those concerns."[3(p19)] White[4] also notes the document's neglect of the population focus and possibilities for modifying the environment. Clearly, nursing has yet to reconcile many of the differences between operationalization of a population-centered practice and policies that define nursing primarily in terms of individual-focused care.

Three theoretic approaches will be contrasted below to demonstrate how they may lead the nurse to draw different conclusions not only about the reasons for client behavior, but also about the range of interventions available to the nurse.

THE DOWNSTREAM VIEW: THE INDIVIDUAL AS THE LOCUS OF CHANGE

The health belief model evolved from the premise that the world of the perceiver determines what he or she will do. The social psychologists[5,6] who outlined this model were strongly influenced by Lewin and the view that a person's daily activities are guided by processes of attraction to positive valences and avoidance of negative valences. From these inceptions evolved a model that purports to explain why people do or do not engage in a preventive health action in response to a specific disease threat. The model places the burden of action exclusively on the client; only those clients who have distorted or negative perceptions of the specified disease or recommended health action will fail to act. In practice, this model focuses the nurse's energies on interventions designed to modify the client's distorted perceptions. Although the process of promoting behavior change may be masked under the premise of mutually defined goals, passive acceptance of the nurse's advice is the desired outcome of the relationship.

Although the health belief model was not designed to specify intervention strategies, it can lead the nurse to deduce that client problems can be solved merely by altering the client's belief system. The model addresses the concept of "perceived benefits versus perceived barriers/costs associated with taking a health action."[6(p563)] Nurses may easily interpret this situation as a need to modify the client's perceptions of benefits and barriers. For example, clients with problems accessing adequate health care might receive counseling aimed at helping them see these barriers in a new light; the model does not include the possibility that the nurse may become involved in activities that promote equal access to all in need.

True to its historical roots, the model offers an explanation of health behaviors that, in many ways, is similar to a mechanical system. From the health belief model, one easily concludes that compliance can be induced by using model variables as catalysts to stimulate action. For example, an intervention study based on health belief model precepts sought to increase follow-up in hypertensive clients by increasing the clients' awareness of their susceptibility to hypertension and of its danger.[7] Clients received education, over the telephone or in the emergency department, that was designed to increase their perception of the benefits of follow-up. According to these authors, the interventions resulted in a dramatic increase in compliance. However, they noted several client groups that failed to respond to the intervention, most notably a small group of clients who had no available child care. Although this study demonstrates the predictive power of health belief model concepts, it also exemplifies the limitations of the model. The health belief model may be effective in promoting behavioral change through the alteration of clients' perspectives, but it does not acknowledge responsibility for the health care professional to reduce or ameliorate client barriers.

In fact, some of the proponents of the health belief model readily acknowledge the limitations of the model and caution users against generalizing it beyond the domain of the individual psyche. In their review of 10 years of research with the model, Janz and Becker[8] remind researchers that the model can only account for the variance in health behaviors that is explained by the attitudes and beliefs of an individual. Melnyk's[9] recent review of the concept of barriers reinforces the notion that, because the health belief model is based on subjective perceptions, research that adopts this theoretic basis must take care to include the subjects', rather than the researchers', perceptions of barriers. Janz and Becker[8] address the influence of other factors such as habituation and nonhealth reasons on making positive changes in health behavior, and they acknowledge the influence of environmental and economic factors that prohibit individuals from undertaking a more healthy way of life.

The health belief model is but a prototype for the type of theoretic perspective that has dominated nursing education and thus nursing practice. The model's strength—its narrow scope—is also its limitation: one is not drawn outside it to those forces that shape the characteristics that the model describes.

THE UPSTREAM VIEW: SOCIETY AS THE LOCUS OF CHANGE

Milio's Framework for Prevention

Milio's framework for prevention[10] provides a thought-provoking complement to the health belief model and a mechanism for directing attention upstream and examining opportunities for nursing intervention at the population level. Milio moves the focus of attention upstream by pointing out that it is the range of available health choices, rather than the choices made at any one time, that is paramount in shaping the overall health status of a society. She maintains that the range of choices widely available to individuals is shaped, to a large degree, by policy decisions in both governmental and private organizations. Rather than concentrate efforts on imparting information to change patterns of individual behavior, she advocates national-level policy making as the most effective means of favorably affecting the health of most Americans.

Milio[10] proposes that health deficits often result from an imbalance between a population's health needs and its health-sustaining resources, with affluent societies afflicted by the diseases associated with excess (obesity, alcoholism) and the poor afflicted by diseases that result from inadequate or unsafe food, shelter, and water. In this context, the poor in affluent societies may experience the least desirable combination of factors. Milio notes that although socioeconomic realities deprive many Americans of a health-sustaining environment, "cigarettes, sucrose, pollutants, and tensions are readily available to the poor."[10(p436)]

The range of health-promoting or health-damaging choices available to individuals is affected by their personal resources and their societal resources. Personal resources include one's awareness, knowledge, and beliefs, including those of one's family and friends, as well as money, time, and the urgency of other priorities. Societal resources are strongly influenced by community and national locale and include the availability and cost of health services, environmental protection, safe shelter, and the penalties or rewards given for failure to select the given options.

Milio notes the fallacy of the commonly held assumption in health education that knowing health-generating behaviors implies acting in accordance with that knowledge, and she cites the life styles of health professionals in support of her argument. She proposes that "most human beings, professional or nonprofessional, provider or consumer, make the easiest choices available to them most of the time."[10(p435)] Therefore, health-promoting choices must be more readily available and less costly than health-damaging options if individuals are to be healthy and a society is to improve its health status.

The opportunities for a society to make healthy choices have been a central theme throughout Milio's work. In a recent book she elaborated on this theme:

> Personal behavior patterns are not simply "free" choices about "lifestyle," isolated from their personal and economic context. Lifestyles are, rather, patterns of choices made from the alternatives that are available to people according to their socioeconomic circumstances and the ease with which they are able to choose certain ones over others.[11(p76)]

Milio is critical of many traditional approaches to health education that emphasize knowledge acquisition and consequently expect behavior change. In addressing the role of public health in primary care, Milio voices concern that "health damage accumulates in societies too, vitiating their vitality. . . . [and charges nurses to redirect energies] so as to foster conditions that help people to retain a self-sustaining physiological and social balance."[12(pp188,189)]

One cannot help but note the similarities between Milio's health resources and the concepts in the health belief model. The health belief model is more comprehensive than Milio's framework in examining the internal dynamics of health decision making. However, Milio offers a different set of insights into the arena of health behaviors by proposing that many low-income individuals are acting within the constraints of their limited resources. Furthermore, she goes beyond the individual focus and addresses changes in the health of populations as a result of shifts in decision making by significant numbers of people within a population.

Critical Social Theory

Just as Milio uses societal awareness as an aid to understanding health behaviors, critical social theory employs similar means to expose social inequities that prohibit people from reaching their full potential. This theoretic approach is based on the belief that life is structured by social meanings that are determined, rather one-sidedly, through social domination.[13] In contrast to the assumptions of analytic empiricism, critical theory maintains that standards of truth are socially determined and that no form of scientific inquiry is value free.[13-15] Proponents of this theoretic approach posit that social discourse that is not distorted from power imbalances will stimulate the evolution of a more rational society. The interests of truth are served only when people are able to voice their beliefs without fear of authority or retribution.[13]

Allen[14] discusses how nursing practice can be enriched by enabling clients to remove the conscious and unconscious constraints in their everyday lives. He states that women and the economically impoverished are especially vulnerable to being labeled by pseudodiseases that are rooted in social formations, such as hysteria and depression. Health care providers often frame such problems only within the context of the individual or, at best, the family. But critical social theory can enable a nurse to reframe such an interpretation to gain an understanding of the historical play of social forces that have limited the choices truly available to the involved parties. Through exploration of the societal forces, traditions, and roles that have created the meanings of health and illness, clients may be freed of the isolation and alienation that accompany individual problem ownership.

At the collective level, Waitzkin asserts that the current emphasis on life style diverts attention from important sources of illness in the capitalist industrial environment; "it also puts the burden of health squarely on the individual rather than seeking collective solutions to health problems."[16(p664)] Salmon[17] supports this position by noting that the basic tenets of western medicine promote the delineation of individual factors of health and illness, while obscuring the exploration of their social and economic roots. He states that critical social theory "can aid in uncovering larger dimensions impacting health that are usually unseen or misrepresented by ideological biases. Thus, the social reality of health conditions can be both understood and changed."[17(p75)]

Because the theory holds that each person is responsible for creating social conditions in which all members of society are able to speak freely, the nurse is challenged, as an individual and as a member of the profession, to expose power imbalances that prohibit people from achieving their full potential. Nurses versed in critical theory are equipped to see beyond the perpetuation of status quo ideas and may be able to generate unique ideas that are unencumbered by previous stereotypes.[14]

Other Examples of Upstream Thinking

Recent nursing literature provides several other examples of upstream thinking. In a thought-provoking commentary on an intervention program for middle-aged women experiencing subclinical depression, Davis[18] (cited in Gordon and Ledray) notes a lack of congruence between the study's portrayal of depression as a problem with societal roots and its instruction in coping strategies as the intervention program. While recognizing the merits of the intervention program, she comments that, "if our principal task as progressive nurses is to develop and utilize interventions that will ameliorate these social problems, then the emphasis in nursing education and practice might well be on those social actions that aim to change basic social factors such as ageism and sexism." [18(p277)]

Chopoorian[19] takes a different tack, emphasizing the concept of environment and suggesting that nurses develop a consciousness of the social, political, and economic aspects of environment. She maintains that a static portrayal of the environment precludes nurses from acting as advocates for people who lack adequate housing and health care and live in intolerable circumstances. She charges nurses to move beyond a psychosocial conceptualization of the environment into a sociopolitical–economic conceptualization. Through this reconceptualization, nurses will see that human responses to health and illnesses "are related to the structure of the social world, the economic and political policies that govern that structure, and the human, social relationships that are produced by the structure and the policies."[19(p46)]

THE NEED FOR ALTERNATIVE PERSPECTIVES

The danger of the conservative perspective lies not within its content, but rather in the omission of other, larger theories that enable nurses to view situations from both a microscopic and a macroscopic perspective. In discussing the dilemmas of "studying health behavior as an individual phenomena [*sic*], rather than in the context of a broader social change phenomena [*sic*]," Cummings[20(p93)] reminds us that the approaches are complementary, and both are necessary to a comprehensive understanding of health promotion. The strengths and utility of each theoretic approach are most clearly revealed through an understanding of alternate approaches.

Nursing needs conceptual foundations that enable its practitioners to understand health problems manifested at community, national, and international levels as well as those at the individual and family levels. The continued bias in favor of individual-focused theories robs nurses of an understanding of the richness and complexity of forces that shape the behavior of populations. The omission of theories that relate nursing to the social context of behavior may leave nurses with a minimal understanding of their responsibilities to facilitate change at this level and without the tools to promote such change in an effective and systematic manner.

Maglacas[21] provides a global perspective on the health conditions of societies throughout the world and draws attention to the gaps in service access between the rich and the poor. She then charges nurses within each society and culture to act in response to the inequities in health within that society. If nurses are to be able to enact change at the societal level, they need to be provided with theoretic frameworks that are consistent with such ends and with theoretic perspectives in which social, economic, and political forces are given equal weight with the interpersonal aspects of nursing. Through these means, nurses gain insight into the social precursors of poor health and restricted opportunities and learn rationales for engaging in social action. By tipping the scales of nursing back toward consideration of theories that address health from a societal perspective, nurses can receive not only a richness of understanding but also the means by which to enact this kind of change.

REFERENCES

1. Dreher MC. The conflict of conservatism in public health nursing education. *Nurs Outlook.* 1982;30:504-509.
2. McKinlay JB. A case for refocussing upstream: The political economy of illness. In: Jaco EG, ed. *Patients, Physicians, and Illness.* 3rd ed. New York, NY: Free Press; 1979:9-25.
3. American Nurses' Association. *Nursing: A Social Policy Statement.* Kansas City, Mo: American Nurses' Association; 1980.
4. White CM. A critique of the ANA social policy statement. *Nurs Outlook.* 1984;32:328-331.
5. Rosenstock IM. Historical origins of the health belief model. In: Becker MH, ed. *The Health Belief Model and Personal Health Behavior.* Thorofare, NJ: Charles B. Slack; 1974:1-8.
6. Becker MH, Maiman LA. Models of health-related behavior. In: Mechanic D, ed. *Handbook of Health, Health Care, and the Health Professions.* New York, NY: Free Press; 1983:539-568.
7. Jones PK, Jones SL, Katz J. Improving follow-up among hypertensive patients using a health belief model intervention. *Arch Intern Med.* 1987;147:1557-1560.
8. Janz NK, Becker MH. The health belief model: A decade later. *Health Educ Q.* 1984;11:1-47.
9. Melnyk KM. Barriers: A critical review of recent literature. *Nurs Res.* 1988;37:196-201.
10. Milio N. A framework for prevention: Changing health-damaging to health-generating life patterns. *Am J Public Health.* 1976;66:435-439.
11. Milio N. *Promoting Health Through Public Policy.* Philadelphia, Penn: F.A. Davis; 1981.
12. Milio N. *Primary Care and the Public's Health.* Lexington, Mass: Lexington Books; 1983.
13. Allen D, Diekelmann N, Benner P. Three paradigms for nursing research. In: Chinn P, ed. *Nursing Research Methodology: Issues & Implementation.* Rockville, Md: Aspen Publishers; 1986:;23-28.
14. Allen DG. Nursing research and social control: Alternate models of science that emphasize understanding and emancipation. *Image: The Journal of Nursing Scholarship.* 1985;17:58-64.
15. Allen DG. Critical social theory as a model for analyzing ethical issues in family and community health. *Fam Commun Health.* 1987;10:63-72.
16. Waitzkin H. A Marxist view of health and health care. In: Mechanic D, ed. *Handbook of Health, Health Care, and the Health Professions.* New York, NY: Free Press; 1983: 657-682.
17. Salmon JW. Dilemmas in studying social change versus individual change: Considerations from political economy. In: Duffy ME, Pender NJ, eds. *Conceptual Issues in Health Promotion—A Report of Proceedings of a Wingspread Conference.* Indianapolis, Ind: Sigma Theta Tau; 1987: 70-81.
18. Davis AJ. Cited by Gordon VC, Ledray LE. Growth-support intervention for the treatment of depression in women of middle years. *West J Nurs Res.* 1986;8: 263-283.
19. Chopoorian TJ. Reconceptualizing the environment. In: Moccia P, ed. *New Approaches to Theory Development.* New York, NY: National League for Nursing:; 1986:39-54. Publication 15-1992.
20. Cummings KM. Dilemmas in studying health as an individual phenomenon. In: Duffy ME, Pender NJ, eds. *Conceptual Issues in Health Promotion—A Report of Proceedings of a Wingspread Conference.* Indianapolis, Ind: Sigma Theta Tau; 1987:91-96.
21. Maglacas AM. Health for all: Nursing's role. *Nurs Outlook.* 1988;36:66-71.

CHAPTER 9

Theory Development in Community Health Nursing: Issues and Recommendations

Patti Hamilton, RN, PhD
Helen A. Bush, RN, PhD

Although community health nursing celebrated its centennial in this country in 1986, a lack of conceptual clarity and relative paucity of theory development persist in this field of nursing. While research has been conducted that has relevance for community health nursing, the research to date is diverse and lacks an explicit focus on development of theory specific to the field. Sills and Goeppinger (1985), in the *Annual Review of Nursing Research,* report only two studies appearing in the nursing literature between 1952 and 1983 in which investigators delimited the community as the target of the practice of nursing. Their finding is particularly disturbing when one considers that many experts propose that to consider the community as client is the distinguishing feature setting community health nursing apart as a unique field of nursing (American Public Health Association, 1982; Freeman, 1970; Robischon, 1975; Spradley, 1986; Watson, 1984; Williams, 1981).

The development of community health nursing has been influenced by social conditions, political changes, economic contingencies, war, and human need. Many public health, and later community health nursing, care practices were based on common sense, intuition, ritual, and tradition, as well as on medical and environmental science.

Efforts of community health nurses, along with progress in medical treatment, immunizations, sanitary conditions, and nutrition, have dramatically improved public health in the U.S. during the past 100 years. Many of the illnesses and health concerns of Americans today, however, are not easily prevented, treated, or ameliorated. Community health nurses face complex health problems such as childhood pregnancy, AIDS, cancer, and heart disease, all with multiple causalities. In addition, community health nurses find themselves in an uncertain economic environment. Shifts in government appropriations and private health care financing arrangements greatly influence the structure, process, and outcomes of community health nursing practice. A sound theoretical foundation for practice is needed if these health concerns are to be adequately addressed. Sills and Goeppinger (1985) warn, however, that the "American society in its present state seems less likely than it was in the 1970s to be willing to invest in the research needed to develop this field" (p. 20).

Efficient, cost-effective, and focused research in community health nursing is a priority need at this time in the U.S. This article presents a variety of strategies for developing community health nursing

Reprinted from *Scholarly Inquiry for Nursing Practice: An International Journal,* Vol. 2, No. 2, with permission of Springer Publishing Company, © 1988.

theory. Researchers are challenged to focus their attention on the generation of sound community health nursing theory and to do so with the most efficient use of the limited resources available for the task. This article does not advocate a singular strategy for theory development in community health nursing, but instead considers the wide range of research strategies and data sources that hold promise in community health nursing theory development.

The term *community health nursing* is used throughout the paper. It is acknowledged, however, that the term *public health nursing* was most often utilized prior to 1970. In addition, the term *generic nursing* refers to all types of nursing other than community health nursing. These terms are used purely for convenience in communication and should not be interpreted as verified distinctions. Part of the needed research in community health nursing is the identification of diagnostic criteria for the field. Until such criteria are identified, the use of distinctions such as setting, role, and client focus should be viewed with caution.

Meleis (1985) determined five strategies for theory development, each based on a different origin of inquiry and different sequence of attention to theory, research, and practice. She called these strategies:

1. theory-practice-theory
2. practice-theory
3. research-theory
4. theory-research-theory
5. modified practice-theory

The merits of these strategies have been analyzed extensively in the literature (Mannoia, 1980; Meleis, 1985; Reynolds, 1980). The discussion here centers on the issues surrounding the consequences of initiating community health nursing development by employing theory, practice, or research.

THEORY AS POINT OF ORIGIN

Using this strategy, the theorist begins with well-defined concepts in an established paradigm. The concepts from the paradigm are applied to practice settings or to the conduct of research, and the theorist describes and explains phenomena using these concepts (Meleis, 1985). When theory precedes research or practice, theorists are much more likely to "see" what they expect to "see," thus limiting the possibilities of identifying useful but overlooked concepts not yet explicated in existing theory. This situation is particularly important in the case of developing community health nursing theory. There are no existing theories for use in community health nursing practice in which the explicit unit term is *community*. Some theories that have been borrowed for use in research and practice within community health nursing have been developed by epidemiologists, anthropologists, community planners, sociologists, program planners, and other public health scientists. Other theories were developed by nurses involved primarily in the care of individuals and/or families. Continuing to depend on existing theory borrowed from other disciplines to guide the development of specific community health nursing theory may result in delay, frustration, and oversights because neither other professionals nor generic nurses have the same role in the community as does the community health nurse.

On the other hand, it may be arguable that the act of taking theory from another discipline and utilizing it within a community health nursing context is sufficient for transforming it into community health nursing theory. This type of theory development is quite logical if community health nursing is perceived as a combination of public health sciences and nursing practice as in the Public Health Nurses Division of the American Public Health Association (American Public Health Association, 1980). This conceptualization could be represented by the following equation:

> If CHN = PH + N, then CHN theory = PH theory + N theory (CHN = community health nursing, PH = public health science, N = nursing

Those working to develop community health nursing theory need to consider which of the following types of theory holds the greatest promise:

1. The sum of two distinctly different types of theory (i.e., public health and generic nursing)
2. the transformation of theory from a non-nursing discipline into community health nursing theory
3. generic nursing theory transformed into community health nursing theory
4. theory derived from a unique community health nursing perspective

Any one or all of these could be useful, depending on how well developed the theory is and what repeated application shows.

Resolution of these theory development issues could have an impact on nursing education, practice, research, and theory development. Depending on the way in which community health nursing is defined and its theory developed, questions similar to the following may arise:

1. Should community health nurses be prepared at the baccalaureate level (which is primarily based on a generic nursing framework) or at the master's level, either in schools of public health, where public health science will build on generic nursing knowledge, or in master's programs that build on a generic nursing base of knowledge?
2. Should there be greater emphasis on joint research with disciplines outside of nursing, thus stimulating complementary disciplines to generate research and theories that can be applied in community health nursing practice?
3. How much of community health nursing practice is generic nursing, and how much, and what part, is uniquely community health nursing?
4. Would society's resources best be utilized by research and theory development in community health nursing paralleling such fields as anthropology, epidemiology, community medicine, or sociology, or do nurses need to develop separate research and theory agendas based on the unique contributions of nursing to community health?

RESEARCH AS POINT OF ORIGIN

Some experts believe that theories evolve from research findings; that, as Bacon (1863) suggested, laws of nature are derived from a careful examination of all the available data. To develop theory by the Baconian approach presupposes two conditions:

1. There is agreement in the field on the major concepts of concern (Meleis, 1985).
2. There are only a few significant patterns to be found in the data (Reynolds, 1980).

When trying to identify the range of concepts of interest to theorists in community health nursing, the task quickly becomes overwhelming. There are concepts related to social systems, economics, politics, biology, anthropology, linguistics, ethics, chemistry, and history, to name only a few. It becomes extremely difficult in a field as broad as community health nursing to delimit variables and discern patterns of phenomena that can be used for description, explanation, and prediction. What results from the research-as-a-point-of-origin strategy can be widely disparate attempts to sample the universe. Indeed, to date there appear to be an accumulation of unrelated, one-time-only studies in community health nursing that have been modeled on the research-first strategy of theory development (Sills & Goeppinger, 1985). Careful consideration should be given to the wisdom of continued proliferation of random inquiry into community phenomena. Without an organizing framework to serve as a guide, the result can be answers to minute questions that are either not central to nursing or are not translatable to patterns that could eventually be connected to theory (Meleis, 1985). The greatest purpose that a community health nursing organizing framework could serve would be the identification of the client of community health nursing practice. Without a delimitation of client focus, community health nursing theory development will continue to encompass (1) clients in communities, (2) clients influenced by communities, as well as (3) clients *as* communities.

Work based on the design of Glaser and Strauss (1968) may hold great promise in research-as-origin of community health nursing theory. Using the grounded theory approach, theorists derive relevant research questions throughout the conduct of the research. In this type of strategy the theorist is guided in inquiry, and the result may be more pertinent questioning and more focused analysis.

PRACTICE AS POINT OF ORIGIN

Dickoff and James (1968) asserted that "theory is born in practice and must return to practice" (p. 197). In reality, the previously stated points of origin of community health nursing theory development (theory and research) likely have their roots in practice. In the strategy to develop theory by beginning explicitly with practice, however, a concerted effort is made by the theorist to use observation and conceptualization based on the meaning of the phenomenon in the context of practice rather than in the context of a predetermined theory or research methodology. Phenomena studied using this strategy would be viewed from a community health nursing perspective, not from the perspective of another discipline or field such as anthropology, public health science, sociology, or generic nursing. There is confusion over where nursing stops and public health science begins, and whether community health nursing is a unique field of nursing or simply generic nursing in a community health setting. This confusion complicates the practice-as-origin strategy, the difficulty being lack of consensus on what constitutes community health nursing practice.

In addition to lack of consensus internally over what constitutes practice, there are external factors that must be considered when using the practice-first strategy. Community health nursing practice is heavily influenced by social, political, and economic factors. What is seen in practice is delimited by external forces. Only certain types of clients are seen in most contemporary community health nursing agencies. Individuals who cannot pay for care are not seen. Conditions requiring care that is not reimbursable are likewise invisible in community health nursing practice settings. Home health care is an example of a practice setting heavily influenced by payment structures and by necessity concerned primarily with providing services that are reimbursable under prevailing market conditions. It is impossible for home health agencies to carry large caseloads of individuals who need care but cannot pay and are not eligible for public or private assistance.

Community health nursing has a philosophy based on concern for whole populations, not just those individuals who receive care (American Nurses Association, 1973). An expanded definition of practice is needed that will include all phenomena of significance to theory development and not merely those observed in current practice settings. In other words, practice as a concept needs to be expanded from community health nursing "as it is" to community health nursing "as it needs to be," thus moving the theorist from practice as a point of origin to theory as a starting place.

SOURCES OF IDEAS FOR THEORY DEVELOPMENT

The point of origin of inquiry (whether it be theory, research, or practice) can have a significant effect on the nature of the theory that is developed in community health nursing. So, too, can the source of the ideas and data examined. The old tale of the blind men examining separate parts of an elephant illustrates the point well. Each tried to describe the whole from his own experience with a different source of data. Perhaps community health nursing, like the elephant, cannot be fully described or its theory developed until a wide range of ideas and data sources are examined and the results analyzed. Each idea or data source has its own unique contributions to make to theory development. Taken alone, however, it is no more than part of the picture. Eight sources of ideas and data are proposed here to point out the diversity of the types of ideas and data relevant to community health nursing. The list of sources, which is representative rather than comprehensive, is presented, and each source is then discussed.

1. history of community health nursing
2. lived experiences of nurses and clients
3. structure of community health nursing practice
4. process of community health nursing
5. outcomes of community health nursing
6. education of community health nurses
7. clients of community health nursing
8. previous research

History

Community health nursing's heritage in the U.S. is extremely rich and diverse and has been well documented by individual writers and by the National Organization for Public Health Nursing (NOPHN), which was founded in 1912. One of the first nurses to write about nursing concerns of interest to community health nurses was Florence Nightingale. Her

Notes on Nursing: What It Is, and What It Is Not (1859) contains numerous references to hygiene, health promotion, disease prevention, the influence of the environment on health, the need for health education, and much more. Her observations are sound and amazingly relevant today. For example, on reading a report that increased childhood mortality in London had prompted officials to found a hospital for children, Miss Nightingale wrote:

> The causes of the enormous child mortality are perfectly well known; they are chiefly want of cleanliness, want of ventilation . . . in one word, defective household hygiene. The remedies are just as well known, and among them is certainly not the establishment of a Child's hospital. (p. 7)

After more than a century, community health nurses still advocate the more responsible use of scarce health care resources to prevent illness rather than to treat its consequences (Hamilton, 1981). Lillian Wald (1867-1940) was another early contributor to community health nursing wisdom. Wald's descriptions of community health nursing as it was developing and being practiced at the time were preserved in her books, *The House on Henry Street* and *Windows on Henry Street.*

Careful examination of the roots of community health nursing practice would reveal the wisdom of our predecessors. The writings of early community health nurses are rich with concepts to be analyzed and clarified. Their reminiscences reveal their lived experiences as community health nurses. Their preserved correspondence traces the development of community health nursing education in this country and the changing organization of community health nursing services.

Early scholarly writings are also potential sources of ideas for community health nursing theory development. Research regarding the most efficient and effective means of organizing and delivering community health nursing was first conducted in 1926 in a comprehensive study of generalized and specialized nursing through the East Harlem Nursing and Health Demonstration in New York City (Williams, 1981). Comparing and contrasting the outcome of this type of research with similar studies today might reveal patterns of influence of external forces on nursing outcomes over time.

Only a few examples of historical sources of data have been suggested here. Theorists could consider these and other sources to be rich sources of insight into the nature and significance of community health nursing. Historical research methods could be applied to all of the data sources that follow.

Lived Experiences of Community Health Nurses and Clients

A number of nurse researchers have used grounded theory, phenomenology, and other qualitative techniques to investigate the nature of nursing. Yet few, if any, have applied these techniques to theory development in community health nursing.

Paterson and Zderad (1976) generated a theoretical formulation whose purpose is to develop humanistic nursing and the human method of nursology (Meleis, 1985). A review of Paterson and Zderad's central concepts reveals some interesting possibilities for application in community health nursing. A few of these concepts include:

relating
mutuality
other human beings
meeting
time
space
We
things
community
environment
choices

Qualitative techniques also can be used to describe the lived experiences of community health nurses. These experiences can then be compared and contrasted with the experiences of generic nurses. Theorists may ask, "Do community health nurses truly experience the nursing of communities, or are their experiences actually an accumulation of interactions with individuals, the sum of which is described as community nursing?" Finally, determining the ways in which communities experience community health nursing would be a methodological and conceptual challenge and might reveal insights into the nature of the practice.

Structure of Community Health Nursing Practice

The structure of community health nursing services includes not only patterns of practice, but also the contextual elements that shape those patterns. The works of Archer and Fleshman (1975; Archer, 1976) are classic examples of investigations of structure of community health nursing practice. Their typologies of practice are in need of replication but can serve as rich sources of concepts for analysis in community health nursing theory development. Theory that distinguishes between nursing in community settings and nursing of communities would be especially useful. Comparisons of practice elements in home health, schools, health departments, and other settings may yield evidence of the essential elements that set community health nursing apart. This comparison may reveal elements of community health nursing that are actually the same as the elements of generic nursing taking place in a novel setting.

Much can be learned about community health nursing by observing and measuring ways in which its practice structure responds to changes in political, social, economic, and legal factors. International comparisons of community health nursing would be especially rich sources of knowledge regarding the unique as well as the common structural characteristics of the field worldwide.

Process of Community Health Nursing

The theorist who wishes to understand community health nursing may find examination of the processes used in practice to be most helpful. The types of questions that may lead to this understanding include:

1. Do community health nurses assess the community as a client?
2. What do community health nurses assess?
3. What diagnoses are commonly derived by community health nurses? (For an extensive analysis of community nursing diagnosis, see Hamilton, 1981.)
4. What types of interventions do community health nurses use in practice?
5. How do interventions differ with client focus?
6. How is community health nursing evaluated?

Many of the problems identified in the discussion of practice-as-origin of theory development apply to the use of the process of community health nursing as an idea or data source. The process used in the nursing of individuals and families in communities, nursing of individuals and families influenced by communities, and nursing of communities may be quite different. Theorists in community health nursing need to recognize these differences and address them in theory development. Also, theorists need to consider which of these processes are unique to community health nursing and which are shared with generic nursing and with other disciplines. If the processes are shared with generic nursing or with other disciplines, should they be described as community health nursing processes, or should investigations focus on identifying only those processes that can be considered unique to community health nursing? While the process of community health nursing clearly is a potential idea and data source of major importance, it is also the source of greatest confusion and controversy. Resolution of this controversy in community health nursing might lead to consensus in the field regarding phenomena of significance and to more focused theory development. Porter (1987), for example, in her article, "Administrative Diagnosis: Implications for the Public's Health," reports developing a factor-isolating theory of population group diagnosis using grounded theory methodology.

One obstacle in community health nursing theory development to date is that the underlying assumptions of researchers and theorists have not been recognized, acknowledged, and critiqued by the nursing community. Assumptions regarding the following questions should be made explicit by those who develop community health nursing theory:

1. Who is the client of community health nursing care?
2. What is the difference between community health nursing and generic nursing?

3. What is the difference between community health nursing and disciplines outside of nursing?

Lack of attention to these assumptions has played a major role in retarding theory development in community health nursing.

Outcome of Community Health Nursing

Because community health nursing is an applied practice activity, the consequences of its application are important in understanding its nature. Measurement of the outcome of care appears to be among the earliest research strategies in community health nursing. The East Harlem Nursing and Health Demonstration (Williams, 1981) and the Child Health Demonstration Program and Policies (Williams, 1981) both compared the outcomes of specialized versus generalized community health nursing practice (Williams, 1981). These early findings indicated that the generalized practice model was more cost effective than the specialized model. Specialized care was disease- or age-specific nursing intervention, while generalized care was nursing of a variety of ages and conditions within a prescribed geographic area. Questions similar to those asked over 60 years ago are still relevant today.

As health care continues to move from hospitals into the home and community, there is a need to define and redefine the community health nursing role. For example, community health nurses in home health would do well to ask: "What are the consequences of organizing care around reimbursement guidelines rather than basing care on family theory or community theory?" The school nurse may question whether it is cost effective to provide specialized care only to students or whether the outcome would be more beneficial (and cost effective) if school nursing were redefined as a blend of child, family, and occupational nursing. Outcome measures will undoubtedly receive a lot of attention during periods when resources are scarce. Outcome measures on at least three levels (individuals, groups, and communities) need to be investigated. Can society afford for community health nursing to focus on individuals and families when total community intervention may bring more cost-effective results?

Education of Community Health Nurses

If one looks at education as the passing on not only of knowledge but also of the memories, myths, rituals, and shared experiences of the expert to the novice, then the potential for theory development would appear great in examining community health nursing education for theory development. Why are certain concepts taught in community health nursing? How is community health nursing education perceived by practicing community health nurses, by students, and by the community? What are the differences and similarities between community health nursing and generic nursing? Do different educational strategies result in different outcomes in practice?

These are just a few of the questions that theorists may want to consider. By observing what educators assert students and community health nurses must know and must do, the theorist can identify a wealth of concepts for analysis and clarification.

Nature of the Client of Community Health Nursing

One of the central domain concepts of community health nursing theory is "client." To understand client in a variety of ways will be essential in community health nursing. Client may be conceptualized as any one or all three of the following (Hamilton, 1983):

1. The individual and family within the community.
2. The individual and family influenced by the community.
3. The community as client.

Studies aimed at discovering the dimensions of the individual and family *within* and *influenced* by the community often explore the effects of culture, environment, and social structure on the individual and family client. Patterns of health and illness are examined using methods of epidemiology, anthropology, and sociology. Sills and Goeppinger (1985), however, found only two community health nursing studies in which the community itself was conceptualized as client. Because the client focus is often seen as the characteristic distinguishing community health nursing from other types of nursing, this area of inquiry is central to the development of community health nursing theory. Arguments regarding the necessity of explicit delimitation of the client of care in any attempt to develop community health nursing theory have been presented elsewhere in this article.

To date, most of the concepts used to think about the community as client have been borrowed from other disciplines such as sociology, urban planning, and epidemiology. Often community assessment guidelines are unwieldy and take a great deal of determination and imagination to apply in a nursing context. The community health nurse collects a great deal of data (i.e., transportation patterns, number of water treatment plants, average annual rainfall, etc.) concerning the community of interest but still does not "know" the community. Community health nursing is in great need of relevant models for knowing communities in order to assess, diagnose, intervene, and evaluate effectively. This is particularly important if the "community as client" is the diagnostic criterion of community health nursing practice.

Previous Research

Archer and Fleshman's (1975; Archer, 1976) typologies of community health nursing practice are more than 10 years old and in need of replication. This replication could contribute greatly to community health nursing theory development. Cruise and Storfjell (1980) and Anderson (1983), the only two studies published to date that explicitly consider the notion of community as client, would be excellent resources for ideas for community health nursing theory development. Depending on the underlying assumptions of the theorist, the numerous studies (both within and outside of nursing) of disease patterns in populations, cultural effects on health, distribution of health resources, social support systems, and health behavior could also serve as fertile fields of inquiry for community health nursing theory development. Regardless of the assumptions of the theorist regarding the nature of community health nursing, previous research should be considered an extremely important source of ideas and data.

If community health nursing is considered to be the nursing of communities, unique, explicit community health nursing theory must be developed for use in practice. There are a variety of strategies for developing community health nursing theory. Each has its own problems and its promise. The sources of ideas and data for use in theory building are also numerous. For this reason, the theorist is warned to examine a wide variety of data and ideas to avoid taking too narrow a view of community health nursing. Researchers and theorists are strongly urged to examine their assumptions, especially those regarding the relationship of generic nursing and community health nursing and the community as the client of community health nursing. These assumptions will be at the center of community health nursing theory development in the future.

A MODEL FOR ANALYSIS

The model presented in Figure 9-1 is proposed for use in analyzing theory for use in community health nursing. The model suggests a continuum extending from nonspecific theory for use in community health nursing to emerging theory developed specifically for community health nursing. It is acknowledged that theory falling anywhere along the continuum can be useful; however, there is a serious gap in theory specifically developed for community health nursing. Specific community health nursing theory will facilitate practice activities and outcomes that are consistent with stated definitions of community health nursing. In addition, theory development specifically for community health nursing has far-reaching implications for health policy.

CONCLUSION

Society needs a discipline that is developing knowledge to prevent illness in communities. When its theory base is sufficiently developed to describe, explain, and predict the health of communities, community health nursing will potentially have a great contribution to make to public policy. Implications for health policy from developing theory-based community health nursing practice include:

1. Increased authority base for nursing in society; therefore, more influence over public policy making.
2. Shift in emphasis in health policy, away from

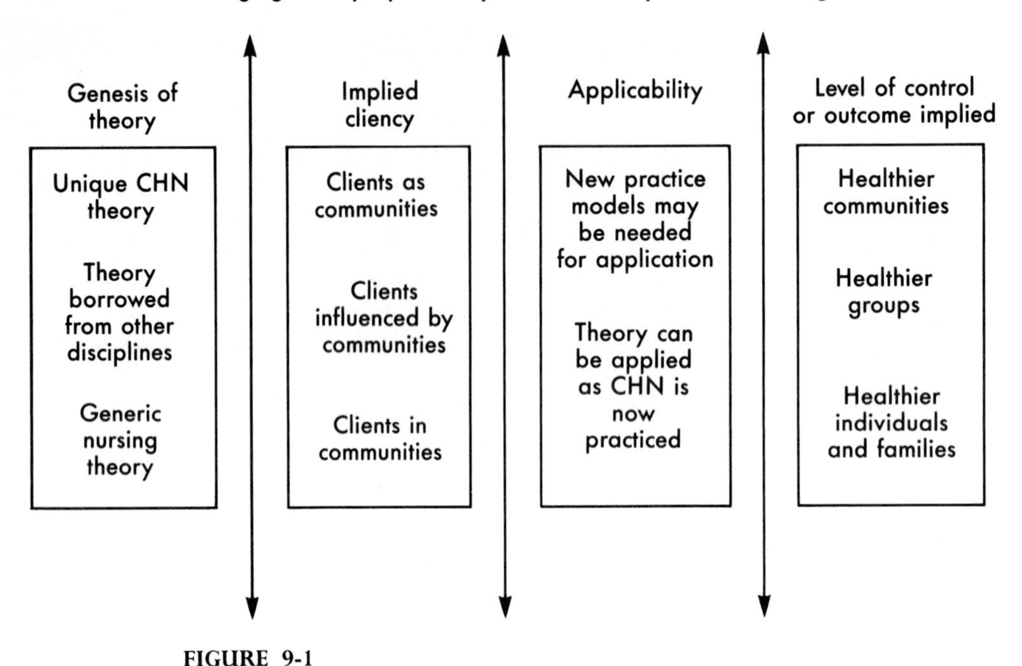

FIGURE 9-1
Framework for analyzing theory for use in community health nursing.

individual illness care toward health promotion and disease prevention.

3. A proactive strategy by this field of nursing to influence its own practice rather than simply to react to the demands and pressures of powerful groups.
4. Stimulation of allocation of health care resources and funds for health promotion and disease prevention.
5. A shift in society's expectations from nursing being accountable primarily to individual clients and physicians toward expectations of nursing being accountable to society for the quality of health of communities.
6. An ideological shift away from a belief in the individual nature of health and illness toward an acknowledgment of the collective nature of these phenomena.

Nursing's influence on community health may well be one of the most important issues facing nursing in the future. This influence rests on sound community health nursing theory. Progress in community health nursing theory development is dependent on the consequent analysis and debate of issues such as the ones raised in this article.

REFERENCES

Anderson, E. T (1983). Community focus in public health nursing: Whose responsibility? *Nursing Outlook, 31,* 44-48.

Archer, S. E (1976). Community nurse practitioner: Another assessment. *Nursing Outlook, 24,* 499-503.

Archer, S. E., & Fleshman, R. P (1975). Community health nursing: A typology of practice. *Nursing Outlook, 23,* 358-364.

Bacon, F. (1863). *Novum Organum* (Vol. VIII). Translated by James Spidding et al. Cambridge, England: Riverside Press.

Cruise, P., & Storfjell, J. (1980). *Community focus model of community health nursing.* Unpublished master's thesis, University of Michigan, Ann Arbor, MI.

Definition and role of public health nursing in the delivery of health care. (1980). American Public Health Association.

Dickoff, J., & James, P. (1968). Theory of theories: A position paper. *Nursing Research, 17,* 197.

Freeman, R. (1970). *Community health nursing practice.* Philadelphia, PA: Saunders.

Glaser, B., & Strauss, A. (1968). *Time for dying.* Chicago, IL: Aldine.

Hamilton, P. (1981). *Health care consumerism.* St. Louis, MO: C. V. Mosby.

Hamilton, P. (1983). Community nursing diagnosis. *Advances in Nursing Science,* 5(3), 21-35.

Mannoia, V. (1980). *What is science?: An introduction to the structure and methodology of science.* Washington, DC: University Press of America.

Meleis, A. I (1985). *Theoretical nursing: Development and progress.* Philadelphia, PA: J. P. Lippincott.

Nightingale, F. (1859). *Notes on nursing: What it is, and what it is not.* London: Harrison & Sons.

Paterson, J., & Zderad, L. (1976). *Humanistic nursing.* New York: Wiley.

Porter, E. J. (1987). Administrative diagnosis: Implications for the public's health. *Public Health Nursing,* 4(4), 247-256.

Reynolds, P. (1980). *A primer in theory construction.* Indianapolis, IN: Bobbs-Merrill Educational Publishing.

Robischon, P. (1975). Community health nursing in a changing climate. In B. Spradley (Ed.), *Contemporary community health nursing.* Boston, MA: Little, Brown.

Sills, G., & Goeppinger, J. (1985). The community as a field of inquiry in nursing. *Annual Review of Nursing Research, 3,* 1-57.

Spradley, B. (1986). *Community health nursing: Concepts and practice.* Boston, MA: Little, Brown.

Standards of community health nursing practice. (1973). Kansas City, MO: American Nurses' Association.

Wald, L. D (1915). *House on Henry Street.* New York: Holt.

Wald, L. D (1934). *Windows on Henry Street.* New York: Holt.

Watson, N. (1984). Community as client. In J. Sullivan (Ed.), *Directions in community health nursing.* Boston, MA: Blackwell Scientific Publications.

Williams, K. (1981). *Major trends in public health nursing 1902-25: The transition from specialized to generalized practice.* Doctoral Dissertation, Teacher's College, Columbia University.

CHAPTER **10**

The Epidemiology of HIV Infection, AIDS, and Health Care Worker Risk Issues

Marguerite M. Jackson, RN, MS, CIC
Patricia Lynch, RN, MBA, CIC

The first documented isolate of the human immunodeficiency virus (HIV) was detected retrospectively in a blood specimen from a young Central African man who had participated in a study in 1959.[1] He was a normal control in the study. The leftover sera from the study were refrigerated and stored. Names of the subjects were not linked to the sera. After the acquired immunodeficiency syndrome (AIDS) epidemic was recognized in 1981 and the HIV antibody test developed in 1984 and 1985, many researchers tested stored, residual specimens from other studies to learn more about the genesis of the epidemic in time and place.

In the years between 1959 and the first reported cases of AIDS in 1981,[2] the epidemic spread silently across the world. This year, 1989, marks the 30th anniversary of the first isolate, but only the eighth year of the recognized epidemic. Two factors kept the epidemic silent for 22 years: the long incubation period between the initial infection in patients and the onset of disease, and the relatively recent intrusion of the virus into developed nations that have systems for detecting, reporting, and analyzing health information.

Reprinted from *Family & Community Health,* Vol. 12, No. 2, with permission of Aspen Publishers, Inc., © 1989.

The silent period of the epidemic also created a situation in which hundreds of thousands of infected individuals unknowingly functioned as sources of infection for others. For example, the majority of present AIDS patients in the United States became infected before the disease was recognized, and so did many of the estimated 1 million to 2 million asymptomatic infected persons.[3]

By the time this article is published, almost 100,000 people in the United States will have been classified as "cases of AIDS," having met the criteria of the Centers for Disease Control (CDC).[4] Most of those persons were hospitalized at least once, and probably all of them received outpatient care more than once over the course of their illness. Additionally, asymptomatic infected people probably receive at least as much health care as the average person in the United States as a whole, since they get sick, have accidents, have babies, and seek care for other reasons. Literally millions of interactions between health care workers (HCWs) and infected patients have occurred over the past 30 years, most of them during the silent period before 1981, or with asymptomatic infected patients who are not recognized as being infected or at risk for infection.

From the moment that HIV was found to be

transmitted by blood, there has been concern about the risk for transmission from infected patients to HCWs. Several questions have been addressed, either by formal studies that evaluate HCWs after various exposures in a somewhat controlled fashion or by looking for results of the great natural experiment that has been taking place since the virus was first introduced into the United States.

THE EPIDEMIOLOGY OF HIV INFECTION IN THE UNITED STATES

The disease we now know as AIDS was first described in 1981 in five sexually active homosexual young men in Los Angeles.[2] Within a short time, similar clusters of infected persons were described from San Francisco, New York, and other major cities. By 1989, cases of AIDS had been reported from all of the states in the United States and almost all countries in the world.

The disease AIDS is defined as a constellation of unusual infections or cancers that suggest a poorly functioning immune system for which no other cause can be found. *Pneumocystis carinii* pneumonia and Kaposi's sarcoma are two of many conditions that meet the criteria for an AIDS diagnosis.[4]

The etiologic agent for AIDS was first identified in 1983 by scientists at the Pasteur Institute in Paris.[5] Subsequently, Gallo and others[6] identified a similar virus at the National Cancer Institute, and Levy and colleagues[7] described a similar virus in San Francisco. By 1985, a test for the antibody to the virus had been developed and was being marketed, mainly to blood banks and plasma centers. The availability of this test for the antibody made it possible to learn about the magnitude of asymptomatic seropositivity in various populations. By 1987 the virus had been named HIV.

Statisticians with the US Public Health Service have used mathematical models to estimate the magnitude of infection with HIV in the United States,[3] which they estimate currently to be a total of 1 million to 1.5 million infected persons. That so many people are infected with a virus that has a latent period of perhaps several years means that there will be numerous newly reported AIDS cases for many years. The CDC[3] estimates that the cumulative case count will reach 350,000 by the end of 1992. More than half of these individuals will be alive and requiring care in 1993, while at the same time an increasing number of newly diagnosed persons will be entering the health care system. Thus, less than four years from now, there will be more than 200,000 persons with AIDS alive in the United States compared to the more than 50,000 persons alive with AIDS by the end of 1989.

Behaviors associated with transmission of the HIV were recognized early in the epidemic, and a number of studies have substantiated the fallacy of casual transmission.[8-10] The three established routes of transmission — sex, contact with blood, and being born to an infected mother — are not equally efficient, however. For example, the transfusion of a single unit of HIV-contaminated blood is very likely to result in infection, and perinatal infection appears to occur in 30% to 50% of all births to infected women. Sexual transmission is most effective when the infected partner is a man who deposits semen into the rectum of the uninfected partner (male or female); sexual transmission from infected women to uninfected men appears to be much less efficient, probably because the concentration of virus in vaginal secretions is less than that in semen. The sharing of needles or other drug-related paraphenalia — not drug use per se — is the risk behavior for HIV infection among intravenous (IV) drug users.[8,10] Although it is estimated that the risk of infection from one episode of heterosexual sex may be about 1 in 200,[8] most people have multiple sexual experiences over time or share IV drug paraphenalia repeatedly. Thus, the risk for infection in the community is rarely limited to a single exposure episode.

In addition to the route of transmission, other factors also appear to influence transmission risk[8]: the dose (inoculum size) of virus transferred, the frequency of exposure, differences in host susceptibility, the infectiousness of the person at the point of the exposure, possible differences in the virulence of different strains of the virus, and the presence of other sexually transmitted diseases (eg, genital herpes) or other cofactors. A number of studies are in progress to answer questions about the contributions of each of these factors to transmission risk.

It is unfortunate that the statistics for the United

States reflect only cases of AIDS, the most serious form of HIV infection. We now know that HIV infection has a spectrum of clinical manifestations, ranging from asymptomatic seropositivity through "full-blown AIDS." Many persons have significant clinical illness prior to meeting the criteria for AIDS, but they are not reflected in the statistics. Thus, it is important for HCWs to recognize that the magnitude of the epidemic is far greater than the CDC statistics report, and that people infected during the silent period of the epidemic will become ill in increasing numbers as we move into the next decade.

The natural history of HIV infection has also been well-defined. It is now estimated that virtually all infected persons will sooner or later become seriously ill with HIV-related disease; however, it may take 5, 10, or even 15 years for this to happen. In the meantime, researchers are actively seeking drugs to abort infection or delay the progression. To date, only one drug (azidothymidine, or AZT) has been licensed as an effective antiviral drug, although a number of other drugs are currently the subjects of clinical trials.[11,12]

The CDC reports cases of AIDS by population group category. Although the absolute numbers in the categories continue to increase, the proportional distribution has changed little since the beginning of the epidemic. The distribution, by category, is:

- Homosexual or bisexual men, 63%;
- Heterosexual IV drug users, 19%;
- Homosexual or bisexual male IV drug users, 7%;
- Heterosexual men and women, 4%;
- Recipients of blood or blood product transfusions, 3%;
- Persons with hemophilia or other coagulation disorders, 1%; and
- Other or undetermined, 3%.[3]

Because of the dominance of cases in homosexual and bisexual men in the United States, the male:female ratio is about 10:1. Among cases in children (persons under 13), almost 80% are in infants born to infected mothers, and most of these pediatric cases can be traced to IV drug use by the infant's mother or her sexual partner. The remaining cases in children are related to blood transfusion or to treatment for coagulation disorders.

AIDS IN HEALTH CARE WORKERS

In April 1988, the CDC[13] reported that HCWs developed AIDS with the same statistical frequency as the rest of the general population. At this point in time, therefore, the number of HCWs who have developed disease as a result of occupational exposure is so small that it is statistically undetectable in the large mass of cases. This does not mean that there is no risk for occupational infection, but only that it is a relatively low risk for most HCWs.

According to the CDC, 41 HCWs with AIDS reported no risk factor other than occupation; however, many of them had not been interviewed extensively at the time of the report, and most of the 41 were men. As most HCWs are women, the proportion of men among the HCWs with AIDS indicates that some of these cases of the disease are probably due to factors other than occupation. Of the 41 HCWs with AIDS, 17 reported needlestick injuries in the years preceding the onset of disease.

A finding that, at worst, only 41 of the more than 75,000 cases of AIDS in the United States at the time of the report were due to the occupational exposure of HCWs provides reassurance, in light of the millions of patient care interactions. However, the numbers of infected people are still growing, not declining, and advances in therapy are extending the lives of people with AIDS so that HCWs will care for more infectious patients year after year. It is important to be clear about the activities that increase risk for HCWs, and these are best determined through formal studies.

HIV INFECTION IN HEALTH CARE WORKERS

Several investigators have serially tested sera from HCWs after needlesticks or mucous membrane exposures from patients who were documented as having AIDS or being HIV positive. By December 1987, 1,176 HCWs were being observed and their data reported by the CDC. Of the 489 with parenteral exposures for whom serum was available to compare time of exposure and status changes subsequently, 3 became HIV positive within 6 months. No nonparenteral exposures resulted in seroconversion.[13]

In another large study, at the University of California in San Francisco, only one seroconversion had been reported by March 1988 in 235 HCWs who had had 644 needlesticks or mucous membrane exposures.[13,14] Similar results have been reported by investigators at the National Institutes of Health,[15] in England,[16] and in Canada.[17]

Two factors affect the likelihood of HIV infection as the result of a single occupational exposure. One, the infectivity of the HIV-positive patient is believed to increase as the immune deficiency increases. Two, the efficiency of delivering the dose of infective material must be greater through punctures than through cutaneous exposures. From a single needlestick with a hollow needle that has had contact with infected blood, the infection rate is estimated to be about 0.5%, or 1 in 200.[13,18]

Unfortunately, occupational exposures occur repeatedly over the course of a career. It is entirely possible for surgeons or technicians to have in their working lifetimes more than 200 to 300 punctures, usually with solid needles or scalpels, which transmit less efficiently than hollow needles. Occupational exposures have transmitted hepatitis B virus (HBV) very efficiently to persons in certain job categories, such as emergency ward nurses, dentists, and surgeons.[19] Thus, it is obvious that patient care practices must be modified in all of the health care professions to increase the safety for the practitioners over their long working lives.

PROTECTING HEALTH CARE WORKERS FROM OCCUPATIONAL HIV INFECTION

The major risk for transmission of HIV to HCWs is associated with handling sharp instruments, and the major preventive effort should be directed at this problem. Sharps injuries result from a combination of factors:

1. design deficiencies. Small-diameter caps for syringes make it difficult to cap used needles without sustaining a puncture. Some laboratory equipment requires the wiping of sharp instruments. Some syringes or procedure needles are very difficult to lock together in use. Correcting these deficiencies would substantially reduce the risk to HCWs, but eliminating all risk is impossible.
2. inadequate training. Personnel perform incorrectly because they learned incorrect methods as students and are still being given incorrect information and taught incorrect practices in the work setting. A major retraining for faculty and inservice educators, accompanied by new textbooks and training materials, is essential to correct the knowledge deficit.
3. lack of appropriate supplies. An adequate supply of clean examination gloves, necessary to keep HCWs from having bare skin contact with bloody body substances, is often unavailable, as are other supplies, because restocking may be inconsistent or not clearly assigned as anyone's responsibility. In addition, during 1987 and 1988, there was a national shortage of examination gloves, and some facilities were unable to obtain adequate supplies from distributors.
4. management attention. Many HCWs are aware of correct practices and have ample supplies, but continue to use unsafe practices for a variety of reasons. Managers must motivate the staff by using tools such as performance reviews to reward or correct performance.

Risk-Reducing Patient Care Practices

The goal of changes should be to reduce the risk of HIV and HBV infection in HCWs without increasing the risk of nosocomial transmission of infectious agents to patients. The precautions used should be generic; that is, they should be applied in all patient care settings, as the "tip of the iceberg" of HIV infection comprises the diagnosed AIDS cases, with a huge portion of asymptomatic cases of HIV infection below the water line.

The CDC has suggested a system of infection precautions[20,21] called "Universal Precautions" (UP) to protect HCWs from HIV and HBV infection. Using UP, HCWs would wear barriers such as gloves, gowns, eyewear, and so forth to prevent their skin or clothing being soiled with bloody fluids from any patient. Traditional isolation precautions would be employed for diagnosed cases of infectious diseases other than HIV, HBV, or any other bloodborne infection. In essence, the UP eliminates the previous guidelines for blood and body fluid precautions, but leaves intact the remainder of the isolation system revised by the CDC in 1983.[22]

Another approach, "Body Substance Isolation" (BSI), uses many of the same precautions as UP but has a slightly different emphasis. BSI is intended to be a complete isolation and precautions system and is used without additional precautions for diagnosed infections.[23-25] In 1983, the CDC offered hospitals three options for isolation precautions: they could retain the "category-specific" system, use a "disease-specific" system, or "design their own system."[23] The BSI system was devised under the third option. The key elements of this system indicate that all HCWs should:

1. Put on clean examination gloves before anticipated contact with the mucous membranes or broken skin of any patient. Change gloves as necessary to ensure this clean surface. When contact with moist body substances is likely, wear appropriate gloves for the task; these may be examination gloves or household gloves.
2. Wash the hands before touching any patient and any time the hands have been soiled.
3. Wear gowns or plastic aprons when it is likely that the HCW's clothing will become soiled with moist body substances.
4. Wear eye protection and masks or face shields for tasks that are likely to generate aerosols.
5. Use private rooms for patients who extensively soil the room with moist body substances or who have airborne communicable diseases, such as chickenpox or tuberculosis. (People with HIV infection do not routinely need private rooms.)
6. Place all used sharps in puncture-resistant containers. Do not recap needles except with recapping devices or using a one-handed technique.
7. Handle all laboratory specimens as if the patient were known to be infected, consistent with P-2 level containment. Mouth pipetting, smoking, and eating at the benches is prohibited.
8. Handle all trash and linen uniformly, by bagging it securely to prevent leaking. It is prudent to autoclave or incinerate sharps, fluid-filled containers, and all laboratory and pathology specimens. It is unnecessary to provide "infectious waste" management for other soiled trash, but local regulations may require this.

Disinfection of Used Items

Reusable instruments should receive the same careful cleaning and disinfection as appropriate for equipment used with all patients. Instruments with hemoaccess should be sterilized between cases; instruments with mucous membrane contact need high-level disinfection or sterilization between cases. Materials in contact with intact skin need routine cleaning and low level disinfection. Special precautions such as double-autoclaving are unnecessary.

MANAGEMENT OF HEALTH CARE WORKERS WITH POTENTIAL EXPOSURE TO HIV

HCWs with open skin lesions should avoid performing or assisting in invasive procedures or patient care in which contact with moist body substances is likely. HCWs with parenteral or mucous membrane exposure to bloody fluids should report the incident to the appropriate department. Similarly, if patients are exposed to bloody fluids from an HCW or another patient, the exposed patient should be informed. The same management is recommended for both groups:[20]

- The donor source should be identified and informed, and the recipient should be evaluated and treated prophylactically for HBV if indicated;
- The donor may be screened for HIV after giving consent; and
- The recipients should be counseled and screened for HIV infection to establish their HIV serologic status at the time of the exposure. Recipients who are HIV negative should be screened again at 6 weeks, 3 months, and 6 months after exposure.[20]

• • •

The President's Commission on the Human Immunodeficiency Virus Epidemic[26] recommended that health care facilities adopt a comprehensive strategy for improving HCW safety. Such a strategy includes improved training, adequate supplies, reinforcement for correct personnel practices, and prompt management of any exposure. The Occupational Safety and Health Administration (OSHA)[27,28] will during 1989 or 1990 complete its rule making, with specific requirements for employers to reduce the risks to HCWs of contact with HIV, HBV, and other bloodborne agents.

REFERENCES

1. Motulsky AG: A University of Washington historical connection: The detection of HIV in Central Africa in 1959, in Motulsky AG (ed): *AIDS: A Guide for the Primary Physician.* University of Washington Medicine, Vol 13, no 1. Seattle, University of Washington, 1987.
2. Centers for Disease Control: *Pneumocystis* pneumonia—Los Angeles. *MMWR* 1981;30:250-252.
3. Heyward WL, Curran JW: The epidemiology of AIDS in the U.S. *Sci Am* 1988;259(4):72-81.
4. Centers for Disease Control: Revision of CDC surveillance case definition for AIDS. *MMWR* 1987;36(suppl 1S):3S-15S.
5. Barre-Sinoussi F, Chermann JD, Rey F, et al.: Isolation of a T-lymphotropic retrovirus from a patient at risk for acquired immunodeficiency syndrome (AIDS). *Science* 1983;220:868-871.
6. Gallo RC, Salahuddin SZ, Popovic M, et al: Frequent detection and isolation of cytopathic retroviruses (HTLV-III) from patients with AIDS and at risk for AIDS. *Science* 1984;224:500-503.
7. Levy JA, Hoffman AD, Kramer SM, et al: Isolation of lymphocytopathic retroviruses from San Francisco patients with AIDS. *Science* 1984;225:840-842.
8. Institute of Medicine, National Academy of Sciences: HIV infection and its epidemiology, in *Confronting AIDS, Update 1988.* Washington, DC: National Academy Press, 1988.
9. Friedland GH, Klein RS: Transmission of the human immunodeficiency virus. *N Engl J Med* 1987;317:1125-1135.
10. Centers for Disease Control: Human immunodeficiency virus infection in the United States: A review of current knowledge. *MMWR* 1987;36(suppl S6):S1-S48.
11. Yarchoan R, Mitsuya H, Broder S: AIDS therapies. *Sci Am* 1988;259(4):110-119.
12. Richman DD: The treatment of infection: Azidothymidine (AZT) and other new antiviral drugs, in Sande MA, Volberding PA (eds): *The Medical Management of AIDS.* Philadelphia, WB Saunders, 1988.
13. Centers for Disease Control: Update: Acquired immunodeficiency syndrome and human immunodeficiency virus infection among health-care workers. *MMWR* 1988;37:229-239.
14. Gerberding JL, Bryant-LeBlanc CE, Nelson K, et al: Risk of transmitting the human immunodeficiency virus, cytomegalovirus, and hepatitis B virus to health care workers exposed to patients with AIDS and AIDS-related conditions. *J Infect Dis* 1987;156:1-8.
15. Henderson DK, Saah AJ, Zak BJ, et al: Risk of nosocomial infection with human T-cell lymphotropic virus type III/lymphadenopathy-associated virus in a large cohort of intensively exposed health care workers. *Ann Intern Med* 1986;104:644-647.
16. McEnvoy M, Porter R, Mortimer P, et al: Prospective study of clinical, laboratory, and ancillary staff with accidental exposures to blood and other body fluids from patients infected with HIV. *Br Med J* 1987;294:1595-1597.
17. Health and Welfare Canada: National surveillance program on occupational exposures to HIV among health care workers. *Can Dis Weekly Rep* 1987;13:163-166.
18. Marcus R, the CDC Cooperative Needlestick Surveillance Group: Surveillance of health care workers exposed to blood from patients infected with the human immunodeficiency virus. *N Engl J Med* 1988;319:1118-1123.
19. Dienstag JL, Ryan DM: Occupational exposure to hepatitis B virus in hospital personnel: Infection or immunization? *Am J Epidemiol* 1982;115:26-39.
20. Centers for Disease Control: Recommendations for prevention of HIV transmission in health-care settings. *MMWR* 1987;36(suppl2S):1S-18S.
21. Centers for Disease Control: Update: Universal precautions for prevention of transmission of HIV, HBV, and other bloodborne pathogens in healthcare settings. *MMWR* 1988;37:377-388.
22. Centers for Disease Control: Guideline for isolation precautions in hospitals, in *CDC Guidelines for the Prevention and Control of Nosocomial Infections.* Atlanta, Centers for Disease Control, 1983.
23. Jackson MM, Lynch P: Infection control: Too much or too little? *Am J Nurs* 1984;84:208-210.
24. Jackson MM, Lynch P, McPherson DC, et al: Clinical savvy: Why not treat all body substances as infectious? *Am J Nurs* 1987;87:1137-1139.
25. Lynch P, Jackson MM, Cummings MJ, et al: Rethinking the role of isolation practices in the prevention of

nosocomial infections. *Ann Intern Med* 1987;107: 243-246.

26. Watkins JD, Commissioners: *Report of the Presidential Commission on the Human Immunodeficiency Virus Epidemic.* Publication No 1988 0-204-701:QL3. Government Printing Office, 1988.
27. US Department of Labor; US Department of Health and Human Services: Joint advisory notice: HIV/HBV. *Federal Register* 1987;52(Oct 30):41818-41824.
28. US Department of Labor; US Department of Health and Human Services: Advance notice of proposed rulemaking. *Federal Register* 1987;52(Nov 27):45438-45441.

CHAPTER **11**

Public Health Nursing Model for Contact Follow-up of Patients with Pulmonary Tuberculosis

Bonnie Kellogg, RN
Charlene Dye, RN, PHN
Karen Cox, RN, PHN
Greta Rosenow, RN, PHN

Public health nurses (PHNs) continuously assess the effectiveness of their role in providing health services to the community. Recently, a PHN in Los Angeles County demonstrated exceptional success in coordinating the industrial contact follow-up for a patient with active pulmonary tuberculosis. Los Angeles County has a higher than average tuberculosis case rate of 18:100,000 (P. Davidson, personal communication 1985), as compared with the nation's rate of 10.2:100,000 (*Nation's Health,* 1985, p. 4). Tuberculosis control is an important function of the district PHN's case load. This includes identifying high-risk contacts and providing appropriate screening such as Mantoux skin testing and chest radiograms for those with positive skin tests (Figure 11-1). An important component of the PHN's follow-up includes health education regarding the disease process and preventive measures. Public health nursing interventions are based on standards established by the health department and theoretical concepts from epidemiology, nursing, and the behavioral sciences such as the health-belief model.

Reprinted from *Public Health Nursing,* Vol. 4, No. 2, with permission of Blackwell Scientific Publications, Inc., © 1987.

PATIENT NO. 1

The PHN received a referral on a 48-year-old male Hispanic with the diagnosis of pulmonary tuberculosis based on a positive sputa concentrate, positive Mantoux reaction, and clinical symptoms of disease. His chest film showed right upper lobe infiltration. Although he lived in another district, he worked in the PHN's district and, based on health department protocol, it was her responsibility to assess the work environment and identify co-workers who may have been exposed to the patient. In communicable disease follow-up, at-risk contacts must be identified and advised of their exposure. Permission was obtained from this patient to conduct an industrial investigation. The nurse contacted his supervisor within six days of the industry learning of the diagnosis. Incorporating the theoretical framework of the health-belief model, the PHN based her interventions and health teaching on the following concepts that may influence compliance:

1. Perceived susceptibility—the person's view of the likelihood of experiencing harmful effects or contracting a disease
2. Perceived seriousness—how threatened the in-

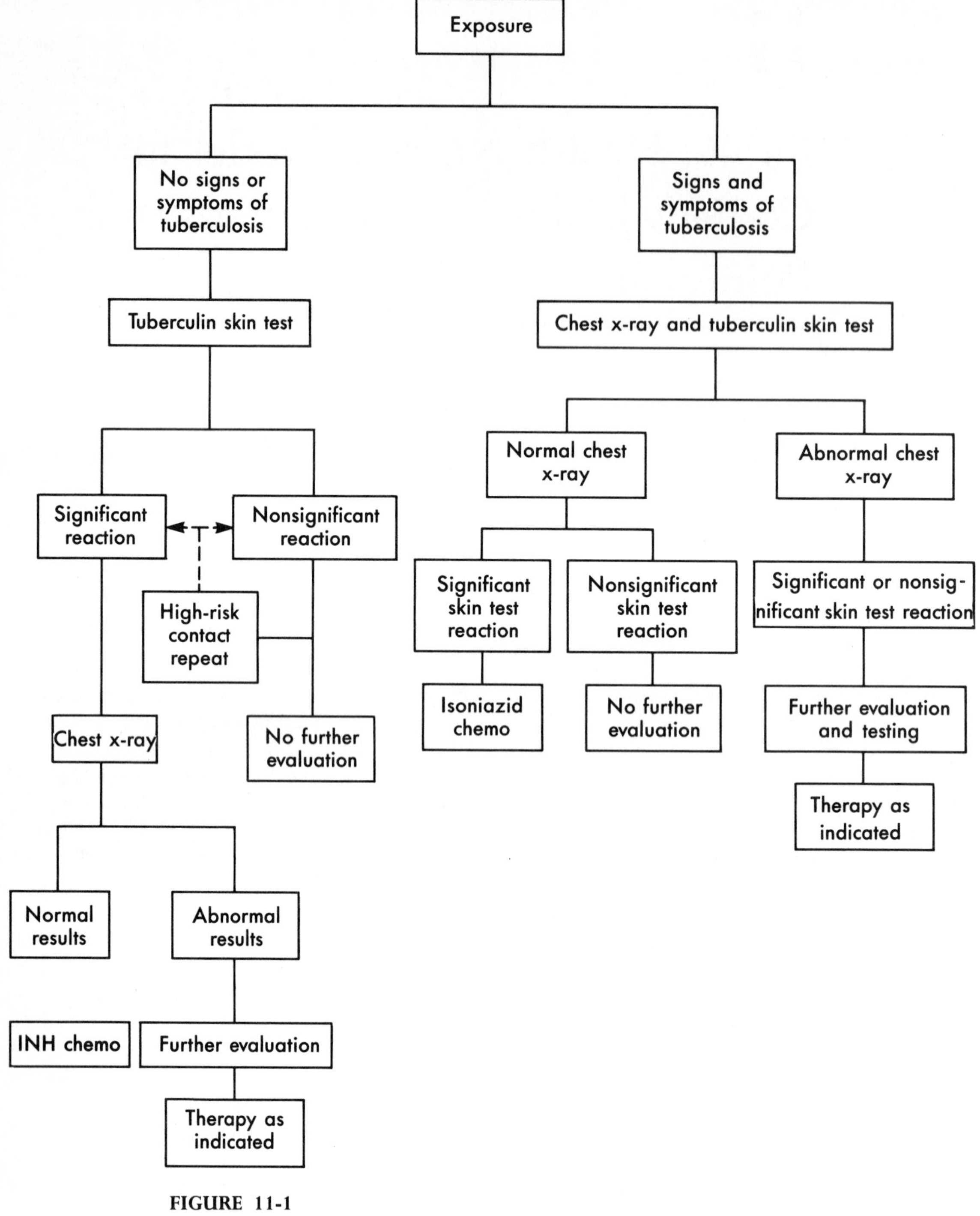

FIGURE 11-1
Contact follow-up. (Modified from the American Thoracic Society, *Control of tuberculosis,* 1983.)

dividual feels the disease is to his or her lifestyle

3. Perceived benefits — how beneficial the specific behavior is felt to be in reducing the individual's risk or threat to the disease
4. Perceived barriers — what negative aspects are anticipated from the behavior (Rosenstock, 1966; Champion, 1984)

Using these four concepts, the nurse developed an intervention strategy to educate the supervisor regarding the disease process, modes of transmission, current treatment modalities, prognosis, preventive measures recommended for at-risk contacts, and the health department's legal responsibility in the control of communicable disease. The PHN stressed the importance of adequate contact screening and the effectiveness of isoniazid (INH) chemoprophylaxis in controlling future cases of the disease. This encouraged the supervisor to accept the need for follow-up of at-risk employees and to assist the PHN in identifying these individuals. Those at greatest risk were screened first.

A Mantoux screening clinic was set up at the industrial site. The plant supervisor assigned his personnel to ensure that all required paper work was in order prior to this and a later screening clinic. This saved a great deal of time for the nurse and the industry, since each employee was off the job for only a short period of time. It also allowed the nurse to review the information necessary and answer individual questions as they arose.

Twenty-two individuals, considered high-risk contacts based on their close proximity and time exposure to the index case, were skin tested. Three days later the skin tests were read. Of the 22, 16 (72.7%) had significant reactions and 6 (27.3%) were negative (Table 11-1). Standards of practice established by Los Angeles County Health Department Tuberculosis Control recommend that moderate or secondary contacts be screened if high-risk contacts have a 30 percent or greater reaction rate. Since the rate was 72.7 percent, a second Mantoux clinic at the industrial site was scheduled and 125 secondary contacts were screened. The skin tests were evaluated three days later and 44 (35%) individuals had a significant reaction; the remainder were negative.

Before the first Mantoux test, the 22 employees were informed that tuberculosis spreads through

TABLE 11-1
High-risk contacts

1 MANTOUX (mm)	2 MANTOUX (mm)	X-RAY	ISONIAZID THERAPY (mo)
+18		Negative	12
+37		Suspect class IV	12
+32		Negative	Refused
+20		Negative	3
+17		Negative	3
+10		Negative	Refused
+22		Negative	3
Negative	+12	Abnormal non-TB	Refused
Negative	Negative		None
Negative	+11	Negative	Refused
Negative	+14	Negative	Refused
+18		Negative	Refused
Negative	+15	Negative	Refused
+28		Negative	?
+16		Negative	3
Negative	Negative		None
+17		Negative	Refused
+20		Negative	Refused
+17		Negative	Refused
+26		Negative	Refused
+24		Negative	6
+10		Negative	3

personal contact with the bacillus, and this information could have stimulated a hypersensitivity response. A third Mantoux screening clinic was scheduled 4 months later to retest the contacts that were negative. Of the 10 high risk contacts that were negative at the first testing, four (66.6%) had a positive reaction to the second test. These individuals were referred to their private physician or to the routine chest clinic for chest x-rays, and isoniazid chemoprophylaxis was recommended.

A total of 155 high-risk and moderate-risk contacts were screened for tuberculosis and all the required documentation was completed within four months. Follow-up of this magnitude often takes six months to a year to complete. The PHN made a total of seven visits to the industrial site and all the legal and epidemiologic documentation was completed and the case was closed within nine months.

Components for Success

Compliance with the screening of at-risk contacts was 100 percent. What made this case so successful? Evaluation of the PHN's interventions identified seven points that became the foundation for the proposed TB follow-up model (Figure 11-2).

The first component was immediate and timely identification of high-risk contacts. The longer the time between diagnosis and initial contact, the greater the chance of noncompliance. In this case, the industry was made aware of the implications of employees becoming ill as a result of work-related exposure. The PHN established follow-up as a priority by initiating screening and by providing literature from the health department and the American Thoracic Society. This gave employees accurate information regarding their potential risks and outlined the appropriate measures available to control or eliminate these risks.

A special x-ray clinic was set up at the health center to accommodate the employees with positive Mantoux skin tests. This allowed the employees to come in as a group for their evaluations during work time, as arranged with the cooperation of the industry. All 60 individuals with positive Mantoux tests received a chest x-ray and were referred to the tuberculosis clinic for chemoprophylaxis. Isoniazid, 300 mg by mouth for nine months to a year, is the recommended

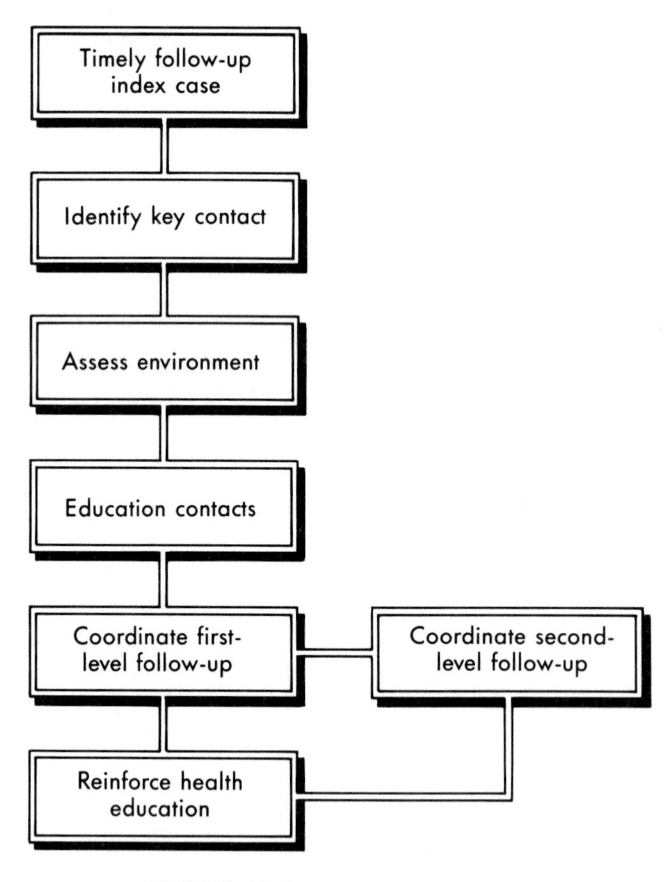

FIGURE 11-2
Tuberculosis contact follow-up model.

regimen. (The Centers for Disease Control recommends isoniazid for Mantoux reactors; however, to date, it is not mandatory.)

The second component was to identify a key contact. This is a significant individual who has the authority or ability to coordinate action for those at risk. In this case, the supervisor, after education by the PHN, was motivated to cooperate with the recommendations of the health department. In other situations, it may be a relative or friend who has access to those at risk and is aware of the need to implement screening procedures. This individual believes there is a potential risk and that something can be done to control the spread of the disease.

The third component used epidemiologic and public health nursing skills in the thorough assessment of the work environment. The assessment focused on identifying individuals who shared proximity with the index case during the infectious stage of disease. Using the concept of the expanding circle of contacts (Figure 11-3), the PHN identified persons who spent a substantial amount of time with the patient in an environment with limited air circulation. The expanding circle of contact allowed the nurse to establish priorities for the risk factors. Individuals at greatest risk were screened first. Because this group had a positive yield, it was important to evaluate the second level, or moderate-risk contacts. Evaluating the risk status of the contacts made the best use of time and resources, since not everyone who came in contact with the patient required screening.

The fourth component of this model involved providing appropriate health education to all those exposed to the source case. This was directed toward the implications of the disease and available preventive measures. Based on the health-belief model, appropriate health education should increase individuals' awareness of their susceptibility to a specific condition and outline actions that may be taken to decrease the risks of disease and eliminate perceived barriers of the screening process. Therefore educational materials related to mode of transmission, prognosis, treatment, and prevention are important to increase compliance.

In the fifth step, the appropriate follow-up services were organized and coordinated. In an effort to reduce potential perceived barriers to participating in follow-up, the PHN set up skin test screening clinics at the industry. This not only saved the employees time and the industry money, it saved the health department many hours of follow-up. By providing the service at a convenient time and location, the nurse was able to test all at-risk contacts. Furthermore, by coordinating with the supervisor, all necessary paperwork and forms were prepared prior to the clinic. The supervisor, with guidelines, had each employee complete the forms and these were available at the time of screening. The cooperation between the health department and the industry ensured that the screening of high-risk contacts proceeded efficiently.

The sixth step involved follow-up of all abnormal results. At this point, the nurse was able to work individually with persons who had greatest needs. The

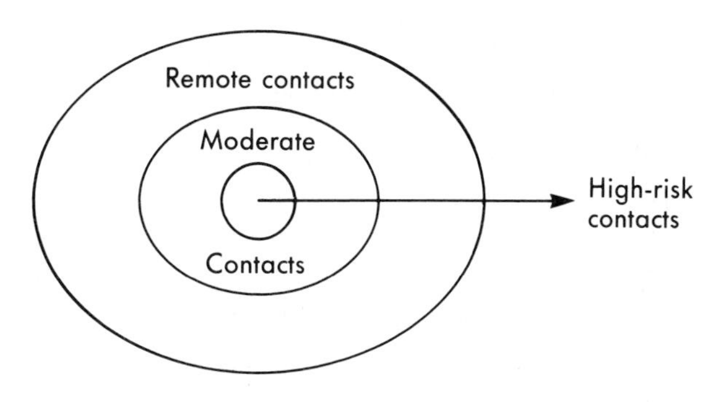

FIGURE 11-3
Expanding circle of contacts.

x-ray follow-up was facilitated and scheduled for the convenience of the industry and the PHN. This extra effort on the part of the health department proved successful and validated the importance of contact follow-up.

In the final component of this model, the nurse and contacts had continuous interaction, with the major focus on expanding and reinforcing the educational aspects of nursing interventions. Reinforcement of the steps appropriate to control and prevent tuberculosis was a continuous part of the nurse's role.

Shortly after the model was identified, the health center encountered a second case of tuberculosis involving industrial contacts. The PHN applied the model again, with some minor modifications.

PATIENT NO. 2

A 31-year-old Hispanic male was referred to the health department by a local hospital where he had been admitted for diagnostic work-up of hemoptysis and a persistent, productive cough. According to the criteria established by the American Thoracic Society, the diagnosis of pulmonary tuberculosis was based on a positive Mantoux reaction, positive sputa concentrate for acid-fast bacilli, and clinical improvement after initiation of isoniazid and ethambutal. The patient's chest film showed left lower lobe infiltrate consistent with pulmonary tuberculosis disease.

Initial industrial contact was made by the PHN within 10 working days after being notified of the diagnosis. The patient was made aware of the need for contact investigation, and with his cooperation, the PHN identified the personnel officer and his immediate supervisor as key contacts. They were provided with a thorough explanation of the importance of contact screening and follow-up. One hundred forty-six potentially high-risk contacts were identified and skin tested at the work site. Forty-seven (33%) were reactive. Since more than 30 percent were positive, the secondary contacts were screened and 137 moderate and remote contacts were tested. Twenty-three (17%) had significant readings on their skin tests.

Those with a significant reaction were x-rayed at conveniently arranged health department clinics or by their private physicians. The plant supervisor arranged for the required paperwork to be completed prior to testing. The PHN was actively involved in providing coordination and health education to the contacts.

The compliance rate of contacts initiating and completing 9 to 12 months of isoniazid chemoprophylaxis was not impressive in the first case. The PHN and the nursing care specialist in the chest service hypothesized that by removing the potential barriers of time, distance, and effort, compliance could be increased if an isoniazid clinic was established at the work site. Therefore using the health department's protocols and standards, a clinic was set up. Of the 47 high-risk contacts who had significant reactions to the Mantoux test, 17 agreed to initiate chemoprophylaxis. Six monthly follow-up clinics were held at the industrial site from 7 to 9 A.M. Of the 17 contacts who started taking isoniazid, 15 successfully completed the recommended regimen. Thus this extra effort on the part of the nurse had a positive effect on the compliance rate of those who initiated chemoprophylaxis.

Implementation of the model resulted in the examination of all identified contacts. Furthermore, it demonstrated that by being creative and resourceful in carrying out nursing interventions, the PHN was working in a cost effective manner and receiving professional satisfaction.

By actively involving the industries in this epidemiologic process, their awareness of the role of public health nursing and the health department in communicable disease control was increased. It is speculated that in the future, these two industries will be more aware of the signs and symptoms of pulmonary tuberculosis and the steps available for early diagnosis and treatment. This will not only shorten the time the patient will be off work, but potentially decrease the exposure of noninfected individuals to pulmonary tuberculosis.

This model provides the PHN with a framework in which to organize management of communicable disease. It also increases the level of interaction among the various disciplines involved in disease control and prevention by their cooperation in facilitating the follow-up services provided to at-risk populations. This model needs further testing and refinement; however, it provides a methodical approach to communicable disease follow-up and incorporates creative and flexible interventions, which are important components of effective public health nursing.

REFERENCES

Anonymous. (1985). Tuberculosis, the historic bane of humankind, on decline again. *Nation's Health, 15,* 4.

Archer, S., & Fleshman, R. (1985). *Community health nursing* (3rd ed.). Monterey, CA: Wadsworth Health Sciences.

Champion, V. (1984). Instrument development for health belief model constructs. *Advances in Nursing Science, 6,* 73-85.

Kearns, T., Cole, C., Farer, L., Leff, A., Reza, R., Slarbaro, J., Stead, W.M. (1985). Public health issues in control of tuberculosis: Surveillance techniques and role of health care providers. *Chest, 87,* 135-138.

Pender, N. (1982). *Health promotion in nursing practice.* Norwalk, CT: Appleton-Century-Crofts.

Rosenstock, I. (1966). Why people use health services. *Memorial Fund Quarterly, 44,* 94-121.

(1983). Treatment of tuberculosis and other mycobacterial diseases. *American Review of Respiratory Diseases, 127,* 790-796.

CHAPTER 12

Current Perspectives in Quality Assurance and Community Health Nursing

Beverly C. Flynn, RN, PhD
Dixie W. Ray, MPA

BASIC CONCEPTS

The process of quality assurance follows the steps in the nursing process or basic problem solving: assessment, analysis of information collected during the assessment, planning to correct or maintain community health nursing practice, taking action according to these plans, and reassessment. The process, cyclical and ongoing, provides information that is useful in decision making.

There are two parts of this process: quality assessment and quality assurance. Quality assessment is the measurement phase of quality assurance and involves identifying what is to be measured, choosing a method of measurement, performing the measurement, interpreting the results, and determining the causes of problems. Quality assurance, on the other hand, involves using the results of quality assessment, taking action on the problems identified in the quality assessment, and reassessment to make certain the action worked.

In reviewing the literature to determine the state of the art in quality assurance, a number of conceptual frameworks and models were found, a few of which are highlighted (Chance, 1980). Perhaps the most widely noted were variations of the systems approach. The structure-process-outcome framework has been utilized in evaluating not only the quality of medical care, but also in evaluating nursing, community health nursing practice, and health services in general (American Nurses Association [ANA], 1976, 1986; Donabedian, 1966; Starfield, 1973). Although the structure-process-outcome framework was widely published, the relationships among the three dimensions remain to be proven. The open systems theory is similar to this and has been applied to hospitals in which inputs, processes, and outputs were studied (Georgopoulos, 1972). An economic model that focuses on two dimensions of the systems approach, inputs and outputs, includes evaluation of resources, money, products, labor, and capacity (Jelinek, 1976). Orem's self-care theory (1971) has been used in quality assessment to develop criteria for process, both the assessment of patient behavior and nursing interventions, as well as patient outcomes (Horn & Swain, 1976; Padilla & Grant, 1982). The nursing process is another framework used in studying the quality of nursing care and was used by researchers at Rush University in Chicago (Hegyvary, Gortner, & Haussman, 1976). A relatively recent approach to evaluating quality of care is participatory evaluation and involves consumers and local people themselves

Reprinted from *Journal of Community Health Nursing,* Vol. 4, No. 4, with permission of Lawrence Erlbaum Associates, Inc., © 1987.

in each stage of the evaluation. It has been used more frequently in the developing world (Feuerstein, 1980; Rahman, 1978), yet it has applicability in community health nursing.

The original structure-process-outcome framework does not really apply to groups and communities, which are essential components of community health nursing practice (ANA, 1976). Therefore, a modification of the framework (Flynn, 1977) is used, building on the work of Neuhauser and Anderson (1972) in the study of hospitals. The modified framework uses a systems approach that shows the interdependence of four major dimensions—environment, structure, process, and outcome. The environment surrounds structure, process, and outcome. The environment we are most familiar with is the community but it may also be a state, region, or a nation. Included in the environment are characteristics of people such as level of health, age ranges, racial and cultural backgrounds, and their life-style habits. Also included in environment are health-care services, health legislation, and geographic conditions including climate, mountains, and rivers.

Structure refers to the organization providing community health nursing services. This may be a home health agency, a school, or industry. Characteristics of structure include staffing patterns, programs, finances, facilities, and size of the organization.

Process involves the interaction between the community health nurse and the client whether it is a patient, family, or community group. Examples of process characteristics are community health nurse's time spent with a client; services provided; place of service such as home, clinic, school, or telephone.

Outcomes are the results of community health nursing services in terms of client's knowledge, health, physical functioning abilities, immunization levels, problem-solving skills, and their abilities to cope with stress and crisis.

None of these dimensions exist alone; structure, process, and outcome are all interacting with one another and with the environment of which they are a part. All four dimensions influence one another. Change in any one part of the system creates change in other parts.

The following examples relate these dimensions. A common event in the community health nurse's day is to teach (process) a diabetic patient and his or her family to give insulin injections, a process aimed at encouraging the patient's independence and stabilizing blood sugar level (outcomes). Another frequent situation is for the community health nurse to work with a group of mothers with infants in a clinic. These mothers have expressed common concerns over their inadequate parenting skills. The focus of community health nursing service in this situation is to provide anticipatory guidance and advice on coping with the developmental needs of young children (process). This will increase the mothers' knowledge of growth and development and will improve their ability to problem solve and to cope with a growing family (outcomes). In the school, the nurse is involved with teachers in case finding to determine the extent of an outbreak of pediculosis. Follow-up includes information for children and parents on appropriate treatment and methods to prevent further spread of the disease (process) resulting in control of the condition (outcome). In the health center of an industry, the community health nurse is involved in a nutritional education program for employees (process) aimed at reducing weight, cholesterol, and blood pressure levels among the workers (outcomes). An example that relates all four dimensions involves immunizations of schoolchildren. A state passes an immunization law requiring all school-age children to be immunized against childhood diseases (environment). An agency providing community health nursing services responds by setting aside finances to establish immunization clinics (structure), which results in an increased number of schoolchildren immunized (process) and the reduction of childhood communicable diseases (outcome).

SELECTED LITERATURE

This framework has also been useful in helping to organize the literature related to quality assessment in community health nursing. The quality assessment criteria and measures can be tabulated by their relevance to each of the four dimensions in the framework (see Table 12-1). A few of the criteria and

TABLE 12-1
Selected quality assessment criteria or measures categorized by the framework

SOURCE	MEASUREMENT			
	ENVIRONMENT	STRUCTURE	PROCESS	OUTCOME
ANA (1976)				X
ANA (1986)		X	X	X
Colorado Department of Health	X	X		
Minnesota Department of Health				X
New Haven VNA				X
Ramsey County Public Health Nursing Service				X
Omaha VNA		X	X	X

measures are highlighted, and, as can be observed, most of the work has been related to outcome.

The ANA (1976) utilized five task forces, one of which represented community health nursing. Each task force identified outcome criteria for three target populations, with outcome criteria and target populations differing for each task force. The well family was one of the target populations for the community health nursing task force. An example of an outcome criteria was that the family "identifies appropriate situation for entry into the health care system" (p. 54). The method of collecting this information was a review of community health nursing family records or record audit.

The recent ANA *Standards of Community Health Nursing Practice* (1986) apply to any community health nursing setting involving care of communities, families, and individuals. The standards are written within the framework of the nursing process and provide clear and concise statements for action in each element of the framework: structure, process, and outcome.

The Colorado Department of Health has been a leader in assessing agency structure since 1971. Its 1979 quality assurance package included guidelines for community assessment, and criteria for agency structure and nine specialty programs including adult-health, child-health, school-health, and migrant-health programs (Colorado Department of Health, 1979). Data collection forms included the criteria, checklists that indicate whether the standards were met, how the evidence was documented, and the reviewer's comments.

The Minnesota Department of Health has developed and implemented outcome criteria for a wide range of target populations (Decker, Stevens, Vancini, & Wedeking, 1979; Minnesota Department of Health, 1979). A criteria, data collection, and distribution system has been established that allows for criteria exchange and reporting on a state-wide basis.

The New Haven Visiting Nurse Association (VNA) utilized a "rehabilitation potential" patient classification system (Daubert, 1979). This system focused on patient outcomes. Generic criteria were utilized to classify all patients admitted to an agency's illness service program into one of five patient groups, based on severity of illness. This system also included a special family record and has been utilized by numerous other visiting nurse agencies.

The Ramsey County Public Health Nursing Service in Minnesota (Choi, Josten, & Christensen, 1983) has further developed the Richmond/Hopkins Family Coping Index (Freeman & Lowe, 1964). The index consisted of nine outcome domains, such as the family's physical independence, therapeutic competence, knowledge of health condition, and hygiene application. Five levels of family coping were described across all nine domains. The index is particularly useful in that a score may be calculated for the patient and family. The Wisconsin Division of Health was also using this index and has combined it with family health status characteristics and community health nursing services (Vahldieck, personal communication, February 1985).

The Omaha VNA developed a system for classifying and recording client problems requiring community health nursing interventions (Simmons, 1980; Visiting Nurse Association of Omaha, 1986). Problems are grouped into four major domains, environmental, psychosocial, physiological, and health-related behaviors. Patient outcomes have been developed according to these problems and have been tested in a number of cities in the United States. A unique feature is that this system has computer capability and provides information that can link structure and process with outcomes.

PROBLEMS, ISSUES, AND GAPS

There are a number of problems, issues, and gaps related to the assessment of quality of care in community health nursing. Some of these problems reflect the technology or state of the art in quality assessment and others are philosophical in nature. Because they affect the direction of quality of care programs they both are considered.

State-of-the-Art Issues

Perhaps the most obvious problem with existing quality assessment criteria and data collection methods is that agencies use different classification schemes for their patient populations, thereby reducing the possibilities for sharing quality assessment methods or for making comparisons across agencies. Some agencies classify patients by diseases, whereas others use problem categories. Along with this are difficulties in classifying and handling multiple problem populations. For example, into what category should a patient who is diabetic, hypertensive, and arthritic be placed? Other problems relate to identifying appropriate criteria for multiple problem cases in that the problems often confound one another. Lists of criteria that are applicable only to very specific patient populations have been developed by many agencies. There are few examples of the development of generic criteria that may be applied to a wide range of patients. One such example is the New Haven VNA, mentioned earlier (Daubert, 1979). Other problems relate to the fact that patient and family records are often cumbersome for use in collecting data in quality assessment. The problem-oriented record system is often suggested as a solution, yet in many agencies implementation of this system is difficult and slow. As if these problems are not enough, very few of the criteria and data collection methods have established reliability and validity. Because of this one does not know what is being measured in quality of care or how consistently it is being measured.

Philosophical Issues

Our orientation to community health nursing is that of the integration of public health principles with primary health care, as defined by the World Health Organization (1978). Due to this orientation, it is relevant to comment on the notion of quality of care within this context. These comments center on the primary health-care concepts of appropriate technology, equitable distribution, health promotion and disease prevention, and community involvement.

Quality assurance is a concept that reflects the need for holding professionals accountable to consumers for their health-care practices. Some professionals have called quality assurance a "Trojan horse" in that it also carries with it an increased emphasis for external intervention in clinical affairs. There is an obvious conflict between the public's demand for quality of care and the professionals' demand for clinical freedom (Markus, 1981).

It has been documented that the level of people's health is only slightly related to the health care they receive (Department of Health and Social Services, 1980; Navarro, 1977; Vuori, 1980). This was clearly pointed out in the Black report on *Inequalities in Health* in Great Britain (Department of Health and Social Services, 1980). This is a particularly intriguing fact in a country that has since the 1950s sought to distribute its health services equitably through its National Health Service. It is obvious that the health-care system can only be held accountable for those population outcomes that are within its control.

In thinking about community health nursing in particular, the focus of practice is not only patient- and disease-oriented care. Practice is focused on communities and population groups with an emphasis on health promotion, disease prevention, and health maintenance (ANA, 1980; Public Health Nursing Section, 1980). Quality assurance programs rarely include these aspects of practice. For example, how often is information about the unserved or underserved populations documented in considering the effectiveness of community health nursing practice? Regretfully, rarely if ever.

The concept of quality of care has also been criticized because most programs are aimed at maximizing the quality of health services, especially the scientific aspects of care (Vuori, 1980). No country can afford to provide all citizens with first class care. Scarce resources would go only to a few, reflecting an example of inappropriate technology. We know that the greatest good to an individual is not necessarily the greatest good for society. Realizing this, many European countries have taken a stand that quality is a luxury that must be kept on hold until adequacy and equity problems are resolved (Vuori, 1980). Surely, the concept of quality needs to fit realistically within a community's and country's socioeconomic and political realities. This is consistent with the primary health-care approach.

Further examination of the concept of quality of care indicates that it has two major components—technical care and art of care (Brook & Williams, 1975). Technical care includes the scientific aspect of care, the diagnostic and therapeutic processes. The art of care relates to the milieu, the manner and behavior of the professional providing care and communicating with recipients of care. These two concepts are interactive, influencing the overall quality of care. Vuori (1980) indicates that quality assurance programs have almost exclusively been concerned with technical care. He suggests more emphasis should be given to the art of care, especially to include consumer views of quality. These considerations were also reflected in an article reviewing public opinions of health-care programs (Kelman, 1976). It was found that providers do not regard consumers as competent to judge the technical aspects of health-care quality. Consumers of care were found to be concerned over the process of health-care delivery, or art of care. That is, the way they are regarded by health-care personnel and the physical and administrative characteristics of these programs. In other words, the process of care aspects of quality can be judged by consumers yet these aspects are neglected by health-care personnel in evaluating quality of care. If consumers are involved at all, it is to obtain their satisfactions with services provided while agency administrators decide on what changes (if any) are made in service delivered. It is rare to find consumers involved in making decisions related to improving the quality of care.

The concept of community involvement requires new relationships for professionals and such relationships are bound to create tensions with the traditional view of professional control of health care. If primary health care is to be successful then consumers themselves must be involved in making decisions about quality of care. These decisions are too important to be left to the professionals alone.

SUGGESTED SOLUTIONS

These problems may appear to be overwhelming. One may question what can be done in a local agency about all of these issues. The answer relates, in part, to developing a sound quality assurance program in the agency and using a process that considers the following guidelines that have been proven useful by others in the field (ANA, 1976; Michnich, Harris, Willis, & Williams, 1976; Taylor, 1974; VNA of Omaha, 1986; Zimmer, 1974).

The first step is formation of a quality assurance committee composed of community health nurses and possibly others. In doing this, consideration should be given to the professional groups that are employed by the agency and should include representatives of all groups that will be evaluated; for example, community health nurses, home health aides, and social workers. Consumers should also be involved in the quality assurance process at this time, especially in the evaluation of the process of care or the art of care. Existing agency goals and objectives need to be clarified. Nursing directors and supervisors can identify areas in which information is needed for decision making so that the quality assurance program is consistent with agency policy making. Use of the quality assessment information and cost considerations are two factors that must be considered before starting the quality assurance program. The evaluation processes currently utilized by the agency should be reviewed, for example, staff evaluation and staff development activities.

Review of the current literature will facilitate

building on the experiences of others. Agencies can include those elements that have been missing from quality assessment—the unserved population. Client characteristics can be compared to population characteristics to determine what portion of potential clients is being served.

When all the information is collected, it must be studied to determine the strengths, problems, and gaps. It is less threatening to start with one area of the agency and to identify strengths as well as problems. Collaboration in quality assessment with other community health nursing agencies and community health nursing educators can produce group expertise not available in any one organization. Such collaboration provides benefits to all participants. Agencies are able to develop quality assessment programs, and community health nursing educators meet the community service and/or research requirements of faculty appointments in universities or colleges.

Throughout the process of establishing a quality assurance program, key principles are to encourage flexibility and creativity; for example, the exploration and development of generic criteria or population and community outcomes with consumer input. Consider how the record-keeping systems will be affected as well as the computer capability of the quality assurance program.

As the quality assurance program evolves, an agency profile may be developed where the information collected represents the environment, structure, process, and outcome components. Once the data are available for more than one dimension, the relationships among the dimensions can begin to be established. This type of information may prove useful in justifying budgets. In other words, how many staff (structure) are needed to provide what quantity of services (process) and to produce what level of population outcomes. Such information may also prove useful in planning and conducting inservice education programs. The quality assurance program can also be used in the continuing development of knowledge through research. And, last but not least, this information should be helpful in improving or maintaining a level of quality of care that is appropriate for the community's health, because consumers themselves were also involved in the decision making.

CONCLUDING CASE EXAMPLE

A case example demonstrates the function of the quality assurance process. A community health nursing agency has an objective to immunize 90% to 100% of kindergarten through 12th-grade students. The nursing director indicates that she needs information about childhood communicable disease rates, the percent of children immunized in the grades, and the costs of the immunization program. The information will be used to support the community health nursing position in the school system.

The agency's quality assurance committee consists of not only representatives of all groups in the agency but also consumers. In reviewing the evaluation processes in the agency the quality assurance committee finds that one staff development program focused on childhood communicable disease control and immunizations. The community health nurses participating in the program were found to have a high level of knowledge and skill in these areas upon completion of the program. Review of the literature supports use of the school immunization records as a reliable source of information (process). The committee found the health department's record of communicable diseases to be the best estimate of the incidence of disease (outcomes). Use of existing data is a cost effective method for quality assessment. The nursing director's budget allocations for the immunization program provide cost data (structure). Because all the information is numerical, computer applications are easily made and permit linking structure, process, and outcome.

REFERENCES

American Nurses Association. (1976). *Guidelines for review of nursing care at the local level.* Kansas City, MO: Author.

American Nurses Association. (1980). *A conceptual model of community health nursing.* Kansas City, MO: ANA Division on Community Health Nursing.

American Nurses Association. (1986). *Standards of community health nursing practice.* Kansas City, MO: Author.

Brook, R. H., & Williams, K. N. (1975). Quality of health care for the disadvantaged. *Journal of Community Health, 1,* 132-156.

Chance, K. S. (1980). The quest for quality: An exploration of attempts to define and measure quality nursing care. *Image, 12*(2), 41-45.

Choi, T., Josten, L., & Christensen, M. L. (1983). Health specific family coping index for noninstitutional care. *American Journal of Public Health, 73,* 1275-1277.

Colorado Department of Health. (1979, October). *Manual for Community Health Nursing Structure Review.* Denver: Community Health Nursing Section.

Daubert, E. A. (1979). Patient classification system and outcome criteria. *Nursing Outlook, 27,* 450-454.

Decker, F., Stevens, L., Vancini, M., & Wedeking, L. (1979). Using patient outcomes to evaluate community health nursing. *Nursing Outlook, 27,* 278-282.

Department of Health and Social Services. (1980). *Inequalities in health: Report of a research working group.* London: Her Majesty's Stationery Office.

Donabedian, A. (1966). Evaluating the quality of medical care. *Milbank Memorial Fund Quarterly, 44,* 166-203.

Feuerstein, M. T. (1980). Participatory evaluation—An appropriate technology for community health programmes. *Contact, 55,* 1-13.

Flynn, B. C. (1977). Research framework for evaluating community health nursing practice. In M. H. Miller & B. C. Flynn (Eds.), *Current perspectives in nursing social issues and trends* (pp. 35-45). St. Louis, MO: Mosby.

Freeman, R. B., & Lowe, M. (1964). *Richmond/Hopkins Family Coping Index.* Mimeographed material developed by the Richmond, Virginia, Instructive VNA and the Johns Hopkins University School of Hygiene and Public Health. (Available from Mary Lou Christensen, Ramsey County Public Health Nursing Service, 910 American Center Building, 150 East Kellogg Boulevard, St. Paul, MN 55101)

Georgopoulos, B. S. (Ed.). (1972). *Organization research in health institutions.* Ann Arbor: University of Michigan, Institute for Social Research.

Hegyvary, S. T., Gortner, S. R., & Haussman, R. K. D. (1976). Development of criterion measures for quality of care: The Rush-Medicus experience. In American Nurses Association (Ed.), *Issues in evaluation research* (pp. 106-114). Kansas City, MO: ANA.

Horn, B. J., & Swain, M. A. (1976). An approach to development of criterion measures for quality patient care. In American Nurses Association (Ed.), *Issues in evaluation research* (pp. 74-82). Kansas City, MO: ANA.

Jelinek, R. C. (1976). *A review and evaluation of nursing productivity* (Publication No. HRA 77-15). Bethesda: U.S. Department of Health, Education, and Welfare.

Kelman, H. R. (1976). Evaluation of health care quality by consumers. *International Journal of Health Services, 6,* 431-441.

Markus, A. C. (1981, February). Quality assurance—Panacea or Trojan horse? *Quality Review Bulletin,* pp. 21-22.

Michnich, M. E., Harris, L. J., Willis, R. A., & Williams, J. E. (1976). *Ambulatory care evaluation: A primer for quality review.* Los Angeles: University of California, School of Public Health, ACE Project.

Minnesota Department of Health. (1979). *Outcome criteria: Public health nursing services and home health care services.* Minneapolis: Office of Community Health Services.

Navarro, V. (1977). Justice, social policy and the public's health. *Medical Care, 15,* 363-370.

Neuhauser, D., & Anderson, R. (1972). Structural comparative studies of hospitals. In B. S. Georgopoulos (Ed.), *Organizational research on health institutions* (pp. 83-114). Ann Arbor: University of Michigan, Institute for Social Research.

Orem, D. E. (1971). *Nursing: Concepts of practice.* New York: McGraw-Hill.

Padilla, G. V., & Grant, M. M. (1982). Quality assurance program for nursing. *Journal of Advanced Nursing, 7,* 135-145.

Public Health Nursing Section. (1980). *Definition and role of public health nursing in the delivery of health care.* Washington, DC: American Public Health Association.

Rahman, A. (1978). A methodology for participatory research with the rural poor. *Assignment Children, 41,* 110-124.

Simmons, D. A. (1980). *A classification scheme for client problems in community health nursing* (Publication No. HRA 80-16). Hyattsville, MD: U.S. Department of Health and Human Services, Bureau of Health Professions, Division of Nursing.

Starfield, B. (1973). Health services research: A working model. *New England Journal of Medicine, 289*(7), 132-135.

Taylor, J. W. (1974). Measuring the outcomes of nursing care. *Nursing Clinics of North America, 9*(2), 337-348.

Visiting Nurse Association of Omaha. (1986). *Client management information system for community health nursing agencies.* Rockville, MD: U.S. Department of Health and Human Services, Bureau of Health Professions, Division of Nursing.

Vuori, H. (1980). Optimal and logical quality: Two neglected aspects of the quality of health services. *Medical Care, 18,* 975-985.

World Health Organization. (1978, September 1-12). *Primary health care* (Report of the International Conference on Primary Health Care, Alma Alta, Union of Soviet Socialist Republics). Geneva: Author.

Zimmer, M. J. (1974). Guidelines for development of outcome criteria. *Nursing Clinics of North America, 9,* 317-321.

CHAPTER 13

A Critical Social Reconceptualization of Environment in Nursing: Implications for Methodology

Patricia E. Stevens, RN, BSN, MA

Nurses claim environment as a central component within their domain of knowledge development.[1,2] One nursing scholar, Chopoorian,[3] challenges nursing's usual conceptualization of the environment as the immediate milieu to which clients must respond and adapt. She suggests that nursing research and theory do not acknowledge or explain persons who reject accommodation to environments that present oppressive social, political, or economic circumstances. She asserts, "Nursing ideas lack an archeology of the social, political, and economic worlds that influence both client states and nursing roles."[3(p41)] She testifies further that the unequal class hierarchies, power relationships, political interests, and economic policies that produce ideologies such as sexism, racism, ageism, and classism interfere with health and cause illness.

If nursing as a discipline wishes to take up Chopoorian's challenge and forge a broader, more comprehensive view of environment and its interaction with persons and their health, how will it go about that? This article will outline the history, assumptions, and tenets of critical social theory and demonstrate how theory might be used as a framework for reconceptualizing the environment in nursing practice, research, and theory building. The discussion will be grounded in an example of critical social analysis of the environment from a nursing perspective. The implications of critical social theory for nursing research methodology will also be discussed.

Reprinted from *Advances in Nursing Science,* Vol. 11, No. 4, with permission of Aspen Publishers, Inc., © 1989.

EARLY CRITICAL SOCIAL THEORY

There is no single critical social theory. Critical ways of knowing are manifested in the tradition of the German scholars of the Frankfurt School,[4] Third World liberation scholarship, and feminist theory. This article will explore in detail the history and development of the Frankfurt School as an example of the genesis and growth of critical social thinking.

In this case, critical social theory refers to a series of ideas that emerged in Frankfurt, Germany in the 1920s and 1930s. These ideas were based on critical Marxist self-understanding and Hegelian dialectics that stressed the principles of contradiction, change, and movement. A program of interdisciplinary research involving philosophers, sociologists, economists, historians, and psychologists emanated from the Institute for Social Research in Frankfurt under the leadership of Max Horkheimer. The distinguished critical theorists at the institute included Theodur Adorno, Friedrich Pollock, Erich Fromm, Franz Neumann, Herbert Marcuse, and Leo Lowenthal.[4]

Critical theorists were concerned about interpreting 20th-century history, especially the effects of World War I, the defeat of left-wing working-class movements, the rise of fascism and Nazism, and the degeneration of the Russian revolution into Stalinism. Their basic belief was that no aspect of social phenomena may be comprehended unless it is related to the historical whole and to the structural context in which it is situated. The primary goals of these theorists were to break the grip of closed systems of thought and to counter the unreflective affirmation of society.[4-7]

Their formulation of problems and analytical style reflected a central, emancipatory value orientation. Horkheimer[8] summarized the process of critical social theory by the following actions:

- constructing a picture of society that exposed the prevailing system of domination;
- expressing the contradictions embedded in the domination;
- assessing society's potential for emancipatory change; and
- criticizing the system to promote that change.

HABERMAS'S CRITICAL SOCIAL THEORY

Critical social theory in the Frankfurt School tradition was rejuvenated in the late 1960s by a second generation of German theorists, the most prominent and prolific of whom has been Habermas. Habermas[9-12] emphasizes communication and the collective coordination of social action. The task of Habermas's critical social theory is to understand how people communicate and develop symbolic meanings, and by means of this process to uncover the distortions and constraints that impede free, equal, and uncoerced participation in society. The ultimate goal of critical social theory is to facilitate liberation from constraining social, political, and economic circumstances. Habermas therefore proposes scientific inquiry into people's lived experience, with a critical eye[10,13] toward exposing patterns of both recognized and undisclosed dogmatic domination of individuals and groups.

According to Habermas, for a social critique to be useful in liberating persons and aggregates from domination it must be aimed at the fundamental structures and ideologies of social systems. The fundamental structures of society include:

- the kinds of work and wages that are available and to whom;
- the meaning of privatized, unpaid work and who does it;
- assumptions about what constitutes family;
- access to education;
- images of women, Blacks, Latinos, and gay people in the media;
- the availability of health care;
- the profit motive of capitalist economies and the distribution of wealth; and
- laws and law enforcement.[14]

Such social structures define how privilege, exploitation, and powerlessness are distributed among persons and groups in the society. Racism, sexism, classism, ageism, and heterosexism are some of the fundamental dogmatic ideologies that are internalized in social structures and thus operate in unexamined ways. These kinds of ideologies both limit the concrete alternatives open to individuals and maximize the life opportunities of some groups by minimizing those of others.[15]

Habermas places critical social theory within a framework of scientific knowledge. He distinguishes types of scientific knowledge by examining critically the interests they serve. His categories of knowledge are (1) empirical/analytical knowledge, which serves the interest in technical control of the environment; (2) historical/hermeneutical knowledge, which has a practical interest in understanding individuals' subjective experiences; and (3) critical social theory, which is interested in liberating persons from unacknowledged circumstances of domination and transforming constraining conditions. He does not question the validity of the first two forms of knowledge, but he does demand that they realign their self-perceptions in relation to each other and to the critique of domination.[10,16]

These epistemologic categories and their relevance within the discipline of nursing have been discussed elsewhere.[17-19] Certainly empirical/analytical knowledge is well established within nursing, and historical/hermeneutical knowledge is developing rapidly, whereas the critique of domination within fundamental social, political, and economic structures and the analysis of how domination affects the health of persons and communities are in their infancy.

THE FRAMEWORK OF CRITICAL SOCIAL THEORY

To provide a theoretical framework within which nurses may reconceptualize their understanding of environment to encompass social, political, and economic worlds, the basic assumptions, concepts, and propositions of critical social theory will be outlined. The various perspectives of critical social theory, including those of the Frankfurt School, Third World liberation scholarship, and feminist theory, share a history of originating within resistance movements against such social conditions as fascism, Third World colonization, and exploitation of women. Although the particular focuses of research and the communities of interest differ, critical social perspectives—whether they be Frankfurt School, liberationist, or feminist—are built upon the same fundamental assumptions, concepts, and propositions. The following are drawn from an integrated review of the literature from all three perspectives.

Assumptions

Six assumptions of critical social theory were gleaned from the literature.

1. All research and theory are political in that the social, economic, and political processes of a society are reflected in the microcosm of scholarly investigation.[20-22]
2. Oppressive structural relations pervade modern industrial society; they usually function automatically, are taken for granted, and remain unexamined.
3. Mythical, religious, scientific, practical, and political interpretations of the world are open to systematic questioning and critique.
4. Social conditions are not interpreted as natural and constant but are rather viewed as created by specific historical situations.
5. Understanding of the changing conditions of human suffering can be gained through an historical study of the development of oppressive arrangements in society.
6. Liberation from oppressive structures is an indispensable condition of the quest for human potential, completion, and authenticity.[23]

Concepts

Seven concepts defined by critical social theory were derived from the literature.

1. *Oppression* and *domination* are used interchangeably to indicate unequal power relations embedded in basic structures and functions of society: oppression, which inheres in the social structuring of life limitations that are not equally experienced across groups, is the systematic abbreviation of possibility by which dominated persons are constrained in their quest for human potential.[15]
2. *Liberation* is freedom from the coercion and constraint of oppressive social structures; the particular freedom of individuals is understood within a social and collective context.
3. *Dogma* or *ideology* is a dominant, authoritative system of ideas whose underlying assumptions and premises have not been sufficiently examined or challenged.
4. *Critique* is a process that consists of several components: (a) oppositional thinking that unveils and debunks oppressive ideology by explaining the implicit rules and assumptions of the historical, cultural, and political context; (b) reflection upon the conditions that make uncoerced knowledge and action possible; (c) analysis of the constraints upon communication and human action; and (d) dialogue.
5. *Dialogue* is mutual interaction that raises collective consciousness by clarifying, affirming, and integrating the historical, social, political, and economic experiences of communities.
6. *Conscientization* is learning to perceive social, political, and economic contradictions and conceiving of ways to take action against oppressive contradictions.[23]

7. *Action* is informed, deliberate, meaningful behavior and verbalization by those experiencing oppression that seeks to bring about social change; it is based on critical insights, reflection, and dialogue.

Propositions

The following seven propositions were derived from the literature of critical social theory.

1. The greater the distortion between dominant ideology and the reality of people's experience, the more vulnerable is the social system to critique.[5]
2. Critique of structural domination that illuminates relationships of power and exposes the unnatural and inharmonious character of existing oppressive relationships potentiates the process of liberation.
3. Critical social theory serves to enlighten persons and groups regarding the positions they occupy and the prevalent interests that are served. If persons recognize themselves in the critical interpretations offered, they are conscientized.
4. Informed by critique, conscientized persons engage in dialogue with one another and reflect critically upon their own situations with respect to oppressive environments. They take context-specific action to bring about social change based on this critical reflection and dialogue. This liberation process can be conceptualized as dialectical, in that action prompts further reflection and dialogue, which in turn generates renewed action.
5. Action for change emanates from groups and communities. Their reflection and dialogue consider: (a) their common interests; (b) the risks they are willing to undergo; (c) the consequences they can expect; and (d) their knowledge of the circumstances of their own lives.
6. The ultimate goal of critical social theory is to facilitate change in structural conditions that (a) distort or inhibit communication; (b) limit life options; (c) constrain action; and/or (d) impose unequal economic, gender, or racial imperatives. Social change is advocated so that persons might enjoy authentic existence free from these oppressive conditions.
7. Critical social theory is concerned with the reasons why and the circumstances under which members of societies collectively mobilize to transform the conditions that thwart their full realization of individual and collective possibilities[7,24]

Summary of Critical Social Theory

Research and analysis within the realm of critical social theory promote conscientization among persons who are impeded by oppressive constraints. They bring about conditions in which oppressive elements are illuminated and a dialogue about action for change can occur. But they do not prejudge or mandate the future actions of persons involved.[11] Offering challenges and identifying possible strategies for action in critical social research and theory can serve to interpret hypothetically the constellations of the struggle for liberation and political change and can open up a liberating perspective. Critical social theory can only aid in the anticipation of strategic action; it does not compel action, because that would elevate those who do the research and theorizing above those who are experiencing the phenomena addressed by the theory, in itself a situation of domination.

EXAMPLE OF A CRITICAL SOCIAL RECONCEPTUALIZATION OF ENVIRONMENT

Using a framework of critical social theory as outlined in this article necessitates that the understanding of environment be expanded to incorporate critical analysis of the social, economic, and political worlds of nursing clients, families, and communities.[25] This critical way of thinking may be experienced as a powerful new lens, a frame of reference or interpretive scheme that is different from conventional nursing scholarship[19] yet clearly in line with nursing's holistic perspective.[26]

To demonstrate the use of this critical social reconceptualization of the environment and its implications for people's health, the dilemmas surrounding the use of the drug Accutane (isotretinoin) will be explored. This situation, which has given rise to a political discourse in the public media (*New York Times,* April 27, 1988, p3; April 28, 1988, p1), readily illustrates the connections between ideology and health. This topical anecdotal situation can be examined from the perspective of an expanded conceptualization of the nursing environment.

Example

Since its approval for marketing by the US Food and Drug Administration (FDA) in 1982, Accutane has proved effective in treating severe recalcitrant cystic acne. However, it was well known even before its approval and release that Accutane causes severe and often lethal birth defects in babies born to women who take it during pregnancy, even in small doses over short periods. According to the Centers for Disease Control, 25% of the babies exposed suffer defects, including facial malformations, missing or misplaced ears, severe mental retardation, and serious heart defects.[27]

The United States was the first country to license Accutane. It may be prescribed by any physician. The medication label contains a warning against using the drug during pregnancy, but its prescription does not require a pregnancy test or informed consent from women of childbearing age. European countries have either placed severe restrictions on the prescription of Accutane, allowing only a limited number of monitored dermatologists to dispense the drug, or have banned its sale altogether.

By comparing the incidence of severe cystic acne in women of childbearing age to the number of Accutane prescriptions written, the FDA concluded in its April 1988 hearings[28-30] that as many as 75% of these women should not have been taking the drug. The FDA also indicated that some women are not made fully aware of the dangers of Accutane or take it without knowing that they are pregnant. Official statistics indicate that in the United States and Canada 62 babies have been born with severe Accutane-caused birth defects. However, studies estimate that, from 1982 to 1986, up to 600 babies were born with Accutane-induced birth defects. The only drug comparable to Accutane in its impact on birth defects has been the sedative Thalidomide, which caused thousands of birth defects in Europe in the 1960s. Thalidomide, which was never licensed for sale in the United States, was withdrawn from the market in European countries when its dangers became clear.

Roche, the manufacturer of Accutane, has aggressively marketed the acne drug and has contested the accuracy of the statistics regarding the number of affected children. The manufacturing company and certain dermatologists argued during the FDA hearings that the drug is urgently needed for the treatment of acne and testified that if it were not sold, desperate acne sufferers would obtain it on the black market. Rather than remove Accutane from the market, restrict its prescription to dermatologists, or mandate informed consent and pregnancy tests, the FDA concluded its investigation by recommending further labeling changes and warnings in larger type and by suggesting that Roche ask physicians to obtain informed consent voluntarily.

Critical Analysis of the Example

Critical social theory holds the key to understanding the constraining environmental factors affecting people's health and provides the potential for transforming the conditions that hinder human potential. Newman[31] asserts that the focus of nursing is the health of persons in interaction with the environment. She defines health as expanding consciousness in which the pattern of openness, diversity, and quality of persons' interactions with the environment are increased. Conditions of freedom and unrestricted choice are essential for health, according to Newman, as they allow for expansion of persons' potential and increase their consciousness about their situation in the world. Her definition of and conditions for health echo the basic assumption of critical social theory, which maintains that liberation from oppressive structures is an indispensable condition of the quest for human potential.

Critical social reconceptualization of the environment involves uncovering and critiquing the oppressive social structures that constrain persons' health, limit their life possibilities, and restrict their equal and fully conscious participation in society. The oppressive, nonegalitarian social structures that underpin the Accutane case include:

- an ideology that weighs youthful cosmetic beauty against the life and well-being of human beings born to Accutane-using mothers;
- an unexamined dogma that the health of child-bearing women is of less importance than the health of men who may require acne treatment (as yet no comparable risks have emerged for males who take Accutane);
- a profit-making motive accomplished through the sale of a "wonder" acne drug that benefits the drug manufacturer and the physicians who prescribe it;
- the unequal concentration of economic and political power in the hands of large drug companies and physician lobbies;
- a lack of consumer representation at FDA hearings;
- improper diagnosis of the severity of acne conditions with inappropriate prescription of Accutane;
- inadequate drug education and warning efforts; and
- a lack of informed consent and safety measures for women of childbearing child-bearing age.

Obviously, severe birth defects limit the physical, social, and economic life possibilities of affected children and mothers. The potential for continuing occurrences of Accutane-caused birth defects through the sustained marketing of the drug impedes women's health in general. Under the present oppressive conditions, women are not made fully conscious of the risks involved in taking Accutane. They cannot be confident that it will be prescribed for only the most severe cases of acne, nor can they be assured that it will never be prescribed during pregnancy.

The more accurately and extensively that individuals are able to perceive and reflect upon their social, political, and economic environment, the more effective they become in interaction with the environment, a condition that is the essence of health. Critical social theory generated by nurses can be instrumental in the development of this critical awareness in clients. A nursing-generated critique can uncover the disparate gender priorities in health, health care delivery, and health care regulatory mechanisms that are embedded in the Accutane example. It can offer an historical analysis of the situation, making comparisons to the ramifications of the Thalidomide birth defects in Europe and the current European restrictions on Accutane distribution. The critique can encompass potential strategies for personal and collective action that women might take to change the oppressive conditions under which Accutane is prescribed and marketed. Coupling an historical social critique with accurate health and medication information targeted at women locally and nationally could be powerfully conscientizing. This task could be accomplished via individual and collective endeavors by practitioners and nursing organizations. They could engage in dialogues with women and disseminate the critique, information, and suggested strategies for action through the news media, local women's organizations, churches, day care centers, and other outlets. A public stance and critical dialogue could also be initiated with legislators and drug regulators.

Intervention by nursing in sociopolitical structures is as essential to promoting health and preventing illness as are activities with individual clients.[32] From a critical social viewpoint on the world, nurses who are committed to human liberation are not afraid to challenge the legitimacy of a status quo that oppresses or coerces groups and communities, are able to analyze historical and present realities with a critical eye, and are willing to enter into dialogue with persons who are oppressed. Nurses facilitate liberating dialogue with individuals, families, and communities by directing it toward consciousness raising about the environmental constraints upon their health and freedom. Through such dialogue nurses

- affirm person's attempts to criticize their social, political, and economic situations from their own perspective;
- facilitate collective confirmation of persons' experiences of oppression; and
- encourage reflection upon the conditions that might lead to liberation from these constraints.

By utilizing a critical social theory framework, therefore, nursing scientists and clinicians can inspire individuals, families, and communities to identify the environmental problems with which they struggle and can encourage their clients to collectivize their experiences through dialogue, in order to plan appropriate action. By virtue of a critical analysis of the environment, nurses can assist in exposing power relations that usually operate unnoticed in concrete situations such as:

- unequal access to health care, jobs, education, law enforcement, political authority;
- ideologies that place paramount value on youth and beauty, male competency, and/or a white middle-class lifestyle; and
- distorted representations of minority racial, ethnic, and sexual orientation groups in media, legislation, science, literature, and religion.

Through a critique of domination, nurses can encourage clients to perceive social, political, and economic contradictions in their own lives, thus setting the stage for conscientized collective action to change oppressive constraints.

RESEARCH METHODOLOGY FOR CRITICAL SOCIAL THEORY IN NURSING

Implementing nursing research within a critical social context is an integral part of the struggle to liberate people from environmental oppression. Within this framework, nursing knowledge is elicited and analyzed in such a way that it can be used by persons to alter oppressive and exploitative conditions in their environment[24]; thus it provides a transforming vision of the future as well as a critically analyzed structural picture of the present. The dialectic of doing and knowing is exemplified by the integration of nursing research with social and political action; thereby knowledge coincides with liberation.[11,23]

A variety of research methods may be used to develop critical social knowledge in nursing science, including quantitative methods in the empirical/analytic empirical/analytic tradition and qualitative methods in the historical/hermeneutic tradition. Any number of quantitative and qualitative methods, when developed from a perspective consistent with the assumptions and premises of critical social theory, can generate liberating nursing research. It is not the mechanical application of any particular method that leads to critical insight but rather the use of methodology in a manner consistent with the philosophy of critical social theory that raises consciousness and catalyzes liberating transformations.[5,25]

Instead of focusing on characteristics of individuals and their immediate milieu, research problems must be reframed so that broader environmental and ideologic factors are examined and structural solutions are sought. Addressing oppressive constraints in the social, political, and economic environment makes the investigation of nursing phenomena broader in scope and more informative about reality.[21]

Reciprocal interaction is a cornerstone of critical social theory and research.[6,33] In place of controlled observation, there is a dialogue between the investigator and those investigated. Hence the research paradigm is no longer simply the observation process; it enlarges to incorporate the dialogue. Examples of a number of methods that expand the research paradigm to include dialogue will be discussed to illustrate the potential for variety and innovation that is inherent within a critical social framework.

The use of quantitative methods can be strategic to action research, a methodology that shares basic assumptions with critical social theory. Quantitatively generated information (such as that about the side effects of Accutane in the example just given) becomes the tool for a critique of domination. A dialogue is initiated with community members in which the quantitative research findings serve to raise consciousness and assist persons to perceive and describe their environments more effectively. Community members are taught methods by which they might generate similar quantitative knowledge about their particular social, political, and economic environment. They will then possess the strategies and information needed to challenge competently the established systems or political interests that oppress them and limit their health and potential.

Participatory research is another type of critical theory investigation[5,22] that applies critique to sources of domination. In this approach, members of the communities under investigation participate in the entire research process. Within natural community institutions such as churches, schools, labor unions, self-help groups, women's organizations, senior citizens' centers, and grass roots political coalitions, the nurse researcher and subjects work together on conceptualization, design, collection of data, data analysis, and posing solutions to problems. The goal is not merely the production of information, but the generation of open discussion and debate that intensifies a community's consciousness of how its health is impaired by environmental constraints. This dialogue helps to mobilize the community to deal with problems. The research acts as a catalyst for conscientization and strategic action toward change.

Several interview strategies expand the dialogic nature of critical social investigation. Making verbatim interview transcripts and preliminary interpretations available to participants prior to follow-up interviews and final reporting provides opportunities for more critical self-reflection, dialogue, and collaboration with the investigator.[33] Shifting the focus away from individual interviews to group interviews guides people to document and analyze their own struggles and collectivize their experiences. Group discussions, particularly at repeated intervals, are not only a means of getting more diversified information, but they also assist participants to overcome structural isolation and understand their individual oppressions, fears, and constraints as collective phenomena that have social, political, and economic origins.[22]

A dialectic, historical nursing investigation of contemporary social phenomena that relates its analysis to the historical whole, to the structural environment in which persons are presently situated, and to unconstrained future possibilities is another example of critical social theory methodology.[25]

• • •

The basic assumptions, concepts, and propositions of critical social theory as outlined in this article can be used as a framework for the reconceptualization of the environment in nursing. The outlined conceptual basis provides a point of view from which to assess and intervene in social, political, and economic environments. It guides the identification of environmental conditions that constrain health and those that potentiate health. Critical social theory in nursing values, above all, human liberation from oppressive constraints that inhibit health and human potential. It seeks to critique, facilitate dialogue, and potentiate changes in oppressive conditions. This critical social reconceptualization of the environment offers not only an organizing perspective but an invitation to action in both nursing practice and research.

Critical social nursing research questions and clinical issues emerge from the concerns of those who are oppressed. Research and practice are organized in line with broadened conceptualizations of the social, political, and economic environment of clients. A critical social nursing research program and its conceptual framework are informed by the struggles of the historical period in which they originate. If environmental struggles against the subordination of women, Blacks, the poor, gays, and lesbians figure among those that are significant in a given age, then critical social nursing theory and research for that time must seek to shed light on the rationale and forms of such subordination. Critical social nursing attempts to describe and explain oppressive environmental effects on health by uncovering the relations of dominance and by demystifying the ideology that rationalizes unequal power relations.[34]

REFERENCES

1. Newman M: The continuing revolution: A history of nursing science, in Chaska N (ed): *The Nursing Profession: A Time to Speak.* New York, McGraw-Hill, 1983, pp 385-393.
2. Yura H, Torres G: *Today's Conceptual Frameworks within the Baccalaureate Nursing Programs* (NLN pub. no. 15-1558). New York, National League for Nursing, 1975, pp 17-75.
3. Chopoorian TJ: Reconceptualizing the environment, in Moccia P (ed): *New Approaches to Theory Development.* New York, National League for Nursing, 1986, pp 39-54.
4. Thompson JB, Held D (eds): *Habermas: Critical Debates.* Cambridge, MA, MIT Press, 1982.
5. Antonio RJ: The origin, development, and contemporary status of critical theory. *Social Q* 1983;24(3):325-351.
6. Connerton P (ed): *Critical Sociology: Selected Readings.* New York, Penguin, 1976.
7. Morrow RA: Critical theory and critical sociology. *Can Rev Social Anthropol* 1985;22(5):710-747.
8. Horkheimer M: *Critical Theory.* New York, Herder & Herder, 1972.
9. Habermas J: On systematically distorted communication. *Inquiry* 1970;13:205-218.
10. Habermas J: *Knowledge and Human Interests,* Shapiro JJ (trans). Boston, Beacon Press, 1971.
11. Habermas J: *Theory and Practice,* Viertel J (trans). Boston, Beacon Press, 1973.

12. Habermas J: *Communication and the Evolution of Society,* McCarthy T (trans). Boston, Beacon Press, 1979.
13. Turner JH: *The Structure of Sociological Theory.* Chicago, Dorsey Press, 1986.
14. Joseph GI, Lewis J: *Common Differences: Conflicts in Black and White Feminist Perspectives.* Boston, South End Press, 1981.
15. Adam B: *The Survival of Domination: Inferiorization and Everyday Life.* New York, Elsevier, 1978.
16. Bubner R: Habermas's concept of critical theory, in Thompson JB, Held D (eds): *Habermas: Critical Debates.* Cambridge, MA, MIT Press, 1982, pp 42-56.
17. Allen DG: Nursing research and social control: Alternative models of science that emphasize understanding and emancipation. *Image* 1985;18(2):58-64.
18. Allen DG, Benner P, Diekelmann NL: Three paradigms for nursing research: Methodological implications, in Chinn PL (ed): *Nursing Research Methodology: Issues and Implementation.* Rockville, Md, Aspen Publishers, 1986, pp 23-38.
19. Thompson JL: Critical scholarship: The critique of domination in nursing. *Adv Nurs Sci* 1987;10(1):27-38.
20. Duffy ME: A critique of research: A feminist perspective. *Health Care Women Int* 1985;6:341-352.
21. MacPherson KI: Feminist methods: A new paradigm for nursing research. *Adv Nurs Sci* 1983;5(2):17-25.
22. Mies M: Towards a methodology for feminist research, in Bowles G, Klein RD (eds): *Theories of Women's Studies.* Boston, Routledge & Kegan Paul, 1983, pp 117-139.
23. Freire P: *Pedagogy of the Oppressed,* Bergman Ramos M (trans). New York, Seabury Press, 1970.
24. Cook JA: Knowledge and women's interests: Issues of epistemology and methodology in feminist sociological research. *Sociol Inquiry* 1986;56(1):2-29.
25. Hedin BA: Nursing, education, and emancipation: Applying the critical theoretical approach to nursing research, in Chinn PL (ed): *Nursing Research Methodology: Issues and Implementation.* Rockville, Md, Aspen Publishers, 1986, pp 133-146.
26. Allen DG: Using philosophical and historical methodologies to understand the concept of health, in Chinn PL (ed), *Nursing Research Methodology: Issues and Implementation.* Rockville, Md, Aspen Publishers, 1986, pp 157-168.
27. Birth defects caused by isotretinoin—New Jersey. *JAMA* 1988;259:2362-2365.
28. Strauss JS, Cunningham WJ, Leyden JJ et al: Isotretinoin, and tetratogenicity. *J Am Acad Dermatol* 1988;19:353-354.
29. Pochi PE, Ceilley RI, Coskey MD, et al: Guidelines for prescribing isotretinoin (accutane) in the treatment of female acne patients of childbearing potential. *J Am Acad Dermatol* 1988;19:920.
30. Zellmer WA: Editorial: Reiterations. *Am J Hosp Pharm* 1988;45:1295.
31. Newman M: *Health as Expanding Consciousness.* St Louis, Mosby, 1986.
32. Moccia P: At the faultline: Social activism and caring. *Nurs Outlook* 1988;36(1):30-33.
33. Kieffer CH: Citizen empowerment: A developmental perspective. *Prev Hum Serv* 1984;3(2/3):9-36.
34. Fraser N: What's critical about critical theory? The case of Habermas and gender, in Benhabib S, Cornell D (eds): *Feminism as Critique.* Minneapolis, University of Minnesota Press, 1987, pp 31-56.

Suggested Additional Readings for Part II

Conceptual models for community health nursing practice

American Nurses' Association: A conceptual model of community health nursing practice, Kansas City; Mo, 1980, The Association.

Berman S: Quality assurance in ambulatory health care, *Quality Rev Bull* 13(1):18-21, 1988.

Boyce WT, Sprunger LW, Sobolewski S, and Schaefer C: Epidemiology of injuries in a large, urban school district, *Pediatr* 74(3):342-349, Sept 1984.

Buchanan BF: Human-environment interaction: a modification of the Neuman systems model for aggregates, families, and the community, *Public Health Nurs* 4(1):52-64, 1987.

Clayton RR and Ritter C: The epidemiology of alcohol and drug abuse among adolescents, *Adv Alcohol Subst Abuse* 4(3-4), Spring-Summer 1985.

Cox CL: The interaction model of client health behavior: application to the study of community-based elders, *Adv Nurs Sci* 9(1):40-57, Oct 1986.

Eliopoulos C: A self-care model for gerontological nursing, *Geriatric Nurs* 5(8):366-369, 1984.

Fawcett J: Analysis and evaluation of conceptual models of nursing, *Nurse Educator* 5(6):10, 1980.

Goeppinger J: Challenges in assessing the impact of nursing service: a community perspective, *Public Health Nurs* 5(4):241-245, Dec 1988.

Lindheim R and Syme SL: Environments, people, and health, *Annu Rev Public Health* 4:335-359, 1988.

Shamansky S and Cherie L Clausen: Levels of prevention: examination of the concept, *Nurs Outlook* 28:104-108, Feb 1980.

Weidmann JoAnn and North H: Implementing the Omaha classification system in a public health agency, *Nurs Clin North Am* 22(4):971-979, 1987.

PART III

COMMUNITY HEALTH NURSING ROLES

Community health nursing is a diverse field that is distinguished by its focus on population groups rather than on individual clients. It synthesizes nursing practice with public health science for the purpose of promoting and preserving the health of populations or aggregates. Community health nursing roles are unique in regard to the *nature* of their implementation, not necessarily the *setting* where they are enacted. Community health nursing requires a variety of roles, due to the diversity of community health problems. Since the focus is on the health of groups, community health nursing is involved in the identification of populations at risk for illness or disability. Once at-risk groups are identified, the community health nurse utilizes the nursing process to plan and implement appropriate nursing interventions to promote health and decrease the risk of illness, disability, or death in the targeted population. Evaluation of nursing care focuses on the effects of the intervention on the identified aggregate or group needs.

Other unique features of community health nursing include community accountability, illness prevention and health promotion focus, promotion of client autonomy and participation in health care, and an emphasis on interdisciplinary collaboration with other health care team members. The community health nurse gives attention to populations at risk and utilizes the knowledge of the dynamic forces that influence change in the promotion of health. The dominant responsibility of the community health nurse is to the population as a whole; nursing care directed to individuals, families, and groups contributes to the health of the total population. For example, a public health nurse may administer immunizations to preschool children to prevent and control communicable disease in the community.

Community health nurses assisting communities, groups, and aggregates in responding to health problems undertake a variety of roles, including occupational health nurse, school nurse, consultant, home health care nurse, and educator. All community health nursing roles adhere to a philosophy of wellness. Community health nurses participate in health planning using the knowledge of social and ecological influences on the health of populations.

Traditionally, community health nurses have functioned in home health and in the management and prevention of communicable disease. As societal needs have changed and the health care delivery system has evolved in complexity, the roles of the community health nurse have also changed. As a result, the settings, roles, functions, and client population have changed to include more diverse practice fields. Although the focus of community health nursing remains health promotion and protection, clinical specializations such as school and occupational health nursing, home health nursing, public health nursing, and transcultural nursing have developed to meet changing societal needs. Functional roles of educator, collaborator, administrator, and consultant also have emerged in response to changing expectations for health care. The articles in Part III present examples of the variety of roles in community health nursing today.

CHAPTER **14**

Health Promotion, Education, Counseling, and Coordination in Primary Health Care Nursing

Marie Annette Brown, RN, PhD, ARNP
Kathleen M. Waybrant, RN, MN, FNP

The founding work of Florence Nightingale embodied the essence of attention to disease prevention/health promotion and provided an important model for community health nursing (Nightingale, 1969). Community health nurses address needs in these areas at both the aggregate and direct patient services levels (Archer & Fleshman, 1985). These direct patient services in the form of primary health care can serve as a vital medium for the exchange of health promotion information. Taylor, Ureda, and Deuham (1982) asserted that "health promotion is most likely to enter the health care arena through the portal of primary care—an approach which involves first contact with a patient, assessment and management of as many problems as possible, provision of continuing and coordinated services and responsibility for serving as patient advisor and advocate" (p. 12).

According to the American Nurses' Association's (ANA) (1985) monograph, primary health care is described as two-dimensional. First is the care the consumer receives in first identifying a health problem to the nurse practitioner (NP). Primary health care on this dimension leads to resolving the problem.

Reprinted from *Public Health Nursing,* Vol. 5, No. 1, with permission of Blackwell Scientific Publications, Inc., © 1988.

Often, however, the patient needs care that is continuous and involves the coordination of several health-related services. This dimension of primary health care encompasses services such as health promotion, prevention of disease, and health-maintenance and coordination activities. It is at this second level that the primary health care nurse practitioner can have a significant impact on patients.

Documentation of this domain of practice is minimal, however, and must be expanded and quantified in order to delineate more accurately the nursing component of the current NP role. Therefore this study was conducted to examine the extent to which coordination, health-promotion, health-education, and counseling activities were reported by nurse practitioners in their practices. More specifically, it addressed the question, What are the most common coordination, health-promotion, education, and counseling activities performed by NPs?

REVIEW OF THE LITERATURE

The early studies of nurse practitioners almost exclusively used medical care standards and outcomes to gauge the effectiveness of this role, rarely acknowledging the nursing care dimensions that were possible. This early phase of NP research, however, was fundamental in building credibility of the role, and now serves as a foundation to delineate more clearly additional elements of the nursing care that NPs offer.

As nursing has worked to specify its comprehensive domain of practice, issues have arisen regarding the overlap of nursing and medical roles, particularly in the area of primary health care. Studies examining this type of advanced nursing practice highlighted differences such as more specific emphasis on health promotion, self-care education, health maintenance, and a holistic approach to the client (Brallier, 1978; Choi, 1981; Leff, 1983; Muhlenkamp et al., 1985). The theoretical potential for primary health care nurses or nurse practitioners to have an individual, nonsubstitutive role in the health care system is emerging in studies of nursing practice (Davidson & Lauver, 1984).

Energies directed toward clarifying the domain of nursing have stimulated an important period of self-examination for the profession. In 1859 Florence Nightingale commented that the laws of health and those of nursing were essentially the same. Schlotfeldt (1972) emphasized that nursing can help motivate persons to seek a healthier state, identify deviations from health, assist clients to mobilize coping mechanisms when their health is threatened, and thus help them to restore their highest possible level of health and functioning. Brallier (1978) saw the nurse as a holistic health practitioner because "nurses . . . have had the best overall view of the patient's life and of his experience of being ill . . . [and] have often led the way in doing the teaching and consultation necessary for preventing illness" (p. 648).

Carnevali (1983) has been a strong advocate for specifically defining the nursing domain and identified two key variables, "daily living" and "health status," as being the basis for nursing's "gestalt approach" toward the client. Nursing is distinguished from other health disciplines in the sense that it has a broader picture of the client, not just focusing on one aspect of an illness. The profession is oriented toward taking the whole into consideration by balancing activities and demands of daily living (with or without pathology superimposed), and the internal and external resources of the client (Carnevali, 1983). The ANA (1980) social policy statement noting that nurses deal with human responses to actual and potential health problems, most succinctly points toward the essence of nursing.

Discussions about traditional activities in the nurse practitioner and general nursing literature emphasize the areas of support, comfort, teaching, preventive care (Ford, 1979), patient teaching, advocacy, counseling (Diers & Molde, 1979), nurturing, understanding, and education provided by nurses (D'Angelo, Reifsteck, & Green, 1984). A study conducted with NP graduates from the University of Vermont compared functions of NPs to those of other professional nurses, and revealed that NPs were more active in several areas of health care delivery. These areas included both medically oriented skills and nursing activities such as patient education and counseling (Vacek & Ashikaga, 1980). This study concluded that ". . . the acquisition of medically oriented functions has not diminished the NP's activity in more traditional areas of nursing" (p. 122).

Several studies of NPs across the country reported that activities performed frequently tended to include teaching, counseling, and disease prevention in conjunction with disease management (Linn, 1975; Wirth, Kahn, & Storm, 1977; Repicky, Mendenhall, & Neville, 1980; Draye & Pesznecker, 1980). Draye and Pesznecker (1980), in the only extensive study of teaching practices of NPs, found that teaching was the intervention most frequently performed in their patients' care and that it was mostly focused on "assisting patients to understand their diagnosis and learn necessary information to participate in self-care" (p. 32). Sullivan (1982) evaluated nurse practitioner research and noted that the increased amount of educational services offered by NPs serves as a major factor contributing to the success of NPs who provide clinical therapeutics. McCarthy, Webster-Stratton, and Glascock (1987) found that pediatric nurse practitioners (PNPs) conducted comprehensive assessments and provided mothers with a wealth of educational information at well-child visits. They noted that 62 percent of the direct patient care performed by PNPs was well child care. The two areas assessed and managed most frequently were cognitive/physical development and nutrition.

Levine et al. (1978) reported that 59 percent of the NPs interviewed in their study on the role of the NP counseled their patients "often" (and 41% "sometimes") in the area of family problems. It was anecdotally reported that many patients find it easier to communicate with NPs than with physicians (Taller, 1979). He stated "NPs are usually able to give more consistent, focused attention to patients' emotional and living problems than are sick-care oriented physicians" (p. 195).

The extent to which NPs are involved in activities recently designated as health promotion remains relatively undocumented. A broad definition of health promotion was developed by the Office of Health Information, Health Promotion, and Physical Fitness, and Sports Medicine: "Any combination of health education and related organizational, political, and economic interventions designed to facilitate behavioral and environmental adaptations that will improve or protect health" (Green, 1979, p. 161). Our study specifically emphasized "those areas categorized by the Surgeon General's report as representing health promotion—nutrition, exercise/fitness, alcohol, drugs, smoking, and stress—all confirmed by epidemiologic studies as important to physical and emotional well-being and optimal function" (Taylor et al., 1982, p. ix).

American medicine, however, has been slow to implement concepts of health promotion (Taylor, 1981). In contrast, nursing authors have emphasized the vital need for nurses to respond to these health care gaps. They assert that provision of these health promoting activities is vital to the growth of the profession (Pender, 1982; Steiger & Lipson, 1985). One study of NPs in a medical clinic of a county hospital revealed that nurses directed more attention than physicians to patients' diets and recommended more changes in daily activities and exercise (Flynn, 1974).

The extent of specific coordination activities undertaken by NPs remains unknown, and studies specifically addressing this area are virtually nonexistent. This vital activity, however, is well documented as an integral part of community health nursing practice. "Health promotion, health maintenance, health education coordination and continuity of care are utilized in a holistic approach to family group and community" (ANA, 1983).

The revised National Association of Pediatric Nurse Associates and Practitioners (NAPNAP) scope of practice also targets activities in this area for PNPs, noting that they provide ". . . important components of primary health care through consultation, collaboration, coordination, and referral" (Mitchell, 1983, p. 200). According to Stumpf (1986), in providing primary health care for the gerontologic clients, nurses must take an active role in coordinating care activities. Thompson (1986) in a discussion of primary health care nursing for women points to the need for nurses to address barriers to providing health-oriented rather than illness-oriented care to women through coordination activities. "We cannot tolerate insufficient, uncoordinated, overlapping or duplicated care, fragmented services, and failure of the system to meet our health and illness expectations forever" (Thompson, 1986, p. 194). Ford (1979) and Diers (1983) emphasized the underused potential of NPs in a "gate-keeping" role, which provides NPs the opportunity actively to coordinate and initiate a variety of health-related services from many providers and agencies. Brunetto and Birk (1972) stressed the vital need for NPs to assume the coordination of health care services to ensure comprehensiveness and continuity of care. Becker, Fournier, and Gardner (1982) reported successful implementation of this idea with NPs managing complex patients requiring extra teaching and attention to complicated medication regimens and social problems. These NPs assumed the responsibility as coordinator of services as a critical part of their role.

Thus, the nursing domain in primary health care is appropriately manifested in the areas of coordination activities and health promotion and health maintenance using teaching and counseling. An urgent need continues, however, for adequate documentation of an attention to these aspects of the NP role.

METHODS

All the graduates from one Pacific Northwest university's family nurse practitioner (FNP) master's degree program were invited to participate in the study. Participation was voluntary and responses were anonymous. Questionnaires were mailed out in batches (on Monday through Friday) and participants were asked to respond about "yesterday" (the method used in gathering information about a specific practice day for the graduates). This technique was used to minimize biases from retrospective reporting. The limitation, however, is that "yesterday" may not represent the usual experience of the NP.

Of the 210 questionnaires sent out, 164 were completed and returned, yielding a response rate of 82 percent. The sample selected for this analysis included only those NPs who were currently working in primary health care, which totalled 110 subjects.

Instrument

The questionnaire consisted of the coordination activities inventory and the health promotion inventory. It also obtained information about individual characteristics and standard demographic data (i.e., age, sex, year of program completion, current employment status), and characteristics of current practice (i.e., types of clients seen).

The two inventories were created by the principal investigator and a group of primary health care faculty colleagues. Face and content validity were based on an extensive review of NP literature and survey of the competencies taught in the master's degree primary health care program. In addition, three currently practicing NPs in the community were asked initially to review and critique the instruments. The questionnaire was then pilot tested by 10 NPs in a variety of clinical areas. They were given the overall purpose of the project, and asked to complete the questionnaire and comment on form and content. The final revision of the inventories was based on extensive feedback obtained during the pilot phase.

Coordination Activities Inventory (CAI)

Participants were asked to check the types of community resources they "typically coordinated" from a list of 15 choices (including "other"). Sample items included food programs, respite services for families, arranging transportation services, mental health services, and vision or hearing services. A total coordination score was created by summing the number of different coordination activities regularly provided by the NP. The internal consistency reliability, using Cronbach's alpha, was 0.85.

Health Promotion Inventory (HPI)

Participants were asked to note the number of times they performed a specific health education/promotion activity on the reporting day. The list of 27 possible activities included the opportunity for participants to add other similar activities. The number of activities was summed for a total health education/promotion score, which had an internal consistency reliability of 0.90 using Cronbach's alpha. In addition, three subscales were formed from the HPI: health promotion (HP), counseling services (CO), and education (ED) (disease- or medication-related information). Sample items for the HP subscale were stress management, exercise counseling, nutrition information, and smoking cessation. The CO subscale included psychologic help for family problems, sexual concerns, anxiety, depression, and crisis intervention. The ED subscale, which addressed education about a specific disease problem or prescribed medication, asked three direct questions about the frequency of these activities on the reporting day. Internal consistency reliabilities for the subscales were 0.87 for HP, 0.68 for CO, and 0.72 for ED.

Sample

The nurse practitioners in the sample were primarily female and Caucasian. Most were employed as family NPs (78%) and worked full time (68%). Over half (65%) worked in urban, suburban, or inner-city communities. The most common work settings in order of frequency were the community clinic, hospital outpatient clinic, and health department.

Practitioners cared for an average of 13.8 clients per day, with a range of 3 to 35. Those who worked part-time reported seeing 11 clients on the reporting day while full-time workers saw 15. The age group most prevalently cared for was 19 to 64 years, while infants, school-age children, and the elderly over 85 years were attended the least. The most common health problems in order of frequency were women's health, upper respiratory, psychological, eye-ear-nose-throat, and musculoskeletal.

RESULTS

The total number of coordination activities that the NPs regularly performed ranged from 0 to 14 with a mean of 6.0 per NP. Referrals for mental health, social work, drug rehabilitation, vision services, alcohol, and hearing services were the most frequent coordination activities (Table 14-1). This suggests that NPs frequently use mental health specialists as an important referral source as they offer primary care services.

The specific health-promotion areas delineated in the questionnaire were divided into the three subscales of HP, ED, and CO. Tables 14-2, 14-3, and 14-4 outline the frequency and standard deviation of each activity. Disease- and medication-specific education activities were most frequently reported. Other activities performed relatively frequently were general screening measures, nutrition education, psychologic counseling, exercise counseling, family planning, and risk factor analysis. The data suggested that almost 60 percent of the sample offered health-promotion services to at least one client that addressed lifestyle modification about exercise, diet, or smoking. In addition, over one-third of the NPs stated that they provided stress management counseling to at least one client during the reporting day.

The NPs offered disease-specific counseling service to an average of approximately seven clients per day. The data suggested that an average of six clients per day were also offered counseling regarding medication. Counseling regarding psychosocial issues such as relationships and sexual problems was common, with about three patients per day receiving this service. Over 80 percent of the NPs reported that at some time during their work day they counseled a patient on these types of issues. Advice about economic and social issues and crisis intervention was given approximately once during the work day.

Contingency tables served as the basis to calculate a ratio of the number of clients receiving the services noted above with the total number of clients seen by each NP on the reporting day (recognizing that any one patient may have had more than one type of service offered). One ratio was classified as an outlier and deleted because it was considerably higher than the other scores. The ratio of mean number of total activities to number of patients was calculated as 4.1 (± 1.68) activities per patient. The HP activity: client ratio was 2.5 (± 1.42), followed by the ED ratio at 1.6 (± 0.48), and the CO ratio with 1.14 (± 0.27).

TABLE 14-1
Coordination activities

ACTIVITIES	NPS REGULARLY PERFORM (%)
Mental health	75
Social worker or drug rehabilitation	67
Vision (i.e., arranging examinations)	66
Alcohol/Alanon referrals	60
Hearing (i.e., arranging examinations)	58
Visiting Nurse	48
Transportation	35
Language services (i.e., interpreter)	34
Food provider	34
Emergency food or shelter	32
Housing services (i.e., home safety evaluations, chores, services for elderly)	26
Dentures (i.e., arranging for refit)	26
Job or retraining services	21
Respite services	17
Other	42

DISCUSSION

The major purpose of this study was to quantify the amount of coordination, health-promotion, disease- and medication-specific education, and counseling activities performed by NPs in the study sample. The study responded to the current quest for further delineation of the activities involved in primary health care nursing and the need to substantiate the use in

TABLE 14-2
Health-promotion activities in order of frequency

ACTIVITIES	SAMPLE MEAN*	SD	NPS PROVIDING HEALTH PROMOTION TO AT LEAST ONE CLIENT ON REPORTING DAY (%)
Screening such as blood pressure, Pap smears, breast exams, diabetes, misc.	4.67	4.17	81.8
Nutrition information (general)	3.66	3.46	82.7
Exercise counseling	2.96	2.96	76.4
Family planning education	2.76	3.60	55.5
Risk factor analysis	2.61	3.49	57.3
Prescriptions for exercise/diet	2.21	2.65	59.1
Stress management	2.20	2.53	36.4
Obesity, weight-control education	2.20	2.53	36.4
Hygiene information	1.99	2.78	55.5
Smoking cessation education	1.89	2.63	57.3
Prescriptions for contraceptive devices	1.76	3.01	42.7
Immunizations	1.66	2.34	49.1
Safety information (hot water, seat belt use)	1.64	2.66	45.5
Child growth and development education	1.59	2.61	40.0
Nutrition information (in pregnancy or lactation)	0.98	2.22	26.4
Nutrition information (elderly)	0.71	1.40	30.0
Education regarding rehabilitation of work-related injury	0.61	1.24	23.6
Totals	36.09	27.80	98.2

*Average number of patients per NP receiving that service on reporting day.

TABLE 14-3
Frequency of NPs providing disease/medication specific education

EDUCATION	SAMPLE MEAN*	SD	NPS PROVIDING EDUCATION TO AT LEAST ONE CLIENT ON REPORTING DAY (%)
Specific disease or problem	6.80	4.31	96.4
Prescribed medication	6.16	4.00	96.4
Totals	12.96	7.71	99.1

*Average number of patients per NP receiving that service on reporting day.

TABLE 14-4
Frequency of counseling activities offered by NPs

ACTIVITIES	SAMPLE MEAN*	SD	NPS PROVIDING COUNSELING TO AT LEAST ONE CLIENT ON REPORTING DAY (%)
Psychologic counseling (including mild depression, family, relationship, sexual, anxiety)	2.97	2.87	81.8
Advice about economic/social issues	1.40	1.84	48.2
Crisis intervention	0.80	1.69	30.9
Totals	5.17	4.96	83.6

*Average number of patients per NP receiving that service on reporting day.

practice of nursing concepts taught in formal educational settings.

Study findings strongly supported the prominent role of patient education and health promotion that NPs perceive in their practices. Almost all (98%) provided at least one of these types of services on the reporting day. Both the mean combined activity score (54.23 activities per day for each NP) and the mean per client activity score (4.1) were also positive indications of the nursing services being offered. These scores were higher than the Draye and Pesznecker (1980) report of an average of 1.5 teaching activities per client, which did not include the counseling activities. Generally, data from the current study support, corroborate, and extend trends noted by those authors.

Coordination Activities

Due to the lack of studies detailing specific coordination activities of NPs, comparisons between our own results and those of others are not possible. It is clear, however, that the NPs were actively engaged in coordinating a variety of different services for their patients. Given the current NP focus of holistic care, it is not surprising that the most frequent referrals were for mental health and social services. Time spent in assessment and screening activities may uncover common psychosocial stresses and allow for the development of a plan of psychosocial intervention beyond what NPs view as their role.

Health-Promotion Activities

Our findings suggested that the most frequently performed activity was general screening, which included blood pressure, Pap smears, breast examinations, etc. This finding was expected in light of nursing's traditional focus on screening and prevention as well as the high frequency of women's health care visits in this sample. Similarly, another frequent service, family planning education, is generally well accepted by consumers as an area of need, and is commonly provided even by NPs in a general family primary care setting.

The second most frequent activity reported was offering nutritional information. The current surge of consumer interest in nutrition in recent years may partly account for this finding. It would be interesting to know whether the nurses spontaneously offer the information or whether the clients request it, but in either case, the NPs provide this important service that might not be readily available from other sources. Because dietitians tend to be available primarily on a referral basis, their expertise may remain relatively untapped and clients may look for more easily accessible information.

Exercise, diet, and weight control were also areas of frequent counseling. These lifestyle habits have a potentially major impact on disease prevention and are areas in which NPs may be able to make their greatest contribution. Ramsey, McKenzie, and Fish (1982) noted that NPs tended to have greater success in managing obesity in their patients than a physician control group. They also noted that NPs showed a preference for managing their own patients, in contrast to the physicians who were likely to refer patients to a dietitian. These interventions in tandem with risk factor analysis, which occurred relatively frequently in this sample, suggest that NPs are attempting to increase clients' awareness of the effect of lifestyle on their health.

Areas of NP activities that received low mean ratings were also of interest. Education related to smoking cessation was the most notable. Perhaps NPs attract clients who tend to be nonsmokers or persons who actively value their health and previously made this lifestyle change. It is also possible that the NPs were uncomfortable in raising this issue to their smoking clients. Another possibility is that if the NPs had a relatively stable group of clients, they may have previously assisted these individuals in quitting smoking.

Other infrequent activities were those related to pediatric care, such as growth and development education and immunizations. This finding most likely results from the smaller number of patients in the pediatric age group cared for by the sample. Research focusing on pediatric practice suggests that PNPs are actively involved in many health-promotion activities as a part of well-child care (Glascock et al., 1985; Webster-Stratton et al., 1986). Because those investigators focused on PNP practice, their findings are more representative than the current study of the NP response to children and families when given the opportunity to provide this education.

The lowest HP activity frequencies dealt with nutrition information specifically geared to pregnancy/lactation and the elderly, and rehabilitation regarding work-related injuries. Again, these types of clients were less prominent in the practice of the current sample of NPs and therefore the finding must be evaluated in that light.

Our results reflecting individually calculated HP activities (2.5 per patient for each NP) also supported active participation in these activities. Draye and Pesznecker (1980) noted that approximately one-third of the clients receiving care from NPs in their sample received instruction about preventive health practices. The Repicky et al. (1980) study did not categorize health promotion specifically, but noted that 7.4 percent of the patients received prescriptions for exercise and diet and 3.4 percent for information on child growth and development. The current study did not allow for the examination of the specific interventions for each client individually, so cross-study comparisons are difficult. Taken collectively, these studies indicate that NPs are actively promoting health.

Educational Activities

Data suggested that disease- and medication-specific educational activities were the most frequently performed by the NPs. It is reassuring that the philosophy of most health care professionals includes providing information that responds to clients' current problems or concerns. A background in professional nursing that emphasizes client participation and attention to dimensions of daily living may further enable NPs to build their illness care on this philosophy.

The individually calculated education score (1.6 education activities per client) may reflect an increased amount of wellness and maintenance care. Women's health care often does not involve a specific problem or medication, instead focusing on health maintenance, for which education is a vital component.

Draye and Pesznecker (1980) and Repicky et al. (1980) reported on frequencies of patient education given to clients in their respective studies. Repicky et al. did not classify the term specifically but indicated that 38.3 percent of the clients received this service. Draye and Pesznecker reported that 87 percent of the clients in their sample received teaching regarding the plan of care or the diagnosis.

Counseling Activities

Our results also suggested that counseling activities were a common part of NP practice. It was interesting to note that 82 percent of the NPs provided psychologic counseling to at least one client on the reporting day, while almost one-half reported giving advice on economic or social issues and slightly under one-third provided crisis intervention to at least one client. The counseling:client ratio indicates most clients cared for by NPs receive counseling. Thus NPs appear to be sensitive to the emotional and social needs of their clients and perceive that they help to meet these needs. Similarly, when the NPs ranked the health problems of their clients, psychosocial problems were third in frequency, reflecting a major part of the NPs' practice.

The two comparison studies had relatively detailed information on the types of counseling activities performed by NPs for the clients in their studies. Repicky, Mendenhall, and Neville (1980) stated that 4.2 percent of the clients received psychologic counseling, 4.0 percent family or sexual counseling, 2.5 percent social or economic advice, and 1.2 percent crisis counseling. Draye and Pesznecker (1980) noted that 6.9 percent of the clients received counseling, which included relationship problems, economic or employment problems, and ways of coping with difficulties.

SUMMARY

Over all, the study findings lend support to the assertion that nurse practitioners perceived they provide their clients with a wide array of coordination, health-promotion, health-education, and counseling services within a nursing framework. In this regard they are functioning in a manner that is complementary to traditional medical practice. It is critical, however, that nurse educators continue to escalate their efforts to strengthen this area of curriculum content and appropriately inform graduate students about this vital aspect of the advanced nursing practice role in primary health care.

Considerable variability existed among the NPs, with some actively involved in health promotion and others only minimally involved. Future studies of characteristics of both the low- and high-performance groups could explore individual and institutional factors that may contribute to the variability of health-promotion services provided. For example, analysis of these data exploring the influence of practice setting on coordination and health-promotion activities of NPs is described elsewhere (Brown & Waybrant, 1987). In addition, further studies extending beyond this group of master's-prepared NPs are necessary, with observation and generalization to corroborate the NPs' self-reports. Delineation of these activities in other groups such as physicians and physician assistants would prove helpful in comparing similarities and differences in their respective practice roles.

The next critical step is to focus on outcome variables to determine whether these nursing services are affecting the lifestyle and health of clients. To the extent that nurses are successful in their attempts to educate patients, preventable diseases and disabilities may be decreased nationally. At present we know very little about the educational content provided by primary health care clinicians or sought by their patients, about the processes involved in the delivery of health promotion/preventive health education, or about associated patient behavioral and attitudinal outcomes. This information gap is particularly true for adult patients. Greater understanding of the content, processes and outcomes of primary health care nursing practice is a vital area for continued attention.

REFERENCES

American Nurses' Association. (1980). *Nursing: A social policy statement.* Kansas City, MO: Author.

American Nurses' Association. (1983). *Standards of community health nursing practice.* Kansas City, MO: Author.

American Nurses' Association. (1985). *Scope of practice in the primary health care nurse practitioner.* Kansas City, MO: Author.

Archer, S.E., Fleshman, R.P. (1985). *Community health nursing.* Monterey, CA: Wadsworth Health Sciences.

Becker, D.M., Fournier, A.M., & Gardner, L.B. (1982). A description of a means for improving ambulatory care in a large municipal teaching hospital: A new role for nurse practitioners. *Medical Care, 20*(10), 1046-1050.

Brallier, L.W. (1978). The nurse as holistic health practitioner. *Nursing Clinics of North America, 13,* 643-655.

Brown, M.A., & Waybrant, K. (1987). Delineation of the nurse practitioner role: The influence of individual characteristics and practice setting on coordination and health promotion activities. *Journal of Ambulatory Care Management, 10*(3), 8-19.

Brunetto, E., & Birk, P. (1972). Primary care nurse: The generalist in a structured health care team. *American Journal of Public Health, 62,* 785-793.

Carnevali, D.L. (1983). *Nursing care planning: Diagnosis and management* (3rd ed.). Philadelphia: J.B. Lippincott.

Choi, M.W. (1981). Nurses as co-practitioners of primary health care. *Nursing Outlook, 29*(9), 519-521.

D'Angelo, L., Reifsteck, S.W., & Green, R.D. (1984). Nurse practitioners: co-providers of health care. *Medical Group Management, 31*(3), 38-44.

Davidson, R.A., & Lauver, D. (1984). Nurse practitioner and physician roles: Delineation and complementarity of practice. *Research in Nursing and Health, 7,* 3-9.

Diers, D. (1983). Nurse practitioners: The new gatekeepers. *American Journal of Nursing, 83*(5), 294-299.

Diers, D., & Molde, S. (1979). Some conceptual and methodological issues in nurse practitioner research. *Research in Nursing and Health, 2,* 73-84.

Draye, M.A., & Pesznecker, B. (1980). Teaching activities of family nurse practitioners. *Nurse Practitioner, 5,* 28-33.

Flynn, B.C. (1974). The effectiveness of nurse clinician service delivery. *American Journal of Public Health, 64,* 604-608.

Ford, L. (1979). A nurse for all settings: The nurse practitioner. *Nursing Outlook, 27*(8), 516-521.

Glascock, J., Webster-Stratton, C., & McCarthy, A.M. (1985). Infant and well child care: Masters and non-masters prepared pediatric nurse practitioners. *Nursing Research, 34*(1), 39-43.

Green, L.W. (1979). National policy in the promotion of health. *International Journal of Health Education, 12*(3), 161-168.

Leff, S.D. (1983). The standard of care question. *Nurse Practitioner, 8*(7), 34-36, 72.

Levine, J.I., Orr, S.T., Sheatsley, D.W., Lohr, J.A., & Brodie, B.M. (1978). The nurse practitioner: Role, physician utilization, patient acceptance. *Nursing Research, 27*(4), 245-254.

Linn, L. (1975). Expectation vs. realization in the nurse practitioner role. *Nursing Outlook, 23*(3), 166-171.

McCarthy, A.M., Webster-Stratton, C., & Glascock, J. (1987). *The scope of pediatric nurse practice: Nursing activities during well child care.* Unpublished.

Mitchell, K. (1983). NAPNAP's scope of practice survey: Results, revisions and issues. *Pediatric Nursing, 9*(3), 199-203.

Muhlenkamp, A.F., Brown, N.J., & Sands, D. (1985). Determinants of health promotion activities in nursing clinic clients. *Nursing Research, 34*(6), 327-332.

Nightingale, F. (1969). *Notes on nursing.* New York: Dover Publications.

Pender, N. (1982). *Health promotion in nursing practice.* New York: Appleton-Century-Crofts.

Ramsey, J.A., McKenzie, J.K., & Fish, D.G. (1982). Physicians and nurse practitioners: Do they provide equivalent health care? *American Journal of Public Health, 72*(1), 55-57.

Repicky, P.A., Mendenhall, R.C., & Neville, R.E. (1980). Professional activities of nurse practitioners in adult ambulatory care settings. *Nurse Practitioner, 5*(2), 27-34, 39-40.

Schlotfeldt, R.M. (1972). This I believe . . . nursing is health care. *Nursing Outlook, 20*(4), 245-246.

Steiger, N.J., & Lipson, J.G. (1985). *Self-care nursing: Theory and practice.* Bowie, MD: Brady Communications.

Stumpf, N.E. (1986). Providing primary health care for the gerontological client. In M.D. Mezey & D.O. McGiven (Eds.), *Nurses and nurse practitioners: The evolution of primary care* (pp. 201-217). Boston: Little, Brown.

Sullivan, J.A. (1982). Research on nurse practitioners: Process behind outcome? *American Journal of Public Health, 78,* 8.

Taller, S. (1979). Where nurse practitioners expand good care. *Patient Care, 13,* 184-212.

Taylor, R.B. (1981). Health promotion: Can it succeed in the office? *Preventive Medicine, 10*(2), 258-262.

Taylor, R.B., Ureda, J.R., & Denham, J.W. (1982). *Health promotion: Principles and clinical applications.* Norwalk, CT: Appleton-Century-Crofts.

Thompson, J.E. (1986). Primary health care nursing for women. In M.D. Mezey & D.O. McGiven (Eds.), *Nurses and nurse practitioners: The evolution of primary care* (pp. 201-217). Boston: Little, Brown.

Vacek, P., & Ashikaga, T. (1980). Quantification of the expanded role of the nurse practitioner: A discriminant analysis approach. *Health Services Research, 15*(2), 105-125.

Webster-Stratton, C., Glascock, J., & McCarthy, A.M. (1986). Nurse practitioner—Patient interaction analysis during well child visits. *Nursing Research, 55*(4), 247-249.

Wirth, P., Kahn, L., & Storm, E. (1977). An analysis of 50 graduates of the Washington University PNP program. Part 3. Perception and expectations of the role in the health care system. *Nurse Practitioner, 2*(8), 16-18.

CHAPTER 15

Collaborative Practice Models in Community Health Nursing

Betty Pesznecker, RN, MN
Mary Ann Draye, RN, ARNP, MPH, FNP
Jo McNeil, RN, MN

One of the hazards of rapid change is that we usually have little time to ponder, much less plan for, the ramifications of that change. Nowhere is this more evident than in community health settings where there has been a rapid change in nursing roles and scope of practice. Public health nursing and the nurse practitioner movement have undergone significant change and innovation in the last decade. Yet, despite several attempts, clear role distinctions between the public health nurse (PHN) and family nurse practitioner (FNP) elude us.[1-3] The result is that nurses in both groups are often unclear about their scope of practice in relation to each other. It is not surprising then that resentments and territorial concerns arise when nurses are questioned about who does what or what types of agencies need which type of personnel.

We believe this is a critical time to examine the roles and relationship between public health nurses and family nurse practitioners, since effective implementation of both roles is essential to comprehensive care in the community. Further, we believe that in the relationship between these two roles lies the essence of nursing's responsibility and contribution to comprehensive, coordinated primary care that focuses on the health of the total community as well as the health of individuals and families within the community. Nursing has a responsibility to its clients as well as to itself to advance the intradisciplinary cooperation. For these reasons, we wish to clarify some of the issues surrounding PHN and FNP roles as well as to make some suggestions, including models for collaborative practice. Our discussion will focus primarily on PHNs and FNPs employed by official agencies.

Reprinted from *Nursing Outlook,* Vol. 30, No. 5, with permission of American Journal of Nursing, © 1982.

EDUCATIONAL PREPARATION

Since the beginning of the nurse practitioner movement in Colorado in 1965, there has been a steady increase in the number of programs preparing nurse practitioners. Estimates are that 12,000 nurses have been formally prepared for this role.[4] In 1979, the U.S. Department of Health, Education and Welfare identified 140 certificate-awarding programs and another 112 programs granting master's degrees. These programs cover a range of nursing specialties—women's health, occupational health, geriatrics, family health.[5] Obviously they differ in admission requirements, length, and program emphasis; however, the majority of them are centered in academe with an increase in the number at the master's level. The shift toward master's preparation is reflected in programs receiving federal support. Figures for 1976, released by HEW, list 17 funded programs: 6 offered master's degrees, and 11 awarded certificates. However, by 1977, 40 new programs were added, 50 percent at the master's level.[6] During this period, nurse practitioner faculty were increasingly better prepared and curricula became more standardized with emphasis on health assessment and delivery of personal health services. In addition, the ANA developed criteria for nurse practitioner curricula. Graduates of certificate and master's programs must meet ANA standards before taking the FNP certification exam.

As of January 1979, nurses employed in community health totaled 81,219, with 41 percent working in local official agencies.[7] Most of these nurses have baccalaureate preparation which is basic to the PHN role. Baccalaureate programs prepare generalists in nursing who have sufficient introductory content in public/community health for entry into professional practice. Curricula include content in epidemiology, community assessment, statistics, family and community health and safety, and community organization. Specialization for community health nursing practice takes place at the master's level and prepares the graduate with breadth and depth of knowledge essential to the provision of public health services. The functional roles of teaching and administration may also be included in master's level preparation, but the current trend in community health nursing graduate programs is to prepare specialists who are well versed in community health/public health principles and concepts.[8,9]

In summary, public health nurses employed by most community agencies are required to have earned a baccalaureate degree in nursing that includes basic content in community health/public health. Nurse practitioners employed by community agencies may have completed either a certificate program or a master's program. Since admission to the former does not require a BSN, graduates of certificate programs may not have had basic community health/public health content.

ROLES AND SCOPE OF PRACTICE

With the expansion of primary health care delivery and the evolution of the nurse practitioner role, there has been considerable confusion about the role and focus of practice of the public health nurse and the family nurse practitioner, particularly when employed by official agencies in the community. Goeppinger noted that part of this confusion has been a lack of distinction between public health and personal health services.[10] Therefore, in order to understand the difference between these roles in community settings, one has to differentiate between public health and personal health services.

Public health services are consistent with the goal of public health—to promote the health of the total community. These services are socially mandated and focus on societal health concerns such as environmental pollutants, the health of school children, the control of infectious disease, and the provision of health care to the indigent. Official agencies, such as health departments, provide the majority of public health services.[11] Personal health services, on the other hand, focus on the health needs of individual members of society and include services to help individuals keep healthy, recover from illness, or learn to live with disability. These services tend to be episodic and are requested by the individual.[12]

Official public health agencies have always been involved in the delivery of both public health and personal health services. However, in recent years, health departments have assumed a larger role in primary care by providing personal health services through publicly financed community clinics and health centers. Responsibilities of public health nurses and nurse practitioners employed by these agencies have focused more and more on the delivery of personal health services in these centers. Because of this shift in emphasis, efforts have been made to upgrade the skills of public health nurses so that they can deliver high quality personal health services.

Who, then, is focusing on the delivery of public health services? If official health agencies are to carry out social mandates for improving the health of the total community, then public health services must be considered. What role do nurses play in this arena and what group of nurses is best qualified? Both PHNs and FNPs provide service to individuals, families, and communities. However, PHNs and FNPs have different priorities for practice as depicted in Figure 15-1. Further examination of the scope of practice and definitions for each specialty will help to clarify differences in priorities for practice.

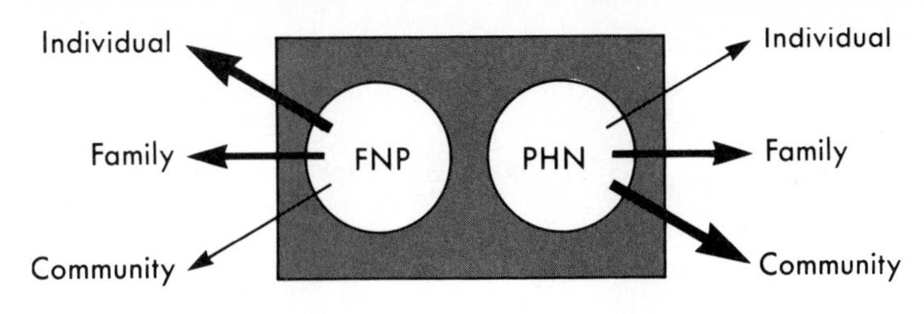

FIGURE 15-1
Priorities for practice–FNP and PHN.

Current definitions of public health nursing place the main focus and scope of practice on public health services, but they also include personal health services. For example, the definition proposed by the American Nurses Association, Division of Community Health Nursing, considers the PHN's responsibility in terms of the population as a whole. Activities such as health promotion, health education, management, coordination, and continuity of care are used to accomplish this goal.[13]

According to the Public Health Nursing Section, American Public Health Association, the focus of public health nursing is the health of the total community or population group. Therefore, the PHN is concerned with identifying and intervening with subgroups or aggregates at high risk for illness and disability in order to direct resources toward these groups for the purpose of improving the health of the total community. All factors impinging on the health of the community are targets for investigation and intervention, including environmental, social, and ecological conditions.[14] Social and political action are also considered important components of PHN practice both at the state and national level.

Inherent in both definitions is the notion that public and personal health services are synthesized in the practice of public health nursing. Current authors tend to corroborate this belief.[15,16]

In contrast to public health nurses, the nurse practitioner's major focus of practice in primary health care is to "coordinate and deliver comprehensive, continuous personalized health care."[17] Primary health care is defined as the care given to individuals at their point of entry into the health care system as well as continued care of individuals and families. In other words, the nurse practitioner provides total patient care, including health promotion and assessment of health status and potential for disease development. The scope of practice also includes assessment, management, and evaluation of disease states, teaching and counseling as well as consultation, referral, and collaboration with other disciplines. Furthermore, nurse practitioner functions and activities are equally appropriate in any setting, including inpatient services, long-term care institutions, primary health care clinics, industry, schools, or jails.

Regardless of the setting in which the nurse practitioner works, the fact remains that she has been specifically prepared to provide highly skilled personal health services to individuals and families. In contrast, the public health nurse is primarily prepared to focus on assessing community health status, identifying populations at risk to health conditions and illnesses, and planning and evaluating community health nursing programs.[18] Fig. 1 illustrates the practice priorities of FNPs and PHNs.

Both nursing roles are essential in relation to the current mission and programs of official health agencies. But are these roles clearly defined in practice and are the functions and activities of both performed? How can nurse practitioners and public health nurses be best utilized to provide both public health and personal health services to communities?

MODELS OF PRACTICE

An official health agency may utilize PHNs and FNPs in differing models of practice depending upon the services it provides. Figure 15-2 depicts one model in which the FNP and the PHN work in separate

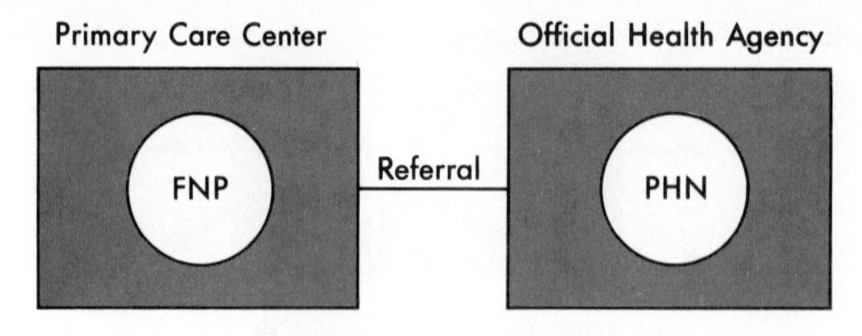

FIGURE 15-2
Separate practice settings.

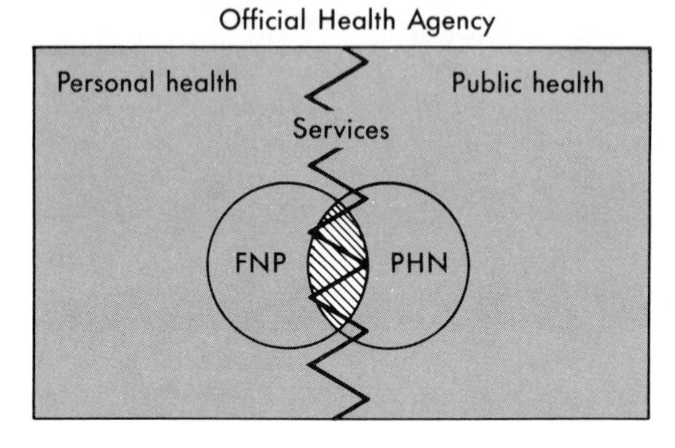

FIGURE 15-3
Combined practice setting with distinct roles.

agencies. For example, the FNP might be located in a neighborhood primary health care center; the PHN might be employed by the local health department.

PHNs traditionally have been the casefinders in the community and consistently have referred individuals with health needs to their family physician or to other sources of care. In this model, the PHN can refer clients to the FNP when appropriate. At the same time, the FNP can refer clients to the PHN for home visit follow up. This may be especially recommended for families needing special teaching, such as a new mother and infant or postoperative clients. Or it may be for detailed assessment of home and family situations or for follow up of communicable disease problems with individuals.

This model would improve continuity of patient care and would also benefit professional nurses because of its network approach. Nurses, primarily women, have not unequivocally accepted the competence of other female colleagues. However, after ten years of expanded education and practice, they are finally beginning to refer clients to one another. Implementation of this model may require some new and innovative relationships between agencies and primary care clinics. For example, if the referral process is to be successful, special attention must be given to referral mechanisms, communication, and follow up.

In the second model shown in Figure 15-3, the FNP and the PHN work in the same agency. Here, the FNP would be responsible for the primary care of individuals who come into the clinic. This care would include personal health service whether it was for health maintenance or an illness condition. In this role, the FNP may be the first to identify problems common to a number of individuals; for example, poor nutrition, teenage pregnancy, alcohol abuse, or other unhealthy life style practices. The FNP could then collaborate with the PHN to plan programs to address some of the problems. For example, one

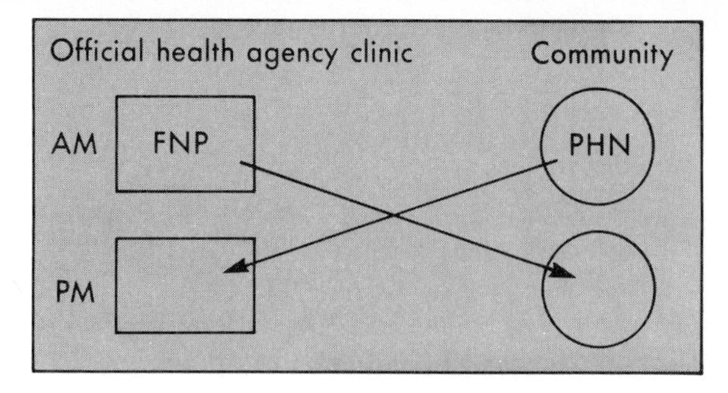

FIGURE 15-4
Combined practice setting with combined roles.

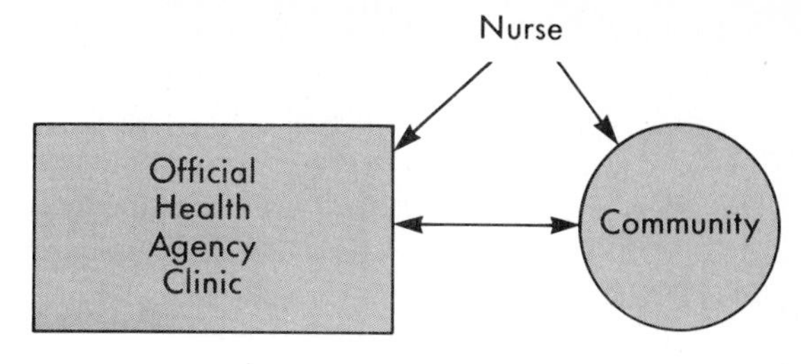

FIGURE 15-5
Rural setting with integrated role.

method might be group teaching in which the FNP, the PHN, or both are involved.

The PHN in this model of practice takes the lead in community organization for the agency. For example, the PHN would use vital statistics to identify subgroups in the community who are at risk for specific health problems, plan and implement health needs assessments, and plan and coordinate citizens' and community agencies' efforts to solve major health problems. The focus or target of practice of the PHN could be groups in the community such as health councils, schools, health and social agencies, senior citizens, workers in industry, and other aggregates of persons with common concerns or health problems. The PHN's major role would be to facilitate community programs aimed at promoting the health of the total community.

Some of the complex agency relationships mentioned earlier may be lessened in this model since both nurses are employed in the same agency. However, such close proximity may intensify problems of role conflict between the PHN and FNP in regard to specific nursing tasks.

Figure 15-4 depicts the combined model in which each nurse wears two caps. Based on this model, more variety and continuity of care can be created in the delivery of both public health services and personal health services. For example, either the PHN or FNP would provide primary personal health services to patients in the clinic in the morning. In the afternoon, that same nurse would go into the community to provide both personal and public health services. Examples of personal health services could include home care, follow up of patients seen in the clinic, or teaching groups or individual clients.

Examples of public health services could include collaborating with local hospitals to provide discharge planning for newborns; consulting with teachers on developing a health curriculum for the school; or meeting with city officials as an advocate for elderly residents of low income housing units. The second nurse would work in the community in the morning and see patients in the clinic in the afternoon. The benefits of the combined model are that only one clinic space is needed, transportation and equipment is shared, and continuity of care is maximized.

The combination of roles as depicted in this model has some limitations, however. First, both nurses must be prepared and experienced in public health and as family nurse practitioners. Although this "super nurse" may be difficult to find at present, the combination of knowledge and expertise may be a worthwhile goal. Second, the switching of roles may prove too exhausting for some; it could mean spreading oneself too thin and lead to role diffusion. Should that occur, public health services might diminish.

Figure 15-5 illustrates a model for rural settings where one nurse practices with minimal back up from other health care providers. In this model, as in the previous one, the nurse needs to be prepared as *both* an FNP and a PHN. This nurse must be able to provide care for all age groups in the clinic, home, and community. The clinic may be a mobile site, especially in areas of geographic isolation. In addition to personal health services, the nurse would be involved in public health services to the community. This could include community screening programs, work with civic leaders to improve emergency transport services, or helping workers recognize occupational hazards. The role diffusion mentioned earlier may be even more significant in this model. The demands of rural practice, especially emergency care, can lead to burnout in even the most dedicated practitioners. Conversely, there is much satisfaction and challenge in being an integral part of a rural community.

CONCLUSIONS

We believe nursing has the ability to provide comprehensive personal as well as public health services through collaborative relationships between FNPs and PHNs. However, implementation of these models poses significant challenges: new organizational relationships will need to be tested and revised, funding mechanisms will need to be altered; and risks will need to be taken. But, the greatest challenge will be to the nurses themselves. Each must respect the other's competencies and be willing to negotiate specific tasks and role conflicts. Preparation for such collaborative relationships should take place early in the education of nurse practitioners and public health nurses. Indeed, by strengthening the intradisciplinary nature of its practice, nursing can provide excellent public and personal health services in the community.

REFERENCES

1. Western Interstate Commission for Higher Education. *Defining Clinical Content, Graduate Nursing Programs; Part 4. Community Health Nursing,* by L. C. Ford and others. Boulder, Colo., The Commission, 1967.
2. Wood, J., and Ohlson, V. Graduate preparation for community health nursing practice. In *Current Perspectives in Nursing: Social Issues and Trends, Volume 1,* ed. by M. H. Miller and B. C. Flynn, St. Louis, C. V. Mosby Co., 1977, pp. 158-164.
3. Williams, C. Community health nursing—what is it? *Nurs. Outlook* 28:250-254, Apr. 1977.
4. Henry, O. M. Progress of the nurse practitioner movement .(editorial) *Nurse Pract.* 3:4, May-June 1978.
5. U. S. Health Resources Administration. *Directory of Expanded Role Programs for Registered Nurses,* 1979. (DHEW Publ. No. (HRA) 79-10) Washington, D.C., U. S. Government Printing Office, 1979.
6. Hedrich V. A national survey: educating for the expanded role. *Nurse Pract.* 3:13-16, Jan.-Feb. 1978.
7. U. S. Health Resources Administration, Nursing Division. *1979 Survey of Community Health Nursing.* Washington, D.C., The Administration, n.d. (Unpublished data)
8. Fonseca, J. D. The pendulum swings. (editorial) *Nurs Outlook* 26:621, Oct. 1978.
9. Ruth, M. V., and Partridge, K. B. Differences in perception of education and practice. *Nurs. Outlook* 26:622-628, Oct. 1978.
10. Goeppinger, J. Community health nursing: primary nursing care in society. In *Current Perspective in Nursing: Social Issues and Trends, Volume Two,* ed. by B. C. Flynn and M. H. Miller. St. Louis, C. V. Mosby Co., 1980, pp. 57-63.
11. *Ibid.,* pp. 70-72.
12. *Ibid.,* p. 57.
13. American Nurses Association, Community Health Nursing Division. *A Conceptual Model of Community Health Nursing.* (Publ. No. CH-10) Kansas City, Mo., The Association, 1980.
14. American Public Health Association, Public Health Nursing Section. *The Definition and Role of Public Health Nursing Practice in The Delivery of Health Care.* Washington, D.C., The Association, Nov. 1981.
15. Skrovan C, and Others. Community nurse practitioner: an emerging role. *Am. J. Public Health* 64:847-853, Sept. 1974.
16. Williams, *op. cit.*
17. American Nurses Association, Primary Health Care Nurse Practitioners Council. *The Primary Health Care Nurse Practitioner: Statement.* (Publ. No. NP-61) Kansas City, Mo., The Association, 1980.
18. Wood and Ohlson, *op. cit.*

CHAPTER 16

Public Health Nursing: The Neglected Specialty

Marla E. Salmon, RN, ScD, FAAN

In fall 1988, the Institute of Medicine released the landmark report of its two-year study, *The Future of Public Health.*[1] The study found that the nation's public health system was in "disarray" and called for major changes in both practice and education. Among the many concerns raised in the report was the lack of public health education among workers in the field. The report called for careful reconsideration of the ways in which we prepare public health practitioners, particularly with respect to their ability to provide leadership in the field.[2]

The IOM report did not specifically address the question of how well nurses are prepared to assume practice and leadership roles in public health. Because nurses constitute the single largest public health workforce category, however, their numbers alone call for careful consideration of the relevance of their education to the needs of public health.[3]

Values and Assumptions

The primary forces shaping educational content are the values and assumptions on which it is based. These values and assumptions constitute the pervasive and frequently unconscious culture that directs all aspects of an organization and determines its membership.[4] The values and assumptions intrinsic to nursing education must be carefully considered if public health nursing education is to be responsive to the needs of practitioners. To understand how these values and assumptions affect public health nursing education, it is essential that they be consciously compared to those of public health and that points of contrast and conflict are clear. Without such an analysis, changes in other aspects of education can only be cosmetic.

Reprinted from *Nursing Outlook,* Vol. 37, No. 5, with permission of American Journal of Nursing, © 1989.

Perhaps the single most important value conflict between nursing and public health is that of primacy of the individual and family versus primacy of society and public good. Nursing education has traditionally oriented its advocacy toward providing comprehensive services to meet the needs and wants of the individual and family.[5] Public health, whose mission is socially and politically derived, is responsible for the overall health of the public and allocating scarce resources to best serve the public interest.

In addition, while the health promotion movement has brought nursing and public health somewhat closer, nursing's primary orientation toward "care and cure" contrasts with public health's broader goals — to prevent health problems from occurring or to detect risk factors and intervene at an early stage.[6] Nursing education at all levels often assumes that the client will come to the nurse's institution with problems, that these problems will serve as the basis for the nurse's actions, and that the institution has the responsibility to provide the resources the nurse needs to practice effectively. The public health educational perspective assumes that the practitioner actively targets at-risk populations, finds members of those populations, generates multi-institutional and community resource bases, and intervenes on a non-institutional or cross-institutional basis.

Nursing and public health differ on professional credibility. Nursing places a high value on its members being technically competent in one-to-one practice. For many educators, the measure of a good nurse is how well he/she performs with individual clients. A public health perspective of competence reflects the indirect roles that public health practitioners play, such as program development, community organization, case finding, surveillance, and political activism. These differing values shape how practitioners are taught and rewarded; they also shape the "vision" educators instill in students regarding their future careers.

Another point of contrast relates to primary disciplinary relationships. For nursing, the educational and professionalization process is strongly nursing-focused; the student's primary teachers and fellow students are nurses. Public health holds that practice is necessarily interdisciplinary and requires an interdisciplinary education. Accreditation requirements for educational programs in nursing schools and schools of public health reflect these differing perspectives in both curriculum and faculty requirements.

For the purpose of this discussion, a final key difference arises from the value placed on uniformity and consensus. Nursing strongly emphasizes the achievement of consensus and the standardization of both education and practice. Within individual nursing programs, this tends to create an organizational culture in which faculty, students, or programs lying outside of the mainstream are frequently not well tolerated, despite their value. Public health necessarily reflects a nonstandardized, form-follows-function perspective. Thus, one finds great variety in public education and practice.[7]

Concepts and Theories

The learning experiences designed by an educational institution are also based on its values and assumptions. The conceptual and theoretical frameworks adopted by educators are the result of the values and assumptions or the culture of that organization. These intellectual structures serve as the sieve through which knowledge and learning experiences are sorted, determining what is included and what is left out. The theories and concepts that reflect the mainstream of nursing education understandably differ from those of public health.

While nursing theorists may, for example, introduce family and, sometimes, community concepts, their conceptualizations generally focus on the individual, as do interventions based on them. For public health, the conceptual and theoretical perspectives reflect the view that the health of people is determined by numerous factors, many of which lie outside of the individual. Therefore, interventions focus on health determinants, which may include the physical and social environment, health services financing and delivery systems, and public policy. The health of an individual may be affected by interventions without any direct public health contact with that person.

A related conceptual and theoretical difference between nursing and public health is the focus for assessment, diagnosis, planning, implementation, and evaluation. Again, nursing's focus for assessment and diagnosis is primarily on the individual client. While community assessment and diagnosis have become parts of some nursing education programs, planning, implementation and evaluation are often necessarily carried out at the individual level. This is reflected in the strong reliance on clinical, one-to-one performance indicators as quality assurance and evaluation measures. For public health, the assessment of morbidity, mortality, and health risk within a community is the departure point for program planning. Community assessment, as an essential adjunct to this epidemiologic assessment, serves as the basis for intervention planning and follow-through at a community level. Evaluation and quality assurance are based on epidemiologic and programmatic measures of performance. For nursing, a guiding principle at all phases of intervention is that the nurse does nursing. For public health, the guiding principle is to do whatever it takes, requiring the fundamental intervention to be interdisciplinary leadership.

The roles for which individuals are prepared are also divergent. In nursing education, role delineation has been a major focus for curriculum development.

Public health, which calls for practitioners to function in multiple roles throughout the course of a career, thus requires multiple role preparation and comfort with ambiguity and uncertainty in role definition.

The difference in how roles are viewed by nursing and public health arises from *who* defines practice. Nurses determine what constitutes good nursing practice, which allows for role standardization and delineation. In contrast, society ultimately determines what constitutes good public health practice, thus demanding a high degree of flexibility and responsiveness in roles and practice modes.

Nursing education and public health are at odds, too, on what constitutes the "core" or discipline-specific knowledge and skills required to prepare effective practitioners. Nursing's core requires nursing knowledge and skills taught by those with nursing expertise. Public health's core requires teachers with expert skills in many disciplines, including epidemiology, environmental health, biostatistics, public policy, management, and program development.

Recurring Problems in PHN Education

Public health nursing education in schools of nursing has been revised repeatedly. The most recent changes have caused it to be subsumed in community health nursing education programs, integrated into the overall curriculum as a curricular thread, or lost entirely as an identifiable specialty. Few nursing education programs have distinct public health nursing tracks or options, despite the continuation of the specialty in practice. The loss of the public health nursing emphasis has led to many problems in preparing public health nurses.

First, nursing theory and content predominate in public health nursing education, largely to the exclusion of public health content. In undergraduate nursing programs, students can graduate without being able to identify the specific public health or public health nursing content in their education. At the graduate level, programs may turn out "specialists" who are ostensibly equipped to function at advanced levels in public health but have little administrative and program development preparation, no environmental health content, and only a sketchy acquaintance with epidemiology or biostatistics. Equally lacking are the ethical and theoretical bases for public health.

Likewise, nursing programs fail to identify and define public health roles and concerns for students. There are deficiencies in public health practice role models for students and faculty, public health agency/program clinical placements, collegial networks with public health leaders, awareness of national and state public health issues and agendas, and general awareness of the field. Coupled with the absence of identifiable and distinct public health content, these deficiencies lead to graduates for whom public health nursing is a nebulous and indistinct practice.

Moreover, the dilution of public health nursing content and the adoption of broad community health nursing concepts in education programs have created multiple standards for faculty teaching community health nursing. Thus, students may have little or no exposure to faculty with expertise or knowledge in public health nursing. In addition, what public health content there is may be taught by a faculty member who has taken only a single course in that area and is only one step ahead of the students.

Ironically, faculty with expertise in public health and public health nursing often encounter major barriers to using their competence in nursing programs. Interpretation of accreditation standards and, in some states, nurse practice acts may preclude nurses with advanced education in public health and public health nursing from teaching in a school of nursing. Because public health nursing is not highly valued in many schools of nursing, the crucial expertise offered by these nurses may not be missed. A dean who must choose between a prospective community health nursing faculty member with advanced nursing degrees and no public health expertise and a nurse with advanced public health nursing education and expertise, will frequently opt for the former.

Nursing faculty with public health nursing expertise frequently encounter additional barriers. Among these are the lack of recognition of their expertise and its value by other faculty members, inadequate curricular time, lack of support for interdisciplinary teaching approaches, lack of colleagues, and lack of rewards for their work. The nursing education system encourages qualified public health faculty to lose contact with the field of public health, which ultimately leads to loss of skill and perspective.

Students, too, encounter educational barriers to involvement in public health nursing careers, such as inadequate preparation for functioning in interdisciplinary settings. Without significant interdisciplinary learning experiences in public health settings, students have little opportunity to master the interdisciplinary leadership and team-building skills needed for public health practice. This not only isolates nurses in public health practice, but also frequently denies them access to career advancement and other professional challenges in the field beyond the direct service and supervisory level. More important, this isolation of nurses limits the contributions they can make at program and policy levels and elsewhere. Further, a specialty that is "invisible" during one's education is generally not seen as a career option later.

Another barrier for students is their lack of credibility in the field. The concept of community health nursing preparation is not widely understood in the public health field, and nurses who are prepared as community health nurses do not have the automatic credibility of those whose preparation is explicitly for public health nursing. Another credibility and career advancement issue is the need for a public health degree. The field of public health recognizes and regards public health degrees as hallmarks of preparation for public health practice.[8] For nurses to assume leadership roles in public health, the public health degree is an important asset.

Leadership preparation in itself is a concern of public health nursing. The leadership roles frequently stressed in nursing programs relate to advancing the profession. As such, being involved in one's professional organization, lobbying for professional survival and development issues, and learning to lead nurses in collective advocacy efforts are all a part of this idea of leadership. The "change agent" role, in which the nurse is seen as a wedge for introducing change in obsolete or unresponsive institutions and systems, is another element of leadership preparation.

What is absent from these concepts is the public health view that leadership is a requisite "clinical" intervention aimed at mobilizing multiple and diverse people and organizations.[9] This view requires that leadership be more than the attribute of a good professional. Rather, it is a primary strategy for accomplishing specific, targeted public health objectives. The leadership preparation that most nurses receive, coupled with the problems of credibility and career advancement in public health, mitigate strongly against their functioning as leaders in public health.

The Future of PHN Education

Education for public health nursing has reached a turning point. Forces both within and outside nursing are creating pressure for change. Recent studies have identified major gaps between the needs of practice and the preparation of nurses for practice.[10,11] The IOM report on public health provides important insights into the needs in the field and calls for development of effective leadership. Nursing education now has an opportunity to carefully construct its future role in preparing public health nurses. The following recommendations provide one way of structuring the discussion and exchanges that must take place at all levels in nursing as part of the building process.

Any effort to reformulate the educational preparation for public health nursing must begin with a new concept of the specialty. The rallying point should be the role of the public health nurse as a leader in public health. This perspective offers public health nurses both the opportunity to contribute at all levels in the field and a career's-worth of growth opportunities.

The role of the public health nurse as leader necessarily calls for critical assessment of any program in which public health nurses are prepared. Evaluation should begin with examination of the program's explicit and implicit educational values and assumptions for solid evidence of public health as well as nursing perspectives. Such scrutiny should then move into a similar examination of concepts, theories, and educational strategies. Are these representative of both nursing and public health? If not, why?

A related, and perhaps more difficult, point of critique should address the underlying issue of nursing education's commitment to public health nursing education. This commitment must be questioned separately from that to community health nursing and answered in a manner that goes beyond an abstract exercise. Commitment includes willingness to commit resources and make changes.

Change for the Better

Through the process of self-examination, challenge, and clarification of commitment, some nursing educators will come to the point of demanding change. Such change requires careful management and should include involved people (nurses and others) with public health knowledge and expertise. They will be invaluable in ensuring the balance of public health and nursing needed to create effective change.

Change should also reflect the actual contemporary issues and practice of public health. Resource material for planning should go beyond nursing's resources, literature, and source material. The IOM study and related public health documents, the *Objectives for the Nation*[12] and other resources relating to the national health agenda are all important.

Change must also involve a commitment to an interdisciplinary learning experience for students, such as multidisciplinary team involvement of both students and faculty, clinical experiences that can be shared across professional programs, and ongoing inter- and multidisciplinary real-world projects.

Collaboration with public health educational resources is another essential element of change. Joint programs, new nursing programs in schools of public health, use of faculty, consultation and courses from schools of public health or preventive medicine programs are all possible outcomes of such collaboration. It is essential that resources not be restricted to those currently existing within nursing programs. Commitment to a public health nursing education that provides both education and, when possible, degree recognition, is necessary to credibility and opportunities for leadership in the field.

Change also requires a conscious recommitment to the field of public health and public health nursing. Consider calling it by its name, (public health nursing), involving its practitioners, and building networks in the field to make it happen. Without this conscious reconstruction of the specialty and its identity, the education itself won't happen. A starting point might be renaming CHN programs to community *and* public health nursing, within which specialty tracks and programs could be developed.

Finally, change in the preparation of public health nurses requires accompanying changes beyond the scope of individual programs. Leaders in nursing and public health must spearhead the development of more supportive national, state, and local bodies affecting education. Among these are professional associations, licensure and testing boards, accrediting bodies, and federal and private funding agencies. An infrastructure that promotes the development and maintenance of public health nursing education is essential.

Nursing education has an important potential role to play in the preparation of public health nurses as leaders in public health. The current common approach to preparation, in which public health and public health nursing are minor or nonexistent components, is part of the leadership problem in public health. If nursing education commits itself to actually preparing public health nurses for leadership in public health, it will be committing itself to self-examination, redirection, and change—change that will necessarily reflect the crucial balance between nursing and public health at all levels.

REFERENCES

1. Institute of Medicine. *The Future of Public Health.* Washington, DC, National Academy Press, 1988.
2. *Ibid.,* p. 157.
3. U.S. Department of Health and Human Services. *Public Health Personnel in the United States, 1980.* (DHHS Publ. No. [HRA] 82-6) Washington, DC, The Department, 1982, p. 43.
4. Sathe, V. Implications of corporate culture: a manager's guide to action. *Organizational Dynamics,* Autumn 1983, pp. 5-23.
5. Nelson, M. L. Advocacy in nursing. *Nurs. Outlook* 36: 136-141, May-June 1988.
6. White, M. S. Construct for public health nursing. *Nurs. Outlook* 30:527, Nov.-Dec. 1982.
7. *Ibid.,* p. 528.

8. Institute of Medicine, *op. cit.,* p. 157.
9. Salmon, M., and Vanderbush, P. Leadership and change in public and community health nursing today: The essential intervention. In *Current Issues in Nursing,* ed. by J. C. McCloskey and H. K. Grace. 3rd ed. St. Louis, Mosby–Year Book, Inc. (To be published)
10. Deiman, P. A., and others. BSN education and PHN practice: good fit or mismatch? *Nurs. Outlook* 36:231-233, Sept.-Oct. 1988.
11. Salmon, M., and others. *Master's Level Community/Public Health Nursing Educational Needs: A National Survey of Leaders in Service and Education.* A report to the National League for Nursing, June 1989. (unpublished)
12. U.S. Health, Education, and Welfare Department, Office of the Assistant Secretary for Health. *Promoting Health/ Preventing Disease: Objectives for the Nation.* Washington, DC, The Department, 1980.

CHAPTER **17**

The Transcultural Nurse Specialist: Imperative in Today's World

Madeleine M. Leininger, RN, PhD, LHD, DS, FAAN, CTN

One of the most significant developments in nursing has been the establishment of the new field of transcultural nursing as a formal, legitimate, and essential area of study and practice. Transcultural nursing was envisioned in the 1950s because of the need for nurses to work with people from widely divergent cultures (Leininger, 1978). Today, the nurse's role is becoming increasingly multicultural, as nurse practitioners are struggling to understand, communicate, and work effectively with clients of many different cultures . . . in hospitals, clinics, and community health agencies. In schools of nursing, faculty have been faced with the dilemma of having nursing students from different cultures who want to retain their own values and identity, and to use relevant concepts, principles, and research that fit with their background.

For a decade and a half, there has been a marked increase in diverse cultures and subcultures in the United States, accompanied by pride in one's cultural heritage and a sentiment that one does not have to change one's name or beliefs as was previously practiced. With the rapid increase of people from different cultures have come cultural tensions, conflicts, and problems in understanding. This is evident in the health field—and especially with nurses, because of their direct and ongoing care to these people. I contend there is a *major crisis in nursing* (even greater than the nurse shortage) in that most nurses are unprepared to function effectively with migrants and cultural strangers. It is difficult for nurses to interpret cultural behavior to know how best to help alien patients. As a consequence, the stress and burnout of nurses occurs and makes them feel inadequate and helpless in their roles. This crisis will increase as nurses work with the politically oppressed, war victims, and immigrants from virtually everywhere in the world. Nurses will be expected to work with even more cultural groups they know little or nothing about.

Even more significant, nurses have become increasingly worldwide travelers seeking new job opportunities, different experiences, and challenges in foreign countries. Some have been lured abroad because of outstanding salary benefits or travel opportunities. Even within their homeland, nurses are migrants or, "nomads," moving from place to place. Many of these roving nurses experience cultural shock in nursing education or practice settings. After the glow of a new place wears off, feelings of frustration, helplessness, incompetence, or discouragement often follow. Nurses begin to realize that they are in a *different* culture and cannot always use their "tried and true knowledge or skills" in ways they thought they could.

Nurses trying to help an Asian, Mexican-American, North American Indian, Amish, or other client in the hospital may find that nothing seems to go well for

Reprinted from *Nursing & Health Care,* Vol. 10, No. 5, with permission of National League for Nursing, © 1989.

either of them. One nurse told how she began to value transcultural nursing while working with an Asian mother who became upset because she removed the child's clothing on admission and put water in the child's ear to clean it. The Asian mother shook her head and took the baby home even though the child was quite ill. This nurse realized that she did not understand this mother or why she seemed so ungrateful for the nurse's care practice. In this instance, the nurse performed her professional activities, but they were offensive to the Asian mother. Likewise, the mother's behavior, including her gestures and actions, seemed strange to the nurse clinician, who was viewed as competent by her peers. Many other examples can be cited, of clients who were slow to recover from illness, wanted to leave the hospital, refused food and medications, and became suspicious of the nurses' actions.

These problems set the background for this article, which focuses on the purposes, characteristics, and role of the transcultural nurse specialist in nursing. The rationale for the role of this new practitioner is discussed, especially in nursing education and service institutions.

Transcultural nursing has truly "come of age" to meet one of the greatest needs in nursing and the health care field. The role of this specialist will grow by the next decade as transcultural nursing and customers of health care increasingly demand and expect respect and effective handling for their cultural values and beliefs. Moreover, the transcultural nurse specialist will be in great demand to initiate new programs in schools of nursing, as students prepare themselves to function in a changing multicultural world. Transcultural knowledge and skills in nursing will be the hallmark for a professional nurse and a basis for quality care to all clients practically all over the world.

Transcultural Nursing: What Is It?

Although the field of transcultural nursing began to take root nearly three decades ago and has become a firmly established field, there are still some nurses unfamiliar with the nature, purposes, and goals of this area of specialization. It has been defined by the author (and founder of the field) as *a formal area of study and practice focused on the cultural beliefs, values, and lifeways of diverse cultures and on the use of this knowledge to provide cultural specific or cultural universal care to individuals, families, and groups of particular cultures* (Leininger, 1978).

The purpose of establishing the field of transcultural nursing has been to prepare nurses through formal educational programs so that they could learn to provide or improve care to people of different cultural backgrounds. Since there was a major and long-standing deficit in cultural knowledge in the profession to care for clients, the goal was to develop knowledge *specific* to diverse cultures. Ultimately, this knowledge base would be used to reach cultural groups, especially minorities who experienced real or perceived conflicts, fears, or problems in using dominant cultural health systems. Nursing programs had virtually no theoretical or practical knowledge to teach students about different cultures, instead, a unicultural (Anglo-American) perspective prevailed in schools of nursing until recently. And in hospitals, cultural imposition, ethnocentrism, and cultural value clashes could be identified as problem areas decreasing quality of nursing care.

It was important that transcultural nursing was established as a formal area of study and practice in order to learn about cultures and to develop transcultural nursing knowledge. The field was perceived to be quite different from the traditionally clinical areas of medical-surgical, psychiatric, maternal-child, and other clinical specialties, as these areas were derived primarily from medicine, the biophysical sciences, and mind-body perspectives. Transcultural nursing was different, as its knowledge base was drawn largely from anthropology, other social sciences, and the humanities (Leininger, 1970). The goal was to develop a body of knowledge and skills needed to provide a holistic and comprehensive view of people—especially about people of different cultures.

The term *transcultural nursing* was deliberately chosen to identify this branch of nursing that focuses on *human care, health (well-being), and environmental context* as the major distinguishing features of the discipline (Leininger, 1988). The term *cross-cultural nursing* was reserved for the traditional use of applied anthropological concepts to nursing. Today, there are nurses (especially some nurse anthropologists) who use "cross-cultural nursing," which accurately reflects their primary focus of applying anthropological concepts and research findings to nursing. Many of these nurses are not committed to developing transcultural nursing knowledge, or to this specialized field in nursing. These differences are important to understand, since they support different goals and purposes.

One of the major goals of transcultural nursing is to prepare transcultural nursing specialists and generalists through educational programs to not only develop new nursing knowledge but also to become skilled practitioners and to perform as researchers and consultants.

Who is the Transcultural Nurse Specialist?

The transcultural nurse specialist is a nurse prepared in-depth in transcultural nursing knowledge, with competency skills, through postbaccalaureate education. This specialist has studied selected cultures in sufficient depth (values, beliefs, lifeways) and is highly knowledgeable about care, health, and environmental factors related to transcultural nursing perspectives. The specialist is able to serve as an *expert* with selected cultures and/or cultural areas as a field practitioner, teacher, researcher, and consultant. She or he is also a nurse who is very involved in theory and development of knowledge within this area of nursing.

The transcultural nurse specialist is often contrasted with the *nurse generalist* in the field. The generalist is prepared mainly through baccalaureate nursing education and focuses her or his work on the *general use* of transcultural nursing concepts, principles, and practices that mostly have been generated by transcultural nurse specialists. He or she has a broad orientation of concepts to serve people of several cultures and is primarily a user of transcultural nursing knowledge in various general nursing contexts.

The transcultural nurse specialist who is prepared through graduate education in transcultural nursing, is able to: (1) develop new knowledge or reconfirm existing knowledge; (2) communicate and disseminate knowledge in the discipline through a variety of means so that other nurses can use the knowledge to care for people; (3) demonstrate through ongoing research and use of theories ways to discover new transcultural nursing knowledge; (4) practice and consult with other nurses about cultures relative to her or his area(s) of expertise; and (5) give noteworthy leadership to advance transcultural nursing practices to improve care to people of different cultures.

While in the program, the transcultural nurse focuses mainly on discovering, building, critiquing, and applying transcultural nursing knowledge about selected cultures with an in-depth, scholarly, and practice viewpoint. The specialist learns about a few cultures rather than attempting to know many. For example, she or he may be a specialist about Arab cultures or Southeast Asian cultures, with a thorough knowledge of the specific cultures or subcultures within these groups. It is a major accomplishment to know the peoples within a culture area. The student completes research related to a care or health problem about a culture under a mentor in transcultural nursing. While in a doctoral program, the student usually does one or two field studies prior to preparing the dissertation. These experiences are valuable learning about specific cultures and give the student excellent experience to understand the ways cultures stay well, become ill, or need human caring.

Qualitative research methods are often chosen to explore unknown aspects of nursing, which requires the development of different research skills than the usual quantitative ones. The specialist learns usually for the first time how to do a qualitative research study such as an ethnonursing, ethnographic, ethnoscience, phenomenologic, or philosophical study of culture care or health domain. Dealing with complex social structures, world views, and cultural values in relation to transcultural nursing necessitates learning in-depth how to tap these areas. Using qualitative research methods is highly rewarding, but it requires new skills and more time in data collection and analysis than quantitative studies. Cultural care is difficult to measure, control, or manipulate as it is focused on understanding naturalistic lifeways of human caring in a culture.

Transcultural nurses are expected to do comparative thinking and analyses of *why* cultures are different or alike regarding human care, health practices, and other nursing aspects. They are prepared to study transcultural nursing problems or concerns in hospitals, clinics, communities, schools of nursing, and other places. Field placement for learning about a culture or conducting research is a major part of the clinical specialist's preparation. Field mentorship under an expert in transcultural nursing is required in order to assure knowledge and skill competencies. The general principle is that the more in-depth and high-quality the field mentorship, the better prepared is the student in research, teaching, and consultation.

It is desirable that the specialist be prepared through doctoral-level work, especially for complex national or international work, although occasionally some transcultural nurse specialists have been prepared through master's degree programs. Research, consultation, and teaching roles are necessary for the specialist because of the nature of transcultural nursing work and the fact that these roles are difficult to separate in transcultural nursing practices in any country. Furthermore, these specialists are cast into these multiple roles in foreign countries and even in the United States. The specialist is also expected to initiate new courses and programs in educational settings. They also learn ways to develop in-service transcultural nursing sessions in hospitals and clinics, often with multidisciplinary groups.

While in the transcultural nursing program, the student takes cognate courses in anthropology, the humanities, and related areas, depending upon his or her special research and theoretical interests. Anthropology and humanities courses are valuable to deepen the specialist's knowledge about cultures and to get multidisciplinary perspectives. Moreover, anthropologists have been most supportive of transcultural nurse specialist and generalist preparation.

Some nurses believe that if they get a master's or doctoral degree in anthropology, this will prepare them as a transcultural nurse specialist. While it can be helpful to have a degree in anthropology, this does not prepare them in the field of transcultural nursing. Unfortunately, some nurses getting advanced degrees in anthropology or related fields never receive transcultural nursing preparation and would not qualify to function as a specialist in that field. This is true for nurses prepared in other nonnursing fields who expect to practice nursing or be experts in a discipline.

Transcultural nurse specialists now, and in the future, are expected to be prepared in the field in which they intend to function. This is a critical issue, since some nurses are pursuing degrees in anthropology or sociology and want to be employed as transcultural nurses. While it was an early evolutionary phase in developing the discipline of nursing to learn about another field, it is no longer feasible today. Moreover, there are still some nurse anthropologists who are functioning as anthropologists rather than as transcultural nurses, and who are not developing knowledge and practices related to transcultural nursing. The new generation of transcultural nurse specialists are excellent role models to help these nurse anthropologists and others gain insight into the importance of being prepared in nursing with transcultural nursing specialization.

A series of sequenced seminars are essential to advance students' knowledge of transcultural nursing phenomenon. These theoretical, research, and clinical seminars help to develop a sound knowledge base, as students discover the meaning and expressions of care, health, and environment from a transcultural viewpoint. Students are actively challenged to transform knowledge derived from anthropology and other fields into a transcultural nursing perspective or to create new nursing ideas. This requires considerable skill and expertise of transcultural nursing faculty, and the use of their research insights. Indeed, transcultural nursing students cannot be borrowers of anthropological knowledge without addressing what these insights mean to the discipline of transcultural nursing. Comparative research and use of theories in the field are valuable to build and use transcultural nursing knowledge.

Transcultural nurse specialists are also expected to have experience in teaching, transcultural nursing, and in developing relevant courses and curricula. Learning different ways to be a consultant and to evaluate clinical and educational programs are part of the student's experiences while in the transcultural nursing program. The program is an intensive one and often requires more field research time than other master's or doctoral programs. But much depends on the student's goals and area in which she or he wants to be competent, plus previous experiences in the field.

Today, a cadre of transcultural nurse specialists has been prepared through master's, doctoral, and postdoctoral programs with in-depth knowledge of particular cultures (or subcultures). These specialists are in great demand, they have substantive knowledge and research skills in transcultural nursing and they value the importance of faculty-prepared mentors to guide them in becoming a specialist. They are specialists who are making significant breakthroughs in nursing and greatly extending or changing traditional views about the base of nursing knowledge and practice.

Certification of Transcultural Nurses

In order to assure competency of safe transcultural nursing practices to people of different cultures, nurses are now being certified by the Transcultural Nursing Society (TNS, 1989). This society is the first to provide worldwide certification of nurses in a specialty field. A certification board with transcultural nurse specialists has worked for a decade to develop criteria, procedures, and examinations for certification. It is open to nurses worldwide who have educational preparation in transcultural nursing or an equivalency, and who meet the other certification criteria. The applicant must also give evidence of basic clinical competency in transcultural nursing. This recent development has been encouraging and exciting to many nurses who have been prepared in, or are working in the field. It is public *recognition* and *protection* of an important new practitioner who is making noteworthy contributions in this country and overseas. For the author, it is a dream fulfilled. In addition, the *Journal of Transcultural Nursing* has been established since 1989 and carries relevant articles on transcultural nursing.

Career Opportunities and Roles of Transcultural Nurse Specialists

Career opportunities for transcultural nurse specialists are continuing to increase as health care and education systems become multiculturally developed. Cultural care clashes, conflicts, and imposition problems necessitate the use of transcultural nurse specialists. Indeed, for the first time in the history of nursing, there are specialists to deal with intercultural problems. The need for such work will increase with greater demands for the transcultural nurse specialist by the turn of the century and beyond.

The nursing profession, however, must take a more active stance to recognize transcultural nursing and invest in preparing specialists and generalists for the field. To date, this has not been the case. Nursing, however, could take an active leadership role in this area, since the groundwork has been well established, along with the idea of and need for transcultural nurses. More such nurses must be prepared, but also marketed with visible and specific role positions to enable them to function effectively. Otherwise, the crisis in cultural care will escalate in nursing.

The role of the transcultural nurse specialist prepared through master's, doctoral, and postdoctoral programs is a model to provide competent services in international education and service arenas. Currently, some transcultural nurse specialists are functioning as clinical specialists in outpatient clinics, hospitals, and community health systems serving those whole areas with respect to cultural problems that are curtailing therapeutic medical and nursing services.

While this is a pressing need with many challenges, it is stretching the one or two specialists very thin within 500-600–bed hospitals. For example, one specialist serves an Arab community hospital. There are far too many critical problems to handle in one shift. She is using her expertise well but needs more nurses like her to meet the critical needs. Another transcultural nurse specialist is working in a hospital where 68 percent of clients are Afro-Americans, as well as many of the staff, but there are also Anglo-American and Philippine nurses and physicians with very different values about care and treatment modes leading to intercultural tensions. This nurse specialist has been extremely valuable to identify and assist with nurse-client cultural problems and many other culturally based problems in the institution.

In another hospital with many Jewish clients, the part-time transcultural nurse specialist, likewise, has been most helpful to support traditional, conservative, and orthodox differential cultural needs that tend to be overlooked in general nursing services. This nurse has also been valuable to improve prenatal care to clients of different cultures who use the hospital. In another setting, where Hispanic clients are the dominant cultural group, they appreciate the fact that the transcultural nurse can assist them with their *culturally based needs and expectations.* In these different hospitals and community settings the transcultural nurse specialist is placed in teaching, enabling, mediating, and supportive roles, so the client's cultural rights are respected and understood as basic human rights in nursing care services.

Many obvious cultural needs may not be recognized by nurses, physicians, and social workers who are culturally ignorant. The specialist plays a major role in problem solving and in identifying *why* the client is upset, noncompliant, or resistant to health personnel expectations. Cultural clashes and tensions are evident among social workers, physicians, nurses, psychologists, administrators, finance officers, receptionists and many others who "can not get clients to comply" or "who must understand our goals if they want to help." Cultural conflicts lead to many unfortunate client-staff consequences.

More often, the transcultural nurse functions as a *crisis manager* for clients of different cultures (especially minority clients) when they refuse to take medications, treatments, or participate in surgery or group therapy. Fortunately, most nurses are kind and try to be helpful, but they gradually become frustrated if the client does not comply. Physicians with virtually no preparation in transcultural health tend to become more impatient and authoritative to client strangers when they fail to comply, such as refusing surgery, or when an Arab family does not want the physician to tell the client they have a disease such as cancer. Cultural reasons for noncompliance, etc., are usually unknown to nurses and physicians, who are eager "to get their job done."

Cultural imposition and *ethnocentrism* prevail in serious ways. Cultural conflicts are difficult to handle because most health personnel have no knowledge of the "why" of the client or family's behavior. They want instant actions and decisions that fit their treatment or care regimes. Explanation of cultural reasons for major value differences between clients and professional staff often requires considerable time and skill. Appropriate explanations and demonstrated ways to help staff and clients are needed, as well as ways to reduce cultural imposition or strong ethnocentric practices of nurses and other health personnel. Currently, problems of noncompliance and the lack of cooperation are the most recurrent problems that make nurses and physicians upset about clients of different or misunderstood cultural backgrounds (Leininger, 1978, 1989).

Transcultural nurse specialists and generalists have an almost incredible task ahead of them because of the great variety of intercultural nurse-client-physician problems. The author has frequently identified as many as 100 such problems in any week in a general hospital. Many of the problems reflect longstanding intercultural tensions and clashes between health personnel that influence the client's care, recovery, and general health status. Many intercultural problems are "swept under the rug" to avoid potential charges of race discrimination. But the problems remain as "smoldering embers" that flareup in different ways and influence quality of care provided.

Needless to say, many of these intercultural client-nurse–staff problems are not unique to U.S. hospitals but can be seen in many other places in the world because of increases in immigration, refugee placements, and unexpected arrivals in a country. In some countries, such as Sweden and Denmark, there are many political refugees from countries that nurses and physicians barely knew existed. Nurses are often forced to work instantly with these people and with no knowledge of their culture. Language difficulties are major hurdles, but understanding the people and their cues are even more troublesome, as well as the nature of the client's oppression. Indeed, nurses can be baffled in ways to work with such culturally different clients.

Recently, the author was a consultant in the Kingdom of Saudi Arabia at a hospital where nurses from 60 different cultures were employed. The majority of the nurses were from a Western country and serving people of the dominant Saudi culture. A Western administrator was keenly aware of the importance of transcultural nursing and of the role of transcultural nurse specialists to assess and improve client-nurse relationships. It was truly like a "United Nations" hospital, with many health personnel representing many cultures. Western nurses had their own professional values that were quite different from the Saudi clients' values, but it was encouraging to see the willingness of the staff to have a transcultural nurse specialist with them and discover areas that provided culturally congruent care, or lack of it in nursing practices. It became a positive experience for learning, discovering, and sharing cultural factors influencing transcultural nursing care. This hospital is an example of what most hospitals will be like in the future in all countries.

While the author has emphasized the transcultural nursing specialist practitioner and consultant's role in hospital settings, the specialist is also expected to have a *teaching career* in many schools of nursing. This specialist is much needed in most undergraduate and graduate nursing programs to develop new courses and programs in transcultural nursing, and new curricula with a multicultural focus. In addition, the specialist has opportunities to provide inservice programs, workshops, and conferences. The latter have increased five fold in the past decade in this country and overseas, but currently there is an insufficient number of well-prepared transcultural nurse specialists to meet this growing demand in the United States and overseas, especially in faculty roles.

The role of the transcultural nurse specialist in community health programs recently has become recognized in alternative, new, and traditional agencies. There is a rich career opportunity for transcultural nurse specialists to develop innovative transcultural health programs where infant mortality is high, and where the homeless and poor exist and do not use available health facilities. This is a critical need in which cultural factors are at last being recognized. For example, in one metropolitan community, the author and some transcultural nursing students took the lead in establishing a transcultural nursing and health community-based program for Arab immigrants and Italians. These projects have been so successful that other cultural groups and hospitals are now establishing similar community-based programs to improve health care and to help members of ethnic groups feel respected and "at home" in the community. There are other similar programs being established on the west, south, and east coasts of the United States with positive outcomes for Vietnamese, Haitians, Puerto Ricans, and others. The author's theory of Culture Care with specific community care programs has helped to increase the use of transcultural knowledge and transcultural nurses in hospitals and clinics (Leininger, 1988). Transcultural nurses are playing a major role in establishing new transcultural community nursing services to reach underserved culture groups and many cultural and subcultural groups in urban and rural communities.

Last, but not least, the transcultural nurse specialist has career opportunities to work directly with many different cultural groups in individual or group therapies in her or his own country and overseas. There are many opportunities to develop new models of health care based on transcultural care needs of cultural groups. There is also the opportunity to work with health anthropologists and members of other disciplines who are now moving into the health field as their "work place." There are opportunities for both inter- and multidisciplinary research to examine nurses' unique contributions with those of others. The field is open and has been tapped only in a limited way when one considers the opportunities to know and serve cultures on a worldwide basis. Education and service programs will increase with transnational policies and practices. The transcultural nurse specialist will play a major role in these endeavors, since she or he is one of the best-prepared workers in this area.

As the founder of and a leader in establishing the field of transcultural nursing three decades ago, and in preparing the largest number of transcultural nurse specialists and generalists, the author has found these experiences rewarding and exciting. However, there have been many hurdles, which a tenacious leader must overcome to see an important goal become a reality.

It is fulfilling to see the genuine enthusiasm of students entering the transcultural field. The field of transcultural nursing is growing markedly, with expanding career opportunities—already it is one of the most popular and attractive fields for nursing students. Transcultural nurse specialists will be well positioned to establish and build meaningful transcultural care programs in consultation, research, and teaching; these specialists in different cultural areas must use their preparation and international experiences to become more active in public policy and administrative decisions. Consumer requests for culturally sensitive care will greatly increase as part of their demand for human rights and ethical and cultural values. Transcultural nurse specialists and generalists will need to lead the way to provide this care, but money and human resources are much needed today and in the future. The National Center for Nursing is becoming more active and supportive of qualitative transcultural nursing research and educational programs; which is a good societal investment for our American multicultural society's health care needs.

The author is pleased that the field has been well established and that there are prepared role models to advance nursing into the future with a transcultural knowledge and practice base.

REFERENCES

Leininger, M. *Care: The essence of nursing & health.* Detroit: Wayne State University Press (first published by Charles B. Slack, 1984).

Leininger, M. (1988). Leininger's theory of nursing: Cultural care diversity and universality. In *Nursing Science Quarterly.* Parse, R. (Ed). Baltimore: Williamson and Wilkins Pub. Vol. 1 No. 4, pp. 152-160.

Leininger, M. (1970). *Nursing and anthropology: Two worlds to blend.* New York: John Wiley & Sons.

Leininger, M. (1978). *Transcultural nursing: Concepts, theories and practices.* New York: John Wiley & Sons, 1978, pp. 1-35.

Leininger, M. (1989). Transcultural nursing field study in hospital settings in an urban community (unpublished study, 1978-1988).

Transcultural Nursing Society Newsletter. (February, 1989). 9, 7. (1988).

CHAPTER **18**

The Primary Care Role in Occupational Health Nursing

Denise C. Murphy, RN, DrPH

Although primary care is generally considered an essential component in the practice of occupational health nursing, its differing definitions have left some nurses wondering how to categorize their services. Additional confusion results from the frequent misuse or misunderstanding of the terms health promotion and prevention.

DEFINING THE SCOPE OF PRACTICE

A review of pertinent primary care literature finds that Brown (1981) is one of the first occupational health nursing authors to use the term primary care. She identified four sets of correlative activities that comprise a comprehensive safety and health program: environmental monitoring, health surveillance, worker education, and primary care which she defines as "the identification of occupational or general health problems [by medical] and/or nursing diagnosis to determine the care required . . . in addition, the management and continued care of the individual as an ambulatory consumer or referral for specialized care and rehabilitation" (Brown, 1981).

Brown points out that there are many definitions of primary care. Some attempt to define primary care in terms of knowledge and skill of the provider. Others include in their definition the prevention of disease and the enhancement of health. Still, others think of primary care as consisting only of the first contact of an ill or injured individual with the provider.

Reprinted from *AAOHN Journal,* Vol 37, No. 11, with permission of Charles B. Slack, Inc., © 1989.

Brown seems to agree that primary care is two-dimensional in that it includes (1) the identification, management, or referral of health problems and (2) the maintenance of worker health by means of preventive and promotional health care actions (American Nurses Association, 1977).

Prevention and Health Promotion

Definitions for the terms health promotion and disease prevention also differ. The author believes, with Pender (1987), that although these terms are often used interchangeably, differences exist in both underlying motivation and goal orientation. (Both, however, seem to come under the umbrella of primary care.)

Pender defines the terms as follows:

- Health promotion: activities directed toward increasing the level of well being and actualizing the health potential of the individual (family, society). For example, initiating an employee fitness and exercise program (Figure 18-1).
- Prevention: three levels consisting of a) Primary—activities directed toward decreasing the probability of specific illness or dysfunction, including active protection against unnecessary stressors—for example, immunization against

Projected Outcomes of Worksite Health-Promotion Programs	
Employee benefits • Increased cardiopulmonary fitness • Weight control • Increased strength and endurance • Decreased stress and tension • Enjoyment	**Employer benefits** • Decreased absenteeism • Decreased health care costs • Increased productivity • Improved corporate image • Improved employee morale

FIGURE 18-1

Projected outcomes of worksite health promotion programs.

Health Promotion	Disease Prevention*
Not disease or health problem specific. Is approach behavior. Seeks to expand positive potential for health.	Is disease or health problem specific. Is avoidance behavior. Seeks to thwart occurrence of pathology.

** Pender uses the terms "prevention" and "health protection" interchangeably.*

FIGURE 18-2

Major differences between health promotion and disease prevention.

tetanus; b) Secondary—early detection and intervention, for example, testing for diabetes mellitus; c) Tertiary—activities with the goal of rehabilitation or restoration to optimal level of functioning, for example, post head injury therapy.

The major differences between health promotion and disease prevention are summarized in Figure 18-2. Using definitions given by both nursing experts (Brown, 1981; Pender, 1987), one can conceptualize the relationship among the terms and the application to occupational health nursing practice (Figure 18-3).

STANDARDS AND LEGISLATION

The extent to which occupational health nurses provide primary care to workers depends on:

- State legislation, for example, both the state workers' compensation law, which may require that the employer provide care for employees with work related injuries and/or illnesses, and the state's nurse practice act, which defines areas of professional responsibility.
- Federal legislation, for example, the Occupational Safety and Health Act (1970). Although this act does not require that employers maintain a health service, it does demand a plan for providing care for employees with work related illness or injury and a surveillance program for workers exposed to specified chemicals. Still, the extent of services provided differs significantly among workplaces.
- Company policy, which clearly defines the type of health services and the extent of care to be delivered by the staff.

It seems clear that primary care is a valid legal responsibility of the practicing occupational health nurse. In addition, nurses are supported in providing

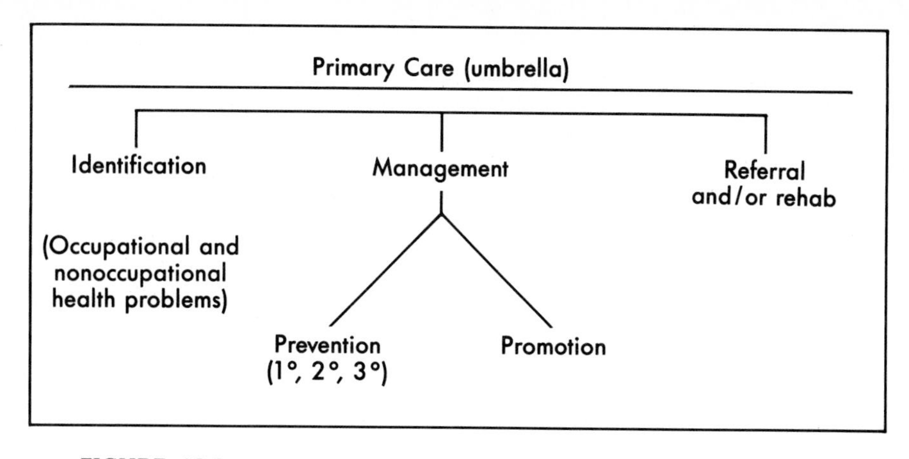

FIGURE 18-3

Using definitions given by nursing experts, one is able to come to an agreement concerning the relationship between the terms.

primary care by their own professional standards. The *Standards of Occupational Health Nursing Practice* (AAOHN, 1988) state that:

> "Occupational health nursing applies nursing principles in promoting the health of workers and maintaining a safe and healthful environment in occupational settings . . . occupational health nursing activities focus on health promotion, protection, maintenance, and restoration of health. The occupational health nurse is primarily concerned with the preventive approach to health care which includes early detection, health teaching, and counseling."

PRIMARY CARE IN ACTUAL PRACTICE

Rossi (1987) has examined the tasks of professional occupational health nurses from an international perspective. She was able to identify five categories of occupational health nursing activities, including curative and primary care, health promotion and preventive care, environmental surveillance, counseling, and administration. A survey of eight countries showed that the major portion of the occupational health nurse's workday was devoted to prevention (40% to 80%) and that treatment and screening dominated these activities (18% and 16%, respectively).

Similarly, the American Board for Occupational Health Nurses conducted a role delineation and validation project in an attempt to define the work activities and tasks of the profession. Burkeen (1984) reported that the two major performance domains and component tasks were 1) Direct care: data collection; assessment of worker health; formulation of nursing diagnoses; implementation, evaluation, and modification of care plans; interdisciplinary collaboration; and documentation of care; and 2) Education/counseling: assessment of worker needs; development, implementation, and evaluation of educational programs; and continuing education to maintain competence.

Recognizing both the professional and legal encouragement for the occupational health nurse to provide primary care, the author attempted to determine the extent to which primary care is actualized in the daily professional activities of practicing nurses.

Workplace Survey

Surveying her own workplace, the author determined that the company provided health promotion and preventive services that are initiated and encouraged by the medical and the nursing staff, and supported by the company administration. The professional staff at the company consists of 2 full time physicians, with specialists who are consulted on site as needed; a full time nursing supervisor; 3 full time nurses on day shift, 1 full time nurse on evening shift, and 1 full time nurse on night shift; and 2 clerical workers.

The purposes of the survey were to assist the staff in identifying how they spend their workday; to compare these findings with those of Rossi; and to stimulate discussion about modifying the daily professional activities of the occupational health nursing staff.

The one page survey (Figure 18-4) revealed information about the daily activities of the nursing staff. Data collection is done through many avenues every day. For example, all new employees undergo a prehiring physical examination including spirometry, vital signs, electrocardiography; chemical screening, urinalysis, and Dole tests (for any illegal drug use); audiometry; chest x-ray; tonometry; and interview. Periodic examinations are also conducted on selected worker groups—for example, vision testing and Dole tests performed on Department of Transportation employees. Also, many employees "walk-in" daily with both occupational and nonoccupational concerns.

At this point, appropriate intervention is performed. It may consist of treatment, education, or referral to an outside health professional. Planning for the care of the client takes place at many levels. It may occur on a one-to-one basis between worker and nurse, on an interdepartmental basis (for example, with the employee relations department, which oversees the employee assistance program); or on an intradepartmental level among health professionals in the health unit. Nurses reported minimal contact with some departments whose responsibilities related to the health of the work force (for example, the safety department), and improvement of communication was among their goals.

Health appraisal is conducted by the nurses, but most information is conveyed in traditional medical

Dear **: Please fill out the information below—it should only take about 10 minutes. Next to each activity, list 1) which activities you do here which fit that category, and 2) how much of your day (of 7 hours) is spent doing it. Be as accurate as possible.

Activity	Yes/No	Examples (my workplace)	# hours/day (out of 7)
1. Data collection (interview, charting, etc.).			
2. Planning health care with client.			
3. Participation in health appraisals (job placement, periodic, etc.).			
4. Participation in identification and treatment of occupational and nonoccupational injury or illness.			
5. Collaborate with other members of team:			
other nurses			
physicians			
safety, industrial hygiene			
other			
6. Counseling and health education:			
individual worker			
group			
7. Plan and implement screening or health promotion programs.			
8. Referrals and consultations.			
9. Use nursing diagnoses.			

FIGURE 18-4

Survey to identify daily work activities.

terminology (in contrast to data collection) with minimal use of nursing diagnoses.

A limited number of special programs are provided, such as a hearing conservation program for employees with high noise exposures, the immunization program for selected worker subgroups, and a combination program consisting of group health education and periodic retinal checks by a consulting ophthalmologist for employees who work with lasers. In addition, some short term programs have been implemented in response to specific situations—for example, when an employee was diagnosed as having Legionnaire's disease, the company arranged for formal health education classes, free literature pertaining to the topic, and blood tests on a worker/physician request basis. Likewise, tuberculin skin testing and chest x-rays were provided when one employee was diagnosed as having tuberculosis.

Summary of Survey Findings

On the basis of Brown's two dimensional definition of primary care and Pender's model, all of the nurses at the company do provide primary care most of their workday. Similarly, the breakdown of their daily professional tasks corresponds with the findings of Rossi. That is, treatment and screening are the two major specific activities conducted at the company. All activities listed in the AAOHN *Standards of Occupational Health Nursing Practice* (1988) are indeed conducted by the full time nursing staff on a daily basis.

The survey also identified areas of concern or interest to the nursing staff such as: increased and improved interactions and communication with some of the other departments, specifically, the safety department; increased involvement by the nursing staff in planning and implementation of health education programs; and increased health promotion activities, in addition to the smoking cessation clinics.

Additional Primary Care Roles

Two additional primary care roles for occupational health nurses are in safety and accident prevention programs and employee assistance programs. Safety and accident prevention programs encourage and assist management and employees to assume an active role in controlling environmental hazards and preventing accidents. Responsibilities of the occupational health nurse may include:

- Understanding what constitutes a safe working environment/making regular safety rounds.
- Being a leader or member of the safety committee and/or accident investigation team.
- Promoting and teaching first aid.
- Making reports/recommendations as needed.
- Utilizing data collected in applicable research.

Employee Assistance Programs (EAPs) have traditionally focused on alcohol abuse, but are now taking a broader approach and addressing emotional, behavioral, family, alcohol/other drugs, and financial and/or legal problems. While EAP services employ a variety of qualified professionals, a role specific to the occupational health nurse may include:

- Identifying troubled employees.
- Motivating employees to seek assistance.
- Referring employees to appropriate resources.
- Assisting supervisors in recognition/handling of troubled employees.
- Knowing a variety of resources.
- Following employees while out of work and assisting employees upon return to the job.

SUMMARY

Over the past decade, the provision of preventive and health promotion services by employers has noticeably increased. Whether the impetus for this interest is generated by legal, economic, or consumer/worker concerns, both employer and employee benefit. Providing such programs at an individual's place of employment offers many advantages, such as convenience of location, positive reinforcement from co-workers, and minimal or no cost to the employee. Also, participation is enhanced, since the workers go to their jobs on a regular basis (O'Donnell, 1984).

This is an optimal time for occupational health nurses to seize the opportunities (such as the examples provided) offered by the current legal, professional, and economic climate by becoming more active in demanding, providing, documenting, and being financially reimbursed for the daily competent provision of these primary care services.

REFERENCES

American Association of Occupational Health Nurses. (1988). *Standards of occupational health nursing practice.* Atlanta, GA: author.

American Nurses Association (ANA), Council of Primary Health Care Nurse Practitioners. (1977). *Operational guidelines.* Kansas City, MO: author.

Brown, M.L (1981). *Occupational health nursing,* p. 28. New York: Springer.

Burkeen, O., Corsico, R., & Harris, A. (1984). The American Board for Occupational Health Nurses Role Delineation and Validation Project. *AAOHN Journal, 32(10),* 522-525.

Occupational Safety and Health Act, 1970, P.L. 91-596.

O'Donnell, M.P. (1984). *The corporate perspective.* In O'Donnell, M.P., & Ainsworth, T. (Eds.), *Health promotion in the workplace (pp. 30-35).* New York: Wiley.

Pender, N. (1987). *Health promotion in nursing practice (2nd ed.),* pp. 4-5. Norwalk, CT: Appleton & Lange.

Rossi, K. (1987). Occupational health nursing worldwide. *AAOHN Journal, 35(11),* 505-509.

CHAPTER **19**

Established and Emerging Roles in School Nursing

Judith B. Igoe, RN, MS, FAAN

This is the 'Age of the Parenthesis.' To paraphrase Naisbett, "Society, is not where it used to be or where it wants to be, but the mind change has occurred. Modifications in behavior, however, have yet to come" (Naisbett, 1984, p. 38). We are in the midst of an interlude, a societal pause during which people take stock of the past and present, and contemplate the future; anxieties rise and there are indications that change is about to begin.

How true these words are today, particularly in terms of our health care trends and policies. The public is becoming increasingly discontented with a health care system that seems to be floundering in the face of spiraling costs, depersonalization, and professional rivalries. Even school health, a frequently overlooked affiliate of the health system, is showing signs of unrest. Throughout the country there are many indications that school boards, parents, and health professionals want a new blueprint for school health (Califano, 1988). However, specific widespread reforms have yet to materialize.

People need and want a more convenient, affordable child health system. By extending the boundaries of the plan for delivery of traditional health care to include school nurse practitioners and school-based clinics, primary health care would be within easy reach of every girl and boy. However, this is a controversial approach and many oppose it (Cormany, 1987). One group argues school-based health services will undoubtedly be fragmented and will interfere with parental rights. Others worry about the increasing tendency to employ nurse practitioners; and what long-range consequences this practice might have for medicine, nursing, and the health care industry, as well as for the consumer. Still others point out that an unprecedented "14% to 19% of children under age 13 have no health insurance coverage" (Children's Defense Fund, 1988) which automatically deprives them of most health services, yet another group cries for the "new public health" and argues that school health should be exclusively health promotion (Kolbe, 1985; Levin, 1987). Therefore the 'Age of Parenthesis' is filled with a number of very serious questions that have implications for health policy.

The health issues of school age youth are increasingly the result of complex social and emotional problems which have divided family life and left children at high risk for: violence related health problems, infections, diseases one assumed were eradicated a decade ago, and with myriad mental health disturbances which will diminish their motivation to do well in school (Conger, 1988). Consequently, those providing health services to this age group will need to be prepared to address not only

Adapted from "School Nursing and School Health" in J. N. Natapoff and R. R. Wieczorek (Eds.), *Maternal Child Health Policy: A Nursing Perspective,* with permission of Springer Publishing Co., Inc., © 1990.

physical health problems but the psychosocial-cultural problems as well. Unfortunately one also needs to wonder if developmental theories which originated in another era under much different social circumstances still hold true today.

THE ROLES OF SCHOOL HEALTH PERSONNEL AND SCHOOL NURSES: AN ARGUMENT IN FAVOR OF CHANGE

Several kinds of personnel are directly and indirectly involved in the operation of the school health programs. Figure 19-1 identifies the professionals most frequently called upon to provide one or more of the care components of school health. With the exception of nurses and physicians, none are expected to gain any special credentials and skill in school health in order to be certified for this type of work. In fact, certification is not a universal requirement for physicians and nurses. They, too, may assume positions with little or no preparation in the field, or any knowledge of the key elements of school health.

Until recently, registered nurses outnumbered other members of the school health team. However, school counselors are increasingly being called upon to assist with the mental health problems school age youth experience, in addition to their responsibilities for academic and career counseling. Department of Education figures indicate the number of school counselors now exceeds the school nurse aggregate by

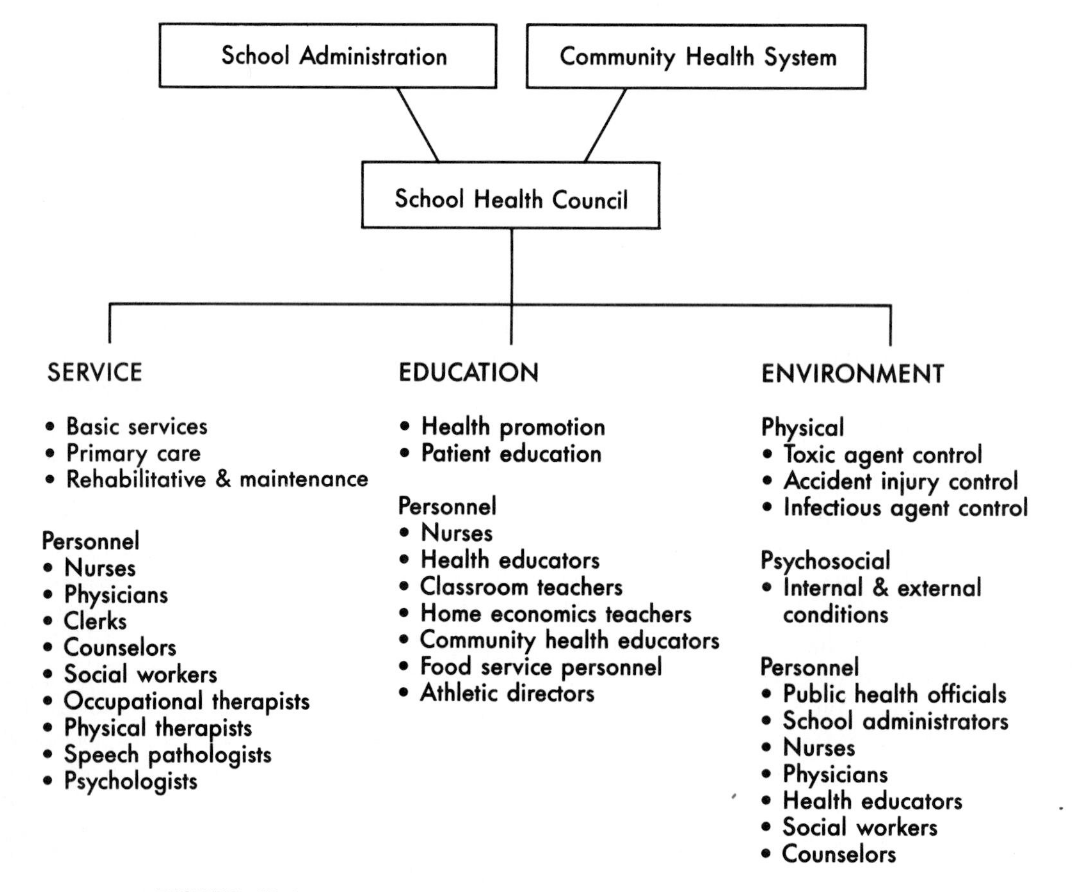

FIGURE 19-1

Nature and organization of school health. (From School Health Programs, University of Colorado Health Sciences Center, 1989.)

approximately 3 to 1 (Hinson, American School Counselor Association, personal communication, March 16, 1988). While there is a growing abundance of school counselors, the situation with school physicians is exactly the opposite. School physicians are almost extinct if the membership records of the American School Health Association for 1987 are any indication. As of 1988, the total number of physician members was 120 (American School Health Association, personal communication, March 16, 1988). The American Medical Association does not keep track of the number of school doctors.

There are two specialty associations with the greatest interest in school health: pediatrics and family medicine. The American Academy of Pediatrics does not keep a record of the number of their members who are in school health. However, there is the suggestion that family medicine physicians are becoming very interested in school health. In a recent survey of 28,000 members of the American Academy of Family Physicians, 75-80% reported they are associated as consultants with school health programs (Zimont, personal communication, March 16, 1988). School health educators are increasing in number and the American School Health Association reports that of approximately 3500 members, approximately 1600 are school health educators (American School Health Association, personal communication, April 13, 1989). However, there evidently is no national estimate of the actual number of health educators working in schools today.

There are a number of unique characteristics which distinguish the specialty of school nursing from other nursing specialties. The school nurse is in what the sociologists call "a boundary dweller position." According to Wall and Adams (1974), "a boundary position is one in which some members of the role set are located in a different system—another unit within the same organization or another organization. An organization member who occupies such a position (boundary dweller) finds himself/herself in a structurally unique position." The natural inclination of most boundary dwellers who are unaware of this phenomenon is to try to rid themselves of any traits which sustain the outsider or boundary dweller image, because this position has limited power and control. In the case of school nurses, the enticement is to take on the characteristics of classroom teachers. Consequently the nurse soon relinquishes her medical terminology, for example, to ease the sense of differentness. Uniforms obviously go because they make one stand out from the crowd. Even the school clinic is relabeled a 'health office' in an effort to become like everybody else. Essentially, every effort is made to stay away from any special health procedures which are obviously out of place because this is a school, not a clinic.

What most people, including school nurses, do not realize is the perilous nature of the boundary dweller position. That is, the conflicting expectations people have toward anyone in this position. There is danger in the school nurse abandoning the nurse role to become a teacher (either informally or formally). They may be suspect in their original organizations and an outsider in the new system. Boundary dwellers who survive gain their power and control within the system/organization in which they are the same as the other members of the role set. If this strategy is used, the knowledgeable boundary dweller will convince this system to exert its power (on behalf of the boundary dweller) on the other organization in which he/she is in the boundary dweller position. In school nursing this may be difficult if the alliance between nursing and school nursing has not been maintained.

Isolation is another experience which interferes with the practice of school and occupational health nursing. As the only member of the health field in a school organization, the school nurse may go for long periods of time without meeting with other school nurses. This kind of isolation certainly contributes to the onset of the boundary-dweller effect.

Over the years nurses in school health received a number of mixed messages regarding the importance of their work. During their own educational preparation as nurses they were very likely told the school health program is secondary to the overall goal of the school which is education. Inherent in this message obviously is the implication that the school nurse is of secondary importance to the organization. We cannot place the blame on education for setting these limits. In reality early public health nursing leaders offered this explanation (Freeman & Heinrich, 1981). Ironically, the National Education Association has maintained, since 1927, that health is the *first* objective of education and consequently placed more importance on the role of the nurse in these settings than nursing leaders did (Brown, 1952).

The 'dilution effect' is yet another example of the ways in which the school-nurse role has been compromised and sapped over the years. By assigning nurses to literally thousands of students in four, five, six, or more schools, the service they can provide becomes so watered down it is meaningless. In these instances nurses are nursing their cars, not the students, as they spend their day driving from school to school. The recommended ratio of school nurses to students in the general school population is 1:750 (ANA, 1983).

An interesting way to illustrate the significance of the dilution effect was recently reported by the medical director of an urban school district in the South. She kept tract of the number of encounters one school nurse had when the nurse/pupil ratio was 1:1000. This figure was then compared with the number of encounters another nurse had with a much higher nurse/pupil ratio. The result was that the nurse with the lower ratio actually saw 66% more students than the nurse with the higher number of schools and students. Obviously many variables need to be taken into account for this investigation. Nevertheless, this creative school physician identified a way to approach the study of the effect of reduced ratios of nurses to students. Hopefully, other school nurses will be intrigued by this idea and pursue it further.

THE SCHOOL NURSE PRACTITIONER ROLE

Over the past 19 years, numerous experimental health programs were launched throughout the United States, the U.S. Virgin Islands, and Department of Defense schools in Europe. In all these programs, the one variable that remains constant is the introduction of the school nurse practitioner (SNP). The school nurse practitioner program originated at the University of Colorado in 1969 under the direction of Ms. Aria Rosner, supervisor of nurses for the Denver Public Schools and Drs. Loretta Ford and Henry Silver from the University of Colorado Health Sciences Center.

Generally, school nurse practitioners are experienced school nurses who have updated their knowledge and skills according to a set of educational guidelines endorsed in 1977 by the American Nurses' Association, the American School Health Association, and the National Association of School Nurses (known then as the Department of School Nurses/ National Education Association). (American Nurses' Association, American School Health Association and Department of School Nurses/National Education Association, 1977). These nurses are prepared to provide:

- Primary health care services such as physical examinations and health histories for well-child check-ups and for the evaluation of sick and injured children. Health counseling and consumer participation are a part of every health care plan. Inherent in these activities are certain duties performed by nurses that distinguish nursing from medicine.
- Neurodevelopmental evaluations for children who fail basic neurological screenings. The evaluations were developed by Dr. Melvin Levine at Harvard Medical School in conjunction with Boston Children's Hospital and are intended to yield descriptive information about the child's strengths and weaknesses in processing information, a neurological skill that is essential to learning.

In considering the functions of the SNP, some observers believe their skill in performing neurodevelopmental evaluations is especially helpful in the efficient screening of children with disabilities. For example, the present method of evaluating these students is a separate comprehensive assessment by every related (or special) services personnel (e.g., psychologist, speech pathologist, etc.); hence the student could be subjected to numerous evaluations. Furthermore, given the number of times health problems are the underlying cause of a suspected learning disorder and have gone unnoticed, many people believe every child should have an initial health evaluation. It might prove more effective, efficient, and economical to have the nurse evaluate the children first. Team members could then use the nurses' evaluations, including the neurodevelopmental data, to selectively decide who else should evaluate the child. This type of approach would individualize the process, probably reduce the cost considerably but unfortunately will be difficult to do because of "turf" issues and state regulations that identify a cadre of professionals whose evaluations are part of the diagnostic work-up to which the child is entitled. Nevertheless it is worth the struggle because it moves children out of the never-ending diagnostic phase and onto some type of remediation. In limited instances in which this type of triage has been tried using SNPs, such as in Gary, Indiana, the professionals who saw a child following the SNP's evaluation also tended to use more complex diagnostic evaluation tools than previously and to develop more specific recommendations for the individualized educational plan.

Between 1979 and 1984, the Robert Wood Johnson Foundation conducted the largest study of school health ever undertaken. Four states were involved: Colorado, North Dakota, New York, and Utah. The overall goal of the study was to determine if school health programs staffed by school nurse practitioners with medical consultation could play a greater role in providing health services to children (Meeker et al., 1986). The findings from the study are summarized here:

- SNPs were capable of handling 87% of the presenting health problems within the school setting.
- 97% of the health problems identified were resolved.
- Overlap in the identification of health problems was minimal.
- The traditional activities of screening and basic-level care were discharged primarily by others, while the school nurse practitioner provided primary level care, immunizations, and physican examinations.
- The cost of school nurse practitioner care ($100/child/year) unfortunately has only been compared with the cost of traditional school health services, the wrong comparison. It makes far more sense to compare the cost of school-based primary health care provided by school nurse practitioners with the cost of primary health care in other community settings. Blim (1986) reported that figure to be $498/year in 1983.

Goodwin summarized the initial studies of the SNP role by reviewing all published research of the new role (Goodwin & Burgess, 1985). She concluded that when considered cumulatively, the data indicate that nurse practitioners in schools are different from regular school nurses in terms of several important process variables including: emphasis on and specificity of assessment and management skills; time devoted to individual students' problem identification skills; attention to children with special physical, behavioral, or learning needs, and number of contacts with parents, school personnel, and other health professionals.

Findings from two studies show that SNPs exclude fewer children from school because of illness or injury. The findings on referral rates have been mixed with one study showing fewer referrals for SNPs, two showing no differences in referral rates between SNPs and regular school nurses, and one indicating an increase in referrals following SNP training, as compared to previously.

As a variable, "referral rate" presents some methodological concerns as the accuracy of the decisions to refer and the outcomes of the referrals actually are the important considerations. The findings from three studies do suggest that SNPs' referrals and exclusions result in more positive outcomes than those of regular school nurses.

Although the process variable data support the belief that nurse practitioners in schools are making valuable contributions to the effectiveness of school health services, the question remains about the influence of institutional factors on nurse practitioner effectiveness. The SNPs perceive a large number of institutional impediments. Meanwhile, the evidence to date suggests that nurse practitioners in schools do increase and improve health services. Susan Sobolewski (1981), a school nurse supervisor, adds to Goodwin's findings with her article on the cost effectiveness of the SNP, concluding that SNPs were cost-effective in her school district in Arizona.

THE ROLE OF THE COMMUNITY HEALTH NURSE SPECIALIST FOR SCHOOL AGE YOUTH

In addition to the role of the school nurse practitioner, there will be a need in schools for a nurse whose skills are in the program management arena. The Robert Wood Johnson study of school nurse practitioners documented the difficulty SNPs had with these skills.

Provided that primary care is institutionalized in schools and school nurses decide they wish to remain in leadership roles in school health, they will need additional human resources. Therefore, a new and different school nurse role has been proposed by the faculty at the University of Colorado. This school nurse would be: (a) a program planner; (b) epidemiologist; (c) case manager; and (d) provider of health promotion services to groups of students (Igoe, 1987). Together, this community health nurse specialist for school age youth (the program manager) and the school nurse practitioner (the clinician) will have the expertise to effectively establish and operate the community nursing organizations for school age youth which have been previously described.

THE ROLE OF THE SCHOOL NURSE WORKING WITH HANDICAPPED CHILDREN

SNPs, along with all school nurses, care for children with disabilities, handicapping conditions, and chronic disease. In 1980 the American Nurses' Association, the National Association of School Nurses, and the American School Health Association defined the role of the nurse in caring for these children as fourfold:

- To develop a specific health care plan as the health component of the individualized educational plan
- To coordinate the health services and information related to the students' functioning at school
- To serve as the children's advocate in ensuring that a safety program exists, as needed
- To serve as a member of the school team evaluating these children and provide the necessary health information to ensure that health problems do not interfere with learning (ANA, 1980).

Currently, more than 4,500 school nurses nationwide have participated in a short-term educational program which offers academic credit and enables them to fulfill this role. The School Nurse Achievement Program (SNAP), offered by the University of Colorado School of Nursing, has had the following effects (Goodwin & Smith, 1982):

- School nurses who took SNAP reported significant increases in their knowledge and skills. For example, skill areas which increased included modification of screening procedures, modification of the school's environment to make it safer for children with handicaps, writing the health component of individual education plans, and evaluating the effectiveness of nursing intervention.
- The nurse's attitudes changed. In fact, 61% of the nurses said SNAP caused positive changes in the way they perceived disabled students, and 42% reported positive changes in their attitudes.
- School principals whose nurses took SNAP were very positive about the course. They said the nurses made clearer and more concise health recommendations, anticipated problems earlier so they could be prevented, and planned earlier to meet the health needs of handicapped children.
- 4,500 children with disabilities, handicaps, and chronic diseases in 18 states received comprehensive care as each nurse followed a child throughout the 8-week course.

While this program does not prepare nurses to become nurse practitioners, it is a step in the right direction in the sense that it is restoring a clinical component to the school nurse role. Currently a new teaching program from the University of Colorado is being prepared for school nurses nationwide. Known as the Center City/USA Project, this course, which is at the graduate level, is intended to improve the program management skills and critical thinking ability of nurses currently employed in school health. A case study format is used for this course of study and school nurses are introduced to numerous learning experiences that are intended to improve their leadership skills.

Conclusion

The role of the school nurse has been ambiguous and of secondary importance in the past; a number of factors have contributed to this dilemma. Change, of course, is inevitable but how and to what end remain debatable issues.

In recent years, there are numerous indications that health and education as societal institutions are blending. Boundaries which distinguish one professional from another are not as clear as previously and the consequences of this situation, coupled with other societal changes, are generally unknown at this time. As all of this occurs, it places confusing demands for change on traditional school health programs. Some teachers, for example, do not and will not provide nursing services and others welcome the opportunity. This leaves school attorneys and policy makers bewildered and confused about what approach to take.

Ideally each school probably needs a nurse. Pragmatically, however, it is doubtful this demand could be met in terms of available nurses and financing required for such an arrangement. Unfortunately, school nurses have been reluctant to consider the use of health clerks in many areas of this country; this limits their ability to extend their efforts through the process of delegation. Given this dilemma, should schools become the next major public health frontier for the delivery of primary health care?

Indeed, the 'mind change' aspects of this Age of Parenthesis are actively underway in the field of school health. School health moved beyond a first aid station and referral agency. New effective roles and practice standards for school nurses have been conceptualized, established, and evaluated. The nature of school health has attracted public attention and is a topic of debate. School nurse and school health organizations have far more visibility these days as they speak on behalf of their membership in support of measures to improve health care in schools. For indeed, the actual need for school health has become painfully apparent as children and youth struggle with a host of new morbidities. The school health program still is not where it needs to be, an effective community-based, nurse-managed health center for school-aged children and youth. It is the exact nature of this change and how to make it happen that makes the future of this area of public health particularly challenging and important to examine at this time. The situation is precarious. Critical questions remain to be answered. The potential benefits for all far outweigh the struggle which lies ahead.

REFERENCES

American Nurses' Association Division of Nursing Practice, the American School Health Association, and the National Association of School Nurses [A Statement]. (1980). *School nurses working with handicapped children.* (ANA Publication No. NP-60).

American Nurses' Association. (1983). *Standards of school nursing practice.* Kansas City, MO: Author.

American Nurses' Association, American School Health Association & Department of School Nurses/National Education Association [Joint Statement] (1977). *Guidelines on educational preparation and competencies of the school nurse practitioner.* Kansas City, MO.

American School Health Association, (March 16, 1988). Personal Communication.

American School Health Association, (April 13, 1989), Personal Communication.

Blim, R. D. (1986). Financing well-child care. *Well-Child Care* (Report of the Seventeenth Ross Roundtable on Critical Approaches to Common Pediatric Problems). Columbus, OH: Ross Laboratories.

Brown, E. S. (1952). The role of the nurse in the school health program. *Journal of School Health, 22,* (8).

Califano, J. A., Jr. (1988, March 20). The health-care chaos. *The New York Times Magazine,* 44, 46, 56-58.

Children's Defense Fund's legislative agenda for the 100th Congress: (1988, February/March). *CDF Reports 9* (9), 6.

Conger, J. J. (1988). *Hostages to Fortune: Youth, values and the public interest. American Psychologist.* 43, 291-300.

Cormany, V. (Ed. Chairman). (1987). School-based clinics [Special Issue]. *School Nurse,* (March/April).

Freeman, R. B. & Heinrich, J. (1981). *Community health nursing practice* (2nd ed.). Philadelphia: W. B. Saunders.

Goodwin, L. D., & Burgess, H. (1985). *School nurse practitioner program: Summary of evaluation activities from 1977-1984.* Unpublished manuscript, University of Colorado, School of Nursing, Denver.

Goodwin, L. D., & Smith, A. N. (1982). School nurse achievement program: Part II evaluation components: *Journal of School Health,* 52, 608-610.

Hinson, B. (March 16, 1988). American School Counselor Association. Personal Communication.

Igoe, J. B. (1987). *The role of community health nursing specialist working with school age youth.* Unpublished manuscript, University of Colorado Health Sciences Center, School of Nursing, Denver.

Kolbe, L. J., (1985, October). Indicators for planning monitoring school health programs. Paper presented for *The Symposium on Indicators of Health Promotion,* University of California, Los Angeles, California.

Levin, L. S., (1987). The school of the new public health. *Health Promotion, 2*(2), 91-94.

Meeker, R. J., DeAngeles, C., Berman, B., Freeman, H. E., & Oda, D. (1986). A comprehensive school health initiative. *Image: Journal of Nursing Scholarship, 18*(3), 86-91.

Naisbett, J. (1984). Megatrends (p. 38). New York: Warner Books.

Sobolewski, S. D. (1981). Cost-effective school nurse practitioner services. *Journal of School Health, 51,* 585-586.

Wall, J. A., & Adams, J. S. (1974). Some variables affecting a constituents evaluations of and behavior toward a boundary role occupant. *Organizational Behavior and Human Performance, 11,* 390-408.

Zimont, C. (March 16, 1988). Personal Communication: Reprinted with permission from *Life Plan,* available through The Center for Corporate Health Promotion, Inc., Reston, Va.

CHAPTER 20

Home Care Nursing Practice: The New Frontier

Molly A. Rose, RN, MSN

Home care nursing as it exists today, denotes different things to different people. Some feel that home care is an ongoing frontier, not necessarily a new one. The demand and need for home care services of various types are extremely evident. Home care is, indeed, a wide frontier to be developed. Home care is an expanding and integral component of the health care delivery system that provides health services to individuals and families, across the life cycle, in their places of residence. The services provided depend on the needs of the individual and the family. These services may include nursing care, medical care, physical therapy, speech therapy, occupational therapy, nutritional counseling, social services, the provision of medical equipment, and the services of home health aides and homemakers. The goals of home care are to promote, maintain, or restore health; to minimize the effect of illness and disability; or to allow for a peaceful death.

Home care is essential for those who are discharged from the hospital in need of skilled nursing care, which is primarily Medicare-reimbursed care. However, there is also a definite need for home care to be more than just a Medicare-regulated type of care. Toward that end, this article will (1) present a brief history of home care nursing to show some similarities between the past and the present home care situations, (2) discuss three of the several issues that affect home care nursing today—the changing practice of home care nursing, the lack of chronic monitoring and supportive and preventive home care, and methods of financing home care, and (3) provide some general strategies to help shape the future of home care, including some examples of innovative home care programs existing today. Other issues concerning home care for the older adult (including care for the chronically ill) are high-technology home care, education, and gaps in services—all of which are discussed in more depth elsewhere in this issue.

Reprinted from *Holistic Nursing Practice,* Vol. 3, No. 2, with permission of Aspen Publishers, Inc., © 1989.

HOME CARE NURSING: YESTERDAY

To better understand the home care climate of today, it is helpful to look at the history of home care nursing. The current health care delivery system is one that encourages divisiveness and competition among providers, which promote fragmentation and a potentially lower quality of care.[1] To what, then, can this disruption in the system be attributed? The history of home care and home care nursing demonstrates that divisiveness and competition, although currently intense, are not unique to today's health care system. History also reveals the origins of creative and innovative home care programs that exist today.

Home care began in the United States in 1796, when the Boston Dispensary provided care at home for the sick poor. In 1877, the New York City Mission and the New York Society for Ethical Culture were the first establishments to hire a graduate nurse (from Bellevue Hospital's first nursing class) to provide nursing care and religious instruction for the sick in their homes.[2] Voluntary (non-government) agencies, later to become visiting nurse associations, opened their doors in Buffalo, Boston, and Philadelphia in 1885 and 1886. The home care nurses provided nursing care to the sick and taught families cleanliness and proper care of the sick. In 1889, the Los Angeles County Health Department became the first official (operated by a local government) agency to provide such services. The Henry Street Settlement House in New York City, which was founded by Lillian Wald in 1893, is an example of an innovative nursing program. Wald and other nurses, who moved into the community in which they practiced, provided home care nursing to the sick poor. In addition to caring for the ill at home, Wald was instrumental in the development of payment by insurance companies for nursing services. In 1909, she helped establish the first home nursing program for workers at the Metropolitan Life Insurance Company. This home nursing component emphasized health promotion, not merely care for the sick worker. She was also politically active, fighting for better living conditions in tenements, pure food laws, better parks and recreation centers, and assistance for immigrants.[3]

By 1912, home care nursing was supported by both public and private funds through state and city boards of health, visiting nurse associations, hospitals, and churches.[4] Divisiveness and competition developed. The official agencies (public, tax-supported organizations such as health departments) and the voluntary agencies (the visiting nurse associations) soon began arguing over who should be providing preventive services to the public. Public health nurses were told by the health officers of the official agencies that if they gave bedside care to the sick, they were not public health nurses and could not teach prevention. Yet, visiting nurses saw caring for the sick as a way to gain access to families in greatest need of health education. Buhler-Wilkerson summed up this confusion of who was providing what type of care in the home by stating that "despite their failed ideal, public health nurses went on caring for at least some of the public — in sickness or in health — but rarely the same nurse for both."[5]

In the late 1940s, hospitals began to enter the home care field. This was probably a result of the discovery of antibiotics and immunizations and the shift of health care problems away from infectious diseases to chronic diseases. The Montefiore Hospital Home Care Program in New York City, one of the first hospital-based home care programs, began in 1947. Soon after the enactment of Medicare in 1966, home care agencies significantly increased because of the ability to receive reimbursement; illness care began to proliferate competition.

HOME CARE NURSING: TODAY

Over the last 20 years, home care agencies have quadrupled in number.[6] The rise in hospital-based programs, health maintenance organization (HMO) programs, and proprietary or profit-making agencies affects competition and the fragmentation of home care today. The prospective payment system (diagnosis related groups) and technological advances encourage an emphasis on an illness-focused type of care in the home.

The Changing Practice of the Home Care Nurse

Nurses in hospitals, because of the acuity of the patients and the shortage in staffing, often do not have the time to teach self-care skills as they once did. People are sent home from the hospital in need of skilled nursing care, which may involve such procedures as providing intravenous antibiotics or chemotherapy and total parenteral nutrition. In a survey of 35 home care agencies, 83 percent reported seeing more acute and less stable patients than in the past, including people discharged home directly from intensive care units with catheters and continuous intravenous lines in place and open or incompletely healed wounds.[7] Home care nurses, who previously cared for less acutely ill patients, have to become efficient in high-technology tasks. Hospital nurses are being recruited into home care because of their high-technology skills. Yet, they often are not familiar with the other activities of the home care nurse (such as teaching, counseling, referring, supervising, documenting, and case managing).

With many home care agencies being reimbursed by Medicare, nurses are facing a high rate of retroactive denials because of the restrictive regulations. This is a major concern of nurses in primarily Medicare-generated home care agencies. To meet Medicare criteria, clients must need intermittent care and be homebound, except for medical visits. Often nurses must discontinue care when needs continue to exist but do not fit the Medicare regulations. This puts nurses in the precarious situation of having to base their nursing care on an illness-focused model, many times leaving the client in the home with unmet health needs. Griffith[8] stated that the home care nurse of today is often penalized for giving the kind of care that historically elevated home care as the alternative to institutionalization.

Lack of supportive and preventive home care

Although Medicare and third party payers emphasize episodic, curative, or restorative nursing care in the home, clients also need to receive supportive care (for the chronically ill) that emphasizes home management and comprehensive services. Clients also need distributive nursing care that emphasizes health promotion and disease prevention activities. Unfortunately, these services are not reimbursable. Andreoli and Musser[9] predict that as the number of older people increases, the need for at-home health promotion and education will flourish. The decrease in extended families and social support systems, the influx of other cultures (such as Latinos and Indochinese refugees), the high infant mortality rates in certain areas, the growing homeless population, and the trend toward greater consumer awareness and interest in self-care also contribute to the need for home care that provides services in addition to the skilled nursing care valued by the third party reimbursement system.

Home care financing

Although the actual number is difficult to ascertain, there are many people in the United States who cannot afford home care services. At present, there are over 37 million people who have no medical insurance or coverage. Seventy percent of these are employed workers and their families.[10] As for the poor, in 1984 Medicaid covered less than 50 percent of persons below the federal poverty level.[11] An example of those who are and will be affected by this concern is people with acquired immunodeficiency syndrome (AIDS), who often lose their insurance benefits or may not qualify for Medicaid and are waiting for Medicare benefits but who have many complex home care needs.

With limited public funds and increased competition, many agencies that once provided home care to the indigent are closing. After providing uncompensated care to the medically indigent since its founding in 1889, the Chicago Visiting Nurse Association was forced to almost entirely close its doors to the uninsured in May 1986. The Association nurses were concerned and frustrated about who would care for the poor in Chicago who need home care services.[12] There are few and sometimes no nonprofit home health agencies or other types of funded programs available, which leaves the indigent without a source of home care services.

HOME CARE NURSING: STRATEGIES FOR A NEW FRONTIER

The possibilities for developing a new frontier in home care are endless for creative nurses providing home care, nurses in home care administration, and other nurses interested in the field. However, this must be done within today's economic and political home care climate.

The Changing Practice of Home Care Nursing

Home care nurses are generalists and provide a variety of nursing activities. They also come from all the types of basic nursing education programs and all types of nursing past experiences. Therefore, home care nurses have varied continuing education needs. Inservice education in home care often involves improving skills in patient assessment, high-technology procedures, health education, and documentation. Public health content also needs to be included. A nurse in Maryland, for example, identified the need to provide public health content (such as community assessment, program planning, policy making, and focus of the nurse in the home) to home care nurses and gave a series of inservice workshops.[13] Home care nursing administrators with baccalaureate and master's degrees should also seek out continuing education that will provide information and skills to develop creative programs that will influence positive changes in the home care field. Nurses must also become politically active and involved in research.

Lack of Supportive and Preventive Care

Nurses in home care must be aware of the home care needs of the community that they serve. The need for home care for the chronically ill cannot be overemphasized. The growing number of homeless individuals and families, the indigent, people affected by the AIDS epidemic, and Indochinese and Hispanic refugees are other examples of those in need of special consideration. Creative strategies to devise innovative programs in home care must be developed. Nurses should look for ways to expand beyond the Medicare population, such as providing case management and home maintenance and finding other sources of funding. Multidisciplinary collaboration, knowledge of potential funding sources, and skill in grant proposal writing are essential. Nurses must also continue to provide health promotion and disease prevention in their practices. The Medicare reimbursement policy for health promotion activities is being studied to determine the need and the frequency with which nurses teach health promotion in home care. It is extremely important for nurses to document all health promotion activities.

Home care nurses must demonstrate that their services make a vital contribution to the health of individuals, families, and the community. This can be achieved by participating in, recommending, and conducting research studies with strong evaluation tools. Examples of relevant research are studies in the home on the outcomes of nursing interventions that promote health, a classification tool that measures types of nursing activities in the home, quality of life changes during or after home care, use of case management models, the effect of home care on identified high-risk groups, the psychological and economic effects of comprehensive programs for the chronically ill, and studies on home care and creative funding sources for the indigent. McKay and Segall[14] recommend the use of ethnomethodology in addition to the usual quantitative data (mortality and morbidity statistics) used in community assessments. Ethnography is a research method that considers the values and perceptions of individuals and society—how people in the community or high-risk groups view their world, an important aspect of health planning.

Home Care Financing

Nurses in home care practice and administration must also use political strategies to influence, develop, and implement health policy. To be an advocate for the actual or potential home care client, the nurse must know the political environment. Lobbying efforts of both state and national home care associations have encouraged directives to federal regulators to devise an equitable reimbursement system based on accurate data.[15] Legislation to allow third party reimbursement for nurses who provide health promotion is important. The bill currently in committee in Congress that requires employers to provide full-time employees with minimal, essential health care coverage might partially help the access problem. It is time for nurses to become politically involved in the enactment of a national health insurance program. This would be a major change in the system that would assure the right to health care (including home care) for everyone.

Examples of Current Innovative Home Care Programs

Home care nursing may involve a wide range of activities, age groups, and service agencies. There are types of home care that tend to be more holistic and use nursing models opposed to medical-illness models. These may include, among others, hospices, home care programs designed around the physical and many psychosocial problems of people with AIDS, maternal-child health programs for the poor, and comprehensive services to prevent early institutionalization of the chronically ill. The Block Nurse Program, an example of such a program, evolved during a project that studied home care for dying children. The use of the nurse who lived closest to the child was tested and found to be a successful method to assign nurses.[16]

The Block Nurse Model of home care for elderly people has been implemented in a section of St. Paul, Minnesota. The program is coordinated through the county health nursing service, which also provides quality control, inservice education, utilization review, Medicaid and Medicare supervision, and administrative services. Of the 40 registered nurses who live in the designated area, 18 chose to be block nurses. They are on call and are paid an hourly rate when actually visiting in the homes. The nurses, in addition to providing direct nursing services for a certain number of people, are also involved in prevention and case-finding activities. They must fulfill a continuing education requirement by completing an additional 60 hours of gerontological nursing courses. Physicians (as backups), peer counselors, and other community resources are involved in the process. The program is paid for largely through a grant (50%); client fee system (23.7%); and Medicare, Medicaid, or third party payments (21.9%).[17]

Innovative home care programs are being developed for individuals who would otherwise be institutionalized. Hawaii's Nursing Home Without Walls (NHWW) is one example of such a home care program. NHWW provides health and social services to Medicaid recipients of any age who are certifiably in need of nursing home care but would rather receive care at home. Sixty percent of the people enrolled in the program are over 60 years of age, and 30 percent are between the ages of 19 and 59 with handicaps such as spinal cord injuries. There are a number of handicapped children under the age of 18 who are also served. The program includes a wide range of services, among which are nursing, rehabilitation, homemaking, home-delivered meals, and transportation. A recent evaluation of patient outcomes compared people participating in the NHWW to people admitted to nursing homes. After three months, the NHWW group improved significantly more than the nursing home group on functional measures of continence, transfer abilities, and the ability to go out of doors. The NHWW also reported significantly more client responses of feeling happier, having more contact with children, and having more support people than the nursing home group.[18]

Maternal-child care has traditionally been a part of home care and continues to be a focus. Nursing visits usually entail antepartal and postpartal care and follow-up of high-risk infants. A home care program where nurses provided both pre- and post-natal care for 400 low-income young women having their first child was recently evaluated. The investigators found that the children of mothers participating in the program had fewer emergency room visits for upper respiratory tract infection and for injuries associated with child abuse than children of nonparticipating mothers.[19]

• • •

Home care is an integral part of the health care delivery system. Although home care has been discussed as a less costly alternative to hospital care, it is quite reasonable to consider the home the primary site for the delivery of health care, with the institution the alternative site.[20] Thus, home care nursing, as the new frontier of health care, does and will continue to involve an array of nursing responsibilities from high-technology skills to case management of the chronically ill patient's multiple needs. There are specific areas that need to be addressed in home care, three of which were included in this discussion. These include the changing practice of the home care nurse, the lack of preventive and supportive services, and home care financing.

Home care nursing has changed since the first sick poor people were visited in their homes by nurses in 1877. It would behoove nurses to try creative ways to reconstruct Wald's model of home care in today's home care system. Nurses in home care must be actively involved in practice (including care of the sick, chronically ill, and those at risk for potential health problems), continuing education, research, and political action. Home care nursing is more than caring for an individual or family at home; it is being aware of and involved in changing the home care climate for a holistic nursing practice.

REFERENCES

1. Humphrey, C.J. "The Practice of Home Care Nursing." *Public Health Nursing* 4, no. 2 (1987):79-83.
2. Bullough, V., and Bullough, B. *The Emergence of Modern Nursing.* New York: Macmillan, 1964.
3. Christy, T.E. "Portrait of a Leader: Lillian Wald." *Nursing Outlook* 18, no. 3 (1970):50-55.

4. Rosen, G. *A History of Public Health.* New York: MD Publications, 1958.
5. Buhler-Wilkerson, K. "Public Health Nursing: In Sickness or in Health?" *American Journal of Public Health* 75 (1985):1160.
6. Brazda, J. "Briefly This Week." *Washington Report of Medicine and Health* 38 (1984):4.
7. Seifer, S. "Impact of PPS on Home Health Care: A Survey of 35 Home Health Agencies." *Caring* 6, no. 4 (1987): 11-12.
8. Griffith, E.I. "The Changing Face of Home Health Care." *Public Health Nursing* 4, no. 1 (1987):1.
9. Andreoli, K.G., and Musser, L.A. "Trends That May Affect Nursings' Future." *Nursing and Health Care* 6 (1985):47-51.
10. Robert Wood Johnson Foundation. *Access to Health Care in the United States: Results of a 1986 Survey.* Princeton, N.J.: Johnson Foundation, 1987.
11. Roemer, R. "The Right to Health Care—Gains and Gaps." *American Journal of Public Health* 78 (1988):241-47.
12. Kilbane, K., and Blacksin, B. "The Demise of Free Care: VNA of Chicago." Paper presented at the American Public Health Association Annual Meeting, New Orleans, La., October 1987.
13. Trotter, J.O. "Home Care: Client or Profit? A Dilemma for Community Nurses." Paper presented at the American Public Health Association Annual Meeting, New Orleans, La., October 1987.
14. McKay, R., and Segall, M. "Methods and Models for the Aggregate." *Nursing Outlook* 31 (1983):328-34.
15. Heyrman, H. "Home Care Provisions of the 1987 Budget." *Home Healthcare Nurse* 5, no. 1 (1987):6-7, 18.
16. Moldow, D.G., and Martinson, I. "From Research to Reality—Home Care for the Dying Child." *The American Journal of Maternal Child Nursing* 51 (1980):159-66.
17. Martinson, I.M., et al. "The Block Nurse Program." *Journal of Community Health Nursing* 2, no. 1 (1985):21-29.
18. Goto, L., and Braun, K. "Nursing Homes Without Walls." *Journal of Gerontological Nursing* 13, no. 1 (1987):7-9.
19. Olds, D.L., et al. "Preventing Child Abuse and Neglect: A Randomized Trial of Nurse Home Visitation." *Pediatrics* 78 (1986):65-78.
20. Stewart, J.E. *Home Health Care.* St. Louis: Mosby, 1979.

Suggested Additional Readings for Part III

Community health nursing roles

Brown MA: Health promotion, education, counseling, and coordination of primary health care nursing, *Public Health Nurs* 5(1):16-23, 1988.

Collis JL and Dukes CA: Toward Some Principles of School Nursing, *J Sch Health* 59(3):109-111, March 1989.

Curtin LL: The nurse as advocate: a philosophical foundation for nursing, *Ans/Ethics and Values*, 1-10, 1979.

Edwards L: Health planning: opportunities for nurses, *Nurs Outlook* 31(6):322-325, 1983.

Flaherty Sr MJ and DeMoya D: An entrepreneurial role for the nurse consultant, *Nurs & Health Care*, 10(5):259-263, May 1989.

Hastings GE, Vick L, Lee G et al: Nurse practitioners in a jailhouse clinic, *Med Care* 18(7):731-744, 1980.

Igoe JB: The School Nurse Practitioner, *Nurs Outlook* 23:381, 1975.

Lamper-Linden C, Goetz-Kulos J and Lake R: Developing ambulatory care clinics: nurse practitioners as primary providers, *J Nurs Adm* 13(12):11-18, 1983.

Parker-Conrad JE: A century of practice: occupational health nursing, *AAOHN J* 36(4):156-161, April 1988.

Tansey EM and Lentz JR: Generalist in a specialized profession, *Nurs Outlook* 36(4):174-178, 1988.

White DH: A study of current school nurse practice activities, *J Sch Health* 55(2):52-56, Feb. 1985.

PART IV

ISSUES IN COMMUNITY HEALTH

Changes in society often require that community health nurses respond with new programs, services, and interventions. Health problems and issues that historically have been associated with communicable disease have evolved into issues regarding lifestyle, risk detection and management, and efficient health care delivery. In an era of shrinking health care resources, now more than ever nurses must assume leadership roles in community health in order to be a part of important decision-making processes. Ethical issues in community health are related to health care priorities and access to services. As persons assume more and more responsibility for their own health status, community health nurses can provide the necessary resources to foster greater client autonomy. This unit provides specific examples of issues relevant to contemporary community health nursing practice and identifies appropriate intervention strategies.

CHAPTER 21

Leadership and Change in Public and Community Health Nursing Today: The Essential Intervention

Marla E. Salmon, RN, ScD, FAAN
Patience Vanderbush, MA, MSPH

The focus of this chapter is on leadership as an essential intervention for change in the practice of public and community health nursing. Leadership has come to mean many things in our society and has numerous definitions. For the purposes of this chapter, leadership is defined as the ability to envision and communicate a changed future and to foster a dynamic that mobilizes and catalyzes the efforts of many toward that end. In this definition the dynamic between leader and follower is "leadership"; it is not simply what the leader does.

Leadership has been a theme in the literature and professionalization of nursing; it is viewed as the hallmark of professional nurses. For nurse administrators and supervisors, leadership is an integral component of the managerial and administrative strategies used to optimize clinical practice. For the overall profession, leadership is seen as a means of advancing the professionalization of nursing. Leadership, however, has not been viewed as a key intervention strategy for the direct practice of nursing. Nursing care plans or other documentation of the nursing process generally do not include leadership as an intervention. With one critical exception, the clinical practice of individual nurses can proceed on a day-to-day basis without any consideration or utilization of leadership as an intervention strategy. The exception is the practice of public and community health nursing.

Public and community health nursing practice differs from all other nursing practices in a number of significant ways. The departure point for practice, particularly for public health nurses, is public mandate and responsibility for the health of the public. This mandate translates into a focus on the prevention of premature death and disability and the preservation of health. The client is the public or community; advocacy is for the public and community good. This form of advocacy and focus of practice demand that interventions involve both the formal and informal structures of society and communities. In other words, the policies, organizations, institutions, and other components of the community infrastructure are the foci for action; the community is the client. The tangible, reassuring, here-and-now character of other types of clinical nursing practice is not a constant dimension of public and community health nursing. While the practice for the entry-level practitioner of public health and community health nursing may involve predominantly hands-on nursing care, the *raison d'être* is the well-being of the com-

Reprinted from *Current Issues in Nursing*, J. C. McCloskey and H. K. Grace, eds., with permission of Mosby-Year Book, Inc., © 1990.

munity and public. Advanced practice, which may appear indirect relative to other forms of nursing, is quite direct in the domain of moving the health status of communities and populations.[18] To accomplish this, nurses must effectively use leadership as an applied clinical strategy.

THE CLIENT'S CURRENT CONDITION

The nature of leadership as an essential strategy for public and community health nurses is best emphasized by examining the condition of the client. Currently there are some key factors or determinants of health in communities and American society in general that seriously affect the health of their members. These determinants constitute the domain of public health and community health nursing practice and require that interventions address them directly, rather than focusing only on the person whose health is affected. The determinants are classified in four general categories:[18] (1) social, (2) medical/technological/organizational, (3) environmental, and (4) human or biological. The common theme in all these determinants is that the ability of individuals to affect them on behalf of communities and society is greatly enhanced by the leadership in public policy and social institutions. For public and community health nurses to play a role in these arenas, leadership must also be their key intervention.

SOCIAL DETERMINANTS OF HEALTH

One significant social trend affecting the health of people today has been the emergence of concern for health promotion and disease prevention. In 1979 the federal government published *Healthy People: The Surgeon General's Report on Health Promotion and Disease Prevention.*[4] It was the first report of its type and clearly outlined a national agenda for health promotion and disease prevention. This report and subsequent related documents reflect two major social phenomena: Americans' realization that lifestyle is a major determinant of health, and the escalating costs of health care, particularly to businesses through health benefits packages.[16]

Although the trend toward health promotion and disease prevention is clearly in keeping with the goal of public health nursing and has given community health nurses new opportunities to expand the scope of their practice, it does pose challenges to the public health nursing leadership. Ostwald and Williams,[12] for instance, have written that community health nurses are in an excellent position to capitalize on national trends toward wellness promotion and cost containment by contracting with local companies to provide health-promotion programs for their employees. However, they also warn that community health nurses must understand the rationale for development of these programs and that the organizational structure of the workplace may compromise individual autonomy and the goal of optimal health. Cost containment and wellness promotion can be, but are not always, complementary; to be so requires significant influence through leadership at policy levels within and outside of the organizations in which such initiatives are formulated.

Cost containment has itself become a major social determinant of health. In recent years U.S. health care costs have risen faster than the inflation rate. Now at 12% of the gross national product, they are expected to reach 15% by the end of the century.[19] The biggest factors in these rising costs have been the costs of advanced technology and hospital care.[16] The ramifications of increasing costs are many. Society will have to consider difficult trade-offs.[19] A challenge for the public health nursing leadership is to become actively involved in that debate, to ensure that the good of the public is paramount in these considerations.

One response to problems of cost containment has been the federal fiscal policy of the Reagan administration, including the Omnibus Budget Reconciliation Act of 1981 (OBRA) and the Tax Equity and Fiscal Responsibility Act of 1982 (TEFRA). According to Milio,[11] this legislation has been the single most important policy action affecting Americans' health in the early 1980s. Linked to the growing federal deficit, the stated aims of this legislation were to bring federal spending under control, to transfer responsibility to the states in the form of block grants, and to reduce regulation to allow the marketplace to efficiently allocate resources and thus reduce health care cost inflation.[11]

As a result of these federal initiatives, cuts were made in many programs. States have commonly responded to these cuts (in concert with recession) by cutting or ending services, the eligibility of certain groups, or provider payments. Over two thirds of the states are now attempting long-term reforms, such as providing home- or community-based care in place of institutional care. These actions reflect leadership at all levels of government; they are examples of opportunities for public and community health nursing involvement that have far-reaching health consequences.

At first glance the consequences of these cost-containment strategies may appear to enhance public and community health nursing practice. An immediate outcome of these actions has been greater reliance on publicly funded health agencies, with an accompanying push toward preventive and alternative health services strategies. Milio contends that these changes may be a cloud with a "silver-yet-gray lining."[11] It is increasingly obvious that restricted state and local budgets are not sufficient to support the rapid development of the alternative preventive and health-promotion strategies that are needed. In addition, those people with existing health problems are often only minimally affected by preventive strategies that only could have worked prior to the onset of the problem. The confusion that has resulted from this shift of financing from the federal government to local and state authorities, with an accompanying shift in the ostensible focus of services from curative to preventive, is also a confusion about who is responsible for providing these services. Those who are lost in this confusion are generally people who have the greatest need for services and the fewest resources to purchase them.

Other social factors affecting the health of communities include some major demographic changes, such as the increase in the older population. With extension of the lifespan and the movement of the baby boomers into middle age, there is a rapidly increasing demand for services relating to chronic and other diseases associated with aging. Another important factor is the increase in minority and ethnic populations in the United States and the need for traditionally white, middle-class institutions to become responsive to the needs of these people. In addition, while resources to support services are becoming increasingly scarce, unemployment, teenage pregnancy and suicide, violence, and drug and alcohol abuse are on the rise in this country. The "shrinking" of the globe and the crucial interrelations with the world community, particularly with respect to peace, also are critically important health considerations. All these and many other social factors determine the condition of the client and what public and community health nurses do. To have any significant impact on these determinants, nurses must be able to master the leadership of society and its institutions.

MEDICAL-TECHNICAL-ORGANIZATIONAL DETERMINANTS OF HEALTH

The nature of medical technology and services and how they are organized and financed reflect the values, resources, and nature of society in general. Too often, however, these factors are not considered to be key determinants affecting the health of communities and their members. Recent rapid and large-order changes in the medical-technical-organizational domain have had major effects on who receives services, who provides services, what types of services are available, and who is responsible for ensuring the quality of such services. The common theme of recent innovations in health services financing and delivery systems has echoed the overall social and political climate: reduce and contain costs! Diagnosis-related groups (DRGs), health-maintenance organizations (HMOs), and emergency care centers[10] are all reflections of the finance-driven nature of the health services systems. An accompanying theme has been the "corporatization" and "commodification" of health services, where health and illness are variables in the equations of the marketplace and are targets for the generation of profit.

These new health care delivery systems provide nurses with practice opportunities in both ambulatory and home settings and thus contribute to the demand for more nurses. But they also challenge public and community health nurses to look at the systems from a broader perspective than their immediate effect on the nursing profession. In the face of a finance-driven delivery system, it is essential to assess more than the savings. The equation must be one of cost-effectiveness (rather than cost efficiency) and must include careful appraisal of the quality of service, the response of providers to these varying economic incentives, and the overall performance (both financial and qualitative) of different types of organizations relative to their social and health-related responsibilities.[19] It is essential that public and community health nurses play leadership roles in these evaluative and regulatory functions; they are key factors in shaping the health of communities. Nurses must, at the very least, be able to do so relative to their own practices.

One area in which these regulatory roles for public and community health nurses are of acute importance is home health services, particularly home care. Prospective payment under Medicare, DRGs, and the expanding elderly population have contributed to a tremendous growth in home care. Although home care has been a traditional domain of community health nursing, both the increasing complexity and extent of home services have provided greater opportunities for nurses in the community. Yet in many states there is little if any regulation of home care, and many experts are concerned that quality may seriously deteriorate as services expand.[6]

One reason the quality of home care is increasingly threatened is the growing need for nurses to have the knowledge and skill to manage seriously ill clients, particularly those requiring high-technology interventions and equipment.[16] Not only have the numbers of patients requiring home care increased, but the majority of them are older, sicker, and require more complex care.[13] Community health nurses are experiencing changes in their clinical, counseling, and coordinating roles,[13] reflecting more sophisticated technical interventions. Clients and their families also require more counseling and teaching, because they are sharing the burden of the complex direct care being provided in their own home. As case managers in the home setting, community health nurses need outstanding organizational and interpersonal leadership skills to effectively patch together a productive collage of services from the myriad of unrelated community resources. This is particularly challenging in cases where financial resources are minimal.

One particularly difficult aspect of this concentration of the need for nursing services in home care is the extent to which this diverts resources from preventive programming, particularly in official public health nursing agencies. The competition for scarce resources between caring for the sick and preventing morbidity and mortality in healthy populations challenges public health nurses to provide leadership in developing creative and collaborative approaches to generating and allocating resources within and outside of their own agencies.

Federal reimbursement systems, while contributing to the growth of home care services, also present a challenge to quality assurance programs.[13] Medicare doesn't pay for most long-term home care—only for skilled assistance, as from a physician or nurse.[6] According to Rogatz, to meet the increased level of need among patients discharged from hospitals, governmental third-party payers must broaden eligibility standards, benefits ranges, and reimbursement levels. Current home delivery models have led to problems of access and fragmentation.[7] The responsibility for seeing that clients are not dropped from care and that they receive maximum reimbursement is being assumed by many staff nurses in home health agencies.[13]

Public and community health nursing leaders must work to ensure that the federal government and others supply sufficient resources to meet the growing demands on health care. One way to do this is to define the elements of a home visit in such a way that it can be priced appropriately for various buyers.[2] Nurses should participate in developing patient classification systems; in describing and measuring clinical care, counseling, coordination, and other activities; and in collecting data on the cost-benefit ratio of prevention to make a compelling argument for resources for preventive practice.[13]

Another challenge to public and community health nursing leaders is in their capacities as advocates for the good of society. The changes in our health care delivery system are already threatening to pit corporate interests against those of the public and society at large. Third-party payers and profit incentives are exerting increasing influence on the for-profit health sector. This pressure has resulted in moves to provide services only to paying clients, dumping high-risk, costly, nonpaying clients into the already straining public sector, and skimming off those clients with resources who could help offset the cost of others. This phenomenon, while contributing to the health of the corporation, is creating a two-tiered care system that is devastating to the overall health of the public.

Vertical integration is a part of this corporatization of health care.[17] Providers are organizing in groups of increasing size, corporations are managing or providing their own health care, and major for-profit entities are taking an increasing share of the health care business or industry.[5] One advantage to nursing may be that because nursing services are more cost-effective than physician services, many cost-conscious health care organizations could be persuaded that nurses get the job done more efficiently.[5] However, this again places nurses in the ethical dilemmas posed by conflicts between the needs of clients and the requirements of the corporation.[19] These dilemmas can only be resolved through creative and responsible leadership at policy levels within and outside of these organizations. Unless nurses are involved in such leadership, the advocacy and social concern required for enlightened decision making may well be lacking.

Another determinant in the medical-technical-organization domain of health is what has been called the "mechanization" of health care. This is defined as the growing orientation of U.S. health care toward technology—the drugs, devices, and medical care and the organizations and supportive systems within which such care is provided. In the current atmosphere of cost containment, there is a greater need to assess whether technology has sufficient advantages to justify its costs, and to explore its social and ethical implications for our health care system.[5] Public and community health nurses, increasingly asked to use new technologies in nonhospital settings, must understand and also be able to evaluate the new technologies, including the broader values, principles, and roles of this technology, if they are to be involved in the decision-making process.[5] They must also be included in forums where the costs and benefits of the technology of "care and cure" are weighed against those of preventive strategies. These discussions, which occur at all policy levels, are critical intervention points that have far-reaching effects on health. The effective practice of public and community health nursing in this context again demands leadership as one of its intervention strategies.

Leadership is also required to ensure that nurses are educationally prepared to practice effectively within this rapidly changing health services system. In their recent study of public health nursing education and practice, Jones and colleagues emphasize the gap between what nurses are educated to do and what their actual practice entails.[8] The Institute of Medicine's 1988 "Study on the Future of Public Health"[3] also emphasizes that current public health workers are generally not prepared in public health. Lack of preparation in public health, including the skills required for leadership intervention, has serious implications for this rapidly emerging finance-driven high-tech health services system.

ENVIRONMENTAL DETERMINANTS OF HEALTH

In terms of impact, the environment may be the single most important determinant of health in the very near future. It is also the determinant about which nurses perhaps know the least. The nursing literature on environmental health and the role of public and community health nurses vis-à-vis the environment is alarmingly sparse. Environmental problems of concern to community health nurses include the disposal of hazardous waste, including toxic industrial waste and radioactive-contaminated materials; acid rain; urban lead poisoning; inadequate solid waste disposal; noise pollution; air pollution; and water pollution.[16] Global concerns include the depletion of the ozone layer, with its accompanying weather changes and warming of the oceans. And most critical of all is the threat of thermonuclear war.

Part of the leadership required of public and community health nurses is the task of educating themselves and others about what environmental health issues are and how to intervene effectively. Clearly, all of the environmental issues relate to the state of environmental policy and regulation. Nurses must learn to insert themselves into the debates surrounding these policies and regulations, at the same time becoming involved in the specifics of environmental exposures in their own clientele. Macinick and Macinick[9] suggest some action guidelines for nurses to begin to help solve the problems of our environment, including the following: being willing to admit to the idea of asymptomatic, subclinical toxicity and the multiple-effects disease model; being aware that environmental toxicology is a politically charged issue involving the world of high finance and corporate egos; being able to accept disbelief and even anger toward not only the message but the messenger; and being aware that almost no research on the synergistic effects of low-level toxins has been done, leading to downplaying of their importance. They suggest that the nurse's most helpful coping mechanism is knowledge, which will also enable the nurse to begin educating the community about the effects of low levels of pollution.

One of the key leadership strategies relating to the environment is that of interdisciplinary, collaborative action. While this is also a key intervention strategy with other health determinants, it is most critical in dealing with environmental issues because of the specialized knowledge required to address and monitor action in this area. Although nurses generally do not possess sophistication in this area, they can provide the generalist leadership and health knowledge necessary to catalyze health-committed action relating to the environment.

HUMAN AND BIOLOGICAL DETERMINANTS OF HEALTH

The human and biological health determinant, probably the most familiar and comfortable to nurses, is one in which significant public health issues have emerged in this last decade. We have observed the appearance of devastating and exotic infectious diseases such as AIDS, toxic shock syndrome, herpes, and Legionnaires' disease. More than any other disease, AIDS,[1] coupled with the reemergence of new strains and epidemics of diseases formerly thought to be under control such as syphilis, gonorrhea, mumps, measles, diphtheria, and flu, has radically altered the course of public health in this nation. The global eradication of smallpox in the 1970s signaled a new era in public health in which there was great optimism that the age of infectious disease was coming to an end. This hope has been erased; public health practitioners are faced with challenges greater than ever in infectious diseases, as well as the challenges of chronic disease associated with growing numbers of the elderly. The increasingly grave and diverse disease picture in public and community health has not been accompanied by an increase in resources or systems to address these problems. Again, the development of effective strategies must involve the leadership of public and community health nurses to be appropriately responsive.

Public health practitioners are also confronted with the promises and threats to society inherent in the reality of genetic engineering. The ethical, moral, legal, social, and economic questions surrounding developments in this area fall squarely in the domain of public health. Society will confront these issues in all arenas: individual, family, community, state, and national. How these issues are resolved depends greatly on who provides the leadership. The inclusion of public and community health nurses in these debates is essential to an outcome sensitive to and respectful of the public good and the public health.

A final concern is the challenge of enabling people to optimize their own health. Although the lifestyle movement certainly provides answers for the middle and upper classes, which have options associated with their financial resources, it does not address the needs of those people who are less fortunate. Questions of how to ensure that all people are equipped with the advantages of a healthy fetal and early childhood experience, adequate nutrition, immunizations, exercise, and the skills of self-development, are not easily answered through most of the current lifestyle programs. Children are still bearing children, destroying themselves and others through drug abuse, suicide, and other forms of violence. These questions clearly cannot be addressed solely at the one-to-one level. They require the leadership of those who are close to the problems, committed to the good of the community, and skilled in understanding the relationship between the health of the individual and the broader society.

THE NEXT STEPS

Although the condition of the client—our communities and society—is clearly grave, it is not without hope or an agenda for action. One of the intriguing and perplexing aspects of the problems that we face today is that we already know many of the answers. Never before have we known as much about health as we do now; what we don't know is how to put this knowledge into action. Again, this requires leadership.

In the July 4, 1988, issue of *Newsweek*[14] a special report portrayed a number of "unsung heroes." The common theme in these stories was the unwillingness of each of these "heroes" to accept the status quo; each took action and effected change. All of them, while not trained to accomplish what they undertook, had a vision of a better situation and pursued this vision with personal commitment and courage. Of all of the attributes of leadership, these are perhaps the most important. Another noteworthy theme in this report was that for each of these individuals, people were the primary means for achieving change. These leaders relied on themselves and others as the means for effecting change; they did not wait for technical or economic answers.

The message here for public and community health nurses is that leadership is necessary and attainable. The lessons from the unsung heroes—vision, conviction, and the courage to act—are an excellent departure point. Another worthwhile lesson was their willingness to work with others. Finally, the reason that these heroes are "unsung" is that they did things in their own backyards and communities; their actions were local, beginning at home.

The next steps for public and community health nursing are to focus on nursing's leadership interventions. Understanding the condition of the client and the factors creating this condition is only the beginning. The future health of the client, our communities and society, relies greatly on the development of leadership as the key strategy for public and community health nursing. The challenge is perhaps best stated by an aphorism from the 1960s: If you aren't part of the solution, you are part of the problem. If public and community health nurses aren't part of the leadership required to enhance the health of society, then we are, in fact, contributing to its decline.

REFERENCES

1. Fineberg HV: The social dimensions of AIDS, Scientific American, p 128, Oct 1988.
2. Griffith EI: The changing face of home health care, Public Health Nurs 4(1):1, 1987 (editorial).
3. The future of public health. Report of the Institute of Medicine Committee for the study of public health, Washington, National Academy Press, 1981.
4. Healthy people: the surgeon general's report on health promotion and disease prevention, Washington, DC, 1979, US Department of Health, Education, and Welfare.
5. Herdman RC: Health care technology and the changing health care system, NLN Publication 41:15, 1985.
6. Hey RP: The challenges of caring for a relative at home, Christian Science Monitor, p 3, May 26, 1988.
7. Humphrey CJ: The practice of home care nursing, Public Health Nurs 4(2):79, 1987.
8. Jones DC, Davis JA, and Davis MD: Public health nursing: education and practice, Springfield, Va, 1987, National Technical Information Service.
9. Macinick CG and Macinick JW: Toxic new world: what nurses can do to cope with a polluted environment, Int Nurs Rev 34(2):40, 1987.
10. McCreight LM: The curriculum of the future: adapting to changing demands in community health, NLN Publications 41:144, 1985.
11. Milio N: Chains of impact from Reaganonomics on primary care policies, Public Health Nurs 1(2):65, 1984.
12. Ostwald SK and Williams HY: Community health nursing in workplace health programs: rationale and ethics, J Community Health Nurs 4(3):121, 1987.
13. Phillips EK and Cloonan PA: DRG ripple effects on community health nursing, Public Health Nurs 4(2):84, 1987.
14. Special report: a holiday for heroes, Newsweek, p 34, July 4, 1988.
15. Rogatz P: Perspective on home care, Public Health Nurs 4(1):7, 1987.
16. Spradley BW, editor: Readings in community health nursing, Boston, 1986, Little, Brown and Co, Inc.
17. Starr P: The social transformation of American medicine, New York, 1982, Basic Books, Inc.
18. White MS: Construct for public health nursing, Nurs Outlook 30(9):527, 1982.
19. Winkenwerder W and Ball JR: Transformation of American health care: the role of the medical profession, N Engl J Med 318(5):317, 1988.

CHAPTER 22

Health, Risk Factor Reduction, and Life-Style Change

John H. Milsum, ScD

HEALTH AND ILLNESS

Probably no disease or illness is caused by any single factor, and correspondingly, no single factor is sufficient to maintain health. This contributes to a continuing controversy in defining health, particularly among the health scientists. One major focus of this debate concerns the attributes to be included in the definition of health.

At the first—and physical—level, human beings are biological organisms who through pathogenic inputs, and possibly through their internal reactive mechanisms, acquire various pathologies that are then defined as particular physical diseases.

At a second level, humans are characterized particularly importantly by a brain or central nervous system whose function involves the mental, intellectual, cognitive, emotional and intuitive qualities that characterize humans so uniquely. It is therefore meaningful to consider mental as well as physical health and illness. Indeed much interest focuses on the psychosomatic nature of illness in the context that mind and body are hardly ever separable in any fully meaningful way. This concept has existed from the most ancient times, as expressed, for example, in the phrase *mens sana in corpore sano* (a "healthy mind in a healthy body"). There seems to be increasing acceptance that the mind is the more powerful controller in regard to health than is the body.

Reprinted from *Family & Community Health,* Vol. 3, No. 1, with permission of Aspen Publishers, Inc., © 1980.

The World Health Organization, in its charter, has defined health as "a state of complete physical, mental and social well-being, and not just the absence of disease or infirmity." This, then, incorporates a third level of health—that of social aspects—and herein lies much controversy. The inclusion of social aspects of health could be taken to imply that an individual's health can be assured only if society provides the right conditions. This in turn might tend subtly to discourage individuals from taking full responsibility for their health. Also, this inclusion could provide a ready justification for society—which in this context largely means government—to intrude upon almost all aspects of the individual's life.

A fourth level of health, one that has even less consensus today, is that of spirituality. Health disciplines do not generally assume more than a secular, mechanistic basis for human nature. Spiritual or religious beliefs are considered the individual's own concern and not of fundamental importance to the practice of medicine and sick care. This attitude also applies to the creative, intuitive, and spiritually related pursuits such as art, music, dance, poetry, and generally all the recreational activities that are recognized as vital for an individual's health. Yet perhaps the greatest practical importance of the spiritual aspect lies in its contribution to the sense of purposefulness of life, and therefore to the will individuals apply to their affairs and to their health.

Health, then, may be characterized for different persons by variously weighted combinations of the four aspects discussed above: physical, mental, social, and spiritual. It may be concluded that the health of a person is in fact intimately related to, if not identical with, the state of that person in his or her entirety. An important question concerns how an individual moves from a particular initial health state, for example, under the influence of stressors.

Physiologically there seems no doubt that humans are constructed as physical-health-oriented, integrated systems, with multiple homeostatic mechanisms to monitor any departure from "healthy" conditions of various parameters (blood pressure, temperature, blood sugar, etc.), and then to bring restoring forces into play to reestablish the desired dynamic equilibrium. Scientifically it is more difficult to infer that this same homeostatic urge to health applies at the mental, social, and spiritual levels.

HEALTH PROMOTION

The apparently inexhaustible "need" for sick care—with costs increasing faster than the GNP—has stimulated consideration of illness prevention and health promotion. However, prevention and promotion constitute a huge and largely unexplored terrain, so that desirable directions must first be agreed upon.

Technological strategies of health promotion, while raising the standard of living, life expectancy, and general health to unprecedented levels, have increasingly assumed much of the individual's healthful functions and responsibilities. Such strategies depend on mass application for their economical benefits and are inevitably inflexible, thus reducing the individual to a passive receiver rather than a challenged innovator of health. As a result, the individual's motivation for self-responsibility atrophies.

"Passive" strategies of health promotion involve the individual as a passive participant or recipient. Two examples are (1) clean water and sanitary sewage systems, to obviate infectious diseases and improve health generally, and (2) introduction of vitamin D in all milk so that young children will not be subject to high risk of rickets when there is little sunlight. Because studies have shown that compliance with individual therapeutic regimens tends to be low, many health professionals argue for passive strategies.[1]

"Active" strategies, in distinction, depend inherently on the individual becoming personally motivated to adopt a given program of health promotion. The most obvious examples involve changes in life style such as (1) adoption of a physical fitness plan and, more broadly, of an energy-balance program; (2) moderation of alcohol use and cessation of smoking; and (3) adoption of a stress management plan.

In all societies the best solution is inevitably a combination of active and passive strategies. However, when sociocultural issues are involved in a political context, there can be much controversy about the optimal balance between these two approaches. This is the situation today, and the best resolutions for societies at different stages of industrialization are not yet clear.

RISK FACTORS AND A MULTIFACTORIAL MODEL OF HEALTH/ILLNESS

The concept of risk factor sets the stage for a modified and deeper understanding of the disease process. Specifically, it allows us to move away from the simple cause-effect (input-output, stimulus-response) model of illness in which a single factor is seen as the basic cause of an illness—for example, the tubercle bacillus as the "cause" of tuberculosis. Perhaps this simple model of disease causality has not fairly represented the understanding with which the good health professional has practiced; but nevertheless it has not unfairly represented the conceptual basis on which most pathology has been taught following the discoveries of Pasteur.

The concept of risk factor has two important implications:

1. *A risk factor merely establishes a probability context;* that is, an elevated risk factor implies that more individuals of a given group will be affected by the risk implied. Even if the risk factor is very high, it does not guarantee that any one particular person will succumb to a particular disease; nor, equally, does it imply that even when the risk factor is extremely low another person may not in fact come down with that disease. In regard to implementing active strat-

egies of health promotion, it is important to explore the underlying mechanisms in individuals. (This is in order to explain why some individuals may be excessively disease prone, given apparently low risk, while others remain obstinately healthy in the face of very high risks.)

2. *The risk factor concept inherently embraces the idea that disease (and conversely health) is overwhelmingly multifactorial in genesis;* that is, the essential responsibility cannot be attributed to any single factor. Furthermore, both the time sequences and the ordering of the particular factors are important in determining the end result. In consequence there can be many patterns that produce the same particular end result. This could explain why so many different and apparently incompatible therapies are offered from time to time, each as "the cure" to a particular disease. Each assertion may in fact be true within its very limited conditions of the other multiple factors. Unfortunately, such assertions are not helpful in synthesizing a satisfying explanation of the underlying mechanisms.

   It should be noted here that there are some genetically determined diseases in which a key process of development, growth, or metabolism may fail because of the absence of a particular substance or configuration. In such special cases, the single-cause theory becomes more plausible.

A further comment concerns the "last straw" phenomenon. The last straw is the contribution from one of the sets of multiple factors that finally triggers a response. This trigger level is technically called a *threshold.* Since stress will be used as the final common factor in pathogenesis, it is convenient to introduce it here as the "effect" variable, corresponding to the multiple factors as joint "cause." Therefore, once stress has exceeded a certain level—"the threshold"—a pathogenic process begins to occur at a highly accelerated pace. The term *highly accelerated* indicates that it may not be the same simple threshold as when water spills over from a bucket once it is full; rather it is used in the context of the bucket that is leaky because of holes in the sides so the outflow begins even before the bucket has been completely filled.

The process of pathogenesis may also require considerable time before it can accumulate the effects of the multiple factors to result in an overt disease or illness—that is, there is a "latent time." Latent times of several decades are frequently quoted, for example, in the development of cancers in response to such factors as tobacco smoking, asbestos particles and other carcinogens.

In any case, the last-straw phenomenon indicates that it is not useful to classify as a cause of the illness the particular factor that contributed the last increment of "causality" before the threshold was surpassed. It is the proximal effect—the last straw, indeed; but in fact it only succeeded because other factors depleted the defense resources almost to exhaustion.

This leads to formulation of a general model for health/illness incorporating multiple factors. Figure 22-1 shows a multiple set of stressors that tend to move the organism away from its homeostatically driven tendency toward sustained health. These stressors can be of many types, and indeed can be categorized into the major aspects discussed above—especially physical, mental , and social. A somewhat different categorization is now used, based upon the concept that the individual's current health/illness condition depends on the state of balance between the strengths of host resistance and the invaders (all the "bugs," notably viruses and bacteria).

1. *Physical stressors* are most easily exemplified by environmental influences—for example, the various outputs from automobiles including carbon monoxide, asbestos particles, rubber particles, heat, and perhaps noise.
2. *Psychological stressors* are most easily characterized by those stressors of civilization so frequently quoted: "the stresses of living." Of course it is impossible to separate physical and psychological stressors exactly. Noise is a typical overlapping example. While noise is inherently physical in the nature of its transmission, its perception and evaluation as a stressor are psychological. Other psychological stressors have been well characterized by[3] Holmes and Rahe in regard to life event units. Their results show, for example, that much of life's perceived stressfulness is related to the changes in an individual's life, with stress resulting almost

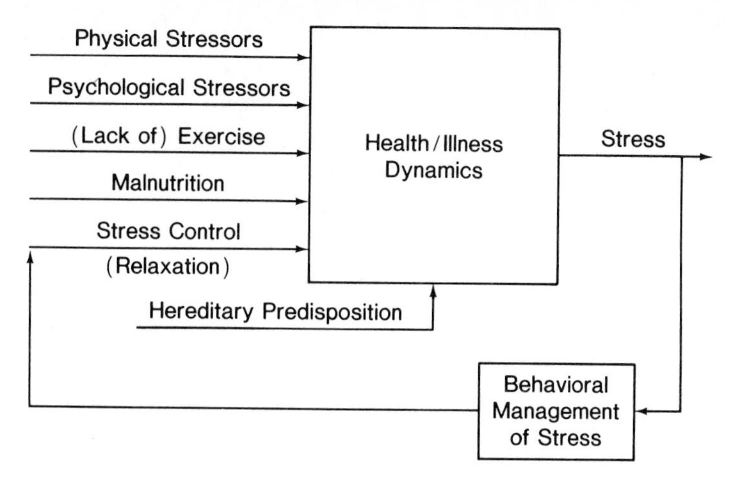

FIGURE 22-1
Multifactorial health/illness dynamics.

as much from "joyful changes" as from "bad changes." "Death of a spouse" is awarded twice as many life event units (100) as marriage (50), while vacation and Christmas are allocated about one-fourth as many (about 12). In the Holmes and Rahe model the accumulated life event units within a period such as two years generate a probability (risk factor) of becoming sick.

3. *Nutrition* or, more strictly speaking, *malnutrition* is shown in Figure 22-1 as another stressor. Presenting it separately underlines that it is a crucially important factor for health.
4. *Lack of physical exercise* or *fitness* is another major factor. At the physical level, work and exercise represent the body's output made possible by appropriate nutrition. Furthermore, however, the fitness so acquired also stimulates the host-resistance factor already referred to.

The combined action of such sets of factors is treated briefly in "Risk Factor Reduction" below.

The outcome of the multiple factors in this present model is an effect on stress level within the individual. Some stress is of course desirable for each individual so that he or she is not a "vegetable"; on the other hand, too much stress is clearly harmful.[4] Therefore optimal health for any individual will involve an optimal level of stress. Unfortunately, no simple ranges for specific measurable biochemicals are available to define the state of stress. In addition, there is much semantic confusion in the literature about the use of these terms (stress, stressor) and others (tension, pressure, strain).

In any case, there is a typical human response to stressors that Selye calls the general adaptation syndrome.[5] It has three phases: alarm, resistance, and ultimately exhaustion—with characteristic physiological correlates. In particular, disease is associated with prolonged resistance and exhaustion. Even more, diseases such as hypertension can arise in a technical, intense, urbanized life just from frequent elicitation of the alarm reaction.[6] This is identically the fight-or-flight response, and its eliciting challenge often allows no civilized release in either fight or flight. Then the response necessarily occurs first internally and ultimately pathogenically.

Fortunately, humans have the potential to perceive their stress level and therefore to complete a behavioral homeostatic loop intended to reduce that stress. Normally they do this in multiple ways: in a short timespan, for example, by resting and sleeping; and in a longer timespan, for example, by modifications of life style and habitat. Indeed the very process of becoming sick may constitute, as one major function, a feedback mechanism to ensure that the patients will relax their stressed condition and will therefore be able to buy time in order to regain their health. Figure 22-1 therefore shows a fifth input: stress management and relaxation. Inserting it on the left-hand side means unequivocally that each individual potentially has the power to reduce stress or to maintain it at a desired level.

Unfortunately, this can of course also work the other way around, and in "pathogenic societies" there can be pressures for individuals to incorporate various factors into their lives that can increase their stress level until a life style of very high risk results. Without getting into extreme examples from social deviance, alienation, and brutal excitements, it may be noted that the order of risk adopted by many people in sports and recreation (for example, private flying and skiing) exceeds by several orders of magnitude that permitted by society for the work environment and commercial transportation.[7]

This stress-relaxation factor covers the whole spectrum — from physical and mental relaxation in an arm chair, through sports and recreation of all kinds (note that this word originally meant *re-creation*), to various spiritual or religious activities. Benson proposes that a "relaxation response" mechanism exists at the neurological level equally as certainly as, and in direct agonist-antagonist relation to, the fight-or-flight response.[8] He offers a simple technique for eliciting this that functionally appears to be the same as classical meditative techniques — except that no underlying spiritual concepts are considered relevant or necessary.

RISK FACTOR REDUCTION

The discussion so far would suggest that strategies of health promotion should aim at risk factor reduction, at the level of both the individual and the community. Before considering this further, however — and bearing in mind the ethical problems implicit in asking people to change life style — it is necessary to have some evidence that risk factor reduction in a set of individuals does in fact result in health benefits. Unfortunately, while the "controlled clinical trials" so strongly recommended by Cochrane for health care research would theoretically provide such evidence — one way or the other — they are not practical in this situation.[9]

Figure 22-2 illustrates the underlying situation. Suppose it is possible to identify, through surveys, that two groups of individuals exist with respectively high and low risk for illness (e.g., for cardiovascular disease). This categorization is based on a set of risk factors that have typically been established through such prospective epidemiological studies as the Framingham study.[10] For example, eight risk factors have been quantified in Health Hazard Appraisal for Death by Heart Attack: (1) systolic blood pressure, (2) diastolic blood pressure, (3) fasting blood cholesterol level, (4) presence of diabetes, (5) family history of heart attack, (6) cigarette smoking, (7) obesity, and (8) physical fitness. Other factors, especially nutrition and stress, are known to be connected with risk of heart attack; but so far, for reasons already mentioned, they have not been successfully quantified as a concise and credible set of risk factors. In order to categorize individuals as indicated in Figure 22-2, it is necessary to combine the many different risk factors to assess a single, composite risk factor for death from any particular disease or group of diseases, or even for general proneness to illness.

Returning to the problem illustrated in Figure 22-2, the basic question to be answered is: if some

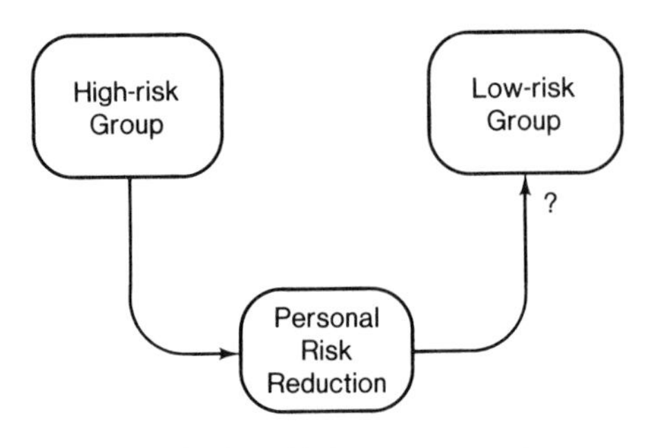

FIGURE 22-2
Membership in risk groups.

individuals currently allocated to the high-risk group should change their life styles in such a way that their risk factors will be appropriately reduced, will they in fact become members of the low-risk group as established by their subsequent mortality experiences? The confounding problem in answering this positively is that there may be predisposing factors—for example, heredity—that are pertinent to membership by people in the high- and low-risk categories, since these can only be arrived at a posteriori by observing their relative mortality or morbidity figures.

Unfortunately, it is impossible to conduct the double-blind cross-over trials considered desirable by modern scientific methodology, as for example in trials using both experimental drugs and placebos. In life-style experiments, the individual will be willfully involved in any life-style changes, so that the placebo concept becomes an impossible dream. Therefore, any attempts to allocate the subject randomly to such regimens as "exercise" and "no exercise" cannot be methodologically valid since the benefits to be derived from such regimens are presumably intricately and intimately bound up with the person's attitude. An example here would be that some of those allocated to "exercise" might resent this and either perform it without spirit or simply cheat. Hence observations on the effects of life-style change are almost always acquired through the integrated results of individuals having voluntarily, but for internal and often obscure reasons, made these life-style changes.

Given the impossibility of the epidemiologically desirable experimentation, it would seem prudent to accept these emerging results in the same context as was done with cigarette smoking: as associative evidence has accumulated, though without conclusively proving causality, the vast majority of both scientists and the population have accepted that cigarette smoking is a highly significant risk factor for many serious diseases.

In this manner, some important data have emerged from the prospective cohort study of Belloc and Breslow on nearly 7000 people in California, in relation to the number of "good health habits" followed.[11] The seven health habits studied are: (1) sleeping 7 to 8 hours regularly; (2) eating breakfast regularly; (3) snacking little or not at all; (4) maintaining near-optimal weight; (5) exercising frequently; (6) moderating alcoholic consumption; and (7) avoiding smoking. They found that the mortality rates of those people who follow 0 to 3 good health habits are about double the rates of those who follow 6 to 7, over all age and sex groups. Thus this study confirms that those with lower risk factors do subsequently show lower mortality rates. Several studies are now underway to explore whether those people who voluntarily remove themselves from a higher risk group to a lower risk group do in fact subsequently show lower morbidity and mortality rates. The study in North Karelia, Finland has apparently produced very encouraging but as yet largely unpublished results,[12] while the Multiple Risk Factor Intervention Trials (MRFIT) in the United States are just starting.[13]

It should also be noted that these studies and the Stanford heart project have shown that public campaigns can be effective in promoting life-style changes among the population to reduce risk factors.[14]

In the context of a multifactorial model, the risk factor approach has value in public campaigns since it helps individuals become aware of the benefits of life-style change. For example, using the specific case of heart attack risk factors, individuals can learn that even if they have high clinical risk factors or a high risk factor due to family history, three of the life-style factors already mentioned (smoking, obesity, and physical fitness) are still under their own control—at least in principle. In part this may stimulate overcoming the sense of helplessness that is engendered in some people who may have a bad family history in this area. In any case, may such a sense of helplessness not constitute a defense mechanism behind which arguments can be made that changing of life style would not make any difference anyway?

LIFE-STYLE CHANGE

Risk factors in the multifactorial model of health/illness are based on the rational concepts of science. The life style chosen by individuals is subjective and unique to each, usually built up over their lifetimes, and is a rather precious vehicle protecting them against many of the difficulties and misfortunes of life.

At this point, then, a fundamental question arises: do rational information about personal risk-factor levels and the potential health benefit of their reduction help to motivate the person to undertake life-style change? Only some general points will be mentioned here.

Present life styles in the United States represent a complex outcome of many personal, interpersonal, environmental, and societal practices. They arise not only from present situations, but also from previous history and heredity. Therefore any life-style changes that are made inevitably involve complete personal Gestalt, both as a present condition and as a dynamic historical process. In this historical process the concept of threshold, already referred to in regard to illness, plays an important part. Thus there is a typical exposure to many different inputs of information, emotional events, and so on, before enough concern can be accumulated to reach threshold for actually initiating change. Many theoretical models for life-style change have been constructed, with one important feature being that they involve multiple stages. A reasonably general synthesis of such ideas is the following hierarchical model, in which each stage must be fulfilled in sequential order:

1. *Awareness and acceptance of risk.* We must be aware that the behavior in question is harmful in the population and, more particularly, accept that this risk applies personally. For example, cigarette smoking is accepted as affecting lung cancer and involves other health risks.
2. *Integration of the knowledge.* We must take the knowledge into our personal self-image so that, for example, we can believe that stopping smoking is quite possible.
3. *Effort and application for change.* We must decide to make a change in behavior and then apply the new knowledge to produce and sustain the actual change.

Because the strength of a chain is indeed only the strength of the weakest link, it is crucial to consider all aspects involved in the health promotional activity, and to plan for each link to be equally strong. Now the promotion of life-style change, as for example in Health Hazard Appraisal, has matured around the concept of the counseling session. Here the emphasis is on the *counselor* presenting and discussing with a *client* the special knowledge made available through the Appraisal and its background methodology, in the hope of reaching a *contract* for life-style change. In other words, the whole emphasis is upon the client as the initiator of, or at least a willing participant in, the process—moving toward more self-responsibility for health in undertaking life-style change. This implicitly requires an underlying belief by the client that through adoption of a life style the state of health or illness in which a person lives is in some measure chosen and controlled.

This concept has significant and salutary implications for the counselor. The current medical model increasingly emphasizes medicine as primarily a scientific enterprise. Medical activities therefore focus on the diagnosis of pathology through scientific tests, and the prescription of precise therapeutic regimens aimed at specific target organs or systems through specific drugs, surgery, or other interventions. In this context physicians may be encouraged to believe that their particular life styles are of no pertinence to the client (patient). Indeed the extreme result of this process is that some physicians may neither perceive nor suggest that improved life style may improve health.

In contrast, the counseling model recognizes that the interaction between patient and professional is in many respects similar to the student-teacher and child-parent relationships; in particular clients are typically more motivated by what the counselors do than what they say. Thus ordering and prescribing may not be effective. Furthermore the counseling session provides a potentially important "teachable moment" in which the clients are able to see, perhaps for the first time, a large amount of information about the effects of their life styles usefully integrated in one document. To capitalize on this, it seems important that the counselor be an exemplar, in order to reinforce the rational message that the information being provided is in fact potentially helpful for the client.

Indeed, all clients will presumably assess their counselors regarding whether they believe in the concepts and information that they are transmitting. This homily may seem to make the whole process of counseling for health very onerous and responsible for the health professional; but actually it should be seen that it only returns the situation to that which existed before the recent development of high technology medicine. At that time it was mutually recognized, if only tacitly, that the physician had few powerful technical interventions available, but that the counsel, empathy, and tender loving care provided by the physician were of basic significance. In a real but extended sense this is another and important example of the power of the placebo.

The exemplar effect may be particularly important in those frequently encountered cases where the life-style changes necessary for risk reduction are already well known by us as clients to be "desirable." That we have not already adopted the changes clearly indicates that we perceive that there are benefits from such high-risk life-style habits that outweigh the hazards. Of the "desirable" life-style changes, the major frequently occurring examples are (1) reduction of overweight (the average North American is approximately 20 pounds over the "desirable weight")[15]; (2) increase of physical activity; (3) cessation of smoking; (4) moderation of alcohol consumption; (5) better nutrition; and (6) more effective stress management. To many individuals these recommendations for change seem; "sentencing to penal servitude," because "everything I like is either illegal, immoral, or fattening." In consequence people often assert, "I would rather live a shorter but happy life than extend it if I have to forego these few pleasures of life." Why then should health professionals take on the role of "do-gooders"—an often thankless task? And if they do, can they successfully counter the accusation that exemplars really are masochists who want their clients to join them in their misery, in order that the high-risk "enjoyable" life styles not provide a constant temptation for the exemplars?

The only convincing answer—and indeed the only justification for health promotional efforts—must reside in an ongoing demonstration that these lower risk life styles do in fact result in more good than bad in the overall balance of the continuing enjoyment of life and health. At present this is to some extent a statement of faith. There does, however, seem reason to hope that further and continuing research will justify it—quite apart from the evidence of increasing numbers of people who are so convinced.

Eventually the success of schemes for risk reduction by individuals will depend upon the viability of these arguments. By now it is clear that mere threats about the economic cost to everyone of an increasingly morbidity-prone society, in a high-technology medical system oriented toward acute care, will not produce the underlying shift in values necessary for such change.

TOWARD THE WHOLE PERSON

It should hardly be necessary to assert that a sense of purpose is essential in the long run for any individual's maintained health. The degradation in behavior of both individuals and nations who have no humane and meaningful purpose has been forcefully demonstrated in the last few decades. (Purpose itself is not a "sufficient" condition, only a "necessary" one; repugnant deeds and wars are also often highly motivated.) The sense of purpose is fostered in an environment having meaning and coherence. In such environments there can blossom all the classic characteristics of healthy individuals and societies—notably stimulation, challenge, love, joy, happiness, laughter, intimacy, service, wonder, and reverence. Those whose bodies are well nourished and well exercised are also those whose brains are more effective vehicles for these aspects to flourish. Indeed the continuing challenge is to realize the necessity for ever-increasing integration of physical, mental, social, and spiritual aspects into a whole person. Fortunately long journeys do indeed begin with a single step, and each successive step achieved makes further progress both less uncertain and more appreciated.

The apparently simple and desirable attempt to implement risk-reduction programs widely may well lead to a thoughtful and long-overdue rediscovery of the need of persons to be whole in order to be healthy. In synergy with other developing social thrusts, this may help stimulate mankind to evolve a more stable, humane, and balanced society.

REFERENCES

1. Sackett, D. L. and Haynes, R. B. *Compliance with Therapeutic Regimens* (Baltimore: The Johns Hopkins University Press, 1976).
2. Antonovsky, A. *Health, Stress and Coping* (San Francisco: Jossey-Bass 1979).

3. Holmes, T. H. and Rahe, R. H. "The Social Readjustment Rating Scale." *Journal of Psychosomatic Research* 11 (1967) p. 213-218.
4. Selye, H. *Stress without Distress* (New York: Signet Books 1976).
5. Selye, H. *The Stress of Life* (New York: McGraw-Hill 1950).
6. Benson, H. *The Relaxation Response* (New York: Avon 1975).
7. Starr, C. "Social Benefit versus Technological Risk." *Science* 165 (1969) p. 1232-1238.
8. Benson. *The Relaxation Response.*
9. Cochrane, A. L. *Effectiveness and Efficiency* (London: Nuffield Provincial Hospitals Trust 1971).
10. Robbins, L. C. and Hall, J. H. *How to Practice Prospective Medicine* (Indianapolis: Methodist Hospital of Indiana 1970).
11. Belloc, N. B. and Breslow, L. *Preventive Medicine* 1 (1972) p. 409-421.
12. Puska, P. "Community Control of Acute Myocardial Infarction in Finland." *Practical Cardiology* (January 1978) p. 94-100.
13. The Multiple Risk Factor Intervention Trial Group. "Statistical Design Considerations in the NHLI Multiple Risk Factor Intervention Trial (MRFIT)." *Journal of Chronic Diseases* 30 (1977) p. 261-275.
14. Macoby, M. and Alexander, J. "Use of Media in Life Style Programs," in Davidson, P. O. and Davidson, J. M., eds. *Behavioral Medicine: Changing Health Life Styles* (Brunner/Mazel 1979).
15. HEW, National Center for Health Statistics. *Advance Data No. 3* (Washington, D.C.: November 19, 1976).

CHAPTER 23

Self-Care Today—In Search of An Identity

Jeanine L. Johns, RN, MS, ANP

Self-care is currently a focus of attention in professional nursing journals. Authors are addressing topics ranging from patient compliance with medication regimens to self-care's role in holistic health. Related conferences abound, and books including self-care in their subject appear on the best-seller lists. Despite this widespread interest, there are substantial differences of opinion regarding self-care's definition, its potential as a means of health-care delivery, its prioritized research needs, and its future role in health care. A look at these issues and at self-care's historical development will bring today's self-care into sharper focus.

HISTORY

Self-care may be viewed as a modern phenomenon. However, throughout much of recorded history, it has been a primary mode of health care delivery. Its decline and recent resurgence are the result of a number of complexly interrelated factors, many of them socioeconomic.

The role of individuals as passive health care consumers is a relatively recent development. In preindustrial societies, all but the elite members produced the majority of their own goods and services. Health care was largely the responsibility of individuals and their families. Formulas for self-medication were popular in seventeenth-century England; the first comprehensive self-treatment guide was published in Scotland during the eighteenth century.

With the beginning of large scale industrialization in the late nineteenth century, a number of changes occurred that contributed to the decline of self-care. One of the most basic changes was the separation of producer from consumer. The advent of the producer-consumer medical model was accompanied by the development of medical technology, concepts, terminology, and equipment at an unprecedented rate. These changes were often foreign to consumers and tended to reinforce their passive roles. As technology became more sophisticated, medical schools emphasized technical skills, often at the expense of personal patient/doctor relationships. These trends resulted in an asymmetrical relationship between health care professionals and patients, contributing to a condition of learned helplessness among many consumers. At the same time, increasingly available public and private health insurance allowed more people than ever access to professionally provided health care.

Just as self-care's decline was influenced by social and economic factors, so also has been its resurgence. In the mid-1960s, social pressures converged on the delivery of health care in the United States. The Kennedy and Johnson administrations emphasized health care, illness prevention, and safe environmental

Reprinted from *Nursing & Health Care,* Vol. 6, No. 3, with permission of National League for Nursing, © 1985.

placement of the aged. From this emphasis came the Medicare, Medicaid, and supplementary Social Security programs. The public became more aware of their health needs as well as the programs available to meet these needs. Consumers actively questioned the nature and the necessity of health care services.

Consumerism is even more prevalent today. Consumer interest groups are stimulating awareness and active participation in health care decision-making. Media coverage of major health problems has furthered their cause. Increased specialization and an emphasis on technology have left many Americans dissatisfied with what they perceive as an impersonal delivery system. This dissatisfaction has been accompanied by a loss of confidence in health care professionals, particularly physicians. Escalating costs compound the situation, contributing to a resurgence of interest in self-care among consumers, public officials, and health care professionals.

DEFINITION

If self-care is to become a major component of our delivery system, it must be defined in measurable terms so that it can be used in planning, resource allocating, and professional preparation. A broad, widely accepted definition does not exist today.

A variety of definitions have been written, ranging from the narrow and personally oriented to the broad and socially oriented. Most authors reflect their specific interests in these definitions, rather than broadly describing the concept and then relating it to those interests. *Patient education, self-help, compliance, adherence,* and *therapeutic alliance* are often used synonomously with self-care.

Lowell Levin defines self-care as "a process whereby a lay person can function effectively on his own behalf in health promotion and prevention and in disease detection and treatment at the level of the primary health resource in the health care system."[1] This definition illustrates both the broad functional nature of the self-care concept and importance of the individual in the system. Both are prerequisite if self-care is to minimize costs and maximize benefits.

Dorthea Orem defines self-care as "the practice of activities that individuals initiate and perform on their own behalf in maintaining life, health, and well-being."[2] This definition includes most activities an individual performs in his or her lifetime. She defines a self-care deficit as inability to perform all the necessary self-care functions. Her definition narrows, though, when she emphasizes the role of the physician in identifying the needed treatments.

Kathryn Dean describes self-care as "the basic level of health care in all societies. It can be preventative, curative and rehabilitative, but is neither contemporary nor reactionary. It includes the range of individual health behaviors: health maintenance/lifestyle, utilization of preventive health services, symptom evaluation, self-treatment and interaction with the professional sector."[3] Dean's description specifically includes provider/consumer interaction, while in Levin's that relationship is implicit.

Barafsky identifies four functions of self-care. The first, and perhaps the most widely perceived as self-care, consists of following a provider's directions for treatment of diagnosed illness. It is most often imposed, reactive, and either temporary or chronic, depending on the illness. In the second form, a person treats his or her symptoms without a health care professional's assistance. This is self-initiated, proactive and episodic. A third form is preventive—reducing life-style risk factors that may affect the onset of disease. This form is sustained, self-initiated, and self-selected. The last form involves regulating physiological processes required for daily living, such as eating, drinking, and physical protection, that are considered health related only in the broadest sense.[4] These behaviors correspond to those in Dean's definition and support a broad conceptual perspective.

CURRENT FORMS

There are many disagreements about self-care's relationship to conventional health care delivery. At the extremes are: those who believe we currently practice a sufficient amount of self-care and that to expand it would lower the quality of health services; and those who consider the present system narrow, coercive, overinstitutionalized, and asymmetrical, and think it requires radical change. Between these extremes is the view that self-care should be further integrated into our system in cost-effective stages.

Although there are some areas of agreement regarding self-care's place in our system, we are not close to a widely-accepted definition. If public and private insurers begin reimbursing self-care, covered activities will be "legitimized." This will develop slowly and will contribute to a limited, narrow definition of self-care. In the absence of a consensus definition, a look at self-care's major forms will provide insight into its scope.

Current forms of self-care fall into three categories: patient education, patient compliance, and self-help. Patient education is primarily the function of health care providers; compliance and self-help are undertaken by consumers with providers' assistance.

Patient education is well established today. It is practiced in some form by almost every health care institution in the United States. The need for patient education is recognized, but the issues of who should receive services, what should be taught, who should teach, and how to evaluate education's effectiveness remain unsettled.

Patient compliance refers to how well a patient adheres to a health professional's directions, particularly in ambulatory settings. Many health care professionals rely on patients' awareness of their expertise and respect for their professional status to stimulate compliance.[5] Studies show that motivation strategies that encourage patients to participate in decision-making are more effective.[6] These include patient education, contracting, and other forms of establishing rapport with patients, emphasizing a personalized, cooperative relationship consistent with a broad definition of self-care.

Self-help involves a small group structure with mutual goals to assist one another in coping successfully. These are most often voluntary peer groups that stress face-to-face contact and member responsibility.

Levy indicates four areas in which these groups are helpful. They are behavioral control, such as Alcoholics Anonymous; shared predicament, such as Ostomy Association; survival-oriented, such as minority organizations; and personal growth, such as creative-thinking groups.[7] Self-help groups that focus on health issues are accepted forms of self-care. Patient education and patient compliance are sometimes seen as extensions of the coercive model of health care delivery, rather than as true forms of self-care. When they exist in a coercive environment, that may be true. However, in more participative contexts, they are legitimate forms of self-care. The disagreement supports the contention that no widely accepted definition of self-care exists and that differences are based on preference, economic interest, and philosophy.

BARRIERS

Our economic situation creates formidable barriers to the integration of self-care into our delivery system. The health care industry is labor intensive and highly capitalized. If the preventive and self-treatment functions of self-care are perceived to result in fewer patients, patient visits, or days spent in hospitals and other institutions, they may seem threatening to health care jobs and to the ability to amortize the costs of physical facilities and high-priced equipment. If health care organizations feel threatened, they will oppose self-care's growth.

Health care professionals, particularly physicians, who are reluctant to change their roles and relationships with consumers, pose another barrier to self-care's expansion. Increasing self-care would lead to consumers questioning and challenging providers more, as well as to self-administering care. Many providers are likely to be uncomfortable with this situation.

Another barrier to self-care is inadequate evaluation of the costs and benefits that its adherents claim. Although some evaluations have been done, both proponents and opponents may continue to state their cases with little hope or danger of well-documented support or refutation.

Other barriers concern the problems associated with outreach and social structure. That health care providers can reach and relate to those populations not already receiving health care—particularly disadvantaged social groups—has not been proven. Neither has the ability of members of those groups to successfully participate in self-care.

In spite of these barriers, strong forces are pushing the delivery system toward adopting a broader role for self-care.

FACILITATORS

Just as some of the strongest barriers to self-care are economic, so are some of the strongest forces in its favor. The United States spends more on health care than on housing, education, or national defense. This rate of expenditure is escalating. In 1982, national health care expenditures were approximately $322.4 billion — 10.5 percent of the Gross National Product. In 1985, those costs are expected to reach $500 billion.

The health care industry has traditionally rewarded providers who have increased costs, not reduced them. The insurance industry-initiated perception of "free" health care is headed for obsolescence. Many companies are requiring employees to bear a larger share of their health insurance costs. Consumers know that high insurance premiums are passed along to them, where possible, in the form of higher prices, and that increased government payments mean increased taxes.

High medical costs strain our economy and cannot be sustained. Structured competition is here. Health Maintenance Organizations, which base costs on fixed payments, have an incentive to reduce costs. Higher co-payment requirements for public and private insurances reduce access to marginal care. Minor emergency care centers compete with hospital emergency rooms by offering prompter, less expensive services. While each of these alternatives has been criticized for possibly lowering quality, price competition *is* creating change that will stimulate self-care.

As the United States moves away from an industrial orientation toward an information orientation, structural unemployment is likely to increase and incomes will fall. Members of the European Common Market are shortening the work week, often with reduced wages, and some American companies have done the same. Studies show that people want to participate in producing goods and services. The combination of increased leisure time, lower income, and that desire to participate may contribute to the rise of "prosumers" — a term coined by futurist Alvin Toeffler in *The Third Wave* referring to people who do for themselves. In *Megatrends,* John Naisbitt indicates this will probably apply to health care as well as other goods and services. With increasing emphasis on health behaviors and on holism, self-care will expand.

IMPACT ON HEALTH PROFESSIONALS

Integration of self-care into the health care delivery system will require changes in health professionals' roles.

Existing health care jobs will be reshaped; new ones will be created. As patients assume more responsibility for their care, professionals will need to engage in patient education. Research is needed to redefine the roles of practitioners and academicians in a system that emphasizes more individual responsibility for health.

Attitudes must also change. As consumers demand a more active role, providers will become less dominant. Providers' expert, legitimate, and, to a lesser extent, normative forms of power will be challenged. For example, patients will want more input into the care process, request justification for , and sometimes challenge diagnoses, and expect to help prepare their records and to have direct access to them.

At first, providers may tend to resist these changes. However, resulting tensions may be positive. Interpersonal and intergroup conflict will lead to positive results if well managed. Potentially, the tensions will help patients and providers understand their capacities and limitations and work to accomplish maximum care levels.

RESEARCH NEEDS

Some of the most productive research areas are self-care's effectiveness, cost-effectiveness, and appropriate place in the overall health care delivery system, as well as the most effective and efficient implementation strategies. Methodologies to support these evaluations need to be established and developed. Present and future attitudes of providers and consumers need to be defined and change strategies developed for implementation. The structure of the health care industry as it relates to barriers and facilitators merits attention, with particular emphasis on the effects of competition and prepaid care. Cross-cultural studies of health care delivery, particularly in emerging countries where traditional self-care is being combined with modern medical technology under conditions where resources are severely limited, would prove instrumental. In light of the limited amount of research now available on self-care, any methodologically sound studies would be useful.

CONCLUSION

The dynamic health care environment, particularly the changing emphasis on self-care, offers challenges and opportunities for health care providers. A failure to meet the challenges or to take advantage of the opportunities will lower the quality of American health care. Facing the challenges head-on may help to produce a more cost-effective system that uses fewer resources to better meet the increasing health care needs of an aging population.

REFERENCES

1. Levin, Lowell, Self-care: towards fundamental changes in national strategies, *International Journal of Health Education,* Vol XXIV, No. 4, 1981.
2. Orem, Dorthea, *Nursing Concepts of Practice,* New York: McGraw-Hill, 1980.
3. Dean, Kathryn, Self-care responses to illness: a selected review, *Social Science and Medicine,* Vol. 15A, 1981.
4. Barofsky, Ivan, Compliance, adherence and the therapeutic alliance: steps in the development of self-care, *Social Science and Medicine,* Vol. 12, 1978.
5. Gannon, Martin, *Management: an organizational perspective,* Boston: Little, Brown & Co., 1977.
6. See note 4 above.
7. Levy, L.H., Self-help groups: types and psychological process, *Journal of Applied Behavioral Science,* 12, 1976.

CHAPTER 24

Home Visits: Effective or Obsolete Nursing Practice?

Dorothy S. Oda, RN, DNSc, FAAN

In recent years, there has been a marked increase in home health services due to earlier discharge of patients from acute care institutions. However, to date, no data exist to confirm that public health nursing (PHN) home visits result in significantly positive outcomes. Therefore, there is a critical need for examination of this clinical practice as the most common mode of providing professional nursing care to clients in the community.

One way to conduct an organized analysis of existing research is the integrated review (Ganong, 1987). Such a review of PHN home visits between 1960-1984 which focused on maternal and child health has already been done (Combs-Orme, Reis, and Ward, 1985). Four studies (of eight) showed positive effects and four others showed no positive outcomes. Replication of such work would merely confirm that findings on home visits are inconclusive.

Thus, this commentary is a combined developmental and research review to clarify the issue of PHN home visits as an effective continuing clinical practice and to demonstrate the tremendous need for innovative research approaches in this growing area of home health services.

DEVELOPMENTAL PERSPECTIVES

Comprehensive articles in current public health nursing periodicals reflect the development of public health nursing from its origins in communicable disease detection and public health protection to prevention-oriented social activism, and finally to primary health care community level expertise (Buhler-Wilkerson, 1985; Buhler-Wilkerson, 1987; Roberts and Heinrich, 1985). Early health visitors' duties involved doing anything that needed doing, emphasizing preventive rather than curative work (While, 1987). Visiting nurse agencies cared for five types of patients: surgical, medical, obstetrical, contagious, and tubercular (Buhler-Wilkerson, 1987). With substitutions of currently common terms such as congestive heart failure, preterm infants, and AIDS, today's list of conditions requiring nurse home visits has much in common with the old one.

The Diagnostic Related Groups (DRGs) have markedly affected acute care institutions. PHNs and visiting nurses, too, have quickly felt these ramifications that have changed the face, but not the nature, of home health practice. That is, home visits now, more than ever, are the vehicle of service provision. However, a higher acuity case mix of clients in the home requires technologically advanced nursing skills and more detailed documentation for reimbursable services. (Phillips and Cloonan, 1987). In turn, home health services have become a burgeoning part of hospital extensions and separate entity organizations (Alford and Stanhope, 1985; Coleman and Smith, 1984; Keating and Kelman, 1988).

Home visits, however, are not the sole domain of public health or visiting nurses. Brooten et al. (1986)

Reprinted from *Nursing Research,* Vol. 38, No. 2, with permission of American Journal of Nursing, © 1989.

concluded that early discharge of very low birth weight infants with follow-up in the home by a hospital-based nurse specialist is safe and cost effective. The net savings for each infant's hospital cost was calculated to be $18,560. Other benefits that are not easily quantifiable in this low-income, low educational level group were: (a) no incidence of failure to thrive due to parental neglect, (b) no reported physical abuse, and (c) no foster placement. These findings were not compared with other home follow-up options by nurses.

In another randomized trial of prenatal nurse home visitation (nurse title unspecified), the results suggested that nurse home visits were responsible for improving women's use of community services, informal social support, and health habits. Heavier weight newborns and reduction of preterm deliveries were also noted (Olds, Henderson, Tatelbaum, and Chamberlin, 1986). In this study, nurses made visits of approximately 1 hour and 15 minutes once every two weeks (average of 9 visits per pregnancy) and also provided developmental screening and transportation. Implementation of this pattern of nurse visits within an existing health care system was not discussed.

The above reports suggest that a nurse who visits a patient in the home with a specific purpose and population can effect a positive outcome depending on the criteria of the study. However, few, if any, studies are available on the efficacy of home visits from a generalized PHN agency by nurses who make home visits to a variety of clients (e.g., chronically ill elderly, high-risk infants) and for various purposes such as communicable disease follow-up.

Precise details of public health nursing field activities are rarely found in articles or documents such as the American Nurses' Association (1980) *Conceptual Framework for Community Health Nursing* or the American Public Health Association (1982) Public Health Nursing Section Statement on the Role of the Public Health Nurse. PHNs themselves often define their role as educator, counselor, advocate, etc. (Gulino and LaMonica, 1986). The provision of care by PHNs is frequently described as comprehensive and holistic. Objectives and benefits of comprehensive care are reported in such terms as "enhance the informal support available to the women," "encourage the women's relatives to participate," "urged to keep prenatal appointments" (Olds, et al., 1986, p. 18). These activities and outcomes are elusive to identify as role components and even more difficult to measure in a rigorous cause-effect manner. Thus, evidence points to the effectiveness of home visits in some studies and lack of evidence in others. The latter does not mean that home visits are *not* effective, only that there is no evidence to show a positive result.

The foregoing indicates that home visits appear to be an enduring mode of clinical practice and a means of nursing care delivery by nurses in community and acute care settings. Barring drastic fiscal or human resource availability changes that can make the cost of home visits prohibitive, it seems likely that more diversified types of nurses will be making visits to patients in their homes.

Nurses in clinical areas other than public health as well as nonnurse health care providers now make visits to patients' homes. Burn unit nurses follow their patients to their homes and schools (Manger, Rahim, and Zettel, 1987). Nurse practitioners are urged to market their services to the elderly in the community (Shamansky and St. Germain, 1987). Physicians, too, are rediscovering house calls as a form of service delivery to the needy (Reuler, Bax, and Sampson, 1986) and medical students are being taught to make home visits (Page, et al., 1988). Home health aides are providing perinatal care for high-risk infants after discharge from the neonatal intensive care unit (Raff, 1986). In England, respiratory health workers visit patients with chronic respiratory disability (Cockcroft et al., 1987).

Differentiation between public (or community) health nursing and home health care nursing has become increasingly unclear. Humphrey (1988) points out that home care is defined variously by organizations. The American Medical Association views it as an extension of the physician's therapeutic responsibility while the American College of Physicians defines home care as the provision of health care services in the patient's home rather than in an institutional or office setting. Humphrey (1988) believes that home care nursing is a new specialty and contends that "professional services constitute home care, and technical services provided in the home rather than in an institution constitute housecalls" (p. 311). Professional home care is explained as that given by any licensed provider and is practice-driven while house calls are product-driven (e.g., home delivery of meals and oxygen supplies).

Overlap of health services for clients in the community is not new and has always required coordination. But problems occur when overlap results in duplication or fragmentation of services. Continuity of care has been a cornerstone of public health nursing (Myers, 1988). However, it is becoming increasingly difficult for PHNs to spend time needed to properly assess the individual, family, and environment for coordination of care, let alone for health and wellness promotion. The emphasis is on quickly completing the assigned task and documenting what was done because "if you haven't written it, you haven't done it" and reimbursement is lost (Morrissey-Ross, 1988).

Before nursing care provided in the home becomes a quagmire of confusion, the nursing profession should examine home care services in light of the client's welfare. PHNs as generalists need to sharpen their focus on the traditional (yet newly relevant) concept of comprehensive care for clients in their roles as caregivers, coordinators, teachers, counselors, and advocates. Although the single specialized approach is a valuable resource and adjunct to the continuing care process, it is an inadequate substitute for a client's overall care.

Moreover, nurses must work together rather than in isolation from one another. Although discharge planning is a step in this direction, a nursing referral network between institutions and agencies that offers acute and community care would be even more beneficial for the client. A regional, or even national, clearinghouse for nursing referrals according to nursing diagnosis or client classification could be a workable system. Based on a uniform method of categorizing client conditions, a nursing plan might be retrieved from a central computerized source. As the process is now developing, nursing seems to follow the medical system of specialized referrals based largely on medical diagnosis, leading to further fragmentation of care.

RESEARCH NEEDED

Because of the complexity of a comprehensive service and the difficulty in identifying sound independent and dependent variables, further research is indicated on the efficacy of home visits by PHNs. Highrighter (1984) points out that research in the community setting is difficult when investigators have little control. Public entitlement programs have regulations that require certain services be given within a specified period, limiting an investigator's study period. What's more, service benefits within a public program have restrictions that can make manipulation of variables almost impossible. Also, design considerations that affect sampling, validity, and generalizability are problematic in conducting experimental studies with federal or state health and welfare programs.

Another complicating factor is the multidisciplinary nature of public health services where PHNs often function in a team relationship. Rigorous design requirements are difficult to fulfill in areas such as counseling and anticipatory guidance, which are fraught with variability and subjectivity. Cost-benefit and cost-effectiveness studies also present methodological problems in PHN interventions such as breast self-exam teaching and use of community resources by the chronically ill.

The review of PHN studies by Combs-Orme et al. (1985) showed inconclusive results, and the more extensive analysis by Highrighter (1984) concluded that the status of public health and community health nursing research did not change substantially over the ten-year review period (1971-1981). Most of the studies were descriptive, with experimental or quasi-experimental design being used in less than a fourth of the studies. Highrighter (1984) called for: development of a theoretical framework for public health nursing; examination of public health nursing activities within this framework; use of experimental and quasi-experimental designs where possible; replication studies; focus on major practice problems; and educational research involving groups of schools.

Collaboration of research-interested parties is basic to the advancement of public health nursing research. Mechanisms to join public health nurses in service with PHN researchers as well as investigators with other investigators must be made available. Too often, nurse researchers produce piecemeal studies in isolation and competition rather than collaborating with fellow researchers. Groups of investigators who can conduct clustered or coordinated studies that complement each other could produce a valuable databank on an area. Clusters might include related interventions or regional trials of the same intervention. Moreover, a theoretical framework is needed that would blend the research components or clusters into a well synthesized whole. The team approach offers the highest potential for solving design and methodological problems inherent in public health nursing research.

The clinical practice of visiting patients in their own environment is both an old (public health and visiting nurses) and a new (nurse specialists) service delivery mode that seems well suited to providing appropriate care to the elderly as well as to the very young. But what nursing needs now is an adequate database of home visit information. In particular, innovative research approaches are sorely needed for this traditional clinical nursing practice that is a vital part of the burgeoning home health care services delivery system.

REFERENCES

Alford, R., & Stanhope, M. (1985). The changing scene in home health care. *Family and Community Health, 8*(2), 66-76.

American Nurses' Association. (1980). *A conceptual model of community health nursing.* Kansas City, MO: Author.

American Public Health Association. (1982). The definition and role of public health nursing in the delivery of health care. *American Journal of Public Health, 72,* 210-212.

Brooten, D., Kumar, S., Brown, L. P., Butts, P., Finkler, S. A., Sachs, S., Gibbons, A., & Papadopoulos, M. (1986). A randomized clinical trial of early hospital discharge and home follow-up of very-low-birth weight infants. *The New England Journal of Medicine, 314,* 924-938.

Buhler-Wilkerson, K. (1985). Public health nursing: In sickness or in health? *American Journal of Public Health, 75,* 1155-1160.

Buhler-Wilkerson, K. (1987). Left carrying the bag: Experiments in visiting nursing, 1877-1909. *Nursing Research, 36,* 42-47.

Chavigny, K. H., & Kroske, M. (1983). Public health nursing in crisis. *Nursing Outlook, 31,* 312-316.

Cockcroft, A., Bagnall, P., Heslop, A., Anderrson, N., Heaton, R., Batstone, J., Allen, J., Spencer, R., & Guz, A. (1987). Controlled trial of respiratory health worker visiting patients with chronic respiratory disability. *British Medical Journal, 294,* 225-228.

Coleman, J., & Smith, D. (1984). DRGs and the growth of home health care. *Nursing Economics, 2,* 391-395.

Combs-Orme, T., Reis, J., Ward, L. O. (1985). Effectiveness of home visits by public health nurses in maternal and child health: An empirical review. *Public Health Reports, 100,* 490-499.

Ganong, L. H. (1987). Integrative reviews of nursing research. *Research in Nursing & Health, 10,* 1-11.

Gulino, C., & LaMonica, G. (1986). Public health nursing: A study of role implementation. *Public Health Nursing, 3,* 312-316.

Highrighter, M. E. (1984). Public health nursing evaluation: Education and professional issues: 1977 to 1981. In H. H. Werley & J. J. Fitzpatrick (Eds.), *Annual review of nursing* (Vol. 2, pp. 165-189).

Humphrey, C. J. (1988). The home as a setting for care: Clarifying the boundaries of practice. *Nursing Clinics of North America, 23,* 305-314.

Keating, S. B., & Kelman, G. B. (1988). *Home health care nursing.* Philadelphia: J. B. Lippincott Company.

Manger, G., Rahim, N., & Zettel, J. (1987). Home and school visits by the burn unit nurse. *Canadian Nurse, 83*(11), 24-36.

Morrissey-Ross, M. (1988). Documentation: If you haven't written it, you haven't done it. *Nursing Clinics of North America, 23,* 363-374.

Myers, M. (1988). Home care nursing: A view from the field. *Public Health Nursing, 5,* 65-67.

Olds, D. L., Henderson, C. R., Tatelbaum, R., & Chamberlin, R. (1986). Improving the delivery of prenatal care and outcomes of pregnancy: A randomized trial of nurse home visitations. *Pediatrics, 77,* 16-28.

Page, A. E. K., Walker-Bartnick, L., Taler, G. A., Snow, D. A., Wertheimer, D. S., & Al-Ibrahim, M. S. (1988). A program to teach housecalls for the elderly to fourth-year medical students. *Journal of Medical Education, 63*(1), 51-58.

Phillips, E. K., & Cloonan, P. A. (1987). DRG ripple effects on community health nursing. *Public Health Nursing, 4,* 84-88.

Raff, B. S. (1986). The use of homemaker/health aides' perinatal care of high risk infants. *Journal of Obstetrics, Gynecologic, and Neonatal Nursing, 15,* 142-145.

Reuler, J. B., Bax, M. J., & Sampson, J. H. (1986). Physician house call services for medically needy, inner-city residents. *American Journal of Public Health, 76,* 1131-1134.

Roberts, D. E., & Heinrich, J. (1985). Public health nursing comes of age. *American Journal of Public Health, 75,* 1162-1172.

Shamansky, S. L., & St. Germain, L. (1987). The elderly market for nurse practitioner services. *Western Journal of Nursing Research, 9,* 87-106.

While, A. E. (1987). The early history of health visiting: A review of the role of central government (1830-1914). *Child: Care, Health, and Development, 13,* 127-136.

CHAPTER 25

Abandonment of Patients by Home Health Nursing Agencies: An Ethical Analysis of the Dilemma

JoAnn Bell Reckling, RN, MN, MA Phil

Today's economic climate is forcing nurses to ration care to patients. This is especially troubling to nurses working in the home health care arena, where some nurse-run agencies are forced to either refuse care to nonpaying patients or go out of business.[1,2] Nurses, knowing that these individuals must often go without needed home health care, may believe they are abandoning their patients and compromising their personal and professional ethical obligations if they discontinue care. What ought a nurse to do when confronted with such a situation? Intense psychological pressure is created by this ethical dilemma, and it contributes to professional and workplace dissatisfaction for nurses, most of whom entered the profession in the first place "to serve people."[1]

A search of current nursing literature reveals that the ethical dilemma posed by the possibility of patient abandonment in the home health care arena has not been addressed. This article explores the ethical and moral aspects of discontinuing provision of home health care, for economic reasons, to patients who, in the nurse's best professional judgment, continue to need such care. Extremely important and complex economic and legal issues are involved in patient abandonment, but this article will not attempt to explicate them in depth. Rather, the focus will be on the ethical aspects of the dilemma, which has been called to the author's attention by colleagues working currently in home health care agencies.

This ethical dilemma will be analyzed following an accepted pattern of rational ethical inquiry.[3-7] Such inquiry involves gathering the facts; examining the choices; reflecting on the values, moral principles, rights, and duties that are applicable in the situation; and arriving at the best possible answer or solution to the question or dilemma addressed. Since "the very nature of ethics is one of dilemmas,"[8(pvi)] and an ethical dilemma is one where "moral claims conflict with one another,"[4(p6)] disagreements and alternative positions may result, but one hopes that the process of ethical inquiry will result in a state of reflective equilibrium, enabling the nurse to select a course of action at least morally tolerable, if not completely satisfactory.

The following definitions will clarify terms used throughout. *Abandon* means "to withdraw protection, support, or help. . . . Abandon suggests that the thing or person left may be helpless without protection."[9(p43)] *Ethics* is a level of activity that implies using a rational process to deliberate among moral principles and concepts or choices to justify a decision or course of action (ie, to indicate what ought to be done).[10] *Morals* are the fundamental

Reprinted from *Advances in Nursing Science,* Vol. 11, No. 3, with permission of Aspen Publishers, Inc., © 1989.

principles and basic concepts deliberated in ethics. The source of such standards is wide ranging, deriving from one's environment, culture, religion, and laws. Many philosophers consider beliefs about moral principles and standards of lesser certainty than absolute knowledge, yet they are stronger and bear a certain consensus and responsibility for action more prescriptive than that of a simple matter of taste or preference.

IDENTIFYING THE PROBLEM AND GATHERING THE FACTS

The ethical dilemma explored in this article is the situation encountered by a nurse-director of a home health care agency when all potential sources of payment for home health care services have denied economic support, yet it is obvious to the nurse that continued home health care services are necessary if the patient is to maintain what the nurse deems a minimum standard of health and well-being. The nurse's immediate choice of action is between two unsatisfactory solutions, leaving a patient without needed home health care, or threatening the economic existence of the agency, leading to potential societal harm by depriving many other patients of such care. Similar economic constraints are being encountered in long-term care institutions as well, but for clarity, the issue in this article will be limited to the home health care environment.

Although the issue unquestionably includes the broader problem of ethics in the arena of public policy, the focus of this article will be on the individual nurse, with inclusion of the broader aspect only as necessary. Further, although the term abandonment is also used in the legal arena, this article's focus will be on the ethical, not legal, aspects of the question of patient abandonment. Is the nurse obligated to continue to provide home health care to an economically destitute patient? Does refusing to provide such care violate personal and professional moral standards of service? Is discontinuation of such service abandonment of the patient?

Such situations are occurring daily and causing considerable consternation among nurses confronted with the dilemma. Evidence of concern about the situation is widespread, and the problem is increasing. Multiple references to the problem appear in recent health care literature.[11-20] According to Droste,[21] approximately 6% of home health care claims today are being denied by Medicare, and it is estimated that this will increase to 8% before it will decrease. The problem of denials escalated in April 1985, when regional offices started pressuring local intermediaries to meet minimum mandated savings rations. Since Medicare provides more than 70% of home health care agency revenue,[11] these denials directly affect the caring relationship between the home health care agency nurse and patient. Other sources of funding, such as private third party payers or community-based resources are sometimes available, but there remain a number of patients who do not meet any such guidelines. Thus, the problem of people without funds requesting home health care is a very real one.

Another factual part of the problem is the question of need for home health care. Medicare's regulations for home health care are not specific[13]: for instance, a patient is eligible for home health care if skilled nursing care is needed. All nurses are aware of the ambiguity of interpretation of the term skilled. Furthermore, under some circumstances, care by a home health aide is funded, but in some instances nurse-run agencies must also deny this level of care to patients they perceive as needing it. The standards allowing or disallowing payment for home health care are not now based on the judgment of professional nurses. This fact contributes heavily to the dilemma nurses face.

While some might perceive the issue of funding separate from the issue of discontinuing care, this author considers it a motivating force of the dilemma. First, the assumption is made that the agency in question is practicing good business management and all possible avenues have been explored to maintain the viability of the agency and still provide care to needy patients who cannot pay. Thus, the problem stems from public policy. If funding were adequate, the dilemma would not exist. Although this article will not attempt to explore the public policy issue in depth, nurses' responsibility for informing the public of the impact of policy on individuals will be addressed as necessary to better analyze the issue of patient abandonment as it is affected by public policy.

EXAMINING THE CHOICES

Social Justice: Allocation of Scarce Resources

The issue of patient abandonment is a problem of social justice (or more accurately, social injustice) and falls in the ethical arena of the allocation of scarce resources. If economic resources were infinite, or distributed in a different manner within the social structure, the patient would receive the needed care and the agency would be adequately compensated. However, since funds are not unlimited within US society, decisions have been made by private organizations and government alike regarding how such funds will be distributed. Currently, priorities for overall health care spending are aimed at acute care and high technology.[15] With the increase in age of the population, and the accompanying increase in the chronically ill, society is going to have to take a hard look at realigning these priorities.

Microallocation and Macroallocation

General distribution guidelines for society's resources on a large scale can be termed macroallocation and include allocation of funds in and among all facets of society, not only within health care. Microallocation decisions occur at a more local level, and usually occur after macroallocation decisions are made. A microallocation decision is made at the individual agency level regarding whether or not to accept a nonpaying patient, using criteria developed by such an agency to ration the resources accorded them at the macro level.

Because the issue confronting the individual nurse at the micro level is affected by allocations at the macro level, resolution of the overriding cause of the conflict must be addressed at the macro level. Macro-level changes that would ensure financial coverage for the patients now facing denial of services would ease the agency's financial plight, but currently the uncomfortable economic reality is that agencies must be reimbursed or they cannot provide services. Since macro-level change processes are usually lengthy, the prospect of immediate resolution of the micro problem is not likely, and the nurse will have to contend with the dilemma for some time to come.

Respect for Human Dignity

Integral to the professional nursing practice is respect for human dignity. Traditionally this respect takes priority over economic considerations. Clearly, the nurse who believes that devaluation of the human dignity of the individual patient is occurring will find his or her moral standard violated. Yet consideration of the human dignity of society as a whole, as well as of individuals, cannot be ignored. Thus the nurse's choice remains whether or not to provide care to nonpaying patients, with either alternative equally unsatisfactory.

PERTINENT ETHICAL THEORY

After identifying the problem, gathering facts, and examining the choices, the next step in ethical inquiry is to engage in reflective deliberation regarding possible moral guidelines that will aid in resolution of the dilemma. This process involves systematically using the process of reason to explore pertinent ethical theory, including values, moral principles, duties, and obligations that apply to any and all aspects of the situation.

Philosophical Perspective of Distributive Justice

Historically, philosophy offers guidelines for just distribution of resources. At least from the time of Plato,[22] philosophers have considered several criteria as options for fair or just distribution of limited resources, assuming equal distribution of a portion to each is impossible. Distribution may be according to merit or desert (entitlement), social worth, need, similarity to another receiving the resource, or even randomly, as in a lottery. But consensus regarding selection of one or more criteria for resource distribution, within society at large and specifically in health care, has not been reached and is a subject of numerous contemporary publications.[23-31]

Currently the criteria used to decide who may receive home health care depend on a combination of the above theoretical possibilities. Those who have accumulated means of payment can buy care.

This can be considered entitlement: such individuals or families presumably have earned or merit the right to receive such care. In one way or another, they have been able to accrue enough resources and have chosen to use them in this way, rather than to secure other goods. In other instances, society decrees desert based on individual need: for instance, care may be awarded to those with certain disabilities, because they reputedly deserve society's help. A debate now centering on social worth is focused on the aged.[32] Although age is named as being a potential criterion for limiting allocation of scarce resources in health care, the underlying implication includes the worth of an aged individual in terms of future societal contribution. It is obvious that requirements for being an eligible recipient of home nursing care vary widely and are not easily manipulated by the nurse or agency on an individual basis. The nurse must therefore look beyond traditional philosophical views regarding distributive justice for moral guidelines that will assist in solving the dilemma presented when his or her agency cannot provide care for such a patient.

Role-designated Moral Guidelines

Significant in the issue of possible patient abandonment are the variety of roles the nurse fills, since conflicting moral standards contribute to the ethical dilemma. First and foremost, a nurse is an individual adult human being, with values and moral standards developed during a lifetime. A significant additional role imposed on this human being is the role of the professional nurse, which carries with it the values, goals, and ethical codes of nursing that influence the nurse's obligations and conduct. The nurse is part (or the entire unit) of both a nuclear and an extended family. He or she is also a member of a larger society, which can be defined and circumscribed in a variety of ways, such as governmental, geographical, ethnic, and religious, all of which entail values, standards, and often obligations to others. And last, but certainly not least, the nurse commonly works for an agency that has its own standards, role expectations, and expectations of conduct.

With such wide-ranging potential sources for moral standards, it is no wonder that conflicts arise. The nurse might then ask the following questions: How can I prioritize moral standards that conflict when I use them to help me decide between the alternatives of continuing care unreimbursed or abandoning the patient? Is discontinuing care truly abandonment? Can discontinuing care be justified ethically? What are a patient's rights to home health care? What are my rights as an individual and as a professional? What are the agency's rights as an institution? What are the rights of society at large to health care? What are the obligations entailed by these rights, as well as those obligations arising from sources other than rights?

Consequentialism

In looking at potential consequences of an action, one usually assigns a good or bad value to those consequences. Since values can derive from a wide variety of sources, it is impossible to arrive at an absolute definition or measure of good and bad, but it is usually possible to ascertain whether consequences are good or bad relative to some standard. Yet one must consider the consequences as they apply to more than one side, or party, when a conflict is involved, and in the question of individual patient abandonment, consequences good for the patient (continuing care) may be bad for the agency (insufficient available resources), and vice versa. For the nurse, consequences of either action may be both good and bad. Continuing care may satisfy strong feelings of moral responsibility and obligation to respect the dignity of fellow humans and to the profession, yet jeopardize a job; discontinuing care may protect the job and enable the agency to continue caring for many other patients who would not be served if the agency did not have adequate resources to do so, yet leave the nurse extremely distraught over failure to meet personal moral and professional expectations. Thus, careful consideration of the consequences of either action for guidance toward resolving the conflict simply perpetuates the conflict. It appears that balancing risks and benefits of consequences will be necessary if any priority is to be established. The nurse needs to consider moral rules and principles as a potential source of help.

Moral Principles

Rules or principles of ethical conduct have been derived from a variety of sources including religion and philosophy. Rules can provide satisfactory solutions in some situations, but in others the rules may be inadequate or even conflict when two or more of them are applied to the same situation.

The following situation is an example of rule conflict and is often used by philosophers to illustrate this point. A German homeowner, hiding Jewish people in his attic during the Hitler regime, is confronted by Nazi storm troopers at the door. If he reveals that there are Jews in his attic, he will certainly be an accomplice to their murder, violating the "Do not kill" rule, yet if he lies he will violate the rule "Do not lie." More pertinent to nursing are situations where information regarding the death of a loved one might be temporarily withheld from a trauma victim in very unstable physiological condition. Lying might be necessary in this instance to prevent possible killing.

The problem of patient abandonment in the home health care arena exemplifies inadequacy rather than conflict of rules: this problem lies in those rules or duties that are impossible to fulfill in entirety. Such duties are designated as "imperfect duties" by Kant in his famous *Groundwork of the Metaphysic of Morals.*[33] According to Kant, perfect duties are usually negative duties, and are fairly easily described. Included in the perfect category are the rules "Do not kill" and "Do not make false promises." These duties are considered perfect duties because it is clear where their boundaries lie, except when they conflict with each other. On the other hand, imperfect duties are positive duties that cannot be carried out to an absolute extent. For instance, "Cultivate your talents to the fullest" and "Help others" (the duty of beneficence) carry infinite possibilities. It is unlikely that anyone could cultivate all of his or her talents. While "Provide food so the hungry do not starve" seems to be a sensible rule to follow, the responsibility of each human being who possesses at least minimally adequate resources toward those who do not is difficult to determine. Unquestionably criteria of distance; family, filial, and civic responsibility; and feasibility enter the picture and prevent absolute fulfillment of such a duty by any one individual.

Agency and nurse responsibility to help others in providing home nursing care is certainly one of these imperfect duties. It is impossible for one nurse or agency to provide home nursing care for everyone in need of such services. Thus decisions regarding allocation of services must be made. Those left without care may be considered to be abandoned.

If one tries to judge the duty of beneficence by the more conservative standards of nonmaleficence, the problem remains. Even the slightly more restricted "Do no harm" rule is open to interpretation: how much deprivation of what degree of quality of care is harm? Thus reliance on moral principles or rules, while somewhat helpful, does not resolve the ethical conflict that arises when it appears economically necessary to terminate or deny home care nursing services.

Consideration of other issues is necessary. Questions of the rights of the patient to some nondesignated quality of health care must be reflected on, as well as the obligations carried by the nurse and agency as members of society, of the nursing profession, and of the human race.

Rights and Obligations

Rights, and the duties or obligations that arise from them, are a complex subject that generates considerable debate among philosophers and lay people alike. The *Encyclopedia of Philosophy*[34] describes the attention paid by philosophers over the years to a variety of rights (religious, legal, moral, human, natural), commenting on the various interpretations and on the relationship of rights to duties or obligations. Some rights entail a duty or obligation on the part of a human being. But human rights are described as basic human needs, and it is noted that they do not obligate any individual or government to supply them; rather, they presuppose a standard below which no human being should fall. It is suggested that coping with meeting such standards must occur in the arena of social justice.

What constitutes fundamental human rights, those rights deserved by virtue of being human, is a subject for argument. For instance, while freedom is often considered one of these rights, it is limited when it encroaches on another's freedom. Another seemingly fundamental human right, the right not to starve to death, is not accepted by all cultures of the world; some societies approve of allowing unwanted infants or the elderly to starve. Neither is this particular right limited to humans: few in US culture would accept someone's right to let a puppy, for example, starve.

Differences also exist over the right to health care. There are those who argue that health care is a fundamental human right and there are those who disagree. Furthermore, since health care is a very broad concept, questions of rights to health care necessarily involve questions of whose rights to what standard of health care. Attempts continue to define a minimally decent standard of care, but again there is a lack of harmony among those who attempt such definition. Standards vary among cultures, governments, and even families on the same block in any US city.

Such indecisiveness regarding rights and standards affects one trying to make a just decision regarding home health care for patients without economic resources. While most nurses would agree that patients involved in this situation would benefit from home nursing care, many would argue that it is not their fundamental right. Usually the idea of protection of a fundamental right involves a more immediate life-threatening situation than deprivation of home nursing care. The American Nurses' Association (ANA)[35] code of ethics discusses protection of human dignity and protection of an individual's right to autonomy in health care, but does not define a right to health care. It appears that the issue of whether a fundamental human right to health care exists is clouded by ambiguity.

Abandonment

The term abandonment is often used in reference to the legal responsibility of health care providers in emergency situations where an individual's life is at risk.[36] Use of the term abandonment implies that the patient is helpless, which in turn implies that harm may occur if help is not rendered. Attention has been focused on standards of acute care, and minimal standards in the chronic care arena are sorely lacking. A minimum standard of harm has not been established. This problem is one of those addressed in the report by the Hastings Center project on ethics and chronic illness.[15]

Collective Obligations

One might ask, if minimal standards for home care could be established and agreed on by all of society, can an agency (as compared to an individual) actually bear a moral responsibility to meet such standards? Consensus within the business and philosophic community seems to lie in the direction of an affirmative answer. DeGeorge[37] and others[38,39] explain that when any collective (a group of individuals, such as an agency's administrators or management persons) engages in rational decision making, (such as making policies or rules within its structure), it generates an obligation to be responsible for the consequences of such decisions. Using this interpretation, a home health care agency might certainly be held responsible for some designated degree or measure of harm occurring to its patients as a result of its decisions. However, if minimum standards of well-being are not designated, and the individuals to whom such standards are obligated are not defined, it can be difficult to assess agency responsibility.

The issue of the obligation of professional nurses to provide quality health care without regard to economic compensation is skirted by the ANA code of ethics. It offers general principles to guide and evaluate nursing actions: "The nurse provides services with respect for human dignity and the uniqueness of the client, unrestricted by considerations of social or economic status, personal attributes, or the nature of health problems."[35(p2)] This statement seems unclear in regard to the phrases "provides services" and "respect": does it mean that the provision of services is unrestricted, or that respect for dignity and uniqueness is unrestricted? The interpretive statement further explains that "need for health care is universal, transcending all . . . economic difference . . . [and] is delivered without prejudicial behavior."[35(p3)] Although the code indicates that respect for the patient must be maintained without regard to economic status, it is unclear regarding any link of provision of services with the nurse's need for direct reimbursement. Thus it appears that there are no clear patient rights or professional nursing obligations that would mandate that the nurse continue to provide home health care services in the face of peril to the agency due to economic resource depletion.

IMPLICATIONS OF MORAL THEORY

Does the home health care nurse have a moral obligation to continue such care? This author argues that the nurse does not. The moral principle of beneficence does not imply that every nurse has to give home health care service to every needy patient. Nonmaleficence is subject to wide interpretation. Minimum standards of health care have not been defined; thus, it is difficult to determine what level of deprivation of care will cause what degree of harm. Obligation to provide care regardless of a person's ability to pay has traditionally been upheld only in emergency situations where the risk of death is imminent if care is not provided.

Is the nurse abandoning the patient? This author believes that discontinuing home nursing care is not abandonment in most situations. Helplessness is implied by the definition of abandonment, and degrees of helplessness are difficult to define or measure. Society does provide safety nets for people in life-threatening situations, and nurses must, of course, refer patients with such dire needs to institutional care.

The problem lies in the differing interpretations of minimum standards of care by funding sources and by professional nurses. Individual and societal consequences of providing care while imperiling the agency are difficult to measure. Declaring one consequence superior to another in terms of respect for human dignity is therefore impossible.

Assignment of rights and the obligations they may entail is ambiguous; thus, rights provide no clear-cut guidelines for resolution of the dilemma. The ANA code of ethics is intended to provide guidance, not ultimata, and its guidelines are general, not specific, regarding nursing obligations to individuals. The code is clearer in the area of responsibility of nurses to society as a collective. It states that (1) "nurses have an obligation to promote equitable access to nursing and health care for all people," (2) "nurses should ensure [adequate] representation [of nursing's values, goals and commitments] by active participation in decision making in institutional and political arenas to assure a just distribution of health care and nursing resources," and (3) "nurses should actively promote the collaborative planning required to ensure the availability and accessibility of high quality health services to all persons whose health needs are unmet."[35(p16)]

• • •

Therefore, no clear moral or ethical obligation exists for the nurse decision maker to continue care of the nonpaying patient. And discontinuation or denial of care, where immediate, life-threatening consequences are not likely, is not abandonment.

Yet, although the nurse is not morally or ethically obligated to provide care for a nonpaying patient who is well enough to be at home and not in immediate life-threatening danger, this does not mean that no professional responsibility exists. Nurses do have a professional responsibility to promote public awareness of the existence of denial of aid to needy persons. According to Evans,[16] change will only occur if and when public sentiment is aroused to the point that society-wide changes are made. In a thorough analysis of health care allocation and rationing decisions, he suggests that only when the public is exposed to micro-level rationing decisions that it feels are contrary to the interest of the persons involved will changes be made at the macro level.

What then should a nurse and a nursing agency do in such a situation? Unless the patient is in an immediate life-threatening situation, the nurse may discontinue care without violating a moral obligation or being considered as having abandoned the patient. However, as suggested by Curtin,[40(p12)] "nursing is a moral art," and wise application of knowledge and skill to benefit human welfare is a moral end of the nursing profession. Curtin further states that "nursing and the individual nurse are in very vital positions to help create a climate respectful of the human rights and needs of patients."[40(p19)] Thus, while maintaining patient confidentiality, the nurse must share information with public policy makers, informing them of micro-level rationing decisions that rest on social criteria for devaluing human lives, so that they can better choose among the options when public policy allocation decisions are made.

REFERENCES

1. Kelly LS: When nurses ration patient care. *Nurs Outlook* 1985;33(3):123.
2. Myers MB: Home care nursing: A view from the field. *Public Health Nurs* 1988;5(2):65-67.
3. Benjamin M, Curtis J: *Ethics in Nursing,* ed 2. New York, Oxford University Press, 1981.
4. Davis AJ, Aroskar MA: *Ethical Dilemmas and Nursing Practice,* ed 2. Norwalk, Conn, Appleton-Century-Crofts, 1983.
5. Jameton A: *Nursing Practice: The Ethical Issues.* Englewood Cliffs, NJ, Prentice-Hall, 1984.
6. Sigman P: Ethical choice in nursing, in Chinn PL (ed): *Ethical Issues in Nursing.* Rockville, Md, Aspen, 1986.
7. Veatch RM, Fry ST: *Case Studies in Nursing Ethics.* Philadelphia, Lippincott, 1987.
8. Chinn PL: *Ethical Issues in Nursing.* Rockville, Md, Aspen, 1986.
9. *Webster's Ninth New Collegiate Dictionary.* Springfield, Mass, Merriam-Webster, 1984.
10. Flew A: *A Dictionary of Philosophy,* ed 2. New York, St. Martin's Press, 1979.
11. Balinsky W, Starkman JL: The impact of DRGs on the health care industry. *Health Care Manage Rev* 1987; 12(3):61-74.
12. Omdahl DJ: Preventing home care denials. *Am J Nurs* 1987;87:1031-1033.
13. Coombs VA: Preventing home care denials is not a simple matter. *Am J Nurs* 1988;88:446.
14. Koren MJ: Home care—who cares? *N Engl J Med* 1986;314:917-920.
15. Jennings B, Callahan D, Caplan AL: Ethical challenges of chronic illness. *Hastings Cent Rep* 1988;18(1)(special supplement):1-16.
16. Evans RW: Health care technology and the inevitability of resource allocation and rationing decisions, in Friedman E (ed): *Making Choices: Ethics Issues for Health Care Professionals.* Chicago: American Hospital Publishing, 1986.
17. Rogatz P: Perspective on home care. *Public Health Nurs* 1987;4(1):7-8.
18. Humphrey CJ: The practice of home care nursing. *Public Health Nurs* 1987;4(2):79-81.
19. Phillips EK, Cloonan PA: DRG ripple effects on community health nursing. *Public Health Nurs* 1987;4(2): 84-87.
20. Kavesh WN: Home care: Process, outcome, cost. *Ann Rev Gerontol Geriatr* 1986;6:135-195.
21. Droste T: Alternate care: Medicare denials threaten the health of home care. *Hospitals* 1987;61(June 5):58.
22. Plato: *The Republic,* Sterling RW, Scott WC (trans). New York, Norton, 1985.
23. Rawls J: *A Theory of Justice.* Cambridge, Mass, Harvard University Press, 1971.
24. Nozick R: *Anarchy, State, and Utopia.* New York, Basic Books, 1974.
25. Calabresi G, Bobbitt P: *Tragic Choices: The Conflicts Society Confronts in the Allocation of Tragically Scarce Resources.* New York, Norton, 1978.
26. Outka G: Social justice and equal access to health care, in Mappes TA, Zembaty JS (eds): *Biomedical Ethics.* New York, McGraw-Hill, 1981.
27. Menzel PT: *Medical Costs, Moral Choices: A Philosophy of Health Care Economics in America.* New Haven, Conn, Yale University Press, 1983.
28. Daniels N: *Just Health Care.* Cambridge, Cambridge University Press, 1985.
29. Engelhardt HT Jr: Rights to health care, in Engelhardt HT Jr (ed): *The Foundations of Bioethics.* New York, Oxford University Press, 1986.
30. Morreim EH, Wenz PS, Menzel PT, et al: Costs and benefits in medicine: Some philosophical views, in Agich GJ, Begley CE (eds): *The Price of Health.* Boston, D. Reidel Publishing, 1986.
31. Silva MC: Ethics, scarce resources, and the nurse executive. *Nurs Economics* 1984;2:11-18.
32. Callahan D: *Setting Limits: Medical Goals in an Aging Society.* New York, Simon & Schuster, 1987.
33. Kant I: *Groundwork of the Metaphysic of Morals,* Paton HJ (trans.) New York, Harper, 1956.
34. *Encyclopedia of Philosophy.* New York, Collier Macmillan, 1967, vols 7, 8.
35. American Nurses' Association: *Code for Nurses with Interpretive Statements.* Kansas City, ANA, 1985.
36. Annas GJ, Glantz LH, Katz BF: *The Rights of Doctors, Nurses and Allied Health Professionals: A Health Law Primer.* Cambridge, Mass, Ballinger, 1981.
37. DeGeorge RT: Can corporations have moral responsibility? *Univ Dayton Rev* 1981-1982;5:3-15.
38. Feinberg J: Collective responsibility. *J Philosophy* 1969;65: 674-688.
39. French PA: The corporation as a moral person. *Am Philosophical Q* 1979;16(3):207-215.
40. Curtin LL: The nurse as advocate: A philosophical foundation for nursing, in Chinn PL (ed): *Ethical Issues in Nursing.* Rockville, Md, Aspen, 1986.

Belloc NB and
status and he
Birmingham JJ: T
Admin Quarterly
Bradstock MK et a
ic heavy alcoh
1985.
Breslow L and Son
program: a prac
Engl J Med 296(1
Dixon JK and Dixo
health and viabilit
Gross D, Frost AD a
of nursing: develo
work, *Nurs Health*
Johnston JE and Clark
mizing medicare re
8(1):45-49, 1990.
Keller MJ: Toward a definition of health, *Adv Nurs Sci* 4(1): 43-52, 1981.
Laffrey SC: Health behavior choice as related to self-actualization and health conception, *West J Nurs Res* 7(3): 279-300, 1985.

101(6):571-580,

Tripp-Reimer T: Reconceptualizing the construct of health: integrating emic and etic perspectives, *Res Nurs Health* 7, 101-109, 1984.
Wallack L and Winkleby M: Primary prevention: a new look at basic concepts, *Soc Sci Med* 25(8):923-930, 1987.
Weisensee MG: Evaluation of health promotion *Occup Health Nurs* 9-14, Jan 1985.

PART V

COMMUNITY-CENTERED NURSING PRACTICE

Community health nursing practice focuses primarily on population/aggregate health. The care that community health nurses deliver to individual clients, families, and groups contributes to improved community health. Because nurses initially learn personal, individual health assessment and intervention, the focus of community health nursing at the aggregate level is sometimes more difficult to understand. This structural perspective begins with an understanding of the concept and definition of community. A community can be a *place* community, defined by geographical boundaries, such as a neighborhood, town or county, or a *nonplace* community, which includes persons who share common interests, problems, and/or features, such as new parents, women over the age of 50, or the gay community. Each definition is valid and useful for the community health nurse in assessing health problems and identifying appropriate interventions.

Assessing a community differs from assessing an individual client. The nurse studies structural variables that influence a community's health, including political, economic, sociological, health, and geographical system variables. The nurse must understand the total community client in order to plan, implement, and evaluate nursing interventions at the community level. Effective planning for present and future responses to health care problems requires that the community client form a partnership with the nurse from the beginning of the nursing process.

The community health nurse works with various groups in the community, from prenatal classes to neighborhood screenings. Successful intervention at the group level requires an understanding of group process and dynamics. Specific high-risk groups are often the target of service for the community health nurse, such as persons with AIDS or the elderly. The identification and management of risk factors in such groups involves appropriate assessment strategies and health promotion interventions aimed at improvement of the total health of the community. Unit V provides selected examples of models of community assessment and methods for intervening at the community level, and articles regarding groups with specific health needs.

CHAPTER 26

Methods and Models for the Aggregate

Rose McKay, RN, EdD
Mary Segall, RN, PhD

The development of graduate programs in community health nursing in the 1980s presents a number of options that deserve recognition and exploration.[1-4]

Two types of issues are important in defining community health nursing as a specialty. The conceptual issue relates to the nature of the aggregate. Empirical issues include the length of the master's program, doctoral program development, and local availability of public health science content.

THE RELATIONSHIP BETWEEN THE CONCEPTS OF AGGREGATE AND COMMUNITY

The nature of the aggregate requires discussion and exploration. Williams defined aggregate as "individuals who have in common one or more personal or environmental characteristics."[5] To focus on the aggregate is to move beyond planning for the care of individuals to "monitoring, protecting and restoring the health of the population."[6]

Aggregates cannot be considered in isolation. The public health model emphasizes the complexity of interactional factors existing in practice. Decision making for the aggregate requires knowledge and skills beyond the clinical proficiency necessary for dealing with individuals. Designing outcome-oriented interventions for population groups should be based on community action.

While the definition of aggregate derived from epidemiology is clear, its relationship to the term community is often obscure because of the various uses of the concept of community in our field. Goeppinger states that nursing has used the term "community" to mean a geopolitical area as well as shared functions in an interactional group.[7] This is supported by Shamansky and Pesznecker, who define community as consisting of people, a time-space dimension and the network of associations and dynamic interplay of power and authority.[8] This flexible approach to the concept of community connects the related tasks and responsibilities of community health nursing, which extend from personal caretaking to subpopulation analysis and community level planning. Whether community is defined as noninteractional aggregate or as interactional group, it is possible to carry out assessment, intervention and evaluation at the same level. Community, however defined, is the target system at all levels of operation (see Figure 26-1).

At other times, "community" is a focus for assessment but intervention and evaluation relate to another level of operation. When this happens, the concept of community is functionally different because it is no longer the target system but has become

Reprinted from *Nursing Outlook,* Vol. 31, No. 6, with permission of American Journal of Nursing, © 1983.

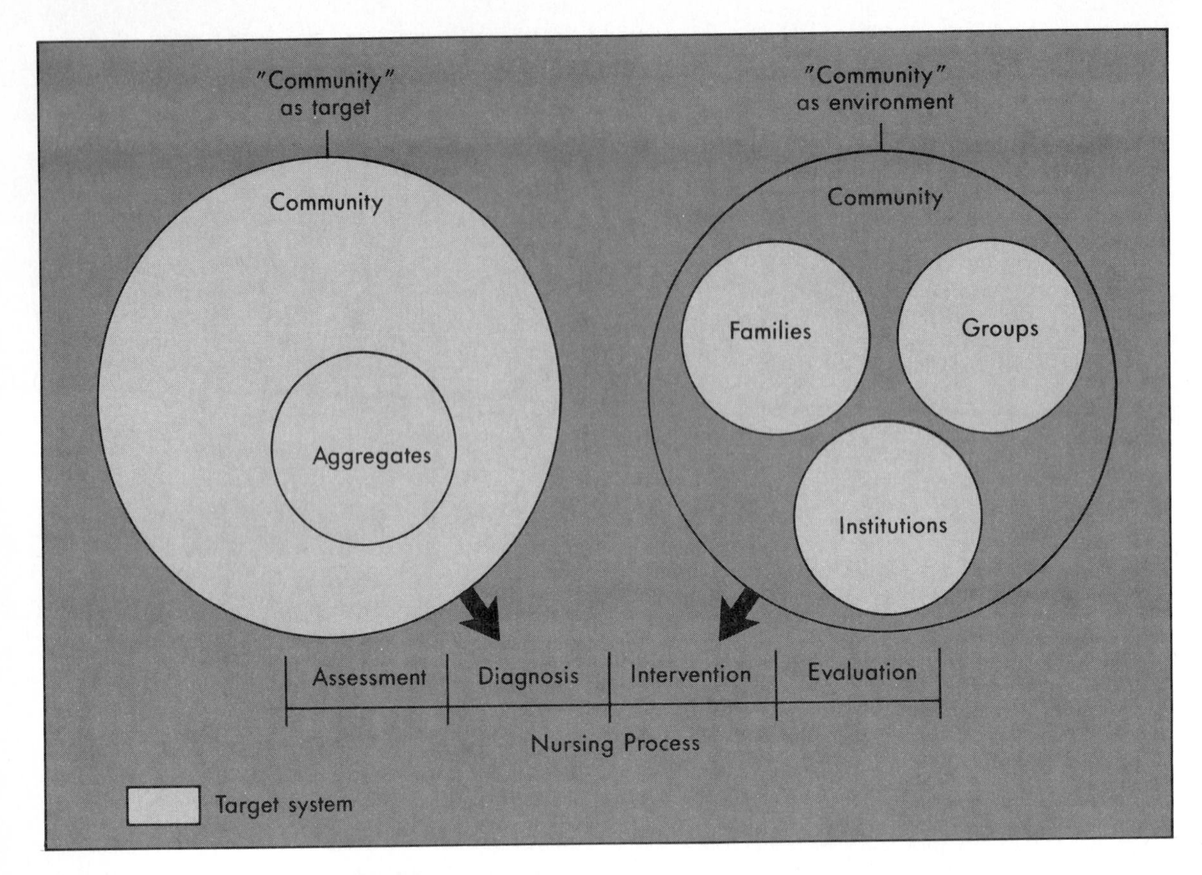

FIGURE 26-1
Comparison of "community" as target or environment.

the environment of the target system. This analysis utilizing components of the nursing process assists in clarifying the use of the same term under varying conditions. The fact that community health nurses are competent in community/aggregate analysis and planning either directly or in developing plans for intervention at another level is what distinguishes them from other clinical specialists and practitioners who give care to individuals or groups.

The inclusion of these two concepts (aggregate and community) is an integral part of program development in community health nursing. Through examination of the relationship of aggregate to other aspects of content, we developed a graduate level community health nursing program. First, we will present the specific community analysis plan we used at the University of Colorado. Following this, we will examine a model that we have developed that describes different possibilities for including the aggregate in community health nursing programs.

DEVELOPMENT OF COMPLEMENTARY METHODOLOGY

During the past two years, we have studied six rural communities, using two complementary methodologies—one quantitative, the other qualitative. The quantitative (epidemiological) approach describes the distribution of health and illness in population groups and clarifies the personal, societal, environmental and health care determinants that increase the risk of illness or death.[9]

The model of health that we have chosen reflects our belief that health must be viewed within a broad context since it is influenced by behavioral and environmental factors and the health care delivery system. In addition, the Dever model includes personal risk factors as a significant influence on mortality. The four primary elements in the Dever model are life style (self-created risks), environment, human biology and health care system.[10]

To begin analyzing the health of the population within a designated geopolitical area such as a city or county, we constructed a data base from multiple published sources (vital statistics, local surveys). The aim of this effort was to identify illnesses and health problems that contribute to the mortality and morbidity of the selected population. First, the leading causes of mortality and illness were described in relation to age, sex, and socioeconomic status. Then each element of the Dever model was assigned a percentage indicating the extent to which it might influence the occurrence of a particular health problem.

For example, a group in Georgia estimated that over 50 percent of deaths from heart disease could be attributed to life style, with proportionately less importance assigned to environment, human biology, and the health care delivery system. While Dever suggests that inferences derived at this point can be used to set priorities, establish health policy and allocate economic resources, these decisions could be premature.

The quantitative data (typically mortality statistics) and the subjective nature of the percentage allocation of the elements do not reflect the values and priorities of a community. In addition, this sort of data base does not identify the kind of problems that community health nurses typically address, such as home health care, family violence or health promotion. Because of these limitations we decided to carry out a second phase of data collection (see box at the top of the next column).

We selected ethnomethodology because of its emphasis on understanding people from their point of view. The goal of ethnography is identification of an individual's point of view and his vision of his world.[11] This approach has been a major research method of anthropology, but increasingly it is also being used by professionals in the health care disciplines.[12] Considering the values and perceptions of individuals and the society they are part of is mandatory for successful health planning.

Steps in community analysis

- Epidemiological Data Base
- Community-Based Interviews
- Content Analysis of Residents Comments
- Construction of Community Profile
- Net Value for Each Area of Community Functioning
- Ethnoclassification and Net Health Status
- Recommendations for Action
- Preparation of Report
- Feedback Opportunity and Report Revision
- Plan for Implementation

Faculty identified communities that were willing to cooperate with the planned ethnographic phase of the analysis. The purpose of this phase of a study is to learn from people what their world is like and what meanings people in a community attach to the events and situations occurring around them and to them. We, the outsiders, learn from our informants; without their assistance we could not understand their needs.

During the assessment phase of a community study, faculty and students focus on nine areas of community functioning: economic, political and legal processes, recreation, transportation, education, religion, family and health. This results in identification of the formal and informal structures of the community. We interview people in the organizations that reflect the nine areas of community function. We interview individuals such as the clergy, politicians, teachers, nurses, physicians, curanderas (faith healers), bankers, bartenders, bus drivers, shopkeepers, sheriffs, and real estate brokers. We talk with people who live in and use the various services in the community. We shop in local stores. We have dinner with senior citizens. We live with local families and share the local life style. While the interviews are open-ended and unstructured, the data base acquired in Phase I gives some direction to the discussions. Discovering the individual's perception and/or reaction to the community health problems and risk factors previously identified is one example. We construct a profile of the community based on residents' comments. This holistic view is a more realistic base for planning than the perspective of an outsider or even a resident with a particular priority such as health, education, or business.

This integrated community profile or description is used to identify strengths, weaknesses, and net values for each area of community functioning. Based on this data, we determine net health status. Using this information, a series of recommendations oriented to each area of community functioning is developed. A report is prepared and a town meeting is scheduled. At this meeting, confirmation of the data, feedback concerning changes and revisions, and plans for implementation of the recommendations are discussed.

To summarize, we have found it helpful to use these two methodologies when conducting a community analysis. The knowledge gained from the analysis of vital records and other data sources identifies patterns concerning the distribution of mortality and morbidity in the population. This knowledge helps to provide a focus in interviewing citizens concerning the quality of their life, their perceptions of health problems, and what priority they give to various health issues affecting their community. These interviews come from a large number of sources (e.g., 160 in Rifle) and are a valuable base from which community problems, priorities and trends may be projected. Health problems that have been identified at the population level are validated at the individual and small group level and then restated in the form of recommendations for action based on the local value system. Since these suggested plans are constructed on the basis of community relevance, support, visibility and identified priority, implementation of the recommendations by the community is likely.

CONCEPTUAL MODELS

When one considers the inclusion of aggregates in community health nursing programs, several patterns may emerge. The four models that follow include several variations. While these designs may represent an idealized version of the pattern, in reality most programs will be able to identify with one of the models or perhaps with a mix of their components. In any case, this structure may help to clarify the range of options available.

Each of the models presented assumes the learner will have core content in nursing and community health nursing research, nursing theory, epidemiology, biostatistics, and social policy. The aggregate emphasis at the core of community health nursing is a strong component in three of the four models. The components used in describing each model are: goal, unit of analysis, nursing process and product. The unit of analysis is the component that identifies the target system and the level at which the nursing process design is implemented. Design details of each model are presented in Table 26-1.

Aggregate Model

This model provides a design to prepare students to plan for solving health problems at the population level. The nursing role includes assessment, diagnosis, intervention, and evaluation of aggregates (populations) in the context of a community.

The content of this program includes mass data analysis, qualitative analysis, program evaluation, political power and pressure groups, and strategies for community organization. Graduates of nursing school programs of this type compete for jobs with individuals prepared at the doctoral level in schools of public health. If graduates of nursing programs expect to achieve leadership positions in health planning, we must have programs at the doctoral level in this area. Doctoral study would provide students the opportunity to develop greater knowledge in these identified content areas to extend their research abilities.

Aggregate/Administration Model

Many of the positions available to nurses with master's degrees in community health require administrative ability. A design that synthesizes aggregate analysis and administrative theory and practice can be developed. The administrative unit is the target system. The ratio of administrative content to clinical content may be adjusted to fit local program needs. For this model, aggregate analysis serves as background data for the administrative function.

TABLE 26-1
Conceptual model

TYPE	GOAL	UNIT OF ANALYSIS	NURSING PROCESS		PRODUCT
Aggregate	Improve the health of the community	Sub-Populations/ Aggregates/ Community	*Assessment:*	Risk factors of population Patterns of health problems Perceived needs and values Community functioning	Community organizer Program planner Evaluator
			Diagnosis:	Deficits relative to areas of community functioning	
			Intervention:	Influences policy and resource allocation Collaborates with others Participant in goal identification of community health needs Implements plans for nursing and health care services Advocate for consumer needs Designs the process for measuring program results	
			Evaluation:	Assess change in health status outcomes and community functioning Program service outcomes Determines match between needs and services	
Aggregate Administration	Efficient and effective functioning of the nursing unit within the health care system	Nursing unit or agency	*Assessment:*	Standards for quality care Staffing needs Range of client needs Sub-Population needs (risk factors) Resource estimation and capital investment Types of services available	Supervisor Administrator Director

Continued.

TABLE 26-1
Conceptual model—cont'd

TYPE	GOAL	UNIT OF ANALYSIS	NURSING PROCESS		PRODUCT
			Diagnosis:	Need for change—deficits and duplication Program planning and implementation Resource procurement and allocation	
			Intervention:	Setting priorities Organizing Staff recruitment and development Increasing power base Collaboration Negotiation Management of change process Influencing legislation	
			Evaluation:	Client care outcomes Risk factor reduction Staff-morale productivity Turnover and absenteeism Resource utilization cost effectiveness Needs vs. demand for services	
Aggregate/Family and group	Optimal functioning Decrease major risk factors affecting health	Family and groups	*Assessment:*	Environmental/aggregate influences Family/developmental stage and interactional patterns Individual physical and psychological status Life style patterns (self-created risks) Priority values and felt needs Stress and coping patterns Group interaction and role taking	Group leader Health teacher/educator Clinician (community health nursing specialists in various settings, e.g., nursing agency, school, industry)
			Diagnosis:	Health deficits due to life style patterns of the family or group Role within the family group Stress tolerance—coping patterns Environmental deficits/hazards	

TABLE 26-1
Conceptual model—cont'd

TYPE	GOAL	UNIT OF ANALYSIS	NURSING PROCESS		PRODUCT
			Intervention:	Advising (giving directions) Behavioral modification Shaping behavior toward self-responsibility Values clarification Teaching Counseling Modeling Referral Different styles of group leadership (support teaching)	
			Evaluation:	Changes in process and behavior among members of family or group Knowledge Attitudes; belief; values (self-motivation for self-care) Goal attainment	
Individual	Promotion and protection of individual	Individual	*Assessment:*	Biopsychosocial and cultural assessment of individual health status	Primary care clinician Practitioner
			Diagnosis:	Health problems and/or deficits	
			Intervention:	Therapeutic protocol implementation Educational teaching, counseling, behavior modification, advising Referral: community health services Management: monitoring of chronic disease states and drug therapy Collaboration with other health care disciplines	
			Evaluation:	Improvement of health status Prevention of complications Maintenance of health status	

Aggregate Family and Group Model

This model emphasizes interacting social groups, especially the family. At the graduate level, it can be used to develop and test theories of family functioning and to advise individuals in families and groups such as people at the work site. The design emphasizes adaptation to new life styles required by health maintenance or health improvement goals.

The aggregate analysis is treated as an influencing system for the target system (family/group). Association between life style choices and impact on health status identified from the aggregate data base is a major orienting perspective in dealing with families and individuals.

How much the community health clinical content can be expanded so that both the aggregate analysis and the family/group focus receive sufficient emphasis is a matter of priorities. The student can be encouraged to pursue an interest such as gerontology, occupational health, mental health, management, or teaching.

Individual Model

Personal health care has characterized much of the growth in community health services in the last few years. Many of these personal health services are offered by nurse practitioners. Some focus on one age group; others care for the whole family. This kind of preparation usually does not include aggregate analysis, but focuses on primary care. Primary care is usually understood to include first contact with the health care system as well as continuity, coordination and comprehensiveness of care.

Primary care, however valuable, does not include the prerequisite community focus and should not be seen as a substitute for community health nursing, but as a complementary practice area. A master's program that includes preparation for both primary care and community health nursing is probably too long to be completed within the usual time frame. Continuing education for both aggregate/community analysis and practitioner preparation should be available. Training for skill in both roles would be efficient for certain kinds of service delivery situations. The relationship between the community health nurse and the practitioner should be carefully examined since their continued association in care delivery is likely.

IMPLICATIONS

Methodology

We believe that the complementary methodologies described in this paper could be used to improve the health of a community.

With the focus on mutual goal setting and planned change shared among all members of the community, possibilities of highlighting programs for health promotion and disease prevention become likely. When the definition of community health includes all areas of community functioning, the result is a more comprehensive assessment of the influence of community resources on health states.

As an educational strategy, this methodology provides some advantages. The community data collection assignment is a time-limited field experience that only briefly interrupts a student's program schedule and offers learning experiences with aggregate/community analysis either limited to assessment and diagnosis or including the complete nursing process.

Models

The conceptual models presented here can clarify educational decision making regarding possible content and roles for shorter master's programs.*

The *aggregate model* emphasizes planning and policy making based on a strong background in public health science areas. When a school of nursing develops this type of program, what is the appropriate nursing content? Is it a doctoral program with emphasis on nursing theory and research? Problems relevant for nursing would be identified at the level of community functioning, and public health science would be a supportive cognate area. Participation in health planning and policymaking would be reinforced by a research base derived from our own field.

* Of 42 community health nursing graduate programs identified in the 1981-82 NLN list of accredited programs, 10 were two-year programs, 19 lasted one calendar year, and 13 programs were three semesters long.

The inclusion of aggregate analysis with *administration* strengthens the program by providing nurse administrators with the skills to develop community health programs. We believe content in analysis of community needs would be desirable for all nurse administrators. The design of this model emphasizes the functional role rather than advanced clinical knowledge.

The *family and group* model includes aggregate/community analysis content. It emphasizes extension of theory and skill in dealing with the family and group in a community context. While the individual is not a primary target of concern, the theories of family and group usually deal with individuals as well as with the family as a whole. This design is suitable for master's level programs.

The *individual model* focuses on primary care to individuals. Do the growing number of primary care practitioners in the community setting and the reduction of support for preventive services suggest that disease prevention and health promotion for individuals will increasingly become the domain of practitioners? If trends in this direction continue, possibilities for role change could move in the following directions: the staff nurse role in community health agencies will be oriented to individuals requiring home health care services; the main concern of practitioners will be the management of individual health problems including preventive services; the community health nurse specialist prepared at the graduate level will design and carry out interventions for groups to support change and lead to improved health. The specialist could also focus on these goals in an administrative role.

The conceptual models developed for this project illustrate one way to integrate nursing and public health content, which will continue to be a major challenge in community health nursing programs. These models, based on concepts of the nursing paradigm, reveal the limitation of existing definitions of health for families and communities. Without a clear view of the desired goal (health), assessment, diagnoses, nursing actions, and evaluation become almost haphazard. It will be easier to define appropriate nursing behaviors when their goal is clarified.

The claim made by nursing for a dominant role in family health care and planning and policy making for community health services is being challenged by other health care providers. By developing associations between the nursing model (person, environment, health and nursing) and public health concepts, the specialty of community health nursing will be strengthened and a sound base for expanded practice roles can be established.

REFERENCES

1. Definition and role of public health nursing practice in the delivery of health care. *Am. J. Public Health* 72: 210-212, Feb. 1982.
2. Flynn, B. C. Research framework for evaluating community health nursing practice. In *Current Perspectives in Nursing; Social Issues and Trends,* ed. by B. C. Flynn and M. H. Miller. St. Louis, C. V. Mosby Co., 1977, Vol. 1, pp. 35-45.
3. Goeppinger, J. Community health nursing. Primary nursing care in society. In *Current Perspectives in Nursing; Social Issues and Trends,* ed. by B. C. Flynn. St. Louis, C. V. Mosby Co., 1979, Vol. 2, pp. 57-63.
4. Woods, Jean, and Ohlson, Virginia. Graduate preparation for community health nursing practice. In *Current Perspectives in Nursing; Social Issues and Trends,* ed. by B. C. Flynn and M. H. Miller. St. Louis, C. V. Mosby Co., 1977, Vol. 1, pp. 158-164.
5. Williams, C. A. Community health nursing—what is it? *Nurs. Outlook* 25:250-254, Apr. 1977.
6. Sheps, C. Crisis in school of public health: the issues. *Body Politic* (School of Public Health at the University of North Carolina, Chapel Hill) 2:3, Aug. 1974.
7. Goeppinger, J., and others. Community health is community competence. *Nurs. Outlook* 30:464-467, Sept.-Oct. 1982.
8. Shamansky, S. L., and Pesznecker, B. A community is . . . *Nurs. Outlook* 29:182-185, Mar. 1981.
9. Ibrahim, M. *Epidemiology-Application to Health Services. Resource Book-Health and Behavioral Sciences.* Washington, D.C., Association of University Programs in Health Administration, 1976.
10. Dever, A. *Community Health Analysis: A Holistic Approach.* Germantown, Md., Aspen Systems Corp., 1980, p. 15.
11. Spradley, J. P. *The Ethnographic Interview.* New York, Holt, Rinehart & Winston, 1979.
12. Glittenberg, J. An ethnographic approach to the problem of health assessment and program planning: project GENESIS. In *Developing, Teaching, and Practicing Transcultural Nursing,* ed. by P. Marley. Salt Lake City, University of Utah Press, 1981, pp. 143-153.

CHAPTER 27

Community Nursing Diagnosis

Patti Hamilton, RN, PhD

The term *diagnosis* has been used in a nursing context for a relatively short period of time. Nursing diagnosis began to appear regularly in nursing literature in the 1950s and was initially applied to the individual client or family. A review of the nursing literature indicates that interest in nursing diagnosis increased during the 1960s with attempts to define and operationalize the concept.

Abdellah's definition of nursing diagnosis is an early attempt to define the term: "Nursing diagnosis is a determination of the nature and extent of nursing problems presented by individual patients or families receiving nursing care."[1(p25)] In 1973, Gebbie and Lavin initiated the first national conference on classification of nursing diagnosis.[2] They viewed nursing diagnosis as a concept critical to nursing, and they asserted that the classification of nursing diagnoses represents "nothing less than the systematic description of the entire domain of nursing."[2(p250)]

In approximately 30 years a new concept has become a part of society's definition of nursing, mandated to form the basis for professional practice by many state nursing practice acts.[3] In addition, the American Nurses' Association's Social Policy Statement published in 1980 states: "Nursing is the diagnosis and treatment of human responses to actual or potential health problems."[4(p9)] Professional nurses now define their practice as being based on nursing diagnosis, and society legally requires it.

Reprinted from *Advances in Nurisng Science*, Vol. 5, No. 3, with permission of Aspen Publishers, Inc., © 1983.

In light of these mandates for practice, it appears essential to develop a clear conceptualization of nursing diagnosis as it is applied in each area of practice. Significant work is being accomplished in regard to nursing diagnosis. Biennially, the National Conference on the Classification of Nursing Diagnosis meets to give direction to inquiry into the nature of the concept. Gordon[5] and Campbell[6] have published references for use in the education of beginning nurses and in the work of those nurses already practicing. Monographs, journal articles, and entire issues of journals have been devoted to the study of nursing diagnosis.

Much of the work concerning nursing diagnosis seems to be more applicable to the care of individuals than to the nursing of entire communities. Many authors make the assumption when writing about nursing diagnosis that conclusions drawn concerning ways to develop, classify, and act on nursing diagnosis will be the same whether nursing relates to individuals, families, groups, or entire communities. This assumption requires testing, and the analysis of the concept in a community context is a critical first step in developing research into nursing diagnoses made by community nurses. Such an analysis should include an investigation of relevant nursing theories, the actual practice of community nursing, and the idea of community as client.

Riehl and Roy,[7] who have worked extensively in analyzing and comparing nursing theories, report that systems theories and models for nursing practice are the ones most widely used in academic settings.

Neuman,[8] Roy,[9] Johnson,[10] Orem,[11] and Rogers[12] are theorists whose work is considered to be based on systems theory. Because of the widespread use of these works and their potential for influence on future nursing practice, these models were reviewed for their relevance to the concept of community nursing diagnosis.

Open systems models, by their nature, consider persons to be constantly exchanging energy, matter, and information with their environment. Although persons and their environment may be conceptualized uniquely by each theorist, it is assumed that environment in some way includes the geographic community. When theorists refer to society, culture, or groups it is assumed that these concepts influence or are influenced by geographic community and are, therefore, related.

Johnson's model of nursing[10] depicts persons as behavioral systems and subsystems. Nursing acts as an external regulatory force to assure balance and stability in both external and internal affairs. The strongest inference that can be drawn from Johnson's model for community health nursing is that the environment, including community, can affect balance and stability in behavioral systems and subsystems. Therefore, it might be concluded that nurses should consider the influence of communities on individuals.

Roy's adaptation model[7] is useful in community health nursing. She claims that "the person and his interaction with the environment are . . . units of analysis of nursing assessment while manipulating parts of the system or the environment is the mode of nursing intervention."[7(p170)] Roy identifies three types of stimuli that affect persons as focal, contextual, and residual, each of which can arise from conditions influenced by environment or community. She sees recognizing adaptation to environment as crucial in understanding the human condition and in directing nursing practice.

In applying Roy's model in a community setting, Schmitz[13] gives the example of a mother caring for an infant experiencing diarrhea. The residual stimuli influencing the adaptation of the mother and child might be "the cultural perception of the meaning of elimination problems."[13(p198)]

Neuman's model[8] depicts individuals as open systems, striving to maintain harmony and balance between their internal and external environments. Using the Neuman model, the nurse would assess human variables of four types: physiologic, psychologic, sociocultural, and developmental. The nurse would then plan intervention in one of three modes: primary, secondary, or tertiary prevention.

Venable considers the Neuman model as congruent with society's expectations of community nurses: "Primary prevention is more frequently seen as a nursing role in public health and community nursing."[14(p140)] Beitler et al[15] applied Neuman's model to community health nursing education and concluded that the stressors inherent in the poverty culture, the intrapersonal, interpersonal, and extrapersonal factors that contribute to the problems of the low-income client, and the primary, secondary, and tertiary forms of prevention, could be the basis for organizing content in a community health nursing course.

Flaskerud and Holloran[16] point out that the Orem self-care model[11] of nursing practice, although an open systems model, does not focus as much attention on interaction with the environment as do the models of Roy, Neuman, and Johnson.[8-10] Nevertheless, Orem clearly states that ways of meeting self-care needs are cultural elements and vary with individuals and larger social groups. The influence of society or community on nursing practice is quite explicit in Orem's writings. She believes that societies "specify the conditions that make it legitimate for its members to seek the various kinds of human services that are provided. These conditions become the criteria that members of the society use in determining whether or not a particular human service can or should be used."[11(p3)]

Orem sees four categories of nursing as a service:

1. home nursing,
2. ambulatory nursing for adults,
3. infant and child nursing in clinics and offices, and
4. nursing of all age groups in long- and short-term care institutions.

Three of the four categories have traditionally been settings of community health nursing practice. Orem also addresses nursing education by describing five disciplines that need to be offered in undergraduate nursing curricula. One of these disciplines, nursing's social field, is especially applicable in community health nursing. She describes nursing's social field as "dimensions of nursing as institutionalized service in social groups under fixed and changing social, cultural, economic, and political conditions."[11(p31)] Orem's work is useful when the community influence in nursing is considered, but her concept of the client seems to be the individual, not the larger community.

On the other hand, Rogers sees the individual and the community as "continuously shaping one another."[12(p124)] Rogers' model of individuals and their environment precludes separating them for consideration. She believes that to deal with a wide range of diverse human problems "requires the seeing of a pattern, a concept of the wholeness of man and his environment, and a recognition of escalating, dynamic evolution."[12(p124)] Rogers addresses community health services directly in explaining the theoretical basis of nursing. She sees a critical need to "incorporate within community based centers services designed to maintain and promote health (not to be confused with disease prevention) and to transmute the present limited ventures into truly community health resources."[12(p130)]

Rogers sees a strong desire of consumers to shape the nature and quality of public services because they are no longer content to be passive recipients of care. A recognition of unity and wholeness of persons and their surroundings pervades Rogers' model and has strong implications for recognizing the importance of the community in any nursing activity.

Based on these systems theories of nursing, the following empirical and analytical generalizations can be made.

- Communities influence the health of individuals.
- Individuals, in turn, influence communities.
- The community is an appropriate setting for nursing practice.
- Communities influence the practice of nursing.

Each of the systems theories has components of use to community health nurses. However, although communities were viewed by these theorists as dynamic forces, the theories contain little to guide the nurse in considering the community as the primary recipient of care. As Stevens points out, "some theories leave room for both individuals and groups as subject matter. More often than not, however, theories that claim this dual approach address only the singular man when they unfold the theory components."[17(p235)]

COMMUNITY NURSING PRACTICE

Theories of singular persons can be used in community health settings such as school, occupational, and home health nursing, in which practitioners deliver nursing care to individuals in much the same way as nursing care is delivered in emergency departments or nursing homes. What, then, are the differences, if any, between community health nursing and other types of nursing? The work of Archer[18] and Archer and Fleshman[19] in developing a typology of community health nursing practice may help in determining the nature of community health nursing. They conducted a 3-year longitudinal study of community health practitioners: those nurses who identified themselves as community health practitioners at a national American Public Health Association meeting. After an initial classification of five functional categories of community health practice, a revised typology was constructed to include six subsystems of practice classified by the nature of client services (Table 27-1).

Subjects in the Archer and Fleshman study[19] responded to open-ended queries to identify their functions as community health practitioners. The

TABLE 27-1
Typology of community health nurse practice*

DIRECT CLIENT SERVICES	SEMIDIRECT CLIENT SERVICES COMMUNITY NURSING	INDIRECT CLIENT SERVICES
1. Primary care	5. Middle management teaching	6. Administration systems management
2. Disease specialty		
3. Population groups		
4. Place or spatial unit		

*Adapted from Archer SE, *Nurs Outlook* 1976; 24:500. Reprinted with permission.

responses were then categorized. In the group studied, the researchers found that 40% of the respondents listed at least one of their functions in the indirect category. Indirect services in the revised typology included administering a nursing division or school of nursing; working for a professional organization; serving as a lobbyist; and participating in health planning, research, and evaluating services.

This typology represents the various foci of community health nursing practice of those individuals studied. The researchers realized the limitation of studying only those who considered themselves to be community health practitioners. There was uncertainty about what was meant by this title. Some of those who responded in the study had associate degrees in nursing, some had bachelor's and master's degrees, and at least two had completed work at the doctoral level.

Nevertheless, it is important to note that almost half of those who participated in the study functioned at a systems level of nursing practice and the implication for the classification of indirect client service appears to be that activities directed at a community system are an indirect means of serving individuals. Before these findings can be generalized to all community health nurses, replication with a different population is necessary. Replication of such a study should also include the analysis of nursing diagnoses made by community health nurses.

Some would argue that nursing is an activity directed to persons, not communities, and that health care cannot be given to a community.[20] Archer and Fleshman[19] counter the argument that community health practitioners involved at a systems level are no longer nurses by stating: "Our feeling is that to the extent that community health practitioners working with systems are involved in advancing the delivery of improved health services to clients, these community health practitioners are very much involved in nursing."[19(p10)] Doster concurs: "Giving health care to a community is essential for the achievement of the highest state of wellness for each individual in the community."[21(p83)]

Perhaps another reason there is uncertainty in the validity of nurses ministering to entire communities is that other disciplines consider community intervention to be their domain. As Fromer points out: "Within the past decade health planning for existing and proposed communities has become such an important factor in society that it has developed into a large academic field with studies leading to a doctoral degree."[22(p159)] Because of the complexity of working with entire communities, some experts in nursing advocate the preparation of nurses at the master's and doctoral levels for this type of specialized practice.[23]

Williams[23] recommends that more attention be given to the distinctions among diagnosis, treatment, and evaluation at the individual level and at the aggregate level. Considering either level alone diminishes the effectiveness of nursing. Although nursing of individuals need not be the only focus of nursing, individual well-being is the ultimate goal.

But a perspective that overemphasizes individual services can be counterproductive. Williams warns that as the components of primary care services are strengthened, individual and family services can monopolize attention and resources. The danger is that this perspective recognizes those individuals who place themselves in the acute care system for existing services and does not consider who needs services but cannot obtain them, which services might be more useful, and whether the services are resulting in a *real* improvement in the health of the community.

Is there adequate justification to assume that general nursing theory is sufficient to serve as a basis for the nursing of communities? Archer and Fleshman submit that community nursing is uniquely different from clinical nursing of individuals: "The core of our uniqueness, we believe, includes our breadth of knowledge of community processes and our expertise in adapting health promotion and health maintenance activities, as well as clients' life styles and environments."[19(p2)] Adapting interventions to environments and life style is addressed in general nursing theory, but degree of knowledge of community processes represents a gap in the existing theoretical bases for nursing.

COMMUNITY AS CLIENT

Current theory gives little direction to the understanding of the type of client of communities. Countless questions are unanswered. What exactly is meant by the term *community?* What are the characteristic similarities or differences among individuals, families, groups, and communities as recipients of nursing? If persons are bio-psycho-social beings, what are the dimensions of communities? Do persons and communities have the same needs and goals?

Current definitions of community health nursing practice seem to assume that these questions have already been answered. Clemen et al say: "In community health nursing the family is the unit of service and the client is the community."[24(p318)] The Nursing Development Conference Group identifies the goal of public health nursing as "the health of a neighborhood, a local, state, national or international community with focus on prevention of disease and disability, promotion and maintenance of health, and comprehensive care of the sick and disabled; and this can be accomplished through assisting communities toward self-care which contributes to the above."[25(p123)] The self-care concept also appears in Fromer's assertion that "the community must recognize and meet its own health needs, but it is the nurse who can lead the way."[22(p152)]

These definitions imply that there is some "whole" of a community that might be different from and greater than the sum of all its parts, an entity capable of decision making and action. There is a need for clarification of whether the community is merely the setting or context of the individual's existence and of nursing intervention or whether it is the primary client. Until nursing theory addresses this distinction, there will be confusion concerning community diagnosis. To illustrate the confusion that exists in community mental health literature over the focus of nursing services, some related terms will be discussed. Each related term has appeared in the literature as the distinguishing focus of community health nursing.

RELATED TERMS

Words that have been used to describe community health nursing clients include individuals, families, aggregates, groups, populations, systems, and communities. Although community nurses use the terms *individual* and *family* in virtually the same way as do other nurses, the terms *aggregate, group, populations, systems,* and *communities* may be used in ways that are unique to community health nursing. Kurtzman et al[26] refer to aggregates as "population groups." In considering the nursing process at the aggregate level, they used elementary school classes and dormitory residents as examples of aggregates.

Another frequently used term to identify the community health nursing client is "group." According to Spradley, "a group is two or more persons engaged in repeated, face-to-face communication, who identify with one another and are interdependent."[27(p288)] Spradley gives classes as examples; people gathered together for support, as in Alcoholics Anonymous; and people who come together to share a task, as in committees. A significant amount of working with a group takes place in community health nursing practice.

Populations can often be distinguished from groups in that face-to-face interaction and interdependence may be lacking. Spradley defines population or population group as "a large, unorganized aggregate of people, based on one or more common characteristics."[27(p289)] She gives adolescent girls, the elderly, and electricians who work in the communications industry as examples. In view of Kurtzman's definition of aggregate,[26] it appears that aggregate and population group are interchangeable terms. On the other hand, group has a connotation of unique personal interaction. When certain populations are identified as having a common characteristic, activity, or attribute that places them in danger of illness, injury, or health problem, they are referred to as a population at risk.[24]

Systems are referred to by some as the clientele of community health nurses.[18,19] The use of the term *system* in community health nursing has often been synonymous with community.

Hanchett says that in community assessment, system refers to "the community itself, no more, no less."[28(p12)] Rapoport defines a system as "a whole which functions by virtue of the interdependence of its parts."[29(pxvii)] Spradley[27] describes a community as having three dimensions: its physical location, its population demographics, and its social system dimensions. She lists as subsystems of a community its social system, communication, health, family, economics, education, religious, welfare, political, recreation, and legal systems. Thus, it appears that to some, system refers to the entire community and to others, it is a unit or component of the community, such as the economic system.

Society is another term that is often associated with nursing in general, especially community health nursing. Some would conceptualize society as being one level above community in a hierarchy of social organization. Weaver says that "society has often been called the suprasystem with regard to community, and as such, is considered to function as an open system as well."[30(p166)]

Nurses and sociologists have investigated the concept of community, and there is much confusion regarding its definition. Experts feel the word community is used so often to refer to diverse phenomena that it now has multiple, ambiguous connotations.[31]

A review of nursing literature reveals a diverse use of the term *community*. The literature mentions a community of need, problem ecology, concern, special interest, viability, resources, action capability, concern, an urban community, a rural community, an academic community, and a professional community, to name a few. It appears that community has been used to refer to both groups of people and to places.

Poplin,[32] a sociologist who has studied communities extensively, prefers to use the term *social group* instead of community when referring to groups of people. One reason that nurses might want to heed his advice is that it is misleading to imply that only community health nurses are concerned with groups (often termed *communities*). Prenatal classes for pregnant women, cardiac rehabilitation programs, and therapeutic groups in mental health facilities are all focused on a group of persons or a community of concerns or needs, yet the nursing intervention involved in caring for these groups is not generally referred to as community nursing.

When taken as a whole, community health nursing literature appears inconsistent and confusing in attempts to describe the focus of its practice. A variety of terms—aggregate, population, systems, groups, and many others—have been used to point out the unique forms of community health nursing. However, rather than clarify, often these terms have created more confusion. What is needed is a conceptualization that incorporates the dimensions of human environment in such a way that the various theories and models of nursing might eventually aid in explicating community nursing practice. One such conceptual model of community has been developed.

A CONCEPTUAL MODEL OF COMMUNITY

Sanders[33] identified four dimensions of communities.

First, Sanders describes "communities as a spatial unit."[33(p26)] This concept includes demographic characteristics, physical location and organization, environment, and technology. Second, the "community as a place to live"[33(p24)] is its qualitative nature in the view of its residents. Some objective measurements might be levels of income and crime rates, but more subjective information would come from interviews. Third, the "community as a way of life,"[33(p27)] an anthropologic view, is a way of defining the unique style of functioning from an ethnographic approach. Finally, Sanders sees the community as "an arena of social interaction."[3(p33)] To study the community from this perspective would require investigation of social systems, the distribution of power and resources, and the struggle to equalize their distribution. Spheres of influence and patterns of change (social field) would be also analyzed.

Using Sanders' model for community assessment, community health nurses might apply the public health sciences of epidemiology, biostatistics, sanitation, and human ecology to determine the levels of health and illness within the community and the identification of populations at risk for health problems. This would be a disease-oriented approach.

Investigation of the ways of life of the community can give insight into methods of making services acceptable and into the cultural meaning of health or illness; it can help to determine ways in which life-style affects health.

The social interaction dimension gives us a great deal of insight into the community of solution, the means of effecting change. An assessment of the dimension may require going beyond the city limits and looking at ways this community interacts with other communities. Clemen et al stated that "a community is a part of a larger society and has patterns of communication, leadership, and decision making which either facilitate or inhibit interactions within the community and between the community and the larger society."[24(p55)]

CRITICAL DISTINCTION

The typology of practice developed by Archer and Fleshman[18,19] helps to explain the unique functions of community health nurses in regard to communities and groups. Although the direct and semidirect care provided to individuals and groups takes place outside hospital walls, it has much in common with the commonly understood general practice of nursing.

Community health nurses functioning in direct and semidirect contact with individual clients and groups could use existing theories and conceptual frameworks for nursing; they could assess, diagnose, intervene, and evaluate outcomes in much the same way as nurses who practice in inpatient institutional settings because it is only the place they are practicing that separates them from other practitioners of nursing. This type of practice might be referred to as nursing *in* the community or as the nursing of individuals *influenced by* the community. Archer and Fleshman did, however, identify the critical element distinguishing community health nursing practice from other types of nursing: the indirect or systems approach to all those factors that impinge on the health of individuals and groups in a community. The critical element is the nursing *of* communities.

COMMUNITY NURSING AT A SYSTEMS LEVEL

Rather than merely taking environmental stressors into account or helping groups to overcome common threats to health, the community health nurse focusing on the overall system works toward implementation of strategies to eliminate or minimize stressors or threats to health on a systems level.

In an effort to identify a term or concept that would communicate this understanding of the importance of community at a systems level for action, the National Commission on Community Health Services[34] coined the term *community of solution*. Health hazards arise from conditions that can be affected by local, regional, state, national, or even international influences. For example, citizens of Canada are concerned with acid rain related to air pollution from American industrial cities. Community health nurses interested in this problem could not effectively limit their assessment to a single geographic community but would have to broaden their scope to the community of solution, which in this case would necessitate action on an international level.

There are those who echo earlier challenges that this type of concern and the types of intervention implied, including political and social action and economic analysis, may fall outside the realm of nursing. On the other hand, this unique form of nursing practice may be the only functional area that sets community health nursing apart from other types of nursing practice. Archer and Fleshman warn: "Unless community nurses can differentiate their area of practice and expertise from the area of those adopting an expanded community orientation within their fields, it is possible that Community Health Nursing could be integrated out of existence."[19(p2)]

Considering the increasing interest in the politics of health care delivery and the widening opportunities for nurses in all practice areas to participate in health planning, it may become an artificial distinction to call some nurses community nurses simply because they focus on the organizations or systems in communities that influence the health of individuals. For the sake of nurses and their clients, it may become imperative that all nurses adopt this broader view of caring.

Nursing theory as applied to individuals guides assessment, implementation, and evaluation. For example, in a model based on adaptation, a nurse can draw inferences about phenomena that exemplify adaptation or maladaptation. But nursing theory has not developed sufficiently to guide community health nurses in assessment, diagnosis, intervention, and evaluation of ways community systems influence health. Community health nurses have used public health science for this guidance, and in some cases, community health nursing is defined as the merging of nursing with public health science.[35]

Williams[23] points out that public health science directs the attention of nursing to the effects by environmental factors on the health of populations. The study of sanitation, communicable diseases, and biostatistics historically developed as public health sciences and these were adopted for use by community health nurses. But considering the views of nurse theorists, primarily Rogers,[12] concerning the unity of persons and their environment and the wholeness of all dimensions of human experience, it is clear that the public health sciences based largely on a biomedical model are inadequate to explain the influence of individuals on communities and of communities on the health of individuals.

Conceptualization of communities as physical/sociocultural/experiential entities provides a framework for assessing the community in terms of functional and structural characteristics. This is a task that Braden et al[36] see as a necessary part of applying the nursing process at a community systems level.

NURSING DIAGNOSIS

The definition of nursing diagnosis accepted at the First National Conference on Classification of Nursing Diagnoses in 1973 stated that nursing diagnosis is "the judgment or conclusion which occurs as a result of a nursing assessment."[2(p250)] In the intervening years, the concept of nursing diagnosis has been expanded and refined. In 1982, Andrews defined nursing diagnosis as "a clear, concise, and definitive statement of the client's health status and concerns that can be affected by nursing intervention." She says: "A nursing diagnosis is derived from inferences of assessed validated data and from perceptions. It follows a careful investigation of the data and results in a decision or opinion."[37(p111)]

Nursing diagnoses have to meet explicit guidelines of form and process. Andrews has outlined four steps to follow in developing a nursing diagnosis.[37(pp116-118)]

1. Determine health status and concerns.
2. Write a nursing diagnosis.
3. Validate the nursing diagnosis and recheck it.
4. Arrange the nursing diagnoses in order of priority.

The structure of the actual nursing diagnosis has been considered by numerous nurse theorists.[3,5,37] Gordon and Sweeney address the structural components of nursing diagnosis by stating that it should be a "concise term representing a cluster of signs and symptoms and describing an actual or potential health problem or state of the patient which nurses by virtue of their education and experience are licensed and able to treat."[3(p2)] They assert that the statement of nursing diagnosis must contain the problem, etiologic factors, and signs and symptoms.

In addition to process and structure, there are conceptual considerations. How to go through the steps of the process and what a nursing diagnosis must include are much simpler to determine than what type of framework is needed to conceptualize a nursing diagnosis. Gordon and Sweeney summarize the work of Soares,[38] Yura and Walsh,[39] and Little and Carnevali[40] to determine a conceptual focus for nursing diagnosis. These major theorists in the field have proposed conflict in needs, deprivation or alterations in meeting human needs, and response to stressors or potential stressors as models to guide nursing diagnosis. As previously demonstrated by the diversity in nursing systems models, the frameworks for assessment and diagnoses might also include adaptation, self-care deficits, and maladaptation patterns of unitary humans.

Again, the community health nurse is faced with using theories and models based primarily on singular persons to organize data gathering and decision making on a community level. Gordon addresses the multiplicity of nursing models for nursing practice by proposing health patterns that she believes transcend most nursing theories and can be applied regardless of the area of practice:[5(p81)]

- health perception-health management,
- nutritional-metabolic,
- elimination,
- activity-exercise,
- sleep-rest,
- cognitive-perceptual,
- self-perception/self-concept,
- role relationship,
- sexuality-reproductive,
- coping-stress-tolerance, and
- value-belief.

If a model such as the Sanders[33] model were applied to community health nursing practice, could the Gordon typology be used as well? At first glance, the model seems to be aimed primarily at assessment and diagnosis of individuals. Yet, some enlightening examples provided by Gordon show that there may be some pertinence to a community focus. Considering the Sanders model, which includes the community as a place to live (the qualitative nature), it is clear that

Gordon's functional patterns of role relationships, coping-stress-tolerance, and self-perception/self-concept are pertinent. But it is not as obvious how this typology would aid the community health nurse concerned with inefficient allocation of health care resources or the rising cost of health care.

Perhaps this is the reason why the diagnoses accepted at the Fourth National Conference on Classification of Nursing Diagnoses are ostensibly appropriate for individuals, not communities. It is more apparent how the nurse might develop a nursing diagnosis of an individual *in* a community setting or *influenced by* a community, rather than a nursing diagnosis *of* a community. If these theorists do not provide an example of a nursing diagnosis of a community, then other sources must be scrutinized.

A unique book by Griffith and Christensen[41] which applies theories, frameworks, and models to the nursing process, includes a helpful section on nursing diagnoses for community health concerns. The following are model cases representing nursing diagnoses *of* communities:[37(p125)]

- increased number of respiratory diseases related to air pollution,
- increased number of dog bites related to inadequate code enforcement,
- increased infant mortality rate related to increased teenage pregnancies,
- increased number of lead poisoning cases in toddlers related to substandard housing or lack of prevention or knowledge,
- decreased communication related to sectionalism,
- lack of neighborhood participation related to apathy.

DIAGNOSTIC AND PROVISIONAL CRITERIA

The criteria that set Andrews' diagnoses[37] apart from nursing diagnoses of individuals *in* the community or individuals *influenced by* the community are as follows:

- They are generated from assessments, not only of the state of individuals, but also of the state of the community as a physical/sociocultural/experiential entity.
- Relational statements imply intervention not by providing direct client services, although these may be the ultimate result, but by instituting some change in the present community.
- The implied direct client is the community; the indirect client is the individual.

In other words the one provisional criterion is the community being the direct client. It is primarily this feature that distinguishes community nursing diagnoses from nursing diagnoses of individuals *in* the community or individuals *influenced* by the community.

EMPIRICAL AND CLINICAL REFERENTS

Sanders' community model[33] can guide in identifying the empirical/clinical referents for nursing diagnoses of communities. To study the community as a spatial unit suggests demographic data collection. Such information as maps, census bureau reports, and morbidity and mortality statistics by area would all be useful.

To consider the community as a way of life, the cultural dimension, lists of civic groups, observations of neighborhoods, and census reports on ethnicity would be examined.

To examine the community as a place to live, opinion polls, oral and written community histories, crime rates, employment figures, and housing and work conditions would be studied.

Finally, to become aware of the social forces at work in a community, personal reports of conflicts and cooperation among groups would be obtained, and community agency directories; city, county, state, and federal budgets; voting records; and newspaper articles would be examined.

ANTECEDENTS AND CONSEQUENCES

Those factors that must be present to facilitate development of nursing diagnoses of communities are similar to the antecedents of other types of nursing diagnoses. Nurses need sound decision-making skills, as well as experiential and educational preparation adequate to enable them to understand all the dimensions of individual-community interaction. There must also be some assessment tool or scheme that can aid in gathering pertinent information. Andrews,[37] in agreement with other nurses, sees diagnosis as a part

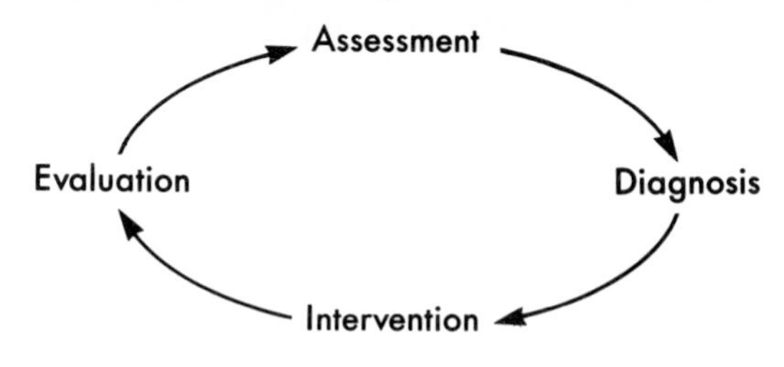

FIGURE 27-1
Diagnosis as part of the nursing process.

of the nursing process as shown in Figure 27-1. She says: "The diagnostic process is never complete as long as there is a nurse-client contact."[37(p116)]

Classification of nursing diagnoses will likely occur in the future, providing insight into the true practice of community nursing. Gordon and Sweeney[3] believe nursing diagnoses can serve to

- guide the education of nurses,
- aid in writing outcomes in quality assurance programs,
- assist in measuring the cost-effectiveness of care, and
- determine staff assignments.

They could also be used to provide a framework for resource allocation.

Some consequences of clearly stating nursing diagnoses of communities can be somewhat threatening. Mundinger and Jauron point out that "it demands risk taking for the nurse, because she is putting her inferences in print to be scrutinized by other chart readers."[42(p98)] Tucker speaks specifically to community health nurses making explicit diagnoses:

> The implication for community health workers is inescapable. The most meaningful preventive actions, those most effective in producing a safe and healthy existence for the community are universalist, that is, political. . . . Participating in these activities will involve some risk.[31(p186)]

RECOMMENDATION FOR RESEARCH

The analysis of the concept of community nursing diagnosis reveals a variety of areas of potential research. First, there is great need for investigation into the nature of communities. Related to this is the question of the type of clients in communities. What are communities like and in what ways do nurses enter into association with communities to work for change in health status?

Studying the scope of effectiveness of nurses with communities as clients would also be worthwhile. This might be accomplished in part by replication and expansion of the typology of community nursing practice begun by Archer and Fleshman.[19]

As the concept of nursing diagnosis is applied by community nurses, perhaps it will become clear if nursing of individuals *in* the community, nursing of individuals *influenced by* the community, and nursing *of* the community are real or artificial distinctions. The assumptions that the nursing of individuals will improve communities and that nursing of communities will improve the lives of individuals are also in need of validation.

REFERENCES

1. Abdellah FG, Levine E: *Better Patient Care Through Nursing Research.* New York, The Macmillan Co, 1975.
2. Gebbie K, Lavin MA: Classifying nursing diagnoses. *Am J Nurs* 1974;74:250-253.
3. Gordon M, Sweeney MA: Methodological problems and issues in identifying and standardizing nursing diagnoses. *Adv Nurs Sci* 1979;2(1):1-15.
4. *Nursing: A Social Policy Statement,* American Nurses' Association publication code NP-63, 35M. December 1980.
5. Gordon M: *Nursing Diagnosis: Process and Application.* New York, McGraw-Hill, 1982.
6. Campbell C: *Nursing Diagnosis and Intervention in Nursing Practice.* New York, John Wiley & Sons, 1978.
7. Riehl JP, Roy C: *Conceptual Models for Nursing Practice.* New York, Appleton-Century-Crofts, 1980.
8. Neuman B: The Betty Neuman health care systems model: A total person approach to patient problems, in Riehl JP, Roy C (eds): *Conceptual Models for Nursing Practice.* New York, Appleton-Century-Crofts, 1980, pp 119-134.
9. Roy CA: A diagnostic classification system for nursing. *Nurs Outlook* 1975;23:91.
10. Johnson DE: The behavioral system model for nursing, in Riehl JP, Roy C (eds): *Conceptual Models for Nursing Practice.* New York, Appleton-Century-Crofts, 1980.
11. Orem DE: *Nursing: Concepts of Practice,* ed 2. New York, McGraw-Hill, 1980.
12. Rogers ME: *An Introduction to the Theoretical Basis of Nursing.* Philadelphia, FA Davis Co, 1970.

13. Schmitz M: The Roy adaptation model: Application in a community setting, in Riehl JP, Roy C (eds): *Conceptual Models for Nursing Practice.* New York, Appleton-Century-Crofts, 1980.
14. Venable JF: The Neuman health-care systems model: An analysis, in Riehl JP, Roy C (eds): *Conceptual Models for Nursing Practice.* New York, Appleton-Century-Crofts, 1980.
15. Beitler B, Aamodt D, Tkachuck B: The Neuman model applied to mental health, community health, and medical-surgical nursing, in Riehl JP, Roy C (eds): *Conceptual Models for Nursing Practice.* New York, Appleton-Century-Crofts, 1980.
16. Flaskerud JH, Holloran EJ: Areas of agreement in nursing theory development. *Adv Nurs Sci* 1980;3(1):1-7.
17. Stevens BJ: *Nursing Theory Analysis, Application, Evaluation.* Boston, Little Brown & Co, 1979.
18. Archer SE: Community nurse practitioners: Another assessment. *Nurs Outlook* 1976;24:499-503.
19. Archer SE, Fleshman RP: Community health nursing: A typology of practice. *Nurs Outlook* 1975;23:358-364.
20. Kinlein ML: Point of view/on the front: Nursing and family and community health. *Fam Community Health* 1978;1(1):57-68.
21. Doster CC: Health index of a community, in *Community Health — Today and Tomorrow,* National League for Nursing, New York, publication No. 52-1768, 979.
22. Fromer MJ: *Community Health Care and the Nursing Process.* St Louis, CV Mosby, 1979.
23. Williams CA: Community health nursing — what is it? in O'Connor AB (ed): *Nursing in Community Health Settings.* New York, American Journal of Nursing Co, 1978.
24. Clemen SA, Eigsti DG, McGuire SL: *Comprehensive Family and Community Health Nursing.* New York, McGraw-Hill, 1981.
25. The Nursing Development Conference Group: *Concept Formalization in Nursing: Process and Product.* Boston, Little Brown & Co, 1973.
26. Kurtzman C, Ibgui DF, Pogrund R, et al: Nursing process at the aggregate level. *Nurs Outlook* 1980;28:737-739.
27. Spradley BW: *Community Health Nursing, Concepts, and Practice.* Boston, Little Brown & Co, 1981.
28. Hanchett E: *Community Health Assessment: A Conceptual Tool Kit.* New York, John Wiley & Sons, 1979.
29. Rapoport A: Foreword, in Buckley W (ed): *Modern Systems Research for the Behavioral Scientist.* Chicago, Aldine, 1968, pp xvii, xiii-xxii.
30. Weaver BR: Conceptual basis for nursing intervention with human systems: Communities and societies, in Hall JE, Weaver BR (eds): *Distributive Nursing Practice: A Systems Approach to Community Health.* Philadelphia, JB Lippincott Co, 1977.
31. Tucker WH: The nature of a community, in Fromer MJ (ed): *Community Health Care and the Nursing Process.* St Louis, CV Mosby, 1979.
32. Poplin D: *The Concept of Community.* New York, Macmillan, 1972.
33. Sanders IT: *The Community.* New York, The Ronald Press, 1975.
34. National Commission on Community Health Services: *Health is a Community Affair.* Cambridge, Mass, Harvard University Press, 1967.
35. American Public Health Association: *The Definition and Role of Public Health Nursing in the Delivery of Health Care: A Statement of the Public Health Nursing Section.* Washington, DC, American Public Health Association, Nursing Section, November 1980.
36. Braden CJ, Nerban NL: *Community Health: A Systems Approach.* New York, Appleton-Century-Crofts, 1976.
37. Andrews PB: Nursing diagnosis, in Griffith JW, Christensen PJ (eds): *Nursing Process: Application of Theories, Frameworks, and Models.* CV Mosby, St Louis, 1982.
38. Soares CA: Nursing and medical diagnosis: A comparison of variant and essential features, in Chaska N (ed): *The Nursing Profession: Views Through the Mist.* New York, McGraw-Hill, 1978.
39. Yura H, Walsh MB: *The Nursing Process: Assessing, Planning, Implementing, Evaluating.* New York, Appleton-Century-Crofts, 1973.
40. Little D, Carnevali D: The diagnostic statement: The problem defined, in Walter J, Pardee G, Molbo D (eds): *Dynamics of Problem-Oriented Approaches: Patient Care and Documentation.* Philadelphia, JB Lippincott Co, 1975.
41. Griffith JW, Christensen PJ: *Nursing Process: Application of Theories, Frameworks, and Models.* St Louis, CV Mosby, 1982.
42. Mundinger MO, Jauron GD: Developing a nursing diagnosis. *Nurs Outlook* 1975;3:94-98.

CHAPTER 28

Psychosocial Support Groups for People with HIV Infection and AIDS

Denise Ribble, RN, BSN, MPA

The diverse communities affected by the human immunodeficiency virus (HIV) infection and acquired immunodeficiency syndrome (AIDS) make it likely that the nurse will be exposed to life styles and behaviors with which he or she is unfamiliar and, possibly, uncomfortable. Some nurses are uncomfortable teaching the basics of heterosexual safer sex and are unable to discuss safer sex for gay men or lesbians. Safer needle use (and drug use in general) are other areas where the client may have a need for knowledge that is not covered by "patient teaching." Professional and therapeutic conduct by the nurse is required in these situations.

Clients with HIV infection or AIDS may break through the barrier of professional denial (e.g., the client is a woman who was sexually infected; she is also an R.N.). This can cause personal risk assessment and anxiety. The risk of infection while working is small and is reduced even further by the use of infectious disease protective procedures.[1] However, the risk cannot be ignored because of the epidemic of fear that surrounds AIDS and the implications fear has in causing provision of substandard nursing care.

HIV infection is tremendously stigmatizing, and nurses working in this field may find that they are also stigmatized. Issues of racism, classism, sexism, ageism, homophobia, and addictophobia in society and in the nurse make advocacy, a traditional nursing role, more difficult. For example, a nurse may feel empathy for the sexually infected partner of an intravenous (I.V.) drug user and advocate strongly for that client. However, when the client who was infected via I.V. drug use comes in, there is less empathy and less advocacy.

A holistic nursing approach includes the use of conventional nursing actions in dealing with HIV infection and AIDS but is not limited by the bounds of pathology. In looking beyond disease and cure, the holistic approach looks at the connections of mind-body-spirit and environment for impact on the client's well-being and healing.

The Japanese concepts of "Shiki shin funi" and "esho funi" describe the relationship of "mind-spirit-body" and "self and environment" as "two, but not two."[2] An analogy would be the head and tail of a nickel—these characteristic parts being viewed separately, but integral to the nickel. It is at the fundamental level of "but not two" that healing is thought to occur.

Healing can be defined as "to make whole," "to reunite," "to make intact."[3] Client care in HIV infection includes prevention of infection or transmission, self-controlled life-style modifications, better self-care, education, health promotion, primary care, prophylaxis, and a high degree of client-nurse interaction directed to the goal of healing. A holistic approach to the nursing process allows for mental,

Reprinted from *Holistic Nursing Practice,* Vol. 3, No. 4, with permission of Aspen Publishers, Inc., © 1989.

emotional, motivational, and spiritual outcomes in addition to physical outcomes.

A holistic nursing approach is particularly useful in HIV infection and AIDS because there is no medical cure available. Therefore, the health care systems many of us work in, which normally prioritize medical concerns and reward medical interventions, are unable to address all of the issues, concerns, and desired outcomes involved in providing care. In my opinion, this makes AIDS nursing territory!

HOLISTIC NURSING AND EMPOWERMENT

In a holistic model, one of the conceptual outgrowths of primary care (facilitating well-being), advocacy, and client teaching is *empowerment.* Providing empowerment for clients with HIV infection is a specific area of challenge to nurses.

Empowerment is a process by which people are supported and valued as they learn about themselves; make decisions; mobilize resources; and accept power, control, and direction of their lives. In assuming that the empowerment process is part of nursing function, several concerns emerge.

First, is the nurse personally prepared to advocate for the diversity of clients with HIV infection? Potential clients are gay men, bisexual men and women, I.V. drug users, drug and alcohol abusers, heterosexual women, adolescents, elders, lesbians, hemophiliacs and blood product recipients, people of color, people who are poor, and the sexual partners of any of the above. Infant and pediatric clients might also be involved.

Second, empowerment is not magically granted by the health care professional (i.e., the nurse waves a magic wand, and suddenly this client who has only basic survival skills is empowered because the nurse told him or her about empowerment). Empowerment of the client is a gradual process, starting with an assessment of the client's unique circumstances and using strategies to move the client toward increasing independence and mobilization of resources. Empowerment is particularly crucial in surviving and healing HIV infection. "Not everyone who is HIV positive will progress to AIDS and not everyone with AIDS will die" states Michael Callen, Director of Publications, People With AIDS Coalition (PWAC).[4] A focus on the positive, less fatalistic aspects of the disease is important. Reconnection to a sense of purpose, a sense of ability to change, to grow, is vital. The idea of inevitable death can be challenged by empowerment.

The concept of a peaceful, dignified death can also be embraced by empowerment. Self-advocacy is encouraged, but empowerment does not preclude asking for help as a way of mobilizing resources. A sense of power, control, and direction applies in physical, mental, emotional, and spiritual aspects of a person's day-to-day life.

EMPOWERMENT AND SUPPORT GROUPS

Haney writes, "The most functional area that people with HIV disease need connecting with, is a support system. One potent support system, that is often underutilized, is the support group. The possibility of hope and strength that is provided in a group is basic to coping with HIV disease."[5(p.252)] Support groups provide social contact; emotional outlet; information sharing; education and health promotion; behavior change information and reinforcement for positive behavior changes; motivation; and psychosocial support (which can occur concurrently in individual therapy, counseling, 12-step programs, families, and communities).

In a study of a three-session psychoeducational group for HIV seropositive individuals by Gross et al., it was found that this support group met the objectives of support, isolation reduction, education, and triage to other community resources.[6]

Stresses related to a lack of empowerment, like disclosure of antibody status, hopelessness, helplessness, and abandonment, were reduced. "Group members were remarkably uniform in affirming the value of the program, citing support gained from making contact with other people in the same situation."[6(p.4)] Connections with peers provided shared experiences. Participants found information about risk reduction, treatments, medical follow-up, and community resources valuable. Although pre- and postgroup symptom checklist-90R scores varied, distress, depression, anxiety, and hostility often decreased significantly.

One consistent criticism was that three sessions were not enough. An unintended outcome was the introduction of participants with little or no previous group experience to the benefits of group work for dealing with their antibody status and feelings.

Other unintended outcomes included the following:

1. In people with different risk histories, the bonds of common experience were more powerful than sociocultural differences. (In my experience, this is true in short-term group meetings that focus on psychoeducational themes. However, in longer-term psychosocial group meetings, these differences can interfere with group process unless specifically addressed.)
2. Participants examined interventions to actively maintain health, explore treatment trials, and evaluate wellness programs.
3. Group leaders were exposed to seropositive issues and felt more empowered to offer care.[6]

In Cobb's study, it was found that social supports can modify life stresses.[7] Included in the life stresses so modified were feelings of hopelessness, helplessness, anger, depression, and concerns about relationships, sickness, and mortality—the kinds of life stresses that HIV infection imposes on clients. Kennedy et al. found that interpersonal relationships mediated stress and promoted positive physiological immunological outcomes[8] and Teshima et al. found that T-cell subsets improved with stress reduction.[9]

The above information indicates that stresses and anxieties have a negative impact on immune function and well-being. When people with HIV infection are empowered through emotional, educational, social, and peer support, some of these negative outcomes are reduced. Positive outcomes of empowerment cover the continuum of mind-body-spirit and environment. They include development and maintenance of hope, behavior changes to reduce risk, wellness activities, and improvements in immune function.

Outline for Establishing Psychosocial Support Groups for People with HIV Infection

The need: What is the purpose of the group?

One of the most frequently stated disenfranchisement issues of people with HIV infection is isolation. Support groups allow members to know that they are not alone. The group may provide emotional support, information sharing, socializing, or political action, whatever is needed to provide its members with empowerment.

When looking at the purpose of a group to reduce isolation and provide support, it is pertinent to look at the value support groups have in different communities. Rodriguez points out that an English-speaking, process-oriented AIDS support group would get little Latino participation because it would violate cultural, language, health belief, and stigma precepts in the community. Furthermore, just having a group in Spanish is not enough when there are issues of poverty, transportation, child care, health care access, and public knowledge. Rodriguez says that the family is the Latino or Latina's major support network and any successful support efforts must include the families.[10]

Rashidah Hassan, Executive Director of BEBASHI (Blacks Educating Blacks about Sexual Health Issues) discusses the importance of the community as a major venue for providing support to blacks through community activists, community awareness, and community resources. She also states that conventional support groups will not meet the needs of blacks if they are insensitive to black issues.[11]

Types of groups: Who is the group for?

Groups can be formed based on diagnosis (worried well, HIV positive, AIDS-related complex [ARC], AIDS) or risk category (needle or other drug user, sexual transmission, hemophiliacs, and so forth). Groups can be formed on the basis of race or ethnicity, class, sex, or language. Some groups are "mixed" according to the above type classifications. Other types of groups are for prevention orientation, bereavement, significant others, care partners, children, and political action. Care providers need support too, to prevent burnout, so care provider groups should also be included.

Facilitation: Who leads the group?

Groups can be facilitated or nonfacilitated. If a leader is available, this person may be present as a consultant, cofacilitator or leader of the group. Whether the person is a professional or lay leader, he or she should have already dealt with his or her own feelings of the unknown, diseases and contagion, sexuality, drug use, empowerment, and death and dying. When selecting leaders, it is important to consider whether there will be a fee for services.

Self-help (nonfacilitated) groups are often run by member leaders on a fixed or rotating basis, such as in the 12-step Alcoholics Anonymous program. Using member leaders provides a broad sense of ownership. Groups can be structured or informal, time limited or ongoing. They can be free standing, independent, organizationally attached, or religiously affiliated. Other concerns to be considered include location, transportation, time and frequency of meetings, availability of child care, size of group, and costs or fees.

Problems That May Be Encountered in Starting and Maintaining Psychosocial Support Groups

One of the main goals of any support group is to reduce the isolation of its members. Because of the stigma attached to HIV infection, clients need to feel safe in coming to a group. This raises the issue of confidentiality.

Some ways of ensuring confidentiality include using false names, using first names only, and not requesting any identification. A telephone tree was developed for people who could not come to the group out of fear of stigma or for health reasons, so that they could still have some contact. Social contact, emotional outlet, information sharing, and psychosocial support generally take place within the group once it has established a sense of trust. However, if the purpose of the group is political action, personal exposure is usually required, and anonymity and confidentiality may be lost.

When looking at types of groups, it is important to plan for empowerment. For example, starting a women's group without considering the need for transportation and child care would prevent some women from participating.

A number of problems can arise with group membership. When I first decided to facilitate a women's group, I wanted to recruit a broad spectrum of women, with differences in diagnosis, route of infection, class, race, ethnicity, and sexual orientation. I was aided in my efforts by the PWAC (which donated space and advertising), the Community Health Project (where I was seeing women clients), and my professional and personal contacts within the Latina, black and lesbian communities. However, the single most important reason that a diverse group of women attended was that it was the *only* support group for HIV positive-ARC-AIDS-diagnosed women at the time.

Other women's groups have started since that first group in 1986, and many of them have a narrower membership focus. There is a "positive ways" Narcotics Anonymous (NA) group for women, a hemophiliac wife group, and even a group for "nice girls" that recruits middle-class, sexually infected women. There are groups for female I.V. drug users, mothers of PWAs, and prostitutes.

In the women's group I facilitate, membership requirements established by the group include the following members:

- must be HIV positive, have ARC or AIDS (anxious at-risks or HIV negatives have different issues and take up too much group time).
- must be clean, sober, or in recovery. Relapses are tolerated, not condoned. Active use of drugs or alcohol is not tolerated.
- are allowed to bring children. (A volunteer child-care person is available.)
- The member can be a female transsexual (post-sex change).

The group actively discusses differences and similarities related to diagnosis, mode of infection, racism, classism, sexism, sexual orientation, and addictophobia.

Another problem with membership arises when individual participants have disparate coping or living strategy skills and individual circumstances or come to the group in a crisis. Empowerment skills can be developed and referrals made within the group setting, but crisis situations (e.g., a woman is about to lose custody of her child) are handled individually by the facilitator, with group work to process the crisis after it has been addressed.

Facilitated groups have the advantage of one person's being responsible to observe and monitor group process, provide feedback, and move the group along if it gets stuck. Disadvantages include the possibility that the facilitator has not addressed personal issues, HIV-related issues, or group process issues or lacks the skills needed for facilitation. (I had to work intensely on my addictophobia issues before facilitating the women's group.) Another disadvantage with facilitators is that they may charge a fee that the group or its sponsoring agency cannot afford. Volunteer professional or lay facilitators need the same skills mentioned above but are not remunerated for them.

Nonfacilitated groups or self-help groups with member leadership have the advantage of providing a broad sense of group ownership. Problems can arise with issues or skills of member-leaders, inconsistency with rotating leadership, and impasses in group process.

Time-limited groups can work well for psychoeducational support but are not ongoing enough for psychosocial support. With ongoing groups, addition of new members at appropriate times is a concern, as is the loss of members related to attrition or death. Ongoing groups also have the potential to "burn out" facilitators and participants. One way of reducing burnout is to take one week off every month and to incorporate "special events" (like a visualization night) in the scheduling cycle.

Finally, the affiliation of a support group is significant. For example, a group sponsored by a religious organization may impose moral guidelines on discussions of sex or drugs. A group sponsored by a drug-free therapeutic community might "process" drug use differently than one formed at a Methadone maintenance clinic. This is pertinent if the affiliation results in changes in the group that inhibit the empowerment process.

The development of a support group involves finding someone to start it; locating a place in which to meet; developing a clear description of the type of group, a format, advertising, leadership, group input, special events, and member self-sufficiency; dealing with loss of group members through attrition or death; adding new members at appropriate times; and acknowledging closure.

How to Help Empower Through Groups

The following are examples of individuals whose lives were changed, and how support groups made a difference.

Case study 1: Behavior change reinforcement

M. is a 19-year old bisexual, Latina I.V. drug user with lymphadenopathy, laboratory abnormalities consistent with immunosuppression (T4 cells less than 200), and no other reported or observed symptoms of HIV infection. Prior to coming to the group, she had gone through three relapses at two-week intervals. When she came to the group, she was attending NA meetings again and had been clean for nine days. She discussed her difficulties with "staying clean" and received encouragement from other I.V. drug users in the group. Over the weekend she "picked up" (used I.V. drugs) and reported this to the group the following week. Members in the group expressed their concerns for her recovery and an attitude of intolerance toward her relapse, yet specifically told her she was accepted in the group as long as she was trying to stay clean. They also expressed concerns for her health.

M. has now been clean for nine months. Her T cells are between 300 and 400. She credits the support group with reinforcing her behavior change in helping her stay clean because "these people barely knew me, but they cared about my health and my life. They accepted me as an I.V. drug user and an HIV-positive woman, and some of them had been exactly in my shoes—and they encouraged me."

Case study 2: Reproductive rights

A. is a 33-year-old, black, heterosexual woman who was sexually infected by her exhusband. She was HIV positive, asymptomatic, and newly married to an HIV-negative man who was aware of her situation prior to their marriage. She wanted to get pregnant but had received counseling from her private medical doctor that pregnancy would cause her to progress to full-blown AIDS and that the child would most likely be born HIV-infected. She wanted information about her risks and the risks to a child and wanted to know what other women thought of her desire to have a baby. This was discussed in the group for several months. Topics that were addressed included:

- anger at the physician for giving A. incorrect information and infringing on her reproductive rights,
- the possibility that the infant would be healthy but A. would get sick or die,

- the possibility that the infant would be HIV positive and get sick or die,
- the possibility that both A and the infant would get sick or die,
- support for the husband, and
- concerns about where A. would get good prenatal care.

Some of the women in the group went with A. to the hospital to look at the HIV-positive boarder infants. Several husbands and boyfriends contacted A.'s husband to talk about their experiences with having a healthy child and losing a child. Prenatal and postpartum care were explored.

After several months, A. and her husband decided to have the infant. A. continued to come to the group, where she was able to offer support to a woman who had decided to have an abortion and another woman who wanted to have a child. After a medically uneventful gestation, she delivered a baby infant who is HIV antibody negative at nine months. A. remains HIV positive and asymptomatic.

Case study 3: Sex and relationships

R. is a 55-year-old lesbian who was infected when she received a contaminated blood transfusion during open heart surgery. She expressed great fears that no one would ever want to touch her or love her and that she would never have sex again. She felt it was harder for her to discuss her HIV-positive status with prospective partners because of the denial about AIDS in the lesbian community.

The group requested that I review safer sex information and practices for women, which I did. This included demonstration and role playing around dental dams, gloves, condoms, and dildos, and role playing around telling a partner, not telling a partner, how to deal with a resistant partner, how to protect oneself, and so forth. After several weeks of discussion, R. admitted it was possible to have safer lesbian sex.

Relationships are an ongoing topic of discussion in the group. Prior to her HIV infection, R. had not had a relationship in seven years, so she had many preexisting relationship issues, which were exacerbated by her HIV antibody status.

The group formulated a relationship motto, "Who's to say I won't have the best relationship in my life—and how do I get started?" around the discussions with R. However, it wasn't until H., another HIV-positive lesbian, brought her HIV-negative lover to the group that R. stated that she wanted a relationship and decided to go for private therapy for her relationship issues.

Case study 4: Change in diagnosis from adaptive denial to focus on internal issues

L. is a 44-year-old heterosexual woman with no known risk factors who may have been infected by a bisexual man. Upon learning of her HIV-positive status (she had a test just to make sure she was okay), she immediately took a positive health-style approach. She improved her diet, stopped her moderate drug and alcohol use, quit smoking, began exercising, practiced safer sex, visualized, meditated, and pursued nontoxic early intervention treatments to maintain and boost her immune system. She stated that these health-promoting behaviors allowed her to feel "in control" and that she felt well (Adaptive Denial). She refused laboratory and physical examination monitoring, despite encouragement from me and the group. Even when asked by group members, she denied anger, fear, uncertainty, or depression.

After L. was diagnosed with *Pneumocystis carinii* pneumonia (PCP) and received outpatient treatment, she came to the group and stated she didn't know whether the group would support her or take an "I told you so" attitude. The group responded by asking her how she was feeling physically and emotionally. Over time, she was able to express feelings of anger, betrayal and loss, fear, grieving, and appropriate depression (Focus on Internal Issues). She made changes in her health care monitoring, health care provider, and treatments. One year post-AIDS diagnosis, she states "I am a survivor."

As a result of this experience, most of the HIV-positive, asymptomatic group members have started processing internal emotional issues about sickness while maintaining some control through adaptive denial. One member stated that having women with AIDS in the group let her fantasize and practice what it would be like to get sick. This included discussions in the group where women with AIDS provided reality feedback on the fantasies. In return for this "practice," several HIV-positive asymptomatic women offer physical and emotional upport to the women with AIDS (e.g., shopping, cleaning, visiting, or going with them to the physician, the movies, or the gym).

Case study 5: Gynecological concerns, health care providers, conventional western and traditional holistic treatment options

S. is a 28-year-old lesbian who believes she was infected by her female lover. Upon initial work-up with her physician, her T4 cells were above 400, and she had no symptoms. After attending the group for four months and discussing her feeling about how she was exposed, she developed a severe vulva-vaginal yeast infection. This yeast infection was resistant to treatment with vinegar and water douches, cranberry juice, and acidophilus, which had worked for her in the past. She was concerned this was related to her HIV infection and requested that her private physician examine her and do a laboratory work up on her immune status. Her physician referred her to a gynecology specialist and told her he would do a complete immunological work up in two months, when she was due for her regular six-month follow-up. S. expressed anger at this in the group and was encouraged to persist in her requests for earlier follow-up by several women who recalled prodromal yeast infections that were not considered HIV related months before ARC diagnosis. S. kept her appointment with the gynecologist, and with treatment her yeast infection cleared. She also persisted with her physician, and he agreed to do a laboratory work up. Her T4 cells were 75.

S. was encouraged by the group to discuss her frustrations and concerns with her health care provider to see whether their relationship could be salvaged. She felt it was valuable to have a physician to consult with about her health care yet wanted to be involved in decision making and wanted to be able to trust her physician. Except for this situation, she felt comfortable with the provider. She stated she would change providers if this one did not respond to her issues. She reported to the group that he apologized to her for not paying attention to her concerns and wanted to be supportive of her health care decisions regarding treatment.

At a "special event" in the group, S. was introduced to acupuncture and Therapeutic Touch. She decided she would like to take trimethoprim and sulfamethoxazole (Bactrim) for PCP prophylaxis and use acupuncture and Therapeutic Touch as her treatment options. After discussing this with her physician and the physician and registered nurse who would would be doing the holistic treatments, all agreed to a six-month trial period of her treatment choice. After six months, her T4 cells rose and stabilized at 380; she has not had any recurrence of yeast infections, and she has not developed any new symptoms. S. states that her treatment choices satisfied her evaluation criteria, and she will continue with her treatments and the monitoring of her health status.

• • •

Conventional models of nursing are often forced to focus on medical management and pathology reduction outcomes. A holistic model of care allows for mental, emotional, motivational, and spiritual outcomes as well as physical outcomes.

Facilitating empowerment for clients with HIV infection is a specific area of challenge in holistic nursing. Support groups can provide empowerment for these clients.

By developing support groups that are planned, implemented, and evaluated using the holistic approach of empowerment, nurses can facilitate the process of healing in people with HIV infection.

REFERENCES

1. Centers for Disease Control. "Recommendations for Prevention of HIV Infection in Health Care Settings." *Morbidity and Mortality Weekly Review* 36, no. 25 (1987): 35-185.
2. "Shiki Shin Funi" and "Esho Funi" *Seikyo Times* 11, no. 328 (1988): 17-18.
3. Strawn J. "Alternative Therapies Taking Healing into Their Own Hands." Paper presented at 2nd National Nursing Conference on AIDS, Nashville, Tenn., sponsored by Nursing Transitions, October 17-19, 1988.
4. Callen, Michael. Personal conversation with author, 15 October 1988.
5. Haney, P. "Providing Empowerment to People with AIDS." *Social Work* 33 no. 3 (1988): 251-53.
6. Gross, M., Bauer, S., Carr, R. et al. "Three-Session Psychoeducational Group for HIV Seropositive Individuals," unpublished manuscript, 1988.

7. Cobb, S. "Social Support as a Moderator of Life Stress." *Psychosomatic Medicine* 38, no. 5 (1976): 300-314.
8. Kennedy, S., Kiecolt-Glaser, J., and Glaser, R. "Immunological Consequences of Acute and Chronic Stressors Mediating Role of Interpersonal Relationships." *British Journal of Medical Psychology* 61, pt. 1 (1988): 77-84.
9. Teshima, H., Sogawa, H., Kihara, H., et al. "Changes in Populations of T-Cell Subsets Due to Stress." *Annals of NY Academy of Science* 10, no. 529 (1988): 459-66.
10. Rodriguez, G. "Hispanics, AIDS, and Self Help: Barriers and Benefits." In *Self Help Groups for People Dealing With AIDS: You Are Not Alone,* edited by A.D. Bernstein. Denville, N.J.: Self Help Clearinghouse, St. Clare's-Riverside Medical Center, 1988.
11. Hassan, R. "BEBASHI: A Model of Activism and Self Help in the Community." In *Self Help Groups for People Dealing With AIDS: You Are Not Alone,* edited by A.D. Bernstein, Denville, N.J.: Self Help Clearinghouse, St. Clare's-Riverside Medical Center, 1988.

CHAPTER **29**

Assessing Community Health Needs of Elderly Populations: Comparison of Three Strategies

Phyllis R. Schultz, RN, PhD
Joan K. Magilvy, RN, PhD

PROBLEM EXPLORED

The problem explored in this paper is how to assess the community health needs of elderly populations. This problem is part of a broader subject in the health and social science literatures, namely, community health needs assessment and diagnosis of a population or aggregate. The specific research questions are: (1) do three research strategies — secondary analysis of data available from the Census of Population and Housing, primary data collection using survey methodology, and primary data collection using ethnography — yield comparable information for assessing the health needs of a sub-population aggregate; and (2) what are the relative strengths and limitations of each strategy.

To answer the research questions posed above, we examined and summarized data from selected Census items of a particular neighbourhood in Denver, Colorado from 1970 and 1980 for which data from a health needs survey and an ethnography also were available. All 'First World' nations have some form of population-level information similar to the United States Census of Population and Housing. All three strategies focused on the Greater Capitol Hill neighbourhood of Denver; residents aged 60 years and older were the sub-population aggregate of interest. Information from the 1970 Denver Census of Population and Housing had been used as the basis for drawing a stratified random sample for the health needs survey (Flaming 1977).

Reprinted from *Journal of Advanced Nursing,* Vol. 13, with permission of Blackwell Scientific Publications, Inc., © 1988.

The purpose of the survey was to assess the health needs of 100 persons aged 60 years and older in the Capitol Hill area as part of a larger effort initiated by elderly persons to improve the delivery of health services in their neighbourhood. This same neighbourhood formed the geographical boundaries of the ethnographic study by the authors in the spring of 1984. For the comparisons reported in this paper, published reports of the 1970 (United States Bureau of the Census 1970) and 1980 United States Census and the Flaming 1977 study were used. Methods are discussed as appropriate in the sections on the health needs survey and ethnography below.

BACKGROUND

Recent texts for students of community health (e.g. students in professional study in the fields of nursing, social work and medicine as well as human services administration and planning) advise a broad conceptual approach to assessing populations focusing on 'people and environment' and deriving a 'community diagnosis' (Dever 1984, Freeman & Heinrich 1981, Geoppinger 1984, Watson 1984). For example, Watson (1984) defined community diagnosis as 'the identification of health problems in communities or populations for the purpose of preventing them at the community or population level.' Freeman & Heinrich (1981) suggested that a 'community health diagnosis' is based on three 'interdependent, interacting, and constantly changing conditions: (1) the health status of the community population including its vulnerability to disease, disability or death; (2) community health capability, or the ability of the community to deal with its health problems; (3) community action potentials, or the ways and directions in which the community is likely to work on its health problems'.

Data Categories

Several types of data useful for diagnosing the health of a community or specific sub-population group are outlined by Freeman & Heinrich (1981). The major categories of data include: 'people' factors such as demographic, morbidity, mortality, and vital statistics as well as high risk groups; 'environmental' factors, including social as well as physical environment; 'health capability' factors such as institutional and human resources; and 'health action potentials', such as the politics and value system of the population. Sources of these data categories can include official vital statistics and census data, surveys (officially or privately initiated), central registries, agency records, historical documents, and systematic observation and interviews. This approach to community health analysis is holistic and is termed an ecological approach (Freeman & Heinrich 1981).

Oreglia (1973) stated that while abundant health data exist of the type Freeman & Heinrich (1981) identified as 'people factors', efficient use of it is precluded by discontinuity of the data sources and by the lack of effective and efficient techniques for collecting, analysing and displaying the data. Some of these problems may have been overcome in recent work by Dever (1984), but three specific problems cited by Oreglia (1973) remain to be resolved:

1. lack of mechanisms for linking diverse health data sources;
2. lack of small-area demographic and socioeconomic data to which data on community (especially neighbourhood) health services needs and utilization as it is collected can be related; and
3. lack of denominator data for the calculation of meaningful health services need.

Of the 'people factor' data, most are available for area units as small as census tracts and for some, census blocks, if the small area is within standard metropolitan statistical areas. The smallest area for which birth and death data are available is the county level. However, a community or population of interest may well be bounded geographically by areas smaller than a county, such as census block or tracts in urban areas or enumeration districts in rural areas.

From the literature and experience of the authors, census data are best used as denominator data with other local or health survey data serving as numerators for calculating rates or proportions. Once rates are calculated, comparisons can be made to similar locales or age, sex, or race-specific sub-populations as evidence for identifying needs and subsequently for planning for health and other human services.

COMPARISON OF CENSUS DATA WITH PRIMARY SURVEY DATA FOR ONE DENVER NEIGHBOURHOOD

Of the factors required for a community needs assessment, several 'people factors' available in the census data for the Capitol Hill neighbourhood included: age, sex, race, marital status, education and income. 'Environmental factors' such as residential characteristics and mobility were also available. Comparable factors included in the primary survey (Flaming 1977) were age, sex, race, marital status, education, income, occupation, housing characteristics, and length of time at present residence. In the comparisons of census and survey data shown in Table 29-1, percentages have been computed for most items based on either the total population base of the eight census tracts or on the total sample drawn for the survey.

From the 1970 census data, a portrait of the Capitol Hill neighbourhood population can be drawn using the nine sociodemographic factors (i.e. 'people factors') suggested in the literature to be relevant to the assessment of health needs in a community. With

TABLE 29-1
Comparison of census findings with survey findings

PEOPLE FACTORS	CENSUS FINDINGS 1970 (%)	SURVEY FINDINGS 1977 (%)	CENSUS FINDINGS 1980 (%)
Persons aged 60+ years	26	100	20
Age categories (of those 60+)			
60–64	23	21	21
65–74	42	41	39
75+	34	36	40
Sex ratio			
(age specific)	51-5	61-1	65-3
Race (white)			
(not age specific)	98-5	94	83-3
*Marital status**			
Single	38	15	47
Married	35	30	22
Widowed	12	38	9
Separated	3	—	4
Divorced	12	12-5	18
*Occupation**			
Professional	21	13-9	9-8
Managers	9	10-6	9-8
Clerical	28	19-5	20-6
Service	12-4	15-5	11-3
*Income**			
% households on social security	25-7	82-5	22
Mean social security income per month per household	$140	—	$303
Mean income per month, all sources	—	$225-249	—
*Education**			
Finished high school	63-3	17-2	78-9
*Residential characteristics**			
Persons per household	1-6	—	1-5
One person occupied units	58	—	66-3
Live alone	—	67	43-7
Rentals	93	73-3	76-5
Mobility			
Of occupied units, moved in 1968–1970	69	—	—
1–3 years at this address	—	36-3	—
Moved in 1979–1980	—	—	53-2

*Figures in these categories for the 1970 and 1980 census were not age specific. Those for the survey were.
Census data obtained from: US Department of Commerce, Bureau of the Census, 1970 and 1980 population data for Denver, Colorado. Census tracts: 26.01, 26.02, 27.01, 27.02, 27.03, 28.01, 32.01, 32.02.

reference to Table 29-1, the population in Capitol Hill could be characterized as slightly more than one-fourth elderly (26%) with fewer males than females by two to one (51/100), largely white (98.5%), with 25.7% of households on social security payments for a mean social security monthly income of $140. Over half of the population had finished high school (63.3%), lived in single person units (58%), rented their housing (93%) and had lived in the unit 2 years or less (69%).

About 65% of the neighbourhood population were either single (38%), widowed (12%), separated (3%), or divorced (12%); these figures probably account for the large number who lived in single person units. One-fifth or so reported occupational categories as professional (21%) or clerical (28%).

By 1980, this profile had changed considerably. Again, with reference to Table 29-1, the population in Capitol Hill was only one-fifth elderly (20%), with an even higher proportion of females (65/100), fewer whites (83.3%), with 22% of households on social security payments for a mean monthly income of $303. Three-fourths of the population had finished high school (78.9%). Over half (66.3%) lived in single person units and more than three-fourths (76.5%) rented their housing. Over half (53.2%) had lived in the unit 2 years or less. Of these several variables, only age and sex were categorized by age groups.

Primary Data Collection

Thus, to learn the extent to which the 20+% of the Capitol Hill population who were elderly reflected a similar profile, primary data collection was necessary. The 1977 primary data survey used a random sample of people aged 60 years and older, and revealed a portrait remarkably similar to the population of the neighbourhood as a whole. Referring to Table 29-1, there were fewer males than females (61/100), slightly fewer whites (94.4%) and the mean monthly income was somewhat greater than the households on social security of the community as a whole ($255-249 compared to $140). As would be expected, a higher percentage of the senior citizens were on social security. The higher mean monthly income may be explained by the greater detail achieved in the survey question than the census data. Also, the amount of social security payments may have been increasing from 1970 to 1977.

The elderly population appeared to be less educated; 17.2% finished high school compared to 63.3% in the population as a whole. This is not surprising when the level of education available to these elders when they were young is taken into account. Sixty-seven per cent of the elderly lived alone, mostly in rental units (73.3%). The elderly lived in their rental units longer than the rest of the population; 36.3% had lived 1-3 years at 'this' address compared to 69% of the total population having moved to their present address 2 years prior to the Census.

Nearly 40% of the elderly were widowed. This figure is much higher than the neighbourhood population as a whole but is not surprising in this age group. A comparison of the 1977 survey findings with the Census data of 1980 revealed a similar portrait with respect to education, living alone, and length of years at the same address. The proportion of widowed elderly remained greater than the percentage in the population as a whole although the occupational structure remained fairly similar. On the variable 'marital status' the portrait of the neighbourhood changed in 1980 to one in which a larger percentage of single (47%) and divorced (18%) persons lived in Capitol Hill than was the case in 1970. The occupational structure of the elderly sample was similar to those in the neighbourhood as a whole with fewer in the professions and in clerical work but slightly more in managerial and service occupations.

Based on these sources, Capitol Hill in the decade from 1970-1980 can be characterized as a neighbourhood with a mobile population of large numbers of single, widowed and divorced persons with fairly low incomes living in rental apartments, predominantly female, high school educated, with a mixture of professional and clerical occupations, managers, and some service workers, either employed or retired. As shown in the comparisons, the elderly reflect this same profile although they didn't change dwellings as often. This conclusion could not have been drawn from the Census data alone because the critical variables are not age specific. Thus, primary surveys are required to learn whether a specific aggregate or sub-population is similar to or different from the population as a whole.

COMMUNITY HEALTH NEEDS

Health needs cannot be inferred directly from the above portrait of the Capitol Hill population nor from the demographic and residential profile of the elderly sample without reference to additional information found in the health literature. Questions of relevance to health needs that are suggested by analysis of the census data are: How is health care paid for by persons with low income? Who cares for the single and widowed when they are ill? Will the low incomes allow enough money for medications and for a healthy diet?

Answers to the above questions are best found by direct inquiry. Such questions were asked in the primary survey. For example, 19% of the elderly respondents in the survey reported that they had been ill enough during the past year to require care by someone else (Flaming 1977). Forty per cent said they had a need for health care services in general, and 14% reported they needed home nursing services, specifically. Seventy-five per cent of the respondents reported they carried Medicare coverage for health insurance. Twenty-two per cent of the respondents said they had problems getting groceries and 5.3% identified the high cost of groceries as a problem (Flaming 1977). Comparable information was not available for the neighbourhood population as a whole from census data.

CONCLUSIONS FROM THE COMPARISON OF CENSUS WITH SURVEY DATA

Many factors identified in the literature as relevant to assessing health status are available from census data for small area analysis such as census tracts, i.e. age, sex, race, education, residential characteristics and mobility. Unfortunately, only age and sex are further categorized such that an age-specific analysis can be conducted. Other important factors relevant to assessing health status are not readily available for area analysis smaller than at the county level. For example, age-specific mortality or disability statistics are not available at the census tract level for analysis in the form of printed reports. Disability statistics are available in the form of computer tapes but the user must have computer capability in order to access this information.

Other 'people factors' such as a prevalence of presymptomatic illness, number and location of vulnerable or special risk groups and number and location of those persons functioning below potential health levels must be ascertained by methods different from either census or typical primary survey approaches. Specifically, assessment of health status by professionals is required. Health-related questions found to be implied in the characteristics of the Capitol Hill neighbourhood such as 'who cares for single and widowed when they are ill' are best answered through the direct inquiry method of a survey.

Problems

Thus, the three problems in using health-relevant information from the Census that Oreglia (1973) identified have been operant in these comparisons. First, some items were not easily compared between census data and survey data (refer to Table 1) due to lack of age specificity, variations in form, content and scoring of the questions asked and the like. Second, important factors such as natality, mortality, and disability are unavailable for small area analysis such as census tracts. A disability rate might have been estimated if a small additional question had been included in the primary survey. For example, one question in the survey was 'During the past year, have you ever been ill enough to need care by someone else?' If a follow-up question to that had been 'About how many days were you ill?', the information would be comparable to a disability question asked in the Census. Third, there is a lack of denominator data on available health services as well as per person rates for incidence of ill days and similar indicators of health needs.

In general, census data can provide the basis for a broad, somewhat superficial picture of a population's characteristics and their environment. These characteristics cannot lead to identification of health needs without the knowledge of how such characteristics correlate with health problems and use of health resources. Such knowledge has been learned through large scale surveys such as Andersen & Anderson's (1974) 'Decade of Health Service Utilization' and the several national health surveys.

THE ETHNOGRAPHIC STUDY

Ethnography as a research method applied to the process of community analysis is a relatively recent strategy. Through ethnographic field methods, the residents of a community are seen as key informants and teachers to the researchers, who, in turn, learn about culture and lifestyle of the community (Glittenberg *et al.* 1981). Applying ethnography to a community analysis is an attempt to understand what it is like to live in that community and to assess health problems, resources and needs from the perspective of the residents initialized in their own terms. Based on ethnographic assessment and from analysis of available epidemiologic and survey data, problem solutions and short- and long-range goals can be proposed to the community. Ethnographic methods provide a very different approach to the process of community analysis. Rather than a statistical portrait drawn on the basis of specific variables, people's cultural patterns, behaviours, and meanings are explored.

For the past several years, faculty and graduate students of the School of Nursing, University of Colorado Health Sciences Centre, have applied ethnographic field methods in combination with available demographic, epidemiologic, and historic sources to the analysis of health status and health problems of several Colorado rural communities, and more recently, to specific aggregates within urban communities (Glittenberg *et al.* 1981, 1982, Magilvy *et al.* 1984, 1985, 1986, Schultz *et al.* 1984). During Spring 1984, the older adult population of the Greater Capitol Hill neighbourhood in Denver was assessed using the GENESIS design with its emphasis on ethnography (Schultz *et al.* 1984). The study was sponsored by the Health Support Council for Capitol Hill Seniors which had previously commissioned the 1977 Flaming survey. Many interesting findings resulted from the analysis, some of which will be compared to findings of the two survey approaches discussed above.

Method

The methods used involved several steps, to be briefly discussed in this section. Available secondary data such as census reports, epidemiological data, survey reports such as the Flaming (1977) study, histories and other literature pertinent to older residents of Denver and Capitol Hill were collected, analysed and collated to provide direction for the ethnographic field study. 'Key' informants were then identified. These individuals were official and informal community leaders and older adults active in community organizations. Key informants interviewed included a person from the city council, clergy, representatives of the mayor's office, officers of senior organizations, and nurses, physicians and other health or social service workers. Information about services, resources, and problems affecting seniors was obtained from the key informants. They also suggested strategies for locating a variety of older residents to serve as primary informants.

Next, 'primary' informants, older people themselves, were identified by key informants or by the researchers doing participant observation in the neighbourhood. Primary informants were interviewed using a typical ethnographic nonstructured interview style in an attempt to learn what life was like for an older person in Capitol Hill, as well as perceptions of health, health needs and services. The researchers attempted to locate a mixture of non-institutionalized older people to serve as the primary sources of information about life and health of Capitol Hill senior citizens. Over 60 informants were interviewed in a variety of settings, such as age-segregated apartments, single-room occupant hotels and boarding homes, age-heterogeneous apartments, and informants' own homes. In addition to home interviews, informants were also interviewed in grocery stores, parks, businesses, clinics, and on the street. During the interview phase of the study, participant observation of activities of older adults resulted in field notes that were combined with tape-recorded interview transcripts and photographs (both with informed consent and confidentiality of informants protected) to provide a more complete portrait of the community.

Secondary data were organized around a variety of community institutions which were thought to broadly impact upon health, such as demographics, religion, transportation, recreation, social support, environment, politics, economics, housing, legal and protective services, and health care services. Analysis of primary ethnographic data to identify major themes and categories revealed many of the same categories, as well as lifestyles, food and nutrition, and health-in-context. Secondary and primary data were then both considered in the formulation of several summary tables for each category, presenting strengths, weaknesses, net health values, and recommendations for solutions to some of the problems identified. Finally, an oral presentation and written report of findings were shared with community members, who responded that the information presented was an accurate picture of their neighbourhood community.

Findings

Due to a large number of variables considered and presented in the report, and limited space in which to discuss these issues, two content areas are presented briefly as illustration: 'Lifestyle' and 'Health-in-Context'. In general, the 'lifestyle' of the Capitol Hill elderly population may be characterized by three groups, divided by background, income level and availability of social support. The first group is single-room occupants, found to be low income, lacking social support, marginally mentally ill, and often lonely. These individuals often 'fall through the cracks' of the social service network and are often transient. Many of this group frequented a meal and socialization programme available in a converted hotel; however, many never availed themselves of any organized services.

A second group consisted of fairly healthy retired persons with limited resources but able to afford medium-priced apartments or their own homes. Subsidized senior citizen apartments and congregate apartments also housed these individuals, many of whom participated actively in a variety of religious, recreational and socialization activities and meal programmes. The third group was made up of retired, well, older adults who sought high quality housing, and had a high degree of social support, were interested in community organizations, and fund-raising, and took leadership roles in the community. Many of this group were retired professionals who maintained an active intellectual and political involvement in their later years (Schultz & Magilvy 1984).

Table 29-2 displays a summary of the lifestyles and nutrition category, including strengths, weaknesses, and net health values resulting from the difference

TABLE 29-2
Lifestyle, food and nutrition

STRENGTHS	WEAKNESSES	NET VALUES
Sense of community. Tolerant, 'live and let live' attitude toward the diverse groups that make up this neighbourhood.	Prejudice of some seniors towards other elderly in the community.	Sense of cohesiveness varies.
Diverse group with many interests.		Interest in different programmes.
Large number of individuals who have lived in the neighbourhood over a long period of time.		Promotes a sense of belonging.
Seniors who are interested and adept in community organizations.	Transient group who lack cohesiveness, coping skills.	Support for programmes varies.
Opportunities for socialization exist through recreation and community organizations.	Isolation imposed by physical limitations, lack of transportation, disinterest.	Some needs are not being met despite number of programmes available.
Congregate meal sites serve as a means of socialization.	Lack of transportation to meal sites. Fear of going out, especially alone. Lack of transportation for convenient marketing.	Those most in need remain isolated.

TABLE 29-3
Lifestyle, food and nutrition—recommendations

1. Provision of transportation to senior meal sites.
2. Community and recreation centre services to homebound elderly.
3. Development of convenient transportation for shopping.
4. Development of home delivery services by supermarkets.
5. Development of shopping services by volunteers or within supermarkets.
6. Increased sensitivity of store personnel to needs of seniors with regard to poor vision, limited physical endurance, limited mobility.
7. Increased homemaking services for cooking, shopping.

between the two factors. From this table, Table 29-3 was then constructed, containing recommendations made by the researchers to the membership of the Health Support Council for improving health status related to lifestyle needs identified.

Problems of the Older Resident

Analysis of the content area 'health-in-context', revealed that acute and chronic health problems of the older resident were being met, by and large, by the traditional health care system. This content area was used to summarize the entire study. It was recognized that the health of a population does not exist in isolation; it is intertwined with the demographic, historical, environmental, political, social and economic forces of the community. Health is interactive with the lifestyle and nutritional characteristics of the population and with transportation, housing, recreation, religion and social support activities of the community (Schultz *et al.* 1984). The key deficit revealed in this broad analysis was health maintenance, especially in the areas not served or reimbursed by the traditional health care system and insurance coverage, such as maintenance of optometric, foot and dental health.

Recommendations reflecting all categories resulting from the ethnographic and secondary data analysis were made as a conclusion to the study. Some of these recommendations, all impacting on the health of the older population, are shown in Figure 29-1.

Recognizing the inter-relationships of all categories, it was revealed that the ethnographic approach to this community analysis provided a rich perspective of life and health from the viewpoint of a community's residents. The picture was holistic and authentic. Primary informants as well as residents not interviewed related positively to the final report. When reflected back to neighbourhood residents, they affirmed its validity in describing the life and health problems obvious to those participating in the 'lived experience' of life in Capitol Hill.

COMPARISON OF THREE STRATEGIES

What can be concluded from these comparisons is that those in charge of constructing items for a new primary survey would do well to be familiar with how census data questions are phrased so that comparable data can be acquired from the survey. Such data provide the information for the numerator over which the information from the Census can serve as denominator. In turn, it would be very useful to health personnel or others interested in health needs assessment if Census data were summarized with age breakdowns for more categories and if specifically health-related data such as natality, mortality, and disability were made readily available for small areas. Uniform data is needed about health resources and resource utilization so that rational assessment, planning, and development of resources can be accomplished. Neither the Census nor the primary survey reviewed in the foregoing discussion yielded information about health beliefs of the population nor about how this neighbourhood community had solved health problems in the past. In other words, census and structured questionnaire type random survey strategies do not reveal the 'lived experience' of a people in their environment. In these content areas, the ethnography is an especially useful strategy.

Of the types of data required to make a health needs diagnosis for a sub-population aggregate such as the elderly, the three strategies described in this paper

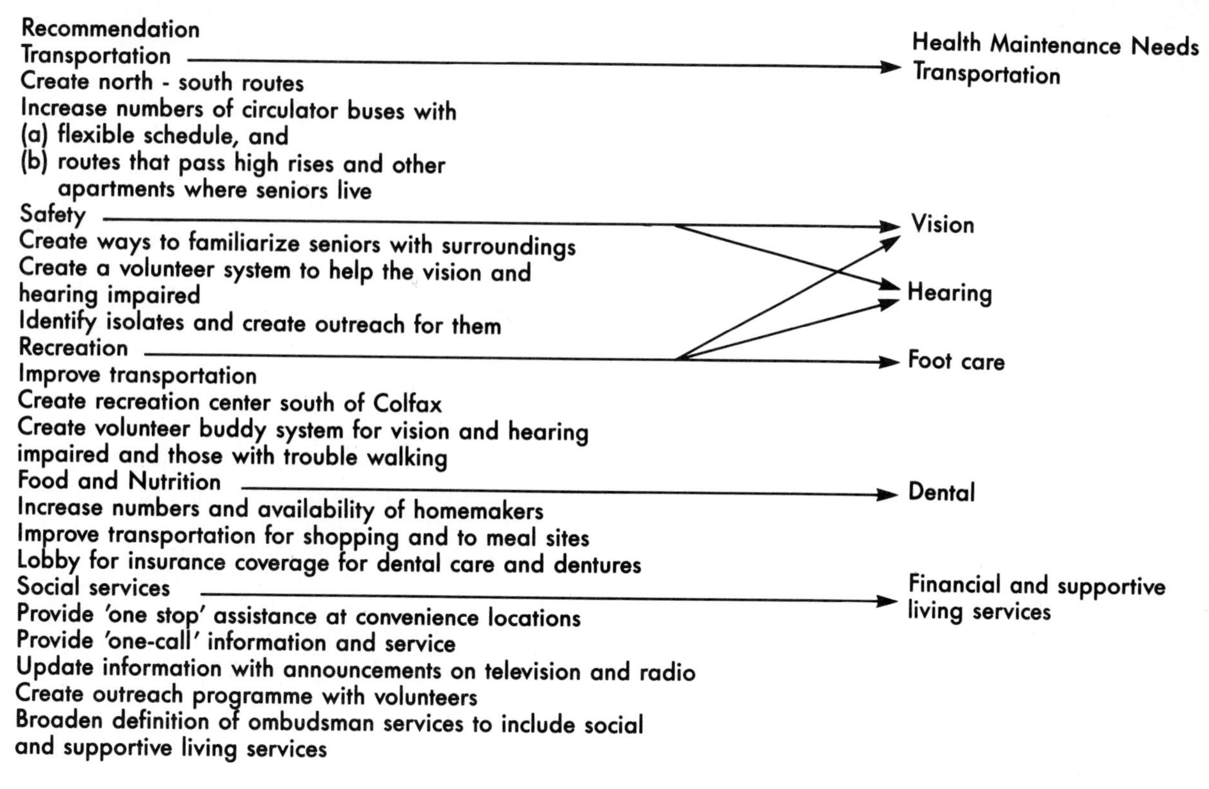

FIGURE 29-1
Health in-context.

yield different types of data as summarized in Table 29-4. The Census of Population and Housing can provide a baseline of information about the elderly when analysed in light of health science generalizations. Primary survey data can extend and specify the Census portrait but are costly to obtain. Framing some primary survey questions to be identical to those in the Census is one way to strengthen a survey because rates can be calculated and comparisons made possible. Ethnography yields more rich detail about the place of health in the whole fabric of the lived experience of a population. When combined with primary and secondary data sources, a closely accurate assessment of needs can be determined.

All three strategies, then, were found to be useful in constructing an analysis of community health needs of a population or sub-population aggregate such as elderly residents of the Capitol Hill neighbourhood in Denver and are recommended for future analysis of this or other populations. With the 1990 Census in preparation, those in charge of such needs assessments can prepare themselves for studies that will complement each other and provide comprehensive information on which to plan programmes well into the 21st century.

TABLE 29-4
Comparison of strategies for data collection

CENSUS	SURVEY	ETHNOGRAPHY
Population	Population	—
Environment	Environment	Environment
—	Resources	Resources
—	Beliefs	Beliefs

ACKNOWLEDGEMENTS

The authors gratefully acknowledge the assistance of Judy Schultz in the preparation of this manuscript. An earlier version of this paper was presented in a Research Brief session at the annual meeting of the Western Gerontological Society, 17-19 March 1985 in Denver, Colorado.

REFERENCES

Andersen R. & Anderson O. (1974) *A Decade of Health Services.* University of Chicago Press, Chicago.

Dever G.E.A. (1984) *Epidemiology in Health Services Management.* Aspen Publications, Germantown, Maryland.

Flaming K. (1977) *CHAPC Health Needs Assessment Survey: Technical Report, Part II and III, Section B.* Applied Sociological Research Team, University of Colorado, Denver.

Freeman R.B. & Heinrich J. (1981) *Community Health Nursing Practice.* W.B. Saunders, Philadelphia.

Glittenberg J. *et al.* (1981) Project GENESIS: La Junta, 1981. University of Colorado School of Nursing, Denver.

Glittenberg J. *et al.* (1982) Project GENESIS: Trinidad, 1982. University of Colorado School of Nursing, Denver.

Geoppinger J. (1984) Community as client: using the nursing process to promote health. In *Community Health Nursing: Process and Practice for Promoting Health* (Stanhope M. & Lancaster J eds). C.V. Mosby, St Louis.

Magilvy J.K. *et al.* (1984) The teenagers of Ft Collins, Colorado: a focused ethnography. University of Colorado School of Nursing, Denver.

Magilvy J.K. *et al.* (1985) Project GENESIS: being older in Brighton. University of Colorado School of Nursing, Denver.

Magilvy J.K. *et al.* (1986) Project GENESIS: across the street: perceptions of the Health Sciences Center Community. University of Colorado School of Nursing, Denver.

Oreglia A. (1973) *The Uses of Census Data for Health Services Planning and Management.* Department of Sociology, Purdue University, Lafayette, Indiana.

Schultz P.R. *et al.* (1984) The seniors of Capitol Hill—a focused ethnography. University of Colorado School of Nursing, Denver.

United States Bureau of the Census (1970) *Census of Population and Housing,* 1970. United States Bureau of the Census, Washington, DC.

Watson N.M. (1984) Community as client. In *Directions in Community Health Nursing* (Sullivan J.A. ed). Blackwell Scientific, Oxford.

CHAPTER 30

Identifying Needs and Community Resources in Arthritis Care

Judith J. Liebman, RN, BS, MSLS, MSN
Alan L. Hull, PhD
Michael Blauner, BA, MA
John Barkey, BA, MA
Paul J. Vignos, Jr., MD
Roland W. Moskowitz, MD

PROJECT GOAL

According to Webster, a need can be defined as "the lack of something requisite, desirable, or useful; a physiological or psychological requirement for the well-being of an organism." In health planning, the concept of need is understood "as the gap between an existing and a desired state of health," which "in the context of social planning can (potentially) be prevented or ameliorated by the use of health services" (Blum, 1981, p. 88). A need can also be defined as a problem arising out of a situation in which goals or outcomes that are valued are not satisfied as expected. While health needs have been defined by professionals as perceptions of situations deviating from expected norms, health needs perceived by individuals themselves are influenced by an awareness of what is wrong with something valued as well as knowledge of the resources available in the community to meet those needs (Blum, 1981).

The factors that influence health service needs therefore include the actual availability and supply of services, the nature and state of the art of the delivery system, the productivity of the providers, and most important, the needs and wants expressed by a particular population. The demand or perceived need for services can actually be affected by the supply offered in the community—the greater the supply, the greater the demand (Blum, 1981, pp. 91-92).

A crucial focus in community health nursing is understanding the nature of a particular group at risk and the resources that exist to address its needs (Shamansky & Pesznecker, 1981). Uncurable but manageable rheumatic disease, for example, affects millions of individuals; in persons 65 years of age and older, 30 percent universally demonstrate symptomatic complaints of osteoarthritis (OA), while in rheumatoid arthritis (RA), the second most prevalent rheumatic disease and by far the most debilitating, a minimum of one million people are affected (Arthritis Foundation, 1983). With the majority of these patients being cared for outside the hospital environment, the two conditions constitute a challenge to community health nursing and the service delivery system. The health gain derived from care provided by health service agencies, however, is frequently difficult to measure because the goals of

Reprinted from *Public Health Nursing*, Vol. 3, No. 3, with permission of Blackwell Scientific Publications, Inc., © 1986.

health care in these situations can be ongoing: to improve quality of life and slow down progression of disease.

The pain and disability associated with OA, RA, and other less prevalent rheumatic diseases can affect many aspects of daily living. Special considerations arise as a result of changes in functional ability and lifestyle. In contrast to acute illness, chronic disease requires a more personal commitment to managing pain and disability over longer periods of time. Individuals with arthritis therefore may have persistent and unrelenting burdens, including financial crises; interference with occupational, educational, and family pursuits; and a continuing demand for medical, nursing, recreational, rehabilitative, and psychologic resources. While many of the health and social needs growing out of these situations are satisfied by family members, others can best be met through the help of formal service agencies in a community.

Many services are often enlisted to deal with an arthritis patient's aspects of daily living—dressing, meal preparation, bathing and toileting, and ambulation in and out of the home, to name a few. Managing recreation, home, and personal relationships in the face of chronicity are also imperatives. Two principal strategies patients with RA are known to employ, keeping up and covering up, are attempts to maintain normalcy, such as job, family activities, and social commitments (Wiener, 1975).

Although community resources are often already in place, identification of needs by the individuals themselves has not always preceded the determination of the compatibility between needs and services. Methodologic dilemmas exist, for example, in developing assessments for identifying needs. Problems relate to individual personality characteristics and variations in responses to illness, as well as scale development (Williamson, 1978).

Despite such problems, expressions of needs by patients can facilitate recognition of health and social problems for further exploration in planning nursing interventions (Aspinall, 1975; Kinlein, 1977). Individuals' perceived needs and preferences, while not always in agreement with views of health professionals, form the basis of self-care practices (Chang, 1980). Collaborating with patients in making theoretical predictions of needs, based on their attributes and their perceptions, is therefore critical in nursing (Roberts, 1982). Assessing the perceptions of patients and the meaning of illness, as well as the nurses' role in providing necessary health care, are inherent in nursing models (Neuman, 1980).

While studies have compared the congruency between nurses and patients about care problems (Roberts, 1982), as far as these authors can tell, none has directly assessed patients' health and social need for community services. We conducted a project to assess and analyze patient perceptions of need in arthritis care. A structured interview was constructed for this purpose and administered to 189 patients. Once the needs were determined, they were analyzed according to categories of priority and later matched with viable community resources in a defined geographic region. Based on the agreement between identified needs and services, an arthritis services directory was then developed to facilitate patient access to community resources.

DEVELOPMENT OF THE STRUCTURED INTERVIEW

Literature Review

A literature review revealed few data with regard to filling perceived health and social needs in arthritis care. Instead, most studies represented health professionals' medical management view, determined on an a priori basis, of what a recipient should require or desire from health and social service professionals. Therefore empirical evidence is required of needs in arthritis care that includes data derived from actual consumers (Pratt, 1978).

In terms of service use, patients with RA who rely heavily on medical care at the same time infrequently employ social and other nonphysician resources. This is evident despite the frequency of psychologic and social changes, and the reductions in recreational and functional activities experienced by these patients (Yelin, Henke, & Epstein, 1977). In addition, suggestions have been made that patient satisfaction with professional health care, as well as how successfully needs are met, may depend on the need-service congruency (Eisenberg, 1976; Williamson, 1978). With the condition of arthritis, furthermore, it has been demonstrated that patients who require a wide array of complex services make economical and efficient service choices once their specific needs have been assessed (Weiler, 1979). Previous research also indicated that patients and families who are capable of expressing needs and are aggressive in obtaining professional care progress the best with illness (Pratt, 1978; Mechanic, 1977).

It would appear helpful therefore for health and social service professionals to have a clear understanding of the perceived needs of those with arthritis, and the care issues they face in the event of long-lasting illness. A common base of understanding between providers and recipients of care of what is important in a person's physical, personal, functional, and social life may contribute to more satisfactory health care management.

Methods

As indicated, the first task in identifying the perceived needs of patients with arthritis was to develop a structured interview that could be easily administered. As the literature was reviewed, several areas of need became evident both intuitively and objectively: (1) Medical and Related Care; (2) Tangible Service; and (3) Psychosocial and Vocational Counseling.

Medical and related care needs referred to care and information provided by health professionals, that is, rheumatologists, arthritis clinics, nursing care, medication information, physical and occupational therapy, and the like. Tangible needs were the necessary materials or task-oriented assistance patients required to function more successfully, including aids and devices, financial assistance, transportation, meals for the home-bound, homemaker services, and others. Examples of psychosocial and vocational needs included mental health counseling for both families and patients, support groups, recreational activities, and employment guidance.

The next step in developing the interview was to validate and expand the list of needs identified in the literature. Sources used, therefore, to develop the comprehensive list included the following:

1. A review of current arthritis literature to identify variables related to patient needs
2. Interviews with patients to obtain their own expressions of needs
3. Health professionals' documentation of need
4. A review of functional assessment questionnaires reported in the literature
5. Interviews with staff members of the local Arthritis Foundation to document needs requested through telephone and mail communication

Needs identified in the arthritis literature

From approximately 200 titles of clinical relevance obtained from a MEDLINE search, many were selected that highlighted medical management issues in arthritis (Baum & Figley, 1980; Fries, Spitz, Kraines, & Holman, 1980; Gross, 1981; Meenan, Yelin, Henke, Curtis, & Epstein, 1978; Pigg, 1974; Wiener, 1975; Yelin, Feshbach, Meenan, & Epstein, 1979; Yelin et al, 1977). The literature surveyed appeared to stress primarily health professionals' medical management of patients and psychosocial and functional status rather than needs articulated by the patients themselves. Medical management and nursing care issues included the importance of rest and activity, nutrition and weight control, understanding and administering medication, and the contributions of physical and occupational therapy to arthritis care. Functional aspects and tangible service needs in the literature reflected activities of daily living problems, transportation, and exercise and mobility. Psychosocial and vocational issues stressed were related to feelings about physical changes in the body, sources of depression, social and personal relationships, and associated disability problems. As a starting point, variables describing patients and patient care issues were selected from the literature and translated into patient needs.

Patients' expressions of needs

Discussions with selected patients during their visits to a weekly arthritis clinic served as a second source. Suggestions made by patients included need for foot care, to be creative through arts and crafts, a "swap shop" for loaning or renting equipment, and support groups. Patients also wanted more information about their diagnoses and diagnostic procedures, what to expect in the future, and ways to pay for care. Several needs were not easily translated into service. For example, a male patient with RA pointed out that assistive devices and rehabilitative aids are usually designed for right-handed individuals and relate primarily to a homemaker's tasks. The workplace activities of men require different types of aids. In addition, a group of young working women with systemic lupus erthematosus (SLE) was concerned with the inability to purchase life insurance once their illness became known. Sensitivity to individual health problems and finding ways to serve such clients are issues for insurance companies, legal personnel, health professionals, and society in general.

In summary, many of the concerns of patients centered on the need for additional knowledge, including more illness information, the creative activities that were available to help them live more satisfying lives, and instrumental help such as financial and legal assistance. The needs were again listed and integrated into the previous cataloged group derived from the literature survey.

Health professionals' documentation of need

An advisory board of health professionals was established to review the needs being identified and to provide assistance to the project. The group included a senior clinical nurse responsible for a musculoskeletal unit in a hospital, two rheumatologists, an attorney working in disability and the law, a pharmacist, occupational and physical therapists, an arthritis care social worker, a medical educator, a vocational guidance and rehabilitation counselor, a patient, and a staff person from the local chapter of the Arthritis Foundation. The board met regularly every six months for two years. Several members were interviewed individually to identify needs specific to their disciplines.

The needs articulated by the advisory board related primarily to management issues in care, although transportation, patient concerns about cost of medications, the desire of patients for more detailed explanations about medication therapy, and the problems inherent in obtaining disability assistance were included. The board also corroborated the needs identified in the medical, nursing, and psychosocial literature, and reviewed the needs list derived from patients and the remaining two sources.

In addition, other groups of health professionals had earlier identified patient needs using two group process methods, the Nominal Group Process (NGP) and the Delphi Technique (DT) (Vanek, Liebman, Amy, Getzy, Moskowitz, & Hull, 1985). Items identified in these included but were not limited to the need for information about referral services (arthritis clinics and rheumatologists), support groups, home health care and transportation resources, where to purchase rehabilitation equipment, financial assistance, and how to obtain occupational and physical therapy. These were also integrated into the prior list.

Review of functional assessment questionnaires

Several functional assessment questionnaires were reviewed. In particular, the Duke Multidimensional Functional Assessment questionnaire (DMFA) provided a thorough approach to identifying both functional aspects (part A) and service needs (part B) of patients (Multidimensional Functional Assessment, 1978).

The DMFA (part B) was relevant because it asked about the kinds of help or services patients used. For example, patients were queried about social and recreational services, transportation, employment services, personal care services, nursing care, physical therapy (occupational therapy was not included in the DMFA), homemaker services, locating housing, and legal assistance.

Three other assessment questionnaires were useful in translating functional issues into needs: the Arthritis Impact Measurement Scale (AIMS) (Meenan, Gertaman, & Mason, 1980). Index of Activities of Daily Living (IADL) (Katz, Ford, Moskowitz, Jackson, & Jaffe, 1963), and the Fries Stanford Measurement of Function (Fries et al, 1980). The AIMS, for example, examines self-care, mobility, transportation, the necessity for clothing that is easy to put on and take off, shopping assistance, and ability to prepare meals. Functional categories from these questionnaires were reviewed, organized into items of need, and cross-matched with the needs cataloged from the preceding sources.

Interviews with staff members of the local chapter of the Arthritis Foundation

Two staff members from the local chapter of the Arthritis Foundation were individually interviewed to collect data related to telephone and written inquiries.

The two staff members consulted were the receptionist who accepted telephone calls and mail requests and the person in charge of the Patient Services Committee, a permanent committee responsible for developing programs and projects related to patient needs. The needs reported by patients were not too dissimilar from those identified in the preceding four sources. The following reflect the substance of needs documented from this source: financial assistance related to medical care costs, information about medication therapy, where to find aids and devices, locations of arthritis clinics and rheumatologists, vocational retraining, counseling for families with children affected by arthritis, support groups, nursing homes, and water exercise programs. Once more these were cross-matched and integrated into the prior lists.

Development of Items of Service Needs for the Interview Questionnaire

Once the needs from the five sources were matched in terms of similarity, they were analyzed and grouped into the content areas earlier noted. Service areas were developed from the content areas and submitted to the advisory board for review. Based on the review, the following service areas were included in the structured interview:

1. Medical and related care
   a. Aquatic exercise programs in public swimming pools
   b. Home health care, including skilled nursing and personal care
   c. Information about arthritis, including explana tions about medications
   d. Medical care, including arthritis clinics and arthritis physicians
   e. Nutritional assistance
   f. Occupational therapy, including use of assistive devices, rehabilitative aids, and easier ways to do home chores
   g. Physical therapy, including exercises and expla nations about balancing rest and activity
   h. Podiatry
2. Tangible needs (material or task-oriented assistance)
   a. Clothing, easy to put on, take off, and fasten
   b. Purchase of aids and devices
   c. Financial assistance including Major Medical, Medicare, Medicaid, disability insurance, General Relief, and equipment reimbursement
   d. Household assistance
   e. Legal assistance
   f. Meal preparation both inside and outside the home
   g. Public building access
   h. Reading materials about arthritis
   i. Respite care to relieve families, including information about nursing homes
   j. Transportation, public and private
3. Psychosocial and vocational counseling
   a. Counseling—family, mental health including sexuality issues and related problems at home, work, and school
   b. Crafts and hobbies
   c. Recreational activities—planned programs
   d. Self-help groups and clubs
   e. Social activities
   f. Spiritual assistance
   g. Vocational guidance and rehabilitation, including working while getting disability benefits; work potential in general

Sixty-six questions were developed across the above areas. The instrument was revised several times based on suggestions made by the advisory board and patients. As a final step, 12 patients similar to the target sample were interviewed to test the clarity of the questions.

In addition to service needs, other information was obtained, such as patient perception of diagnoses, chart diagnoses, length or arthritis illness, current medications, other physical problems, demographic information, and functional ability as measured by the Stanford Measurement of Function (Fries et al, 1980). Open-ended questions were also included, asking patients what agencies helped them the most and, when appropriate, why they did not seek help if they needed it. A final open question asked patients if any needs were not listed.

For ease of administration, the following stem question was used for each of the 66 items: Because of your arthritis, have you ever needed help in finding . . . ? A response to the question included "never needed" to "often needed" on a scale of 1 to 5.

For each item, patients were also asked: Have you ever tried to get help? If the answer was "yes," a question was asked concerning the extent of satisfaction with the help they had received. A five-point scale from no satisfaction to very satisfied was used. The interview took an average of 45 minutes to complete.

Training Interviewers

Interviewers were hired as part of the project. Meetings were held to assist them in the interview process. A written guideline was prepared to aid them in understanding the nature of rheumatic disease, the interactive process they were to use in interviewing patients, and the importance of recording patient comments related to each question. Project staff and interviewers met several times to give everyone the opportunity to ask questions, clarify issues, and offer suggestions. A termination meeting allowed interviewers to discuss the project as a whole and summarize the recognized needs of patients with arthritis.

Identifying Patients

The structured interview was administered by several interviewers trained by the staff. A convenience sample of patients with rheumatic disease, the majority of whom received care from two urban health care centers, were asked to participate in the project. Of the 189 patients interviewed, 62 (33%) were obtained through suburban physicians. Thirty-three (17%) patients were identified as home-bound (Table 30-1). Except for these participants, patients with a primary problem of arthritis were directly referred on site to the interviewers after medical appointments with their physicians. In some cases, patients preferred to be interviewed at home and these request were

TABLE 30-1
Characteristics of the sample

CHARACTERISTIC	NUMBER (%)	CHARACTERISTIC	NUMBER (%)
Age (yrs)		Sex	
Median	66	Females	154 (81)
Range	28–92	Males	35 (19)
Race		Marital status	
Black	115 (61)	Married	76 (40)
White	72 (38)	Widowed	64 (34)
Other	2 (1)	Divorced	24 (13)
Totals	189 (100)	Single	13 (7)
		Separated	10 (5)
		Not available	2 (1)
Income ($)		Education	
Less than 6999	110 (58)	Grade 11 or less	158 (84)
7000-9999	22 (12)		
10,000-16,999	22 (12)		
Greater than 17,000	27 (14)		
Not available	8 (4)		
Totals	189 (100)		
Patient status		Patient interview sites	
Ambulatory	156 (83)	Urban clinics	127 (67)
Homebound	33 (17)	Private physicians' suburban clinics	62 (33)
Totals	189 (100)	Totals	189 (100)

honored. Two women, similar in characteristics to the sample as a whole, refused to participate. According to the interviewers, patients generally enjoyed the process, eager to have the opportunity to talk about their health problems and activities.

Results of The Structured Interview

Knowledge about diagnosis

Although a chart review indicated 90 (48%) patients with osteoarthritis (recorded sometimes as degenerative joint disease or arthritis), only 25 (13%) could label their disease as OA (Table 30-2). It is interesting to note also that 86 (45%) participants attached no specific name to their disease, despite the chart diagnosis.

Comparison of function

In terms of disability, the functional outcome measurements obtained in this patient group were compared to the RA sample of Fries and co-workers (1980). In that group, function was initially assessed through both interview and self-administration formats in order to test the reliability of the scale. For making comparisons here, however, only the results of the interview are used to highlight differences between the current sample and Fries's (Table 30-3). When comparing only patients with RA in both samples, our group functioned less well than the patients in the Fries's sample.

Needs analysis

A subsequent factor analysis of the survey responses to the 66 items revealed three significant need:

1. General information
2. Personal care and medical services
3. Assistive devices and equipment

The instrument used was judged by the authors to be both reliable and valid. The use of several sources to identify the scope and type of items to be included suggested that the full domain of content was included. The sources were diverse enough to assume full coverage of the subject, since they included patients and professionals who provided information through several processes, including interviews, meetings, other instruments, and publications. The internal consistency of the items was estimated by computing a Chronbach's alpha statistic for the items in three major categories. The alpha coefficients for the items in each index were all above 0.88. (Additional data on these analyses are available from the authors.)

Table 30-4 provides some further insights into the needs of this population group. The percentages of patients indicating a need of two or more on the scale 1 to 5 are illustrated across items used in the interview.

TABLE 30-2
Diagnoses

DIAGNOSES	NUMBER (%)	DIAGNOSES	NUMBER (%)
Chart diagnoses		Perceived diagnoses	
OA	83 (43)	OA	25 (13)
RA	54 (28)	RA	67 (35)
SLE	5 (3)	SLE	29 (1)
Gout	2 (1)	Gout	7 (4)
OA + Gout	3 (2)		
RA + OA	4 (2)		
RA + SLE	1 (1)		
RA + Gout	1 (1)	Do not know	86 (45)
Other	10 (5)	Other	1 (1)
Not available	26 (14)	Not available	1 (1)
	189 (100)		189 (100)

TABLE 30-3
Stanford measurement of function[a]

FUNCTION	CURRENT STUDY[b] RA PATIENTS	CURRENT STUDY[b] ALL PATIENTS	FRIES STUDY[b,c] RA Patients
Dressing and grooming	1.38 (1.03)	0.91 (1.01)	0.98 (0.73)
Arising from straight chair without using arms for support	1.60 (1.30)	1.31 (1.14)	0.53 (0.62)
Eating (cutting, lifting cup to mouth)	0.92 (0.93)	0.40 (0.73)	0.55 (0.76)
Walking (outdoors on flat ground)	0.98 (1.13)	0.70 (0.86)	0.80 (0.88)
Hygiene (washing, bathtub use, toileting, able to turn faucets on and off)	1.68 (1.21)	1.07 (1.11)	1.33 (1.00)
Reach (above head, comb hair)	1.78 (1.25)	1.26 (1.23)	1.43 (1.00)
Grip (use pen or pencil, open previously opened jar)	1.58 (1.17)	0.94 (1.09)	1.30 (0.95)
Activity (run errands and shop, drive)	1.63 (1.24)	1.47 (1.12)	1.05 (1.13)

[a]Patients were scored on a scale of 0 to 3 as follows: 0 = without difficulty; 1 = with difficulty; 2 = with some help from another person or device; and 3 = unable to do.
[b]Means (standard deviations).
[c]Fries et al, 1980.

RESULTS AND CONCLUSIONS

The results of the structured interview reflected the perceived need for service of one group of patients who desire to live more comfortably and independently; thus outcome should not be generalized to other populations. Health care needs regarded as important to patients are often viewed from the perspective of health professionals who may claim that patients' own expressions of need are related to wants and therefore are not always medically important. Empirically derived information from those who are actual consumers of health care, however, is essential to match needs with available community service agencies.

In addition, measurement of patient needs can add significantly to our understanding of the consequences of illness, provide a basis for nursing actions, contribute to planning programs, and involve patients in their own health care destiny. Maslow (1968) pointed out that illness in a person's life is a central concern that can alter perceptions of needs by reordering priorities. In arthritis, for example, information about rest and activity and dealing with physical changes in general can take precedence over usual activities of daily living and social interactions.

The definition of a need, however, is a personal judgment about a human condition or life situation that has a valued goal and requires some action to satisfy it. A subsequent behavior or action to fulfill the need may not always follow. Personal experiences with service agencies can play a major role in whether one perceives a need and will seek help from the community to meet it. Patient problems may be unresolved or needs unperceived if no assistance is forthcoming from an agency. As mentioned earlier, health needs can be influenced by the resources in a community capable of responding to them (Blum, 1981).

Issues that confronted the project staff in developing questions for the structured interviews centered on, for example, health professionals expressing the need of patients for physical and occupational therapy as such, forgetting that patients often do not understand the role of therapists. Questions relating to

TABLE 30-4
Expressions of needs

EXPRESSIONS OF NEED AS A RESULT OF ARTHRITIS	PATIENTS REPORTING PROBLEM NUMBER %
Medical and Related Care	
Help with understanding medications	106 (56)
Explanations of special exercises (physical therapy)	106 (56)
Arthritis doctor	98 (52)
Explain type of arthritis	98 (52)
Explain rest and activity	85 (45)
Podiatric care	87 (46)
Aquatic arthritis exercise programs	68 (36)
Help with bathing at home	60 (32)
An easier way to do home chores (occupational therapy)	51 (27)
Help with personal care	40 (21)
How to prepare healthful meals (nutrition)	32 (17)
Care during day and night	11 (6)
Skilled nursing care	9 (5)
Care during day	9 (5)
Care during night	8 (4)
Tangible Needs	
Reading materials about arthritis	93 (49)
Help for household chores	87 (46)
Someone to clean house	85 (45)
Help with shopping for food	85 (45)
Canes and crutches	84 (44)
Comfortable shoes	70 (37)
Public transportation	68 (36)
Private transportation	68 (36)
Help with rights as disabled person	66 (34)
Find out about disability insurance	55 (29)
Money for arthritis care	55 (29)
Where to buy special assistive aids for dressing	50 (26)
Building access	50 (26)
Clothing easy to put on, take off, and fasten	49 (25)
Find out about Medicare	45 (24)
Find out about Major Medical	43 (23)
Tangible Needs—cont'd	
Bathroom aids	43 (23)
Aids to prepare food	43 (23)
Respite for family	42 (22)
Meals outside the home	42 (22)
Reimbursement for equipment	42 (22)
Preparation of food in the home	36 (19)
Find out about Medicaid	34 (18)
Find out about General Relief	34 (18)
Home-delivered meals	26 (14)
Locate wheelchairs	26 (14)
Help find a lawyer	25 (13)
Neck collars	24 (12)
Help find out about good nursing homes	23 (12)
Blocks to raise beds	19 (10)
Back braces	19 (10)
Resting splints	8 (4)
Psychosocial and Vocational Counseling	
Self-help support groups	91 (48)
Someone to talk to about things that make me nervous	74 (39)
Someone to talk to about personal problems	66 (35)
Someone to talk to when feeling down	60 (32)
Someone to talk to about living with arthritis at home	60 (32)
Crafts and hobbies	60 (32)
Recreational activities	53 (28)
Someone to talk to about religious feelings	51 (27)
Explain work I can do	42 (22)
Help with arthritis problems at work	38 (20)
Planned social activities	34 (18)
Help with sexual relationships	34 (18)
Explain work I can do while getting disability	30 (16)
Help with arthritis problems in school	8 (4)

occupational and physical therapy therefore were phrased in the terms of the skills those professionals offered: "someone who can teach you an easier way to do home chores," or "someone who can explain how much rest and activity you need."

In addition, because interview items were obtained through several sources, it was necessary to refine carefully and cross-match the selected characteristics. The notable overlap of items among the five perspectives added to the validity of the 25 content areas selected.

Finally, data that were gathered through the structured interview were, as part of the analysis, formed into a matrix of needs and matched with community service resources identified through several different sources, that is, available computerized listings of health and human services, consumer telephone directory, and information from project staff. Agencies selected for inclusion in the service directory were telephoned and received written communications. The directory is published and has been distributed to participating patients, community leaders, and health care and social work professionals who have frequent contact with persons with arthritis. We believe, and already have written documentation, that such a directory facilitates access to needed resources in a community.

SUMMARY

The method used to identify and classify the perceived needs of persons with arthritis served as a necessary mechanism in the first phase of a project to match needs with community resources. The process may be of interest to others assessing patients' self-preceptions. Prior research demonstrated the numerous sources that can be used to develop questions for documenting patient characteristics and needs—review of the literature, expressions of health professionals and patients, critical examination of functional assessment characteristics, and data gleaned from the experience of relevant nonprofit agencies (Davis, Hull, & Boutaugh, 1980). By using several sources, one can be assured that many areas are considered. Also, divergent views between health care professionals and patients reported elsewhere (Lorig, Cox, Cuevas, Kraines, & Britton, 1984; Potts, Weinberger, & Brandt, 1984; Roberts, 1982) in relation to needs may become more congruent during such assessments.

ACKNOWLEDGMENT

This work was supported by grant AM 20618 from the National Institute of Arthritis, Musculoskeletal and Skin Diseases (NIAMS).

REFERENCES

Aspinall, J. (1975). Development of a patient-completed admission questionnaire and its comparison with a nursing interview. *Nursing Research, 24*(5), 377-381.

Baum, J., & Figley, B. A. (1980). Psychological and sexual health in rheumatoid diseases. In E. W. Kelley, S. Ruddy, S. Sledge, & E. Harris (Eds.), *Textbook of rheumatology, Vol. II.* Philadelphia: W. B. Saunders.

Blum, H. L. (1981) *Planning for health: Generics for the eighties.* New York: Human Sciences Press.

Chang, B. L. (1980). Evaluation of health care professionals in facilitating self-care: Review of the literature and a conceptual model. *Advances in Nursing Science, 3,* 43-58.

Davis, W. K., Hull, A. L., & Boutaugh, M. L. (1980). Diagnosing the educational needs of the chronically ill. *New Directions for Continuing Education, 7,* 65-72.

Eisenberg, L. (1976). Delineation of clinical conditions: Conceptual models of physical and mental disorders: Their interactions. In *CIBA Foundation Symposium No. 44. Research and medical practice.* Amsterdam: Elsevier.

Fries, J. F., Spitz, P., Kraines, K. G., & Holman, H. R. (1980). Measurement of patient outcome in arthritis. *Arthritis and Rheumatism, 23*(2), 137-145.

Gross, M. (1981). Psychosocial aspects of osteoarthritis: Helping patients cope. *Health and Social Work, 6*(3), 40-45.

Katz, S., Ford, A. B., Moskowitz, R. W., Jackson, B. A., & Jaffe, M. W. (1963). Studies of illness in the aged. *Journal of the American Medical Association, 185*(12), 914-919.

Kinlein, M. L. (1977). *Independent nursing practice with clients.* Philadelphia: J. B. Lippincott.

Lorig, K. R., Cox, T., Cuevas, Y., Kraines, R. G., & Britton, M. C. (1984). Converging and diverging beliefs about arthritis: Caucasian patients, Spanish-speaking patients, and physicians. *Journal of Rheumatology, 11*(1), 76-79.

Maslow, A. H. (1968). *Toward a psychology of being.* New York: Van Nostrand Reinhold.

Mechanic, D. (1977). Illness behavior, social adaptation, and the management of illness: A comparison of educational and medical models. *Journal of Nervous and Mental Disease, 165*(2), 79-87.

Meenan, R. F., Gertman, P. M., & Mason, J. H. (1980). Measuring health status in arthritis: The arthritis impact measurement scales. *Arthritis and Rheumatism, 23*(2), 146-152.

Meenan, R. F., Yelin, E. H., Kenke, C. J., Curtis, D. L., & Epstein, W. V. (1978). The cost of rheumatoid arthritis: A patient-oriented study of chronic disease costs. *Arthritis and Rheumatism, 21*(7), 828-833.

Multidimensional Functional Assessment. (1978). *The (OARS) older Americans resources and services methodology* (2nd ed.). Durham, NC: Center for the Study of Aging and Human Development, Duke University Medical Center.

Neuman, B. (1980). The Betty Neuman health care systems model. In J. Riehl & C. Roy (Eds.), *Conceptual models for nursing practice* (2nd ed.). New York: Appleton-Century-Crofts.

Pigg, J. (1974). 50 helpful hints for active arthritis patients. *Nursing 4*(7), 39-41.

Potts, M., Weinberger, M., & Brandt, K. D. (1984). Views of patients and providers regarding the importance of various aspects of an arthritis treatment program. *Journal of Rheumatology, 11*(1), 71-75.

Pratt, L. V. (1978). Reshaping the consumer's posture in health care. In E. B. Gallagher (Ed.), *The doctor-patient relationship in the changing health scene.* Washington, DC: U.S. Department of Health, Education, and Welfare.

Roberts, C. S. (1982, September). Identifying the real patient problems. *Nursing Clinics of North America, 17*(3), 481-489.

Rodnan, G. P. & Schumacher, H.R., eds. (1983). *Primer on the rheumatic diseases* (8th ed.). Atlanta: Arthritis Foundation.

Shamansky, S. L., & Pesznecker, B. (1981, March). A community is . . . *Nursing Outlook, 29,* 182-185.

Vanek, E. P., Liebman, J. J., Amy, C. K., Getzy, L., Moskowitz, R. W., & Hull, A. L. (1985) Identification of needs of health professionals in arthritis patient care using two group process techniques. *Clinical Rheumatology in Practice, 3*(1), 32-35.

Weiler, P. G. (1979). *Problems in obtaining services and possible solutions in public policy and chronic disease.* In DHEW Public Policy and Chronic Disease: *A forum sponsored by the national arthritis advisory board.* U.S. Dept. of Health, Education, & Welfare, Public Health Service (NIH Publication No. 79-1986) Bethesda, Maryland: NIH.

Wiener, C. L. (1975). The burden of rheumatoid arthritis: Tolerating the uncertainty. *Social Science and Medicine, 9,* 97-104.

Williamson, Y. M. (1978, May-June). Methodologic dilemmas in tapping the concept of patient needs. *Nursing Research, 27*(3), 172-177.

Yelin, E. H., Feshbach, D. M., Meenan, R. F., & Epstein, W. V. (1979) Social problems, services and policy for persons with chronic disease: The case of rheumatoid arthritis. *Social Science and Medicine, 13c,* 13-20.

Yelin, E. H., Henke, C., & Epstein, W. V. (1977). Resources for the care of arthritis in a non-metropolitan community. *Arthritis and Rheumatism, 20,* 45-57.

Suggested Additional Readings for Part V

Community-centered nursing practice

Archer, S. E. (1982). Synthesis of public health science and nursing science. *Nursing Outlook,* Sept/Oct, 442-446.

Bell, D. M., et. al. (1989). Illness associated with child day care: A study of incidence and cost. *American Journal of public health,* 79(4), 479-484.

Dean, P. G., Expanding our sights to include social networks, *Nursing & Health Care,* Dec 19?, pp. 545-550.

Gloss, E. F. and S. B. Fielo. (1987). The nursing center: An alternative for health care delivery. *Family and Community Health* 10(2), 49-58.

Goeppinger, J., & Baglow, A. G. (1985). Community competence: A positive approach to needs assessment. *American Journal of Community Psychology,* 13(5), 507-523.

Goeppinger, J., Lassiter, P. G., and Wilcox, B. Community health is community competence. *Nursing Outlook,* Sept/Oct 1982, pp. 464-467.

Miller, J. T. (1987). Wellness programs through the church. *Health Values* 11(5), 3-6.

Popp, R. A. An overview of occupational health promotion, *AAOHN Journal,* April 1989, Volume 37, Number 4, pp. 113-120.

Rogers, S. S. (1984). Community as client—a multivariate model for analysis of community and aggregate health risk. *Public Health Nursing,* 1 (4), 210-222.

Schultz, P. (1987). When client means more than one: Extending the foundational concept of person. *Advances in Nursing Science* 10(1), 71-86.

Williams, C. A., and Highriter, M. E. (1978). Community health nursing: Population focus and evaluation. *Public Health Reviews,* VII, (3-4), 197-221.

Zapka, J. G., and Love, M. B., College health services: Setting for community, organizational, and individual change, *Family & Community Health,* May 1985, pp. 18-34.

PART VI

CULTURE AND COMMUNITY HEALTH NURSING PRACTICE

The social and health behavior of individuals is greatly influenced by the culture in which they live and interact. Culture refers to the beliefs, values, and behavior shared by members of an interacting society. The ways in which an individual reacts to illness and seeks health care is determined to a great degree by cultural influences. Culture is a blueprint or design for living, including customs, norms, folkways, and ways of thinking. For the community health nurse to deliver appropriate nursing care, the cultural context must be assessed and the knowledge utilized to plan, implement, and evaluate care.

In the U.S. we share many common characteristics as a society; however, there is a rich and varied sociocultural heritage which exists in our subcultures. Many subcultures, such as Mexican-Americans, Native Americans, and Black Americans, have retained many traditional cultural aspects. Cultural differences, however, are not confined to ethnic groups. Much cultural diversity exists in regional differences, such as Appalacia and the American South.

Because of the focus in community health nursing on prevention and health promotion, awareness of cultural dimensions in community health nursing practice is essential to appropriate and effective assessment and intervention at the community level. The following articles provide the community health nurse with specific guidance and examples for working with diverse cultural groups in the U.S.

CHAPTER 31

Beyond the Concept of Culture; Or, How Knowing the Cultural Formula Does Not Predict Clinical Success

Toni Tripp-Reimer, RN, PhD, FAAN
Stephen S. Fox, PhD

In the nineteenth century concepts from the biological sciences were introduced into nursing and were followed by contributions from psychology and sociology. More recently concepts from anthropology have been introduced into the mainstream of nursing education and practice. However, the incorporation of cultural concepts into the discipline of nursing has not generally occurred in such a way as to optimize the relationship between professional and layperson. Specifically, an overemphasis on units of culture and cultural differences fosters the alienation of nurse and patient.

In this chapter we briefly trace the historical evolution of the inclusion of cultural dimensions within nursing education and practice. We point out how this approach could be assistive, but how it is generally misapplied. Specifically, we contend that nursing approaches to cultural dimensions have tended to foster ethnic stereotypes. The assessment and treatment of patients based on specified characteristics of their culture emphasizes the differences between nurse and patient and promotes a separation from the patient. We further propose that the intent underlying this approach stems from an agenda in which concern for therapeutic compliance, rather than for the person, holds primacy. Finally, we propose an approach that transcends cultural distinctiveness or categories.

Reprinted from *Current Issues in Nursing*, J. C. McCloskey and H. K. Grace, eds., with permission of Mosby Year-Book, Inc.

THE EVOLUTION OF A CULTURAL APPROACH IN NURSING

In the discipline of nursing, concern with the culture of the client dates at least to the beginning of the twentieth century. This early interest is particularly evident in public health nursing, where a major impetus for considering the client's cultural context was the need to work with immigrant groups. Early in the century a series of articles appearing in the *Public Health Nursing Quarterly* gave cultural overviews of various immigrant groups such as Italians, Russians, and Portuguese. However, the majority of this early literature was parochial in its intent to homogenize (assimilate) the immigrant groups. That is, different European nationalities were described not for the purpose of tailoring culturally sensitive care, but to assist nurses and social workers in transforming foreign beliefs and customs so that the group could be blended in the proverbial "melting pot."

In areas of nursing other than public health, the cultural dimension was generally ignored until World

War II. At that time anthropologists and other social scientists, national organizations and foundations, and the educational reform movement were instrumental in moving cultural content into nursing. For example, the National Nursing Council commissioned the anthropologist Esther Lucille Brown to conduct a study of nursing education. Her findings, containing recommendations for nursing education, were published in the 1948 book *Nursing for the Future,*[3] which spearheaded the movement for midcentury educational reform in nursing.

As a consequence, schools of nursing were progressively integrated into university settings where there was a closer relationship between nursing faculty and social scientists. The content of nursing education in its new collegiate setting was characterized by increased attention to content from the social sciences.[2,6] The social sciences (specifically psychology and sociology) provided a theoretical base for what nursing had previously done intuitively.

Addressing the National League of Nursing Education in 1949, Birdwhistell[1] identified some of the uses of the anthropological approach to the problems of nursing. Other national nursing groups invited speakers such as Brown, Margaret Mead, and Lyle Saunders to address their organizations.

An example of the interplay among anthropologists, nurses, and national foundations may be seen in the 3-year experimental project on the application of the social sciences to nursing conducted at the Cornell University School of Nursing from 1954 to 1957 and supported by the Russell Sage Foundation. In this course a number of anthropologists and sociologists (Mead, Renee Fox, Rhoda Metraux, August Hollingshead, and others) presented lectures highlighting the importance of cultural and social concepts in the practice of nursing.[5]

As nursing became concerned with its professional definition, there was increasing appreciation that nurses deal primarily with those aspects of a person's life shaped by cultural practices such as diet, family patterns, communication styles, and rituals. Subsequently there was greater interest in the influence of the patient's culture. In 1949 Margaret Huger initiated the first nursing research project concerned with the cultural component in the delivery of health care. She conducted a year-long hospital field study of Italian-American patients' responses to the nursing situation.[8]

Similarly, in 1954 the University of North Carolina School of Nursing received a training grant from the National Institute of Mental Health (NIMH) to incorporate concepts from social science into the undergraduate program in nursing. Gracia McCabe, a psychiatric nurse and research assistant, conducted a subproject for the grant by investigating cultural factors to be considered when providing nursing care to African-American patients.[7]

The National League for Nursing (NLN) was also instrumental in the incorporation of culture content into nursing. In 1927 the NLN recommended that social sciences be included in nursing curricula; this recommendation was strengthened in 1937 when the NLN suggested that nursing students enroll in at least 10 semester hours in the social sciences. Movement toward inclusion of the social sciences was furthered by the 1942 organization of the Joint Commission on Integration of Social and Health Aspects of Nursing in the Basic Curriculum by the NLN and the National Organization for Public Health Nursing. Finally, in 1977 the NLN mandated for accreditation the inclusion of cultural content in nursing curricula.

With the advent of the federally funded Nurse Scientist Program, nurses began to obtain doctoral degrees in increasing numbers, and several nurses obtained doctoral preparation in anthropology. In 1968 sufficient interest had developed to form the Council on Nursing and Anthropology in relation with the Society for Medical Anthropology. Subsequently other organizations were formed: the Transcultural Nursing Society, in 1974, and the American Nurses' Association's Council on Inter-Cultural Diversity (later called the Council on Cultural Diversity in Nursing Practice) in 1980.

In part these events may be seen as stemming from the work of nurses, anthropologists, and organizations. In part they also stemmed from the civil rights and affirmative action movements of the 1960s and 1970s, in which some groups of minority nurses emphasized minority rights and nursing care for "ethnic people of color."

Since that time the cultural aspects of clinical care have experienced an explosion of interest. Several special issues in nursing journals have been devoted to cultural considerations in clinical practice and research. Amplification of this history may be found in Dougherty and Tripp-Reimer.[4]

Nursing seldom acknowledges any specific culturally based theoretical orientation, even though a wide array of theoretical orientations are available from anthropology (including cultural evolutionism, functionalism, cultural materialism, neoevolutionism, culture ecology, and structuralism). On the few occasions in which theory is invoked, it is generally a narrowly applied functionalist approach that errs by stressing the specifics of individual cultural components rather than their interrelationships. Stripped of cultural theory, nursing is left with only a set of atheoretical components (primarily in the form of customs or beliefs such as dietary habits or health beliefs and practices). Nursing has moved as if an understanding of the workings of the whole culture can be revealed by the progressively evolving distinction of cultural components. As a consequence nursing is left with culture lists, for example, with typologies of "folk" illness beliefs (witchcraft, spirit possession, object intrusion, breach of taboo).

The rich matrix encountered when a whole culture is embraced has little in common with the fragments left as a result of viewing the concept of culture through a narrow focus on discrete components. Although nursing attempts to deemphasize this discrepancy by invoking the concept of holism, it contradictorily emphasizes distinctions among cultural components and treats these distinctions as if they, not the patient, were important.

It is commonly proposed that by knowing cultural characteristics, nurses will be able to provide more culturally sensitive approaches to health care. However, if notions of culture arising from the integration of nursing and anthropology are conceptually restrictive, a stereotypic or inauthentic approach to patients is fostered. This designation by category emphasizes differences and promotes a separation from the patient.

Nursing education reflects this stereotypic approach, evidenced by the routine textbook inclusion of transcultural concepts as a means to identifying "typical" characteristics of particular ethnic groups. The underlying assumption is that if only the "right" formula or recipe were known to nursing, it would be possible to tailor interventions to maximize patient compliance. Texts often contain lists of characteristics of African-Americans, Hispanics, Native Americans, Asians, and Euro-Americans—as if cultural traits are held uniformly and are static. This approach may be likened to the pathogenic analogy from microbiology where clinicians, in an attempt to identify pathogenic organisms and the most effective therapy, order "culture and sensitivity" laboratory tests.

Nursing has been exhorted to treat the client, not the disease. That is, we have come to appreciate the difference between treating "the cholysystectomy in Room 407" and treating Mrs. Golden. However, treating Mrs. Golden as an Indian (or African-American or Hispanic) is just as depersonalizing. Nursing may wish to transcend this static stereotypic view of culture.

THE PROBLEM OF CATEGORIES

Thus far we have presented the history of the evolution of a cultural perspective in nursing and have discussed ways that this cultural perspective has been incorrectly adapted by the profession. There is, however, an even broader problem that goes beyond those incurred by a stereotypic approach. The broader problem is that, without caution, *any* categories that nursing creates may serve to objectify the patient.

In Western science a tradition holds that understanding can be derived from distinction and categorization. Scientists create scales of difference through objectification and categorization, and often fail to realize that the process of producing categories is structured and therefore limited by specific assumptions. Understanding through distinction by difference requires methods for the detection of differences; in the end, these are only projections from the standpoint of the observer's own culture.

The process of producing categories reflects the desire to struggle against all others, to understand the self (as distinct from the other) in the guise of understanding the other. Such a paradigm of understanding by delineation of categories of difference does not unify conceptions of human diversity. While it attempts to exhaust that diversity, it fails to take into account the separating and alienating effects of the method, and is therefore a paradigm of distance.

The problem is not a matter of an ill-defined category but a matter of the origin of the category. We propose that stereotypy results not merely from the imposition of too general or imprecise categories. Rather, stereotypy resides in the imposition of the category itself, regardless of how detailed or refined such categories may become. This point of view implies that stereotypy is not overcome by the proliferation of additional appropriate categories, but rather that all categories imposed on the patient's culture are simply statements arising from the nurse's culture and are therefore inherently objectifying.

Nursing may advocate advancing beyond stereotypes. However, there is not a clear understanding of what form this advancement might take. The elimination of stereotypes does not occur through the proliferation of differences. For example, the few nursing texts that advocate cultural sensitivity without stereotypic response usually illustrate the necessity of doing so by describing the diversity within minority groups. For example, the broader category "Hispanic" is broken into populations of Mexican-Americans, Puerto Ricans, Cubans, and others. Further distinction is made between new immigrants and those who have lived in the United States for several generations. Additional distinctions are made between characteristics of urban and rural Hispanics as well as those who are Catholic, Protestant, or other. Emphasis is also placed on the importance of characteristics that correlate with income levels (the difference between Hispanics of the lower and middle classes). If these distinctions are pursued to their logical conclusion, nursing would prescribe different nursing actions if the patient is low income, urban, Catholic, and Puerto Rican than if the patient is middle income, urban, agnostic, and Cuban.

However, in making these finer distinctions nurses fail to see the error inherent in the entire process. The problem is that all these distinctions arise from the point of view of the nurse's culture. These are distinctions that nurses think have meaning. They fail to understand that these even finer distinctions do not allow greater access to the patient. All distinctions are just that: facets that separate the patient from the nurse, facets that allow the nurse the illusion that the patient is other (not related to self), is an object.

Nurses must confront not merely the fact that they make such cultural distinctions, but also that the disposition to differentiate is part of the attempt to create the self, using the products of such distinctions. This is the unexamined and unconscious agenda of the ontological use of cultural difference. The prediction of effective care on an understanding of categories of difference has given rise historically to the dilution of the concept of care through emergent theories of distinction.

Attempts have been made to recognize and reverse this trend by a reconstruction of "holistic nursing care." However, the recombination of the disparate parts into larger cognitive units effectively preserves the process of distinction. Identification as division and recombination does not enhance patient acceptance. Rather, this reduces the patient to a set of categories that ultimately objectifies and alienates patient from nurse, nurse from patient, and nurse from self.

Nursing's concern for human respect and its recognition of the creative implications of diversity mean that it is naturally drawn to a discipline such as anthropology, which, on the surface, has done much to support and preserve human diversity in a world of progressive homogenization and under the undue influence of dominant cultures. However, diversity as defined by the categories imposed by the dominant observer culture at the same time undermines recognition of diversity's value and positions the observer culture as the "namer" or "definer" of the object culture. By breaking down and superimposing their categories, nurses disembody the patient's culture.

TRANSCENDING CATEGORIES OF DIFFERENCES

Nursing is faced with the option of predicating care on categories of difference or, alternatively, on those that address the core of all humanity, independent of form. This latter approach, that of convergence, implies not the naive elimination or disregard of difference but the displacement of the locus of difference from the object to the observer. Individuals are cared for beyond and within the expression of difference, since they exist differently only as manifestations of their sameness and commonality.

Cultural specificity is not excluded and cultural sensitivity is not devalued. They are lived contextually within the life of the nurse; they are not means to particular ends. Nursing now must choose between these two approaches: that of understanding others through the analysis of categories of difference, or that of unconditional acceptance, regardless of form. Nurses may consider, for example, whether the objectification of African-American culture has created greater limitations or greater access to patients?

We propose a recognition of diversity of different forms without the subsequent formulation of a set of fixed categories that predict at the level of the individual. With this approach nurses could come to see that all people face the same human dilemmas; the specifics vary and their consideration is important, but the human dilemmas remain the same. Cultural expression is not ignored or excluded, but is elevated beyond any formulated objectification of cultures. The caveat is not to allow differences in form to be misinterpreted as differences among people. We remember that the relation that we have with anyone who we perceive as culturally distinct will be just that: distinct, objectified and separate. Alternatively, difference may be recognized but remains unknown and unknowable in its separateness.

A different relationship thus transpires: an unconditional concern for and affirmation of that which is universally human. This formulation is more consistent with nursing than that of distance and differentiation. Although nurses can consider cultural form a relevant dimension of treatment, we must also recognize that an understanding of *no* difference is the true basis for care. Nursing's attitude toward cultural diversity can be an attitude of compassion, not distinction.

REFERENCES

1. Birdwhistell R: Social science and nursing education, Annual Report of the National League for Nursing Education, New York, 1949, National League for Nursing.
2. Bridgeman M: Collegiate education for nursing, New York, 1953, Sage Foundation.
3. Brown EL: Nursing for the future, New York, 1948, Sage Foundation.
4. Dougherty MC and Tripp-Reimer T: The interface of nursing and anthropology, Annual Review of Anthropology, 14:219, 1985.
5. MacGregor FC: Social science in nursing: applications for the improvement of patient care, New York, 1960, Sage Foundation.
6. Martin HW: The behavioral sciences and nursing education: some problems and prospects, Social Forces 37:61, 1958.
7. McCabe GS: Cultural influences on patient behavior, Am J Nurs 60(8):1101, 1960.
8. Mead M: Understanding cultural patterns, Nurs Outlook 4(3):260, 1956.

CHAPTER 32

Is Health Care Racist?

Sheana Whelan Funkhouser, RN, MN
Debra K. Moser, RN, MN

In American society, many health care inequalities exist along racial lines. Blacks are 1.3 times as likely to die of heart disease, 2 times as likely to die of stroke, 2.2 times as likely to die of diabetes, 3.2 times as likely to die of kidney disease, and 6 times as likely to be murdered as are their white counterparts. Hypertension, a probable contributor to several of these diseases, strikes one quarter of the black population while affecting only one tenth of the white population. Cancer is detected later and has a higher mortality rate in blacks than in whites. Black women are three times as likely to die in childbirth as are white women, and indicative of the alarming black infant mortality rates is the finding that a black infant is two times as likely to die before age 1 as is a white infant. Black teenagers are twice as likely to become pregnant and six times as likely to be killed as are white teenagers. Of the 15 leading causes of death in the United States, blacks have the highest death rates for all but 2 of them[1-3]; blacks are more often uninsured than are whites.[4] Although heredity may be a factor in many of these conditions, the significance of these statistics in conjunction with socioeconomic considerations suggests a multifactorial answer with poverty exerting a major influence in producing disparities in health care.

The purpose of this article is to heighten the reader's awareness of the inequalities involved in health care access. Included in this discussion are examinations of the significance of black-white racial conflict in a historical perspective, health care access for the medically indigent, and the failure of traditional solutions.

Reprinted from *Advances in Nursing Science,* Vol 12, No. 2, with permission of Aspen Publishers, Inc., © 1990.

HISTORICAL OVERVIEW OF RACIAL CONFLICT IN AMERICA

Black Americans occupy a unique place in American history. To understand and appreciate the present situation of the black poor and health care, a brief historic overview of race relations between blacks and whites will be helpful. Prior to this discussion, several terms need to be defined. The box[5,6] summarizes the authors' definitions of racism, prejudice, discrimination, and class divisions as they apply to this article.

Wilson[6] argues that there are three major periods in American race relations, each of which has been shaped by economic systems of production as well as by laws. The first period is the preindustrial era. This period was characterized by the slave-based plantation economy of the South from the early to mid-1800s. In this system, a relatively small, elite group of white planters developed enormous regional power. Because free white workers were not central to the labor supply, slavery became a mode of increasing production and the economic power of the white plantation owners. Race relations assumed a paternalistic quality, specifying duties, norms, rights, and obligations of slaves and masters. Racial antago-

Definitions of terms used in the discussion of race and class conflict

Racism: the subordination of people of color by white people; at the very least, this subordination involves power plus prejudice.[5]

Prejudice: preconceived ideas or opinions about an individual or group based solely on race, sex, or national origin.

Discrimination: when opportunities or choices are limited to people because of race, sex, or national origin.[5]

Class: any group of people who have similar goods, services, or skills to offer for income in a given economic order and who therefore receive similar financial remuneration in the marketplace.[6]

Lower class: a population that represents the very bottom of the economic hierarchy and includes not only those workers whose incomes fall below the poverty level, but also the more or less permanent welfare recipients, the long-term unemployed, and those who have dropped out of the labor market.[6]

Underclass: the more impoverished segment of the lower class.[6]

nism can be explained by the deliberate exploitation of the slave-labor blacks by the capitalist whites.

After the Civil War, despite the abolition of slavery, racial antagonism continued. This may also be explained by an economic theory, but one different from that of the preindustrial era. In the late 19th and early 20th centuries, industrialism flourished. The white working class and the urban blacks were competing for similar jobs. White workers increased their power through unions (which blacks could not join) and demanded higher wages and more fringe benefits. As a result, managers used blacks as strikebreakers or permanent replacements for white workers. The more management used blacks to undercut white laborers, the more racial conflict arose between the two groups. Added pressures came from racial competition for housing, neighborhoods, and recreational areas. Thus capitalists exploited the black workers with low wages and created an atmosphere of competition between the two groups (black and white workers), which fueled racial antagonism.

The postindustrial-modern period extends from the 1940s to the present. The patterns of race relations of this time do not fit either of the above eras. Once racial barriers were broken down in unions, blacks and whites presented a more united front to management, thus decreasing competition and racial tension. In the 1960s, unprecedented civil rights legislation was passed, giving blacks greater political and social equality in the areas of education and job opportunities. According to Wilson,[6] the ultimate basis for the current racial tension is the deleterious effect of basic structural changes in the modern economy on black and white lower-income groups. These changes include uneven economic growth, increasing technology and automation, and industry relocation out of urban areas. Blacks are disproportionately represented in the underclass population, in that about one third of the entire black populace resides in the underclass.[6] Also, since 1970, poor blacks and poor whites have evidenced little progress out of the underclass. Hence, Wilson posits that economic class is now a more important factor than race in determining job placement and life chances for blacks. What does this mean for the underclass in terms of health care?

HEALTH CARE ACCESS

Scope of the Problem

Access to basic health care or, more accurately, lack of access is an urgent issue currently troubling society. Organizations such as the International Council of Nurses and the World Health Organization (WHO) devote much attention to this issue.[7] Because of this concern for the delivery of adequate levels of health care, WHO set forth the goal of "the attainment by all peoples . . . of a level of health that will permit them to lead a socially and economically productive life."[8(p8)] Attainment of this goal will require two kinds of action. The first type of action, the delivery of primary health care, involves such strategies as improved management of health care resources, health education, and health development. But, as Hindson[8] points out, this type of action can be expected to have little effect on improving health unless a second type of action, the "defeat . . . of the anti-health forces"[8(p9)] such as poverty, suppression, and dehumanization, is undertaken.

Basic to this idea are the concepts that certain societal aspects such as poverty, lack of access to resources, and unequal life chances are foundational causes of poor health and the inability to obtain adequate health care and that these issues must be addressed if the goal of adequate health care for all is to be achieved. Ironically, the United States is one of the richest countries in the world, yet it is experiencing what some call a crisis in health care delivery. Areas of critical concern are access to health care for the indigent and access to health care for the uninsured or underinsured. Just what is the extent of this crisis?

Although medical indigence and lack of access to health care are areas often neglected in reports, the problem is still known to be enormous. Conservative estimates of the number of people who face problems in obtaining access to health care due to a lack of any health insurance coverage begin at 35 million to 45 million.[4,9] This number doubles when those who are underinsured are taken into account and reaches 100 million when the elderly who frequently do not have coverage for extended service needs are included. These estimates place two out of every five members of the population at some risk for not being able to obtain health care in a time of need. The uninsured are not necessarily the unemployed. Half of the medically uninsured are full-time employees and their dependents.[10]

Merely having insurance, however, does not assure access to needed health care. Hayward and associates[11] studied 7,633 adults to determine patterns of health care access. Predictably, the uninsured had lower access to health care. More surprising, though, was the finding that problems with access to health care exist among insured (Medicaid included) working-age adults. Even greater problems in access to health care exist among the insured poor, black, or Hispanic persons. Indeed, being black, poor, or Hispanic were independent predictors of inadequate access. Possible reasons for these findings posited by Hayward et al[11] include

- copayments, high deductibles, and other restrictions that may deter the poor from pursuing health care;
- physicians who may fail to provide care to Medicaid recipients due to poor reimbursement;
- lack of transportation, medical facilities, and caregivers in poor, ethnic communities that may make access problematic; and
- cultural and bureaucratic hostilities or outright discrimination that may set up institutional barriers to obtaining health care.

Federal programs designed to provide access to health care for the poor or "health care poor" have never completely met the needs of the medically indigent. In this era of increased budget deficits and an administration that advocates a minimal role for the federal government in providing this care,[10] the crisis in health care access can only be expected to deepen. Poverty and the numbers of poor and near poor are increasing and are projected to continue to increase while health care funding for the poor has declined.[12,13] The results, under the present administration's "new federalism," include reduced funding for Medicare, Medicaid, and other programs such as nutrition funding for women and children, and a shifting of responsibility for these programs to the state governments.

These changes have had great impact: The number of people eligible for Medicaid significantly decreased as eligibility was linked to qualifications for such programs as Aid to Families with Dependent Children (AFDC). At the same time, more stringent criteria for AFDC eligibility were created. The net result was to disqualify large numbers of indigent people (generally single-parent women and children) from both AFDC and Medicaid. In any case, Medicaid always excluded certain groups of the poor such as single adults, childless couples, intact families, and the near poor. The last, despite their slightly better-sounding designation, often have less access to health care because they are ineligible for assistance despite demonstrated need and the inability to afford other health insurance. In 1988, more than 50% of US citizens with incomes at or below poverty level were not eligible for Medicaid.[9]

In addition to reducing funds, new federal policies that give more responsibility to the states have changed patterns of fund administration and thus adversely affected health care access. The diversity of the states' responses to these policies prompted one author to comment, "eligibility and administration vary so much from one state to another that inclusion, scope of coverage, and access to care may be an accident of residence."[14(p288)] Additionally, the majority of states have reduced Medicaid funding and made requirements for eligibility more stringent.[4]

Where does the medically indigent person who requires hospitalization go? The role of providing uncompensated care has largely fallen on public hospitals. Previous methods of providing uncompensated care (cost shifting and dependence on the federal government) have fallen to the demands of economic pressures.[15] Profit and nonprofit hospitals utilize only approximately 3% to 5% of their revenue for uncompensated health care[16]; and as the for-profit sector increases, there are burgeoning concerns over the provision of uncompensated care. Large numbers of public hospital closures and the closure of hospitals serving urban minority communities have potentially serious implications for access to health care for the medically indigent as these hospitals are large providers of indigent health care.[4] Thorpe and Brecher, in studying access to health care and the public hospital, conclude that an operating public hospital "does not simply reduce the burden on private hospitals in a city; it is also likely to be a net addition to the volume of care available to the medically indigent."[15(p322)] Closure of public hospitals or lack of public hospitals in an area thus adversely affects health care delivery to the poor because private hospitals do not compensate for the loss or lack of health care.[15]

In addition to concerns over lack of access to health care for the medically indigent, there are concerns over the quality of health care provided to the poor. Lack of access to preventive or primary health care, lack of adequate referrals or follow-up, lack of access to many services and usual diagnostic procedures, and inappropriate emergency department transfers from private to public hospitals contribute to a reduced quality of health care for the poor.[13,16]

Relationship Between Medical Indigence and Race

As may seem obvious, the medically indigent confronted with problems obtaining access to health care are most often those people living in poverty or near poverty. Simply stated, poverty seriously limits access to adequate health care. Additionally, those families in which the main wage earner is unemployed or sporadically employed are uninsured or underinsured and thus face the hazard of medical indigence. People under age 24 are often uninsured. Finally, members of racial minority groups, particularly blacks and Hispanics, are more at risk than whites for medical indigence.[4]

Descriptions of those living in poverty and facing the potentially serious consequences of medical indigence reveal that blacks are disproportionately faced by this threat.

Approximately 27% of all Americans live in poverty or near poverty, whereas 36% of all blacks live in poverty.[17] Although figures vary depending on the source, census figures from 1962 to 1982 estimate that the percentage of blacks living below the poverty level for all of this 20-year period was at least twice the percentage of whites living below the poverty level.[18] Black children and female-headed black households have been hit particularly hard by poverty. Almost 50% of black children are poor, and the poverty rate for female-headed families nears 57%.[17,19]

Unemployment, sporadic employment, and employment in low-paying jobs all put people at risk for medical indigence because they do not provide a high enough income with which to purchase health care and health insurance. Again, blacks are particularly affected in this area. Black unemployment rates are significantly higher (often double) than those for whites; median black family income is significantly lower; and blacks (especially black women) are frequently employed at lower-paying jobs without benefits or insurance.[2,18,19]

In summary, those at special risk for medical indigence include those people living in poverty and those people with limited or no employment opportunities. Because blacks are overrepresented in the ranks of the poor, unemployed, and low-wage employed, they are particularly in jeopardy of medical indigence, lack of access to health care, and the consequences.

Consequences

The relationships among poverty, access to health care, health status, and race are complex, but that there are relationships seems clear. Gordon-

Bradshaw[2] notes that advances in health care have failed to correct the "serious inequities in the health care system and health status for the most vulnerable . . . poverty wreaks havoc on people of color because of their limited resources and lack of access to health care, and lends credence to the adage 'those who suffer most get the least.'"[2(p254)]

Blacks in this country have increased mortality and morbidity for a number of diseases and illnesses.[1] Genetic predisposition has been implicated as the source of much of the problem in increased black mortality and morbidity, especially in the case of hypertension and its sequelae. Increasingly, however, the evidence points to the contributions of life-style risk factors such as poor nutrition, inadequate and delayed health care, exposure to excessive health risks, inadequate living conditions, and stress.[1,2,14] These high-risk life-style factors are, in many cases, attributable to "a legacy of economic deprivation and social oppression."[1(p126)] As Mechanic[14] points out, "throughout the life span poverty and poor health reinforce one another."[14(p283)]

Good nutrition, early and continued prenatal care, and adequate postnatal care can reduce the alarming maternal and infant mortality rates among blacks. Early detection and adequate treatment of cancer, hypertension, and their sequelae can contribute to reductions in black morbidity and mortality in these areas. Proper nutrition can contribute to reduced morbidity and possibly reduced mortality and can reduce the risk factors for the development of hypertension and heart disease. Improved living conditions and less exposure to environmental hazards can reduce morbidity and mortality from many causes. But these measures can be expensive and are prohibitive for many poor or near-poor blacks. Access to health care and access to the means of acquiring and maintaining health are simply out of the reach of those not able to pay for such access.

WHY TRADITIONAL SOLUTIONS HAVE FAILED

Traditional solutions to the health care problems of the poor have their roots in the phenomenon known as "blaming the victim."[20] In this phenomenon, the victims of societal inequities such as inadequate health care, rather than the societal structures themselves responsible for the problems, are targeted for change or action. Although the destructive effects of poverty are recognized, the problem (and thus the solution) is said to reside within the victim. On the surface this ideology appears well-meaning, even humanitarian.[20] Problems are recognized and studied, and solutions are recommended and acted on. However, the result of this sort of action is that the root causes are never addressed and, thus, long-lasting solutions are not forthcoming. As Ryan writes,

> They turn their attention to the victim in his post-victimized state. They want to bind up wounds, inject penicillin, administer morphine, and evacuate the wounded for rehabilitation. They explain what's wrong with the victim in terms of social experience *in the past,* experiences that have left wounds, defects, paralysis, and disability. And they take the cure of these wounds and the reduction of these disabilities as the first order of business. They want to make the victims less vulnerable, send them back into battle with better weapons, thicker armor, a higher level of morale." [20(p332)]

Better weapons, thicker armor, and a higher level of morale in the war against poor health and inadequate health care in the underclass translate into health education and assisting individuals and families to cope with poverty and its consequences. It cannot be denied that health education is important, but health education alone fails to address the fundamental issue, which is lack of resources. Education concerning proper and healthful nutrition, the importance of early health care, and risk factor reduction is of relatively little use to the individual or family too poor to purchase healthy food, obtain preventive health care, or take advantage of risk factor reduction strategies. Teaching people to cope with poverty and inadequate health care blames the victims for their problems and fails, again, to address the rudimentary issues of the failure of society to provide certain individuals with the opportunities and life chances to avoid poverty. Attempting to teach people to cope with poverty "unwittingly or not . . . reinforces the thinking that poverty is unavoidable. Historically, the poor have been held responsible for their own plight. Because the poor are disproportionately people of color and women, such an explanation easily assumes racist and sexist overtones."[17(p20)]

It can be argued that one of the driving forces for allocation of resources for research, education, practice, and theory development for professions such as nursing and medicine is the philosophy of science that those professions choose to embrace. What the appropriate and significant research questions are for a discipline, what constitutes theory,[21] and what direction education and practice should take are all determined largely by the scientific philosophy adopted by the discipline. The current predominant philosophy in the health care field (although not exclusively) is that of the so-called "received view" or logical positivism.[22,23] Research, education, and practice driven by this philosophy have failed to identify the fundamental issues in the provision of health care for the poor and have failed to derive meaningful solutions to the problem. Usually, either health education, health promotion, or low-cost health care is seen as the solution. In reality, health education and health promotion will most likely do very little to change the outcomes because the economic crisis of the lower class is the root of the problem. Even when low-cost health care is provided to poverty areas, many cannot afford to take leave of a menial-paying job, cannot afford transportation to the health care clinic, or have no resources to pay the low-cost fee. In this day of cost containment and competition in health care, the amount and type of charity care offered by health care providers are shrinking, concomitant with a swelling underclass population.[4,12]

The logical positivist would argue that the problems of poverty, social structure, and access to health care are sociopolitical problems, not scientific problems, and as such do not present questions appropriate for scientific inquiry. Poverty and its health care implications are wide-ranging, resource-consuming, seemingly perpetual problems confounding not only society in general but also nursing and other health care disciplines. That it is a problem suitable for concerted scientific inquiry seems clear. Perhaps a scientific philosophy that embraces problem solving as its core[24] is immanently more suited to addressing the unsolved issues of inadequate and inaccessible health care for the indigent.

• • •

Is health care racist? There are no doubt individual instances of racism in the delivery of health care. There are recent disturbing reports of disproportionate medical treatment along racial lines,[25] and underrepresentation of blacks in clinical trials of new drugs.[26] However, the authors would argue that the problem of inadequate health care for blacks is largely due to socioeconomic constraints rather than race.

Lasting solutions to the problems of poor health in the indigent and the provision of access to quality health care will involve a restructuring of the health care delivery system that will ensure access to adequate and timely health care for all. Most importantly, fundamental changes must be made in the societal structures and policies that contribute to poverty. One reason for failure to solve the problems of poor health status and inadequate health care access in the indigent may be due to the predominating philosophy of science that does not regard these issues as legitimate pursuits of science. Most current theories concerning improvement in these areas are based on describing the relationships between health education, coping with poverty, and improved outcomes in health status. The failure of these theories to propose lasting solutions to the problems may be due to failure to adequately and accurately conceptualize the problem as one of poverty and unequal life chances.

REFERENCES

1. Foley D. Being black is dangerous to your health. In: Rothenberg PS, ed. *Racism and Sexism: An Integrated View.* New York, NY: St Martin's Press; 1988:125-129.
2. Gordon-Bradshaw RH. A social essay on special issues facing poor women of color. *Women Health.* 1987;12: 243-259.
3. *Los Angeles Times.* The right start. October 24, 1988: II,22.
4. Bazzoli G. Health care for the indigent: Overview of critical issues. *Health Serv Res.* 1986;21(3):353-393.
5. Rothenberg PS. Introduction. In: Rothenberg PS, ed. *Racism and Sexism: An Integrated View.* New York, NY: St. Martin's Press; 1988.
6. Wilson WJ. *The Declining Significance of Race.* 2nd ed. Chicago, Ill: University of Chicago Press; 1980.
7. Bergman R. Nurses as a social force. *J Adv Nurs.* 1985; 10:197-198.
8. Hindson P. The "anti-health forces." *Hygie.* 1985;4:8-9.
9. Ginzberg E. Medical care for the poor. *JAMA.* 1988;259:3309-3311.
10. Darling H. The role of the federal government in assuring access to health care. *Inquiry.* 1986;23:286-295.

11. Hayward RA, Shapiro MF, Freeman HE, Corey CR. Inequities in health services among insured Americans. *N Eng J Med.* 1988;318:1507-1512.
12. Curtis R. The role of state governments in assuring access to care. *Inquiry.* 1986;23:277-285.
13. Popp R Sr. Health care for the poor: Where has all the money gone? *JONA.* 1988;18:8-11.
14. Mechanic D. Health care for the poor: Some policy alternatives. *J Fam Pract.* 1986;22:283-289.
15. Thorpe KE, Brecher C. Improved access to care for the uninsured poor in large cities: Do public hospitals make a difference? *J Health Polit Policy Law.* 1987;12:313-324.
16. Light DW. Corporate medicine for profit. *Sci Am.* 1986;255(6):38-45.
17. Moccia P, Mason DJ. Poverty trends: Implications for nursing. *Nurs Outlook.* 1986;34:20-24.
18. Rothenberg PS. Blacks in America. In: Rothenberg PS, ed. *Racism and Sexism: An Integrated View.* New York, NY: St Martin's Press; 1988:82-84.
19. Wilson WJ. *The Truly Disadvantaged: The Inner City, the Underclass, and Public Policy.* Chicago, Ill: University of Chicago Press; 1987.
20. Ryan W. Blaming the victim. In: Rothenberg PS, ed. *Racism and Sexism: An Integrated View.* New York, NY: St Martin's Press; 1988:324-333.
21. Silva MC. Philosophy, science, theory: Interrelationships and implications for nursing practice. *Image.* 1977; 9:59-63.
22. Kemeny JG. *A Philosopher Looks at Science.* Princeton, NJ: Van Nostrand; 1959.
23. Popper K. Science: Conjectures and refutations. In: *Essays in Philosophy of Science.* Chicago, Ill: University of Chicago Press; 1979.
24. Laudan L. *Progress and Its Problems: Towards a Theory of Scientific Growth.* Berkeley, Calif: University of California Press; 1977.
25. Wenneker M, Epstein A. Racial inequalities in the use of procedures for patients with ischemic heart disease in Massachusetts. *JAMA.* 1989;261:253-257.
26. Svensson C. Representation of American blacks in clinical trials of new drugs. *JAMA.* 1989;261:263-265.

CHAPTER 33

Cultural Values and the Decision to Circumcise

Chandice Harris Covington, RN, PhD

That it is right and proper to be circumcised is an assumption of the dominant American culture. The majority of males born are circumcised before they leave the hospital, even though in 1975 the American Academy of Pediatrics reaffirmed the stance:

> There is no absolute medical indication for routine circumcision of the newborn . . . circumcision of the male neonate cannot be considered an essential component of adequate or total health care. (p. 610).

The Academy's edict along with research that demonstrates the fallacy of the procircumcision argument makes circumcision at best a questionable health practice and at worst a costly, life-threatening ritual. Even more important are the cultural processes that influence the circumcision decision and serve to "disenfranchise" males based on the presence of a foreskin.

Circumcision is the most frequently performed surgical procedure in the United States. Currently, in the U.S., 80 to 90 percent of newborn males are circumcised (Wirth, 1980), though Wiener (1980) reports a low of 30 percent for infants born at home or in alternative birth settings. Still, these rates far surpass those in other countries where circumcision is viewed as being unnecessary, for example, in Canada, England and Sweden (Wirth, 1980). This study addresses the research question, "What variables influence parents' decisions to circumcise or not to circumcise their newborn?"

This article is slightly edited and reprinted with permission of the publishers, from P.N. Stern (Ed.) (1986), *Women, health, and culture.* New York: Hemisphere Publishing Corporation. The author thanks Dr. Phyllis Stern for her assistance in the development and realization of this research project. Reprinted from *Image: Journal of Nursing Scholarship*, Vol. 18, No. 3, with permission of Sigma Theta Tau, © 1986.

BACKGROUND

In 1859 Florence Nightingale (1859/1970) promoted the idea that nursing is concerned with discovering and reinforcing nature's "law of health" (p. 60). One such "law of health" is that the uncircumcised state is a natural, not pathologic, condition. There now exists ample scientific evidence to discard the idea that circumcision is a health practice. Not so clear are the cultural processes that influence the social need for circumcision. Because maternal-child nursing practice requires teaching and counseling clients about their circumcision choice along with assisting with the procedure, scientific as well as transcultural enlightenment of the nurse is necessary (Harris & Stern, 1981).

At present many health professionals act as "cultural imposers" by denying circumcision to some subcultures who desire the procedure and by promoting circumcision to others who are uncertain as to the need for the procedure (Aamodt, 1978; Leininger, 1979). In fact, many doctors and nurses in the study asked, "Why research circumcision? It's such a little thing . . . " (no pun intended). This "little thing" acts as an additional stressor, especially during the postpartum period, when parents are trying to make a decision that they feel will affect their child for a lifetime. Furthermore, Dickoff, James, and Semradek (1975) suggest that "Nursing reality from the consumer's view point is a madhouse world of horrors" (p. 86). They propose that nursing research be evaluated as to "payoff," that is, research in nursing that results in improved patient care processes in the health care system.

REVIEW OF THE LITERATURE

Around the turn of the century the status of circumcision changed from a religious rite to a common surgical procedure. In 1891, a physician, Remondino (1891/1974) stated that the foreskin was a "dangerous relic of a far-distant prehistoric age," designed to protect unclothed early man from "bark, brambles, and insect bites" (p. 34).

The five main reasons for circumcision include (a) an adolescent initiation rite of passage and test of manhood through torture and pain, (b) a personal sacrifice in religious ritual, (c) an act to mark, torture and humiliate slaves and defeated warriors, (d) conformity with hygienic and cosmetic values, and (e) a response to the antimasturbation hysteria of the late 1800s (that is, if the child has to wash under the foreskin, he might learn to masturbate). Even today many of these reasons are used but with a slightly different context in language and custom. Woven through the history of circumcision is ritual, psychoanalytic theory and stigma.

Ritual

Rituals are rich in symbolism. The symbolism of circumcision hinges on the absence of a foreskin, which implies that more than a simple operation has taken place. Especially in America, it suggests that a well-accepted "ritual" has occurred. The term "ritual," according to Gluckman (1975), is used to describe many different kinds of phenomena of a repetitive, almost obsessive nature. When approved by a certain culture, ritual can become standardized, repetitive and prescribed; that is, cultural rules command that the ritual be performed. Such rules were especially evident in past years when hospitals routinely circumcised newborns, often without informed parental consent.

Most rituals signify a rite of passage and convey a sense of belonging. When a culture accepts a ritual of another culture, it signifies a desire for status passage, or "keeping up with the Joneses." In the United States, "the Joneses" are the norms, beliefs and values of the dominant American culture (Glaser & Strauss, 1971); this includes the tradition of circumcision.

Psychoanalytic Theory

Another aspect of circumcision is embodied in the Freudian theory of psychologic processes existing between the mother, child and father. Shrouded in misogyny, these suppositions explain circumcision as a ritual of matriarchal control, a measure to resolve the Oedipal conflict and a symbolic solution to man's envy of the womb and fear of that envy (Bettelheim, 1954; Gluckman, 1975; Kitahara, 1976; Ostow, 1970).

Stigma

In subtle and overt ways the uncircumcised male is stigmatized by the dominant American culture. Fear of stigma leads American parents to elect circumcision. As Cogan (1981) points out, the American Academy of Pediatrics did not offer any guidelines on the management of cultural pressures and potential identity problems generated in the locker room or in the family system because of this stigma.

Clearly, the brunt of the stigma is experienced by the child, not by the parents who made the choice. In the words of one of my chief informants, who is an uncircumcised urban white, "I think there is psychological trauma when you are not circumcised. I went through gym class, being in the locker room. There were not remarks, but I felt different." But not all uncircumcised men who were interviewed felt this way. Some related a feeling of superiority, that they possessed something better than being circumcised. Goffman (1963) in *Stigma,* explains this attitude:

> It seems possible for an individual to fail to live up to what we effectively demand of him and yet be relatively untouched by this failure; insulated by his alienation, protected by identity beliefs of his own, he feels that he is a full-fledged normal human being, and that we are the ones that are not quite human. (p. 6)

Those uncircumcised males or parents of uncircumcised males who feel stigmatized by the dominant American culture, Goffman suggests further, may attempt to "cover," or restrict the display of the stigma, similar to the person undergoing a rhinoplasty or mammoplasty. The usual situation is the "circumcision rider" attached to another surgical procedure. Examples of this include the 4-year-old who receives a circumcision along with a tonsillectomy or the 40-year-old who is circumcised along with a vasectomy. What often results is the absence of a fully formal status; that is, a circumcised male but one who is, according to Goffman, "someone with a record of having corrected a particular blemish" (p. 102). It is the old horror story. "He had to be circumcised at 40!"

Major influences on the development of the foreskin stigma are the myths that make circumcision a necessity. Research exposes these myths, yet the findings are neither well distributed nor accepted by the dominant American culture. Concisely, these findings are summarized as follows, (Harris & Stern, 1981):

1. Newborns are born with fused foreskins.
2. The foreskin gradually separates. Complete separation may not occur until near puberty.
3. Smegma is most often nonexistent in children.
4. Forced retraction of the foreskin (often done by caretakers) produces scar tissue.
5. Scar tissue produces adhesions.
6. Adhesions make circumcision necessary (a "Catch 22" situation).
7. Cancer of the prostate, cervix, and penis is directly related to personal hygiene, not to the presence or lack of a foreskin.

METHODOLOGY

This study was conducted using a naturalistic approach to develop grounded theory. According to Stern (1980), qualitative research is particularly useful when a new perspective on a familiar situation is needed. Especially in America, the circumcision of newborns is a familiar situation. However, a new perspective is now needed because of the American Academy of Pediatrics' stance on circumcision.

Data Collection

The majority of the data represent approximately 60 hours of participant-observation study in north Louisiana. The interviews were conducted at numerous sites and times at the convenience of the subjects. At first, the interviews were open free-flowing; as the process emerged they became more directed. The interviews were written down verbatim and later typed for analysis.

Sources of the Data

Initially the sources of the data were new parents, nursery nurses and pediatricians. As the processes of the theory emerged, theoretical sampling included pregnant women and couples, parents of older children, urologists, obstetricians, general practitioners, pediatric nurse practitioners, community health nurses, certified nurse midwives and men and women of various ages. The literature, additionally, provided an important source of information.

It is important to emphasize that the data from the grounded theory approach is qualitative, not numerative, with hypotheses generated but not tested. Therefore demographic data, personality factors and intelligence quotients are not relevant to the study.

Data Analysis

With grounded theory, analyzing the data is a constant, comparative, cognitive process similar to a matrix computer-analyzed design; that is, each da-tum is examined in reference to all other data and to the emerging categories and processes. As themes are discovered, further data collection serves to strengthen and refine these themes. According to Wilson (1977), data are interrelated for "causes, contexts, contingencies, consequences, covariances, conditions, mutual effects, cutting points, degrees, and types" (p. 109). The resultant hypotheses yield a molecular rather than a direct causal relationship. The theorists of grounded theory, Glaser and Strauss (1967), refer to this as a "dense" theoretical schema. The credibility of this resultant schema is advanced by the "goodness of fit" that the theory has for the real world. Glaser (1978) claims that it is the "integration, relevance and workability" of the theory that promotes its significance.

FINDINGS

In this study, the substantive area is circumcision of newborns under conditions existing in the lay and health culture. The categories named circumcision reasoning, cultural decisionmaking and cultural franchising were discovered and are shown in Figure 33-1.

Circumcision Reasoning

The major reasons to circumcise one's child are balanced out by the same reasons to avoid circumcision; for instance, the reason "medical advice" is used in both instances. However, the way in which these reasons are defined by the parent differs markedly from family to family and culture to culture. MacKay (1978) explains that cultural patterns are designs not only for reality perceptions, but also for constructing that reality. The subjects in the present study gave evidence of how they had constructed their reality through their reasons for and against the practice of circumcision. Their answers were categorized into nine main reasons and are shown in the box below. The emphasis of this report focuses on these reasons for choosing circumcision.

Sign of manhood

The most common reason to circumcise was "So he will look like his daddy (or brother)." An additional theme in this line of reasoning was explained by one father's words, "Even if it hurts, he has to go through it . . . One day he'll thank me." It was interesting to observe the strong emotion evoked, especially in the Anglo male, when he was told that circumcision was no longer recommended. As one informant stated, "It's part of being a man in a man's world . . . My father was circumcised, I am, and my son will be." This need for circumcision as a sign of manhood was reflected in the words of one of the chief informants, "Men are put down by those who have [been cir-

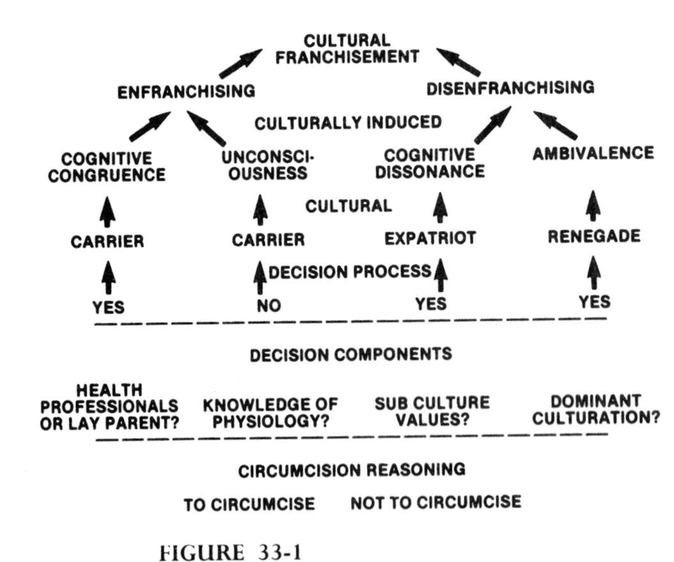

FIGURE 33-1

Components of circumcision reasoning.

Balance of factors in circumcision reasoning
Circumcision reasoning

To Circumcise	Not To Circumcise
1. Sign of manhood	1. Sign of manhood
2. Culturally induced unconsciousness	2. Culturally induced unconsciousness
3. No harm, no pain	3. Traumatic/ dangerous
4. Sex worries	4. Sex worries
5. Hygienic/cosmetic/ comfort	5. Hygienic/cosmetic/ comfort
6. Guidance from Bible	6. Guidance from Bible
7. Playing it safe	7. Playing it safe
8. Cultural/ sentimental order	8. Cultural/ sentimental order
9. Medical advice	9. Medical advice

cumcised]. All males should be; then they have things in common."

Culturally induced unconsciousness

The existence of culturally caused or induced unconsciousness was evident in the data (Aamodt, 1978). Such reasoning was "You don't stop to question what has always been done" and "We didn't even talk about it, we just assumed it would be done." Most parents are never in a position to think about, discuss or question circumcision. There is no need. The child will be circumcised, period.

No harm, no pain

As one informant stated, "There are less problems if it's done early. It's bad on a grown man. It can cause him to have problems with sex." Or as another said, "It's better to do it when they're a baby, it doesn't hurt." And, "There are no nerve endings. Babies don't feel it like a grown man does."

Contrary to these beliefs, research demonstrates that during and following circumcision, newborns show behaviors that when observed in an adult are diagnosed as pain. These include crying, changes in sleep-wake states and feeding patterns and significant increases in the endocrine response (Anders & Chalemian, 1974; Talbert, 1976). However, since newborns are unable to verbalize this distress, even some health professionals believe that pain is not experienced during the procedure.

The issue of harm to the newborn is also usually denied. The fact is that 1 out of 500 circumcisions threatens the life of the neonate; while few (less than two per million procedures) actually result in death. However, these numbers are being challenged as a result of the connection between circumcision and neonatal sepsis, a leading cause of neonatal death (Cogan, 1981; McHugh, 1981).

Indeed males who undergo circumcision later in life report marked physical and psychologic suffering. It is postulated, however, that this response occurs because in America, adult circumcision is a mistimed cultural event. Ozturk (1973) reports that in Turkey, children between three and seven years of age are circumcised without anesthesia. Contrary to the predictable psychologic effects of the operation at this age, namely castration anxiety, Ozturk discovered that the societal preparatory experience and meaning overrode such effects. The dominant American culture ignores, exaggerates or makes this experience the brunt of jokes. Meanwhile it is interesting that a similar invasive procedure, female episiotomy, has not (until recently) received the notoriety of adult male circumcision. Whether this is because of a woman's "long-suffering role" or the cultural sanction of episiotomy is not clear.

Sex worries

Frequently mentioned reasons for advocating circumcision referred to sexual concerns, both for the adult sexuality of the child and his relationship to his mother and father. Circumcision was viewed most often as a method of preventing masturbation or promiscuity in sexual matters. One father stated, "It will make it last longer." A mother related, "I had him circumcised when he was two because he started playing with himself." And from another, "Men who are circumcised are able to control themselves; it prevents premature ejaculation." It is interesting that a similar operation, female circumcision, is prescribed in America for the opposite effect, namely to cure frigidity (Wollman, 1974). Conversely, in Egypt, female circumcision is practiced to attenuate the female sexual response (Assaad, 1980).

The idea of sex also concerned the mothers who were then caring for their sons. As best explained by one female informant, "The child might remember his mother cleaning under the foreskin. Mother has no business doing that." This theme, found across cultures, exposes the fear of incest attached to the uncircumcised state.

Hygienic, comfort and cosmetic

The argument for circumcision for reasons of hygiene, comfort and "beauty" is greatly supported by the dominant American culture. First, hygiene can be a problem, especially for individuals who do not practice adequate hygiene either because of cultural factors or because of lack of bathing facilities and supplies. As one 56-year-old male informant explained, "We took a bath a week and you best not be caught washing below the water line. And Mom certainly didn't [help with hygienic care]. It wasn't right."

War-associated conditions were also mentioned by some informants: the lack of opportunity to cleanse the body during World War II or the Korean and Vietnam conflicts. However, one urologist interviewed claimed that circumcised males suffer equally in such circumstances because of irritation of the glans and of the perineal area in general.

The need for hygiene relates to the occurrence of smegma. Smegma is composed of both a lubricating fluid secreted by the glands of the inner surface of the prepuce (or clitoral hood) and desquamated epithelial cells. This composition has been implicated as being carcinogenic; however, recent studies have failed to demonstrate this causal relationship. It is important to point out that women also produce smegma.

Nurse informants discussed the poor hygiene practices of elderly males. As one said, "A man of 70 is not worried about cleaning himself." Elderly females suffer some of these same problems, but with more available female caretakers, female hygienic care is provided without the taboo associated with a female nurse caring for a male.

Comfort reasons included the idea that a "tight" foreskin "bothered" the child. One mother stated that as her son was toilet training, he would "grab at his penis" when he needed to urinate. This she attributed to a "tight skin." However, even after circumcision, the child continued this behavior until full bladder training was achieved.

Finally, the cosmetic appeal of circumcision is best explained as "beauty being in the eye of the beholder." In America, the beholder is the dominant culture that has advanced the notion that the circumcised penis is more aesthetic. It is as Leitch (1970) states, "The exposed glans is the fashion" (p. 59). However, in other countries, circumcision is viewed as a barbarous practice that leaves the male disfigured. This is much the same view that an American might have toward female circumcision practiced in other cultures.

On an historical note, the Greeks (A.D. 14-37) in their quest for Christianity, balked at the rabbinical direction to undergo circumcision. To meet a consumer need, a "decircumcision" procedure was developed to reconstruct the prepuce after the Greek male was circumcised. This need related to the Greek's love of the natural beauty of the human body (Rubin, 1978).

Guidance from the Bible

Many informants cited the teachings of the Bible as their motivation for circumcision. One informant stated, "My mother regretted not having my four brothers circumcised. She believes from the Bible . . . Boy babies having to be [circumcised] or they're unclean. She worries about what the Bible said. She prays for my brothers to go to heaven anyway."

The Jewish biblical heritage of the covenant of circumcision addresses the chosen people:

> And God said unto Abraham . . . This is my covenant, which ye shall keep, between me and you and thy seed after thee; Every man child among you shall be circumcised . . . And the uncircumcised man child whose flesh of his foreskin is not circumcised, that soul shall be cut off from his people; he hath broken my covenant (Gen. 17:9-14).

One can appreciate the importance of the act to the Jewish people. This covenant has been a source of confusion, especially when interpreted to apply to individuals not of the Jewish faith. The cirumcision law was recorded in the Bible when the Jews suggested that the lack of circumcision among the Gentiles excised them from the faith. Apostle Paul's advice in the New Testament cleared up this concern:

> And put no difference between us [the Jews] and them [the Gentiles], purifying their hearts by faith (Acts, 15:9).
>
> Is any man called [to the faith] being circumcised: Let him not become uncircumcised. Is any called in [to the faith] uncircumcised: Let him not be circumcised (I Corinthians, 7:18).

These passages implied that God wanted evidence of faith, not merely circumcision, from the Gentiles—the concept of "circumcision of the heart." It is interesting, then, that one of the main reasons given by parents today who are not Jewish is, "It says to do it in the Bible, doesn't it?"

Playing it safe

Some parents elect to have their sons circumcised even when they are uncertain as to the need. This need to "play it safe" was evident when one mother stated, "I know that it's not needed, but I worried. I decided to have it done just in case something went wrong." There are many other examples of "playing it safe," for example, infant baptism by agnostic parents or an educated woman who is careful not to raise her hands above her head during pregnancy. Playing it safe allows the individual to "ward off" danger or bargain with fate: "If I have my son circumcised, he won't have problems." This reasoning is closely associated with the next reason—sentimental order.

Cultural sentimental order

Sentimental order is an emotional attachment to familiar ways of doing things (Stern, 1982). Sentiment compels one to ascribe. For example, one couple interviewed was on the waiting list to adopt a boy baby. In this area the relinquished infant is circumcised before his adoptive parents are notified. Since this adoptive father had not been circumcised and was adamantly against circumcision, the couple changed their preference to a girl baby.

Health professionals also "suffer" from the effects of sentimental order. One pediatrician, whose spouse was pregnant, said, "I don't know what I'll do if it's a boy. It just seems right to circumcise my son, even though I know it's not necessary to do it." Some of the health professionals, to save professional "face," placed responsibility on the spouse for electing circumcision for their son. In fact, all of the pediatricians interviewed stated that they were against circumcision; and yet their children were circumcised.

Meeting one's sentimental order through circumcision provided comfort to parents and their friends and relatives. Failure to experience this sentimental order led to such associated feelings as uneasiness, guilt, regret, grief and a sense of courting disaster.

Medical advice

While no longer advocated by the Academy, circumcision is still valued very much by some physicians and nurses. One nurse interviewed stated, "I encourage all my friends to have it done when they have a boy. It solves a lot of problems." Some general practitioners, obstetrician-gynecologists and urologists interviewed supported either circumcision or forced retraction. As one general practitioner stated, "You have to free the foreskin, then teach the mother to keep it back. But some women just won't do it. So the baby has to be circumcised later." However, forced retraction is not a therapeutic intervention. The two opposing epithelial surfaces tend to seal together following forced retraction and adhesions form (Harris & Stern, 1981).

Many health professionals interviewed mentioned parent and staff pressure to have the circumcision performed. As one physician said, "The nurse is my worst enemy on this. I get the parents agreeing not to have it done, and before I can get back to my office the nurse has talked them into wanting it again. So it's just easier to go ahead and do it." A nurse-mother of boys informed me of intense pressure from her obstetrician to have the circumcision done. "I really had to stand my ground on this," she reported. Health ethnocentrism, which is the health professional's belief that their factual and value systems are always correct, frequently governs medical advice (MacKay, 1978). In the case of circumcision, many professionals do not accept the findings that eliminate the need for the procedure. As a urologist stated, "I've never seen a circumcised man with penile cancer. They can't tell me it [circumcision] doesn't prevent cancer."

The reasons to circumcise are varied and have different meanings for each individual parent. None of the reasons are based on fact. Value systems and cultural beliefs form the framework of the reasons.

Cultural Decision-Making Process

As Cogan (1981) suggests:

> Whatever its origin and meaning, circumcision represents a difficult area of decision-making for many prospective parents today, except where unambiguous cultural tradition facilitates decision-making (p. 1).

Most parents experience a decision-making process that hinges on four main states of nature: (a) Is the parent a health professional? (b) Does the parent understand the physiology of the foreskin? (c) Does the parent's subculture value circumcision? (d) Does the parent value and ascribe to such dominant American culture prescriptions as circumcision? This process is depicted in the cultural decision-making model in Figure 33-2.

To use the model, the health professional first determines whether the parent is a lay person or is affiliated with a health profession. Second, knowledge about physiology of the prepuce as well as about myths is assessed. When given such information, many parents in the present study were surprised, and it made the decision more difficult. Knowing does not assure the valuing of such information. As Aamodt (1978) states, "Common sense ways of acting on health and healing situations may appear either to be related or unrelated to a cultural belief system" (p. 10).

Third, the subcultural beliefs about circumcision are determined. Groups such as the American Indians and Hispanics have not traditionally practiced circumcision; therefore it is not part of their sentimental order. Similar to an ethnic subculture is what Stern (1982) describes as "individual family culture"—the nuclear and extended family's unique sentimental orders and cultural heritage. While a parent may be part of the dominant American culture, there are special influences from individual family cultures.

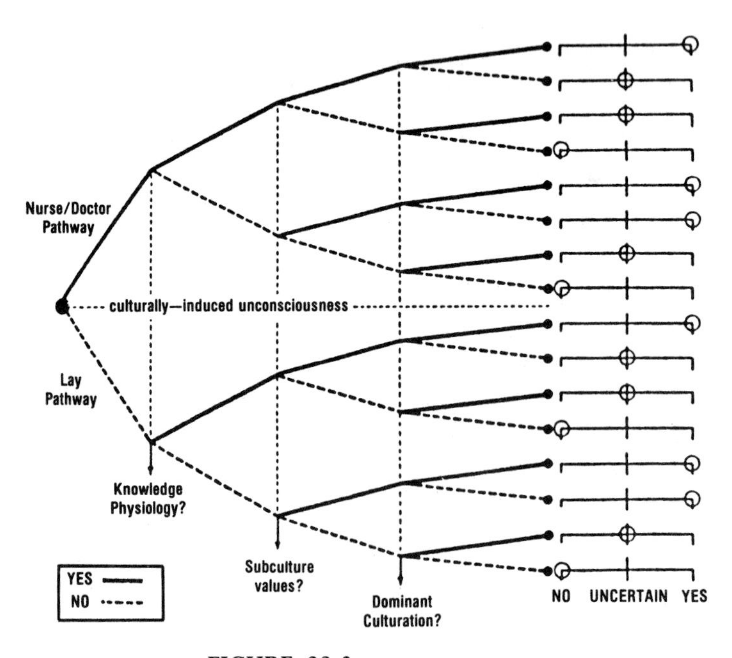

FIGURE 33-2

Cultural decision-making model.

Finally, the parent's relationship to the dominant American culture is assayed. Valuing the dominant American culture's prescription in general implies cultural change or acculturation of the subculture parent.

By tracing the pathway through determination of lay status, knowledge, myths, and culture influences, one arrives at a decision to circumcise, a decision not to circumcise, or uncertainty over the decision. The model predicts the decision-making pathways that individuals take in response to the described determinants. The value of this model lies in the opportunity that it affords health professionals to assess as well as intervene based on client knowledge and cultural values.

Cultural Franchise

As the research process in this study advanced, the construct of cultural franchising (see Figure 33-3) became evident. Parents who elected to have their sons circumcised were accepted, or "franchised," by the dominant American cultural network of family, friends, associates and even health professionals. Those who resisted or did not follow the cultural network were pressured and criticized, or "disenfranchised." Some sought later circumcision for their child to relieve these pressures.

The outcomes of the decision to circumcise or not to circumcise led to a classification of three main archetypical cultural actors:

1. *The cultural carrier.* One who follows and promotes cultural norms (Aamodt, 1978), for example, the urban white.
2. The cultural expatriot (ate). One who is denied access to practice cultural norms, for example, the indigent Southern Black.
3. The cultural renegade. One who purposively does not practice cultural norms, for example, the Hispanic or naturalist parent.

The decision of these actors invoked feelings either of cognitive congruence, dissonance or ambivalence. Congruence is simply agreement between cultural norms and actions. Dissonance implies nonagreement between cultural norms and actions, along with such associated feelings as uneasiness, guilt, regret and a sense of courting disaster. Finally, ambivalence is the alternating emotion of being drawn to, yet at the same time, repelled by cultural norms and actions.

In response to the circumcision choice, the parent and child are enfranchised or disenfranchised by their subculture as well as by the dominant American culture. The franchise is cultural credibility; it may be described as a cultural credit card—the "American Express" in the locker room. The best example of this

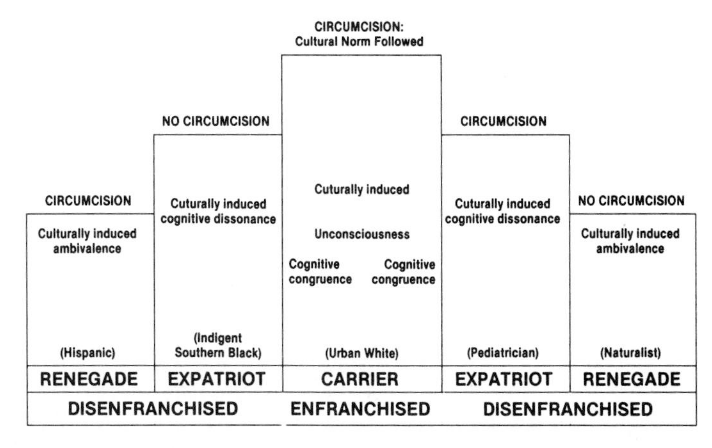

FIGURE 33-3

Critical junctures of franchisement.

disenfranchised process was given by a circumcised Anglo father who elected not to have his son circumcised:

> When we brought the baby home, my neighbor came over and noticed during a diaper change that my son was not circumcised. He asked me about it. When I told him that we had decided not to have him circumcised, he gave me all the reasons why we should. He said, "Only poor black and farm boys aren't." Once he saw that his pleading was doing no good, he got angry and left.

The two main processes of the Cultural Franchise theory, then, are (a) enfranchising, or the process of extending cultural credibility in response to acceptable behaviors and attitudes, and (b) disenfranchising, the process of denying this cultural credibility when cultural norms are not observed.

CONCLUSION

A transcultural health setting is defined by Aamodt (1978):

> one in which health professionals and clients informed by different cultural, health, and healing systems communicate and resolve their differences in order to meet the needs of the client (p. 9).

As demonstrated in this study, those needs vary in regard to circumcision.

Two clear stances guide client care. One is in Zimmer's (1977) words: "When a physician disagrees with the parents on performing the operation but goes along with their decision, this is not medical leadership" (p. 505). This viewpoint directs health professionals to inform parents and encourage them strongly not to have their child circumcised and even not to offer the procedure.

The second viewpoint allows a less rigid alignment with scientific knowledge; that is, circumcision is an acceptable practice based on cultural values. As Leininger (1979) suggests:

> Ritualized ethno-caring activities can have highly therapeutic benefits to clients and their families and should not be readily modified or disbanded as "too routine" and "nontherapeutic" caring measures (p. 24).

Therefore, since circumcision is a relatively safe practice, culture might be the deciding factor. The teaching, anticipatory guidance and actual procedure must be in tune with "cultural boundedness," namely the "relationship between a cultural system and a cultural carrier" (Aamodt, 1978, p. 8). In this way, the health professional is a caring and perceptive cultural broker. The assessment needed to provide this harmony can be completed using the described cultural decision-making model.

The theory of the cultural franchise is grounded in the experience of parents, health professionals and the child. Finally, a major discovery of this study was that the truly disenfranchised individual is the circumcised son of the enfranchised parent. He has no options and no freedom to change his state.

REFERENCES

Aamodt, A. (1978). Culture. In A. Clark (Ed.), Cultural-childbearing-health professionals. Philadelphia: Davis.

American Academy of Pediatrics (1975). Report of the ad hoc task force on circumcision. Pediatrics, 56, 610-611.

Anders, T., & Chalemian, R. (1974). The effects of circumcision on sleep-wake states in human neonates. Psychosomatic Medicine, 36, 174-179.

Assaad, M. (1980). Female circumcision in Egypt: Social implications, current research,and prospects for change. Studies in Family Planning, 11(1), 3-16.

Bettelheim, B. (1954). Symbolic wounds: Puberty rites and the envious male. New York: Free Press.

Cogan, R. (1981). Circumcision. ICEA Review, 5(1), 1-7.

Dickoff, J., James, P., & Semradek, J. (1975). 8-4 Research, Part I: A stance for nursing research-Tenacity or inquiry. Nursing Research, 24(2), 84-88.

Glaser, B. (1978). Theoretical sensitivity. Mill Valley, CA: Sociology Press.

Glaser, B., & Strauss, A. (1967). The discovery of grounded theory: Strategies for qualitive research. Chicago: Aldine.

Glaser, B., & Strauss, A. (1971). Status passage. Chicago: Aldine.

Gluckman, M. (1975). Specificity of social-anthropological studies of ritual. Mental Health Society, 2, 1-17.

Goffman, E. (1963). Stigma: Notes on the management of spoiled identity. Englewood Cliffs, NJ: Prentice-Hall.

Harris, C., & Stern, P. (1981). Care of the prepuce in the uncircumcised child: Reinforcing nature's law of health.

Issues in Comprehensive Pediatric Nursing, 5(4), 233-242.

Kitahara, M. (1976). A cross-cultural test of the Freudian theory of circumcision. International Journal of Psychoanalytic Psychotherapy, 5, 535-546.

Leininger, M. (1979). Transcultural nursing. New York: Masson.

Leitch, I. (1970). Circumcision: A continuing enigma. Austrian Pediatrics, 6, 59.

MacKay, S. (1978). Cultural factors as a source of influence on the health professions. In M. Hardy & M. Conway (Eds.), Role theory: Perspectives for health professionals. New York: Appleton-Century-Crofts.

McHugh, M. (1981). Circumcision: Is it ever necessary? Irish Medical Journal, 74(2), 55-56.

Nightingale, F. (1859/1970). Notes on nursing: What it is, and what it is not (2nd ed.). London: Duckworth.

Ostow, M. (1970). Parent's hostility to their children. Israel Annals of Psychiatry and Related Disciplines, 8(1), 3-21.

Ozturk, O. (1973). Ritual circumcision and castration anxiety. Psychiatry, 36, 49-59.

Remondino, P. (1891/1974). History of circumcision from the earliest time to the present. Philadelphia: Davis & AMS.

Robin, J. (1978). Celsus' decircumcision operation: Medical and history implications. Urology, 16(1), 121-124.

Stern, P. (1980). Grounded theory methodology: Its uses and processes. Image, 12(1), 20-23.

Stern, P. (1982). Conflicting family culture: An impediment to integration in stepfather families. Journal of Psychosocial Nursing, 20(10), 27-33.

Talbert, L. (1976). Adrenal cortical response to circumcision in the neonate. Obstetrics Gynecology, 48, 208-210.

Weiner, R. (1980). Circumcision. Mothering, 16, 35-40.

Wilson, H. (1977). Limiting intrusion-social control of outsiders in a healing community: An illustration of qualitative comparative analysis. Nursing Research, 26(2), 103-111.

Wirth, J. (1980). Current circumcision practices: Canada. Pediatrics, 66(5), 705-708.

Wollman, L. (1974). Female circumcision. Journal American Society Psychosomatic Medicine, 20(4), 130-131.

Zimmer, P. (1977). Modern ritualistic surgery. Clinical Pediatrics, 16(6), 503-506.

CHAPTER 34

Hospice: Concept and Implementation in the Black Community

Louisa M. Lundgren, RN, MS
Shu-Pi C. Chen, RN, DrPH

The true roots of the hospice stretch back to medieval times and even earlier. The early hospices were generally located along the routes of the crusaders, pilgrims, and other medieval travelers and were run by religious orders. Stoddard (1978) described the ancient hospice:

> It offered an open door of welcome not only to the sick and dying, but to the hungry wayfarer, the woman in labor, the needy poor, the orphan, or the leper with his bell. The common base or denominator of the offering was hospitality in its original sense of protection, refreshment, "cheryssing," and fellowship, rather than the demand of a patient for a cure. (p. 7)

In the late 1800s Sister Mary Aikenhead and the Sisters of Charity founded a home for the dying in Dublin. In 1889 Catherine McParlan and a group of Irish Catholic laywomen established the House of Calvary in lower Manhattan.

Credit for the founding of the contemporary hospice movement is attributed to the work of Dr. Cicely Saunders in England, who conceptualized the idea in 1948. Dr. Saunders combined the older elements of care for the dying with modern pain control care for the entire family, bereavement counselling, coordinated day and home services, and multidisciplinary teams. In 1967 Dr. Saunders's concept took shape in the form of St. Christopher's Hospice. Every hospice established since that time has taken direction from the St. Christopher's program.

The basic components of hospice are coordinated home care with inpatient beds under a central autonomous hospice administration, control of symptoms, physician directed services for treatment of physical symptoms, provision of care by an interdisciplinary team, services available 24 hr a day 7 days a week, patient and family regarded as the unit of care, provision of bereavement follow-up, use of volunteers, structured personnel support and communication systems, and patients accepted the program on the basis of health-care needs rather than ability to pay (Lack & Buckingham, 1978).

INSTITUTIONAL FORMS OF HOSPICE

Three forms of hospice care have emerged: (a) home-care programs, (b) hospice with hospital affiliations including hospice teams and palliative care

Reprinted from *Journal of Community Health Nursing,* Vol. 3, No. 3, with permission of Lawrence Erlbaum Associates, Inc., © 1986.

units, and (c) completely autonomous hospices.

Home-care programs either have been developed to work in cooperation with other community agencies or have been established as adjuncts to already licensed home health agencies. Home-care programs provide supportive services for families to enable terminal patients to die at home. These services will generally be given only if there is a primary caretaker at home. Because of their financial feasibility and capacity to use volunteers, many community-based hospices started out as home-care programs.

Hospices with hospital affiliations serve those individuals who require admission to control new symptoms or to provide respite for the family members providing care. Inpatient hospice facilities provide home-care services either through their own social service departments or through community-based agencies (McCabe, 1982). Hospital-based hospices will likely proliferate due to the excess of hospital beds available throughout the country. A major objection to this development is the conflict in philosophies between acute and palliative care. Although the hospice concept sometimes carries over to the acute area, those in the acute settings frequently fail to appreciate the unique dimension of hospice care.

The completely autonomous hospice is generally modeled after St. Christopher's Hospice in England. It provides home-care, day-care, inpatient, and 12-month bereavement services. Although the autonomous hospice may provide greatest patient care continuity, there are major problems. There is the difficulty of licensure and reimbursement because hospices have not been recognized as unique institutions by many state licensing laws. Some people feel that until cost efficiency of the hospice program has been determined, no new care facilities should be built. This would force hospice care to be integrated into the mainstream of medicine.

HOSPICE CARE AND ETHNICITY

Research related to the need for hospice service among individual ethnic groups is minimal (Benoliel, 1983). Gordon and Rooney (1984) suggested that the cultural and religious background of a family may significantly influence its response to the crisis of serious illness. The ethnicity literature (McGoldrick, 1982) suggests that a person's cultural frame of reference leads to differences in the experience of pain, what the person labels as a symptom, how the person communicates about pain or other symptoms, beliefs about the cause of illness, attitudes toward helping professionals, and what treatment is desired or expected.

Black families have unique skills for coping with stress and crisis. These include reliance on a lifelong extended kinship network (Hines & Boyd-Franklin, 1982) and the black church (Wimberley, 1982). Research has not been done to assess the extent to which the church network remains operative within the black community. However, movement from the multigenerational extended family to two-generational or one-generational nuclear families leads to discontinuity of traditional values and supports (Wimberley, 1982).

Bereavement following the death of a family member represents a major disruption of the survivor's intimate network and severely tests the strength of remaining supports (Walker, MacBride, & Vachon, 1977). Wimberley (1982) indicated that historically the black church has provided a unique set of support systems. These include black worship, the black world view, care groups such as prayer meetings and burial societies, and the rituals of baptism and funeral. Thus, it is possible that elements of the hospice concept could be integrated with supports already available in the black church to strengthen the social networks present during times of grief and bereavement.

ISSUES FOR HOSPICE IN THE BLACK COMMUNITY

Assessing the Need

As the hospice concept has become more widely accepted, an assumption has emerged that most people would use hospice once they are aware of this type of service (Perrollaz & Mollica, 1981). Hospice of Columbus, Ohio found that its caseload was predominantly white, although community residents were primarily black (Creek, 1982). A hospice serving a largely black population on Chicago's south side has maintained an annual caseload of about 30 patients over 3 years, not all of whom have been black. This low rate remains in spite of concerted promotional attempts with community physicians and social workers.

Strong Memorial Hospital, in Rochester, New York, indicated that an urban population of 300,000 or a combined urban and suburban population of 750,000 would form a critical mass of target population to be served by a hospice care unit (DuBois, 1980). This formula for determining hospice needs in the Anglo community cannot be automatically applied to the black community. Kalish and Reynolds (1976) reported a 2:1 preference among randomly selected blacks in Los Angeles for dying at home rather than a hospital. Anglos reported a 4:1 preference.

There is no clear answer on how best to determine the need for hospice in a community. Random samples of a population do not represent the target group most likely to use hospice services. Consumer adoption theory posits that once awareness has been aroused, concrete steps must be taken to maintain interest, help individuals evaluate whether the program meets their needs, and make it easy for new prospects to sample the new program (Kotler, 1982). Individuals who respond in support of hospice should they need it at some later time will not likely use this service in the absence of further marketing efforts.

Data gathered from hospice clients may suffer from two sources of bias. First, those interviewed have already accepted the hospice philosophy in order to be admitted as patients. Their needs, then, might be different from those of the general public. Second, families responding to surveys on satisfaction with hospice services may have less difficult illness experiences overall than those who fail to respond (Bass, 1983). Services based on findings from less complicated cases would not meet the needs of the general public.

A large-scale survey of supports and services already available and used by the terminally ill has the advantage of identifying a base on which to add new programs. It is often both difficult and time-consuming, however, to find willing participants.

Issues for Hospice in General

Hospice care in the urban black community shares general problems of the hospice movement (Lack & Buckingham, 1978):

> Two fundamental difficulties faced—and continue to confront—the New Haven hospice: first, the status quo for terminal care in the American medical community, and second, the problem of fitting hospice into the bureaucratic maze of American health care without changing its purposes and nature . . . Despite the benefits of the hospice program to patients and families, these characteristics make hospice care a square peg to be fitted into the round holes of Medicare, Medicaid, certification, various reimbursement plans, and physician referral systems. (pp. 19-20)

For growth of any agency to proceed beyond the initial charitable voluntary stages, hospice management must combine the management functions of any health-care organization with flexibility and responsiveness to the needs of dying persons. The financial future of specific services tends to follow the existence of third-party reimbursement (Hackley, 1979). Hackley also asserted that if the hospice concept is to become widely available in the United States, financial feasibility is critical.

Barriers to Hospice Use in the Black Community

A number of potential sources of resistance to hospice use may exist within the black community. These include lack of availability, lack of community awareness, lack of trust of social service providers, and misperceptions of the role of hospice services.

In many areas, hospice services are not yet available. Where such services do exist, community awareness programs have been inadequate in explaining the purpose of hospice care, what it is, what it can and cannot do, and how to gain access to it. Educational programs have been conducted largely with health-care providers serving the black community rather than local churches and service organizations through which individuals receive information.

Historically, there has been a lack of trust of social

services within the black community (Wimberley, 1982). Hines and Boyd-Franklin (1982) contended that reliance on a lifelong kinship network, not necessarily drawn along "blood lines," remains a major coping mechanism. Wimberley (1982) also contended that the black church has traditionally fulfilled many of the political, social, educational, recreational, economic, medical, and mental health needs of the black person as a result of segregation. It is likely that individuals and families at the crisis time of impending death would turn to familiar sources of support. Strangers from an agency such as hospice, whether professional or volunteer, may not be allowed into the home. In addition, the requirement that there be a primary caretaker in the home may eliminate the use of hospice by those in greatest need of supplemental support systems.

The grieving process has been described by several authors as passage through phases of anger, shock and denial, intense grief, bargaining, and a final stage of acceptance of death or loss. The goal of hospice is to provide palliative and supportive care when cure is no longer considered possible and death is viewed as probable within a short time by patient, family, and professional caretakers. Findings among black Americans suggest a high acceptance of life that may be inconsistent with their perception of hospice philosophy. Hospice care might be viewed as giving up on life rather than aggressively prolonging it. On the other hand, misperceptions also might lead to a view that hospice represents an attempt to interfere with a process that should be left to God and personal faith. Swanson and Harter (1971) summarized interviews of 20 older black men and women: "They have never considered that life might not be worth living, nor can they conceive of a situation with which they, themselves, or with the help of the Lord, cannot cope" (p. 216).

DISCUSSION

Hospices in general operate under medical direction largely due to the need for specialized pain control management, especially in the case of terminal cancer patients. For the most part, however, the actual coordination of patient care services is performed by nurses. It is therefore up to nursing to identify and address the larger issues relative to the hospice movement, in addition to the individual needs of the dying patient.

Formal and informal studies among professionals and community members indicate that care for the terminally ill is inadequate in the black community. Strong barriers, however, may prevent the use of hospice services as we currently know them.

Satisfaction with institutions as a place to die appears stronger in the black community than among other ethnic groups. For many, there remains a strong belief in the power of medical treatment to cure all illnesses. This coincides with a view of life and death that values longevity and the will to survive. Reluctance to accept personal care from those outside the extended family, whether lay or professional, would make the provision of hospice services difficult.

Hospices in mostly white communities have frequently started as in-home agencies only later expanding to institutional facilities. The reverse may be more appropriate in the black community. Hospital staffs working with terminal patients must be educated about the hospice philosophy of care and encouraged to adopt a more holistic approach. If the perceived safety and objectivity of the hospital or nursing home can be enhanced by family-centered holistic care and symptom control, understanding and acceptance of the hospice philosophy may be attained. Family teaching available from in-house staff may then reduce the anxiety of family members toward caring for the terminally ill in the home. It might also serve to increase acceptance of hospice professionals and volunteers into the available support network. Hospitals would have the financial and administrative resources to permit Medicare certification for hospice care. Patients would thus have fewer concerns about the cost of care. Patients without family members to serve as primary caregivers in the home could receive hospice services in the institutional setting.

If hospice is to develop within the black community, the support systems already available must be identified to design a model of care based on actual needs. The multigenerational extended family and the black church traditionally have served these needs. The nature of the crisis, the personal resources within the social network for support to persons in crisis, and the resources within the local church must be considered in planning individual care.

Although it is not known to what extent the church is still viewed as the center for comfort and support, it seems the logical base for in-home services. Many black churches already have committed volunteers recognized as providers of spiritual and physical care. Additional training would be required in specialized support of the terminally ill and in documentation. Coordination and supervision would need to be established with professional caregivers. Recipients of care would therefore not necessarily view themselves as terminally ill, but as part of the overall caring community of the church.

Hospice care in its medieval form served all those in need, rather than those dying of terminal illnesses alone. It is possible that a return to this global approach would be useful in the black community. Support services are needed for families of those who die unexpectedly as much as for those with known diagnoses. Bereavement services should be available to all, whether or not the deceased was admitted as a hospice patient. This is especially true in cases where multiple deaths have occurred in the family within a short time.

Kalish and Reynolds (1976) found that with increasing education in the black community came greater expectations of help from relatives during bereavement and less reliance on nonfamilistic supports. They suggested that this might be a function of age because the young tend to be more educated. With its emphasis on enabling the family to become caregivers for the patient, hospice may become increasingly acceptable as educational levels rise. Consumer adoption theory also suggests that younger, more highly educated individuals tend to try new services earlier than others in their communities (Kotler, 1982). It is possible, then, that as young middle-class blacks become more aware of hospice services, the need for hospice care may grow. Such care, however, would still need to be tailored to the unique needs of the community.

Research is needed in all areas relevant to the provision of care to the terminally ill in the black community. Nationwide studies should be conducted to determine which agencies are serving the black community, to demonstrate their effectiveness, accessibility, availability, acceptability, and efficiency. Comparisons of the relative effectiveness of the various institutional forms of hospice might provide answers to the controversy over home-based versus inpatient care settings.

Study of the grief and bereavement process as indicators of future health-care needs would provide vital information to both health-care providers and reimbursement institutions. Comparisons of the stages of grief between white and black populations might indicate unique counselling approaches needed in the black community. Research on symptom control issues specific to this community is also needed: the perception of pain, indigenous forms of symptom control, fear of addiction, a felt need to endure hardship.

Because people's views of life and death are in large part culturally determined, one model of hospice care for the terminally ill cannot be universally applicable. Unique support systems already available in each community must be clearly identified and used as the basis for additional care.

REFERENCES

Bass, D.M. (1983). Response bias in studying hospice clients' needs. *Omega, 13*(4), 305-319.

Benoliel, J.Q. (1983). Nursing research on death, dying and terminal illness: Development, present state, and prospects. In H. H. Werley & J. Fitzpatrick (Eds.), *Annual review of nursing research,* (Vol. 1, pp. 101-123). New York: Springer.

Creek, L. V. (1982). A homecare hospice profile: Description, evaluation, and cost analysis. *Journal of Family Practice, 14*(1), 53-58.

DuBois, P. (1980). *The hospice way of death.* New York: Human Sciences Press.

Gordon, A., & Rooney, A. (1984). Hospice and the family: A systems approach to assessment. *American Journal of Hospice Care, 1,* 31-33.

Hackley, J. (1979). Financing and accrediting hospices. *Hospital Progress, 60*(3), 51-53.

Hines, P.M., & Boyd-Franklin, N. (1982). Black families. In M. McGoldrick, J. Pearce, & J. Giordano (Eds.), *Ethnicity and family theory* (pp. 84-107). New York: Guilford.

Kalish, R. A., & Reynolds, D. K. (1976). *Death and ethnicity: A psychocultural study.* Los Angeles: Ethel Percy Andrus Gerontology Center.

Kotler, P. (1982). *Marketing for non-profit organizations.* Englewood Cliffs, NJ: Prentice-Hall.

Lack, S., & Buckingham, R. (1978). *First American hospice: Three years of home care.* New Haven: Hospice.

McCabe, S. (1982). An overview of hospice care. *Cancer Nursing, 5,* 103-108.

McGoldrick, M. (1982). Ethnicity and family therapy: An overview. In M. McGoldrick, J. Pearce, & J. Giordano (Eds.), *Ethnicity and family therapy* (pp. 3-30). New York: Guilford.

Perrollaz, L., & Mollica, M. (1981). Public knowledge of hospice care. *Nursing Outlook, 29*(1), 46-48.

Stoddard, S. (1978). *The hospice movement: A better way of caring for the dying.* New York: Stein & Day.

Swanson, W. C., & Harter, C. L. (1971). How do elderly blacks cope in New Orleans? *Aging and Human Development, 2,* 210-216.

Walker, K. N., MacBride, A., & Vachon, M. L. (1977). Social support networks and the crisis of bereavement. *Social Science and Medicine, 11,*35-41.

Wimberley, E. P. (1982). *Pastoral counselling and spiritual values: A black point of view.* Nashville: Abingdon.

CHAPTER 35

Health and Health Services Among the Navajo Indians

Sixten S.R. Haraldson, DrMed, MPH

INTRODUCTION

The World Health Organization (WHO) program, "Health for All by the Year 2000" should be understood primarily as an appeal for improved health and health services in rural areas, in both the rich and the poor world. WHO is well aware of the often incredible maldistribution of health services, favoring urban areas and more or less neglecting extreme rural areas with scattered populations of low density and great distances. Such groups have been called "adversely situated" people. Sometimes nomadic but more often sedentary minorities, these are difficult groups of people to reach for modern education and efficient delivery of health services, for geographical, socio-economical, political, as well as cultural and linguistic reasons. These issues have been previously discussed in relationship to the developing nations.[1,2,3]

In developed countries, ethnic minorities are often among the most economically disadvantaged and the ones with the least access to the nation's health care resources. However, it must be kept in mind that the provision of health care alone and without economic growth and social advantage will not sustain their general well-being. This paper presents the results of more than 30 years of socio-medical development among an adversely situated population, the Navajo Indians, of the United States. The progress made in physical health measures is clear, but the most instructive component may be the apparent absence of a concurrent internal societal synthesis, providing multi-sector improvements, whereby the people might establish ownership for their continued welfare.

Reprinted from *Journal of Community Health,* Vol. 13, No. 3, with permission of Human Sciences Press, Inc., © 1988.

American Minorities-Native Americans

Of the almost 227 million people counted in the 1980 United States Census,[4] ancestry by self-identification provided the following single or mixed ethnic backgrounds: 188 million European, 21 million black, 10 million Hispanic, 7 million Native American, and 4 million Pacific Islander and Asian. Within the total count of Native Americans, a term encompassing the indigenous tribes of Indians as well as the Aleuts and Eskimos of Alaska, almost 2 million claimed Native American single ancestry, a number which is less than one percent of the total U.S. population. Each of the 50 states collects natality and mortality data, categorized as "white," "black" and "other races," which are transmitted to the National Center for Health Statistics. States may choose to elaborate on race/ethnicity and 28 of the 50 States do identify American Indian and Alaskan Native on certificates of vital events.

Because the Native American people are well represented in the national trend to migrate to urban areas for employment, in 1980 less than 1 million lived in regions considered traditional residence and served by federally funded health and education programs specifically organized for Indian and Eskimo people. In addition to some tribal and federal employment in Alaskan Native villages and western U.S. trust lands ("reservations"), cultural identity as well as emotional and spiritual affinity to tribe and place are important factors for those who choose to reside in areas without the usual amenities and resources found in most inhabited regions of the United States. Each of the more than 300 tribes, in fact different groups within a tribe, experience varying levels of socioeconomic development, but for the most part, the almost 1 million Native Americans residing on federally administered regions represent adversely situated people within an affluent country. Demographically, this portion of the population differs from the total U.S. population in several ways. It is estimated that 40% live below the poverty level. The median age of Native Americans is 22 years, that for all Americans is 30 years. The total fertility rate is almost four times higher for Native Americans. Life expectancy is somewhat lower: 75 years for females and 67 years for males, as compared to 77 years for all U.S. females and 70 years for all U.S. males.[5]

THE NAVAJO TRIBE

The Navajo tribe, the "Dineh" in their own language, constitute the largest Indian tribe north of Mexico, with an estimated population in 1986 of 171,097[6] who reside on and near the Navajo Reservation.

History and Geography

The Navajo belong to the Athabascan language group which includes Apaches and some tribes of Alaska and Western Canada. They migrated away from the northern Athabascans into the south-western United States between 1000 and 1400 AD. The Spanish explorers documented their encounters with the Navajo in the early seventeenth century. The dispersed settlements and migratory ways of the Navajo were well suited to the needs of the horses, sheep, and cattle which the Spanish brought to the semi-arid environment, and it was from the Spanish and Pueblo Indians that the Navajo learned silversmithing and vertical loom weaving of wool. Close contact, including intermarriage with the Pueblos led to the adoption of additional religious ceremonies, crops, ritual attire, and perhaps the matrilineal-matrilocal social organization which is still practiced to some extent.

In 1848, after acquiring additional land from Mexico, various Indian tribes, including some 18,000 Navajos, were forcibly settled. Broken treaties and continued warfare led to the incarceration of the Navajos in a military installation (Fort Sumner) in 1864. Their numbers dropped to 6,447. Upon their release in 1868, a new treaty established the present Navajo Nation. The Nation, or Reservation, now consists of 63,000 square kilometers, which is about the size of present-day Hungary. It is located in northwestern New Mexico, northeastern Arizona and in small portions of southern Utah and Colorado. The land is high semi-desert, at an average altitude of 2,000 meters, with forested mountains and large areas of eroded steppe interrupted by dramatic red sandstone and canyons. The average annual precipitation is between 125 and 625 millimeters, making some areas a real desert.

Economy and Tribal Government

Due to low rainfall and poor soil conditions, most of the Navajo land is unfit for stable cultivation and with rapid population growth, the 300 year old pastoral livelihood has been impossible for the majority of families since the 1920's. At that time the marginal land was overgrazed, resulting in desertification. A very unpopular livestock reduction program was implemented by the federal government. Total management of the limited grazing and most other land use is now within the tribal government's own jurisdiction.

For the past 50 years the Navajo tribe has administered increasingly more of its own affairs under leadership of an elected tribal chairman and about 100 elected council members representing geographic constituencies which form the smallest unit of government structure. Of a $158 million operating tribal budget in 1983, two-thirds were derived from the federal government in grants and contracts, and one-third from earned revenues, mostly oil, coal, and uranium mining leases to private corporations. Allocations of this budget included: 26% to social welfare,

22% to locally operated health programs, nine percent to tribally operated school programs, and seven percent to early childhood development.[7]

Across the reservation, social and economic change has been uneven and generalizations can be rather inaccurate. A general description of the smaller economic picture reveals a 1980 per capita income of $2,300 when the national amount was almost $10,000. Unemployment is very high (about 40%), with the tribal and federal governments providing the majority of salaried jobs. Wool production, rug weaving and silver-smithing still figure in local finances, as relatively small sources of income. A Ford Foundation study released in 1986 found that McKinley County New Mexico and Apache County in Arizona, both predominantly Navajo, contained the first and second highest numbers of rural poor among all counties in the United States.[8]

During a mid-1970 household survey, it was found that half of the adults had attended less than four years of school, while seven percent had attended college.[9] The majority of Navajos under 40 speak English either as a primary or secondary language. Older people mostly speak Navajo. Basic schooling is compulsory but the dropout rate is high. In 1980, 35% of Navajo youth graduated from the 12th grade of high school.[9] On the other hand, many of these graduates excel. In 1985, 9 of 12 fully credentialed Navajo medical doctors formed the "Council of Navajo Physicians" to serve as an advisory group to the tribal government and the Navajo Area Indian Health Service.

Spirituality and Cultural Practices

Beginning with the Spanish exploration and current today, numerous Christian missionary endeavors have been active on the Navajo reservation. This had usually resulted in a "partial conversion" and more recently, a resurgence of pride in traditional spiritual belief and practice has taken place. The result is a variable adherence to traditional practices which transcend "religion" and are more of a life-view which has actually bridged the gap between the old ceremonial ways and new patterns of thought responding to the demand of the modern world. Membership in the Native American Church is high both among those who belong to a Christian denomination as among those who do not. The Native American Church has restored self-esteem in its distinctly Indian group process. It is a blend of the ancient Mexican Indian rites utilizing the hallucinogenic cactus, peyote, all-night ceremonies with some "fundamentalist Christian elements, and pan-Indian moral principles."[10]

Coexisting with this Christian influence are traditional Navajo rituals, most of which are curing ceremonies accompanied by group social functions. Diseases and injury are ultimately traced to the breaking of taboos and the individuals who understand this causal relationship are shamans or medicine men (or women) who include singers, curers, prayer makers, and diagnosticians. Relief from illness may require hiring several of specialists which may become very expensive. Traditional and western medicine now frequently complement each other. In Chinle, in the center of the reservation, the new hospital which opened in 1983 has a specially constructed room for traditional healing ceremonies.

Demography and Health

Broudy and May[11] view the Navajo population as being in the second stage of a demographic transition. While mortality has declined, fertility remains high, yielding a 1978 growth rate of 2.7%. This means a doubling of the population in 23 years. With half of its people under the age of 22, the Navajo population graph depicts the classical pyramid shape of a developing nation. Although the birth rate has declined, in 1978 Navajo women gave birth to a total average of 4.4 children while all U.S. women gave birth to a total average of 1.8 children.

Data on migration patterns to and from the reservation are not readily available. This is partly due to the unwieldy sociopolitical structure of the reservation. The smallest geographic unit is the "chapter" of which there are about 100, forming the basis for tribal government representation. People are registered to vote in the chapter from which their family traditionally came, even though they may not currently live there. The limited availability of on-reservation jobs has created clusters of residences in unincorporated and otherwise unorganized settlements, while those who are ranchers, unemployed, or elderly tend to live in the most remote areas. Generally the people are scattered in the vast area with an average population density of only 2.6 per square kilometer.

THE INDIAN HEALTH SERVICE (IHS)

The United States has no organized national health system. There is however, a comprehensive federal health program for Native Americans. The origins of this program go variously back to treaties made with Indian tribes, the purchase agreement for Alaska, and the national government's legal trust responsibility. In 1955, the Congress responded to documentation of poor health care, demonstrated by a raging tuberculosis epidemic in Alaska and infant mortality rates of 80 to 100 per 1000 throughout Indian areas, by establishing the "Indian Health Service." It was administratively placed within the U.S. Public Health Service.

The program is supplemental to other health services which Native people might be entitled to by virtue of their U.S. citizenship and local residence. The operating funds available to the IHS are not based on any legally required capitation formula nor any documented benefit package of health services. The beneficiary population is likewise not fixed nor clearly defined and could potentially include all those descended from Indian people. Currently services are provided to, and utilized by, about 900,000 persons predominantly residing on Reservation Lands. This financing arrangement has required the IHS, over the years, to prioritize its services, to form an efficient operational program linking community and environmental health with primary care and to a referral system for specialty services.

Recruitment and retention of medical staff for the often remote and isolated sites of the IHS program has been a challenge. Initially, duty to the military service could be fulfilled in the U.S. Public Health Service, (assigned to the Indian program) and was an effective incentive. With cancellation of the military draft in the U.S., forgiveness of Medical school loans for work in the Indian Health Service has attracted an adequate number of new physicians. Retention is a problem as the living situation is often too culturally isolated for the family and schooling inadequate for older children. Medical specialists, in particular, feel professionally isolated and earn significantly less than they would in an urban private practice. Nevertheless, having once experienced the challenges and rewards of caring for the medically underserved, and learning to love the natural beauty of many of the reservation sites, a considerable number of young physicians are choosing the IHS for a career.

The general shortage of nurses in the US is particularly felt in all rural and remote areas and may yet be the most difficult health care manpower issue to deal with.

By 1985, the IHS had grown to encompass 12 administrative "Areas," (Table 35-1) containing 48 hospitals and 72 health centers. Primary medical services consume the major share of the approximately $900 million annual budget, but there are also programs in environmental health, community health nursing, dental care, mental health and alcoholism treatment. All of this is now carried out with the maximum management input and employment of Native American people. Since 1975, the Tribal organizations have had the opportunity to take over from the Federal Government the management of their own programs. As Native American people have gained training and experience in health care administration and delivery, partial or complete take-over has occurred in 47 tribes.

Navajo Area Indian Health Service

The Navajo Area Indian Health Service (NAIHS) is one of the 12 administrative regions of the Indian Health Service. The Navajo Area is divided into eight Service Units for the local organization and delivery of health care. Six of these have hospitals, while two offer ambulatory care only. Today, a system of paved main roads, telephone communication, and air travel link them all together. In a typical Service Unit, community and home health services are provided by public health nurses, assisted by a Navajo driver/interpreter. Travel to homes is difficult, on unmarked dirt roads which are often extremely rough, and communication is hampered by lack of telephones. The drivers, through years of translating and observing, have actually become unofficial medical auxiliaries. Emphasis is on maternal and child health as well as care of the elderly.

TABLE 35-1
Indian Health Service administrative areas 1986 service populations

IHS AREA NAME	MAJOR LOCATION	POPULATION	% OF TOTAL
Aberdeen	North & South Dakota	74,781	7.5
Alaska	All of Alaska	75,461	7.6
Albuquerque	Part of New Mexico & Colorado	53,771	5.4
Bemidji	Minnesota, Wisconsin, Michigan	49,550	5.0
Billings	Montana & Wyoming	42,594	4.3
Navajo	Parts of Arizona, New Mexico, Utah	171,097	17.3
Oklahoma	Oklahoma & Kansas	200,488	20.3
Phoenix	Parts of Arizona, Utah, California & Nevada	86,826	8.8
Portland	Washington & Idaho	101,275	10.3
California	Part of California	75,306	7.7
Tucson	Part of Arizona	18,843	1.9
Nashville	Maine, New York, Florida, Mississippi, No. Carolina	37,025	3.9
	TOTAL	987,017	100%

Data compiled from USPHS, Indian Health Service, Rockville, Maryland, 1986 Chart Series.

As roads improved and standards of medical care increased, the surgical and other specialty components have tended to become centralized at a few sites. The Gallup Indian Medical Center, situated just at the eastern reservation boundary, provides primary care to its surrounding Service Unit of 30,000 people, and referral care in surgery, otolaryngology, ophthalmology, orthopedics, obstetrics, intensive neonatal care, radiology, and specialized laboratory services to the entire reservation health system. Patients requiring a tertiary level of care are transported usually by air, to a University affiliated hospital in Albuquerque, New Mexico or Phoenix or Tucson, Arizona.

Morbidity/Mortality Patterns

Crude death rates for Navajos have declined to levels below the general U.S. population. When the effect of the younger population is removed by age-adjusting, mortality rates show that the Navajo mortality is actually 1.2 times greater than that of the total U.S. Table 35-2 indicates that accidents are the chief cause of death, followed by heart disease, malignant neoplasms, influenza and pneumonia. Deaths from tuberculosis are all in older age groups indicating residual problem. Eight to ten percent of infant deaths are due to diarrheal disease (a Total of five or six cases per year). Unlike the situation in many developing countries, malnutrition does not appear to be a contributing factor to the infectious disease death. Immunization rates of over 90% account for the absence of measles, polio, diphtheria and pertussis. Approximately 40% of Navajo deaths are the result of social and environmental pathologies (in categories of mental illness accidents, suicide and homicide). Fifty percent of male deaths and 27% of female deaths were overtly social or behavior-related.[11] The reported Navajo age-adjusted alcoholism death rate is 20 times that of the total U.S. rate.

Hospitalization morbidity data are presented in Table 35-3. Although this is proportionate data, some trends are evident. Infectious diseases have declined while the proportion of hospitalizations for injuries has remained constant. Childbirth constitutes about one-third of all discharges. The need for inpatient medical services has declined and ambulatory care has expanded. In such a young and remotely situated population, pediatric care remains a most important service. With the decline in early childhood diseases, a high immunization rate and improved medical

TABLE 35-2

Age-adjusted mortality rates, rank ordered for Navajo, 1980-82, compared to total IHS population and total U.S. 1981* (rates per 100,000 population)

CAUSE	NAVAJO RATE	TOTAL IHS RATE	TOTAL US RATE	NAVAJO/US RATIO
Accidents/Injuries	165.7	136.3	39.8	4.2
Heart Diseases	77.3	166.7	195.0	0.4
Malignant Neoplasms	76.6	98.5	131.6	0.6
Pneumonia/Influenza	28.6	26.6	12.3	2.3
Liver Disease/Cirrhosis	21.4	48.1	11.4	1.9
Cerebrovascular Disease	17.1	33.8	38.1	0.5
Homicide and Legal Intervention	15.1	21.2	10.4	1.4
All Causes	656.3	778.3	568.2	1.2

*Adapted from: Congress of the United States, Office of Technology Assessment, *Indian Health Care*, p. 94, Washington D.C., April 1986. Data originally from U.S. Public Health Service, National Center for Health Statistics and Indian Health Service computer tapes.

TABLE 35-3

Selected discharge diagnoses; percent of all discharges, Navajo Area Indian Health Service hospitals*

PRINCIPAL DIAGNOSIS AND ICD-9CM CODES**	1959	1968	1977	1982
Pregnancy and Childbirth 630-676 and V27	n/a	22.2	n/a	32.0
Accidents, Injuries, and Violence 800-999	15.4	18.4	18.3	16.5
Gastrointestinal 520-579	13.7	12.8	7.8	13.6
Respiratory 460-519	19.0	16.3	10.0	10.2
Infective and Parasitic 001-139	5.2	4.8	8.7	3.0
Neoplasms 140-239	1.5	1.6	2.7	2.5
				77.8% in 1982

*Adapted from Kunitz & Temkin-Greener; *Changing Patterns of Mortality and Hospitalized Morbidity on the Navajo Indian Reservation*, Rochester, NY, University of Rochester, 1980 and data from Navajo Area Indian Health Service Statistics Branch, 1984.

***ICD-9-CM. International Classification of Diseases.* 9th Edition. Vols I & II, Ann Arbor, Michigan, Commission on Professional and Hospital Activities, 1978.

Note: for comparison purposes. In 1984, the Navajo IHS Four Leading Discharge Rates per 10,000 population (compared to U.S. short term care hospitals in parentheses) were: 391 (206) for Pregnancy & Childbirth, 143 (148) for Accidents, Injuries, & Violence, 117 (184) for Gastrointestinal, and 100 (144) for Respiratory. Data from U.S. Congress, Office of Technology Assessment, *Indian Health Care*, p. 107, Washington D.C., April 1986.

coverage, pediatrics too has become mainly an outpatient activity. The proportion of hospitalized patients below ten years of age (excluding newborns) has declined from 33% in 1959 to 19% in 1982.[9]

The Navajo Area perinatal program illustrates the type of organized network that has been possible within the Indian Health Service. Written guidelines for standards of perinatal care and policies and procedures have been agreed to by all the health care providers, (a "standardization" which is not common

TABLE 35-4
Navajo and total U.S. infant mortality rates (deaths below 1 year, per 1,000 live births)

YEAR	NAVAJO RATE*	U.S. RATE**
1965	46.2	26.0
1970	31.2	20.0
1975	27.8	16.1
1978	15.2	14.0
1980	13.0	12.5
1984	11.8	10.8

*Navajo Area IHS Vital Statistics Reports.
**National Center for Health Statistics.

in the predominantly private U.S. medical practice). Referral patterns are planned *a priori* for various "high risk" conditions and specialists are on stand-by at the medical centers for consultation and service. Results are gratifying with a premature (less than 2500 grams) birth rate of five percent, a neonatal mortality rate of 4.5% and a maternal mortality of zero. All of these perinatal statistics are better than the U.S. total rates.[12]

Table 35-4 shows the steady decline in the Infant Mortality rate. It remains slightly higher than the U.S. rate, due to increased deaths in the post-neonatal period. These excess deaths are generally linked to social and environmental factors.

As community development proceeds, the IHS environmental health staff aims at assuring safe water and waste disposal. In the Navajo Area the task is monumental and 40% of households are still without piped water supply. Rodent control is important as plague is endemic in the wild population.

FUTURE PROSPECTS

As far back as 30 years ago, a few Navajo community leaders began to encourage Navajo citizens to participate in modern health care efforts, in particular with the Tuberculosis control program of that time. This "unofficial" work expanded into an organized Tribal Health Department, with efforts concentrated in the areas of prevention and health education. The tribal government has allocated some of its health budget to employ Community Health Representatives, lay workers who collaborate with the public health nurses, sanitarians and clinics. They form vital links with the families and communities and interpret their health needs and demands back to the Navajo Indian Health Service program. A group of concerned Navajo people formed a family planning association and have been teaching the values of child spacing.

However, as can readily be seen in the tables, the now dominant socio-medical problems are not as easily influenced by either the tribal or federal health care programs. The problems are the products of behavioral factors—in turn, largely a result of changes.[1]

The rapid changes in mortality due to infectious causes, reduction of infant mortality as well as extension of life expectancy among the Navajos has all been accomplished mainly through the provision of public health interventions such as immunizations and sanitary engineering, and an organized system of clinical care provided with funding through the U.S. Public Health Service. At the same time the Navajo have experienced improvements in transportation, communication, housing and education which all contribute to health maintenance—*but* not without some cost to previously held values and lifestyles. While several Native American tribes or corporations, most notably in Alaska and Oklahoma, have exercised their prerogative to manage their health care systems themselves by developing government contracts, the Navajo health care administrators have for the most part joined the federal Indian Health Service. It appears that this is mostly due to the huge geographic expanse, making potential tribal centralization of health care delivery and policy more difficult than in the smaller Alaskan and Oklahoman service areas.

The current behaviorally influenced morbidity and mortality patterns will be the greatest challenge to future health programs among the Navajos. Further improvements in these patterns will require significant changes in lifestyle and behavior, and will extensively depend upon internal tribal interest and activities. It is expected that the Navajos themselves will increasingly manage more of health programs in the concerned fields—although continuing to rely on the U.S. Government to provide significant funding.

The Navajo people are scattered within their reservation. Their disinclination to develop a community infrastructure—and even conglomerations of a few families even in those places where new housing has been constructed to accommodate for the job market, seems likely to counteract favorable development. It also adversely affects the now dominating health problems, and their taking of greater responsibility for public health and preventive peripheral services. As has been experienced in other places such as Alaska, a decisive participation in and the running of small village health units or community health aid stations seems to constitute a *sine qua non* for development in the direction of full health. Intensive local contributions from native communities and individuals are a necessity, particularly for control of socio-mental and behaviorally influenced disorders.

The present situation among the Navajo and other reservations in the field of environmental sanitation including "aesthetic sanitation," which is under the Navajos own control, does not indicate sufficient local interest or initiatives.

The very idea of "reservation" may constitute an obstacle to both an intensified cooperation in health services and a changed way of life. It is difficult to see how the existing socio-mental health problems could be solved in the future without a more active integration of Indian Natives with other Americans.

REFERENCES

1. Haraldson, SSR: *Health planning in sparsely populated areas.* Dissertation. University of Gothenburg, Sweden, 1975
2. Haraldson, SSR: *Role of education in preserving of traditional cultures and as development factor.* Amsterdam. Elsevier Science Publishers. Health Policy and Education, 3, 1983 (pp 289-305)
3. Haraldson, SSR: What expectations do we have in respect of front-line health services for adversely situated populations. *Circumpolar Health 84 Proceedings of the Sixth International Council on Circumpolar Health,* edited by R. Fortuine, Seattle, University of Washington Press, 1985. (pp 17-21)
4. U.S. Department of Commerce, Bureau of Census: *1980 Census of Population Ancestry of the Population by State;* Pub #PC80-S1-10; U.S. Government Printing Office, Washington, D.C. 20402
5. U.S. Department of Health & Human Services, Public Health Service; *HHS News,* July 3, 1984, Rockville, Maryland
6. U.S. Department of Health & Human Services, Public Health Service, Program Statistics Branch, *Indian Health Service Chart Series Book, April, 1986.* Rockville, Maryland, 1986
7. Tribal Council Compromises, *Gallup Independent Newspaper,.* Gallup, New Mexico, September 22, 1983, p. 1
8. Apache County 2nd-poorest in U.S., *The Arizona Daily Star,* Tucson, Arizona, March 26, 1986
9. Fischler, R. and Fleshman, C.: Comprehensive Health Services for Developmentally Disabled Navajo Children; *Journal of Developmental and Behavioral Pediatrics,* 1985, 6:1-14
10. Dutton, Bertha: *Navajos and Apaches: The Athabascan Peoples,* Englewood Cliffs, N.J. Prentice-Hall Publishers, 1975
11. Broudy, D. and May, P.: Demographic and Epidemiologic Transition Among the Navajo Indians, *Social Biology:* 1984;30:1-15
12. Wegman, M.: Annual Summary of Vital Statistics—1984, *Pediatrics,* 1985;76:861-871

CHAPTER **36**

The Health Care Beliefs and Values of Mexican-Americans

Bonita R. Reinert, RN, MSN, ANP-C, PhD

According to the 1980 census, there were (at that time) 8,740,500 persons of Mexican origin in the United States, which makes them the second largest and fastest growing minority group in this country.[1] However, these figures do not include the rapidly growing numbers of migrant and undocumented workers who often remain totally outside the dominant American culture. Even among the Mexicans who have been in this country a relatively long time, most of them have steadfastly maintained their traditional Hispanic identity despite pressures to conform to the prevailing American culture. Various factors have been responsible for their slow acculturation, including the self-imposed isolation of many of them in crowded Hispanic barrios. Their voluntary segregation has encouraged both group identification and the preservation of many traditional folk beliefs.[2]

Although the largest concentrations of this ethnic group are in the Southwest, Mexican-Americans have been dispersing to other parts of the country. For this reason, health care providers need to understand something about the blend of folk medicine beliefs and philosophical ideas that make up the health care expectations of this group. Such an understanding will ensure that they render both sensitive and acceptable care to their Mexican-American clients—care that is consistent with this group's cultural beliefs and values.

Reprinted from *Home Healthcare Nurse,* Vol. 4, No. 5, with permission of J. B. Lippincott Co., © 1986.

Practitioners who refuse to accept the significance of Mexican-American traditional ideas about illness may alienate these clients, reinforce their mistrust of Anglo health care professionals, and affect their future decisions about seeking and complying with health care treatment regimens.

MEXICAN-AMERICAN HERITAGE

Few other ethnic minority groups have been as persistent in maintaining their language, cultural beliefs, and traditions as have the Mexican-Americans.[3] Many of their folk medicine beliefs date back to 16th century Spain, where there was a widespread belief in humoral pathology. Humoral pathology, which originated with Hippocrates, was based on the belief that the body was composed of four "humors"—blood, phlegm, black bile, and yellow bile. Illness, therefore, was viewed as an imbalance among these humors, and treatment was directed at restoring balance.

In 1519 Hernán Cortés and his conquistadores brought these beliefs (as well as Catholicism) with them when they came to the New World. During the following 300 years of Spanish military rule, the presence of thousands of Spanish settlers and soldiers led to the gradual assimilation of many of these views by the native Indians. The Spanish-Catholic tradition and Indian heritage produced a mixture of humoral and herbal medicine, which was then passed down from mother to daughter through successive generations.[4] Although most Mexican-Americans probably no longer adhere exclusively to the folk medicine of their ancestors, some folk medicine beliefs have been incorporated into their overall culture. Several authors have noted that there appears to be a strong correlation among low socioeconomic status, low level of acculturation, old age, and a belief in folk medicine.[5-7] Mexican-American folk medicine endures in the United States today primarily as an alternative to scientific medicine for minor medical problems, psychosocial problems, and chronic problems that continue despite treatment by a physician.

ACCESS TO HEALTH CARE

"Language differences, religious affiliation, low income, limited vocational opportunity, and traditional values and beliefs [have contributed to] the cultural distance of Mexican-Americans."[5] Negative stereotyping by other Americans has also added to the isolation of this group. Cultural distance is reflected in Mexican-Americans' access to health care. Many of them are not familiar with available health care services, and many communities do not have bilingual health services. Transportation to clinics that provide low-cost health care is often a problem, as are the complexities and inaccessibility of our indigent health care system. This lack of access for Mexican-Americans is especially important in light of several recent studies. Data from these studies indicate that members of this group frequently experience serious health problems associated with the high stress and frustration of living in poverty. For instance, approximately one third of Mexican-Americans are overweight, their suicide rate has been increasing rapidly, and few of this group are being treated for diagnosed hypertension.[8] The incidence of diabetes among Mexican-Americans is five times the national average, and diabetes-related complications are frequent.[9] Severe diarrhea is common among Mexican-American infants, and children whose parents are poor are at increased risk for flu, pneumonia, otitis media, conjunctivitis, and parasitic infections. Their illnesses are not treated as early, and secondary complications are more frequent (when compared with the general population).[6]

ILLNESS IN THE MEXICAN-AMERICAN FAMILY

The woman is the initial primary health care provider for the Mexican-American family. Medical information is passed down from mother to daughter, and the woman must decide when an illness is beyond their ability to treat it and requires outside help.[10] If she decides that outside help is needed, she usually discusses the symptoms first with family and friends, then she may utilize folk healers, and finally she may consult a physician. Utilization of both traditional and scientific health care providers is not uncommon.

The traditional Mexican belief is that illness results from an imbalance (or disharmony) in the body, and the degree of imbalance will determine the severity of the condition. The imbalance may exist in food, water, air, between man and God, or in the concept of "hot" versus "cold." Therefore, treatment by the woman or a local folk healer entails balancing the disturbing element by means of traditional home remedies. Curanderos (religious healers) attempt to correct imbalances by using prayers, pledges *(mandas)* to religious or supernatural forces, and rituals that utilize candles and artifacts. Yerberos (herbalists) employ home remedies in the form of diets and herbs. Sobadoras (masseuses) massage or manipulate bones and joints to correct musculoskeletal imbalances, and relatives or friends may advise over-the-counter medicines.

The curandero, one of the most frequently utilized folk healers, believes his power comes from God. He is generally a member of the nuclear family or of the extended family network, which includes godparents and close family friends. Although his prescribed treatments may be scientifically questionable, the patient seems to benefit psychologically from the focused attention he receives from the curandero during the healing process.[11] Frequently, the curandero's approach is simply to listen while the family decides on the best course of treatment and then to offer his support. From the perspective of the Mexican-American family, this treatment differs radically from that of the physician, who asks embarrassing questions, ignores family viewpoints and concerns, and then dictates what the treatment will be. The actual care and treatment provided by a curandero takes place in the community, is not limited to certain business hours, and is usually paid for in the form of a donation. This type of health care is, therefore, generally within the means of indigent families when compared with scientific medicine and its expensive treatments and medicines.

If the illness is quite serious or resists treatment, the woman may seek outside help from a physician or utilize help from several sources simultaneously.[12] "Usually, two symptoms are considered in determining the severity of an illness — pain and the appearance of blood."[10] Illnesses that do not follow typical patterns may also be considered serious enough to require outside help.

Many Mexican-Americans believe that some disorders are natural since they have frequently been experienced by others; these disorders are viewed as harmless or minor problems. Other, less common, disorders are thought to be the will of God *(sea por Dios)* or punishment for wrongdoing. This etiology may be assigned to disorders that are not well understood, thus making early treatment and prevention regimens a low priority among most Mexican-American clients.[13] A long-term illness such as a chronic cough may be believed to be part of one's destiny (destino) and, therefore, something that simply must be endured stoically.

COMMON CLINICAL SYNDROMES

Four of the most common clinical syndromes among Mexican-Americans are *caida de la mollera, empacho, mal de ojo,* and *susto.*

1. Caida de la mollera ("fallen fontanelle") is a condition that can occur in any infant until the anterior fontanelle (or soft spot) closes. The traditional Mexican belief is that this disorder arises from bouncing or dropping the infant or removing the nipple too roughly from its mouth. Symptoms associated with the condition include diarrhea, restlessness, an inability to suck or grasp firmly with the mouth, and occasional fever. Folk treatment includes prayers, pushing up the palate from inside the infant's mouth, holding the child by the feet over a pan of tepid water, and applying eggs or warm salted olive oil to the skull. Since the usual cause of this condition is *severe* dehydration (about 10%), proper medical treatment is essential. Scientific medical treatment usually includes carefully balanced intravenous fluids to correct the fluid and electrolyte imbalance as well as the hyperosmolar state.

2. Empacho ("blocked intestine"). According to ethnographic research, individuals of any age can be affected, but infants, children, adolescents, and women in the immediate postpartum period are at highest risk for this condition.[17] The traditional Mexican view holds that this disorder is due to a bolus of food that has become stuck to the abdominal lining. Symptoms include abdominal pain, vomiting, lack of appetite, or crying. Treatment consists of massage and drinking herbal cathartics. Cathartics are routinely used to prevent *empacho* and keep the stomach clean, but this practice can lead to laxative abuse and chronic bowel problems. Furthermore, potentially toxic substances have been used in the Southwest as part of the folk treatment for this condition.[14]

3. Mal de ojo ("evil eye") can affect people of all ages, but certain individuals are thought to be particularly susceptible, especially pregnant women and young children. Persons thought to have this power can cause illness or misfortune by gazing admiringly or enviously at others. Symptoms associated with this disorder include headaches, weeping, high fever, fretfulness, aches, and pains. The traditional view is that family members should first try to locate the individual who caused the problem. The simplest treatment is to have the person with the evil eye touch the victim. This touch is supposed to break the evil bond and relieve the symptoms. When the person responsible cannot be found, treatment consists of placing an egg in water under the head of the bed where the patient sleeps in order to draw out the evil force. While the folk treatment is being attempted, the family is not likely to seek scientific medical care.

4. Susto ("fright sickness") can affect people of all ages. The traditional Mexican view is that this condition is due to a frightening or upsetting experience. Its symptoms include languor, listlessness, and anorexia. Treatment by a curandero consists of rubbing the patient's body with special herbs, administering herbal teas and sugar water, and prayers. Rubel and associates found that patients suffering from susto may have a serious disease and should be carefully evaluated.[15]

RENDERING APPROPRIATE HEALTH CARE

Although it is important to understand Mexican-American clients' ideas about disease, it is equally important to understand what they view as appropriate treatment and acceptable behavior on the part of health care providers. For example, Mexican-Americans have strong family ties; the family is a large, closely knit group consisting of both nuclear and extended members. The male is the traditional head of the family and his sense of machismo requires that he be consulted before decisions are made and that he be included in any counseling sessions. Health care providers should be sensitive to the fact that Mexican-American males find it difficult to tolerate any loss of authority or self-esteem, even in the presence of their immediate family.

Important decisions may require consultation among the entire family. Family decisions can supersede the priorities set by the health care provider. However, the family also serves as a strong, natural support system for the patient, which can help him cope with illness or disability. Any extended hospitalization is likely to cause high levels of anxiety and stress for both the patient and the family. If the hospital is located some distance from the patient's hometown, housing arrangements should be made (if possible) so that the family can remain close to the patient.

Modesty is important for the Mexican-American patient. Consulting a scientific medical practitioner can be embarrassing. Mexican-American patients may feel ill at ease in discussing sexual matters with a health care provider of the opposite sex. For Spanish-speaking patients, it is essential that the translator (if one is used) be of the same sex as the patient. The patient should be kept covered as much as possible during the physical exam, and all procedures should be explained in advance. Males may refuse parts of a physical exam or treatment if it threatens their modesty. Women may be reluctant to undertake patient care at home if it means they must touch a male's genitalia, even if the male is their son. Health care providers need to be aware of these considerations when they examine patients or explain home treatments.

Finally, it is particularly difficult to explain symptomless illnesses to Mexican-American patients. "Mexican-Americans perceive illness as a state of physical discomfort. The most common criteria of good health are a sturdy body, the ability to maintain a high level of normal physical activity, and the absence of persistent pain and discomfort."[7] Illnesses such as early diabetes, hypertension, or cancer may not present initially with pain or require any restrictions on activities. Therefore, the Mexican-American patient may refuse to comply with treatment. These illnesses should be explained in simple physiologic terms using diagrams and illustrations if possible. An explanation of secondary complications (eg, sores that heal slowly) can improve patient understanding and compliance. A thorough description of the pathophysiology of a disorder and the reasons for treatment can prevent future misunderstandings and confusion.

CULTURAL SENSITIVITY

If health care providers have a working knowledge of the culture of an ethnic group, they can more accurately interpret and influence their patient's behaviors. "Cultural sensitivity evolves from learning about the values, beliefs, and attitudes from which behavior arises as opposed to esoteric cultural patterns of behavior."[16]

If there are no more than two or three minority groups in a given community, one way to learn how to work with them is through the use of a cultural awareness workshop.[17] The workshop should include primary health care providers and representatives of the several minority groups. Spokespersons from each group should be asked to present information on such topics as their folk medicine beliefs, their group's access to health care, and the cultural factors that have influenced their health care beliefs. The participants should then be divided into small (culturally mixed) groups and given scenarios for discussion. These scenarios might deal with areas where cultural misunderstandings could arise, such as the importance of the family, the responsibilities of the patient and the provider in a health care relationship, the significance of specific physical symptoms, the significance of different types of medical treatment, and office routines that could prove embarrassing to the patient. After a specified time, these discussions should be continued in the larger group for general clarification.

A specialist in communication techniques might be invited to explain effective communication patterns, and videotaped interactions might be presented for discussion. Enough time should be allowed for the participants to practice communicating through the use of role-playing.

Finally, the participants might be encouraged to offer suggestions on health care services needed in their area. A general plan could then be developed using these suggestions. Volunteers from each group might be selected to review the plan and discuss how it could be implemented.

When working with minority groups, health care providers should try to incorporate their traditional cultural beliefs into scientific medical treatments. For example, fever is sometimes believed to be caused by an imbalance involving too much heat. If the patient needs to consume a large amount of cool fluids, this could be explained as a means of correcting the prevailing imbalance. Some folk treatments are actually less harmful than over-the-counter medications; for example, the use of herbal tea is preferable to a drug for promoting sleep. Such remedies should be encouraged. Other treatments that are not dangerous should be allowed if they provide mental comfort for the patient and family; for example, the practice of wearing religious articles to drive away evil spirits. Finally, in caring for Mexican-American clients, health care providers should try to learn a little medical Spanish. Even a few words will help the patient feel more at ease and will help to bridge the communication gap. Many educational opportunities are lost when the health care provider cannot speak directly to the patient.

SUMMARY

The most important tools that the health care provider can develop to ensure successful interactions with clients of a different cultural background are good communication skills and an understanding of their cultural beliefs and values. The client's definition of his illness will directly affect his willingness to seek help and his acceptance of treatment.

Although not all Mexican-Americans believe in the full range of folk medicine practices or utilize the services of folk healers, it is important for health care practitioners to understand this group's traditional beliefs regarding the etiology of health problems. Whenever possible, medical treatment should incorporate these cultural beliefs. By developing cultural sensitivity, health care practitioners can provide a humane and holistic form of health care.

REFERENCES

1. US Dept of Commerce: *1980 Census of Population: Persons of Spanish Origin by State.* Supplemental Report PC80-S1-7. Washington, DC, 1980.
2. Munhart NT, McCaffery M: *Pain: A Nursing Approach to Assessment and Analysis.* Norwalk, Conn, Appleton-Century-Crofts, 1983, pp 119-127.
3. Moore JW, Cuellar A: *Mexican American.* Englewood Cliffs, NJ, Prentice-Hall, 1970.
4. Chesney AP, Thompson BL, Guerara A, et al: Mexican American folk medicine: Implications for the family physician. *J Fam Pract* 1980;11(4):567-574.
5. Sandler AP, Chan LS: Mexican American folk beliefs in a pediatric emergency room. *Med Care* 1978;16(9):778-784.
6. Rodriguez J: Mexican Americans: Factors influencing health practices. *J Sch Health* 1983;2:136-139.
7. Abril IF: Mexican American folk beliefs: How they affect health care. *Am J Matern Child Nurs* 1977;2(3):168-173.
8. Clayton WE: Hispanic health linked to culture. *Houston Chronicle* 1985 (Nov 20):6.
9. Special Committee on Diabetes Service in Texas: *Special Report to the 68th Legislature,* State of Texas, 1983.
10. Gonzalez-Swafford MJ, Gutierrez MG: Ethnomedical beliefs and practices of Mexican Americans. *Nurse Pract* 1983;(6):29-34.
11. Maduro R: Curanderismo and latino views of disease and curing. *West J Med* 1983;139(12):868-874.
12. Tamez EC: Curanderism: Folk Mexican-American health care system. *JPN and Ment Health Serv* 1978;12:34-38.
13. Scheper-Hughes N: Curanderismo in Taos County, New Mexico—A possible case of anthropological romanticism. *West J Med* 1983;139(12).
14. Trotter RT: Folk medicine in the Southwest. *Postgrad Med* 1985;78(8):167-179.
15. Rubel AJ, O'Nell CW, Collado R: *Susto: A Folk Illness.* Berkeley, Calif, University of California Press, 1984.
16. Chaney H, Poteet G, Saydjari CA: Management of culturally diverse employees, in Vance C (ed): *Group Processes in Nursing.* To be published.
17. Poteet GW: Ethnic diversity. *J Nurs Adm* 1986;16(3):6.

Suggested Additional Readings for Part VI

Culture and community health nursing practice

Airhihenbuwa, C.O., Health education of African Americans: A neglected task, *Health Education,* Volume 20, Number 5, 1989, pp. 9-14.

Anderson, G. and Tighe, B., Gypsy culture and health care, *American Journal of Nursing,* Feb 1973, Volume 2, pp. 283-85 or 256-262.

Anesnensel, C.S., Fielder, E.P. & Becerra, R.M. (1989). Fertility and fertility-related behavior among Mexican American and non-hispanic white female adolescents. *Health and Social Behavior, 30*(1), 56-76.

Bernal, H. and R. Froman. (1987). The confidence of community health nurses in caring for ethnically diverse populations. *Image 19*(4):201-3.

Braithwaite, R.L., Murphy, F., Lythcott, N., Blumenthal, D.S., Community organization and development for health promotion within an urban black community: A conceptual model, *Health Education,* Volume 20, Number 5, 1989, pp. 56-60.

Davis, K., Lillie-Blanton, M., Lyons, B., Mullan, F., Powe, N., and Rowland, D., Health care for black Americans, the public sector role, *Mailbank Quarterly,* Volume 65, Supplemental 1, 1987, pp. 213-247.

Doyle, E., Smith, C.A., Hosokawa, M.C., A process evaluation of a community staff base health promotion program for a minority target population, *Health Education,* Volume 20, Number 5, 1989, pp. 61-64.

Flaherty, Sr. M.J., Seven caring functions of black grandmothers in adolescent mothering, *Maternal-Child Nursing Journal,* Fall 1988, Volume 17, Number 3, pp. 191-207.

Iskander, R. (1987). Developing a black consciousness . . . health needs of black communities. *Nursing Times 83(42):66-69.*

Leininger, M.M., Leininger's theory of nursing: Cultural care diversity and universality, *Nursing Science Quarterly,* Volume 1, Number 4, pp. 152-160.

Leininger, M.M., Transcultural eating patterns and nutrition: Transcultural nursing and anthropological perspectives, *Holistic Nursing Practice,* Nov 1988, Volume 3, Number 1, pp. 16-25.

Miller, S.M., Race in the health of America, *Mailbank Quarterly,* Volume 65, Supplemental 2, 1987, pp. 500-531.

Smith, K.G. (1986). The Hazards of migrant farm work: an overview for rural health nurses. *Public Health Nursing 3(1):48-56.*

PART VII

FAMILY AND COMMUNITY HEALTH NURSING PRACTICE

The family is the oldest and most basic of all social institutions. Through the family, children are socialized to norms, values, behavior, language, and beliefs. As such, the family influences health beliefs and behavior. The family functions as a unit and can be viewed as a client by the community health nurse. The family has developmental tasks, just as the individual members do; it also performs specific functions, such as physical and emotional care of its members. The assessment of family functioning and its ability to meet the health needs of its members is an important aspect of the community health nurse's practice. The family's level of functioning will greatly influence the nurse's plan of care. A family made up of an unemployed single mother and three small children may have a low level of functioning which influences each one of its members' physical, emotional, and social health.

The American family has undergone significant and profound changes. The familiar stereotype of a family composed of a husband who works, a wife who stays at home, and two children is no longer the norm. In fact, it constitutes less than eight percent of U.S. families. Women are working outside the home in record numbers, people are choosing to postpone marriage and parenthood, families are growing smaller, and there has been a significant increase in the number of one-parent families, generally those headed by women. In addition, families are more frequently assuming responsibility for care of aging patients. All of these trends continue to have important influences on the family's ability to maintain its level of health functioning. Various aspects of family life are addressed in Part Seven. Articles included provide the nurse with assessment methods along with specific examples of various family issues related to community health nursing practice.

CHAPTER 37

Family-Based Practice: Discussion of a Tool Merging Assessment With Intervention

Cheryl Ann Lapp, RN, MPH, MA
Carol Ann Diemert, RN, MS
Ruth Enestvedt, RN, MS

FAMILY ASSESSMENT GUIDELINES: DISCUSSION OF A TOOL FOR USE WITH FAMILIES

Making a Family-Focused Approach a Reality in Professional Practice

The family forms the basic unit of our society; it is the social institution that has the most marked effect on its members.[1] It seems logical, therefore, that caregivers should be equipped to use an orientation to the family whenever professional practice claims to serve families. In nursing, for example, the family as a whole has been an early and enduring focus of care. From the very foundation of professional nursing, written evidence can be found of patient care considered within the context of family life. In the 1850s Florence Nightingale's vision of nursing encompassed more than organizing care for patient "soldiers"; she worked to see that the sick wives and children of soldiers were included in her written justification to improve hospital accommodations. She discussed the privacy and financial needs of families when they joined the soldiers at military camp, and she wrote detailed directions to the army for the improved treatment of the women and children in military camps.[2]

In keeping with the importance of viewing people in context, a comprehensive family intervention guide has recently been designed for professionals working with families. It uses theory to direct data gathering and explores desired behavior change with family members. In this way family members can be actively engaged in the process of decision making regarding self-health priorities. The family perspective serves to expand the scope of practice, to increase insight, to allow for case finding, and to move health intervention to a more holistic dimension. Empirically, people actively engaged in practice professions have realized that quality of family life is intertwined with the health of its members. However, there has been less clarity among professionals about how to support and to promote such complex interaction.

To carry the nursing example further, despite its historical traditions, practice today frequently deemphasizes the family as the foundational perspective. People are often portrayed as passive recipients of care, completely helpless and isolated from the social context of family, friends, neighbors, or pets. But

Reprinted from *Family and Community Health,* Vol. 12, No. 4, with permission of Aspen Publishers, Inc., © 1990.

ironically, now more than ever, nursing practice needs to encompass the family to continue to meet societal needs for a healthy citizenry.

Familism Versus Individualism

Society has a predominant cultural view that minimizes collective need in favor of individualism. Illness-based reimbursement is but one example of the current health care system that directs our practice but that runs counter to public health convictions about serving the public good.

One possible way to improve professional practice is to change the way professionals are being educated. Undergraduate students especially may have difficulty making a connection between giving care to individuals and then viewing these individuals in their relational context as members of families. The problem is how to shift student learning from an individual to a social unit of analysis. The educational process may be flawed when sequenced learning, in which clinical skills are taught in isolation from an early introduction to family theory and contextual information, occurs. Another factor not to be overlooked is the influence of the mainstream cultural orientation in North America that contributes to the perceptual struggle between individualism and "familism," which refers to the deep importance attached to the family by its members.[3] Today's student professionals may acknowledge familism, yet they consistently fall back into an individualistic perspective.[4]

Family assessment guidelines: intervention with families

Family/social network
- Family tradition
- Developmental stages—life events
- Living environment/household constellation
  1. Space/privacy
  2. Physical safety/comfort/accessibility
  3. Animal companionship/protection

Neighborhood environment
- Stability and direction of change
- Degree of homogeneity
- Proximity and access to essential services

Family health: Family perceived
- Strengths and limitations
- Satisfaction with health behaviors—maintenance/disruption of life patterns

Social and financial resources
- Social support—open *v* closed system
- Availability and choices regarding leisure time
- Adequacy of income sources of economic stability
- Management of financial, legal, and protective affairs

Life style
- Values/goals
- Communication/decision making
- Role/flexibility
- Use of resources

Priority issues
- Further exploration
- Summary

FAMILY ASSESSMENT GUIDELINES: FAMILIES AS PARTNERS

One way to assist students of community health to "think family" was to develop family assessment guidelines (see the box). These guidelines are presented with an emphasis on family as partner in health care decision making, a philosophic position consistent with an interpretation of self-care in which decisional control belongs within the realm of the consumer.[5] In keeping with our interpretation of the self-care perspective, the authors view the primary responsibility for health and life choices as ultimately resting with the client family. The authors see the main responsibility of the professional as ensuring that those choices were made on the basis of the most complete information possible while facilitating self-discovery of strengths and resources already existing for a family. With this interpretation of the practice role, these guidelines were designed for use together with families so that all aspects of information gathering would be "family perceived" as well as "professional perceived." The intent of the partnership here is to clarify discrepant views and to discover fresh alternatives for action.

In a partnership context, assessment becomes intervention as new insight and understanding emerge for both the family and practitioner. Active participation is important at every step of the clinical judgment process, beginning with information gathering. But the assessment phase of professional decision making is not a separate preliminary task to be completed before moving to intervention. Rather, assessment and intervention make up a dynamic process that occurs simultaneously.

THEORETICAL CONTRIBUTIONS TO FAMILY ASSESSMENT

Another factor influencing the development of the guidelines was the use of valued content in family theory. After several classical theoretical perspectives had been reviewed and discussed, students were able to apply major relevant concepts in their processing of information. They saw how the theoretical foundations could, at times, assist them in understanding family life in their familiar cultural context. Selected theoretical perspectives that were incorporated into this family assessment included structural-functional theory,[2,6] family developmental theory,[2,7] systems theory,[8] interactional theory,[6] and conflict theory.[9]

While conducting home visits, community nursing students were often able to use each one of these contributing perspectives as they generated their interview questions in an open-ended format. The actual areas of concentration were sequenced to progress from the structural and the least invasive to the more analytic and value laden in recognition of the needed opportunity for family members to establish a trust level on which to base a therapeutic relationship. The guidelines do not prescribe the questions to be asked of families but instead allow for an exploratory and interactional experience in which the content and pace is mutually defined.

Clients benefit by becoming energized and affirmed when actively engaged in a meaningful relationship focused on their own decision making about family health priorities. The "visitor" discovers that a built-in component of validating professional judgment is family perception, a key element providing direction for mutual agreement as to which family goals will be pursued. For both parties the qualitative nature of the information gathering lends to the interaction a richness and depth facilitated by the attainment of trust and rapport. The data itself, true to the strengths of the qualitative style, is dynamic and powerful, in contrast to the limitations of fixed-response format frequently seen in questionnaires and flow sheets.

From the standpoint of educators, this mutual experience engages inductive reasoning.[10] The authors value this approach because students can move from the particular information presented by families to appropriate theoretical perspectives that reflect what examination of the data reveals. The less desirable alternative would be for the student to artificially mold family data to fit a preselected framework.

ASSESSMENT COMPONENTS

Family/Social Network

When considering what constitutes family, in its variety of configurations, family can sometimes be characterized as an "attitude" revealing identification with significant others.[11] One cannot underestimate the importance of social networks of informal support. Particularly for the elderly, friends and neighbors respond to three types of needs: socialization, conducting the tasks of daily living, and assisting in times of need.[12] These closely parallel the classic functions that families are charged with fulfilling for dependent members: social, physical, and affectional.[13] As Peters and Kaiser[12] point out, "there are often cases of long-lived friendships in which the friends actually think of one another as being like relatives and not just as friends."[12(p131)] Although much is yet to be learned about the role of friendship, neighboring, and confidant relationships in social support, research suggests that the role of friendship takes on added importance at certain times in the life course, appears to hold different meaning for women than for men throughout adult life, and may vary with different ethnic group conceptions of friendship.[12]

Once the family boundaries have been clarified, the task unfolds to describe its structure. This is frequently accomplished by using a tool called the family genogram. Its origins are found in the discipline of cultural anthropology, and it usually consists of a three-generational "picture" of a family depicting such things as sex, age, birth order, and lineage.[14] Other basic data can be added to depict such things as religious practices or hereditary conditions. When beginning to explore a family system with family members, the genogram is a "warming" mechanism. As an introductory strategy, it is a relatively noninvasive way to obtain a great deal of information quickly. It is also an activity where participation by family members is frequently enjoyed. Family members tend to ask questions of one another about their parents and grandparents, taking renewed interest in information that has been rediscovered. The structure is diagrammed according to a coded "legend." Such legends may also reveal the existence of family members who are currently absent from the household or those who are deceased but for whom a perceived "presence" is still maintained. The genogram activity is useful for providing insight into cultural factors, acknowledgment of unique family rituals, and family traditions that may be formalized through intergenerational transmission. Usually family members who helped construct the genogram value the experience enough to want a copy left with them.

Once the structural configuration of the family is outlined in genogram form, the developmental stage of the family can be observed and validated with family members. Family developmental theory would direct us to look at the progress of the oldest child or the activity of the breadwinner to discover the positioning of the family in the life cycle. However, in the application of these concepts to assessment and intervention, it is helpful to consider which stages may be occurring simultaneously. Very seldom, if ever, can families progress through the life cycle neatly, completing each task before proceeding to the next. It is important to consider with the family how many of the developmental stages have been successfully completed and for each stage which tasks are considered by the family to be accomplished.

The category "life events" encompasses an area that may not have been logically included in consideration of developmental stages but nevertheless may signify important turning points. One may refer to events that require family accommodation or adjustment, such as a move to a new home or a change in employment. The important feature to keep in mind is the view of family as a social system. General systems theory is based on the premise that all parts are interrelated and that anything affecting one component will influence the family as a whole due to the interdependent and dynamic nature of the system's structure. Therefore if one accepts systems theory, one may project that anything experienced as a significant life event to any one family member will, to some degree, be significant for the family as a whole. In practical terms, this gives us a perspective on the reality that in routine home-visit situations, even though not all family members are likely to be present, the impact of absent members can be felt.

Consideration of living environment and household constellation reminds one to consider the immediate physical environment of the family as it responds to the existing structural-functional configuration. As stated earlier, functional theory holds the family responsible for providing the physical necessities — space, safety, and comfort — for the survival and nurturance of its members. This leads us to assess the internal environment for its safety and support to family members of all ages, offering opportunity for immediate intervention if unsafe situations or conditions are recognized.

Neighborhood Environment

In seeking to work with families, it is important to appreciate the contextual data of the surrounding community. Attention should be given to sociologic features of human group life such as relative stability or transiency and gentrification or deterioration of neighborhoods. The degree of homogeneity, with regard to demographic data and trends toward integration, may give us a clearer picture of such features as ethnic enclaves and how these may serve to enrich or to complicate a sense of the common bond of community life. Especially important environmental factors are perceptions about access to essential services as access is experienced by representative groups such as the elderly.

Family Health: Family Perceived

A major philosophic and practical strength in the intervention guide has to do with the position of family partnership in the decision making regarding self-health priorities. Family perceptions of health are basic, along with professional judgments, to the exploration of any described behavior change in family members. Family strengths,[15] awareness of resources, and satisfaction with health behaviors are explored together with family members.

Social and Financial Resources

Familiarity with the resources available to the family, both material and human, is needed in conjunction with exploration of appropriate and realistic options for intervention. These are increasingly personal areas of data gathering; thus the interviewer would be well advised to review the reasons for requesting such information. For example, insight may be gained regarding the social system's openness to informational exchange. Family choices in the management of resources as they pertain to economic realities and leisure time will reveal the family power structure inherent in structural-functional theory, where role expectations are prescribed and interpreted with the goal of maintaining the unit.

Life Style

The area of life style encompasses decisions over which people have some control. Life-style choices are greatly affected by a family's values as well as by its access to resources.[16] Values expressed are largely determined by cultural background but are mediated by numerous other factors, hence the wide variation in values held among families sharing a common culture. The emphasis on internal dynamics of family life described within interactional theory describes shared meanings and how communication by and within families may be interpreted.[6] Where resources are considered finite, conflict theory focuses on social justice and human nature in its perpetual struggle to balance self-interest against the needs of others. Conflict theory is particularly useful in examining the sexual division of labor in the home and work place, analyzing family life based on social class interests and unequal gender-related access to limited resources.[9]

Priority Issues

Based on information gathered with the family, decisions can be made that incorporate both family and professional perception of need. It is important once again to compare and to contrast these perceptions, for this process may point to the criteria by which priority issues will be decided. For example, the potential for success of any identified goal will largely depend on such things as family commitment to behavior change, awareness of resources, or sources of power within the family. Key issues may be classified as long-term or short-term according to the estimated time frame of action. Some goals established may be amenable to immediate intervention, some may be beyond immediacy and may require consultation or referral, while others may be transferred completely to families within the self-care realm of responsibility.

• • •

The guide for family intervention was developed with nursing application as a frame of reference. It has also been tested since 1985 by senior baccalaureate nursing students. In the tradition of public health nursing that primarily serves disadvantaged populations, students have been working with client families who frequently make up vulnerable groups. Many of these are low-income, socially isolated, mentally confused, minority, functionally disabled, or elderly persons. In the authors' experience to date, these family assessment guidelines appear to accommodate culturally and socially diverse groups.

This family assessment perspective need not be restricted to nursing. It may well be that if a tradition of care is enriched by emphasizing mutuality with the family, this contribution could also extend to other professionals, such as social workers, clergy, and counselors/therapists, who strive for a family-based orientation.

REFERENCES

1. Friedman M: *Family Nursing: Theory and Assessment,* ed 2. Norwalk, Conn, Appleton-Century-Crofts, 1986.
2. Whall A: The family as the unit of care in nursing: A historical review. *Public Health Nurs* 1986;3(4):240-249.
3. Friedman M: Keynote address. International Family Nursing Conference, Calgary, Alberta, Canada, May 25, 1988.
4. Dreher M: The conflict of conservatism in public health nursing education. *Nurs Outlook* 1982;30(9):504-509.

5. Levin L: Patient education and self-care: How do they differ? *Nurs Outlook* 1978;26(3):170-175.
6. Nye F, Berardo F (eds): *Emerging Conceptual Frameworks in Family Analysis.* New York, Praeger, 1981.
7. Duvall E: *Marriage and Family Development.* Philadelphia, Lippincott, 1971.
8. Hazzard M: An overview of systems theory. *Nurs Clin North Am* 1971;6(3):385-393.
9. Burr W, Hill R, Nye F, et al: *Contemporary Theories about the Family,* vol 2. New York, Free Press, 1979.
10. Glaser B, Strauss A: *The Discovery of Grounded Theory: Strategies for Qualitative Research.* Chicago, Aldine Publishing, 1973.
11. Tufte V, Myerhoff B (eds): *Changing Images of the Family.* New Haven, Conn, Yale University Press, 1979.
12. Peters G, Kaiser M: The role of friends and neighbors in providing social support, in Sauer W, Coward R (eds): *Social Support Networks and the Care of the Elderly.* New York, Springer, 1985.
13. Murray R, Zentner J: *Nursing Concepts for Health Promotion,* ed 2. Englewood Cliffs, NJ, Prentice Hall, 1979.
14. Starkey P: Genograms: A guide to understanding one's own family system. *Perspect Psychiatr Care* 1981;19(5&6): 164-173.
15. Otto H: A framework for assessing family strengths. *Fam Proc* 1972;2:329-339.
16. Steinman M, Lapp C, Mowery A: Community health nurses battle economic crunch by matching services to needs. *Nurs Health Care* 1985;6(10):553-557.

CHAPTER **38**

Health Promotion in the Family: Current Findings and Directives for Nursing Research*

Mary E. Duffy, RN, PhD

THE FAMILY

The family influences the lifestyles—health and non-health behaviors—and health status of its members. As the basic unit of health care management, the family assumes responsibility for at least 75% of all health care provided to its members—health promotion, disease prevention, early intervention, and rehabilitation. Nursing research is contributing to the development of a knowledge base which describes the interaction between family dynamics and the prevention and treatment of diseases. However, researchers have neglected to study with comparable zeal the health promotion activities of the family. Although the family is a client of nursing (American Nurses' Association 1980, World Health Organization 1985) the majority of health promotion research reported in the nursing research journals are studies of individuals. The purposes of this paper are to review the current nursing research findings on health promotion within the family and to provide directives for future research.

HEALTH PROMOTION

According to Pender (1982) health promotion is those 'activities directed toward *sustaining* or *increasing* the level of well-being, self-actualization, and personal fulfillment.' In contrast to disease or primary prevention—the specific protection from a health threat—the purpose of health promotion is a generalized enhancement of well-being. The generalized nature of health promotion suggests it is or should be an integrated component of the lifestyle of individuals and families and of the environment created by the social structure. Health promotion behaviours are used to increase the level of adaptive health for an individual or group and not to remove a specific threat to health. This latter health goal defines disease or primary prevention behaviours. For example, an individual may begin a health programme of jogging and weight loss. If the goal is primary prevention, the health behaviours might be undertaken specifically to decrease the risk of heart disease. However, if the goal is health promotion, the same health behaviours could lead to an enhancement in overall healthiness: emotional, feelings of exuberance; physical, increased strength and stamina; and social, improvements in the quantity and quality of relationships. Similarly, the family that applies the principles of health promotion to its lifestyle may prioritize

*This paper was adapted from an earlier version presented at the International Nursing Research Conference, Edmonton, Canada, May 1986.

Reprinted from *Journal of Advanced Nursing,* Vol. 13, with permission of American Journal of Nursing, © 1988.

family recreational time since it is an opportunity for the individuals to spend time in an activity that is enjoyable for them and brings them closer together physically and emotionally.

At the environmental level, health promotion is the development of an environment which is conducive to overall healthiness. These conditions are more than the essential characteristics of an environment designed to eliminate specific health problems such as smallpox, lead poisoning, adolescent suicide, or smoking behaviours. Instead, health promotion alters the underlying social structure which creates the stressors that lead, eventually, to specific health problems. These stressors include economic and social policies which affect the distribution of basic resources including food, shelter, sanitation and safety. 'Current assessment of world health policy indicates that lack of basic needs is the primary barrier to wellness' (McFarlane 1985).

While health promotion and disease prevention behaviours are not mutually exclusive activities, it is important to differentiate between the two concepts. Since health promotion has a broader focus than primary prevention, the definition of health changes in the health promotion framework. Health is not merely the absence of disease or the risks of disease but it is 'a dynamic state of being in which the developmental and behavioural potential of an individual is realized to the fullest extent possible' (ANA 1980). When these conceptual distinctions are applied to research, the ensuing directives for health promotion research and those for primary or disease prevention research are quite varied (Merritt 1986). Health promotion research addresses the general health of the population and the development of that population to its fullest potential. Disease prevention research investigates factors specific to a particular illness, disability or condition and the interventions necessary to prevent the problem.

Lifestyles

In practice and in research, the study of health promotion is inseparable from the study of lifestyles, typical ways of life. The behaviours associated with health promotion are the components of the family's lifestyle. Exercise, good nutrition, stress reduction, hygiene, and rest become part of the family's daily routine, a lifestyle shaped by a philosophy of health. This integration between a philosophy of health and the family's lifestyle does not develop in isolation within the family. Societal factors influence the health perceptions of family members and the emotional, physical and material ability of the family to incorporate health promotion into its lifestyle.

According to Milio (1985), health instruction works; that is, behaviour change results, when individual or family education is reinforced by a social and political climate which supports a healthy environment. Issues of concern at this level include media portrayals of violence, alcohol use, and smoking; the distribution of material resources; access to health care; and the provision of basic human needs; housing, food, employment, etc. Individuals, families, and societies that practice health promotion behaviours are concerned with the impact of all their activities — from individual decisions to societal policies — on the health of individuals, families and the community. Therefore, a research agenda on family health promotion must look at the effects of the internal and external environments of the family on their health promotion behaviours.

NURSING AND HEALTH PROMOTION

The conceptual distinction between health promotion and primary prevention is very important in nursing since nurses provide a large part of health care, not medical care, in most countries (WHO 1985). Health promotion guides the nurse and client away from a definition of health as the absence of disease and towards a concern with generalized well-being. This latter concern directs the focus of care and research to the lifestyle and environment of the client. The enhancement of well-being in the presence or absence of disease becomes a legitimate arena for nursing practice, research and education.

The following examples describe health promotion issues that are concerns of nursing at the local, national and international levels. For example, in western countries lifestyle contributes over 50% to the development of chronic illnesses (Dever 1980) and for many children these lifestyle patterns have led to the development of at least one risk factor for cardiovascular disease before the age of 12 years (William *et al.* 1981). The affluence which leads to the diseases of excess in the developed countries overshadows the grave conditions of the poor in these same countries. In the United States there are 35 million poor Americans and 13.3 million of those poor are children. The State of Maine Child Death Survey estimated that 10,000 American children die each year from poverty (Children's Defense Fund 1985). The report indicates that each year poor children are three times more likely to die than non-poor children. More specifically, poverty in American children is concentrated in certain ethnic groups: 48% of the poor children are black, and 38% are hispanic, compared to 17% who are caucasian.

These same contrasting patterns of excess and impoverishment seen in the United States are present between developed and developing countries. Lifestyle patterns and the environment threaten well-being throughout the world. In developing countries insufficient environmental resources perpetuate lifestyles characterized by inadequate nutrition, unsanitary conditions, mobility, and other factors which prevent families from realizing their potential well-being. These families can only be concerned with survival in environments which perpetuate malnutrition and disease.

The international arena becomes a significant environment for families in poor countries. The willingness of resource rich countries like the United States to contribute to the development of poorer countries is a political decision. Yet it is the financial and people power assistance that many countries need to supplement their own plans and actions. In a recent issue of *The Nations Health,* a newsletter of the American Public Health Association, Ruth Roemer (1986), the association's president, reported on the health promotion outcome in a poor, developing country of Asia when money from the community and central government was combined with multilateral and bilateral foreign aid. The result was the construction of structures which make available safe water and ventilated pit-latrines for each household. This example of international co-operation describes health promotion at its most rudimentary level in a developing country.

Nursing is in a position to have an impact on the decisions made in each of the preceding situations. Through research focused on health and health promotion, nurses can create an improvement in the well-being of individuals, families and communities. Since the family is the basic unit of health care, the study of health promotion activities in the family should be a critical area of concern for nurse researchers. If 'health for all' is to be reached by the year 2000 (WHO 1979), health promotion in the family must be prioritized on the nursing research agendas.

HEALTH PROMOTION RESEARCH: THE NURSING RESEARCH JOURNALS

Current findings indicate that research of health promotion in the family is, for all essential purposes, non-existent in the nursing research journals. Four nursing research journals—*Nursing Research, Research in Nursing and Health, Western Journal of Nursing Research* and *International Journal of Nursing Studies*—were reviewed to identify the number and types of studies related to health promotion in the family which were published between January 1980 and June 1986. Health promotion in the family was defined as follows: those health activities undertaken by a unit consisting of at least one adult caretaker and one child for the purposes of sustaining or enhancing the level of physical, emotional, and social well-being of the family and its individual members. This research analysis included studies of societal and family factors which influence the practice of health promotion in the family.

The review was done by the articles' titles and abstracts. First, each article title was reviewed. If a title indicated even a remote relationship between the study purpose and health promotion in the family, the abstract was read. If further clarification was needed the article was read.

The results of this review of 105 issues of the journals yielded five articles (4.8%) which addressed health promotion activities in the family. One article was instrument development, one looked at the provision of child care services through the types of day care the children attended, and three articles were family studies. These latter articles investigated aspects of family dynamics and the practice of health promotion behaviours. For example, O'Brien (1980) researched the relationships between mother–child communication and the child's exploratory behaviour and self-differentiation. She found a positive and significant correlation between the overall pattern of parental acknowledgement of the child and the child's differentiation of self. Among the non-significant findings reported by O'Brien (1980) was a trend which indicated differing expectations by mothers for boys and girls.

A study of one-parent families headed by women found the general lifestyle patterns of the mother influenced the practice of health promotion behaviours in the family (Duffy 1986). The more psychological growth experienced by the woman as an outcome of her status as a solo parent, the more the family tried new health promotion behaviours for the purpose of enhancing personal well-being.

Other studies of health promotion reported in these journals focused on individuals. In fact, the overwhelming majority of the studies used the individual as the research participant and studied either disease prevention or intervention behaviours. These findings were not unexpected since it has been reported elsewhere that despite the practice emphasis on families, nursing research has continued its individual orientation (Murphy 1986) and, until recently, its selection of families from populations identified as pathological or abnormal (Feetham 1984).

Without further nursing research on health promotion in the family, practitioners will not have a sufficient body of knowledge to influence public and health policy and to work with individuals and families in the promotion of their health. According to O'Brien (1980):

> The literature abounds with speculation as to the kind of parental behaviours that facilitate the child's developmental progress. Yet, there is a paucity of research on parent-child communication and its relation to child development using subjects drawn from populations of 'healthy' parents and children. Such research is needed in order to build a substantive body of knowledge for health promotion.

Fortunately the empirical knowledge on health promotion in the family is not limited to what exists in the nursing research journals. The range of health promotion studies is rather extensive since health promotion is concerned with lifestyle behaviours and the family's environment. These studies include, but are not limited to, the development of health promotion attitudes and behaviours in family members; the influence of the media, especially television, on viewers; the impact of social policies; nutrition; and parent-child communication. In the next section of this paper some of the current findings on health promotion in the family will be used to provide directives for future nursing research.

DIRECTIVES FOR STUDYING HEALTH PROMOTION IN THE FAMILY

Health promotion in the family is the result of an interaction between the internal environment of the family and the external environment which impinges upon it. Family dynamics, the interrelationships among the family members, are the internal conditions which affect health promotion behaviours. The external environment consists of several influences: kinship network, neighborhood, community, and the larger society. The research directives which follow will be discussed in two categories: family dynamics and the external environment.

Family Dynamics

The study of health promotion in the family begins with family dynamics. The influence of the mother—specifically her level of education, her health attitudes, and her health practices—has been documented in several studies to be a significant influence on the health practices of her children. For example, in a follow-up study of childhood symptomatology, Mechanic (1979) found that young adults who reported fewer symptoms remembered their parents emphasizing self-care and health promotion. In a study of Chilean children (McFarlane 1985), the researcher found that children with one or more infections, when compared to healthy children, were more likely to have a mother who was healthy, educated, and older—at least 35 years of age. For these children, characteristics of the mother directly influenced their health status.

The family's influences on the development of

health promotion practices is both direct and indirect. While the family is the major socializer of preschool and school-aged children, their influence goes beyond the obvious promotion of health — food choices, exercise, hygiene, sleep, etc. The family establishes a norm which directs the decision-making of its members in areas of friendships, media, recreation, work, school, etc. (Mullen 1983). For example, parents can either encourage, tolerate, discourage, or forbid children from watching television violence. Research indicates that television does influence its viewers and appears to be related to increased aggressive behaviour (Pearl *et al.* 1982). Socialization toward an active consumer role, and perceptions of the 'real' world that parallel the television stereotypes (Rubinstein & Brown 1985). On the other hand, television can be used as a positive influence on health (Milio 1985). Parents are in a position to differentiate between these various effects of television and to decide for themselves and their children the type of viewing that is permissable. Yet, parents and the family are not the sole influencers on the child. At varying degrees of intensity through the child's life, age, peers, school, television, and medical care temper the family's influence (Mullen 1983).

Decision-making or problem-solving is another dimension of parenting that contributes to health promotion practices of children. Lewis & Lewis (1982) found that children with poor health-related decision-making skills had difficulty making decisions in other areas of their lives. This same decision-making pattern was seen in a study of one-parent families headed by women (Duffy 1984). The women who made general lifestyle decisions which were growth oriented and motivated towards change, practised and encouraged health promotion behaviours for themselves and their children. Women who made decisions by default — letting what happens happen — or maintained routine behaviours, used the same pattern in their health practices. These women did not seek new health information or attempt to change their behaviour patterns. For example, the latter group of women and their children may have brushed their teeth or practised good hygiene because it was an established routine but they did not attempt to learn new health promoting behaviours that could enhance their well-being.

Parenting style itself can enhance health practices. The use of autonomy, reward and reason had a positive influence on the health practices of children (Pratt 1973, 1976). A study by Laskey & Eichelberger (1985) found that children whose parents transferred health self-care decision-making to them in a progressive and developmentally appropriate manner did practise self-care behaviours and could relate the reasons for practising these behaviours. Much more research is needed on these patterns of decision-making and their transfer from parents to children.

Directives for Future Research

There are several directives for future research on health promotion in the family which concern the family's internal dynamics. Table 38-1 lists the major research questions. To begin with, research which describes the health promotion behaviours in families is needed. This type of study could identify patterns of behaviours occurring in families. The richness of these data would be enhanced if the family studies were longitudinal so that changes in parental and child behaviours could be studied together and over time.

TABLE 38-1
Health promotion: directives for family research

1. What are the family health promotion behaviours?
2. What changes occur, over time, in the family's health promotion behaviours?
3. What are the family's definitions of health and health promotion behaviours?
4. What is the value placed on health and health promotion behaviours? How does that value compare to other values in the family's life?
5. What is the influence of parenting style on the development of health promotion behaviours by children?
6. What is the influence of fathers on the health promotion behaviours of children?
7. What is the effect, if any, of various family characteristics on the family's health promotion behaviours?
8. What methods of intervention are most effective in encouraging health promotion in the family?

Some research questions are: What are the health promotion practises and patterns in the family as a unit? What happens to the group interaction—the influence of the members on each other—and health promotion practices over time?

There are several research questions which investigate the family's perceptions of health and health promotion behaviours. The family's definition of health and health promotion, their perceptions of health promotion practices, and the value placed on health and health promotion behaviours are three areas of study. It is important to understand the family's definition of health promotion behaviours, otherwise the behaviours studied will be those identified by professionals only. In Duffy's (1986) study the families included washing clothes, hygiene, nutritional supplements, praying for health, and dressing for the weather in their lists of health promotion behaviours. This approach requires the researcher to ask families what they do to feel good and to improve their health rather than limit the inquiry to a list of behaviours for the family to respond to.

The value of health and health promotion behaviours within the context of the family environment needs study. An understanding is needed of the various stressors in families which distract families, even those with a commitment to health promotion, away from health promotion practices. Coeytaux (1984) recommended that researchers ask why some parents are more concerned about prevention (health promotion) than other parents and what accounts for the difference.

Parenting is a major research area in health promotion research. Areas for study include parenting styles which facilitate or prevent health promotion behaviours, parental methods for teaching health promotion to children, and parental decision-making styles and their relationship to health promotion behaviours. These areas of research can build upon works previously cited. For example, the relationships between decision making, in general and in specific, for health need further study. How do the parents' general patterns of decision making influence the child's pattern and what are the effects of health behaviour decision making? Does the use of autonomy in the parent-child relationship encourage health promotion practices throughout childhood or is it developmentally specific?

While the mother continues to be an important part of family health care, many fathers have become involved in this role. A dearth of knowledge exists regarding the relationships between characteristics of fathers and the practice of health promotion behaviours in families.

The findings from each of these research areas will, most likely, be affected by the characteristics of the family and in order to assist families in practice, knowledge about the influence of various family characteristics on their health promotion behaviours must be understood. These characteristics include family type (single or two parent); age of the family members; numbers of children; income; employment status; education; place (country) of residence; and so forth. An example of the dearth of information on family type and health is evident when the literature on single parent families and health is reviewed. Despite the fact that 23% of all children in the United States are living with one parent and 90% of those children are living with their mothers, studies of female headed, single-parent families are virtually non-existent in the literature on family and health (Loveland-Cherry 1986).

Psychological Characteristics

In addition to demographic characteristics, an understanding is needed of the family's psychological characteristics. Do the family members believe they can impact their health by practising health promotion behaviours? How much control do family members believe they have over their own lives and how effective, do they believe, are their attempts to make changes in their lives?

Once a rich descriptive data base is available, research on interventions to encourage the practice of health promotion behaviours in families should occur. These interventions need to be tailored to the families and not reflect a Western, middle-class bias. For example, Butrin & Newman (1986) looked at time orientation and hemispheric dominance to assess the type of health promotion teaching programmes appropriate for a rural population in Zaire. In Haiti, a study was conducted of visual literacy among non-literates (Gustafson 1986). Both studies provide knowledge that can be used in the development of health promotion education programmes for families that are less likely to be responsive to didactic teaching. The research questions should investigate methods of transmitting health knowledge that build upon but are not limited to conventional health education approaches.

Other intervention studies can build on the family's role as a natural support group since support groups can encourage health promotion behaviours. Related research questions are: How does the family function as a support group in the promotion of health among its member? What types of support are needed by the members?

As stated earlier, the family exists in a larger social environment and is not immune from the influences of that environment. Therefore, it is necessary to study the family-environment interaction in order to understand the practice of health promotion behaviours in families.

External Environment

However influential the family is on the practices of health promotion by its members, the family cannot be studied in a vacuum. The influence of the larger society is pervasive in all countries regardless of the country's level of economic development. As the options for health promotion available to the family decrease, the focus on society as the unit of intervention increases. For example, in countries in which the majority of people suffer from malnutrition, the family has few opportunities for health promotion since their struggle is to meet a basic human need (Maslow 1962). Society has the responsibility to help these children to meet their basic needs.

> However over-burdened or inefficient the individual parent, the health of the children is society's responsibility: it should not be *possible,* whatever the circumstances, for children to remain unimmunised (without conscientious objections) or to suffer the unnecessary worsening of chronic conditions (Blaxter and Patterson 1983).

In an intergenerational study of mothers and daughters, these same researchers reported that environment of poverty rather than the health behaviours and attitudes of mothers contributed to the accidents in the families. Poverty is the greatest threat to health promotion since it decreases the family's options, thus contributing to many of the health problems faced by the poor (Sidel 1986). However, societal interventions can facilitate health promotion in low-income families by providing needed services. A study in Bogata, Columbia found that a state run preschool enhanced the well-being of the mothers and the children (de Ramos 1984). The mothers felt the benefits of this quality day-care programme were: (1) the possibility of improved income since the mother could look for employment while the child was at daycare, (2) socialization for mothers who were primarily isolated because of their demanding schedules, and (3) the alleviation of guilt experienced by mothers who leave their children at day-care.

Regardless of economic level, society establishes norms which facilitate or impede health promotion (Dwore & Kreuter 1980). For example, in the United States, there has been a noticable decrease in smoking on television (Rubinstein & Brown 1985), a decrease which parallels the general decline in smoking among the population. Yet the commitment to prohibit smoking in the United States remains tenuous and as a result, smoking continues to be a problem within certain segments. Finland has demonstrated the effectiveness of a societal commitment to end smoking through governmental regulation in combination with health education and media intervention (Milio 1985).

Regulation and media are only two variables of the environment which impact family health promotion behaviours. The empirical study of the relationships between health promotion in the family and environmental conditions is fertile since little work has occurred in this area. Most health promotion research and practice targets the individual and the individual's responsibility to maintain her or his health. Yet it is difficult to separate the lifestyle behaviours of the individual from the environmental factors which shape those behaviours.

A few of the research questions to be asked are listed in Table 38-2. These questions include: How do the norms of society facilitate or impede the practice of health promotion behaviours in families? How

TABLE 38-2
Health promotion: directives for research of the external environment

1. What role is society able and willing to play in the promotion of health in families?
2. What societal interventions can decrease the impact of poverty in families?
3. What are the societal norms regarding health promotion behaviours?
4. What are the effects of societal institutions on the practice of health promotion behaviours in families?

does society define health? What support — financial, emotional, practical — does society offer for families to encourage health promotion? What are the effects of the societal institutions — political climate, religious tolerance, economic wealth — on the practice of health promotion behaviours in families? What role does health policy play?

Answers to these questions will help us to understand the role of society in the practice of health promotion behaviours in families. Abdicating the responsibility for health promotion to families and individuals has not worked. 'Until the perceptions and values and norms of the larger society change, we cannot rationally expect individual behaviour to alter significantly' (Sidel 1986).

CONCLUSION

Nursing practice has recognized the importance of health promotion in the family to the improvement in individual and community health. However, there is a dearth of nursing research to guide these practitioners. The review of four nursing research journals provided the evidence of this dearth of knowledge. The advancement of family health promotion to the forefront of the nursing research agenda is needed.

Health promotion in the family is the study of the enhancement of well being. Internal family dynamics and external environmental factors interrelate to affect the health and health promotion behaviours of families. In this paper directives were discussed for the study of the relationships between the family's internal and external environments and their practise of health promotion behaviours.

REFERENCES

American Nurses' Association (1980) *A Social Policy Statement.* American Nurses' Association, Kansas City.

Blaxter M. & Patterson E. (1983) The health behaviour of mothers and daughters. In Families at Risk (Madge N. ed.), Heinemann, London, pp. 174-196.

Butrin J. & Newman M.A. (1986) Health promotion in Zaire: time perspective and cerebral hemispheric dominance as relevant factors. *Public Health Nursing* 3(3), 183-191.

Children's Defense Fund (1985) *A Children's Defense Budget: An Analysis of the President's FY 1986 Budget and Children.* Children's Defense Fund, Washington DC.

Coeytaux F. (1984) *The Role of the Family in Health: Appropriate Research Methods,* WHO, Geneva.

de Ramos E.B. (1984) Working mothers of pre-school children in an underdeveloped society. *Women's Studies International Forum* 7(6), 415-422.

Dever G.E.A. (1980) *Community Health Analysis: A Holistic Approach,* Aspen, Germantown, MD.

Duffe M.E. (1984) Transcending options: creating a milieu for practicing high level wellness. *Health Care for Women International* 5, 145-161.

Duffy, M.E. (1986) Primary prevention behaviors: the female-headed, parent family. *Research in Nursing and Health* 9, 115-122.

Dwore R.B. & Kreuter M.W. (1980) Reinforcing the case for health promotion. *Family and Community Health* 2, 103-119.

Feetham S. (1984) Family research in nursing. In *Annual Review of Nursing Research,* Volume 2 (Wesley H.H. & Fitzpatrick J.J. eds.), Springer, New York.

Gustafson M.B. (1986) Research among Haitian village women: implications for the nurse's role in health evaluation. *Public Health Nursing* 3(4), 250-256.

Laskey P.A. & Eichelberger K.M. (1985) Health-related views and self-care behaviors in young children. *Family Relations* 34, 13-18.

Lewis C.E. & Lewis M.A. (1982) Determinants of children's health-related beliefs and behaviors. *Family and Community Health* 4(4), 85-97.

Loveland-Cherry C.J. (1986) Personal health practices in single parent and two parent families. *Family Relations* 35, 133-139.

Maslow A.H. (1962) *Toward a Psychology of Being.* Van Nostrand, Princeton, NJ.

McFarlane J. (1985) Use of an ecologic model to identify children at risk for infection and to quantify the expected impact of the risk factors. *Public Health Nursing* 2(1), 2-22.

Mechanic D. (1979) Correlates of psychological distress among young adults. A theoretical hypothesis and results from a 16 year follow-up study. *Archives of General Psychiatry* 36, 1233-1239.

Merrit D. (1986) The national center for nursing research. *Image: Journal of Nursing Scholarship* 18(3), 84-85.

Milio N. (1985) Health education = health instruction + health news: media experiences in the United States, Finland, Australia, and England. In *The Media, Social Science, and Social Policy for Children* (Rubinstein E.A. & Brown J.D. eds), Ablex Publishing, Norwood, NJ.

Mullen P.D. (1983) Promoting child health: channels of socialization. *Family and Community Health* 5, 52-68.

Murphy S. (1986) Family study and nursing research. *Image* 18(4), 170-174.

O'Brien R.A. (1980) Relationship of parent-child communication to child's exploratory behavior and self-differentiation. *Nursing Research* 29(3), 150-156.

Pearl D., Bouthilet L. & Lazar J. (1982) *Television and Behavior: Ten Years of Scientific Process and Implications for the Eighties* (Volume 1). US Government Printing Office, Washington, DC.

Pender N.J. (1982) *Health Promotion in Nursing Practice.* Appleton-Century-Crofts, Norwalk, CT.

Pratt L. (1973) Child rearing methods and children's health behavior. *Journal of Health and Social Behavior* 14, 61-69.

Pratt L. (1976) *Family Structure and Effective Health Behavior.* Houghton Mifflin, Boston.

Roemer R. (1986) APHA members support more international health work. *The Nation's Health* 16(12), 2.

Rubinstein E.A. & Brown J.D. (1985) Television and children: a public policy dilemma. In *The Media, Social Science, and Social Policy for Children.* (Rubinstein E.A. & Brown J.D. eds). Albex Publishing, Norwood, NJ.

Sidel R. (1986) *Women and Children Last: The Plight of Poor Women in Affluent America.* Viking Penguin, New York.

William C., Carter B. & Wynder E. (1981) Prevalence of selected cardiovascular and cancer risk factors in a pediatric population. *Preventive Medicine* 10, 121-132.

World Health Organization (1979) *Formulating Strategies for Health for All by the Year 2000.* World Health Organization, Geneva.

World Health Organization (1985) *A Guide to Curriculum Review for Basic Nursing Education: Orientation to Primary Health Care and Community Health.* World Health Organization, Geneva.

CHAPTER 39

How Values Affect the Mutual Goal Setting Process With Multiproblem Families

Ruth Carey, RN, MPH

There is an underlying assumption in much of the education of health-care professionals in this country that they, by virtue of their expertise and knowledge, know what is best for their clients. In community health nursing, this assumption leads to a behavioral process in which the nurse sets goals for clients without receiving adequate input from the clients.

There is an alternative assumption that clients have the ultimate responsibility for managing their own lives. In terms of community health nursing, this assumption leads to the process of mutual goal setting.

The writings of Imogene M. King are relevant to the issue of mutual goal setting. Some of the assumptions King (1983) cited are that:

1. Perception of nurse and of client influence the interaction process.
2. Goals, needs, and values of nurse and client influence the interaction process.
3. Individuals have a right to knowledge about themselves.
4. Individuals have a right to participate in decisions that influence their life, their health, and community services they utilize.
5. Health professionals have a responsibility to share information that helps individuals make informed decisions about their health care (p. 228).

King (1986) wrote,

> Through purposeful communications they [nurse and client] identify specific goals, problems, or concerns. They explore means to achieve a goal and agree to means to use to reach the goal. When clients participate in goal setting with professionals, they interact with nurses to move toward goal attainment in most situations. (p. 70)

What does this mean for the nurse in day-to-day practice? It means (a) understanding values and how values differ, (b) having respect for others' values, (c) developing both philosophic and pragmatic views of why mutual goal setting can be effective, and (d) learning when and how to work within a mutual goal setting context.

UNDERSTANDING VALUES AND ETHNOCENTRICITY

A value is a "principle, standard, or quality considered inherently worthwhile or desirable" (The *American Heritage Dictionary,* 1985). Values are those concepts that we believe and hold dear.

Reprinted from *Journal of Community Health Nursing,* Vol. 6, No. 1, with permission of Lawrence Erlbaum Associates, Inc., © 1989.

"Everything we do, every decision we make and course of action we take, is based on our consciously or unconsciously held beliefs, attitudes and values" (Simon, Howe, & Kirschenbaum, 1972, p. 13). Like everyone else, both the nurse and the client will make decisions and take courses of action based on their values.

Our values are shaped by the culture in which we develop. Often values are so deeply a part of us that we assume everyone has the same values as we do, and our values are universally accepted truth. In fact, part of the process of acculturation often includes the belief (value) that our culture of origin and its values are better than others, that "my way is the best and only way to do things." This belief in the superiority of our own values is called *ethnocentrism.*

If we make an unbiased examination of the cultures of other countries and various socioeconomic groups within countries, including our own, it is clear that people hold different beliefs and values.

However, sometimes we do not take into account the facts regarding differing values and the behaviors that grow from them. In other words, we proceed from an ethnocentric mind set.

This issue is discussed by Melanie Dreher (1982) in her article "The Conflict of Conservatism in Public Health Nursing Education." She pointed out that there is an ethnocentric element in many of the models used in nursing education. She reminded us that Maslow's concept of self-actualizing does not take into account the economic barriers to such growth. She wrote that Erickson's "integrity vs. despair" developmental task of the elderly is based on middle-class values and does not take into account that some elderly people have a better chance of achieving integrity because of social and economic advantage. Her discussion of Kubler-Ross's models of the stages of grief or response to death showed the failure to take into account statistics showing that members of certain population groups have a higher probability for survival based on factors such as race, economic status, or occupation. Nevertheless, Dreher wrote, we sometimes take these models based on studies of the middle class and apply them as though they are universal.

Majorities within a society often impose their values on minorities. An example commonly cited in this country is the public education system which is based heavily on the needs of White middle-class children and which teaches the value of White culture and language.

My own early years of teaching, I am chagrined to say, were often fraught with an ethnocentric approach. Back then, I felt that all students should perform at the top of their capacity, and that a student capable of getting "A"s should get them. Of course, I communicated this to my students, and in doing so was imposing my values regarding performance on my students. I was disregarding the fact that some students did not want to perform at the top of their capability level for various reasons such as stress, energy level, health, and other interests. In other words, I was practicing ethnocentrism—wanting my students to do their best because I thought doing the best one could was a good thing. Over the years, as I recognized this tendency to impose my ethnocentric viewpoint on others, I tried to change my approach. I try now to keep in mind that the students, not I, are in charge of their own learning. I try to remember that my role is to help students be clear about their own values regarding performance, and then I try to function within that framework as a resource, support, facilitator, and guide. I attempt to validate students' values even though they do not necessarily converge with mine.

RESPECT

The essence of a nonethnocentric approach is respect for others. If I respect you, then I trust that you have the ability to determine what is best for you, that you are capable of making good decisions for yourself based on your values. One value that is probably universal is the desire to be respected, to be considered worthwhile.

Another example from my own teaching experience illustrates the whole concept of respect. One of my students was working with a mother and her 3-year-old son, who had failed to thrive since birth and who had been hospitalized at least twice. A major outcome of these hospitalizations was that the mother was clearly aware that the professional hospital staff thought she was a bad mother. She was quite angry about not being consulted regarding her child's hospital care and said she felt very neglected and uncared about by the staff. The child's growth patterns did not alter significantly.

I suggested that the student use an approach modeled after Fraiberg and Fraiberg's (1980) work, which focused mainly on caring about and for the mother in a nurturing and supportive way which, in turn, would guide the mother in nurturing her child. During initial visits to the client's home, the student listened to the mother rather than attempting to carry out the details of the health-care plan. The young mother shared her own childhood experiences of being abandoned, not being well-cared for, the pain of growing up without appropriate nurturing. The student concentrated on listening and then on helping the mother see the things she was doing well as well as how to recognize the evidence of her child's affection for her. Nurse and client established a relationship of mutual caring, and the child gained weight.

The student reported that she was able to accept the family "where they were" and to work with them rather than working on them by defining for them what they should do. She said that part of the reason she was able to be accepting and respectful was that she herself had felt accepted and respected by her faculty.

REASONS FOR MUTUAL GOAL SETTING

The student had been shown respect and thus had developed a similar attitude of respect for other people. The behavior that grew out of that respect was listening to the mother and hearing what she wanted in relation to her child. An informal system of mutual goal setting had evolved. There appeared to be a clear correlation between the respect and mutual goal setting and the child's improved health status.

From a pragmatic perspective, as demonstrated in the aforementioned example, mutual goal setting is a positive avenue of interaction with clients.

One explanation as to why mutual goal setting often is effective is that people tend to resist being told what to do and therefore are more likely to work toward goals they choose and support rather than goals selected by someone else. Another explanation is that people who make decisions tend to be accountable for them. When they feel goals are their own, they also feel they have invested in achieving those goals and therefore work to achieve them.

If one pragmatic perspective on mutual goal setting in health care is that it appears to work, another pragmatic perspective is that practicing unilateral goal setting based on ethnocentrism does not work or at least carries significant negatives. These can include: lack of client trust in the effectiveness of health-care practices based on lack of trust in the providers inaccurate information provided by clients attempting to tell health-care workers what the clients believe the providers want to hear, and alienation of clients to the point of withdrawal from health care systems. The result can be that certain population groups do not receive adequate health care.

Speaking philosophically rather than pragmatically, there are additional reasons to practice mutual goal setting. If we are proceeding from a value system in which we value respect for others' beliefs, then it follows that it is "wrong" for us to set goals for others.

O. Carl Simonton, author of *Getting Well Again* (1978), addressed this issue in a presentation to health-care professionals (Simonton, 1981). Speaking of working with dying patients, he stressed that we need to work toward the quality of death the client wants instead of working toward the quality of death we think the client should have. Rather than being invested in the outcome for our clients, he says, we need to let go of the need to control the outcome.

ELEMENTS OF THE MUTUAL GOAL SETTING PROCESS

If we are committed to the principles of understanding and respecting other people's values and to the mutual goal setting process which is the behavioral outgrowth of these kinds of principles, then we need to (a) be aware of and learn to avoid the pitfalls which often impede the mutual goal setting process in community health nursing and (b) understand the process and procedure of mutual goal setting.

The first pitfall is our own ethnocentrism. We can avoid blundering into this pitfall by being watchful for ethnocentric attitudes—warning signs—in ourselves such as assuming we understand another's culture, showing lack of respect for others' values and needs, feeling we need to control outcomes, and feeling we need to convince someone else to adopt our values.

A second pitfall is an outgrowth of our own extensive knowledge base. As nurses, we develop good assessment capabilities and are well-equipped to determine the health status of clients. We are well-versed regarding the kinds of interventions which can be helpful in preventing or correcting certain deviations from health. We know how to select viable options for care, and we know how to communicate these options to clients. Few people would dispute the fact that the competent community health nurse (CHN) operates from an extensive knowledge base. However, the positives of that knowledge base can become the negative pitfall of elitism if we become too impressed with it, if we insist on making things happen just because we know how to make them happen.

A third pitfall involves the human tendency to remain in our comfort zone by operating within the status quo and thus to resist the discomfort incurred by change. Most CHNs are used to unilaterally setting goals for clients and are unaccustomed to mutual goal setting. Often, it is easier to do what has always been done, simply because it is a familiar pattern. We are accustomed to begin working with families by assessing the situation and then by defining, based on the assessment, goals to work toward with a client. If we are committed to mutual goal setting, then we need to think and behave in new and different ways. And, because we are used to thinking and behaving in a unilateral goal setting mode, we need to make a conscious effort to think and behave differently.

A fourth pitfall can be a reluctance to deal with the probability of our own anger. Sometimes when clients state their values and the goals which grow from those values, and as we see how much the values and goals diverge from our own, we feel the clients have, in effect, rejected our value system and/or our expertise. We may feel angry about that perceived rejection. Also, we may feel angry when a family exhibits less energy and ability to work toward goals than we would like—for instance, when a family fails to keep an appointment or carry what we feel is the family's share of responsibility.

We need to be prepared to deal with our anger. We need to be prepared to accept the feelings and to understand the difference between feeling angry and acting in an inappropriate angry way. By recognizing our anger and the reasons for it, we can then manage the anger and express it in ways that do not hurt the client. Often when we examine our anger, we see that it goes back to our own expectations and our own need to control outcomes.

Understanding in advance these possible pitfalls, we are better prepared to carry out our commitment to mutual goal setting.

A mutual goal is one which is shared by both the family and the CHN. This means that the family and the nurse agree on the need for the goal, and they agree to work toward its attainment.

There are two basic approaches to the mutual goal setting process. The first is to ask families what they feel they want or need to work on. This approach tends to work well with clients who have the ability to identify their own problems, to assess their own status. In these kinds of situations, the nurse can provide assistance in matters such as breaking down problem areas into more manageable subproblems, prioritization, goals clarification, and establishing feedback points which can provide the families with positive reinforcement when goals are reached and also can serve as signposts as to when to start working toward a new goal. The second approach is used with less functional families who may not yet have the ability to identify needs and/or who ask for specific kinds of help. With this approach, the nurse shares the assessment/diagnosis, suggests possible goals, and then carefully checks with the family to see if the client shares the concerns identified and if the client wants to work toward the goals suggested by the nurse. If the family's concerns are different from those of the nurse, and/or if the family seems uninterested in the goals presented, then the nurse needs to lead the family "back to square one." This procedure can mean using the nurse's original suggestions as points to which the family can react. Often, the client's responses will provide strong suggestions of the family's perception of the situation. The nurse then can verbalize and feed back the apparent perceptions until the client indicates that a problem and/or goal has been identified.

The mutual goal setting process has two major thrusts with the CHN having significant roles to play in each. In the first, the goals are identified and achievement methods are selected. During this part of the process the nurse: (a) provides accurate information regarding perceived problem areas and feasible solutions, information that will enable the family to make informed decisions; and (b) acts as facilitator in establishing goals. In the second part of the process, family and nurse work together to achieve goals. During this phase of the process the nurse: (a) provides guidance in locating and using community resources; and (b) becomes an advocate, if need be, on behalf of the family in negotiating community health systems.

Throughout the process the nurse provides compassionate emotional support. This is partly achieved by the nurse's continuing physical presence and by ongoing words of encouragement. Compassionate emotional support is particularly effective when the nurse communicates to the family an acceptance of the family "where they are"—in other words by letting the family know that their values are accepted and respected, that the nurse has relinquished attempts to control outcomes, and that the family is ultimately responsible for its own well being.

In other words, compassionate emotional support can mean active commitment to the mutual goals process. It can mean understanding and respecting families' values enough to participate with them throughout the mutual goal setting process and then caring enough to let go.

An example of mutual goal setting is an experience one of my students had which profoundly affected her . . . and me.

The family was one of scarce economic resources and no extended family for support. The husband abused the wife, and she often hit their three small children. She seldom touched them except to dress or punish, and her verbal interactions with the children were usually loud commands. The children's responses to their mother indicated they expected her to hit them when their behavior deviated from her rules.

The student nurse, following the Selma Fraiberg model (Fraiberg & Fraiberg, 1980), focused on nurturing the mother. The nurse directed her attention and care to the mother, especially offering to assist the mother with needs she herself identified. What the student was doing, although she did not label it as such, was working within the mother's value system in an informal mutual goal setting process. As the process progressed slowly throughout the semester, the mother asked for more and more assistance and allowed the nurse to help.

Toward the end of the term, one of the children accidentally knocked an ashtray off the table and broke it. Frightened, the child stood rigidly still and waited for his mother to hit him. Instead, she walked over to him and put her arm around him chuckling, "You know you should be more careful."

Astounded, the student nurse commented that she had never seen the mother respond with understanding rather than anger. "Why did you do that rather than hit him?" she asked. The mother's reply was, "I've never had anyone care about me before."

When the student related that incident to me, I was once again struck with the importance of proceeding from a base of compassion, and I was reminded that when that compassion generates even a limited amount of mutual goal setting, positive change is likely to occur.

Mutual goal setting, in a way, generates a paradox, because as we respect others' values and needs and let go of our own need to control outcomes based on our values, the outcomes seem to be positive in observable changes in families' emotional and physical health. By resisting our own tendencies to impose our values and goals on others, we ultimately achieve our own goals of improving the health status of those who are in our care.

REFERENCES

The American Heritage Dictionary. (1985). New York: Dell.

Dreher, M. C. (1982). The conflict of conservatism in public health nursing education. *Nursing Outlook, 30,* 504-509.

Fraiberg, S., & Fraiberg, L. (Eds.). (1980). *Clinical studies in infant mental health.* New York: Basic Books.

King, I. M. (1983). Imogene M. King: A theory for nursing. In J. Fitzpatrick & A. Whall (Eds.), *Conceptual models of nursing* (pp. 221-244). Bowie, MD: Prentice-Hall.

King, I. M. (1986). *Curriculum and instruction in nursing: Concepts and process.* Norwalk: Appleton-Century-Crofts.

Simon, S. B., Howe, L. W., & Kirschenbaum, H. (1972). *Values clarification.* New York: Hart.

Simonton, O. C. (1978). *Getting well again.* Los Angeles: Tarcher.

Simonton, O. C. (1981). *Presentation to health care providers.* Paper presented at the Conference for Caregivers Working With Terminally Ill Patients, Ann Arbor, MI.

CHAPTER **40**

Strategies for Change: The One-Parent Family

Mary E. Duffy, RN, PhD

The escalation in the number of one-parent families from 3,808,000 in 1970 to 8,544,000 in 1984, a 124% increase,[1] has forced a change in the perception of the one-parent family from a deviant family type to a legitimate family unit. However, the acceptance of the one-parent family in the mainstream of society does not mean this family type is without unique characteristics and problems. One significant characteristic is found in the family's structure: 90% of one-parent families are headed by women. A major consequence of a family structure headed by a woman is a lower socioeconomic level for the family. A serious economic gap continues to exist between the incomes of men and women. On the average, women earn 65 cents for every dollar earned by men. Child support has failed to bridge the economic gap between the female-headed, one-parent family and the family headed by a male or a married couple. This economic gap in the female-headed, one-parent family is a concern to health professionals because of the increased health risks associated with a lower income.

THE FAMILY'S RESOURCES

Although children experience stressors based on the loss of a two-parent family, the intensity of those stressors is mediated primarily by the ability of the parent to cope and respond,[2-5] since few children receive adult help from other family members, friends, or community.[6] The personal and community resources of the woman can facilitate or impede the adjustment of her children and herself to the crisis of separation, divorce, or death. Three types of resources—economic, social, and psychologic—are especially relevant to this adjustment. Economic resources provide the income or the potential to earn an income to maintain the family at its desired socioeconomic level. Social resources are the support systems the woman has or develops to provide her with emotional and physical help. Last, the woman's psychologic resources, especially her sex-role attitudes, influence her functioning. These attitudes direct her definitions of appropriate and inappropriate roles for women and, most importantly, for herself.

Economic Resources

The economic resources of a person emerge from a complex interaction between the individual's abilities and ambitions and the economic structure of a society. The female-headed, one-parent family is the largest growing population in poverty, mainly because the economic structure of society has not adjusted to this change in family structure.[7] Economic policies continue to be based on the nuclear family: the breadwinner father, the homemaker mother, and two

Reprinted from *Family and Community Health,* Vol. 10, No. 2, with permission of Aspen Publishers, Inc. © 1987.

children. This family structure accounted for less than 7% of all families in 1986. In contrast, 68% of working women are sole wage earners for themselves or their family unit.[8]

The median income for female-headed families was $11,789 in 1983 compared with $32,107 for families with an employed husband and wife and $21,845 for the male-headed family. The lower income for women is attributed to occupational segregation, a pattern that has changed little since the turn of the century.[9] Seventy-five percent of employed women are concentrated in female-dominated occupations. These occupations are low-paying service positions that offer little potential for advancement and are inadequate to support a family. The average college-educated woman earns less than the average male high school dropout. For women, marriage provides the financial security they cannot find through employment and education. One study[10] found that separated and divorced women experienced more psychological problems than married women and that 71% of the difference in the number of problems was attributable to a difference in material conditions, the financial advantage of marriage. The researchers concluded that women continue to rely on marriage for material gains. This same pattern is seen in the remarriage behaviors of divorced women. In contrast to divorced men, financially secure women remarry less often and less quickly than those women who are more financially dependent.[11]

Outside of marriage, child support is meant to lessen the economic burden of women as they raise their children. However, many fathers fail to pay any child support and the majority of fathers do not pay the full amount awarded. According to Maury and Brandwein, "Divorcing mothers, on the whole, cannot expect to count on ex-husbands for income. . . . A reliable ex-husband should be regarded as a great (if perhaps temporary) comfort to the mother."[4(p199)] Recently, federal and state governments have responded to problems in child support with changes in public policies, yet the problem remains. As a consequence, women do not have sufficient economic resources to meet their needs and those of their children.

Not only is the availability of an adequate income important to the mental health of women, the source of that income also is important. Women who earn the majority of their family income through employment report higher levels of psychologic well-being than women who depend on another source for that income.[12,13] Child support, welfare, or other assistance perpetuates the dependence of women on their former spouses, the state, or some other person or group. A woman perceives a lack of control and uncertainty when she relies on another person for her support. Therefore, it is important to assess the source and amount of a woman's income.

Social Support

The availability of social support is an important predictor of functioning[5,12] and can decrease stress[14] for the woman heading a one-parent family. Separation, divorce, or the death of a spouse is a crisis that forces a woman to redefine herself in a world that may be less certain to her than before the crisis.[15] The social support network functions as a buffer during this adjustment period.

Social support is defined in many ways. Included in these definitions are emotional support (eg, the listening ear, the provision of services and information), babysitting, advising, housekeeping, and the offer of money, as well as the affirmation of the woman's personal worth as a human being. How these types of support are provided and which types of support are needed can only be determined individually. There is no ideal social support network. Each woman's network is a result of what is available to her and her astuteness in pursuing the types and amounts of social support she needs to attain her goals.

Patterns of social support networks have been discerned.[16,17] The network in which a woman adds new friendships, mainly women, to her existing or pre-single-parent network, appeals to women seeking personal growth and change. These women are attracted to support groups, role models, political action organizations, and other groups that support their commitment to "making it on their own" and establishing their personal identity. In contrast, stability is perpetuated by a network that provides security but little opportunity for a woman to interact outside her immediate network of family and friends. These women have the listening ear of their support persons but do not receive direct help or the push to pursue a goal. The two women described in the following paragraphs typify the contrasts in these network patterns.

The first woman, in her late 30s, wanted to attend college but did not believe her 17 years as a homemaker prepared her to succeed as a student at the university. A friend took her to the admissions office at the university, helped her to complete the necessary admission forms, listened to her fears, and encouraged her by telling her she could succeed at her studies. When interviewed, this woman was in her third year at the university and in the honors program. Her friend has continued to support her, and at the time of the interview, they were discussing plans for graduate school.

A motivating support person is not available to all women. Another woman, interviewed at the same time, did not have the benefits of a motivating support system. This woman, a mother of three teenagers, received a lot of emotional support from her friends but no practical assistance as she attempted to complete a day care workers training program. She needed care for her own children while she was away, transportation to school, and other help. Her friends empathized with her difficult situation, assured her that things were bad for all of them, and concluded that there was nothing they could do about it.

Different types of support networks benefit women who desire stability and women who seek change. However, a crucial question is: Do most women select a support network that will help them to attain their personal goals, or do the women who achieve their personal goals do so because they have, by chance, one or more members in their support network who motivate them? This question invites a philosophic debate about individual control. A more practical problem for clinicians is to help each woman identify a social support network that meets her needs. As Lindblad-Goldberg and Dukes have stated, "Persons who fail to acquire critical skills in social network construction while they are growing up will be both severely affected by their social networks and be unable to build supportive social networks."[12(p57)]

Psychologic Resources

Research evidence suggests that sex-role orientation is associated with the degree of psychologic well-being in the female-head of a one-parent family. Women with less traditional sex-role orientations experience more psychologic well-being than women with traditional orientations.[18,19] A sex-role orientation is a person's beliefs and values about appropriate behaviors based on gender. The traditional sex-role orientation is based on the belief that women are homemakers and men are providers. The nontraditional sex-role orientation prescribes an equality between men and women both in the home and in the work place. For the nontraditionalists, it is individual differences rather than gender that determine roles. Women with nontraditional sex-role orientations are usually college educated and career minded. These women are determined to "make it on their own" when they become single parents.

When the women with nontraditional sex-role orientations become single parents, they have several resources that help them adjust to the change in their family structure and grow from the experience. Attitude is a major asset. Job skills and education are immediate resources. Traditionally, men have benefited from the luxury of having more alternatives when a relationship ends. These alternatives have given men more power.[20] However, nontraditional women share in the advantages of more available options.

Although the adjustment to being a single parent may be easier for women with nontraditional sex-role orientations, women who have more traditional orientations can and do change as they accommodate their new status as a single parent.[19] Women discover personal resources and societal barriers they previously were unaware of. For example, women who return to school or full-time employment express personal satisfaction with their abilities to succeed and excel. However, these same women confront discrimination at many levels and face stressors on a daily basis. Included among the stressors are the perception of their children as disadvantaged, the cost and inconvenience of day care, their low wage potential, and the lack of personal time.

Maury and Brandwein suggested that women must become less feminine if they are to assume control over their lives as they head one-parent families: "Active control and integration often go along with behavior that is not traditionally defined as feminine. This assertive behavior goes against the grain of feminine socialization, and was acquired slowly and painfully through the many experiences divorced women have taking charge of their own psyches and of their families."[4(p203)] Unfortunately, many women remarry before they reach this point of self-development.

Women who remain in an environment that promotes stability maintain more traditional sex-role orientations. Until these women remarry or enter into another partnered relationship, they often experience depression, low self-esteem, anxiety, and ambivalence. A change in sex-role orientation to a more nontraditional orientation is experienced by women who seek and are encouraged toward growth and change.

It is important to note one emerging group of female single parents; women who choose to become parents either through pregnancy or adoption but without entering into a partnered relationship with a man. Little is known about these women. However, emerging patterns suggest that this group of women have more resources to facilitate their role transition. They are nontraditional in their sex-role orientation and in most instances have the benefits of education and job skills. These women determine beforehand that they are capable of raising a child in a single-parent family and make a thoughtful decision to do so.

For the majority of women heading one-parent families and their children, the lack of resources increases their risks for health problems.

THE FAMILY'S HEALTH RISKS

The first risk to the woman heading a one-parent family is to her mental health. The formation of her single-parent status was precipitated by a crisis: separation, divorce, or death. The congruence between her own self-identity and her position as head of a household will influence her psychologic well-being. The woman who is comfortable with her identity as a household head and accepts this position as an appropriate role for women will not suffer the anxiety and depression experienced by the woman who not only rejects the position for herself but also for all women. This personal reaction to the role of household head will be further influenced by the responses of each woman's social support network. In addition to self-identity, a woman's financial assets can either lessen or heighten her initial anxiety.

A woman's psychologic well-being influences the family's health behavior. A study[16] of one-parent families showed a relationship between women's psychologic well-being, sex-role orientation, and social support network and the families' practice of primary prevention behavior. Women who transcended the options typically available to women heading one-parent families held sex-role orientations that were more nontraditional than the norms for women heading one-parent families. These women reported high levels of self-esteem and control over their lives. The desire for personal growth directed their life styles, including their health practices. A woman who typifies this category would perceive herself and her children as healthy. She would read and research health issues and make informed decisions about prevention practices. The family's daily routine would incorporate a variety of health promotion and primary prevention behaviors. Changes in those behaviors would occur if the woman believed they would further enhance the health of the family members.

At the other extreme were the women who were choosing the options typically available to them. These women were the traditionalists who sought security and stability in their lives. This need for stability created a rigid family environment which affected health practices. For example, aversive control of children, with authoritarian and strict disciplinary practices, has been shown to be associated with fewer personal health practices by the mother and her children.[21] In addition to fewer health practices by the family members, there was a pattern to those practices. The health practices were primary prevention behaviors the women had learned in their childhood. These behaviors were life-style routines (eg, brushing teeth, personal hygiene) and not perceived as health related. The most frequent response to the question, "What do you do to maintain or improve your family's health?" was "nothing."[16]

A middle group of women were seeking other options. These women were receptive to change, and with the appropriate support network, they made changes in their life styles and health practices. These women were motivated by growth but, unlike the women who had transcended the options, they needed a great deal of support to sustain the growth they were experiencing.

Other health risks in the female-headed, one-parent family are attributable to the low income of many of these families and are complicated by the fact that they occur in one-parent families headed by women.[8] The cost of health care contributes to decreased utilization of health care resources by one-parent families, especially for prevention or routine care.[22] Often the mother, in an attempt to save money, avoids or delays seeking care for herself. Less frequent care is not always a health risk but can be if the woman fails to receive the needed prevention and treatment. One study[23] found that some women had neglected getting a Pap test for themselves or immunizations for their children. They could not afford private care and were unfamiliar with the less expensive or free services available through the health department or other agencies providing low-cost health care services.

All low-income families experience some stressors to health because they do not have the money to purchase the necessary health products. In addition to health care, money is not available for healthy lifestyle patterns, such as good nutrition, safe housing, and adequate health care.[24] The impact of income on health goes far beyond the ability to purchase health care services and products. For example, the ability to purchase a home made a difference in mental health for some women heading black, low-income, single-parent families.[12]

The availability and function of a support system not only influences personal growth but also affects health practices in the one-parent family. Children with more extensive social support networks practice more personal health behaviors.[21] A support person who engages in a particular health practice (eg, jogging, walking, dieting) with a woman motivates her to continue with the behavior and to incorporate it into her life-style routine.[23]

The influences of economics, social supports, and sex-role attitudes on the health of women heading one-parent families and their children are enormous. Each of these resources interacts to influence the health practices, health risks, and subsequently the health of all members of a one-parent family headed by a woman.

STRATEGIES FOR CHANGE

According to a report on women's health by the US Department of Health and Human Services, good health requires a "safe and healthful physical and social environment, an adequate income, safe housing, good nutrition, access to preventive and treatment services appropriate to the groups to be served, and a population that is educated, and motivated to maintain healthful behaviors."[8(p8)] An adequate income is a prerequisite to attaining good health, according to this definition. Yet, low income is endemic among the population of female-headed, one-parent families. Change is needed, but it is difficult to know where the change should occur. Should it occur with the family or at the level of public policy development?

Clinicians work with individuals and families to effect immediate change. Long-range planning and social action are ongoing processes that are needed to change social policy but are slow to evolve. Both approaches are necessary, and suggestions for change at both levels are proposed.

The following proposed strategies for change are designed to facilitate change in sex role attitudes and social support networks with the expectation that these factors will affect economic well-being. The ultimate goal is to improve health.

Facilitating an Environment for Change

Change is more than adaptation to one's circumstances. The model of growth and change discussed in this article is based on the concept of transcendence. Conventional therapeutic intervention is aimed at encouraging the crisis of single parenting.[25] The transcendence model proposes change strategies aimed at higher levels of personal development. As a result, societal norms that direct the behavior of individuals and groups may be called into question because the norms may place unnecessary limits on personal growth. For example, the perpetuation of the two-parent family model as ideal creates perceptual blocks to acknowledging that the desire for long-lasting, successful functioning of the one-parent family is as normal an aspiration as the desire to remarry.

The facilitation of growth for each woman begins with a thorough assessment of her goals, dreams, and aspirations. In one study,[23] every woman interviewed articulated one or more goals of self-development. These goals related to education, employment, interpersonal relationships, and recreational pursuits. Often, the women felt a lack of support from friends, relatives, and therapists as they pursued their goals.

Women's groups, specifically consciousness-raising groups, provide an environment for women to assess not only their capabilities for working toward their goals but also the societal discrimination that may impede women who attempt to make major life-style changes. Maury and Brandwein described the stereotypes confronting all female heads of one-parent families: "There are no positive expectations of divorced women — successful divorced women are seen as a contradiction in terms. The choice to remain single and yet be a mother remains a nonlegitimated role. The may be defined by her parents and friends as emotionally or financially needy; by school authorities as potentially inadequate in raising her children; by the bank as a poor risk; and by an employer as either expendable labor or as unreliable because of her child care responsibilities."[4(pp197-198)]

Women-centered support groups share a bond based on gender and often on common experiences. These consciousness-raising groups were the backbone of the women's movement in the 1960s and 1970s and can serve a useful purpose now for the woman experiencing personal changes as she becomes a single parent. Clinicians working with women should resurrect this type of group and facilitate accessibility for minorities and low-income women.

There are several benefits a woman can obtain from a woman's group. First, role models emerge, and women learn from other women. Second, support is available both to motivate the woman toward her goals and to reaffirm her worth as a person. Third, networking becomes available as women begin to help other women. Babysitting, employment opportunities, and social contacts can be arranged. Last, women learn to recognize common problems faced by all single parents, and they may unite to address those issues in the political arena. Examples of successful legislation include job training programs, day care services, and child support enforcement. The unique characteristic of these groups, whatever their primary focus, is their emphasis on growth and change for each woman.

Integration into a woman's group can be the basis of a facilitative social support network. However, other support persons may be needed. Each woman should learn to develop a support system that enhances her growth either through emotional support or direct aid. Clinicians can help women learn to develop compatible support networks. To begin with, they can teach women what is known about the effect of the network structure on their likelihood of maintaining stability or achieving growth and change.[17] Often, a support network is not perceived as a group of people a woman chooses to associate with. Instead, the network is constructed over time by default and includes friends, relatives, and colleagues. These people do not always support change in a woman.

A woman can learn to seek out specific types of people she admires or with whom she shares a common struggle. For example, a woman interested in becoming a therapist talked about associating with other people who were therapists and could provide her with direction and assistance as she began graduate school. She described one woman as a role model and mentor, someone who had "made it" in the profession she was trying to enter. She talked about learning from this woman and benefiting from the professional contacts her mentor arranged (M. E. Duffy, unpublished data, 1987).

Compatibility between the woman's own attitudes and those of her support groups enhances her feelings of psychologic well-being. At this point, she becomes more receptive to health instruction for herself and her children. Before, she was too preoccupied with the changes in her life style to prioritize health. Clinicians should recognize the need for women to develop other areas of their lives before they are ready to engage in health-promoting behaviors. Brown-Bryant cautions, "Do not assume that patient education services for women must focus on reproductive health concerns or emotional concerns. Be prepared to deal with problems that are related to a woman's work, her children's health problems, as well as her overall health."[26(p64)]

Facilitating Social Change

Another route to changing the poverty and multiple stressors faced by women heading one-parent families is through social change. Other women and the poor share with female-headed, one-parent families many common areas of need.[27]

These common problems can be addressed slowly, but often more productively, through social action. Women as well as clinicians who are aware of these problems can become activists. Some changes have occurred legislatively, but many are still needed. Political action is one method of allowing a woman to put her experiences to beneficial use.

There are several areas in which social change is needed. Issues related to day care, child support, and sick leave need to be addressed in the political arena. Other areas in need of social change focus on the socialization of children to gender roles. Girls must learn to develop an identity in a role besides motherhood. Preparation for adult employment is essential for all people, not just men. The changes in society and the family are not temporary aberrations. The fact remains that most women will be employed and dependent on their own income.

Changes in sex-role attitudes, support networks, and ultimately the income of women should improve the health behaviors and the health status of women and their children. Changes in these resources are necessary if the goal is enhancement of the health and well-being of the members of the one-parent families headed by women. Changes in individual women will benefit their families, and social changes will benefit the larger group of women and their children. As Toeffler suggests, "To make the new diversity work for us instead of against us, we will need changes on many levels at once, from morality and taxes to employment practices. In economic and social life, individuals cannot enjoy the benefits of widened family options as long as laws, tax codes, welfare practices, school arrangements, housing codes, and even architectural forms all remain implicitly biased toward the Second Wave (nuclear) family."[7(p204)]

REFERENCES

1. *Statistical Abstract of the United States: 1986.* US Bureau of the Census, 1985.
2. Combrink-Graham L, Gursky EJ, Brendler J: Hospitalization of single-parent families of disturbed children. *Fam Process* 1982;221(2):141-152.
3. Felner RD, Farber SS, Ginter MA, et al: Family stress and organization following parental death or divorce. *J Divorce* 1980;4(2):67-76.
4. Maury EH, Brandwein RA: The divorced woman: Processes of change, in Nadelson CC, Polansky DC (eds): *Marriage and Divorce.* New York, Guilford Press, 1984.
5. Norbeck J, Sheiner M: Sources of social support related to single-parent functioning. *Res Nurs Health* 1980; 5:3-12.
6. Wallerstein JS, Kelly JB: *Surviving the Break-up: How Children and Parents Cope with Divorce.* New York, Basic Books, 1980.
7. Toeffler A: *Future Shock.* New York, Bantam Books, 1980.
8. *Women's Health: Report of the Public Health Services Task Force on Women's Health Issues,* US Dept of Health and Human Services publication No. (PHS) 85-50206. Government Printing Office, 1985.
9. Rytina NF, Bianchi SM: Occupational reclassification and changes in distribution by gender. *Monthly Labor Rev* 1984;107(3):11-17.
10. Gerstel N, Reissman CK, Rosenfield S: Explaining the symptomatology of separated and divorced women and men: The role of material conditions and social networks. *Social Forces* 1985;64(1):84-101.
11. Ambert AM: Separated women and remarriage behavior: A comparison of financially secure women and financially insecure women. *J Divorce* 1983;6(3):43-54.
12. Lindblad-Goldberg M, Dukes JL: Social support in black, low-income, single-parent families: Normative and dysfunctional patterns. *Am J Orthopsychiatry* 1985;55(1): 42-58.
13. Pett MA, Cole BV: Economic independence: The impact of income source and security in post-divorce adjustment of custodial parents. Read before the Research and Theory Section, National Council on Family Relations, San Francisco, Calif, Oct 16-20, 1984.
14. McPhee JT: Ambiguity and change in the post-divorce family: Towards a model of divorce adjustment. *J Divorce* 1984;8(2):1-15.
15. Parker CM: Psycho-social transitions: A field for study. *Soc Sci Med* 1971;5:101-115.

16. Duffy ME: Transcending options: Creating a milieu for practicing high level wellness. *Health Care Women Int* 1984;5:145-161.
17. McLanahan SS, Wedemeyer NV, Adelburg T: Network structure, social support, and psychological well-being in the single-parent family. *J Marriage Fam* 1981;43: 601-612.
18. Bloom BL, Clement C: Marital and sex role orientation and adjustment to separation and divorce. *J Divorce* 1984;7(3):87-97.
19. Brown P, Manela R: Changing family roles: Women and divorce. *J Divorce* 1978;1:315-328.
20. Levinger G: A social psychological perspective on marital dissolution. *J Soc Issues* 1976;32(1):21-47.
21. Loveland-Cherry CJ: Personal health practices of single parent and two parent families. *Fam Relations* 1986;35: 133-139.
22. Patton RD, Harvill LM, Michal ML: Attitudes of single parents toward health issues. *J Am Med Wom Assoc* 1981; 36:340-348.
23. Duffy ME: Transcending options: Creating a milieu for practicing high level wellness. *Dissertation Abstr Int* 1983;44:748B.
24. Guidubaldi J, Cleminshaw H: Divorce, family health and child adjustment. *Fam Relations* 1985;34:35-41.
25. Duffy ME: The concept of adaptation: Its limitations on the study of nursing phenomena. *Scholarly Inquiry For Nursing Practice: An International Journal,* in press.
26. Brown-Bryant R: The issue of women's health: A matter of record. *Fam Community Health* 1985;7(4):53-65.
27. Brown CA, Feldberg R, Fox EM, et al: Divorce: Change of a new lifetime. *J Soc Issues* 1976;32:119-133.

CHAPTER **41**

Domestic Violence and Community Health Care Ethics: Reflections on Systemic Intervention

Wayne A. Ewing, MDiv, PhD

Until recently, violence in the American home had come to be accepted as a way of life. Domestic violence is presently perceived, however, as a perpetuation of life-threatening behaviors, beliefs, and attitudes of epidemic proportions. This threat has been perceived as being of such magnitude as to elicit new community interventions and prevention strategies—interventions and strategies that advocate stopping violent behavior and instilling nonviolent behavior. However, because they are enmeshed in their own social fabric, it has been difficult for health care providers to realize how innovative, even revolutionary, their caring responses to domestic violence have been.

This recent response to domestic violence is representative of a newer ethic in community and family health care and deserves some deliberation. There is an emerging consciousness that intervention means something more than just curing the problem. Intervention in domestic violence is becoming an advocacy for change of such social significance that the movement toward this change can be characterized as political. Political, that is, in the comprehensive sense of the word: change directed to the overall exercise of individual rights and privileges within the community at large. Health care providers are not accustomed to thinking of themselves as being engaged in political action when they are intervening for the health and well-being of citizens of their communities. Those who intervene in domestic violence, however, have become increasingly aware of the political nature of their positions in the community.

Reprinted from *Family and Community Health,* Vol. 10, No. 1, with permission of Aspen Publishers, Inc., © 1987.

CLINICAL BEHAVIOR AND POLITICAL ACTION: AN INITIAL PREMISE

Community interventions in family abuse and domestic violence are fairly recent phenomena. The first shelter for battered women appeared only in 1972, in England, under the direction of Erin Pizzey. In Denver, the first service program for battered women appeared in 1974. As was the case in England, this program appeared in response to, and at the demand of, female victims of spousal abuse. Many family health care practitioners take part in the services provided as part of the Denver program. The program continues to take its inspiration and form from an activist community of women and men who refuse to adapt any longer to the social tolerance and civic advocacy of violence as the conflict resolution technique of choice in family affairs.

Domestic violence appears in every socioeconomic, racial, and ethnic group in the United States with equal frequency. Some studies suggest that one in two families experience an episode of physical abuse annually.[1,2] Therefore, intervention in family violence represents a commitment to change, not only in individual lives, but in the sexual and political fabric of American culture as well. To be engaged in the delivery and provision of services for the health and well-being of victims and perpetrators of domestic violence is to be engaged in a value-laden political action that is directed toward change. The change can be summarized as a shift from the value and belief that "violence works" to the value and belief that "nonviolence works."

If professional intervention in domestic violence is a direct engagement in a value-laden community enterprise, then several questions arise in regard to appropriate health care ethics. What standard of excellence is the basis for this professional activity? What suggests that the feminist protest to patriarchal overreach in the violent style of spousal battering finds an authentic response in community health care services oriented to intervention in this epidemic and to the prevention of its cross-generational spread?

These and similar questions in health care ethics are being worked through and answered in the development of domestic violence services. These value-laden concerns are resulting in the development of a new way of thinking about and ethically delivering health care services.

TWO WAYS OF THINKING ABOUT INTERVENTION

The traditional way of thinking about intervention in life-threatening epidemics seems to be marked by particularly militant metaphors. Consider, for example, the range of epidemic disorders that have been, or are currently being, attacked: medical (tuberculosis, acquired immune deficiency syndrome [AIDS]), social (child labor, child abuse), religious (heresy, prolife and prochoice confrontations), and psychologic (hysteria, depression). The principles of attack intervention are organized around quarantine, battle, defeat, and victory strategies. These behaviors and results are thought of as wars on the disorder and chaos in our midst. They are guided by disciplines that are honed to the skills of militant confrontation. The ethic of attack intervention appears to be fairly impositional.

Certainly, one family member physically abusing another member is a particular instance of disorder and chaos. However, the victim of this disorder, who has already been imposed upon by the perpetrator, is vulnerable to additional maltreatment in a health care environment marked by an impositional ethic. Health care professionals may exacerbate the already damaged condition of the victim by thinking about interventions in militant terms. In other words, the cure can be worse than the disease, particularly if the cure is placed in a frame of reference that counters violence with violence. In domestic violence intervention and service provision, the treatment behavior syndrome of impositional ethics is known as "blaming the victim."

Victims and perpetrators of abuse spill increasingly into health care systems as battered women, beaten babies, bruised elders, sexually assaulted women and children, substance-addicted persons, and battering men. If not consciously and deliberately contending with the epidemic of abuse, most health care practitioners are at the very least drawn into the perimeter of this particular disorder and chaos. Given the violent nature of the ills to which practitioners are called on to respond, it is understandable that particularly militant, belligerant ways of thinking about intervention might continue.

However, one aspect of recent interventions in domestic violence that is not included in the militant tradition is the dimension of restoration. There has always been some sense of a return to an original organic, social, spiritual, or mental balance in the warlike metaphors for service delivery. However, the militant way of thinking about intervention mostly subverts restoration under a hierarchical scheme of conquerer and conquered. The militant strategies of curing seem less invested in restoration than in submission and conquest.

An alternative way of thinking about intervention is built more deliberately on restoration. The chaos of the catastrophic disorder—violence at the hands of a loved one—is met by a commitment to restore an integrity of personhood both to the victim and to the perpetrator. A distinctive mark of this alternative way of thinking is to focus on working *with* the disordered reality, rather than *against* it. The confrontation emphasizing militancy is replaced by a confrontation emphasizing compassion. Institutionalized efficiency, in which cost cutting equates with reduction of care, is replaced by efficient, at least creative, institutions, new to our society, in which care equates with a communitywide collaboration toward change. The context of healing in domestic violence, as differentiated from curing or the provision of symptomatic relief, is as broad as the community that permits, tolerates, and advocates violence. There is no distinctive enemy to attack, or as the cartoon character, Pogo, put it so many years ago, "We have met the enemy, and he is us." The militant way of thinking, with its need to isolate or detach in order to destroy, is not adequate to complete the task of working within the social fabric of violence to create a new value and ethic of nonviolence. The alternative way of thinking about intervention that embraces restoration presents some hope that a communitywide, interdisciplinary response to the epidemic of domestic violence can turn the entitlement to abuse (violence works) into the enactment of healing systems (nonviolence works).

AMEND: A COMMUNITY RESPONSE TO DOMESTIC VIOLENCE

An application of the alternative way of thinking about intervention is found in the Denver-based treatment program, AMEND, the acronym for Abusive Men Exploring New Directions. AMEND provides long-term group therapy for men who batter their spouses and lovers. While positioned in the private sector, AMEND serves the public sector as well, in its capacity as a primary referral for the city's court-mandated, sentence-deferral psychotherapeutic treatment of batterers. Initiated in 1976 on an untested premise, AMEND now actively treats over 300 men in 30 to 35 small groups. The majority of these groups are composed of men who volunteer for treatment; a smaller number of the groups are composed of men who are referred for treatment by the criminal justice system. Four metropolitan area counties also have AMEND-coordinated treatment programs.[3]

The origin, development, and delivery of care in the AMEND program illustrate a number of the features of the emerging integrative community model for constructing and enacting the ethics of a restorative community health care environment in response to family violence. A review of the program may be useful for others who are piloting and shepherding domestic violence intervention projects in other parts of the country.

Origins and Development

AMEND began with a vague notion over a decade ago. That vague notion was that sheltering female victims would not eliminate male violence. The contentions that men who batter *can* be treated and that men who batter are *worthy* of psychotherapeutic treatment began to appear on the local community level. These informing principles were born in the crucible of a cross section of community life in Denver and its suburbs.

AMEND was based on a community interest in restoration. Restoration as the mode of intervention is value laden. A motif of declarative ethics—"It is wrong to hit"—provides the basis for treatment. Assault is not met with assaultive treatment but rather with a counter-value that originates within the community of the assaulted. Victims and victim advocates (ie, those most directly affected by the contagion of domestic violence) were the initial body of the community that compassionately confronted domestic violence. The desire to heal was born from within; curing was not imposed upon the affliction from without. No single professional group decided to "assault" the epidemic of violence in the family. Rather, the epidemic was brought to the attention of the community by its primary victims.

By being willing to counter the values that promote violence in the family, an authentic community emerged to enact restorative alternatives to violence in the family. The entitlement to abuse was and is countered by the advocacy of the cessation of violence and the right to safety in one's own home. The premise that violence works as a conflict resolution technique was and is countered by the dismantling of the civic advocacy of violence in the home. The belief that physical attack is justified was and is countered by criminalizing assault in the home. What the community would not tolerate from stranger to stranger now includes, under the law, an intolerance for spousal and lovers' assault. The countering of belief with belief, value with value, has been an integral part of the origins of a restorative intervention in family violence.[4,5]

These alternative beliefs and values emerged in Denver in a political movement in community and family health care. In the early 1980s a community coalition of health care service providers, attorneys, concerned citizens, and other victim advocates formed around the mutual interest in establishing justice for abused women. The city administration, in what could have become an adversarial, combative situation, collaborated with this coalition. For example, arrest and arraignment procedures were changed to account for a changed community consciousness about domestic violence. When there is probable cause, the responding police officer on the scene of a violent act within the family is directed to arrest the perpetrator, and the city attorney is empowered to prosecute the perpetrator with or without the victim filing charges. An alternative sentencing program provides for the perpetrator being screened to determine the need for, and being assigned to, psychotherapy. Thus while on the surface the contention that men who batter can be treated looks like it might simply be a clinical judgment, the contention has been part of a broader political, social movement affecting many aspects of city life. Perhaps any community debate about who can be treated in domestic violence interventions is really a political debate about the ethics of health care delivery. The actual contention is that men who batter *should* be treated. In that movement of consciousness in the community, the journey of an ethically informed, value-laden commitment to restorative intervention in the family disordered by violence is directly underway.

AMEND's participation in this community effort has resulted in a continuing refinement of a treatment program for men who batter. Again, the mark of AMEND has been that the desire to heal was born from within: The therapist *and* the client in the AMEND treatment program work toward the dissolution of violence within the community. Insofar as health care professionals are caught up in the epidemic of domestic violence, they are not free of the affliction being treated. The civic advocacy of violence, countered by the political contention that there are restorative alternatives accessible to all people, moves person by person to a civic advocacy of nonviolence. Health care professionals were among the initial population of persons to be so moved; therefore they represent the ethics of this way of thinking about community intervention.

It has been important for the intervening person to be clear about his or her own feelings concerning violence and violent relationships. Insofar as violence is fed by beliefs, the persons who intervene in domestic violence are asked by AMEND to examine their own beliefs about violence. Might the beliefs of the person who intervenes perpetuate the attitudes and beliefs being addressed by the intervention? For example, no matter how subtle, the belief that a victim can cause or provoke the violent act directed against her obscures the reality of the abusive partner's responsibility and accountability. The intervening person must review and rehearse his or her beliefs about interpersonal violence. This has become essential to the development of effective, restorative treatment interventions in domestic violence.

AMEND has struggled to develop a clinically effective program based on political contentions that continue to be tested in the work of the facilitators of therapeutic intervention. The shared work of therapists with groups of men, and occasionally of women, who batter is a form of collaboration with the victims of violence. The particular aim of this collaboration is to restore to victims, victim advocates, perpetrators of violence, and psychotherapists those human sensibilities that are lost in acts of violence. Victims have lost their self-esteem. In some instances, they have lost basic physical abilities. Some have lost their lives. All have lived in terror. Victim advocates, while engaged in the service of empowering victims to reclaim their lost personhood, share in the loss by attachment to the issues of escape, safety, and shelter.

AMEND treatment groups discover over and over again that men who batter, batter from some place of loss. They have translated untended mourning and grief (more often than not originating in childhood deprivations and victimizations[4]) into anger, anger into rage, rage into abuse, and abuse into physical violence. Effective treatment intervention, therefore, does not stop with didactic and therapeutic work focused on anger management. Treatment proceeds to the place of loss itself so that the restoration of personhood within the perpetrator can begin. The psychotherapist is also a party to loss. Whatever moments and energies are given to intervention are moments and energies removed from the therapist's life. This is not ordinary work; it is an extraordinary exercise of commitment to change, to restoration, and to healing. The intervening activity of therapists in the realm of domestic violence is nonetheless also a place where loss is freely shared. The community of healing and restoration is as broad as the community of loss.

Delivery of Care

AMEND's treatment goals are threefold: cessation of the abuser's violence; expansion of the batterer's emotional repertoire beyond anger, to include feelings of sadness, fear, and joy; and provision of an alternative environment within which violence is not reinforced, and within which nonviolence is reinforced. The program's success is measured by its realization of these goals.

The primary mode of treatment is group therapy. A treatment group of 7 to 12 men can be understood as the community of violence meeting itself. The previously secretive, chaotic act is now revisited in a public, ordered environment. The isolation of the explosive episode, and the isolation of the perpetrator and his victim, are denied in this structured setting. The first session in group therapy for men who volunteer themselves for treatment is the initial public accounting for their choice of violent behavior directed against a spouse or lover. For men who are directed to treatment by the court, the initial public accounting has taken place within the criminal justice system. Both environments, therapy groups and courts, embody a value that counters violence, a belief system that challenges the assumed right to batter in the home and an ethic of gender equality and restorative intervention.

The lengths of treatment programs vary. For court-mandated attendees, the group may meet weekly for 24, 36, or 48 weeks. Volunteers remain in treatment for one to five years. It is AMEND's modest goal to see to it that a number of the batterers who successfully complete the court-mandated treatment continue voluntarily with AMEND programs and services. In any event, the length of the group experience is important to building an authentic community of change. There is no short-term treatment solution to this long-term affliction, affected as it is by both social learning and egodynamic dysfunction.

While individual therapist's styles differ, all share in the urgency of commitment to teach and to heal. The urgency of the service provided is always present. The men being served are lethal; domestic violence is a highly dangerous reality. In the population of men AMEND has served over the years, the homicide rate runs 100 times higher than it does in Colorado's general population; the suicide rate is 200 times higher than it is in the nation's general population. Police are killed and maimed in the course of their interventions; one in four officers who die in the line of duty are killed in the course of domestic violence calls. Attorneys and judges are threatened, and sometimes the threats are shockingly realized. Shelters and shelter staffs are sometimes hunted by abusers and sometimes found. AMEND therapists have had their lives threatened. In two incidents in the AMEND treatment program, clients were involved in contract homicides, one of which was carried out by the batterer himself. The commitment of the therapist to heal and to teach compassionately and confrontively is, in the face of all this, an integral part of restorative health care. A collaboration with the victim of violence becomes a purposeful encounter with the perpetrator, the intention of which is to regain the human.

A programmatic acknowledgment of this struggle for the human is found in AMEND's insistence that therapists frequently experience the community. Therapists meet with each other, with AMEND coordinators and supervisors, with the voluntary Board of Directors, with psychiatric and clinical psychologic supervisors, and with the immediate community of service providers, primarily shelter personnel, on a regular and routine basis. The purposes of these frequent meetings include seeing each other in a mutually supportive environment, celebrating the human in the midst of a massively chaotic disruption of the human, and being involved directly in each other's restoration from loss to wholeness.

COMMUNITY RESPONSE AND COMMUNITY ETHIC

Perhaps this sketch of one organization's intervention environment illustrates the manner in which a restorative way of thinking about health care delivery to the violent family is a community enterprise. The referral of batterers for treatment in the voluntary program depends on victims, victim advocates, and metropolitan area service providers, such as hospital emergency room teams, primary care providers, social workers, and child protective services personnel, clergy, teachers, employers, and employee assistance programs. For the involuntary program, the state's entire law enforcement and criminal justice system is added. Police, sheriff's departments, city and district attorneys, judges, probation officers, family members of both victims and perpetrators, and additional city agencies all have an active role. The comprehensive nature of this intervention strategy and implementation of it seems to approach the comprehensive nature of domestic violence itself. As in the microcosm of a single AMEND therapy group, so too in the macrocosm of the programmatic system, the community meets itself and works in service to itself.

This kind of systemic intervention can be understood as generating from an ethic that is collectively self-serving. Rather than divide and conquer, the strident tone of a militant model of health care marked by impositional ethics, the motif of communitywide intervention in domestic violence is restoration of the human in interpersonal relationships. Intervention for restoration is actually a peace-making venture, a broad-based political movement to renounce violence. The movement is away from the heartlessly patriarchal "rule of thumb" (the old English law whereby a husband could beat his wife without retributive consequence as long as the switch he used was no thicker than his thumb). The movement is toward a gender equality within the social fabric, the most visible result of which is the intolerance of violence within the home and the civic advocacy of nonviolence as the environment for conflict resolution. The community response to domestic violence, inspired by its victims, is engendering a newer community ethic: a change in belief, values, and behavior from violence to nonviolence.

LANGUAGE AND CHANGE: A FINAL REFLECTION

Language both reflects and creates individual and community reality. Ordinary discourse remains a vital signal at any given time to the pace of change and the construction of new ways of thinking. It is significant in this time of community transition from the civic advocacy of violence to the civic advocacy of nonviolence that health care practitioners lack a clear and precise language for the resolution sought for the disorder and chaos of domestic violence. (Intention grapples for a new set of words and symbols and behaviors. Even "violence" is countered only by a "non" and a hyphen.) A challenge to the creative energies given to domestic violence interventions in communities is the explication of what those energies are dedicated to, in a language of fresh possibilities for the ordinary meanings of nurturing, caring, safety, security, mutuality, intimacy, collaboration, growth, justice, and peace.

The most effective intervention is undoubtedly accompanied by preventive strategies. Perhaps one of the most effective preventive strategies is to learn how to speak about violence to one another in the community, within schools and families, and across professional disciplines. The destructive chaos of violence in the family is only worsened by the way of thinking about intervention that incorporates assaultive militancy and impositional ethics. Perhaps the more irenic belief represented in a restorative health care model will enable communities to work from within for systemic change. A language befitting this emerging alternative model will have to be created and learned. Perhaps the language of war and war-like ways of thinking can remain in the arena of war, and vacate the premises of family, intimate relationships, sex, love, marriage, child care—and health care.

REFERENCES

1. Strauss M, Gelles R: *Behind Closed Doors: Violence in the American Family.* New York, Doubleday, 1980.
2. Walker L: *The Battered Woman.* New York, Harper & Row, 1979.
3. Ewing W, Lindsey M, Pomerantz J: *Battering: An AMEND Manual for Helpers.* Denver, CO, AMEND, 1984.
4. Miller A: *For Your Own Good: Hidden Cruelty in Child Rearing and the Roots of Violence.* New York, Farrar, Straus and Giroux, 1983.
5. Miller A: *Thou Shalt Not Be Aware: Psychoanalysis and Society's Betrayal of the Child.* New York, Farrar, Straus and Giroux, 1984.

CHAPTER **42**

Rural Determinants in Family Health: Considerations for Community Nurses

Angeline Bushy, RN, PhD

Extensive citations are available on families, their health status, and the determinants in their health care-seeking behaviors. However, the focus has primarily been on urban/suburban samples, while rural counterparts have been ignored. Rural families address similar life situations, but their experiences are often colored by the somewhat unusual nature of rural values and life styles.[1,2] The reader may ask what is unique about rural settings. The descriptions in the literature of rural-urban differences vary, but there is a consensus that rural residency is not synonymous with farm residency. A commonly agreed upon definition is that a rural community has less than 2,500 residents. Of the total US rural population, 5% live in rural communities but less than 2% live on farms.[3]

Despite the lack of a specific definition, the literature reiterates that the health status of a rural community often is directly impacted by the primary economic resource of a region, such as farming, ranching, lumbering, and mining. Inasmuch as recent news headlines focus on the economic farm crises, only a few citations allude to the social impact on the lives of residents in surrounding communities, and minimal attention has been given to the health status of families who live there.[4,5]

Reprinted from *Family and Community Health,* Vol. 12, No. 4, with permission of Aspen Publishers, Inc., © 1990.

CULTURAL BELIEFS: A DETERMINANT IN HEALTH PERCEPTIONS

Sociologists are inconsistent as to the existence of a unique rural culture. Nevertheless, they agree that there are social, economic, and geographic differences that extend along a continuum from the most rural to the most urban community. For instance, in comparison to urban communities, rural communities generally are slower to change traditional cultural values and are reluctant to adopt mass societal influences. They also prefer less organized bureaucracy, valuing instead a locally focused government. Likewise, less populated areas have limited employment opportunities and fewer special-interest organizations. Finally, rural people are described as being more self-reliant and express greater reluctance to seek assistance from others.[6-8]

Health is a relative concept; therefore rural-urban factors also influence a particular population's perceptions of health. Logically, then, one must consider the rural definition before delineating deviations of health or health care-seeking behaviors in that population. Researchers at the Montana State University[9,10] and the University of Oklahoma[11] found that rural people defined health as the ability to work and to do what needs to be done. In essence, the cosmetic, comfort, and life-prolonging aspects of health are rarely viewed as important. Instead, being able to work is more important than being helped to be pain free, attractive, or in better overall health. Consequently the inability to work may also influence rural population's use of health care services.[9,10]

Interestingly, in several studies with rural populations, mental health was not included in the definition of health. They reported having less time for leisure activities and identified fewer mental health symptoms. A proposed rationale for this finding may be that emotional symptoms are not equated with a mental health problem; thus there is no need to seek mental health services. This also might account for health professionals' persistent reports of untreated chronic depression and anxiety in rural populations. Thus it becomes obvious that cultural values are a determinant of a rural population's health perception, which in turn influences their health care-seeking behaviors.[12-16]

RURAL VALUES: A DETERMINANT IN HEALTH BEHAVIORS

Rural people tend to maintain traditional values, which ultimately impact the health status of various subgroups. For example, rural women describe the ideal life style as being married with children but without employment outside the home. Furthermore, in a small community the identity of a woman is based on her relationship to someone else. A rural woman is viewed as the wife, mother, daughter, or sister of another person, which contributes to low self-esteem and a poor self-concept. Ultimately this also may influence a rural woman's health-promoting behaviors.[17-20]

Two additional child-rearing responsibilities assigned to rural mothers are those of being keepers of the culture and carriers of collective healing experiences. The first transmits cultural values, while the latter perpetuates self-care strategies to offspring.[21] Consequently one must speculate whether the popular theories used to explain female role socialization are appropriate for rural women. In turn, variations also can ultimately influence their life style and health behaviors.[22]

Cultural attitudes regarding marriage and family also may be reflected by fertility rates, which have declined for rural and urban populations. Even though the gap is narrowing, fertility rates continue to be higher among rural women. Moreover, women in rural settings have their first pregnancy earlier in life. These biometric statistics also may be a factor in the higher infant mortality rates consistently reported in rural settings.[22]

RESIDENCY: A DETERMINANT IN SOCIAL SUPPORT SYSTEMS

In rural communities local residents usually are acquainted with personnel in local governmental and health care institutions. Likewise, they also demonstrate greater resistance to outsiders' ideas and prefer to interact with people they know and view as similar to themselves.[8] This value is further evidenced in the "old timer–newcomer (outsider)" label that has ramifications for those who enter a community. The label infers that long-time residents are reluctant to establish a close tie with newcomers to the community. For instance, the effects of labeling have an impact on women who marry "a local fellow" or on a health care professional who accepts employment in a small community. Labeling such as this also is a serious concern when assignments to outreach sites are made on a rotating basis among personnel in a particular health care agency. This policy perpetuates professional alienation, which, in turn, promotes numerous deterrents to providing efficacious health care.[9-11]

HEALTH CARE-SEEKING BEHAVIORS: OTHER DETERMINANTS

Surprisingly, logistic barriers generally are *not* identified by rural families as a major deterrent to seeking health care. For example, in spite of the proclaimed familiarity with personnel employed in local social agencies, this has been identified as a deterrent for some families to seeking available services. This is evidenced by the large number of rural families perceived as needy by social service professionals who do not apply for any public assistance even though services are available.

Two repeatedly cited fears of rural residents with respect to their reluctance include (1) the fear of receiving insensitive treatment by an agency's employees and (2) the fear that friends, relatives, or neighbors may find out about the family's request.

These fears also are projected toward community nurses but not to the same degree as human services' personnel. The fears may be realistic when one considers that a family burdened with economic hardship, guilt, and depression is likely to perceive even the slightest display of insensitivity as an unwarranted attack.[23,24]

An attitude of self-reliance and the rural work ethic may also deter some families from seeking health care. An inherent belief in these two long-standing values is that those who are unable to support themselves are morally deficient or undeserving. For some rural families, going on welfare may be so unpalatable that they choose to live without any assistance. In many instances, though, the decision not to seek assistance is made by the male head of household at the expense of other family members.[25,26]

Another deterrent to seeking assistance may be related to functional illiteracy (reading level below the fifth grade), which often remains undetected in more isolated populations. A person who is unable to read may be reluctant to risk the humiliation associated with not having the ability to complete an application form or having insufficient proof of financial need.[27]

Even though logistic barriers generally are not identified as major deterrents in obtaining health care, geographic remoteness is associated with suboptimal professional work force/population ratios. Specialized services for women and children are especially lacking. This, combined with a number of predisposing, high-risk perinatal conditions, places rural families in the category of "at-risk populations."

Predisposing perinatal risks of rural populations include low socioeconomic status, high fertility rates, lack of medical insurance, and young pregnant women residing great distances from an obstetrician (eg, in some instances more than 100 miles). Another health care dilemma confronting rural populations relates to the astronomic costs of obstetric malpractice insurance that further restricts physicians from providing obstetric services in these areas.[28,29]

A recent descriptor of low population density in a large geographic area is termed "rural frontier." Considering the expansive distances between geographic sites that exist in some north central and western states, residents' perception of space and time also may assume different connotations. Couched in other terms, a family living five miles from the nearest neighbor may be perceived as being close, and traveling 100 miles to the obstetrician may not seem like a great distance. This view evidences adaptations in rural life style. Another adaptation is exemplified by residents who have a health concern. They first confer with a local nurse, who is usually "a neighbor woman." Furthermore, registered nurses consistently are identified as primary providers for prenatal care in the frontier region. For this reason factors such as time, distance, cost, isolation, and transportation also must be considered from ruralities' perspective when planning health care delivery in rural communities.[28-30]

RURAL ECONOMIC STRUCTURES: DETERMINANTS OF FAMILY STRESS

In rural communities one finds greater numbers of small, intergenerational family businesses (eg, grocery stores, service stations, banks, dairy services, farms, and ranches). A family business may promote positive family life; however, this phenomenon also may promote family stress. For instance, a family's income often is directly dependent on the financial success of a region's major industry. When a region's economy is depressed, small local businesses also suffer. In other cases individual family members may have multiple role expectations, or there may be subjugation of an individual's goals for the family's enterprise.[30]

The recent farm crises have resulted in other major community transitions, creating additional family stress. This is evidenced by the persistent increase in the number of reported cases of unemployment, accidents, domestic violence, child abuse, and neglect among rural populations. In the last five years, deaths among young males have steadily increased, and in several small communities adolescent suicides have become epidemic. One must emphasize, however, that determining whether a death is accidental or intentional is often impossible. Nevertheless, be the death accidental or intentional, a family is left to deal with the consequences. Yet there is no research addressing the impact of such tragedies on a family, particularly female heads of households who must assume unfamiliar roles without support services.

RURAL SOCIAL STRUCTURES: DETERMINANTS IN FAMILY HEALTH STATUS

Similar to urban women, the recent economic situation also has forced traditional rural housewives to seek employment outside of the home. However, particularly for women, rural communities have a narrower range of occupational choices. For this reason women with advanced degrees tend to seek employment in settings where opportunities and salaries are commensurate with their educational preparation. Nonetheless, a few elect to return to their home community. These women frequently are underemployed.[31] For example, those prepared in business may only find a secretarial or an office receptionist position; teachers may only find teacher aide positions; while the career options for nurses may be limited in scope or nonexistent. In part this is due to minimal personnel turnover. Consequently there are few opportunities for either upward or lateral career mobility, and this contributes to feelings of helplessness and depression among rural residents, especially women.[32,33]

Older women have additional concerns. Traditionally, rural women have been expected to contribute equally in labor efforts to both domestic activities as well as the family enterprise. Yet these efforts generally do not produce a salary, social security, insurance, or retirement benefits. Because of these practices, stories prevail of poverty-stricken, middle-aged housewives who have been displaced by either their spouse's death or by divorce. Census data further reveal that women in rural communities tend to be living under conditions of greater economic need than their urban counterparts; ultimately this has an impact on the health status of rural families.[34]

SELF-RELIANCE VERSUS DEPENDENCE: DETERMINANTS OF SOCIAL SUPPORT

Social support networks can be a mediating influence on a person's self-concept as well as on the coping strategies employed by a family to resolve life events. An underlying theme of rural culture is preference for family and community support. Even place of residence may dictate the degree of accessibility to formal and informal systems. In other words, social support may vary in quantity and quality, depending on population density. Families in sparsely populated areas, therefore, may employ different coping mechanisms for contending with life transitions, resulting, perhaps, in different outcomes than for those residing in more populated surroundings.[23]

Rural families are believed to be more self-reliant, performing more services for themselves as opposed to relying on specialists. Concomitantly, rural communities also tend to have fewer formal organizations than urban communities. This may be related to rural demographic profiles that may not be conducive to participation in formal organizations.[26] For example, rural residents have fewer years of formal education and lower family income, and rural households tend to be larger, having extended family members of several generations represented. Also, rural communities have a greater representation of elderly people, fewer children, and a higher ratio of females to males. From these figures one can speculate that social activities may be more family focused, or one might question whether individuals have the time, interest, or energy to participate in formal organizations.

Women's organizations, however, are an exception, particularly rural homemakers' clubs in which women often remain active for most of their adult years. Over decades that include numerous life events, the members provide support to each other. Women's organizations also are identified as a primary source of health education. Therefore health care professionals may not be ruralities' preferred information source.[9,10] Even so, long-standing homemakers' clubs are rapidly disappearing in rural communities. Several factors may be responsible for this occurrence, including an aging female population, increased numbers of women seeking employment outside the home, and younger families leaving their community of origin to seek gainful employment elsewhere.[18,20]

Concomitantly, rural women consistently identify a smaller social network. Therefore the disruption of traditional networks, such as a long-established homemakers' club, has particular relevance for rural families. Women's literature indicates that they often assume the role of family buffer; but rural women are socialized to keep their feelings to themselves. They state they are ashamed of their little problems, try to resolve their concerns alone, and believe there is nothing to complain about if one has a healthy husband and children. One must speculate, however, on how long a wife/mother can bear the brunt of her family's emotions and at what cost? Considering the additional burdens imposed on this traditional feminine role, the question must then be raised of whether the recent transitions have resulted in greater vulnerability in the health status of rural families than reported in the media.[33]

Sociologists describe three levels of self-reliance/social support in all populations. The first level does not involve an exchange of money and is provided by individuals or families. The second level is volunteered by informal organizations such as church groups and the previously described homemakers' clubs. The third level of support requires financial reimbursement. These services are provided either by government agencies or the private business sector.[8]

Rural families tend to rely more on the first two levels for social support, while urban counterparts use more services at the third level. Even though there are fewer formal organizations in rural communities, these groups become involved in a variety of activities that change, depending on a community's needs. With the recent transitions in rural communities, however, there has been an increase in the use of third-level services. In essence, rural residents have been forced to interact on a more global level without the support of traditional social systems during personal and family crises.[8]

PRIMARY HEALTH CARE: COMMUNITY NURSES AS PROVIDERS

Even though rural women, particularly nurses, usually are assigned the cultural expectation of perpetuating self-care, coupled with rural residents' preference for someone they know to care for them, many rural communities are without community nursing services. Furthermore, women's work (including nursing) is considered to be a voluntary service. For example, local nurses are expected to provide care without compensation to people who drop by their homes, to respond to accidents, and, in some cases, to provide follow-up care to chronically ill patients living in the community. A small community expects a nurse to provide care to all types of patients voluntarily; therefore nurses assume multiple roles and usually do not have an opportunity to specialize.[2,9,20,29]

Recent employment data show that nurses in rural settings have less professional education than those employed in agencies within a metropolitan area. Lacking access to current information, they have been known to provide outdated information that in some cases has proved to be detrimental to the advice seeker's health.[35] Consistent with the previously discussed employment patterns of women having advanced education, nurses also do not seek employment in a rural community. Those who remain usually have a nuclear and extended family in the area.

Recently researchers at Montana State University noted that similar to rural women in general, nurses do not have an identity of their own.[9,10] This reality and the social and economic climates of rural health care institutions make recruiting and retaining nurses extremely problematic. It is not unusual for a county to have insufficient funds to hire a community nurse; if they do hire one, the salary is very low. In some regions one nurse may be responsible for providing care to three or more counties spanning a large geographic area. Furthermore, community nurses in rural settings tend to have minimal formal education in community nursing. Many have been prepared at the associate or diploma level.[36,37]

In addition to having less professional preparation, educational opportunities for nurses in geographically isolated areas are limited. It is difficult for a rural agency to maintain professionally competent nurses. Participating in continuing education also is a problem due to the high cost of traveling extensive geographic distances to attend programs. This is complicated by having to pay salaries for replacements while other nurses attend a conference. Consequently insufficient numbers of prepared nurses have a negative impact on the health status and the health care-seeking behaviors of rural populations.[10]

• • •

Nurses play a significant role in providing primary health care to rural families. For this reason resources must be allocated to develop innovative programs that can make nursing education, including a focus on community nursing, accessible in remote areas. Professional knowledge must be upgraded to include theory about rural populations. The recent social and economic transitions, however, have caused a decline in well-established natural support systems through which health information historically has been provided. For this reason other educational strategies should be developed to disseminate health information to health professionals and consumers alike (eg, electronic media, outreach programs, and self-study learning modules).

Rural nurses in general and community nurses in particular must become actively involved in recruiting and retaining members of the profession, since they are in a position to identify incentives that will encourage others to practice in small towns. Incentives might include higher salary; but there may be other incentives that may be more enticing, such as providing housing or child care services, encouraging flexible scheduling, providing additional vacation days with access to outdoor recreational facilities, reimbursing for advanced education, and providing opportunities for continuing education or professional development. The "nonidentity" of women also must be addressed so that nurses can be recognized as a community health resource (ie, having monetary worth).

Nurses should become politically active at the local level to effect change in employment opportunities and salary structures for rural women. The scarcity of child care services must be addressed by creating innovative programs that take into consideration rural social and economic structures such as adopt a grandparent program, babysitting cooperatives, or on-site child care services. Ultimately by improving the economic status of women, their families' health will also improve.

The health of a rural community is influenced by traditional rural value systems, such as adhering to traditional gender role behaviors and demonstrating stoic self-sufficiency. Nurses, as primary care providers, must be knowledgeable of these values as well as of their impact on individuals', families', and communities' health and health behaviors. However, additional research is needed that specifically addresses rural residency in relation to life events such as marriage, parenthood, unemployment, foreclosure of businesses, departure of long-time friends, closing of schools, reorganization of school districts, middle age, retirement, and death.

Finally, the unique aspects of the various rural populations must be considered if effective, culturally specific health care is to be provided. Health professionals as well as those who develop public policy should be cognizant of the relationship between rural families and local, state, and national organizations so that formal services mesh with existing informal helping systems. Instead of implementing a new (outside) health care service, greater acceptance by a group can be anticipated if these services are integrated with an established and trusted community resource. Because of rural communities' limited resources, concerted interdisciplinary effort and collaboration are necessary to make holistic health care a reality for families who live there.

REFERENCES

1. Andrews M, Burdick Q: Letter from U.S. Senate Committee on Appropriations Establishing a Rural Health Caucus. Washington, DC, June 17, 1985.
2. Cordes S: Rural America: Preparing for the next century. Presentation at the Dakota Conference on Rural Health, Bismarck, ND, March 1989.
3. Glenn N, Hill L: Rural-urban differences in attitudes and behavior in the United States. *Ann Am Acad Pol Soc Sci* 1977;429:36-50.
4. Haney W: Women, in Dillman D, Hobbs D (eds): *Rural Society in the US: Issues for the 1980s.* Boulder, Colo, Westview Press, 1982.
5. McCormick J: America's third world. *Newsweek,* August 8, 1988, pp 21-24.
6. Rogers E: *Social change in rural societies.* Englewood Cliffs, NJ, Prentice Hall, 1983.
7. US Bureau of the Census: *General Population Characteristics.* Hyattsville, Md, NCHS Series 10, no. 160, 1987.
8. Warren R: *The Community in America.* Chicago, Rand McNally, 1972.
9. Long K, Weinert C: Understanding the health care needs of rural families. *Fam Rel* 1987;36(11):450-455.
10. Shannon A: Educators innovative to match changing needs: Preparing nurses for rural health care. *Am Nurse* 1989;21(2):10.
11. Stein H: The annual cycle and the cultural nexus of health care behavior among Oklahoma wheat farming families. *Culture Med Psychiatry* 1982;6:81-99.

12. Beason P, Johnson D: A panel study of change (1981-1986) in rural mental health status: Effects of the rural crisis. Presented at the National Institute of Mental Health National Conference on Mental Health Statistics, Denver, May 19, 1987.
13. Brown G, Prudo R: Psychiatric disorder in a rural and an urban population. *Psychol Med* 1981;11:581-599.
14. Flax J, Ivens R, Wagenfeld M, et al: Mental health and rural America: An overview. *Community Ment Health Rev* 1978;3:3-15.
15. Palmer C: Overview of Iowa's state mental health authority response to rural life crisis. Presented at the National Mental Health Association Rural Action Commission Forum, Des Moines, December 2, 1987.
16. Wilkening E: Farm families and family farming, in Coward R, Smith W (eds): *The Family in Rural Society.* Boulder, Colo, Westview Press, 1981.
17. Swedlund P: Report of Northeast Colorado ARCH Consortium: Drug and alcohol abuse in rural Colorado (funded by Kellogg Foundation). Presentation at the Dakota Conference on Rural Health, Bismarck, ND, March 1989.
18. Bigbee J: Rurality, stress and illness among women: A pilot study. *Health Care Women Int* 1988;9(1):43-61.
19. Flora C, Johnson S: Discarding the distaff: New roles for American women, in Ford T (ed): *Rural USA: Persistence and Change.* Ames, Iowa, Iowa State University Press, 1978.
20. Kernoff P, Mansfield D, Crawford C: Rural-urban differences in women's psychological well being. *Health Care Women Int* 1988;9(4):289-304.
21. Battenfield D, Clift E, Graubarth R: *Patterns for Change: Rural Women Organizing for Health.* Washington, DC, National Women's Health Network, 1981.
22. Proceedings of the National Conference on the Delivery of Family Planning Services in Rural America. New York, Alan Guttmacher Institute, 1977.
23. Hanson N, Paulson C: *Farm Stress: Learning to Cope.* Bismarck, ND, Mental Health Association, 1987.
24. Lee G, Cassidy M: Kinship systems and extended family ties, in Coward R, Smith W (eds): *The Family in Rural Society.* Boulder, Colo, Westview Press, 1981.
25. Schaefer J: Teardrop time at trail's end. *Newsweek,* December 5, 1988, p 100.
26. Schumm W, Bollman S: Interpersonal process in rural families, in Coward RT, Smith WM (eds): *The Family in Rural Society.* Boulder, Colo, Westview Press, 1981.
27. Quanrud T: For those who can't read there is a way out. *Bismarck Tribune,* September 9, 1988; 1B.
28. Associated Press: Finding doctors a problem: South Dakota too rural to attract medical graduates. *Bismarck Tribune,* January 10, 1988, 10A.
29. Bushy A: Body image and self-esteem in pregnant women: A comparison of rural and urban populations. Ann Arbor, Mich, University Microfilms International; 1987.
30. Danes S: Jobs mean farm wife overload. "Farwest," *Bismarck Tribune,* March 1, 1989, p 7.
31. Dunne F: Occupational sex-stereotyping among rural young women and men. *Rural Sociol* 1980;45:396-415.
32. Sweet J: The employment of rural farm wives. *Rural Sociol* 1972;37:553-577.
33. Tevis C: Farm wife is family's escape valve: Where does she go to let off steam? *Success Farm* 1979;77:22-23.
34. US Department of Labor: *Employment Programs for Rural Women.* Publication No. 491-543/46210. Government Printing Office, 1985.
35. AACN: Facts with impact. *AACN Newslett* 1988;14(1):4.
36. Thornton J: Developing a rural nursing clinic. *Nurs Educ* 1983;8(2):24-29.
37. Mossefin C: The challenge of rural nursing. *Focus Rural Health* 1987;4(2):4.

Suggested Additional Readings for Part VII

Family and community health nursing practice

Allen JR and Allen BA: Violence in the family, Fam Community Health 4(2):19-33, Aug 1981.

Angel R and Worobey JL: Single motherhood and children's health, Health Soc Behav 29(1):38-52, 1988.

Baldwin KA and Chen SC: The effectiveness of public health nursing services to prenatal clients: an integrated review, Public Health Nurs 6(2):80-87, June 1989.

Baranowski T, Nader PR, Dunn K, and Vanderpool NA: Family self-help: promoting changes in health behavior, J Commun 32(3):161-172, Summer 1982.

Bernhardt JH: Potential workplace hazards to reproductive health: information for primary prevention, J Obstet Gynecol Neonatal Nurs 19(1):53-62, Jan-Feb 1990.

Clark J: Supporting the family . . . heading off a breakdown. Nurs Times 82(32):33-34, 1986.

Collins C and Tiedje LB: A program for women returning to work after childbirth J Obstet Gynecol Neonatal Nurs 246-253, July-Aug 1988.

deChesnay M: How healthy families cope with stress AAOHN J 36(9):361-364, 1988.

Helton A, McFarlane J, and Anderson E: Prevention of battering during pregnancy Public Health Nurs 4(3): 166-174, 1987.

Richardson SF: Child health promotion practices, J Pediatr Health Care 2(2):73-78, March-April 1988.

Robinson K: Older women who are caregivers, Health Care Women's Int 9(4):239-249, 1988.

Robinson KM: A social skills training program for adult caregivers, Adv Nurs Sci, 10(2):59-72, 1988.

Rosenfield S: Family influence on eating behavior and attitudes in eating disorders: a review of the literature, Holistic Nurs Practice, 3(1):46-55, Nov 1988.

Ross CE and Mirowsky J: Child care and emotional adjustment to wives' employment, Health and Soc Behav 29(2): 127-138, 1988.

Torres A and Kenny AM: Expanding medicaid coverage for pregnant women: estimates of the impact and cost Fam Plann Perspect 21(1):19-24, 1989.

Walker LO: Stress process among mothers of infants Nurs Res 38(1):10-16, Jan-Feb, 1989.

Whall AL: The family as a unit of care in nursing: a historical review, Public Health Nurs 3(4):240-249, 1986.

Wong DL: Helping parents select day care, Pediatr Nursing 12:181-187, 1986.

PART VIII

HEALTH CARE OF VULNERABLE POPULATIONS

The concept of risk is an important consideration as the community health nurse prioritizes health care at the aggregate level. As communities experience changes in the nature of their health problems, community nurses respond accordingly. Declining financial support for health programs at the national and local levels has dramatically affected the most vulnerable groups in society. Children, the elderly, and other high-risk groups are especially vulnerable to changes in health care accessibility and availability.

Community problems related to unemployment, deteriorating economic conditions, illiteracy, and unstable family functioning continue to affect our society's productivity. Although identified risk factors have changed over the past fifty years, some continue to present problems for vulnerable populations in spite of health care system responses and technological efforts. Communicable diseases such as AIDS, other sexually transmitted diseases, and tuberculosis, continue to threaten our population's health. U.S. infant mortality rates rank twenty-third in the world community, while pollutants threaten the water that we drink and the air that we breathe. Increased rates of substance abuse affect our nation's stability and productivity, and the elderly and those caring for children must compete for scarce health resources. In some cases social stigma increases the vulnerability of certain groups, such as the disabled, the homeless, and lesbian and gay aggregates. All of these risk factors affect intervention as well as assessment. The articles chosen for Part Eight focus on only a few of the U.S.'s most vulnerable populations. Barriers and solutions to care are presented in the context of community health nursing practice.

CHAPTER **43**

Infant Mortality and Public Health Nursing: A History of Accomplishments, a Future of Challenges

Marla E. Salmon, RN, ScD, FAAN
Mary Peoples-Sheps, RN, DrPH

Infant mortality in the United States has improved dramatically in this century. In 1930, 65 out of every 1,000 infants died during the first year of life.[1] By 1986, that number had decreased to 10.4 per 1,000.[2] The magnitude of this change is encouraging, but infant mortality remains a significant problem for the United States. In 1986, this country ranked 19th from the lowest rate of infant mortality in the world (in Sweden), behind such relatively underdeveloped areas as Singapore and Hong Kong.[3] Within the United States, the picture is grim. Differences between the "haves" and the "have-nots" are clearly reflected in infant mortality rates (IMR). The geographic areas that are poor, such as the southeastern states, have much higher infant mortality rates than wealthier states. In 1986, for example, when the IMR for the country was 10.4, the IMR for the eight southeastern states in USDHHS Region IV was 11.7. Particularly appalling, and a likely cause of the disproportionately high rate of infant mortality in the South and some other rural and inner-city areas, is the large gap between white and nonwhite rates in the United States. The nonwhite IMR in 1986 was 15.7; the rate for whites was 8.9.[2] Moreover, infant mortality is only the tip of the iceberg; for every baby who dies, many more survive the first year with serious physical, psychological and cognitive handicaps.[4]

Fortunately, these trends in IMR and associated problems have been recognized by several influential groups. The National Commission to Prevent Infant Mortality recently released a number of important recommendations for preventing infant mortality.[5] The commission, created by an act of Congress in November 1986, consisted of 15 members, including experts in maternal and child health and representatives of state and federal government agencies. Their recommendations include opportunities for public health nurses in both traditional and nontraditional roles. Many of these recommendations mirror those made by other organizations, including the Southern Governors' Association, the Institute of Medicine, and the American Nurses' Association in conjunction with the Federal Bureau of Maternal and Child Health and Resources Development.[6-9]

Reprinted from *Nursing Outlook,* Vol. 37, No. 2, with permission of American Journal of Nursing, © 1989.

TRADITIONAL PHN APPROACHES TO PREVENTING INFANT MORTALITY

For almost a century nurses have played pivotal roles in the prevention of infant mortality. Early in the century, it became apparent that many infant deaths were associated with infectious diseases, and that proper hygiene at home and better packaging and storing of perishable foods could prevent the spread of infections. With this knowledge, some visiting nurses began to shift their role from care of the poor sick in the home to home-based preventive education. The latter area was one of significant concern to public health departments, which were increasingly able to hire public health nurses. As more public health nurses joined the disease prevention campaign, they inadvertently moved away from the autonomy of the privately owned and nurse-managed visiting nurse associations. A major side effect of that shift was that "the concerns of nurses in most official agencies were confined to the teaching of prevention."[10] But although education may have been the entree, public health nurses developed extensive skills in identifying individuals in need and helping them gain access to appropriate services. By exercising these responsibilities, public health nurses came in contact with other specialized nurses, especially those with skills that transcended traditional hospital nursing roles, such as nurse practitioners and certified nurse midwives. In some cases, the roles of these different specialties overlapped in the same person, as demonstrated so well through Kentucky's Frontier Nursing Service.[11]

Public health nurses have contributed to the reduction of infant mortality in other less obvious and less glamorous ways. As members of administrative teams in health departments and other agencies that provide care to pregnant women and infants, particularly at program levels, they have provided leadership, organization, and supervision to the public health nurses for whom they are responsible.

Traditionally, public health nursing and other nursing specialties involved in the prevention of infant mortality have been limited to individual or family care, primarily through education and clinical interventions. It has become increasingly clear, however, that neither the scope nor the magnitude of interventions in behalf of mothers and their infants is enough to reduce infant mortality. Infant mortality is a complex social problem with known social, behavioral, and environmental determinants as well as biomedical factors.[5] The determinants of infant mortality are not limited to individuals or families; rather, they are often forces embedded in communities, large and small, and some of them result from the fragmentation of the U.S. health care system.

The role of nursing in the reduction of infant mortality has been significant, particularly in providing direct services for mothers and babies. The challenge facing public health nurses now is to conquer the other forces that contribute to infant mortality.

FRAMEWORK FOR ANALYSIS OF PHN PRACTICE

To address factors that lie beyond the individual, it is helpful to understand how public health nursing practice has influenced these factors and how it may do so in the future. The White construct for public health nursing practice provides a systematic inventory for analysis.[12] It includes four key determinants of health: biological, environmental, social, and medical/technological/organizational factors. The construct was designed as a framework for examining where public health nursing interventions have been focused and where they may be directed in the future. The White construct is based on one of the principle underpinnings of public health: the public good. With public good as the goal, practice issues are not limited to assuring the health and safety of the individual mothers and infants served; rather, they are broader in scope, encompassing the well-being of all mothers and infants in the United States (or in a community closer to home).

Let us, for example, reconsider the preceding discussion of traditional approaches to preventing infant mortality. For years, nurses have provided clinical MCH services to women and their infants. These interventions focus almost exclusively on biological and medical/technological factors that affect infant mortality. Traditionally, public health nurses have provided these interventions themselves or arranged for their patients to receive them. Public health nurses have also sought to improve the social and environmental conditions of the mothers and infants they serve. They have understood that biology and technology alone are not enough to prevent infant mortality. But, while embracing a broader mandate for nursing practice, traditional public health nurses have usually been constrained by policies and perceptions of what a nurse "is," a situation that has prevented them from extending their skills beyond the individual to the community and thus addressing the problem of infant mortality as a whole.

Public health nurses have increasingly focused on one-to-one interventions, adopting the overall professional trend of using nursing diagnoses and evaluating effectiveness on the basis of single-case care process and outcome. This focus is useful, but it must be expanded. The point of departure of White's construct, the public good, is largely lost when effectiveness is measured by counting only those who are reached and ignoring those who are not. The latter, unfortunately, are too often those who are at greatest risk.

There is, of course, some comfort in the realization that nurses have been in the forefront in providing maternal and infant care to disadvantaged populations. It is at the policy-making level of society and of institutions, however, where programs are created and resource levels are set, that nursing involvement has been minimal. And yet nurses have much to offer the policy-making process. To really decrease infant mortality in the last decade of this century, public decisionmakers must approach the problem as an issue worth the risk of their political careers. The actions they must take to have an impact on this problem include defining the present situation as intolerable and pushing for interventions that can produce tangible improvement. Among these interventions are legislation creating entitlement to services, refusal to ignore the problem, and regulatory and financial incentives necessary to assure program success. Public health nurses are among the few health professionals with the expertise to encourage and hold accountable the legislators and other public officials involved in realizing the "public good." Both direct and indirect contributions to this process of aligning public policy with public good should be major elements of public health nursing practice.

NEW CHALLENGES FOR PHNS

Public health nurses must now expand their roles and activities if they are to be a force in the improvement of infant mortality. This is not to say that the previous and current roles should be abandoned; rather, they should begin to describe only part of what nurses do to decrease infant mortality. The emerging or "new" roles described here should be complementary to and fully incorporated into the range of practice options for which nurses are prepared.

Case Management

Nurses have traditionally felt most "at home" at the clinical, one-to-one level of practice when providing most maternal and infant services. What happens to clients who have not obtained nursing services or who are not eligible for programs covering nursing services has not been an area of primary responsibility for them. The consequences of our disjointed, "fall-through-the-cracks" system of services are often most apparent during gestation and infancy. The ability of nurses to provide continuing, accessible, appropriate, and accountable services to pregnant women and infants is, in itself, a key determinant of infant outcomes. While nurses have often played a role in managing this process (frequently without sanction or resources), recognition of the need for and potential cost-benefit of this type of "brokerage" is becoming increasingly important. What has been an ad-hoc role for nurses now promises to play a prominent role in service delivery. Nurses are the ideal providers of this service. Accepting a direct care role without accepting responsibility for the overall care of the client is providing only a partial service. The clinical effectiveness of public health nurses depends largely on their ability to manage the total care of the client.

Targeted Programming

Targeted intervention programs are the single most important public health strategy for optimizing health outcomes and resource allocations on a large scale. Traditionally, targeted programs have grown out of political awareness of a serious problem for which solutions or interventions were, in fact, available. This awareness is generally the result of grass-roots recognition of the problem and/or epidemiologic surveillance translated into political pressure or activism by special interest groups. Although nurses have played key roles in the operational aspects of program development, they have remained largely uninvolved in the grass-roots, epidemiologic and political origins of these programs. The value of the perspective that nurses can bring to these aspects of program development has been vastly underemphasized. Neither our education nor our practice has adequately encouraged or prepared nurses to move into such roles as community organizer, epidemiologist or political activist. Unfortunately, these roles are too often viewed in nursing as "outside" of nursing practice because the practice of and education for such roles is interdisciplinary (not "pure" nursing). Without recognition of the role that nurses can play in creating responsive programs, their ability to use their knowledge and skills fully in providing direct services to clients will be limited. Without such nursing involvement, the crucial decisions about who receives services and who remains unserved—the most critical decisions of all in the effort to lower infant mortality—will continue to be made primarily by others.

Administration

Public health agencies and programs providing infant mortality prevention services have traditionally been administered and managed by non-nurse personnel (primarily physicians). Although nurses have provided the bulk of services to clients and are closest to the actual problems, few nurses are involved in the leadership of these organizations. Part of the problem is the division of graduate preparation of nurses into clinical and administrative tracks. In infant mortality programs, both clinical and administrative knowledge are essential. The preparation of nurses with MCH-administration expertise is an important way of providing skilled, knowledgeable, and less costly administration for such programs. To accomplish this, however, nurses in both service and education will have to stop using "clinical competence" as the sole measure of professional expertise. Moreover, nursing will have to embrace the notion that it is both legitimate and essential for nurses to serve as leaders in interdisciplinary programs and agencies, and obtain interdisciplinary preparation to accomplish this.

Information Systems

A key area in which public health nurses can improve the effectiveness of infant mortality programs and services is information systems development and management. These systems literally define the problems to be addressed, shape the nature of programs, and describe their effectiveness and costs. All too frequently, however, they are the product of information-technology expertise that does not include knowledge of health, health services, or client needs. It is essential that nurses who work in infant mortality programs be prepared to work effectively with information systems at all levels. A basic knowledge of epidemiology, computers and existing data systems concerned with infant mortality is a good beginning point. The involvement of nurses who have advanced expertise in these areas would improve these systems even more. Because nurses are the single largest category of public health workers, particularly in programs related to infant mortality, it is essential that nurses become key players in these information and surveillance systems.

Health Education

Another role for nurses in preventing infant mortality is in health education and behavior change. Nurses have been effective in one-to-one client education, but at the community or institutional level, health education has become the province of educators employed by health departments. Nurses who have moved into health education roles have frequently been criticized by their nursing colleagues for "leaving nursing." This limitation of the roles that nurses can play in providing services has limited their effectiveness in decreasing infant mortality.

School Health Programs

School health programs are playing an increasingly important role in lowering infant mortality through services to adolescent girls, particularly through the development of comprehensive, school-based clinics.[8] The traditional role of nurses in schools has been primarily to provide direct client services. With increasing school health resources and a heightened awareness of the school services designed to prevent infant mortality, the school health "team" is becoming a highly sophisticated interdisciplinary group requiring knowledgeable and skilled leadership. This need for leadership has given nurses an opportunity to make a great impact on infant mortality and other school health problems. To do so, nurses must acquire adequate interdisciplinary preparation in school and public health, school health administration and interdisciplinary leadership.

Research

One of the most intriguing ironies in all of public health is that although nurses provide the majority of services to clients, these services are the least well understood of any. We know very little about the efficacy of public health nursing services. While we know "intuitively" that home visiting is an important component of services aimed at infant mortality, only preliminary investigations have been made regarding the content and impact of such visits.[14] The involvement of nurses in this and other types of research relating to infant mortality is an essential element of making advances in services.

Other

History and basic educational preparation have equipped nurses to move into various health service roles with minimal additional preparation. There will undoubtedly be many roles for nurses to play in addition to those mentioned above as the campaign against infant mortality continues to evolve. If nurses are to continue to play a key role in decreasing infant mortality, a number of traditional biases must be overcome. Among these is the professional exclusivism that has defined nursing by limitations rather than possibilities. Nurses must begin to support rather than reject colleagues who perform services outside of the one-to-one clinical domain. Nurses must also recognize the value of educational preparation that lies outside of nursing and view it as a means for enhancing nursing rather than an exit from the profession.

Nursing must also be active in its encouragement of ethnic and racial diversity in its membership. Infant mortality is not restricted to white, middle-class people. Until the profession includes members of the groups with the highest infant mortality rates, its ability to relate to and reach these groups will be compromised.

CONCLUSION

Nurses have been and will continue to be important in the campaign against infant mortality. The problem of infant mortality demands that nurses expand their involvement into both new roles and roles traditionally held by others. To do so, nurses in both education and practice will have to change traditional attitudes, alter definitions of and preparation for practice, and provide support for nurses in these new roles. Nursing must also embrace ethnic and racial diversity in its ranks and interdisciplinary diversity in its practice. Nurses are in a unique position to provide the leadership necessary to significantly decrease infant mortality. To do so, however, requires immediate change in both nursing education and practice.

REFERENCES

1. U.S. Select Panel for the Promotion of Child Health. *Better Health for Our Children: A National Strategy. Vol. 3. A Statistical Profile* (DHHS [PHS] Publ. No. 79—55071). Washington, DC, U.S. Government Printing Office, 1981.
2. Region IV Network for Data Management and Utilization. *Consensus in Region IV: Perinatal Indicators for Planning and Assessment.* Chapel Hill, NC, RNDMU, 1988.
3. Hughes, D., and others. *The Health of America's Children: Maternal and Child Health Data Book.* Washington, DC, Children's Defense Fund, 1987.
4. McCormick, M. C. The contribution of low birth weight to infant mortality and childhood morbidity. *N. Engl. J. Med.* 312:82-90, Jan. 10, 1985.
5. National Commission to Prevent Infant Mortality. *Death Before Life: The Tragedy of Infant Mortality.* Washington, DC, The Commission, Aug. 1988.

6. Southern Regional Task Force on Infant Mortality. *Final Report for the Children of Tomorrow.* Washington, DC, Southern Governors' Association, Nov. 1985.
7. U.S. Institute of Medicine. *Preventing Low Birthweight.* Washington, DC, National Academy Press, 1985.
8. ________________. *Prenatal Care: Reaching Mothers, Reaching Infants.* Washington, DC, National Academy Press, 1988.
9. Curry, M. A. *Access to Prenatal Care: Key to Preventing Low Birthweight. Report of Consensus Conferences* (Publ. No. MCH-16). Kansas City, MO, American Nurses' Association, March 1987.
10. Buhler-Wilkerson, K. Public health nursing: in sickness or in health? *Am. J. Public Health* 75:1155-1161, Oct. 1985.
11. Dammann, N. *A Social History of the Frontier Nursing Service.* Sun City, AZ, Social Change Press, 1982.
12. White, M. S Construct for public health nursing. *Nurs. Outlook* 30:527-530, Nov.-Dec. 1982.
13. U.S. Department of Health and Human Services. *Public Health Personnel in the United States* (DHHS [PHS] Pub. No. 82-6). Washington, DC, U.S. Government Printing Office, 1982.
14. Peoples-Sheps, M., and others. *Home Visiting and Prenatal Care: A Survey of Practical Wisdom* (to be published).

CHAPTER **44**

Poverty and Early Childhood Parenting: Toward a Framework for Intervention

Robert Halpern, PhD

The apparent links among poverty, inadequate parenting, and compromised child development have long been a source of concern for American social reformers *(Grubb & Lazerson, 1982)*. Historically, the dominant intervention thrust has been to supplement or compensate for parental care in an effort to assure low-income children an equal opportunity for educational and occupational success. But there have always been organized efforts to strengthen such care as well; for example, the "moral guidance" provided by the nineteenth century friendly visitors, the settlement house workers' advice and assistance on child-rearing matters, and the family casework of the first child and family service agencies *(Lubove, 1968; McGowan, 1988)*. In the past 25 years especially, interventions designed to provide child-rearing guidance, advice, and psychological support to low-income families with young children have proliferated *(Weiss & Halpern, 1988)*.

Why has the relationship between poverty and child rearing been such a compelling and persistent source of social concern? There is unquestionably something to that concern, but the relationship between these two complex variables remains far from clear *(Sameroff, Seifer, Barocas, Zax, & Greenspan, 1987)*.

Reprinted from *American Journal of Orthopsychiatry*, Vol. 60, No. 1, with permission of American Orthopsychiatric Association, Inc., © 1990.

This paper will draw on available literature in an effort to establish a useful conceptual approach to studying the relationship between poverty and early childhood parenting, and to discuss implications for service-oriented intervention strategies. It will be argued that poverty creates a number of characteristic obstacles to attentive and nurturant child rearing; at the same time, it will be argued that the effects of poverty on the parent-child relationship are mediated by the interaction of situational factors, personal developmental history, and cultural affiliation. The appropriate emphases of helping strategies depend on the nature of the defining stresses and vulnerabilities in a family.

CONSTRAINTS TO A REVIEW OF POVERTY AND PARENTING

It is generally difficult to establish causality, and even to decide on a focus, in studying relationships between individuals and the social systems in which they are embedded. In the case of poverty and early childhood parenting, empirical problems are compounded by theoretical differences about how to approach the subject. It has been argued, for example, that it is inappropriate to evaluate parenting in low-income, especially low-income minority, populations by standards that reflect only mainstream cultural norms, opportunities, and situational demands *(Ogbu, 1987)*. Patterns of care and nurturance can only be evaluated in relation to the characteristics of the sociocultural context in which they occur.

From the perspective of mainstream developmental psychology there is substantial agreement about the attributes of parental care that promote healthy development in young children *(Clarke-Stewart, 1973, 1977; Escalona, 1981; Musick & Stott, 1990; Rapoport & Rapoport, 1980)*. Children need to be protected from physical and psychological harm, and provided adequate nourishment. Beyond these basics, in infancy children need frequent holding, touching, smiling, and talking; in a word, nurturing. They need a parent who is a mediator of environmental stimulation, a parent who is sensitive to and accepting of their moods, responsive to their cues, consistent in behavior, and available in the most fundamental sense. For toddlers and preschoolers, additional attributes such as expanding and elaborating on play activities; a cognitively rich physical and social environment; firm, consistent, and yet flexible control strategies; and an absence of restrictiveness have been noted to be important.

Critics argue that mainstream notions of nurturant parenting derive from the study of a particular (i.e., white, middle-class) social world, requiring particular child competencies *(Ogbu, 1985, 1987)*. Children from low-income, especially low-income minority families, face different demands, threats, and opportunities in the immediate physical and social contexts of their daily lives; these require different parental care and nurturance strategies *(Laosa, 1979; LeVine, 1974; Ogbu, 1985)*. Parents interpret and respond to their young children's actions not only in a manner consistent with their individual psychological structures, but in a manner consistent with their belief systems and the sense of what skills their children will need to survive and compete *(Laosa, 1979)*. The evaluative problem, then, is that patterns of care and nurturance designed to prepare low-income children for the immediate contexts of their lives may not always be consonant with those that mainstream psychology defines as optimal. This conflict will be addressed at greater length later.

A different sort of complicating factor in studying the relationship between poverty and early childhood parenting arises from the very act of studying this relationship. It has been argued that by focusing so excessively on child rearing in efforts to understand the reasons for poor outcomes in low-income children, researchers are implicitly placing responsibility for such poor outcomes on parents themselves *(Sigel, 1983)*. The decision to focus on the relationship between poverty and parenting creates a dynamic in which parents are found responsible for any child and family problems observed. In general, according to this argument, we have overemphasized the role that the micro-environment of the family plays in determining child development, and underemphasized the role of the macro-environment in which the family is embedded *(de Lone, 1979)*.

Obviously, parenting is not the only path through which poverty can act to influence child development. Poverty denies young children adequate housing, medical care, nutrition, and, increasingly, safe environments in which to play. The schools that low-income children attend have fewer resources to devote to children's development, and all too often are pervaded by low expectations for their students' achievement. An increasing proportion of low-income children are growing up in neighborhoods of concentrated poverty, neighborhoods devoid of the institutions, role models, and organized activities that serve as a foundation for socially valued adult outcomes *(Wilson, 1987)*. Nonetheless, in early childhood, parents constitute children's primary environment. The specific patterns of interaction that develop between parent and young child are the basic material from which the child constructs a sense of self (i.e., of agency, physical integrity, relatedness) and a particular way of adapting to events in life *(Massie, Bronstein, Afterman, & Campbell, 1988; Stern, 1985)*. Further, parents play an important role in mediating between children and the larger social environment, protecting children from threats to their well-being, seeking out such community resources as early childhood education programs, interpreting and giving meaning to that environment *(Musick, 1987)*.

POVERTY AS AN ORGANIZING INFLUENCE ON CHILD REARING

A large number of factors influence parents' ability to meet their young children's developmental and socialization needs. As Belsky *(1984)* has noted, parenting is multiply determined, with child characteristics, parents' personal characteristics, situational factors, community characteristics, and broader sociocultural factors all playing a role. Each individual determinant of parenting—for example, a child's birth order and skill in eliciting attention, a parent's personal history of being reared and cared for, the degree of material hardship a family experiences—finds its own distinct expression in the parent-child relationship. But each is also linked to the others, modifying their effects *(Pawl, 1987)*. In that light, the influence of poverty is only one of numerous influences, one that not only mediates but is mediated by the others. Why, then, does poverty seem to underlie so much of the caregiving "casualty" that children experience in American society *(Pelton, 1978; Sameroff & Chandler, 1975; Sameroff, Seifer, Barocas, Zax, & Greenspan, 1987)*?

In the first place, the presence of poverty increases the likelihood that other personal and situational determinants of parenting will act as risk factors rather than protective factors in children's and parents' lives *(Rutter, 1987)*. The chronic stress, material hardship, and all too frequent dehumanization that define the experience of poverty in the United States exert a negative potentiating influence on other determinants. Poverty produces its own risk factors, such as dilapidated, overcrowded housing. It also uncovers and magnifies the effects of pre-existing personal vulnerabilities, for example a poor nurturance history *(Solnit, 1983)*. The ways in which poverty potentiates risk can be seen in numerous domains. For example, low-income women are twice as likely to have a low-birthweight baby, with the attendant challenges and stresses for parenting *(Goldberg, Brachfeld, & Divetto, 1980; Starfield, 1986)*. They are less likely to be married; when they are married, they experience more marital conflict than do their more economically-advantaged peers, undermining a key source of social support. Other sources of social support are themselves likely to be struggling with poverty-related stresses, undermining their ability to provide practical and emotional support for parenting *(Belle, 1983)*. Low-income parents are three times more likely than other parents to begin child rearing during adolescence, and thus to face unique challenges *(Kamerman & Kahn, 1988)*. Low-income women have among the highest rates of depression of any group in American society *(Belle, 1982)*. Mothers who are depressed are less responsive and nurturant, less aware of their children's moods, and more restrictive with their children *(Belle, 1982; Siegler, 1982)*.

The effects of any one or even a few risk factors can be mediated by the presence of protective factors elsewhere. But poverty increases the likelihood that numerous risk factors will be present simultaneously—in the child, the parents, the family's informal support system, and the neighborhood; as a corollary, poverty reduces the likelihood that protective factors will be present somewhere in those systems. For example, low-income women are not only more likely than more economically-advantaged peers to experience high risk pregnancies, they are less likely to have access to high quality prenatal care. Low-income parents are not only more likely than more economically-advantaged peers to have experienced poor or erratic nurturance as children, they are less likely to have access to services to help them deal with the harmful consequences of such histories for mental health and parenting. They are not only more likely to lack a marital and extramarital support system that is free from drain, they are less able to purchase support in the marketplace.

Most critically, the chronic and pervasive quality of poverty increases the chances that the impact of early risk factors will be "carried forward" over time, and ultimately internalized; further, risk factors will be more likely to accumulate over time in children's and families' lives, creating an increasingly inexorable pull toward poor outcomes *(Birch & Gussow, 1970; Meisels, 1990; Schorr, 1988)*. For example, the effects of low birthweight on child, parents, and family system tend to reverberate over a longer period in low-income families than in more economically-advantaged ones. The unhealthy physical environments in which low-income families live—for example environments high in ambient lead—exacerbate the biological health risks associated with low birthweight, turning acute problems such as respiratory vulnerability into chronic problems. A fussy, disorganized low-birthweight infant is more likely to overtax the limited physical and emotional resources of an already overstressed mother; parent-infant relationships that get off to such a poor start often become increasingly difficult to redirect *(Beckwith, 1988)*.

SOCIAL TRENDS

Exacerbating the inherent dynamics of risk accumulation for low-income families in American society are the particular correlates of poverty in the late 1980s, correlates that make it increasingly difficult for families to find a path out of poverty however and whenever they are drawn in. These include single parenthood, inadequate wage rates for unskilled jobs, inadequate income supports for parents who cannot or who choose not to work, and a growing geographic concentration of low-income families in socially isolated inner-city neighborhoods.

In 1960 only about 20% of low-income families were female-headed; currently, more than half are *(Halpern, 1986)*. Single mothers with young children are particularly likely to experience their life situation as stressful and out of control, and their options as unpalatable *(Kamerman & Kahn, 1988)*. If they choose to work, can find a job, and can find adequate, affordable child care, they may not earn enough to escape poverty. A single mother with just one child, working full-time all year at a minimum wage job cannot earn enough to escape poverty *(Reischauer, 1986)*. If a single mother chooses or is forced to rely on welfare, poverty is almost guaranteed. Even when their total value is combined, the package of means-tested family supports lifts fewer than 10% of participating families out of poverty *(Reischauer, 1986)*. Moreover, the dehumanization and loss of control that so often accompany welfare dependency in American society bear a personal cost in physical and mental health that undermines the opportunity created to devote oneself to the care and nurturance of one's children *(Belle, 1982)*.

A social trend of growing importance is the increase in the concentration and absolute number of low-income families with young children in inner cities. Poverty is becoming increasingly a big-city, central city phenomenon *(Wilson, Aponte, Kirschenman, & Wacquant, 1988)*. This trend is related to two other long-term trends that are suddenly receiving a good deal of public attention—the loss of jobs and the accompanying emigration of all but the poorest families from the inner cities. These in turn are making it increasingly difficult to sustain traditional institutional sources of authority, support, identity and mobility—churches, neighborhood associations, schools, businesses—in inner city neighborhoods *(Comer, 1989)*. Informal support systems are also "thinning out" and become less protective and nurturing *(Musick, 1987)*. Less effective support systems, critical lack of resources, and the dearth of paths out of poverty are producing and intensifying patterns of survival-oriented coping, decision-making, and relating; these are accompanied by a downward adjustment of expectations and hopes. As Comer *(1989)* noted,

> . . . although minimal income is not an absolute deterrent, desirable family functioning is nonetheless more difficult to sustain without a reasonable threshold of economic opportunity. (p. 110)

PARENTAL CHARACTERISTICS

It would seem to require extraordinary effort not to communicate feelings of futility and hopelessness to one's children under the extreme conditions facing growing numbers of low-income families. But, indeed, some parents do manage to help their children defy the odds. Who are these parents? One can argue that they are the parents with fewer, healthier, and more easy-going young children, better marital and extramarital supports, and more supportive neighborhood environments *(Garbarino & Sherman, 1980; Werner & Smith, 1982)*. But first and foremost they appear to be parents with greater personal resources. Clark *(1983)*, in a study of the influence of early family environment on school success among low-income, urban black children, found that while almost all parents in the sample had been exposed over long periods to discrimination, disparagement from dominant institutions, and constant worries about getting by, parents varied significantly in how they experienced, interpreted, and managed such difficulties. The high-achieving students' parents were realistic about the world, but faced it in a purposeful, serious way. These parents

> . . . possessed a belief in their own ability to see to it that somehow their children's needs would be provided for. . . . [also] deep self-pride and personal integrity, a sense of the salience of the needs of their children. *(Clark, 1983, p. 116)*

Looking into the personal histories of those parents who managed to create a predictable, nurturant home environment under difficult life circumstances, Clark found strong extended families characterized by plentiful practical assistance, a pervasive, consistent current of emotional support among extended family members, and family pride in not becoming "victims" of their life situation. Other studies have documented how some young adults with difficult, even painful, life histories are able to keep the child caring dimension of their functioning autonomous and protected from stress and strain in other areas *(Polansky, Chalmers, Buttenwieser, & Williams, 1981)*. Such adults often have experienced and internalized the care and nurturance of a special figure at least at some point during their own formative years. They may have acquired a set of strongly held beliefs or values that make life seem coherent and manageable, even in adversity *(Werner & Smith, 1982)*.

At the other extreme are young adults in whom personal characteristics seem to exacerbate the effects of situational stresses associated with poverty. For this group of parents, obstacles posed by stressful living conditions and inadequate services are compounded by lack of "self" resources, and struggles for their own personal development *(Egeland, Jacobvitz, & Sroufe, 1988; Musick, 1987; Newberger, Hampton, Marx, & White, 1986; Wieder, Jasnow, Greenspan, & Strauss, 1987)*. The expression of such double vulnerability varies. It may result in increased social isolation. For example, in neighborhoods in which physical danger already tends to isolate families in their own apartments, young parents who feel depressed or overwhelmed are less likely to seek out and develop a support system for their child rearing *(Belle, 1983)*. It may result in lack of investment in the parenting role, due to lack of physical and psychic energy, basic lack of capacity, or the urgency of the parent's own needs. Conversely, it may result in an inappropriate reliance on children for the love and gratification that was not forthcoming from one's parents. Increasingly, it may include serious drug abuse.

The proportion of low-income parents in this psychologically and situationally vulnerable group is simply not known. Worsening social conditions in the inner cities certainly create a context that fosters such double vulnerability. The direct roots of this vulnerability are often found in personal histories marked by important losses and disruptions, and, at the extreme, by abuse or neglect. For example, 70% of the women referred to one clinical infant intervention program because of difficulties with mothering had experienced major disruption of significant relationships before age 12 *(Wieder, Jasnow, Greenspan, & Strauss, 1987)*. Egeland, Jacobvitz, and Papatola *(1987)* reported that 70% of the women in their low-income longitudinal sample who had experienced abuse as children were maltreating their own children. In a study of child neglect in a low-income urban population, Polansky, Chalmers, Buttenwieser, and Williams *(1981)* found that childhood "abuse was reported by over three-fifths of the neglect mothers but by less than a fifth of the non-neglect" (pp. 152-154); likewise, 41% of the neglectful versus 7% of the non-neglectful mothers had experienced long-term removal from their natural parents. Neglectful parents' history of loss, disruption and abuse "conspired" to keep them from developing supportive, intimate relations with persons who could have helped prevent abnormal parenting.

Brooks-Gunn and Furstenberg's longitudinal study *(1987)* of the consequences of adolescent childbearing in a sample of 300 low-income Baltimore families documented the compounding effects of personal and situational stresses—and, at the same time, the buffering effect of even a few protective factors—under generally difficult life circumstances. The study found "tremendous diversity" in both long-term adaptation to early childbearing and long-term outcomes for parents. On the other hand, regardless of parental outcomes, the adolescent mothers' preoccupation with their own developmental struggles during their children's formative years bore tremendous costs for those children.

In a follow-up in which sample members were in the mid- to late-30s, the investigators found significant variability among sample parents in school completion, subsequent reproductive careers, and long-term economic self-sufficiency. For example the sample divided evenly among those on welfare, the working poor, and those with moderate and even relatively high incomes (over $25,000). About one-fifth never had another child; two-fifths had one additional child; 31% had two additional children;

and 8% had three more children. The variability that Brooks-Gunn and Furstenberg found in adult outcomes appeared to be in part related to characteristics of adolescents' biological families at the time they initiated childbearing, in part to the number of additional live births after the target child, and in part to marital history. Long-term outcomes were poorest for those in the sample whose own parents had a low level of education or a history of welfare dependency, and for those who had two or more additional children within five years of the target child. The investigators speculated that, alone or together, such factors decreased the likelihood that the adolescent would return to school to complete her education.

The same factors appeared to work intergenerationally to predict child outcomes. But even when the parents in the sample struggled successfully to overcome the impediments to personal development that early childbearing had brought, such struggle seemed to levy costs on their children. Lack of maternal attention was compounded by "the high rate of marital dissolution, the relatively large number of women who never married, and the frequency of short-term cohabitation relationships," which translated into "fleeting and unpredictable presence of adult men for the children" (p. 181). For these and related reasons, regardless of parents' personal achievements, the majority of target children in the Baltimore sample had very troubled school careers, with high rates of retention in grade (50% at least once), suspension (40% at least once), and truancy; and high rates of specific behavioral problems. One explanation was continuity in children's developmental trajectories from early childhood, which was almost inevitably a difficult period for mothers and children, through adolescence. As Brooks-Gunn and Furstenberg noted, "once a trajectory was set, in terms of preschool academic or behavior problems, it was likely to continue" (p. 184).

ADAPTATION TO POVERTY

While poverty produces and exacerbates many types of vulnerabilities in families, it is also a reality to which children and families adapt. Moreover, adaptations to poverty occur within the framework of the attitudes, beliefs, and behavior characteristic of the sociocultural group to which a young parent belongs. Families' nurturing and socialization strategies are deeply embedded in their cultural and ethnic identities, and deeply rooted in the historical experience of the sociocultural group to which they belong. Intergenerational continuity in such strategies provides a measure of control and stability in the face of uncertainty and lack of control over a hostile external environment. At the same time, adaptively-rooted child-rearing and coping strategies can be an additional source of vulnerability in children and families.

Such vulnerability may be due to a disjunction between the child-rearing strategies of the group and the norms of the larger society. For example, the historical pattern among black families of promoting strong bonds between children and nonparental kin is often overlooked by the child welfare system as a protective factor in black children's lives *(Stack, 1984)*. Yet it continues to serve to protect children physically and psychologically from such poverty-induced uncertainties as forced mobility in housing arrangements. Children with strong secondary attachments may experience temporary separations from parents as less distressing than they would have otherwise. Vulnerabilities may be created also by disjunction between the child-rearing strategies of the group and the psychological or social demands of settings outside the purview of the group. It has been reported, for example, that Mexican-American socialization patterns produce a "more passively and internally-oriented style of coping with problems and challenges in life" *(Lauderdale, cited in Garbarino & Ebata, 1983, p. 775)*. Such coping styles, evolved over centuries of poverty and oppression, may not be well-suited to the extraordinarily competitive environment of modern technological society, nor to the greater social isolation of families in such a society.

Disjunction between societal norms and demands and historically-rooted sociocultural adaptations is perhaps greatest in families going through the early stages of acculturation to American society—notably Southeast Asian, Mexican, Central American and Carribean, and especially Haitian immigrants. In the first place, such families experience a host of situational stresses that undermine child rearing, including economic and legal uncertainty, language difficulties, ineligibility for many social services, loss of traditional sources of informal support, and, in some cases, discrimination and exploitation. But the effects of these stresses are often compounded by the conflict generated when patterns of child rearing that were adaptive in communities of origin are considered maladaptive and even deviant in their new communities *(Laosa, 1981)*. For example, a study of recent Haitian entrants noted the traditional Haitian belief that the good infant and child is quiet, undemanding, and obedient, and the complementary belief that infants are not capable of cognition *(Widmayer, Peterson, & Larner, undated)*. Such beliefs yield children who are often ill-prepared for the demands of formal schooling in the American context. The parents are then blamed for neglecting their children's development, and may be put in the position of struggling to behave in ways that are discordant with deeply-rooted attitudes and feelings, as well as their lifelong experience.

Early parenting strategies designed to prepare children to cope and compete in inner-city environments characterized by grossly inadequate resources, chronic violence, and pervasive distrust may not be consistent with those strategies promoted in the larger society. In such environments interpersonal and cognitive behavior valued by the larger society may be perceived to be dysfunctional *(Raven, 1987)*. Comer *(1989)* cited as a case in point the inner-city child who comes home and complains about being beaten by other children and is told that if he or she does not fight back there will be another beating at home. This child is learning behavior that may be functional for survival; but such behavior is likely to get the child into difficulty upon arrival at school. It has been observed that inner-city minority mothers place a high value on unquestioning obedience and discourage curiosity, because the dangerous circumstances in which such families live leave little room for mistakes in judgment on the part of children *(Escalona, 1981; Silverstein & Krate, 1975)*. A number of observers have posited a pattern of early childhood parenting among inner-city minority mothers characterized by early withdrawal of emotional support, coupled with an emphasis on aggression in early play, early independence and self-reliance (in toileting and other self-care activities), distrust of nonfamily, and a competitive relationship between mother and child *(Escalona, 1981; Ogbu, 1985; Poussant, 1987)*.

Ogbu *(1985)* has argued that these observed patterns of behavior are organized adaptations, evolved over time to prepare children for success in inner-city environments. But it is equally plausible to argue that the powerlessness, personal experiences of injustice, and lack of nurturance from family and broader social world that characterize many low-income parents' own lives can spill over in many less deliberate ways into child rearing. Parents whose own primary needs have not been met may have a very difficult time recognizing or gratifying their children's needs. For example, when a low-income mother insists on immediate obedience or fails to respond to a young child's bid for attention, it may be adaptive; but it can also be interpreted as a response to the debilitating effects of chronic stress. Studies have observed that women experiencing such stress are often conscious of the limited effectiveness of their interactions with their children but lack physical and psychological energy to behave more effectively *(Jeffers, 1967; Zelkowitz, 1982)*.

Whether deliberate or not, adaptive patterns of parental care may not only conflict with those promoted in the larger society, but bear their own distinct costs to children. Restrictive parental behavior or premature assumption of responsibilities for self-care and protection can undermine a young child's developing sense of his or her value as a person, or the child's ability to recognize the importance of reciprocity in relationships. For some children, there may be a point at which such maternal behavior as encouragement of early independence and self-reliance, or lack of parental energy to respond to dependency needs, will be experienced as disapproval or even rejection. Further, patterns of parental behavior take on a symbolic life of their own at some point, and may be transmitted intergenerationally independent of specific situational demands and opportunities *(de Lone, 1979)*.

CONCLUSIONS

Dockecki *(1975)* has argued that having one characteristic in common — lack of financial resources — does not necessarily imply the common possession of other characteristics, for example, particular psychological traits. Families can and do cope adaptively with the stresses associated with poverty; they can and do rear their children protectively and nurturantly under the most difficult conditions. But in the current social context, the stressful and often demoralizing effects of our haphazard patchwork of institutional family supports are increasingly compounded by a deterioration in the social fabric holding low-income communities together, a fabric that traditionally provided at least a measure of support and nurturance for low-income families. As a consequence, the experience of poverty almost invariably brings with it a host of psychological injuries. Personal, situational, and systemic forces can combine to undermine low-income parents' immediate intentions and long-term aspirations, both for themselves and for their children. For a few parents, unique strengths or deficits in their own past nurturance define the parenting situation, and indeed their life situation. But, for better or for worse, most parents who live in poverty don't beat the odds; they reflect the odds.

While poverty is in some ways too global a variable for explaining specific processes in families' lives, it is nonetheless a powerful variable. Hamburg *(1985)* has summarized well the role of poverty:

> While many causes underlie the developmental problems of the young, the most profound and pervasive exacerbating factor is poverty. Poverty does not harm all children, but it does put them at greater developmental risk, through the direct physical consequences of deprivation, the indirect consequences of severe stress on the parent-child relationship, and the overhanging pall of having a depreciated status in the social environment. (p. 4)

Implications for Intervention

Granting that worsening poverty among young families is producing or exacerbating stresses that make parenting difficult, especially for parents with few personal resources to draw upon, how should we as a society respond? At one level, the answer seems straightforward. We must address the contextual factors that impinge on parenting and child development—dangerous neighborhoods; dilapidated, overcrowded housing; unstable, poor quality day care; geographic and social isolation. But directly addressing these factors would require a significant reorientation of social arrangements and public priorities. Such a reorientation does not appear to be forthcoming. While public awareness of the fragile situation of families with young children is growing, the social and political will to address this unfortunate situation is barely discernible *(Hart, 1989)*. That leaves what de Lone *(1979)* has called "secondary strategies." These are predominantly the personal helping services designed to promote individual well-being, adaptation, and development.

The exclusive reliance on personal helping services to address social concerns heightens the importance of clearly articulating what can and cannot be expected of particular service emphases and strategies. With respect to the nexus of poverty, parenting, and child development, the clarification of expectations is especially critical. Parenting interventions should not be viewed as a vehicle for social reform, as a means, for example, to alter significantly the life chances of low-income children. It is both unacceptable and unrealistic to place the burden of social problem-solving on those experiencing the brunt of social problems. On the other hand, there is evidence that helping services that provide additional social resources for parents can alter their subjective experience of a difficult life situation, facilitate their efforts at personal development, and, under some conditions, set the parent-child relationship on a slightly more positive course *(Weiss & Halpern, 1988)*.

During the past decade, a set of child and family services has emerged (or, more accurately, re-emerged) that offers promise of strengthening social resources for low-income as well as other families. The helping principles and strategies of family support programs are especially well-suited to the needs of hard-pressed but adequately coping low-income families. These programs provide sustained and responsive support, addressed to the range of concrete, social, and psychological needs of low-income families with young children. Family support programs have proven adept at providing helping services that do not undermine low-income parents' sense of competence and worth; at providing a direct and knowledgeable link to a range of community resources; and in serving to mediate between the child-rearing norms of a family's reference group and those of the larger society *(Weiss, 1987)*. In the process, family support programs extend the idea of helping and support well beyond the boundaries defined by the current human service system.

A major challenge facing these as well as other community-based helping services in coming years will be the creation of intervention strategies appropriate to the needs of young adults embarking on parenting with poor nurturance histories, compounded by little experience of success in other areas. This growing group of families will need far more sustained and skilled helping services than their better coping peers. Such services will have to attend simultaneously to pressing family survival needs, parents' own significant nurturance needs, a vulnerable parent-child relationship, and, in many cases, the special needs of young children with individual vulnerabilities. Such a multifocused approach is far from new; indeed, it basically describes clinical child and family casework at its best *(Polansky, Chalmers, Buttenwieser, & Williams, 1981)*. But it has been made potentially more potent by enormous progress in the understanding of both normal development and developmental risk in infancy and early childhood, and the accompanying translation of this knowledge into clinical helping principles and approaches *(Bertacchi & Coplon, 1989; Greenspan, 1987)*.

In principle, then, the model that increasingly seems necessary for young families is one that provides a flexible mix of concrete, clinical, and supportive services in a nonbureaucratic, family-like context. It has to be a model that can work simultaneously and comfortably at multiple levels: from the immediacy of getting the heat back on in an unheated apartment to the gradual building of trust in a young adult whose life has been marked by a series of losses; from the simplicity of providing a safe place for relaxation to the subtlety of responding to "the re-awakening of unconscious, preverbal issues stemming from a parent's own experience of infancy and toddlerhood" *(Bertacchi & Coplon, 1989, p. 2)*. There is evidence that such a multifaceted approach can be effective *(Provence & Naylor, 1983; Seitz, Rosenbaum, & Apfel, 1985)*. But it will require a resource commitment far beyond that which has been available for community-based programs up to the present—and a much greater willingness on the part of the most skilled professionals to work in low-income communities. Moreover, multifaceted service models have yet to be implemented on anything like the scale that would be necessary to reach even a modest proportion of those young families who might benefit.

If the earlier sections of this paper suggest an overarching need for a comprehensive, multifaceted approach to helping, the later sections point to the importance of a locally-appropriate, population-specific set of emphases and services. Specific populations of low-income families differ in a number of ways relevant to the design of early parenting interventions. They differ in beliefs and behavior with respect to child rearing; in life-cycle stage and developmental needs; in availability and use of social support and patterns of help-seeking. Communities differ in the availability of formal supports and services, and in the sensitivity of formal helping institutions to cultural and linguistic differences *(Halpern & Larner, 1988)*.

In addition, programs will have to be sensitive to adaptive patterns of child rearing, however functional they may or may not appear to be. It is not always easy to discern the particular dimensions of parenting critical to the prevention of adverse outcomes for children under different community conditions *(Rutter, 1987)*. Those who live in a community 24 hours a day, day-in and day-out, are best equipped to understand what is tolerable, desirable, and possible for them. Families should not just be recipients of services, however individualized, but should contribute to program design and emphasis. Ethical issues aside, when families help to shape parent education and other programs in which they will be participants, it is more likely that they will link the content of these support programs to the challenges they see their children facing.

Finally, successful programs will have to construct a coherent vision of competent child rearing, reflecting both the current reality of families' lives and a sense of what kind of children might grow up to transform that reality. They will also have to construct a vision of where and how they see themselves influencing the host of environmental forces impinging on child, parent, and family. As Slaughter *(1983)* has pointed out, while low-income families may not be self-conscious about the ecology surrounding their behavior, programs serving those families must focus on these contextual factors in order not to put further strain on already stressed lives.

REFERENCES

Beckwith, L. (1988). Intervention with disadvantaged parents of sick preterm infants. *Psychiatry, 51,* 242-247.

Belle, D. (1982). *Lives in stress.* Beverly Hills, CA: Sage Publications.

Belle, D. (1983). The impact of poverty on social networks and supports. In L. Lein & M. Sussman (Eds.), *The ties that bind: Men's and women's social networks.* New York: Haworth Press.

Belsky, J. (1984). The determinants of parenting: A process model. *Child Development, 55,* 83-96.

Bertacchi, J., & Coplon, J. (1989). The professional use of self in prevention. *Zero to Three: Bulletin of the National Center for Clinical Infant Programs, 9*(4), 1-7.

Birch, H., & Gussow, J. (1970). *Disadvantaged children: Health, nutrition and school failure.* New York: Harcourt Brace Jovanovich.

Brooks-Gunn, J., & Furstenberg, F. (1987). Continuity and change in the context of poverty: Adolescent mothers and their children. In J. Gallager & C. Ramey (Eds.), *The malleability of children.* Baltimore: Paul H. Brookes.

Clark, R. (1983). *Family life and school achievement.* Chicago: University of Chicago Press.

Clarke-Stewart, A. (1973). Interactions between mothers and their young children: Characteristics and consequences. *Monographs of the Society for Research in Child Development, 38,* 6-7 (Serial No. 153).

Clarke-Stewart, A. (1977). *Child care in the family.* New York: Academic Press.

Comer, J. (1989). Poverty, family and the black experience. In G. Miller (Ed.), *Giving children a chance.* Washington, D.C.: Center for National Policy Press.

de Lone, R. (1979). *Small futures.* New York: Harcourt Brace Jovanovich.

Dockecki, P. (1975). Minority children and families. In N. Hobbs (Ed.), *Issues in the classification of children.* San Francisco: Jossey-Bass.

Egeland, B., Jacobvitz, D., & Papatola, K. (1987). Intergenerational continuity of abuse. In R. Gelles & J. Lancaster (Eds.), *Child abuse and neglect: Biosocial dimensions.* New York: Aldine.

Egeland, B., Jacobvitz, D., & Sroufe, L. (1988). Breaking the cycle of abuse. *Child Development, 59,* 1080-1088.

Escalona, S. (1981). Infant day care: A social and psychological perspective on mental health implications. *Infant Mental Health Journal, 2,* 4-17.

Garbarino, J., & Ebata, A. (1983). The significance of ethnic and cultural differences in child maltreatment. *Journal of Marriage and the Family, 45,* 773-783.

Garbarino, J., & Sherman, D. (1980). High risk families and high risk neighborhoods. *Child Development, 51,* 188-198.

Goldberg, S., Brachfeld, S., & Divetto, B. (1980). Feeding, fussing and play: Parent-infant interactions in the first year as a function of prematurity and perinatal medical problems. In T. Field (Ed.), *High risk infants and children.* New York: Academic Press.

Greenspan, S. (Ed.). (1987). *Infants in multirisk families.* Madison, CT: International Universities Press.

Grubb, N., & Lazerson, M. (1982). *Broken promises.* New York: Basic Books.

Halpern, R. (1986). Key social and demographic trends affecting young families: Implications for early childhood care and education. *Young Children, 42,* 34-40.

Halpern, R., & Larner, M. (1988). The design of family support programs in high risk communities: Lessons from the Child Survival/Fair Start initiative. In D. Powell (Ed.), *Parent education as early childhood intervention.* Norwood, NJ: Ablex.

Hamburg, D. (1985). *Reducing the casualties of early life: A preventive orientation.* President's Essay, Annual Report of the Carnegie Corporation, New York.

Hart, P. (1989). Investing in prevention: Tomorrow's leaders and the problem of poverty. In G. Miller (Ed.), *Giving children a chance.* Washington, DC: Center for National Policy Press.

Jeffers, C. (1967). *Living poor.* Ann Arbor, MI: Ann Arbor Publishers.

Kamerman, S., & Kahn, A. (1988). *Mothers alone.* Dover, MA: Auburn House.

Laosa, L. (1979). Social competence in childhood: Toward a developmental, socioculturally relativistic paradigm. In M. Kent & J. Rolf (Eds.), *Primary prevention of psychopathology, Vol. III: Social competence in children.* Hanover, NH: University Press of New England.

Laosa, L. (1981). Maternal behavior: Sociocultural diversity in modes of family interaction. In R. Henderson (Ed.), *Parent-child interaction: Theory, research & prospects.* New York: Academic Press.

LeVine, R. (1974). Parental goals: A cross-cultural view. *Teachers College Record, 76,* 229-239.

Lubove, R. (1968). *The professional altruist.* Cambridge: Harvard University Press.

Massie, H., Bronstein, A., Afterman, J., & Campbell, B.K. (1988). Inner themes and outer behaviors in early childhood development: A longitudinal study. In A. Solnit, P. Neubauer, S. Abrams, & A. Dowling (Eds.), *The psychoanalytic study of the child* (Vol. 43, pp. 213-242). New Haven: Yale University Press.

McGowan, B. (1988). Family-based services and public policy: Context and implications. In J. Whittaker, J. Kinney, E. Tracy, & C. Booth (Eds.), *Improving practice technology for work with high-risk families: Lessons from the Homebuilders social work education project.* Monograph No. 6, Center for Social Welfare Research, School of Social Work, University of Washington, Seattle.

Meisels, S. (1990). Who should be served? Identifying children in need of early intervention. In S. Meisels & J. Shonkoff (Eds.), *The handbook of early childhood intervention.* New York: Cambridge University Press.

Musick, J. (1987, December). *Psychosocial and developmental dimensions of adolescent pregnancy and parenting: An interventionist's perspective.* Paper prepared for the Rockefeller Foundation.

Musick, J., & Stott, F. (1990). Paraprofessionals, parenting and child development: Understanding the problems and seeking solutions. In S. Meisels & J. Shonkoff (Eds.), *The handbook of early childhood intervention.* New York: Cambridge University Press.

Newberger, E., Hampton, R., Marx, T., & White, K. (1986). Child abuse and pediatric social illness: An epidemiological analysis and ecological reformulation. *American Journal of Orthopsychiatry, 56,* 589-601.

Ogbu, J. (1985). A cultural ecology of competence among inner-city blacks. In M. Spencer, G. Kerse-Brookins, & W.R. Allen, (Eds.), *Beginnings: The social and affective development of black children.* Hillsdale, NJ: Erlbaum.

Ogbu, J. (1987). Cultural influences on plasticity in human development. In J. Gallagher & C. Ramey (Eds.), *The malleability of children.* Baltimore: Paul H. Brookes.

Pawl, J. (1987). Infant mental health and child abuse and neglect: Reflections from an infant mental health practitioner. *Zero to Three: Bulletin of the National Center for Clinical Infant Programs,* 7(4), 1-9.

Pelton, L. (1978). Child abuse and neglect: The myth of classlessness. *American Journal of Orthopsychiatry, 48,* 608-617.

Polansky, N., Chalmers, M., Buttenwieser, E., & Williams, D. (1981). *Damaged parents.* Chicago: University of Chicago Press.

Poussant, A. (1987, October). *Black children: Coping in a racist society.* Fidele Fauri Memorial Lecture, School of Social Work, University of Michigan, Ann Arbor.

Provence, S., & Naylor, N. (1983). *Working with disadvantaged parents and their children.* New Haven: Yale University Press.

Rapoport, R., & Rapoport, R. (1980). *Fathers, mothers & society.* New York: Vintage.

Raven, J. (1987). Values, diversity and cognitive development. *Teachers College Record, 89,* 21-37.

Reischauer, R. (1986, Fall). The prospects for welfare reform. *Public Welfare,* 4-11.

Rutter, M. (1987). Psychosocial resilience and protective mechanisms. *American Journal of Orthopsychiatry, 57,* 316-331.

Sameroff, A., & Chandler, M. 1975. Reproductive risk and the continuum of caretaking casualty. In F. Horowitz (Ed.) *Review of child development research,* Vol. 4. Chicago: University of Chicago Press.

Sameroff, A., Seifer, R., Barocas, R., Zax, M., & Greenspan, S. (1987). Intelligence quotient scores of 4 year old children: Socioenvironmental risk factors. *Pediatrics, 79,* 343-350.

Schorr, L. (1988). *Within our reach.* New York: Anchor-Doubleday.

Seitz, V., Rosenbaum, L., & Apfel, N. (1985). Effects of family support intervention: A ten year follow-up. *Child Development, 56,* 376-391.

Siegler, A. (1982). Changing aspects of the family: A psychoanalytic perspective on early intervention. In E. Zigler & E. Gordon (Eds.), *Day care: Scientific and social policy issues.* Dover, MA: Auburn House.

Sigel, I. (1983). The ethics of intervention. In I. Sigel & L. Laosa (Eds.), *Changing families.* New York: Plenum.

Silverstein, B., & Krate, R. (1975). *Children of the dark ghetto.* New York: Praeger.

Slaughter, D. (1983). Early intervention and its effects on maternal and child development. *Monographs of the Society for Research on Child Development, 48,* 4 (Serial No. 202).

Solnit, A. (1983). Foreword. In S. Provence & A. Naylor (Eds.), *Working with disadvantaged parents and their children.* New Haven: Yale University Press.

Stack, C. (1984). *Cultural perspectives on child welfare.* Unpublished manuscript, Duke University Institute of Policy Studies and Public Affairs, Durham, NC.

Starfield, B. (1986). *Children at risk: The impact of policy on child health.* Unpublished report, Johns Hopkins School of Hygiene and Public Health, Division of Health Policy, Baltimore.

Stern, D. (1985). *The interpersonal world of the infant.* New York: Basic Books.

Weiss, H. (1987). Family support and education in early childhood programs. In S. Kagan, D. Powell, B. Weissbourd, & E. Zigler (Eds.), *America's family support programs.* New Haven: Yale University Press.

Weiss, H. & Halpern, R. (1988, April). *Community-based family support and education programs: Something old or something new?* Paper prepared for the National Resource Center for Children in Poverty, Columbia University.

Weissbourd, B., & Kagan, S. (1989). Family support programs: Catalysts for change. *American Journal of Orthopsychiatry, 59,* 20-31.

Werner, E., & Smith, R. (1982). *Vulnerable but invincible.* New York: McGraw-Hill.

Widmayer, S., Peterson, L., & Larner, M. (undated). *Intervention with Haitian entrants in South Florida.* Unpublished manuscript, Broward General Medical Center, Ft. Lauderdale, FL.

Wieder, S., Jasnow, M., Greenspan, S., & Strauss, M. (1987). Antecedent psychosocial factors in mothers in multirisk families: Life histories of the 47 participants in the Clinical Infant Development Program. In S. Greenspan (Ed.), *Infants in multirisk families.* Madison, CT: International Universities Press.

Wilson, W. (1987). *The truly disadvantaged.* Chicago: University of Chicago Press.

Wilson, W., Aponte, R., Kirschenman, J., & Wacquant, J. (1988). The ghetto underclass and the changing structure of urban poverty. In F. Harris & R. Wilkins (Eds.), *Quiet riots: Race and poverty in the United States.* New York: Pantheon.

Zelkowitz, B. (1982). Parenting philosophies and practices. In D. Belle (Ed.), *Lives and stress.* Beverly Hills, CA: Sage Publications.

CHAPTER **45**

A Nursing Model for Addressing the Health Needs of Homeless Families

Andrea S. Berne, CPNP, MPH
Candy Dato, RN, CS, MS
Diana J. Mason, RN, C, PhD
Margaret Rafferty, RN, MA, MPH, CS

Homelessness in the United States is a major social problem, directly affecting an estimated three million persons, of whom 30 percent are families. Of these families, 85 percent are headed by single women, a disproportionate number of whom are minorities. While families were the last subgroup to join the ranks of the homeless, they are now the fastest growing segment of that population. It is projected that in the near future a majority of the United States' homeless will be single mothers with children (City of New York Human Resources Administration, 1986a, 1986b; Institute of Medicine, 1988; Molnar, 1988).

ETIOLOGY OF FAMILY HOMELESSNESS

Homelessness is a relative condition that exists worldwide in both developed and underdeveloped countries, although it expresses itself differently in different parts of the world (Patton, 1988). It encompasses Britain's growing poor who are housed in the bread and breakfast rooms in London that have been described as the equivalent of third-world shantytowns (Clines, 1987). It includes the Ethiopian refugees in the Sudan and other countries where war and politics have uprooted entire communities (Smith, 1989). It can be seen in the increasing number of young adults sleeping in hostels and shelters in Denmark, Austria and Belgium (Hope & Young, 1987a; Tennison, 1983; Thomas, 1985). It is evident in the explosion of slums in the cities of developing nations such as the Philippines, Mexico and India (Busuttil, 1987). And it can be seen in the so-called hidden homeless in Hungary—the growing number of people who are doubled-up in the dwellings of friends or families or who are living in decrepit housing (Hope & Young, 1987b). In 1985, the United Nations reported that 100 million people worldwide had no shelter, and it proclaimed 1987 as the International Year of Shelter for Homeless (Ramachandran, 1988).

Homelessness used to occur predominantly in third world countries where material resources were underdeveloped or scarce. Its rise in developed countries suggests a maldistribution of existing resources. Nowhere is this more evident than in the United States, where homelessness is primarily caused by the lack of affordable housing and increasing poverty.

The lack of affordable housing in the United States is the result of several factors:

- Gentrification, or a process in which low-income housing is replaced by middle-income and high-income housing.

Reprinted from *Image: Journal of Nursing Scholarship,* Vol. 22, No. 1, with permission of Sigma Theta Tau, © 1990.

- A freeze on the welfare shelter allowances in most states, resulting in an allowance that has not kept pace with the rising cost of renting an apartment.
- The Reagan Administration's decision to withdraw the federal government from its prior commitment to build and maintain low-income housing (Report of the Committee on Legal Problems of the Homeless, 1989; Institute of Medicine, 1988).

Since most of the homeless would not be without permanent housing if they could afford to pay the rents on the housing that is available, homelessness in the United States is largely a by-product of the increasing gap between the rich and poor. From 1980 to 1984, family income for the poorest 20 percent of the population declined by almost 8 percent, while that of the wealthiest 20 percent of families increased by almost 9 percent (United Auto Workers, 1985). The poorest three fifths of all families received only 32.7 percent of the total national income, while the wealthiest two fifths received 67.3 percent of the income; these were, respectively, the lowest and highest percentages recorded since 1947 (Bureau of the Census, 1985). The relative nature of poverty that is associated with homelessness is illustrated by data indicating that 35 percent of homeless mothers and fathers outside of New York City work, but their incomes are insufficient to pay for the rising cost of housing (Schmitt, 1988). Indeed, a recent study found that the poor are paying an increasing percentage of their income on housing—now 63 percent, as opposed to the standard of 30 percent that is deemed the "affordable" limit by the Department of Housing and Urban Development (Dionne, 1989).

FAMILY HOMELESSNESS AS POVERTY: A MODEL FOR NURSING

Pesznecker (1984) synthesized the literature on poverty and delineated an interactional, adaptational model of poverty (see Figure 45-1). It postulates that one develops health-promoting or health-damaging responses to the stress of poverty, which are shaped by interactions between the individual/group and the environment—interactions that are further mediated by factors such as public policy. It presents the poor as individuals and groups who are continually faced with multiple and chronic stressors, including frustration over few employment options, inadequate and unsafe housing conditions, repeated exposure to violence and crime, inadequate child care assistance and insensitive attitudes and responses of social service and mental health agencies. The coping abilities of the poor are strained by the unpredictable and unrelenting accumulation of these stressors. Mastery may be diminished so that a sense of helplessness develops with the resulting decrease in motivation as well as a sense of helplessness and hopelessness. The stigmatization of being poor in a society that measures one's worth by income only adds to the stress of poverty and makes it difficult to maintain any semblance of self-esteem or self-efficacy. Anxiety, depression and feelings of powerlessness are thus predictable concomitants of poverty.

The experience of homeless families can be described within this context. Pesznecker's (1984) model provides a basis for being particularly concerned about the children of these families and the bleak present and future that they face. It incorporates the effect that the stigmas of poverty and homelessness can have on people who are often stigmatized also by their race and gender in a society that continues to contain covert and overt sexism and racism. It also provides a basis for nurses to incorporate social activism in their role as advocates and providers of care for homeless families.

HOMELESS CHILDREN

The research on homeless children is limited, but the data that are available suggest that homelessness is not an experience to which one can adapt positively. Wright and Weber (1987) reported that 16 percent of the homeless children have various chronic physical disorders, double the rate among patients in the general population. Asthma, anemia and malnutrition were among the most common. In the same study, many common acute pediatric problems were reported at inordinately high rates (upper respiratory infections, skin ailments, gastrointestinal problems, ear infections, eye disorders and dental problems). Data from Bellevue Hospital in New York City revealed that 50 percent of homeless children living

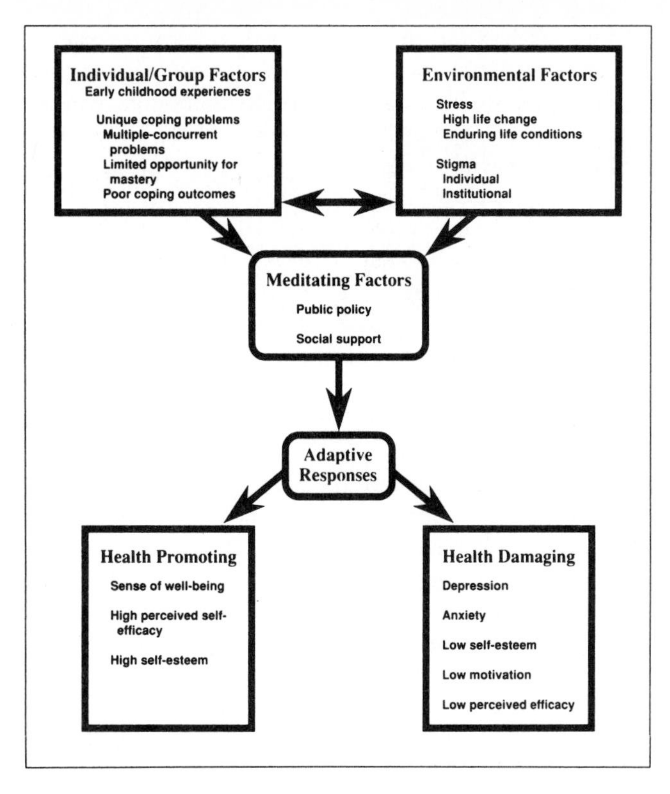

FIGURE 45-1

Adaptational model of poverty. (Modified from Pesznecker E: The poor: a population at risk, Public Health Nursing 1(4):237-249, 1984.)

in welfare hotels had immunization delays (Acker, Fierman & Dreyer, 1987).

Homeless infants living in welfare hotels in New York City had an infant mortality rate of 24.9 per 1000 live births in 1985. This was twice the overall city rate of 12.0/1000. Pregnant women living in welfare hotels in New York City were twice as likely to give birth to low-weight infants than were women living in the "city projects" (Chavkin, Kristal, Seabron & Guigli, 1987).

However, the effects of homelessness are even more profound on the mental health of the children. Bassuk and Rubin's (1987) study of children in Massachusetts shelters found that 47 percent of preschool children were delayed in at least one area of language, gross motor, fine motor and personal/social skills and development. One third of these children demonstrated problems in more than two areas. Almost half of the school-age children showed depression and anxiety, with the majority voicing suicidal ideation. The children were also noted to have sleep problems, shyness, withdrawal and aggression. Gewirtzman and Fodor (1987) reported that children in families left homeless after fires often exhibit these symptoms as well as isolation, disorientation, confusion, grief, psychosomatic complaints and regression. These problems are similar to those found in children of migrant workers and refugees and have been described as manifestations of posttraumatic stress disorder (PTSD) (Eth & Pynoos, 1985). PTSD is a reaction to some kind of psychological trauma and until recently was described mostly among war veterans. A psychologist in New York City reported that PTSD is the most common diagnosis among homeless children that she encounters (J. LeClair, personal communication, May 15, 1989).

Shelter life is stressful and shameful, compounding the children's problems. All school children are sensitive to dressing below peer standards, but homeless children may also face discriminatory remarks made by teachers and classmates, making them a "minority within a minority" (Gewirtzman & Fodor, 1987). Poor attendance and truancy are major problems for this population. School attendance among 10-year-olds to 16-year-olds at the Martinique Hotel, the largest welfare hotel in New York City, was less than 40 percent. In one study, 43 percent of the children had failed at least one grade; 24 percent were in special education classes; 50 percent were failing (Bassuk & Rubin, 1987).

Children without parents in New York City fare worse than do homeless children with parents. Instead of being placed in individual foster homes, these children increasingly are housed in congregate shelters — dormitory-like facilities — that have recently been critically exposed and condemned in a study by the Public Health Interest Consortium of New York City (Brooklyn Health Action Committee, 1989). Unsanitary conditions, spoiled food, blatant fire and safety hazards and inadequate staffing predominate in these facilities. The "orphans" are shuffled from shelter to shelter, their emotional needs are ignored and they endure conditions that are often debilitating and sometimes life-threatening. The study reports that in one review of childhood immunizations, only 22 percent of the children were adequately immunized. Some of the children are HIV-positive and are at great risk for communicable diseases that easily spread in the congregate facilities:

> The children in the shelters then are in profound psychological distress, and the custodial care they receive fails to lessen their pain. The harm to these children goes beyond their immediate suffering, however. It extends to their longterm emotional development. (p. 10)

The data on homeless children suggest that predominant responses of homeless children to their experience with poverty are ones that Pesznecker categorizes as health damaging. The future for these children may be short-lived and without much hope for a better life. Longitudinal studies are needed to examine the long-term effects of a childhood experience with homelessness and the extent to which homelessness is an experience that precludes health-promoting responses to poverty.

HOMELESS MOTHERS

There is a paucity of research on the health problems of homeless mothers. They are a neglected population. The experience of one of the authors (A. B.) is that the mothers wait for health care until they are so acutely ill that they need emergency treatment. They may not seek health care for themselves since they tend to view themselves as the least important person in the household. Their schedules may also preclude attendance at clinics.

When the homeless mothers are seen, as they were in the Health Care for the Homeless Demonstration Project from June 1985 to September 1987 (Wright & Weber, 1987), it was confirmed that they suffer from most physical disorders at higher rates than do the general population. In addition to numerous chronic illnesses, the rate of tuberculosis among the homeless exceeds that of the general population by a factor of 25 to perhaps several hundred. Anecdotal reports from public health nurses in New York City suggest that AIDS is increasingly prevalent among homeless families and progresses more rapidly in these poor women. The overcrowded conditions of shelters and welfare hotels clearly impact on the health of the homeless mothers, as does inadequate diet, substandard bathing facilities and multiple chronic stressors.

It is evident that these same stressors contribute to the mental health problems of homeless mothers, although there is little research in this area as well. The research that has been done coincides with studies of poverty that repeatedly describe an increase in mental health problems — particularly anxiety and depression — with increasing poverty (Belle, 1982; Dohrenwend & Dohrenwend, 1974; Hollingshead & Redlich, 1958). Bassuk's (1986) study of 82 families in 14 Massachusetts shelters reported that the majority of the mothers had a limited number of relationships, with 43 percent reporting no or minimal support, and 24 percent seeing their children as their major emotional support. Of the 82 families, 18 were being assessed for potential child abuse. As children, one third of the mothers had suffered physical abuse, while one in every nine were victims of sexual abuse. The mothers' histories showed a significant amount of major family disruption, loss of parents, lack of work skills and residential instability (Bassuk, Rubin & Lauriat, 1986). The data suggested intergenerational aspects of family disruption and emotional difficulties. Another study estimated that 24 percent of homeless families in New York City were victims of domestic violence (Victim Services Agency, 1989).

Homeless mothers need to be distinguished from another subgroup of the homeless, the homeless mentally ill. Homeless mothers are not psychotic any more frequently than is the general population, and the etiology of their homelessness lies in poverty rather than a combination of poverty and mental illness. Bassuk's (1986) study did find 71 percent of homeless mothers had personality disorders; however, both advocates for the homeless and Bassuk herself criticized this finding as being an exaggeration of the degree of psychopathology. The diagnostic labels do serve to indicate severe functional impairment and the need for help.

One of the health-damaging responses that some of these mothers may have to coping with homelessness is substance abuse, although documenting the prevalence of the problem and whether it is antecedent to or a product of homelessness are difficult. The study of the foster children in New York City (Brooklyn Health Action Committee, 1989) identified parental drug abuse as "the single biggest underlying factor in child abuse and neglect" (p. 34) that results in children being removed from their families. Bassuk (1986) found 10 percent of the mothers to be substance abusers, while New York City public health nurses have estimated that between 80 percent and 90 percent of the mothers in some shelters use crack. Crack has intensified the problem of drug abuse because of its high potency and rapidly addictive qualities. Crack has become a cause of homelessness in New York City, as addicts use money for the drug instead of housing. Other health and mental health problems are expanded with substance abuse, and one would suspect that some of the character disorder problems seen in Bassuk's study were drug related.

As with homeless children, the data suggest that homelessness is a correlate of poverty that overwhelms the physical and emotional resources of homeless mothers. Pesznecker (1984) noted that poverty involves an interplay between environmental and individual factors. The poor encounter more stressors, especially surrounding money, social isolation, stigmatization and parenting, all of which can be exacerbated by homelessness. Coping positively with this multiplicity of persistent stressors becomes increasingly difficult, particularly if one is repetitively unable to change them. Depression, anxiety and feelings of powerlessness readily ensue. Under Pesznecker's model, the mental health problems of homeless mothers are most appropriately viewed as health-damaging responses to harsh environmental conditions that breed demoralization, hopelessness and despair. The model also suggests points of intervention that can foster health-promoting responses to homelessness.

HEALTH CARE SERVICES FOR HOMELESS FAMILIES

Access to health care has been a major problem for homeless families (Institute of Medicine, 1988). For example, a survey of sheltered children in Seattle revealed that 59 percent of the children had no regular care provider. The same group used emergency rooms at a rate of two to three times the rate of the general pediatric population in the United States (Miller & Lin, 1988). Although substance abuse appears to be a growing problem among homeless mothers, there is a paucity of drug treatment programs in the United States, particularly those that provide long-term treatment with a family focus.

Three traditional approaches that have been used to provide health care services to homeless families are the traditional out-patient department (OPD) or clinics, onsite services and comprehensive outreach.

The Clinics

Ambulatory care for the poor is generally delivered in "clinics." While funding from the national government and a nationwide grant from a private foundation have resulted in some outreach services to

Imagine you are homeless...

Imagine you are a 33-year-old woman with three children. Your apartment burned down six months ago. You and your children had been living with your sister in her cramped apartment until she had another baby, and now there simply was not enough room for everyone.

You sleep in your car at night. During the day, you walk the streets with your children trying to find an apartment you can afford. Finally, you go to the department of social services to try to find shelter for the night and are told that your children may have to be placed in foster care if a place cannot be found for all of you. Knowing that the foster care system in this city is unreliable and sometimes unsafe, you agree to spend the first night in an overcrowded warehouse-type shelter, where you end up sleeping on the floor.

You and your children have no privacy here. Many of the children and adults have colds and you hear that tuberculosis has been an increasing problem among the homeless. When the opportunity arises, you agree to move into one of the single-room occupancy hotels that the city is using to house homeless families "temporarily." That temporary shelter becomes your home for 13 months.

The temporary shelter consists of one 10 by 10 ft. room. You have no kitchen, no refrigerator, no stove or cooking facilities. There is one bed for you and your three children.

You pull the mattress off the bed at night to make room for all of you to sleep and then pull the sheets off the bed in the day to eat on the floor.

You use running water to keep your baby's milk cool and you do the dishes in the tub where you bathe and store things.

There is no place for your children to play, no place to sit, no place to do homework. When they try to play in the hall, they are approached by drug dealers and sometimes even pimps.

This is what life is like for you and your children. Imagine the gradual dissipation of your own and your children's self-esteem and the isolation and depression that eventually overwhelm you. Imagine having a future without space, without privacy, without hope.

homeless families, most continue to lack access to anything except emergency room care. This has resulted in a woeful lack of prenatal care for homeless women who then present at the emergency room in labor and are at greater risk for maternal and infant morbidity and mortality (Chavkin et al., 1987).

Even homeless people who do have access to routine health care services often have difficulty negotiating the system. Families are usually sheltered outside their neighborhood of origin so that they are unfamiliar with and apprehensive about new health care providers. For families that are moved multiple times, it is difficult, if not impossible, to establish a stable relationship with a primary provider. Many hospital clinics have long waits for appointments, lack continuity of care and often are understaffed. There have been many reports of families with "hotel addresses" being treated poorly. The clinic staff may blame the homeless for lack of immunizations and records and missed appointments, labeling them "noncompliant." In addition, families often do not keep appointments because of fear of being reported to the Child Welfare Bureau for neglect and/or abuse related to being homeless. For these reasons, the clinic system increases the stressors and stigma with which homeless families must cope and fosters health-damaging responses such as anxiety, low self-esteem and low motivation.

On-Site Services

In some settings, visiting health teams have set up shop. The goal of many of these projects is to mainstream the families into existing clinics. While this is conceptually pleasing and congruent with the goal of establishing coordinated comprehensive care for all, this approach has limitations. The efforts of two or three health providers on site are inadequate to offset the stress and stigma of this extreme level of poverty. On-site providers have become frustrated by some of the same problems that the families are up against with the system as it presently exists, as they try to refer the families to existing services. There are transportation problems, delays in getting appointments and inadequate care. "Homeless providers" fall victim to the same discrimination that the homeless themselves face. The level of effort is inadequate to make a significant difference, but it is often used by politicians to demonstrate that they are "doing something" when, in fact, they are not. On-site services are too often a bandaid approach to the health problems of homeless families.

Comprehensive Mobile Outreach Services

One model program has enough resources to mitigate some of the effects of the poverty that underlies homelessness. The New York Children's Health Project has expanded on the concept of on-site services by providing comprehensive pediatric care with mobile medical units to children living in hotels and shelters in New York City. This project works collaboratively with the public health nurses and city social workers who are on-site at the hotels five days a week doing intake and casefinding. The public health nurses visit the families as they enter the system and take an initial health assessment. They identify children in need of immunizations, mothers in need of prenatal care and a wide variety of other acute and chronic health care needs. By knocking on doors, they attempt to cross the impenetrable boundary that exists between the family and the outside world.

Acute and chronic medical problems are diagnosed and treated by nurse practitioners and physicians. School, day care and camp forms and Women, Infant and Children certifications are frequently completed by the nurses, which has made an enormous impact on enrollment in such programs. In addition, nurses discuss routine health maintenance issues such as growth and development and nutrition as well as strategies for hotel living.

This project essentially provides "middle-class" pediatric health care to the poorest of the poor. Because of the intensive supports built into the program, there is a 70 percent to 80 percent compliance rate, which is comparable to middle-class compliance. The project demonstrates the mitigating effects that public policy and social support—the mediating factors in Pesznecker's model—can have on the ongoing stressors confronting homeless families.

DESIGNING EFFECTIVE INTERVENTIONS FOR HOMELESS FAMILIES

This is not to suggest that comprehensive health services for the homeless are the magic tonic for the problems of homelessness. These families have an enormous number of problems of which health problems are only one small part. Indeed, nursing interventions with homeless families must reflect an understanding of the connections between health and other life and societal conditions. Pesznecker's Adaptational Model of Poverty reflects this understanding. It also is distinguished from most poverty frameworks that actually "blame the victim"—an approach that is contrary to nursing's view of health as a human-environment interaction (Mason, 1981). Her model provides direction for interventions with homeless families that address both the individuals and families and the environment and society.

Pesznecker's model suggests that homeless families can best be assisted through strategies that empower them to develop the skills and self-esteem to recognize and act on opportunities for moving out of homelessness and poverty as well as to cope more positively when those opportunities are not present. Approaching the homeless mothers and children with caring and respect is prerequisite to countering the stigmatizing attitudes that they face in other encounters with society. Additionally, homeless families need tangible and intangible support to cope with the multiple stressors in their lives. Such supports range from adequate public assistance and shelter subsidies to having a network of friends and professionals who will provide both mental and material support during times of crisis. In many communities, homeless families are removed from their community of origin and may be moved through a variety of communities during their experience with homelessness. Maintaining relationships with friends or providers becomes almost impossible. Policies that required each community to have a plan for maintaining families who need emergency housing would enable the maintenance and development of such support systems.

There has been a tendency for health care providers to view psychotherapy as a necessary intervention for homeless families; particularly given the mental health problems outlined earlier. Pesznecker's model suggests that stress management training may be an instrumental intervention. Support for this proposition is evident in two stress reduction projects with women in the United States and Canada who were on public assistance (Resnick, 1984; Tableman, Feis, Marciniak & Howard, 1985). Unfortunately, these approaches are seldom included in the health and social services that are available to homeless families.

Several model projects such as the Henry Street Settlement House in New York City and Trevor's Place in Philadelphia provide safe, clean shelter and supportive on-site services to families. These supportive services include 24-hour on-site staff, day care, after-school tutoring, job training for mothers, assistance with entitlement, and assistance with relocation. These projects have found that the mental outlook of both parents and children improve dramatically under these stable conditions. Children start attending school again; grades and behavior improve. This approach to homelessness both increases coping options and provides some stability so that referrals for self-help groups, stress reduction techniques or traditional psychotherapy services for the homeless who have major functional psychiatric disorders can have some hope for success.

Most health care services for the homeless are really secondary and tertiary prevention. True primary prevention of homelessness demands social policies that call for:

- Affordable housing
- Education and job training
- Meaningful work at an adequate wage
- Adequate levels of public assistance for families that cannot sustain themselves including adequate shelter allowances
- Accessible and adequate child care
- Access to health prevention and promotion including education about preventing pregnancy and substance abuse and coping with stress
- Drug treatment on demand

And if homelessness on an international level is considered, nursing's advocacy for primary prevention of homelessness would include efforts to promote world peace and improved means for resolving intranational and international political disputes.

Nurses can influence and shape policies that deal with homeless families through political advocacy. The American Nurses' Association has included homelessness among the issues it advocates in Washington, D.C., and many other state nurses' associations have done likewise. In New York City, the local district nurses' association adopted a position on homelessness that calls for affordable housing, adequate temporary shelter and accessible health care services.

If the nursing community is committed to primary prevention for homeless women and children, then we must participate in the debate regarding whether or not housing is a human right (Burns, 1988) and recognize the connections between the health of homeless women and children and the broader social, economic and political issues of our times. Such a perspective demands that we also understand that we truly are one world community and that these connections extend beyond geographic boundaries. We challenge the nursing community worldwide to join together in calling for conditions and policies that are health sustaining instead of health damaging, that are supportive and nurturing of families and that make housing a basic human right, without which one cannot ensure health.

REFERENCES

Acker, P., Fierman, A. H., & Dreyer, B. P. (1987). Health: An assessment of parameters of health-care and nutrition in homeless children (abstract). American Journal of Diseases of Children, 141, 388.

Bassuk, E. (1986). Homeless families: Single mothers and their children in Boston shelters. In E. Bassuk (Ed.), The mental health needs of homeless persons: New directions for mental health services. San Francisco: Jossey-Bass.

Bassuk, E., & Rubin, L. (1987). Homeless children: A neglected population. American Journal of Orthopsychiatry, 57(2), 279-286.

Bassuk, E., Rubin, L., & Lauriat, A. (1986). Characteristics of sheltered homeless families. American Journal of Public Health, 76, 1097-1101.

Belle, D. (1982). Lives in stress: Women and depression. Beverly Hills: Sage.

Brooklyn Health Action Committee. (1989). Inexcusable harm: The effect of institutionalization on young foster children in New York City. New York: Public Interest Health Consortium of New York City.

Bureau of the Census. (1985). Money income and poverty status of families and persons in the United States: 1984. Washington, DC: The U.S. Government Printing Office.

Burns, L. S. (1988). Hope for the homeless in the U.S.: Lessons from the Third World. Cities, 5, 33-40.

Busuttil, S. (1987). Houselessness and the training problem. Cities, 4, 152-158.

Chavkin, W., Kristal, A., Seabron, C., & Guigli, P. (1987). The reproductive experience of women living in hotels for the homeless in NYC. New York State Journal of Medicine, 371, 10-13.

City of New York Human Resources Administration (1986a, October). A one-day "snapshot" of homeless families at the Forbell Street Shelter and the Martinique Hotel. New York: The Administration.

City of New York Human Resources Administration. (1986b, October). Characteristics and housing histories of families seeking shelter from HRA. NY: The Administration.

Clines, F. X. (1987). For poor, bed and breakfast at $34 million a year. The New York Times, October 22, 3.

Dionne, E. J. (1989). Poor paying more for their shelter. The New York Times, April 17, A18.

Dohrenwend, B. S., & Dohrenwend, B. P. (1974). Stressful life events: Their nature and effects. New York: John Wiley and Sons.

Eth, S., & Pynoos, R. (1985). Post-traumatic stress disorder in children. Washington, D.C.: American Psychiatric Association.

Gewirtzman, R., & Fodor, I. (1987). The homeless child at school: From welfare hotel to classroom. Child Welfare, 66(3), 237-245.

Hollingshead, A. B., & Redlich, F. C. (1958). Social class and mental illness: A community study. New York: John Wiley and Sons.

Hope, M., & Young, J. (1987a, August). Homelessness in Austria rising, although social programs help. Safety Network, 4(12), 2.

Hope, M., & Young, J. (1987b, December). Housing privitization in Hungary—Will it cause more homelessness? Safety Network, 5(3), 2.

Institute of Medicine. (1988). Homelessness, health, and human needs. Washington, D.C.: National Academy Press.

Mason, D. (1981). Perspectives on poverty. IMAGE, 13, 82-85.

Miller, D. S., & Lin, E. H. B. (1988). Children in sheltered homeless families: Reported health status and use of health services. Pediatrics, 81(5), 668-673.

Molnar, J. (1988). Home is where the heart is: The crisis of homeless children and families in New York City. New York: Bank Street College of Education.

Patton, C. V. (1988). Spontaneous shelter: International perspectives and prospects. Philadelphia: Temple University Press.

Pesznecker, B. (1984). The poor: A population at risk. Public Health Nursing, 1(4), 237-249.

Ramachandran, A. (1988). International Year of Shelter for the Homeless. Cities, 5, 144-162.

Report of the Committee on Legal Problems of the Homeless. (1989). The record of the Association of the Bar of the City of New York, 44(1), 33-88.

Resnick, G. (1984). The short and long-term impact of a competency-based program for disadvantaged women. Journal of Social Service Research, 7(4), 37-49.

Schmitt, E. (1988, December 26). Suburbs cope with the steep rise in the homeless. The New York Times, 1.

Smith, S. (1989). People without land. American Journal of Nursing, 89(2), 208-209.

Tableman, B., Feis, C. L., Marciniak, D., & Howard, D. (1985). Stress management training for low-income women. Prevention in Human Services, 3(4), 71-85.

Tennison, D. C. (1983). Homeless people grow numerous in Europe, despite welfare states. The Wall Street Journal, 80, April 25, 1+.

Thomas, J. (1985). The homeless of Europe: A scourge of our time. The New York Times, October 7.

United Auto Workers of America. (1985). Building America's Future. Detroit: UAW.

Victim Services Agency. (1989). The screening and diversion of battered women in the New York City emergency housing system. New York: The Agency.

Wright, J. D., & Weber, E. (1987). Homelessness and health. New York: McGraw-Hill.

CHAPTER **46**

Stigma, Health Beliefs, and Experiences with Health Care in Lesbian Women

Patricia E. Stevens, RN, BSN, MA
Joanne M. Hall, RN, MA

Nursing claims as its distinguishing core the concept of care (Leininger, 1984). Authentic presence in interaction, in which the nurse is aware of and open to each client as a unique and worthwhile being, is essential for nursing to offer humanizing care (Paterson & Zderad, 1976). If each human being is a valued "whole," authentic, humanizing care necessitates that nurses broaden and deepen their knowledge about specific client populations. Good and Good (1981) suggest that illness and wellness be conceived of as a coherent network of meaning and experience that is linked to the deep semantic and value structures of a cultural aggregate. To offer culturally sensitive care to lesbians in a way that allows them to feel respected and regarded, nurses need an understanding of the cultural experience of being lesbian, a knowledge of what illness and wellness mean for them and a comprehension of their experience in health care interactions.

For lesbian women, the cultural meanings of illness and wellness are linked to lesbian identity, which is an immutable quality that permeates and differentiates the self. Lesbian identity is not limited to sexual activity but is a totality that encompasses a primary orientation toward women and a way of being that is women-relating (Ponse, 1978). As a cultural group lesbians share developmental experiences (Cass, 1979; Dank, 1971; Di Angi, 1982; Kus, 1985), value orientations, community identification (Ponse, 1978), argot (Warren, 1980), characteristic family construction (Krestan & Bepko, 1980) and literature, art and music (Nixon & Berson, 1978).

Reprinted from *Image: Journal of Nursing Scholarship,* Vol. 20, No. 2, with permission of Sigma Theta Tau, © 1988.

REVIEW OF THE LITERATURE

Culture is the symbolic system of a people. Wellness and illness, a group's subjective perception of health (Tripp-Reimer, 1984), are patterns of behavior having significance in cultural terms. What it means to be well or ill in a particular cultural context is negotiated by the members within the belief system of that group. The accumulated wisdom and experience of groups yield informal bodies of codified knowledge about wellness and illness called folk theories (Fabrega, 1979).

The concept of health includes the capacities and activities of individuals in cultural enterprises (Smith, 1981). It is a multidimensional process involving the well-being of whole persons in the context of their psychosocial and cultural environment (Ahmed, Kolker, & Coelho, 1979). Value orientations differentiate cultural groups and affect the ways that health, illness and health care are viewed by members of a group (Hartog & Hartog, 1983).

A core element in the cultural experience of lesbians is the phenomenon of stigmatization. There is abundant historical and sociological evidence that lesbians are viewed negatively in this society, encountering discrimination, social distancing, antilocution and defensiveness. They sustain the damage of others' anger, hostility, fear, anxiety, aversion, excitement and ambivalence (Aguero, Bloch, & Byrne, 1984; Hudson & Ricketts, 1980; Irwin & Thompson, 1978; Laner & Laner, 1980; Levitt & Klassen, 1974; Millham, San Miguel, & Kellogg, 1976; Minnigerode, 1976; Morin, 1981; Nungesser, 1983; Nyberg & Alston, 1977; Weinberger & Millham, 1979).

Goffman (1963) defined the stigmatized as having an identity "spoiled" by a discrediting attribute, which leads to their disqualification from full social acceptance. The concept of stigma requires a relational perspective because only in interaction does stigma become apparent. According to Goffman, there are two groups of stigmatized individuals, the "discredited," whose stigmatizing feature is immediately apparent to others, and the "discreditable," whose attribute may be concealed but is at risk of disclosure in social situations. In dealing with stigma, the task for the "discredited" is to minimize the impact of the stigmatizing feature during social interaction, whereas the task for the "discreditable" is to manage information so that others do not become aware of their discrediting attribute.

Lesbian identity has been conceptualized by numerous sources as a "discreditable" stigma (Fein & Nuehring; 1981; Jandt & Darsey, 1981; Plummer, 1975). Therefore, the "mark" of lesbian identity conspicuously affects interactive outcomes (Jones et al., 1984). Lesbians cannot take for granted that they share the world with others who hold congruent values, interpretations and behaviors; nor can they assume that they will be evaluated according to their own personal qualities. They must always consider the implications of their stigmatized lesbian identity as they anticipate their participation in all areas of life including health care. While self-disclosure is generally considered to be necessary in the formation of authentic interpersonal relationships (Jourard, 1971), the potential negative consequences in the behavior of others often act as effective deterrents to self-disclosure by lesbian women (Brooks, 1981).

Persons formulate ideas of themselves and take action in light of what they encounter in the action of others (Blumer, 1969). Cues about lesbian identity—the "mark"—(Becker, 1973; Fein & Nuehring, 1981) may be available in interactions even though they are not stated or confirmed. The beliefs of lesbians about their degree of identifiability is a basis on which they interpret the responses of others toward them. Self-schemata, the cognitive generalizations that organize the processing of self-related experience (Markus, 1977), are linked to an individual's sense of well-being and health. The degree to which illness and wellness may be assumed to correlate with stigmatized identity is related to the perceptions of lesbians about how identifiable they are to others.

There is a dearth of research regarding lesbian folk theories about health, lesbian identifiability and lesbians' experiences interacting with health care providers. Brooks (1981) found that stress tended to be lower for those who believed that only other lesbian/gay people could identify them as lesbians and higher for those who felt visible to the larger society. Ponse (1978) and Painter (1981) described lesbian folk theories about the ability of lesbians to recognize each other in social interaction. Unfortunately there are no studies about the perceptions of lesbians about how recognizable they are within society as a whole. The few studies that have been done on the interaction of lesbians with health care providers suggest that lesbians found them to be judgmental, nonsupportive and negatively responsive when the identity of the lesbians was known (Chafetz, Sampson, Beck, & West, 1974; Smith, Johnson, & Guenther, 1985). Many wished that they could be open about their lesbian identity in health care situations but never were, fearing that it would hinder the quality of health care (Glascock, 1983; Johnson, Guenther, Laube, & Keettel, 1981). The status of the research in this area means that those who care for lesbians must rely on common sense and intuition with all the potential pitfalls of myth, speculation and antipathy entailed in such an approach (Chafetz et al., 1974).

The present study was undertaken in an attempt to begin to fill these gaps in knowledge. The purposes were (a) to investigate the perceptions of lesbians of their identifiability and the ways in which they feel their identity is communicated to others; (b) to investigate the cultural beliefs of lesbians about wellness and illness; (c) to hypothesize about relationships between health and identifiability in lesbian women, and (d) to investigate the experience of lesbians in interaction with health care providers.

METHODS

Culture must be seen through the eyes of those who live it (Edgerton & Langness, 1974). Qualitative research seeks the insider's view and is more reflective of the complexities of the natural world (Lofland, 1971). Interviewing provides a means of reality reconstruction in which an aggregate's folk theories and experiences regarding their identity, behavior and relationship to the rest of society emerge (Schwartz & Jacobs, 1979).

A semistructured interview guide was constructed using open-ended questions about lesbians' identifiability, health strengths and vulnerabilities and interactions with health care providers. The term "health care provider" was used in the interview to allow participants to describe freely their experiences with any health care professional; however, their responses differentiated between nurses, physicians and others. The participants were asked to speak not only for themselves but also to describe the identifiability, health and experience of lesbians in general because it is often easier to talk about others than about oneself (Van Maanen, Dubbs, & Faulkner, 1982). This technique was also designed to allow comparisons of self versus all of the members of the cultural group, and thus provide a richer source of data (Agar, 1980). Content validity was supported through a review by experts in the areas of qualitative nursing research and gay studies.

Twenty-five self-identified lesbians participated in interviews lasting approximately two hours. Their confidentiality was protected throughout the process. They were solicited through a snowball design by flyers and by word of mouth from the lesbian community in Iowa City, Iowa. Most were college educated, white and employed. Ages ranged from 21 to 58 years with a mean of 30 years. A potential bias in this self-selected sample was inclusion of a majority of women who were more vocal, who openly disclosed and accepted their lesbian identity. However, such a sample is desirable for qualitative research because spokespersons are sought, rather than a random, representative sample (Agar, 1980).

One interviewer and one recorder conducted all of the interviews, writing down the verbatim responses and later transcribing them onto a computer. To gauge reliability, the co-investigators also used field notes about the interview process, including nonverbal responses and consistency of affect, cognition and behavior. The degree of consensus among participants was high, consensus being the primary means of verification in qualitative research. Adequate time was spent with participants in a comfortable setting, and positive evaluations of the experience and rapport with the interviewers enhanced the accuracy of the data (Bruyn, 1966).

Content analysis was used for interpretation of the interview data. The investigators analyzed the data independently, categorizing and coding individual items of information, differentiating discrete pieces of data and determining their relationship to each other and the whole, identifying general themes and establishing consensus. Initial interrater reliability for data coding ranged from 92 percent to 97 percent. Discrepancies were clarified and items recoded until interrater reliability was 100 percent.

FINDINGS

Identifiability

Identifiability was defined as the belief that one is known to others as a lesbian without a verbal disclosure. There was a range of belief about personal identifiability: 48 percent of the participants thought they were clearly recognizable to everyone as lesbians; 32 percent thought that other lesbians could tell that they were lesbian, while the general public could not; and 20 percent thought that nobody could tell. Their opinions about the identifiability of lesbians as a whole were similar.

About half of these women believed that, in social interactions, their lesbian identity was readily apparent to all. It has been assumed in the literature that the task for lesbians in managing stigma is to conceal information so that others do not become aware of the attribute. However, the present findings suggest that at least some women perceive themselves to be readily recognized as lesbians so that their task becomes minimizing the negative impact of the stigma. Consequently, a lesbian's perceived social vulnerability is related to her beliefs about her own identifiability.

The means by which the participants believed lesbians were identifiable to others formed a gestalt of physical appearance, personality, interaction and association. Participants thought themselves to be more androgynous in appearance. They believed themselves to be differentiated from other women by a more purposeful carriage; a less "affected," more natural walk; a stronger, more athletic body; open, definite body gestures; and a more casual mode of dress and hair style. They believed that their degree of independence, self-reliance, assertiveness, confidence, persistence and strength of will distinguished them, making them recognizable as lesbians. They referred also to the perception that some men feel intimidated by them and are more likely to conclude that they are lesbians.

The participants believed that lesbians are marked also by their interactional style and patterns of association. They believed it was noticeable that they do not defer to men, do not form intimate relationships with men and, in general, pay less attention to them. In contrast, they felt lesbians establish more eye contact with other women, stand and sit closer to women, are more likely to touch women as they socialize and ordinarily associate more with women. Speaking about and affiliating with such political concerns as feminism and minority rights helped to identify them as lesbians as did talking about women partners and friends, rather than husbands and boyfriends. A verbal style that sought clarification and offered criticism was also indicated as a distinguishing factor. Participants believed that a constellation of physical, psychological and social factors — as opposed to a single characteristic — combined to distinguish them. These results suggest that for those women who believe they can conceal their lesbian identity and avoid stigmatization, comprehensive management of that information involves vigilance about the intimate details of who they are, how they act, how they look, what they say, who they are with and where they are. Such a task is extremely complex and not replicated in the experience of nonlesbian women.

Health Beliefs

Participants conceptualized health in a wholistic fashion, discussing wellness as a composite of emotional, physical and social elements and envisioning health strengths in lesbians as well as serious health concerns. They focused on independence and self-reliance as the primary components of wellness. A positive self-concept, an affirming attitude toward life, purposeful work toward emotional health and an ability to manage stress were frequently cited as the participants identified the healthiest things about themselves as lesbians. There was consensus about a number of physical health strengths including athleticism, involvement in physical exercise and good nutrition. Social factors identified as common to lesbians and sources of well-being were group cohesiveness that lends social support, ethical responsibility that prompts political action and a tendency to value mutuality in relationships. A predilection for alternative healing strategies such as massage, homeopathy, chiropractic, and acupuncture as well as the avoidance of mainstream allopathy were also viewed positively.

Substance abuse was frequently mentioned. Some participants remarked positively that many lesbians are recovering from substance abuse or simply choosing not to use drugs or alcohol. Others focused on the belief that abuse of substances is more likely to occur in lesbians than in nonlesbian women and is of serious concern.

These women were distressed about aging, viewing it as a loss of physical, economic and social autonomy and as an impairment of athletic capabilities, all of which were so vitally important to their definition of wellness. They feared being dependent on others as they grow older yet isolated from social support. Most had contemplated being old and anticipated alienation, seeing no present social structures supportive of older lesbians. They also feared increasing involvement in the mainstream allopathic health care system because of an overwhelming mistrust of its ability to care adequately and safely for lesbians.

Another health concern identified specifically was the stress of socioeconomic discrimination suffered by women, particularly lesbian women. They described its impact on them much as Adam (1978) did, when he theorized that structural limitations are placed on the alternatives open to stigmatized individuals, so that one dominant group maximizes its life chances by minimizing those of another group. Internalized stigma was recognized by the participants as a health risk for lesbians, verifying Maylon's (1985) finding that the sequence of events in the development of a lesbian identity results in the introjection of antilesbian ideas before the realization of sexual/affectional orientation.

Identifiability in Relation to Health

These lesbian women conceived of the concepts of both identifiability and health as an amalgam of physical, psychological and social components. Several hallmarks of lesbian health were also primary qualities that they believed identified them as lesbians. It may be hypothesized that the challenge of coping with stigma engenders a strong self-concept and underlies many of the attributes of lesbian health, but the factor of identifiability mediates the process. The means by which a lesbian believes her identity to be revealed may affect how she values such aspects of herself as body image, associations and personality characteristics. Her attitude toward the degree of identifiability she attributes to herself may be related to the degree of self-affirmation that she has as a lesbian. Her sense of control over the disclosure of her lesbian identity may be related to the level of stress that she experiences. For example, both the woman who believes that she can conceal her lesbian identity and the woman who behaves as though she is highly identifiable may experience a sense of control and thereby reduce stress.

Interactions with Health Care Providers

Experience in health care interactions was also related to stigmatized identity. Participants discussed health care contacts in which they were known to be lesbians. They identified circumstances in which they were identifiable to health care providers by their behavior, interaction, appearance and associations or by verbal disclosure of lesbian identity. The majority (72%) recounted negative responses from health care providers after their identity was known. They described being responded to with ostracism, invasive personal questioning, shock, embarrassment, unfriendliness, pity, condescension and fear. They reported instances in which nurses did not answer their call lights and doctors stopped talking to them. They felt that their partners had been mistreated; their confidentiality breached. Rough physical handling and derogatory comments were also perceived as being related directly to their disclosures. Of the respondents, 36 percent described situations in which they had had to terminate the interaction or not return to that provider because of events following disclosure. A few of their comments serve to illustrate:

> As soon as I said I was a lesbian, the nurses started giving me disgusted looks. They were nasty to my partner. They rough-housed me. They were not gentle like they would be to a straight woman. They treated me like I was "one of those," like they might catch something.

> The reaction was a subtle thing, an air of pity and fear. A wall went up. I read the shocked facial expressions, and they were saying, "That's too bad." But they made no remarks. They just acted real nervous.

> One of the doctors I told turned completely different colors. He left the office saying he had to get equipment and returned with two nurses like he had to have protection from me.

> In the course of the discussion with the counselor, it became more like voyeurism than therapy. She was obviously curious about the life-style and asked a lot of inappropriate sexual questions.

> I was in the hospital and the nurses would never come down to my room. I was told later that they had specifically talked about not wanting to care for me because I was a lesbian. I was surprised. I am always surprised when these things actually happen.

Negatively perceived interactions occurred in a variety of settings including hospitals, emergency rooms and community clinics. Of particular distress to these lesbians were interactions that involved gynecological health care. They felt harassed by persistent questioning about birth control and pregnancy. As two women put it:

> When you go for a pap test they always ask if you are sexually active. If you say no, they don't believe you. If you say yes, you get badgered about how you should use birth control. If you are stuck with the birth control lecture you disclose just to avoid all that. But I've never done it voluntarily. I've always felt forced to disclose.

> When I was having abdominal pain, they asked me at the emergency room if I was pregnant. When I told them I was sure I was not pregnant, they kept asking me over and over until I got angry and said, "No, I can't be pregnant, I'm a lesbian."

Questions asked by health care providers assumed that their female clients were heterosexual, their partners were male and their sexual activity involved intercourse. Overwhelmingly, participants found that there was no routine, comfortable way to let health care providers know that heterosexual assumptions were not applicable to them as lesbians. To avoid being referred to persistently as something they were not, to avoid upbraiding about irrelevant issues and to obtain pertinent health teaching, many participants felt forced to "make an announcement" of their lesbian identity.

Every participant identified circumstances in which it would be important for her providers to know about her lesbian identity so that they might deliver optimal, comprehensive care. For instance, several feared being hospitalized for a serious condition in which visitation and treatment decisions were relegated to "immediate family" and said that they would definitely disclose in this situation so that their partner or a significant friend could be involved in their health care.

Nearly all (96%) of the women in this study anticipated situations in which it could be harmful to them if their health care provider were to know that they were lesbian. Although they believed that there were frequent specific health care situations in which they wanted to disclose, they described having to assess each individual encounter for both potential antilesbian sentiment and personal vulnerability. In potentially harmful situations, if they were identifiable, they would attempt to minimize the impact of their lesbian identity during health care interactions. On the other hand, if they were to believe that they were not identifiable, they would not disclose and would attempt to manage the information so that health care providers would not become aware that they were lesbian. Their sensitivity to these risks seemed to have developed over a lifetime of dealing with the larger stigmatizing society.

> Society says it is not okay to be a lesbian. We face rejection based on that all the time. Not having access to health care in which it is safe to disclose is just a small part of the larger picture.

When they disclosed or were otherwise identifiable in an unsafe health care situation, they feared danger, infliction of pain, inadequate care, withdrawal of concern for their welfare and pathological assumption, "where your health problem is seen as a pathological extension of the fact that you are lesbian." Several women addressed these fears:

> I think some caregivers leave that room of margin. They put limits on how far they will go to help lesbians, just decide to give you only the minimum care.

> You'd get poorer care if they knew you were lesbian. If they thought it was bad they wouldn't care if you didn't get well. They could relax during surgery. They could give you bad drugs.

> If the environment isn't safe for disclosure, I'm not going to be taken care of. I might even get hurt.

> It would be very damaging if you got into interactions with health care providers in which you are considered deviant. Some people have very negative, very violent reactions. I don't think they can separate from their personal prejudices. It is like putting your life in someone's hands who really hates you.

The most dominant feature of positive health care experiences reported by these women was the perception that providers accepted the knowledge of their clients' lesbian identity as a matter of routine. This was demonstrated by providers' treating them "like anybody else" and maintaining a calm, supportive demeanor. These lesbian women wanted to feel accepted, respected and welcomed by health care providers. They did not want to be questioned when they chose to have their lesbian partners included as their significant others in health care interactions. They felt more comfortable with women and appreciated the availability of female health care providers.

Lesbians take action in light of what they encounter in the behavior of others. Given their negative experiences in interaction with health care providers and their fearful perceptions that harm could befall them, 84 percent described a general reluctance to seek health care. According to the participants, dispelling heterosexual assumption and eliminating prejudicial attitude and action is the responsibility of health care providers so that health care can be made more accessible to lesbians. They suggested the use of inclusive language and the education of providers about lesbian culture and health concerns to accomplish these goals. With empathy and accurate information about lesbians, participants felt it would be possible for health care providers to overcome their negative responses. However, they wanted providers to have dealt with the issue before that moment when it comes to providing care to them.

CONCLUSION

Lesbians share common beliefs and experiences with identifiability, health and health care. They often do not feel comfortable seeking health care, have experienced nonempathetic responses when they did and even feel at risk of harm in some health care situations. The commitment of nursing to wholism and advocacy in the care of women and vulnerable cultural groups and lesbians' preference for female providers makes nursing a logical health care profession to facilitate lesbians' positive involvement in health care. Only when the recipients of care can report feeling respect and regard from caregivers is that commitment to care genuinely fulfilled. This study points out a burden of responsibility for nursing as a profession and for nurses as individual clinicians, educators and researchers to evaluate the adequacy of its knowledge base and reassess the quality of health care offered to lesbian women.

REFERENCES

Adam, B. (1978). *The survival of domination: Inferiorization and everyday life.* New York: Elsevier.

Agar, M. (1980). *The professional stranger: An informal introduction to ethnography.* New York: Academic Press.

Aguero, J. E., Bloch, L. & Byrne, D. (1984). The relationship among sexual beliefs, attitudes, experience and homophobia. *Journal of Homosexuality, 10*(1-2), 95-107.

Ahmed, P. I., Kolker, A., & Coelho, G. V.(1979). Toward a new definition of health. In P. I. Ahmed & G. V. Coelho (Eds.), *Toward a new definition of health: Psychosocial approaches* (pp. 7-21). New York: Plenum Press.

Becker, H. S. (1973). *Outsiders: Studies in the sociology of deviance.* New York: The Free Press.

Blumer, H. (1969). *Symbolic interactionism: Perspective and method.* Englewood Cliffs, NJ: Prentice-Hall.

Brooks, V. (1981). *Minority stress and lesbian women.* New York: D.C. Heath.

Bruyn, S. T. (1966). *The human perspective in sociology: The methodology of participant observation.* Englewood Cliffs, NJ: Prentice-Hall.

Cass, V. (1979). Homosexual identity formation: A theoretical model. *Journal of Homosexuality 4*(3), 219-235.

Chafetz, J., Sampson, P., Beck, P., & West, J. (1974). A study of homosexual women. *Social Work, 19*(6), 714-723.

Dank, B. (1971). Coming out in the gay world. *Psychiatry, 34,* 180-197.

Di Angi, P. R (1982). Grieving and the acceptance of the homosexual identity. *Issues in Mental Health Nursing, 4,* 101-113.

Edgerton, R. B., & Langness, L. L. (1974). *Methods and styles in the study of culture.* San Francisco, CA: Chandler and Sharp.

Fabrega, H., Jr. (1979). Disease and illness from a biocultural standpoint. In P. I. Ahmed & G. V Coelho (Eds.), *Toward a new definition of health: Psychosocial dimensions* (pp. 23-50). New York: Plenum Press.

Fein, S. B., & Nuehring, E. M. (1981). Intrapsychic effects of stigma: A process of breakdown and reconstruction of social reality. *Journal of Homosexuality* 7(1), 3-13.

Glascock, E. (1983). *Lesbians growing older: Self-identification, coming out, and health concerns.* Paper presented at the American Public Health Association Annual Meeting, Dallas.

Goffman, E. (1963). *Stigma: Notes on the management of spoiled identity.* Englewood Cliffs, NJ: Prentice-Hall.

Good, B. J., & Good, M.D. (1980). The meaning of symptoms: A cultural hermeneutical model for clinical practice. In L. Eisenberg & A. Kleinman (Eds.), *The relevance of social science for medicine* (pp. 165-196). New York: D. Reidel.

Hartog, J., & Hartog, E. A. (1983). Cultural aspects of health and illness behavior in hospitals. *Western Journal of Medicine, 139*(6), 910-916.

Hudson, W. W., & Ricketts, W. A. (1980). A strategy for the measurement of homophobia. *Journal of Homosexuality, 5*(4), 357-372.

Irwin, P., & Thompson, N. L. (1978). Acceptance of the rights of homosexuals: A social profile. *Journal of Homosexuality, 3*(2), 107-121.

Jandt, F. E., & Darsey, J. (1981). Coming out as a communication process. In J. Chesebro (Ed.), *Gayspeak: Gay male and lesbian communication* (pp. 12-27). New York: Pilgrim Press.

Johnson, S., Guenther, S., Laube, D., & Keettel, W. (1981). Factors influencing lesbian gynecologic care: A preliminary study. *American Journal of Obstetrics and Gynecology, 140*(1), 20-28.

Jones, E. E., Farina, A., Hastorf, A. H., Markus, H., Miller, D. T., Scott, R. A., & French, R. de S. (1984). *Social stigma: The psychology of marked relationships.* New York: W. H. Freeman.

Jourard, S. (1971). *Self-disclosure: An experimental analysis of the transparent self.* New York: Wiley-Interscience.

Krestan, J., & Bepko, C. S. (1980). The problem of fusion in the lesbian relationship. *Family Process, 19,* 277-289.

Kus, R. (1985). Stages of coming out: An ethnographic approach. *Western Journal of Nursing Research, 7*(2), 177-198.

Laner, M. R., & Laner, R. H. (1980). Sexual preference or personal style? Why lesbians are disliked. *Journal of Homosexuality, 5*(4), 339-356.

Leininger, M. (1984). *Care: The essence of nursing and health.* Thorofare, NJ: Charles B. Slack.

Levitt, E. E., & Klassen, A. D. (1974). Public attitudes toward homosexuality: Part of the 1970 national survey by the Institute of Sex Research. *Journal of Homosexuality, 1*(1), 29-43.

Lofland, J. (1971). *Analyzing social settings: A guide to qualitative observation and analysis.* Belmont, CA: Wadsworth.

Markus, H. (1977). Self-schemata and processing information about the self. *Journal of Personality and Social Psychology, 35*(2), 63-79.

Maylon, A. (1985). Psychotherapeutic implications of internalized homophobia in gay men. In J. C. Gonsiorek (Ed.), *A guide to psychotherapy with lesbian and gay clients* (pp. 59-69). New York: Harrington Pack Press.

Millham, J., San Miguel, C. L., & Kellogg, R. (1976). A factor-analytic conceptualization of attitudes toward male and female homosexuals. *Journal of Homosexuality, 2*(1), 3-10.

Minnigerode, F. A. (1976). Attitudes toward homosexuality: Feminist attitudes and sexual conservatism. *Sex Roles, 2*(4), 347-352.

Morin, S. F. (1981). Psychology and the gay community: An overview. *Journal of Social Issues, 34*(3), 1-6.

Nixon, J., & Berson, G. (1978). Women's music. In G. Vida (Ed.), *Our right to love: A lesbian resource book* (pp. 252-255). Englewood Cliffs, NJ: Prentice-Hall.

Nungesser, L. G. (1983). *Homosexual acts, actors and identities.* New York: Praeger Publishers.

Nyberg, K. L., & Alston, J. P. (1977). Analysis of public attitudes toward homosexual behavior. *Journal of Homosexuality, 2*(2), 99-107.

Painter, D. S. (1981). Recognition among lesbians in straight settings. In J. Chesebro (Ed.), *Gayspeak: Gay male and lesbian communication* (pp. 68-79). New York: Pilgrim Press.

Paterson, J., & Zderad, L. (1976). *Humanistic nursing.* New York: John Wiley & Sons.

Plummer, K. (1975). *Sexual stigma: An interactionist account.* Boston, MA: Routledge and Kegan Paul.

Ponse, B. (1978). *Identities in the lesbian world: The social construction of self.* Westport, CT: Greenwood Press.

Schwartz, H., & Jacobs, J. (1979). *Qualitative sociology: A method to the madness.* New York: Free Press.

Smith, E., Johnson, S., & Guenther, S. (1985). Health care attitudes and experiences during gynecologic care among lesbians and bisexuals. *American Journal of Public Health, 75*(9), 1085-1087.

Smith, J. (1981). The idea of health: A philosophical inquiry. *Advances in Nursing Science, 3*(3), 43-50.

Tripp-Reimer, T. (1984). Reconceptualizing the construct of health: Integrating emic and etic perspectives. *Research in Nursing and Health, 7,* 101-109.

Van Maanen, J., Dubbs, J., & Faulkner, R. (1982). *Varieties of qualitative research.* Beverly Hills, CA: Sage Publications.

Warren, C. A. B. (1980). Homosexuality and stigma. In J. Marmor (Ed.), *Homosexual behavior* (pp. 123-141). New York: Basic Books.

Weinberger, L. E., & Millham, J. (1979). Attitudinal homophobia and support of traditional sex roles. *Journal of Homosexuality, 4*(3), 237-245.

CHAPTER **47**

Barriers to Health Promotion for Individuals with Disabilities*

Alexa K. Stuifbergen, RN, PhD
Heather Becker, PhD
Dolores Sands, RN, PhD

Participation in health-promotion activities may lead to lower mortality rates, a higher quality of life, and lower health care costs.[1] Important as these benefits are for the nonimpaired population, they may be even more significant for disabled individuals, whose quality of life and ability to continue living independently are often heavily dependent on maintaining what DeJong and Hughes[2] have termed their "thinner margin of health."

Although health-promotion activities have been investigated in a number of groups, including working adults, recovering cancer patients, and the elderly, the health promotion of disabled people has not been a focus of research or practice for health care professionals. It is not surprising, therefore, to find that there is a lack of knowledge about disabled adults' perceptions of how various factors may act as barriers to healthy life styles, thereby interfering with their ability to take care of their own health.

Barriers are a particularly salient topic for people with disabilities. Although architectural barriers have received much attention, barriers continue to exist in other areas, such as employment, transportation, housing, education, insurance, and entitlement programs. For example, a Harris poll,[3] commissioned in 1986 by the International Center for the Disabled, found that although two thirds of their 1,000 disabled respondents wanted to work, only 32% of the sample group were currently employed. Respondents identified lack of education, training, accessible transportation, adaptive equipment, appropriate jobs, and medical treatment, as well as employers' attitudes and the disability itself as barriers that kept them from working. Social Security regulations also provide disincentives for working. Moreover, lack of appropriate housing and accessible personal services (eg, readers, interpreters, attendant services) has led to inappropriate institutionalization for many disabled persons. Transportation barriers not only restrict employment possibilities but limit social and community activities as well. Finally, gaps in services provided to people with disabilities, along with the fact that most services are organized according to the traditional medical model, also contribute to the barriers that disabled people experience as they attempt to live more independently in the community.[3]

The National Council on the Handicapped underscores the problems in the following way:

> Whatever the limitations associated with particular disabilities, people with disabilities have been saying

*This study was supported by the US Department of Education National Institute on Disability and Rehabilitation Research (Grant G008720217) — Dr Dolores Sands, principal investigator, Dr Heather Becker, coprincipal investigator.

Reprinted from *Family and Community Health,* Vol. 13, No. 1, with permission of Aspen Publishers, Inc., © 1990.

> for years that their major obstacles are not inherent in their disabilities, but arise from barriers that have been imposed externally and unnecessarily.[3(p11)]

Such barriers affect disabled adults in one of the most important spheres of their lives—the maintenance of their health.[4] Much work is needed to assess factors that might inhibit disabled adults from taking care of their own health and to educate disabled people and professionals about the health-promotion needs of disabled persons.

REVIEW OF RELATED RESEARCH

Barriers to Health Care Services

Much of the literature relating to barriers has addressed factors that inhibit use of the health care system rather than the performance of health-promoting behaviors. In a critical review of the literature, Melnyk[5] grouped barrier variables as structural barriers and as individual barriers. Structural barriers to health care identified in previous research were time, distance, cost, availability of services, organization of services, and discrimination, as well as aspects of the provider-consumer relationship. Individual characteristics identified as potential barriers included demographic characteristics (limited education, limited income, age), personal attitudes, ignorance, effort, cultural factors, and family characteristics. Melnyk[5] concludes that there is considerable confusion surrounding barriers on both theoretical and empirical levels. Operational definitions have varied widely, and most published research does not refer to a conceptual framework. Melnyk suggests that future research explore the notion of barriers as a subjective phenomenon and address the effect of perceived barriers on health behavior.

Disabled people have also identified barriers to the use of health care services. Nosek[4] argues that health care professionals harbor misperceptions about the health of people with disabilities and that these misperceptions lead to inappropriate treatment methods, which create barriers to the maintenance of good health status by disabled people. She further states that health care professionals tend to focus so heavily on the disability itself that they fail to look beyond the disability to consider other factors in their diagnosis or their treatment strategy. Consequently they often fail to discuss life-style changes that might prevent secondary disabilities and enhance health promotion. In other instances, their lack of knowledge of the subtle effects of many impairments leads them to either overtreat or undertreat disabled persons. For example, physicians may not realize that standard medication dosages may need to be adjusted for persons whose mobility impairments cause them to be more sedentary than the average patient. Finally, Nosek[4] points to subtle attitudinal factors that create barriers to disabled people becoming independent in the health sphere. She proposes that the attitude among health care providers that disabled people are sick has led disabled people to think of themselves as passive participants in their own health care rather than as individuals responsible for their own well-being. Similarly, Vertinsky and Auman[6] suggest that the attitude among physicians that old age is a disease demanding medical attention has perpetuated dependency and negative body images among elderly women and has served as a barrier to wellness behavior.

Other researchers have focused on the problems disabled people face in gaining access to knowledgeable health care professionals. In a recent survey of mobility-impaired persons living in the Washington, DC area, Batavia and DeJong[7] reported that 45% of the spinal-cord-injured respondents reported difficulty finding knowledgeable physicians. Warms[8] described the source and content of health care services received by 59 individuals with a spinal-cord injury. Results indicated that discussions at health care visits were overwhelmingly disability related, that participants desired health-promotion services more frequently than disability-related services, and that participants were specifically interested in access to services relating to exercise, nutrition, and stress management.

Barriers to Health-Promoting Behaviors

Pender[9] has identified "perceived barriers" as one of the cognitive-perceptual factors that exert a direct influence on the predisposition to engage in health-promoting behaviors. Barriers are defined as perceptions regarding the unavailability, inconvenience, or difficulty of a particular health-promoting option. They may arise from people's internal cognitions, from significant others, and from the environment.

A number of studies have examined factors that create barriers to health-promoting behaviors for the general population. Dishman et al[10] reviewed the empirical literature on known determinants of regular exercise and physical activity. Factors negatively associated with participation in exercise programs included blue-collar occupation, smoking, being overweight, ignorance of the beneficial effects of exercise, age, intensity of activity, and perceived exertion.

Champion[11] investigated the relationship between attitudinal variables and the intention, frequency, and proficiency of self-examination of breasts in 380 women aged 35 years and over. In this study perceived barriers (eg, embarrassment, unpleasantness, and difficulty) were negatively related to intent to practice breast self-examination ($r = -.47$), and these barriers were the most powerful predictor of frequency of breast self-examination.

The primary prevention behaviors of 59 female-headed, one-parent families and the barriers that deterred practice of these behaviors were examined by Duffy.[12] The most important health behaviors identified were nutrition, rest, and exercise. Lack of time was the most frequently stated barrier, followed by feeling lazy, lack of money, and needing someone's support. Other factors that occurred as part of the participant's life circumstances and that were perceived as negative influences on the family's ability to practice primary prevention behaviors included economics, day care, parenting, inadequate support systems, and low self-esteem.

In a study of health-promoting behaviors among disabled persons, Dai and Catanzaro[13] explored the relationship between an individual's health beliefs regarding skin care and compliance with a skin-care regimen in a group of 20 outpatient paraplegics. Compliance with skin care consisted of knowledge of skin-care strategies and report of actual performance of skin care. Perceived efficacy of skin care was the strongest correlate of compliance ($r = .62$), followed by perceived severity of pressure sores ($r = .56$) and perceived barriers ($r = .33$; the fewer the barriers the higher the score).

In summary, existing literature documents barriers to health care services for both disabled and nondisabled people. Although some literature addresses barriers to engaging in health-promotion activities for the general population, only one study of disabled people was located that examined barriers in relation to taking care of one's health. The concept of barriers, operationalized in different ways, has been related to participation in exercise programs, practicing self-examination of the breasts, and the primary prevention behaviors of rest, nutrition, exercise, and skin care. The limited literature that exists suggests that barriers have important implications for engaging in health-promotion behavior and supports the need for a structured method to measure barriers to health-promoting behavior.

DEVELOPMENT OF THE BARRIERS SCALE

As part of a larger study of the health-promoting attitudes and behaviors of adults with disabilities, the authors were challenged by the project's advisory committee (rehabilitation experts and service providers) to develop an instrument to measure perceived barriers to health promotion. The new instrument the authors developed is the Barriers to Health-Promoting Activities for Disabled Persons Scale. Items for the scale were generated from three sources: (1) a review of the literature, (2) content analysis of interview data from a pilot study undertaken to test the feasibility and appropriateness of the methods proposed for the larger study, and (3) expert consultation. The process of developing a tool to measure barriers to health-promotion activities, the initial findings from use of the tool with a sample of 135 disabled adults, and the implications of these findings will be described.

Content Analysis of the Interview Data

While the literature on barriers to health promotion provided general guidance about the factors that should be included in a barriers measure, the authors decided that more specific information about health promotion and barriers, from the perspective of disabled people, was needed to guide content development. Consequently, a major source of items for the Barriers Scale was interview data from the pilot study. Participants for the pilot study were recruited through a newsletter distributed to disabled students registered at a large southwestern university. Eight men and 10 women participated in this pilot. Their average age was 32.9 years; 60% had at least a bachelor's degree. Participants reported a variety of disabilities and chronic conditions, including diabetes and visual, hearing, and mobility impairments.

Respondents were asked how they would define health for themselves. While a few responses referred to the absence of disease or pain, the majority emphasized a more functional or self-actualized definition of health. Respondents mentioned "being able to take care of myself," "being independent," "leading a normal, productive life," "not having anything interfere with day-to-day living," and "body not being a hindrance." Another respondent focused on what one needs to stay healthy, such as exercise, rest, and being conscious of the body's signals. Two individuals emphasized that being healthy is their responsibility and something that they actively pursue. Of particular interest in respondents' definitions of health was that there was little mention of specific disabilities.

When asked what they did to maintain or to improve their health, approximately three fourths cited diet or exercise. A number of respondents mentioned stress management and self-monitoring of their health. Avoiding negative health practices (smoking, overuse of alcohol or drugs), getting enough rest, cultivating social support, and following the recommendations of those in the wellness field were also reported.

In response to a question about who or what helps them maintain their health, most respondents emphasized their own responsibility. One individual stated the following:

> I feel that basically the struggle is mine and it's my responsibility and I don't think that anybody really understands what I'm going through and that's why I constantly struggle to understand it. And constantly work at it.

Others emphasized their own motivation and self-monitoring in maintaining or improving their health. A number of students pointed out that by working at staying healthy (ie, not overdoing, continuing to exercise, staying on special diets) they avoid problems, and that was incentive enough to keep them attending to their health. One respondent put it as follows:

> Nobody in the real world thinks about how they're eating, how they're sleeping; they just run until they are dead. But if I do that, the consequences are that I don't have rejuvenation, the sort of energy, that other people have.

A few individuals mentioned other people, such as family and friends, who were helpful to them. While four respondents cited health care professionals, others specifically stated that physicians, particularly those with a traditional approach to health care, were not helpful, and so they avoided them.

Time limitations were the most frequently reported barrier to improving or to maintaining health. Other factors were the lack of accessible and convenient exercise facilities or transportation to get to such facilities. To help improve or maintain their health, some students suggested making exercise facilities more convenient or designing nutrition or exercise programs specifically for disabled students. There appeared to be some conflict, however, between the recognition of the need for special assistance and the desire to avoid programs aimed exclusively at people with disabilities.

Expert Consultation

The review of the literature and the content analysis of interview data yielded 15 factors that were identified as potential barriers to taking care of one's health. Two consultants from the Independent Living Centers, one health-promotion researcher, and one special education/rehabilitation professional then reviewed the content of the tool. The experts indicated that all of the items were relevant barriers to health promotion for disabled adults. One additional item, concern about crime, was suggested by a consultant and was added to the Barriers Scale before it was used with the larger sample of adults with disabilities.

Structure of the Barriers Scale

The Barriers to Health-Promoting Activities for Disabled Persons Scale is a 16-item summated-rating scale. Participants were asked to rate each of the 16 items on a 4-point scale (1 = never, 4 = routinely) indicating how often each of the problems kept them from taking care of their health. Only one item ("Impairment keeps me from doing what I want to do") was specifically related to having a disability. Individual item scores were summed to yield a total score.

INITIAL USE OF THE BARRIERS SCALE

Setting

The Barriers Scale was initially used as part of a larger study of the health-promoting attitudes and behaviors of adults with disabilities. Participants were recruited through contacts with two urban independent living centers (ILCs) in the southwestern United States. The goal of ILCs is to improve the quality of life for disabled individuals by assisting them to achieve and to maintain more independent lives in their communities.[14] The ILCs provide a broad range of community-based services to consumers with a variety of disabilities. These services include information and referral, assistance in locating housing, the recruitment of personal-care attendants, training in independent living skills, advocacy, and peer counseling.

Procedures

Participants were recruited through newsletters, personal contacts with ILC staff, and community agencies that serve disabled consumers. The study was explained by the ILC staff to their consumers. The staff reported that virtually all who were approached about the study chose to participate. After informed consent was obtained from the participants, the ILC staff and counselors administered a set of questionnaires (including the Barriers Scale) and conducted brief, semi-structured interviews audiotaped with the subject's permission. To facilitate administration, questionnaires and consent forms were translated into Braille, reproduced in large print format, read aloud, and interpreted in sign language.

Sample

One hundred thirty-five individuals (76 men, 59 women) participated in this phase of the larger study of the health-promoting attitudes and behaviors of disabled adults. Participants reported a wide range of disabilities, including visual impairments (n = 11), hearing impairments (n = 13), neuromuscular impairments (n = 53), neurocognitive impairments (n = 40), and chronic medical conditions (n = 18). The neurocognitive group included 18 head-injured persons, 8 learning disabled persons, 6 persons with mental or emotional disabilities, 7 persons with epilepsy, and 1 mentally retarded person. Therefore, 47% of the sample (n = 64) listed either a neurocognitive or neurosensory impairment as their primary disability. The mean length of disability was 17 years, and 20% of the participants reported more than one disability. The average age of participants was 36 years (range 19 to 85 years). The majority of the sample was white (62%) and unemployed (76%). Seventy-three percent of the participants had completed 12 grades of school.

Results

Quantitative data

Table 47-1 lists each item from the Barriers Scale and the mean rating obtained in this sample. A higher rating indicates that a particular item interferes more frequently with disabled people taking care of their health. The participants rated lack of money, being too tired, the impairment itself, and concern about crime as the most frequent problems. Interestingly "lack of support from family and friends" and "no one to help me" were perceived as infrequent problems.

Internal consistency reliability (Cronbach's alpha) for the 16-item scale was .82. A principal-components factor analysis of the scale was performed on the data from the 135 respondents in this study. A three-factor solution accounted for 48% of the variance. On examination of the item clusters, the first factor included attitudinal items, such as "doesn't help," "no interest," "can't do correctly." The second factor contained disability-related items ("impairment interferes," "lack of transportation," "no support," and "lack of accessible facilities"). The

TABLE 47-1
Mean item ratings of Barriers Scale items for impaired adults ($N = 135$)

ITEM	MEAN
Lack of money	2.62
Too tired	2.25
Impairment interferes	2.24
Concern about crime	2.23
Lack of time	2.13
Lack of convenient facilities	2.09
Lack of transportation	2.05
Cannot do things correctly	2.03
Lack of information	2.02
Interferes with other responsibilities	1.99
Embarrassment about appearance	1.90
Feeling what I do doesn't help	1.90
No one to help me	1.88
Not interested	1.85
Difficulty with communication	1.76
Lack of support from family or friends	1.76

Items rated on a 4-point scale from 1 = never a problem, to 4 = routinely a problem.

TABLE 47-2
Bivariate correlations between demographic variables and Barriers Scale

VARIABLE	CORRELATION
Age	.01
Gender	.01
Married/not married	−.22*
Education	−.10
Socioeconomic status	−.12
White/nonwhite	.07
Black/nonblack	.20*
Hispanic/non-Hispanic	−.22*
Visual disability	.18†
Neuromuscular disability	−.24*
Neurocognitive disability	.12
Hearing/deaf-blind disability	.11
Other chronic conditions	−.05

Dichotomous variables: 1 = member of this group; 0 = not a member of this group.
*$P < .01$
†$P < .05$

third factor contained other external barriers such as "lack of money," "concern about crime," "interferes with other responsiblities," and "lack of time."

Correlations were used to examine the relationship between the Barriers total score and other variables in the larger study. As Table 47-2 indicates, there was a significant, negative relationship between scores on the Barriers Scale and marital status ($r = -.22$, $P < .01$), that is, unmarried participants perceived greater barriers to taking care of their health. The three categories of ethnic status were recoded into three dichotomous variables: white, nonwhite; black, nonblack; and Hispanic, non-Hispanic. There was a positive relationship between being black and scores on the Barriers Scale ($r = .20$, $P < .01$) but a negative relationship between being Hispanic and scores on the Barriers Scale ($r = -.22$, $P < .01$); that is, being black was associated with greater perceived barriers, and being Hispanic was associated with lower scores on the Barriers Scale. Participants with visual impairments had higher Barriers scores than those without visual impairments ($r = .18$, $P < .05$). Participants with neuromuscular impairments perceived fewer barriers than those without a neuromuscular impairment ($r = -.24$, $P < .01$). While all of these correlations were significant, given the large sample size in this study, all represent small-effect sizes.

Scores on the Barriers Scale were significantly correlated with five other attitudinal measures used in the larger study: perceived health status,[15] perceived self-efficacy,[16] likelihood of engaging in health-promoting behavior as measured by the Health-Promoting Lifestyle Profile,[17] and the Chance and Powerful Others externality scales of the Multidimensional Health Locus of Control.[18] As indicated in Table 47-3, higher scores on the Barriers Scale were associated with lower perceptions of health status and self-efficacy and decreased likelihood of engaging in health-promoting behavior, in particular the psychosocial components. Stronger beliefs that health was controlled by chance were associated with more frequently perceived barriers. The correlations of the Barriers Scale with the attitudinal factors, particularly

TABLE 47-3
Bivariate correlations between attitudinal variables and Barriers Scale

VARIABLE	CORRELATION
Self-efficacy	−.48*
Perceived health status	−.29*
Internal health locus of control	−.10
Chance health locus of control	.22*
Powerful others health locus of control	.25*
Health-promoting life-style profile	−.29*
Life-style profile subscales:	
Self-actualization	−.36*
Interpersonal support	−.24*
Stress management	−.33*
Health responsibility	−.09
Exercise	−.19†
Nutrition	−.07

*$P < .01$
†$P < .05$

self-efficacy, were stronger than the correlations with the demographic factors.

Interview data

During the interview each participant was asked, "What prevents you from improving and maintaining your health?" Although the ILC staff interviewed all respondents, only 48 interviews were tape recorded. The subsequent analysis of interview data was based on 44 tape-recorded interviews; the other four interviews were eliminated because of incomplete data or the respondents' lack of understanding of the questions. Two research assistants listened to the taped interviews and independently listed the descriptive statements made by participants. The investigators then categorized the content into themes, and the research assistants recorded the responses into the established categories. Disagreements between the two raters were resolved by a third rater. Overall 79% agreement was obtained on the question concerning barriers to health promotion.

Responses to the interview questions were brief. Approximately one third of the respondents mentioned themselves and their own motivation as preventing them from improving and maintaining their own health, while another third indicated that there were no barriers. Other barriers identified by the respondents included their disability and external factors such as weather, lack of money, and lack of exercise equipment.

DISCUSSION AND IMPLICATIONS

Participants in this study identified a broad array of barriers to taking care of their health. Virtually all of the participants indicated that at least one of the items on the Barriers Scale presented a problem for them, and two thirds of those interviewed cited a specific factor/barrier to improving and to maintaining their health. While not all of the barriers cited in the interviews and endorsed on the Barriers Scale are directly amenable to change, some certainly are. If lack of money translates into lack of access to low-cost community-health facilities, then mechanisms for funding memberships in the YMCA or other community services could enhance these individuals' ability to improve their health. The fact that the items most strongly endorsed included internal barriers (too tired, lack of time) as well as the externally imposed barriers frequently cited in the literature about disabled adults suggests that a variety of strategies, designed to change both individual perceptions and characteristics of the environment, may be needed to reduce barriers and to increase the likelihood of health-promoting behaviors.

Although there were statistically significant relationships between the Barriers Scale and marital status, ethnicity, and disability groups, the magnitude of the correlations was small and therefore of limited practical significance. It may be that other impairment-related characteristics, not measured in this study, such as functional limitation, may obscure the relationship between background variables and barriers to health promotion for disabled adults. In reality this group labeled "adults with disabilities" really comprises many subgroups with different life experiences, different health-promotion needs, and probably different perceived barriers.

The traditional approach to research in this area, dividing the individuals into groups on the basis of their diagnosis (eg, head injury, mobility impairment), is too simplistic and counter to the data, indicating that individuals do not define themselves or their health primarily in terms of their disability. Future research efforts that incorporate a measure specifically designed to assess how participants perceive the impact of the disability on their daily lives, including the practice of health behaviors, might provide more meaningful information about relatively homogeneous subgroups of people with disabilities.

The Barriers Scale was negatively related to measures of health status, health-promoting behavior, and perceived self-efficacy. Those who perceived more barriers to taking care of their health also perceived themselves as "less healthy" and were less likely to engage in health-promoting behaviors, particularly the psychologic components of health promotion. Because this is a correlational study, no causal relationships can be established. These results do suggest a strong relationship, however, between barriers and various health-attitude measures.

The Barriers Scale correlated most strongly with perceived self-efficacy—an individual's judgment of how well he or she can execute a course of action required to deal with prospective situations.[19] This finding is consistent with previous reports that self-efficacy is a consistent predictor of short-term and long-term success in health-related practices and that experimental manipulations of self-efficacy have been consistently powerful in initiating and maintaining change in health behaviors such as smoking, exercise, and nutrition.[20]

The pattern of negative correlations between barriers, self-efficacy, and engaging in health-promoting behavior has important implications for future research and practice. These findings add to an accumulating body of knowledge suggesting that simply providing people with information about good health practices may not be enough to effect changes in behavior.[21] If, as Bandura[19] suggests, it is an individual's efficacy expectations rather than his or her abilities or capabilities that often influence behavior, then new studies testing the effects of interventions enhancing disabled people's self-efficacy should be designed. Interventions that enhance self-efficacy and that lower perceived internal barriers might be most effective in increasing health-promoting behaviors for disabled adults.

Anecdotal comments from ILC staff during the course of this study suggest that the attitudes of health care providers may also be an important factor in enhancing health-promoting behavior. Some professionals who are heavily grounded in the traditional medical model, with its emphasis on "curing" the patient, may find it frustrating to work with people they cannot "fix." Others may believe that disabled persons are unable to take an active role in their own health promotion. Such negative attitudes could undermine efforts to provide effective health-promotion services to persons with disabilities. Future initiatives with health care providers should, therefore, address attitudes of practitioners as well as the skills and knowledge necessary to work with disabled persons.

• • •

While enhancing health-promoting behavior may not have been a priority for programs that serve people with disabilities in the past, it should receive as much emphasis as other forms of life and work-skills training. Because health promotion emphasizes self-care rather than expert care, it promotes an active, independent attitude toward health care. In addition, its expanded definition of health enables the disabled person to draw strength from other areas of life, thereby balancing the stigmas centering around the disability.[22] Finally, disabled individuals are at risk for secondary disabilities and rehospitalization. The "thinner margin of health" described by DeJong and Hughes[2] makes many of these individuals more susceptible to acute and chronic disturbances of their health. Secondary disability, rehospitalization, and disturbances in health status all increase the direct and indirect costs of disabilities. Therefore, interventions aimed at decreasing barriers to health promotion and at increasing health-promoting behavior would not only enhance quality of life but could also reduce the ultimate costs of health care for adults with disabilities.

REFERENCES

1. *Healthy People: The Surgeon General's Report on Health Promotion and Disease Prevention.* Washington, DC: Public Health Service; 1979. US Dept of Health, Education, and Welfare publication 79-55071.

2. DeJong G, Hughes J. Independent living: methodology for measuring long-term outcomes. *Arch Phys Med Rehabil.* 1982;63:68-73.
3. *On the Threshold of Independence.* Washington, DC: National Council of the Handicapped; 1988.
4. Nosek MA. *Relationships Among Measures of Social Independence, Psychological Independence, and Functional Abilities in Adults With Severe Orthopedic Impairments.* Austin, Tex: The University of Texas at Austin; 1984. Unpublished doctoral dissertation.
5. Melnyk A. Barriers: a critical review of recent literature. *Nurs Res.* 1988;37(4):196-201.
6. Vertinsky P, Auman JT. Elderly women's barriers to exercise, part II: the physician's role. *Health Values.* 1988; 12(4):20-23.
7. Batavia J, DeJong G. Results of managed health care feasibility study. Presented at the Primary Health-Care Needs of Persons with Physical Disabilities Conference; September 29, 1988; Washington, DC.
8. Warms CA. Health promotion services in post-rehabilitation spinal cord injury health care. *Rehabil Nurs.* 1987;12(6):304-308.
9. Pender NJ. *Health Promotion in Nursing Practice.* 2nd ed. Norwalk, Conn: Appleton & Lange; 1987.
10. Dishman K, Sallis JF, Orenstein DR. The determinants of physical activity and exercise. *Public Health Rep.* 1985; 100(2):158-171.
11. Champion VL. Attitudinal variables related to intention, frequency, and proficiency of breast self-examination in women 35 and over. *Res Nurs Health.* 1988;11(5): 283-291.
12. Duffy ME. Primary prevention behaviors: the female-headed, one-parent family. *Res Nurs Health.* 1986;9(2): 115-122.
13. Dai YT, Catanzaro M. Health beliefs and compliance with a skin care regimen. *Rehabil Nurs.* 1987;12(1):13-16.
14. Buddle JF, Bachelder GL. Independent living: the concept, model, and methodology. *J Assoc Persons Severe Handicaps.* 1986;11(4):240-245.
15. Lawton MP, Moss M, Fucomer M, Kleban MH. A research and service oriented multilevel assessment instrument. *J Gerontol.* 1982;37(1):91-99.
16. Sherer M, Maddux JE, Mercandante B, Prentice-Dunn S, Jacobs B, Rogers RW. The self-efficacy scale: construction and validation. *Psychol Rep.* 1982;51:663-671.
17. Walker SN, Sechrist KR, Pender NJ. The health-promoting lifestyle profile: development and psychometric characteristics. *Nurs Res.* 1987;36(2):76-81.
18. Wallston BS, Wallston KA, Kaplan GD, Maides SA. Development and validation of the health locus of control (HLC) scale. *J Consult Clin Psychol.* 1976;44: 580-585.
19. Bandura A. Self-efficacy mechanisms in human agency. *Am Psychol.* 1982;37(2):122-147.
20. Strecher VJ, DeVellis BM, Becker MH, Rosenstock IM. The role of self-efficacy in achieving health behavior change. *Health Educ Q.* 1986;13:73-91.
21. Byham LD, Vickery CE. Compliance and health promotion. *Health Values.* 1988;12(4):5-12.
22. Brooks NA. Opportunities for health promotion: including the chronically ill and disabled. *Soc Sci Med.* 1984; 19:405-409.

CHAPTER **48**

The Tragedy of Old Age in America

Robert N. Butler, MD

What is it like to be old in the United States? What will our own lives be like when we are old? Americans find it difficult to think about old age until they are propelled into the midst of it by their own aging and that of relatives and friends. Aging is the neglected stepchild of the human life cycle. Though we have begun to examine the socially taboo subjects of dying and death, we have leaped over that long period of time preceding death known as old age. In truth, it is easier to manage the problem of death than the problem of living as an old person. Death is a dramatic, one-time crisis while old age is a day-by-day and year-by-year confrontation with powerful external and internal forces, a bittersweet coming to terms with one's own personality and one's life.

Those of us who are not old barricade ourselves from discussions of old age by declaring the subject morbid, boring or in poor taste. Optimism and euphemism are other common devices. People will speak of looking forward to their "retirement years." The elderly are described respectfully as "senior citizens," "golden agers," "our elders," and one hears of old people who are considered inspirations and examples of how to "age well" or "gracefully." There is the popularly accepted opinion that Social Security and pensions provide a comfortable and reliable flow of funds so the elderly have few financial worries. Medicare has lulled the population into reassuring itself that the once terrible financial burdens of late-life illnesses are now eradicated. Advertisements and travel folders show relaxed, happy, well-dressed older people enjoying recreation, travel and their grandchildren. If they are no longer living in the old family home, they are pictured as delighted residents of retirement communities with names like Leisure World and Sun City, with lots of grass, clean air and fun. This is the American ideal of the "golden years" toward which millions of citizens are expectantly toiling through their workdays.

But this is not the full story. A second theme runs through the popular view of old age. Our colloquialisms reveal a great deal: once you are old you are "fading fast," "over the hill," "out to pasture," "down the drain," "finished," "out of date," an "old crock," "fogy," "geezer," or "biddy." One hears children saying they are afraid to get old, middle-aged people declaring they want to die after they have passed their prime, and numbers of old people wishing they were dead.

What can we possibly conclude from these discrepant points of view? Our popular attitudes could be summed up as a combination of wishful thinking and stark terror. We base our feelings on primitive fears, prejudice and stereotypes rather than on knowledge and insight. In reality, the way one experiences old age is contingent upon physical health, personality, earlier life experiences, the actual circumstances of late-life events (in what order they occur, how they occur, when they occur) and the social supports one receives: adequate finances, shelter, medical care, social roles, religious support, recreation. All of these are crucial and interconnected elements which together determine the quality of life.

Old age is neither inherently miserable nor inherently sublime—like every stage of life it has problems, joys, fears and potentials. The process of aging and eventual death must ultimately be accepted as the natural progression of the life cycle, the old completing their prescribed life spans and making way for the young. Much that is unique in old age in fact derives from the reality of aging and the imminence of death. The old must clarify and find use for what they have attained in a lifetime of learning and adapting; they must conserve strength and resources where necessary and adjust creatively to those changes and losses that occur as part of the aging experience. The elderly have the potential for qualities of human reflection and observation which can only come from having lived an entire life span. There is a lifetime accumulation of personality and experience which is available to be used and enjoyed.

But what are an individual's chances for a "good" old age in America, with satisfying final years and a dignified death? Unfortunately, none too good. For many elderly Americans old age is a tragedy, a period of quiet despair, deprivation, desolation and muted rage. This can be a consequence of the kind of life a person has led in younger years and the problems in his or her relationships with others. There are also inevitable personal and physical losses to be sustained, some of which can become overwhelming and unbearable. All of this is the individual factor, the existential element. But old age is frequently a tragedy even when the early years have been fulfilling and people seemingly have everything going for them. Herein lies what I consider to be the genuine tragedy of old age in America—we have shaped a society which is extremely harsh to live in when one is old. The tragedy of old age is not the fact that each of us must grow old and die but that the process of doing so has been made unnecessarily and at times excruciatingly painful, humiliating, debilitating and isolating through insensitivity, ignorance and poverty. The potentials for satisfactions and even triumphs in late life are real and vastly underexplored. For the most part the elderly struggle to exist in an inhospitable world.

Are things *really* that bad? Let's begin by looking at the basic daily requirements for survival. Poverty or drastically lowered income and old age go hand in hand. People who are poor all their lives remain poor as they grow old. Most of us realize this. What we do not realize is that these poor are joined by multitudes of people who become poor only after growing older. When Social Security becomes the sole or primary income, it means subsistence-level life styles for many, and recent increases do not keep up with soaring costs of living. Private pension plans often do not pay off, and pension payments that do come in are not tied to inflationary decreases in buying power. Savings can be wiped out by a single unexpected catastrophe.

It has been estimated that at least 30 percent of the elderly live in substandard housing. Many more must deprive themselves of essentials to keep their homes in repair.

The American dream promised older people that if they worked hard enough all their lives, things would turn out well for them. Today's elderly were brought up to believe in pride, self-reliance and independence. Many are tough, determined individuals who manage to survive against adversity. But even the tough ones reach a point where help should be available to them.

Age discrimination in employment is unrestrained, with arbitrary retirement practices and bias against hiring older people for available jobs. Social Security penalizes the old by reducing their income checks as soon as they earn more than $2,400 a year. Job-training programs don't want the elderly (or the middle-aged, for that matter), so there is no opportunity to learn new skills. Employers rarely make concessions for the possible physical limitations of otherwise valuable older employees, and instead they are fired, retired or forced to resign.

It is obvious that the old get sick more frequently and more severely than the young, and 86 percent have chronic health problems of varying degree. These health problems, while significant, are largely treatable and for the most part do not impair the capacity to work. Medicare pays for only 45 percent of older people's health expenses; the balance must come from their own incomes and savings, or from Medicaid, which requires a humiliating means test. A serious illness can mean instant poverty. Drugs prescribed outside of hospitals, hearing aids, glasses, dental care and podiatry are not covered at all under Medicare. There is prejudice against the old by doctors and other medical personnel who don't like to bother with them. Psychiatrists and mental-health personnel typically assume that the mental problems of the old are untreatable. Psychoanalysts, the elite of the psychiatric profession, rarely accept them as patients. Medical schools and other teaching institutions find them "uninteresting." Voluntary hospitals are well known for dumping the "Medicare patient" into municipal hospitals; municipal hospitals in turn funnel them into nursing homes, mental hospitals and chronic disease institutions without the adequate diagnostic and treatment effort which might enable them to return home. Persons who do remain at home while in ill health have serious difficulties in getting social, medical and psychiatric services brought directly to them.

Problems large and small confront the elderly. They are easy targets for crime in the streets and in their homes. Because of loneliness, confusion, hearing and visual difficulties they are prime victims of dishonest door-to-door salesmen and fraudulent advertising, and buy defective hearing aids, dance lessons, useless "Medicare insurance supplements," and quack health remedies. Persons crippled by arthritis or strokes are yelled at by impatient bus drivers for their slowness in climbing on and off buses. Traffic lights turn red before they can get across the street. Revolving doors move too quickly. Subways usually have no elevators or escalators.

Old women fare worse than old men. Women have an average life expectancy of seven years longer than men and tend to marry men older than themselves; so two-thirds (six million) of all older women are widows.* When widowed they do not have the same social prerogatives as older men to date and marry those who are younger. As a result, they are likely to end up alone—an ironic turn of events when one remembers that most of them were raised from childhood to consider marriage the only acceptable state. The income levels of older working women are generally lower than those of men; many never worked outside the home until their children were grown and then only at unskilled, low-paying jobs. Others who worked all their lives typically received low wages, with lower Social Security and private retirement benefits as a result. Until 1973, housewives who were widowed received only 82.5 percent of their husbands' Social Security benefits even though they were full-time homemakers.

Black, Mexican-American and American Indian elderly all have a lower life expectancy than whites, due to their socioeconomic disadvantages. Although the life expectancy of 67.5 years for white men remained the same from 1960 to 1968, the life expectancy for black men *declined* a full year during that time (from 61.1 to 60.0). Blacks of all ages make up 11 percent of the total United States population, but they constitute only 7.8 percent of the elderly. The life expectancy for Mexican-Americans is estimated at 57 years, and for American Indians at 44 years. Most do not live long enough to be eligible for the benefits of Social Security and Medicare. Poverty is the norm. Scant attention is paid to their particular cultural interests and heritage.

Asian-American elderly (Chinese, Japanese, Korean, Filipino and Samoan) are victims of a public impression that they are independently cared for by their families and therefore do not need help. However, patterns of immigration by Asian-Americans to this country, the cultural barriers, language problems and discrimination they have faced have all taken a toll of their elderly and their families. This is particularly true of older Chinese men, who were not allowed to bring their wives and families with them to the United States or to intermarry.

MYTHS AND STEREOTYPES ABOUT THE OLD

In addition to dealing with the difficulties of physical and economic survival, older people are affected by the multitude of myths and stereotypes surrounding old age.

The Myth of Aging

The idea of chronological aging (measuring one's age by the number of years one has lived) is a kind of

*Twenty percent of American women are widows by 60, 50 percent by 65, 66⅔ by 75.

myth. It is clear that there are great differences in the rates of physiological, chronological, psychological and social aging within the person and from person to person. In fact, physiological indicators show a greater range from the mean in old age than in any other age group, and this is true of personality as well. Older people actually become more diverse rather than more similar with advancing years. There are extraordinarily "young" 80-year-olds as well as "old" 80-year-olds. Chronological age, therefore, is a convenient but imprecise indicator of physical, mental and emotional status. For the purposes of this article old age may be considered to commence at the conventionally accepted point of 65.

We do know that organic brain damage can create such extensive intellectual impairment that people of all types and personalities may become dull-eyed, blank-faced and unresponsive. Massive destruction of the brain and body has a "leveling" effect which can produce increasing homogeneity among the elderly. But most older people do not suffer impairment of this magnitude during the greater part of their later life.

The Myth of Unproductivity

Many believe the old to be unproductive. But in the absence of diseases and social adversities, old people tend to remain productive and actively involved in life. There are dazzling examples like octogenarians Georgia O'Keeffe continuing to paint and Pope John XXIII revitalizing his church, and septuagenarians Duke Ellington composing and working his hectic concert schedule and Golda Meir acting as her country's vigorous Prime Minister. Substantial numbers of people become unusually creative for the first time in old age, when exceptional and inborn talents may be discovered and expressed. What is most pertinent to our discussion here, however, is the fact that many old people continue to contribute usefully to their families and community in a variety of ways, including active employment. The 1971 Bureau of Labor Statistics figures show 1,780,000 people over 65 working full time and 1,257,000 part time. Since society and business practice do not encourage the continued employment of the elderly, it is obvious that many more would work if jobs were available.

When productive incapacity develops, it can be traced more directly to a variety of losses, diseases or circumstances than to that mysterious process called aging. Even then, in spite of the presence of severe handicaps, activity and involvement are often maintained.

The Myth of Disengagement

This is related to the previous myth and holds that older people prefer to disengage from life, to withdraw into themselves, choosing to live alone or perhaps only with their peers. Ironically, some gerontologists themselves hold these views. One study, *Growing Old: The Process of Disengagement,* presents the theory that mutual separation of the aged person from his society is a natural part of the aging experience. There is no evidence to support this generalization. Disengagement is only one of many patterns of reaction to old age.

The Myth of Inflexibility

The ability to change and adapt has little to do with one's age and more to do with one's lifelong character. But even this statement has to be qualified. One is not necessarily destined to maintain one's character in earlier life permanently. True, the endurance, the strength and the stability in human character structure are remarkable and protective. But most, if not all, people change and remain open to change throughout the course of life, right up to its termination. The old notion, whether ascribed to Pope Alexander VI or Sigmund Freud, that character is laid down in final form by the fifth year of life can be confidently refuted. Change is the hallmark of living. The notion that older people become less responsive to innovation and change because of age is not supported by scientific studies of healthy older people living in the community or by everyday observations and clinical psychiatric experience.

A related cliché is that political conservatism increases with age. If one's options are constricted by job discrimination, reduced or fixed income and runaway inflation, as older people's are, one may become conservative out of economic necessity rather than out of qualities innate in the psyche. Thus an older person may vote against the creation of better schools or an expansion of social services for tax reasons. His property—his home—may be his only equity, and his income is likely to be too low to weather increased taxes. A perfectly sensible self-interest rather than "conservatism" is at work here. Naturally, conservatives do exist among the elderly, but so do liberals, radicals and moderates. Once again diversity rather than homogeneity is the norm.

The Myth of "Senility"

The notion that old people are senile, showing forgetfulness, confusional episodes and reduced attention, is widely accepted. "Senility" is a popularized layman's term used by doctors and the public alike to categorize the behavior of the old. Some of what is called senile is the result of brain damage, but anxiety and depression are also frequently lumped within the same category of senility, even though they are treatable and often reversible. Old people, like young people, experience a full range of emotions, including anxiety, grief, depression and paranoid states. It is all too easy to blame age and brain damage when accounting for the mental problems and emotional concerns of later life.

Drug tranquilization is another frequent, misdiagnosed and potentially reversible cause of so-called senility. Malnutrition and unrecognized physical illnesses, such as congestive heart failure, may produce "senile behavior" by reducing the supply of blood, oxygen and food to the brain. Alcoholism, often associated with bereavement, is another cause. Because it has been so convenient to dismiss all these manifestations by lumping them together under an improper and inaccurate diagnostic label, the elderly often do not receive the benefits of decent diagnosis and treatment.

Actual irreversible brain damage, of course, is not a myth, and two major conditions create mental disorders. One is cerebral arteriosclerosis (hardening of the arteries of the brain); the other, unfortunately referred to as senile brain disease, is due to a mysterious dissolution of brain cells. Such conditions account for some 50 percent of the cases of major mental disorders in old age, and the symptoms connected with these conditions are the ones that form the basis for what has come to be known as senility. But, as I wish to emphasize again, similar symptoms can be found in a number of other conditions which are reversible through proper treatment.

The Myth of Serenity

In contrast to the previous myths, which view the elderly in a negative light, the myth of serenity portrays old age as a kind of adult fairyland. Now at last comes a time of relative peace and serenity when people can relax and enjoy the fruits of their labors after the storms of active life are over. Advertising slogans, television and romantic fiction foster the myth. Visions of carefree, cookie-baking grandmothers and rocking-chair grandfathers are cherished by younger generations. But, in fact, older persons experience more stresses than any other age group, and these stresses are often devastating. The strength of the aged to endure crisis is remarkable, and tranquility is an unlikely as well as inappropriate response under these circumstances. Depression, anxiety, psychosomatic illnesses, paranoia, garrulousness and irritability are some of the internal reactions to external stresses.

AGEISM—THE PREJUDICE AGAINST THE ELDERLY

The stereotyping and myths surrounding old age can be explained in part by lack of knowledge and by insufficient contact with a wide variety of older people. But there is another powerful factor operating—a deep and profound prejudice against the elderly which is found to some degree in all of us. In thinking about how to describe this, I coined the word "ageism" in 1968:

> Ageism can be seen as a process of systematic stereotyping of and discrimination against people because they are old, just as racism and sexism accomplish this with skin color and gender. Old people are categorized as senile, rigid in thought and manner, old-fashioned in morality and skills. . . . Ageism allows the younger generations to see older people as different from themselves; thus they subtly cease to identify with their elders as human beings.

Ageism makes it easier to ignore the frequently poor social and economic plight of older people. We can avoid dealing with the reality that our productivity-minded society has little use for non-producers — in this case those who have reached an arbitrarily defined retirement age. We can also avoid, for a time at least, reminders of the personal reality of our own aging and death.

Ageism is manifested in a wide range of phenomena, both on individual and institutional levels — stereotypes and myths, outright disdain and dislike, or simply subtle avoidance of contact; discriminatory practices in housing, employment and services of all kinds; epithets, cartoons and jokes. At times ageism becomes an expedient method by which society promotes viewpoints about the aged in order to relieve itself of responsibility toward them. At other times ageism serves highly personal objectives, protecting younger (usually middle-aged) individuals — often at high emotional cost — from thinking about things they fear (aging, illness, death).

The elderly's part in eliciting the kind of response which they receive from the young and from society at large is often a subtle but powerful factor in the public's generally disparaging views of them. They collaborate with their ostracizers. Some individuals act "senile"; others may deny their true feelings in an attempt to "age graciously" and obtain the approval which is otherwise denied them. Psychologist Margaret Thaler Singer observed similarities between the Rorschach test findings in members of a National Institute of Mental Health sample of aged volunteers who were resigned in the face of aging and those in American GI prisoners of war who collaborated with their captors in Korea.

Other self-sabotaging behavior can be a refusal to identify oneself as elderly at all. One sees older persons who affect the dress and behavior patterns of the young, pretending like Peter Pan that they have never grown up. Older women can be seen engaging in sad, frantic attempts to appear young, as if this would ensure appreciation and acceptance in the eyes of others.

A significant minority of older people conceal their age from themselves as well as from others. In a study of 1,700 elderly persons, Taves and Hansen found that one-sixth thought of themselves as old between the ages of 54 and 69, one-third between the ages of 70 and 79, and only 40 percent by age 80 and over. About one person in seven said they never thought of themselves as old.

In a study by Tuckman and Lorge that queried over 1,000 persons from 20 to 80, those under 30 classified themselves as young, and of those between 30 and 60, most classified themselves as middle-aged. At age 60 only a small proportion classified themselves as old, and at age 80 slightly over half called themselves old. A small percentage of the 80-year-olds persisted in describing themselves as young.

Of course, considering oneself "young" is not simply a prejudice or a delusion. Healthy older people do feel strong and vigorous, much as they did in their earlier days. The problem comes when this good feeling is called "youth" rather than "health," thus tying it to chronological age instead of to physical and mental well-being.

Lack of empathy is a further reaction by the elderly to their experiences in the larger culture. Out of emotional self-protection many healthy, prosperous, well-educated old people feel no identification with or protectiveness toward the poor elderly. A lack of compassion is of course not unique to the aged, but it has a special irony here with the advent of catastrophic illnesses or the exhaustion of resources that goes with a long life, they too run a high risk of finding themselves among the poor, facing similar indifference from their wealthier peers.

Older people are not always victims, passive and fated by their environment. They, too, initiate direct actions and stimulate responses. They may exploit their age and its accompanying challenges to gain something they want or need, perhaps to their own detriment (e.g., by demanding services from others and thus allowing their own skills to atrophy). Exploitation can backfire; excessive requests to others by an older person may be met at first, but as requests increase they are felt as demands — and may indeed be demands. Younger people who attempt to deal with a demanding older person may find themselves going through successive cycles of rage, guilt and overprotectiveness without realizing they are being manipulated. In addition to his "age" the older person may exploit his diseases and his impairments, capitalizing upon his alleged helplessness. Invalids of all ages do this, but older people can more easily take on the appearance of frailty when others would not be allowed this behavior. Manipulation by older people is best recognized for what it is — a valuable clue that there is energy available which should be redirected toward greater benefit for themselves and others.

It must also be remembered that the old can have many prejudices against the young. These may be a result of their attractiveness, vigor and sexual prowess. Older people may be troubled by the extraordinary changes that they see in the world around them and blame the younger generation. They may be angry at the brevity of life and begrudge someone the fresh chance of living out a life span which they have already completed.

Angry and ambivalent feelings flow, too, between the old and the middle-aged, who are caught up in the problems unique to their age and position within the life cycle. The middle-aged bear the heaviest personal and social responsibilities since they are called upon to help support — individually and collectively — both ends of the life cycle: the nurture and education of their young and the financial, emotional and physical care of the old. Many have not been prepared for their heavy responsibilities and are surprised and overwhelmed by them. Frequently these responsibilities trap them in their careers or life styles until the children grow up or their parents die. A common reaction is anger at both the young and the old. The effects of financial pressures are seen primarily in the middle and lower economic classes. But the middle-aged of all classes are inclined to be ambivalent toward the young and old since both age groups remind them of their own waning youth. In addition — with reason — they fear technological or professional obsolescence as they see what has happened to their elders and feel the pressure of youth pushing its way toward their position in society. Furthermore, their responsibilities are likely to increase in the future as more and more of their parents and grandparents live longer life spans.

STUDYING THE OLD

We have put precious little work and research into examining the last phase of life. What research has been done has concentrated primarily on studies of the 5 percent of elderly who are in institutions. The few research studies on the healthy aged living in the community have produced exciting new looks at the possibilities and problems of this age group. But on the whole medicine and the behavioral sciences seem to have shared society's negative views of old age and have quite consistently presented *decline* as the key concept of late life, with *neglect* forming the major treatment technique and research response.

Ultimately interest must focus on clarifying the complex, interwoven elements necessary to produce and support physical and mental health up to the very end of life rather than our present preoccupation with "curing" ills after they develop. Understanding what interferes with healthy development throughout the life cycle gives us a chance to prevent problems, instead of rushing frantically and often futilely to solve them after they occur. Life is a continuing process from birth until death and it seems strange that it so seldom occurs to us to study life as a whole.

Finally, from a philosophic view, a greater understanding and control over the diseases and difficulties of later life would hopefully make old age less frightening and more acceptable as a truly valuable last phase of life. The relief of human suffering has merit in itself, but it also releases human beings from the fears and defenses they build up around it.

WHOSE RESPONSIBILITY ARE THEY?

Are older Americans entitled to decent income, health, housing, transportation and opportunities for employment as well as to social status and participation in society? Who should see to it that they get them? Why can't they manage their lives themselves? The struggle to decide on the place of the old in a culture has been familiar throughout history. Cultural attitudes have ranged from veneration, protectiveness, and sentimentality to derogation, rejection, pity and abandonment.

Older Americans of today — indeed the old people in any society — contributed to the growth of the society in which younger people live. One might assume that they would have a justifiable expectation of sharing in what is referred to as America's affluence. All of us, whatever our age, are now contributing taxes and services to our nation and are collectively preparing for our own old age. What will the future bring for us? Will anyone help us if we cannot adequately help ourselves?

The Depression of the 1930s convinced many rugged individualists that forces beyond the control of the individual could bring widespread devastation and poverty. A legislative landmark of Roosevelt's New Deal was the inauguration of Social Security in 1935, a consequence of many pressures. . . . Perhaps the final impetus came from the need to have the old retire in order to provide employment for the young. Thus, years after most Western European industrial nations had introduced it, the United States made its decision for the collective insurance-policy form of income maintenance for the disabled and retired. Eighty-five cents ($0.85) of every federal dollar now expended annually for programs for the elderly derive from Social Security trust funds to which we all contribute — as did the majority of the present elderly themselves in their working days.

Social Security, Medicare and federal housing programs have helped to gain for the elderly *some* income security, *some* health care and *some* housing. But the task has not been finished and the efforts do not match the needs.

Suggested Additional Readings for Part VIII

Health care of vulnerable populations

Breakley WR: Treating the homeless, Alcohol Health & Res World 11(3):42-47, 90+, Spring 1987.

Durell J and Bukoski W: Preventing substance abuse: the state of the art, Public Health Rep 99(1):23-31, Jan-Feb 1984.

Govoni LA: Psychosocial issues of AIDS in the nursing care of homosexual men and their significant others, Nurse Clin North Am 23(4):749-65, Dec 1988.

Kulbok PP, Earls FJ, and Montgomery AC: Life style and patterns of health and social behavior in high-risk adolescents, Adv Nurs Sci 11(1):22-35, Oct 1988.

Lavietes RL: Crisis intervention with ghetto children: mythology and reality, Am J Orthopyschiatry 44:241-45, 1974.

Martin M and Henry M: Cultural relativity and poverty, Public Health Nurs 6(1):28-34, 1987.

McElmurry BJ and LiBrizzi SJ: The health of older women, Women's Health 21(1):161-171, March 1986.

Meyer KA: The hospice concept integrated with existing community health care, Nurs Admin 4(3):49-54, Spring 1980.

Oda DS: The imperative of a national health strategy for children: is there a political will? Nurs Outlook 37(5): 206208, Sept-Oct 1989.

Phillips LR: The fit of elder abuse with the family violence paradigm and the implications of a paradigm shift for clinical practice, Public Health Nurs 5(4):222-229, 1988.

Praeger SG, Bernhardt GR: Survivors of suicide: a community need, Fam Community Health 8(3):62-72, Nov 1985.

Roe DA: Nutritional needs of the elderly: issues, guidelines, and responsibilities, Fam Community Health, 12(1):59-65, May 1989.

Ropers RH and Boyer R: Homelessness as a health risk, Alcohol Health & Res World (11)3:38-41, 89+, Spring 1987.

Silver BJ, Goldston SE, and Silver LB: The 1990 objectives for the control of stress and violent behavior, Public Health Rep 99(4):374-384, 1984.

Skinner PV et al: Home management of the patient with Alzheimer's disease, Home Healthcare Nurse 7(1):23-27, 1989.

Turner SL, Bauer G, McNair E, McNutt B and Walker W: The Homeless experience clinic: building in a community health discovery-learning project, Public Health Nurs 6(2):97-101, June 1989.

Weinreb LF and Bassuk EL: Substance abuse: a growing problem among homeless families, Fam Community Health 13(1):55-64, May 1990.

Williams GO and Dueker DL: The nonuse of free health-screening by rural elderly, Am J Prev Med 1(4):52-57, 1985.

Index